Sold on Radio

ALSO BY JIM COX AND FROM MCFARLAND

Radio Journalism in America: Telling the News in the Golden Age and Beyond (2013)

Musicmakers of Network Radio: 24 Entertainers, 1926–1962 (2012)

Rails Across Dixie: A History of Passenger Trains in the American South (2011)

American Radio Networks: A History (2009)

This Day in Network Radio: A Daily Calendar of Births, Deaths, Debuts, Cancellations and Other Events in Broadcasting History (2008)

Radio Speakers: Narrators, News Junkies, Sports Jockeys, Tattletales, Tipsters, Toastmasters and Coffee Klatch Couples Who Verbalized the Jargon of the Aural Ether from the 1920s to the 1980s — A Biographical Dictionary (2007; paperback 2011)

The Daytime Serials of Television, 1946–1960 (2006; paperback 2010)

Music Radio: The Great Performers and Programs of the 1920s through Early 1960s (2005; paperback 2011)

Mr. Keen, Tracer of Lost Persons: A Complete History and Episode Log of Radio's Most Durable Detective (2004; paperback 2011)

Frank and Anne Hummert's Radio Factory: The Programs and Personalities of Broadcasting's Most Prolific Producers (2003)

Radio Crime Fighters: More Than 300 Programs from the Golden Age (2002; paperback 2010)

Say Goodnight, Gracie: The Last Years of Network Radio (2002)

The Great Radio Audience Participation Shows: Seventeen Programs from the 1940s and 1950s (2001; paperback 2009)

The Great Radio Soap Operas (1999; paperback 2008)

SOLD ON RADIO

Advertisers in the Golden Age of Broadcasting

Jim Cox

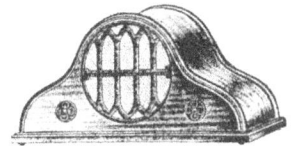

McFarland & Company, Inc., Publishers
Jefferson, North Carolina, and London

The present work is a reprint of the illustrated case bound edition of Sold on Radio: Advertisers in the Golden Age of Broadcasting, *first published in 2008 by McFarland.*

Photographs provided by Photofest

LIBRARY OF CONGRESS CATALOGUING-IN-PUBLICATION DATA

Cox, Jim, 1939–
Sold on radio : advertisers in the golden age
of broadcasting / Jim Cox.
p. cm.
Includes bibliographical references and index.

ISBN 978-0-7864-7518-6
softcover : acid free paper ∞

1. Radio advertising — United States — History — 20th century.
2. Radio broadcasting — United States — History — 20th century.   I. Title.
HF6146.R3C69 2013   659.14'20973 — dc22   2008014538

BRITISH LIBRARY CATALOGUING DATA ARE AVAILABLE

© 2008 Jim Cox. All rights reserved

No part of this book may be reproduced or transmitted in any form or by any means, electronic or mechanical, including photocopying or recording, or by any information storage and retrieval system, without permission in writing from the publisher.

On the cover: Ralph Edwards hosting "Truth or Consequences" for Procter & Gamble's laundry detergent Duz (Photofest); radio © 2013 Shutterstock

Manufactured in the United States of America

*McFarland & Company, Inc., Publishers
Box 611, Jefferson, North Carolina 28640
www.mcfarlandpub.com*

To the memory of
Willard K. (Daddy) Weeks
E. Odell Crowe
and
Chauncey R. Daley

*three men whose mentoring
profoundly shaped my life
and the lives of my contemporaries*

Acknowledgments

No author acts independently. I've said it before and I'm saying it again: were it not for a handful of individuals who supplied information and verified tenuous facts, a project like this would never be completed. With a diverse contingent of resources at my fingertips, I still lean heavily upon the expertise of a handful of confidantes who have proven themselves as reliably accurate as they are dependable, competent and gracious with their time and substance.

At the head of the list is research colleague Irene Heinstein whose ability to discover obscure details about individuals, enterprises and events is mesmerizing. Tirelessly, proficiently, profusely she labors, never satisfied until the most infinitesimal nagging quest is satisfied. Irene possesses the uncanny ability to find and furnish reams of substantive documentation on any topic and does so with dispatch and — I believe — glee. A whole lot of the data in this book passed before her eyes, much of it originating with an august array of factoids she can summon at a moment's notice. I am enduringly grateful for her commitment and am privileged to acknowledge it here.

My chum Charlie Niren came to my rescue several times with tapes of shows and their commercials that were helpful in completing the manuscript. I was profoundly dependent on a similar series of MP3 discs provided by Gary Mercer which he labeled *Encyclopedia of Radio & TV: A History of Radio & TV*. Cope Robinson, a veteran of Newell-Emmett ad agency in "those days," read significant portions of the manuscript and offered priceless comments along the way. He, Chris Chandler, Ted Meland and Jim Widner evaluated my original theme for the project and rendered helpful reactions before I launched into the venture. Several others supplied information, answers and assistance when summoned: Conrad Binyon, Claire Connelly, Jack French, Russell Hudson, Bill Jaker and Lee Munsick.

I'm indebted to a few colleagues who motivated me with their own often unheralded journalistic pursuits in the preservation of vintage radio. My pals include editors Bob Burchett, Steve Darnall, Jack French, Jay Hickerson, Ken Krug, Patrick Lucanio and Mike Utz. Tom Heathwood and Walden Hughes, a couple of stalwarts on the air, lent empathy to these endeavors.

Once again, I'm indebted to my lifelong companion, Sharon Cox, for her willingness to share me with my pursuits into the days of yesteryear. All of my family does likewise, in fact, and I am deeply grateful to each one.

I'm also thankful for you, dear reader — for your interest, encouragement and cheer. You are the reason I do this. I trust you will be rewarded with the outcome of these modest endeavors.

Contents

Acknowledgments vii
Preface 1

PART I. THE COMMERCIALIZATION OF AMERICAN NETWORK RADIO

1. Ancestors of Radio Advertising 7
2. Commercializing the Ether 17
3. Ad Agencies: They Held the Whip Hand 32
4. Audience Measurement Services: Counting the House 41
5. Commercial Copywriters: Persuasive Penmanship 52
6. Commercial Spokesmen: They Delivered the Goods 60

PART II. PATRONAGE OF AMERICAN NETWORK RADIO

American Home Products 73
American Tobacco Company 79
Andrew Jergens Company 88
Bristol-Myers Company 95
Brown & Williamson Tobacco Company 101
Campbell Soup Company 106
Coca-Cola Company 113
Colgate-Palmolive-Peet Company 121
Ford Motor Company 129
General Foods Corporation 136

General Mills, Inc. 146
General Motors Company 156
Kellogg Company 164
Kraft Foods Company 171
Lever Brothers Company 177
Liggett & Myers Tobacco Company 184
P. Lorillard, Inc. 192
Miles Laboratories, Inc. 197
Philip Morris Company 205
Procter & Gamble Company 212
Quaker Oats Company 221
R. J. Reynolds Tobacco Company 228
Standard Brands, Inc. 234
Sterling Drug, Inc. 240

Appendix A: 100 More Advertisers in Radio's Golden Age 249
Appendix B: Variants That Impacted the Radio Commercial 273
Appendix C: A Glossary of Advertising and Broadcasting Jargon . . . 296
Chapter Notes 303
Bibliography 313
Index 317

Preface

"Whatever happened to Peet?" The inquiry, posed by a crony who threw it out to no one in particular as he sauntered in to a gathering of our local vintage radio club, caught us off guard. "Who is Peet?" mused another member in contemplative response. "You know," the instigator expounded. "Colgate-Palmolive-Peet! Whatever happened to Peet?" (For the uninitiated, the Colgate-Palmolive Company bore a triple-pronged moniker for years, with Peet winding it up. But Peet vanished decades ago; hence the question lingering in my chum's mind.)

I admitted that I didn't know. With an inborn wonder about such trivia amplified by a professional background in advertising, marketing and public relations, my instincts had ruminated over that very question some time before our confederate proffered it aloud. Yet I had never pursued it to a satisfactory resolution.

When I finally got around to penning the volume you hold in your hands — having considered a book on radio advertising for some years — the matter of the missing Peet resurfaced. Not only did I have a reason to find what became of Peet but also to discover what or who Peet really was. (Those findings are reported in the chapter on Colgate-Palmolive-Peet Company.)

As it turned out, there were plenty of added revelations during my investigations that were equally stimulating. Did you know, for example, that — for several years — a single individual served a couple of behemoth U. S. corporations at the same time as chairman? It was, for sure, an anomaly in the practice of most unrelated international players. (Hint: See the General Motors chapter.) Could you guess where and when the first radio jingle aired, and what very familiar product now on retail shelves it espoused? This event, by the way, occurred before the manufacturer — Washburn Crosby Company — renamed itself in 1928.

Candidly, there were many bits of unforeseen trivia tucked into the annals of the prominent advertisers of network radio during its golden age. This volume attempts to fill a niche that has, until now, been substantively disregarded by radio historiographers of my acquaintance. Nonetheless, in American radio, had it not been for advertising, a component of the majority of ethereal series, we would have been denied access to most of those superlative features during the halcyon days of network radio. Paid advertising was the means by which broadcasting paid its bills in order to provide free access to a cornucopia of seemingly unending treats dialed by far-flung audiences of millions of listeners.

There were, to be sure, other methods of underwriting a coast-to-coast radio service. For several years, they were hotly and vociferously debated by pioneer broadcasters and Washington officials. Among them, submitting to the government subscription of the airwaves, thereby relinquishing control over programming content (the predominant European style). Another technique incorporated phasing in some type of payment system for services rendered, charging listeners for the privilege of tuning in. (Several schemes were proposed.) Still another, which was attempted for a while, was an indirect approach, a semi-advertising model in which a sponsor's name or slogan was applied to a program title, an orchestra, or an entertainer performing on its series. In this half-hearted approach that usually denied advertisers further remarks promoting their goods and services, the sponsors really weren't gaining a whole lot for their advertising dollars. Sponsorship was sure to diminish after the novelty dissipated. Each of these modes and others had drawbacks. Although it took a few years after radio's launch before the airwaves were turned into a commercial zone, the outcome seemed superior to whatever alternatives had been devised.

In this volume, my attempt is to finally give radio advertising its due: to recognize its contribution and acknowledge those who provided it, to reveal the logistics of on air product promotion, and a variety of sample commercials from long ago. I have deliberately concentrated on a timeline extending from the mid–1920s to the early 1960s, a period dubbed by informed scholars as radio's golden age. In that epoch, four major chains delivered their programming to waiting ears. For the first time, all of the nation's citizens could be concurrently educated, entertained and exhorted in a cost-effective manner.

To clarify, before proceeding further, *advertising* is *any openly sponsored offering of goods, services or ideas through any medium of public communication.* For centuries, the human voice was the principal means of hawking commodities for barter or sale. That changed in the mid-fifteenth century with the emergence of the printing press. A defining breakthrough, it's cited by media historians as a promotional intersect from which the modern age of advertising descended. For a while, the drumbeats of the human voice were overshadowed by messages appealing almost exclusively to the eye. During that era, the tools available to the modern advertiser progressed from crude handbills, signs and posters to circulars, newspapers, magazines, billboards, transit signage, direct mail, film, business publications, and so forth.

The ingenuity of human discovery and invention had to coalesce before audible communications reappeared, making a spectacular comeback through the airwaves of radio.

When did the first radio commercial air? Conventional wisdom, backed by an array of authoritative sources, and a preponderance of vintage radio hobbyists, proposes that the first advertisement aired on WEAF in New York in 1992, when the station broadcast something closely akin to an infomercial late in the summer. The long-held belief is challenged by my findings, however, which support earlier sales messages transported across the ether by more than one entrepreneurial vendor. Stay tuned for details (in Chapter 2).

This book is subdivided into multiple slices. There are two principal parts: Part I delves into the commercialization of American network radio, including radio advertising's place in history and how it became successful. Part II explores 24 major players in the corporate world that underwrote the radio fare of the era.

In preparing Part II, I scoured a variety of reliable sources to determine the organizations that were most active in proffering their products, services and ideas on the national airwaves in the period under study. Based on time purchased (including series and number of seasons aired), a dozen led the list. In descending order, they are:

1. Procter & Gamble
2. General Foods Corporation
3. Sterling Drug, Inc.
4. General Mills, Inc.
5. American Home Products
6. Colgate-Palmolive-Peet Company
7. Lever Brothers Company
8. Miles Laboratories, Inc.
9. R. J. Reynolds Tobacco Company
10. Standard Brands, Inc.
11. Quaker Oats Company
12. American Tobacco Company.

That 12 — plus another dozen — comprise Part II, where the leading corporate players in American radio advertising the most active underwriters of national chain broadcasting from the mid–1920s to the early 1960s are spotlighted. I knew from the start that some of those 24 are operating today under a different moniker from when they were active in network radio. While eight are still working independently under their same — or only slightly revised — appellations, eight others are identified by significantly altered monikers. One, Quaker Oats Company, employs its old nomenclature but persists as a subsidiary of another corporate giant. Yet another, Andrew Jergens Company, also an acquisition, is still operating but under a parent firm's appellation, having lost its self-identification.

The six remaining organizations that expansively patronized radio can no longer be found in business anywhere save for the remnants of product lines still being manufactured and distributed by the surviving heirs of their properties. These leviathans of yesterday, once familiar in the domiciles of millions of American denizens, are now themselves history. In the evolving extension of domestic and international commerce, their corporate identities have been silenced. They include the American Tobacco Company, Brown & Williamson Tobacco Company, General Foods Corporation, P. Lorillard, Inc., Miles Laboratories, Inc., and Standard Brands, Inc.

The book ends with a trio of appendices. The first documents 100 key additional advertisers in golden age radio; the second introduces some of the devices, techniques and systems that uniquely impacted radio commercials; and the third is a lexicon of advertising and broadcasting terminology.

While researching this text, it was also intriguing to stumble upon numerous entertainers who worked for a paycheck without any presumptive regard for organizational loyalty. The same supposition may be made of the firms that hired them. An artist or a program went on for one sponsor and returned in a subsequent season for a competitor. Benny Goodman's big band appeared for Camel cigarettes (R. J. Reynolds) for three seasons and then played for Old Gold (P. Lorillard) after a brief time-out. Dinah Shore sang for Ford in 1946 to 1947 and from 1953 to 1955 she trilled for Chevrolet (General Motors). Showman Eddie Cantor hawked Camel and Philip Morris cigarettes (Reynolds, Philip Morris) over his lengthy air span. One Friday afternoon in 1946, the daytime serial *Big Sister*, which — for a decade — proffered Rinso detergent and Lifebuoy soap (Lever Brothers), signed off the air only to return the following Monday for an archrival sponsor. For the next six years, *Big Sister* plugged Ivory soap and Dreft detergent (Procter & Gamble). Was there no shame in Radioland? Obviously there wasn't when the bottom line was affected — either for the sponsor or for the performer.

The neophyte in old time radio who picks up this book will find it helpful to know that the National Broadcasting Company operated dual networks between early 1927 and 1943. They were referred to as the Red and Blue chains (based on the hues of lines drawn on a national map showing their affiliate connections). Between 1943 and 1945, the second of those chains was spun off, thanks to a directive by the Federal Communications Commission which cited the NBC empire as a broadcast monopoly. That web was known in that era as the Blue network, often without any alphabetical connotation. It became the American Broadcasting Company (ABC) in 1945. In the meantime, NBC Red persisted simply as NBC; the Columbia Broadcasting System (CBS) had been operating since 1927; and the Mutual Broadcasting System (MBS) was launched in 1934. The four units comprise the network radio chains tracked in this volume.

John Wanamaker, proprietor of retail emporiums dating from 1876 in Philadelphia, who substantially invested in newspaper space and added sales promotional formats available to him, confessed: "Half the money I spend on advertising is wasted; the trouble is, I don't know which half." In most of the successful commercial ventures you'll encounter in these pages, you'll meet entrepreneurial types like Wanamaker who — in a sense — threw caution to the wind, pouring money profusely into marketing their goods and services. When radio came along, many of the most triumphant didn't hold back there either, committing vast sums of revenues into putting the people and shows on the air that America loved best. When those salesmen did so prudently, the return on their investment was well worth the expenditure. This is their story about a message, a medium and how the two united to entertain a nation with open purse strings.

PART I

THE COMMERCIALIZATION OF AMERICAN NETWORK RADIO

1

Ancestors of Radio Advertising

Thunder's rumble and the whistling wind, a waterfall's roar and a trickling stream formed earth's original motivational force, alleges a marketing pacesetter. Nature is ascribed with providing a helpful warning system to all living creatures while simultaneously exhibiting an intoxicating majesty of terrestrial wonders. The very sounds of the native environment can be properly dubbed "the first advertiser," asserts Charles Wolfe.[1] That din foretold both man and beast of uncertainties and grandeur on their horizon.

Man's own initial attempts to employ resonance in persuading a mass audience were less imposing but nonetheless effective, Wolfe maintains. A jungle savage signaling distant tribesmen with the reverberations of his tom-tom may have provoked a response. Yet it took an enterprising merchant to actually *trade* commodities, moving beyond the concept of purely transmitting signs, gestures, communications and ideas. During the ancient Babylonian epoch, that marketing capitalist hired stentorian-voiced hawkers to shout at people passing by his shop, enumerating his wares inside. In pursuing that quest — for possibly the very first time in all of history — the human voice became an instrument of direct sales. What a novel inspiration!

Was this to be the start of something grand?

The town crier was the successor catalyst to surface in advertising's progressive lineage. Initially appearing in Egypt before the settlers occupying the banks of the Nile River, couriers proclaimed the arrival of ships laden with spices, wines and precious metals. In the centuries beyond, amid the ruins of Pompeii, archaeologists discovered wall posters and sales letters. Those same ancient Egyptians had crudely scrawled them on papyrus leaves. The abundant papyrus plant, incidentally, native to the Nile valley, supplied an early and reliable form of cellulose paper that was consequently to be adapted to scrolls. Collectively, the Egyptians are thought to have been mankind's earliest professional marketers, making valuable use of both spoken and written language.

As the Greeks supplanted the Egyptians and became the world's next dominant civilization, they too relied on papyrus as a principal method of propagation. In fact, both the Greeks and *their* successors — the Romans — turned to papyrus to advertise lost-and-found items, scientific anthropologists discovered. But similar to the Egyptians before them, they were multidimensional entrepreneurs, while exhibiting a flair for creativity: those Grecian purists procured Demosthenes-skilled orators to make the rounds of inhabited communities, audibly publicizing their slave and animal auctions.

Following the spread of literacy in ancient Rome, however, oral advertising was subdued for a while, outdistanced by penmanship almost altogether. During this period, promotion scribbled or painted on walls, signs, rocks and doors made the spoken word seem just a tad archaic. Commercial advertising via rock and wall painting caught on elsewhere, too: the practice of wall painting can be tracked to Indian rock-art around 4000 B.C., for instance, while examples of the ancient marketing form still broadly exist in Africa, Asia and South America.

But after the Romans declined and the Dark Ages approached, advertisers went on a recycling binge: they revived the all-but-abandoned Babylonian custom of the shouting hawker. The practice became the marketing campaign ritual in England, in fact, as well as throughout southern Europe. The hawker's limited geographical territory was expanded as the Middle Ages neared. Once again the attention-seeking town crier came into vogue, roaming entire hamlets with notices favoring area merchants, tavern-keepers and auctioneers. The heritage left by the earliest PR men had, by then, come full circle.

As a case in point, during the thirteenth century in Paris, some 400 criers fanned out over the city at one time spreading their wide-ranging appeals. A vivid description of a typical crier's functions on behalf of a pub owner at the pinnacle of commercial crying was documented like this[2]:

> Having singled out the audience he wanted to reach, the crier first attracted attention by tooting his horn, playing an instrument, or ringing a bell. To build interest and a responsive attitude he shouted the latest news. His audience properly warmed up, the crier delivered his sales message and capped it off by passing out free samples of his sponsor's product from a bucket of wine.

Those communal hawkers, however, were ill-equipped to deal with the rapidly advancing development of industry and technology going on in the same era. Their jobs withered completely in time, a result of the emergence of the printing press in the mid-fifteenth century. That resulted in advances in reading skills and literacy, which became commonplace a couple of centuries hence. Handbills, posters and newspapers were the tangible culprits. In a vicious tinge of unmistakable irony, a dirty trick had been played on the messengers who relied wholly on their vocal cords for livelihoods: an apparatus for multiplying the written word appeared almost 500 years before the discovery of one that could reproduce the spoken word to mass audiences over still greater distances simultaneously.

After shouting themselves hoarse on behalf of Babylonian traders during the interlude from ancient times to the conclusion of the Middle Ages — a period embracing Egyptian shipping magnates, Roman entrepreneurs, Greek slaveholders, English merchants and French tavern-keepers — the town criers were banished as if they were people of ill repute. As prey to an insipid conspiracy that wasn't of their own making, they lost out to a succession of printing innovations that simply overwhelmed their centuries-honed skills. Until a succession of electrical discoveries resulted in contraptions with the ability to transmit the human voice over widespread territory, they were absolutely dispensable. Not until then, in *their finest hour*, would spokesmen have another turn at cracking the advertising arena. They would do so magnificently, of course, surpassing every other media form they competed with to accomplish their commercial mission. But the time was not yet, and the ink didn't dry for a very lengthy interval between.

The hand-cranked printing press with its movable type arrived about 1450.[3] It was a method that — with refinement and increased mechanization — was adopted as the principal means of copy reproduction, certainly so until late in the twentieth century. Invented by German goldsmith and businessman Johannes Gutenberg (ca. 1397–1468), no other device in the history of humankind has so thoroughly imbued earth's population, according to certain well-informed scholars. The printing press redeveloped communication into a more feasible, sophisticated and modern course.

The new technique generated profound implications for advertising, making possible mass distribution of posters and circulars for the very first time, for example. A handbill announcing a prayer book for sale in 1472 ostensibly was the first advertisement in English. Conversely and somewhat surprisingly, it would take newspapers — which were coming soon — another two centuries before latching onto the scheme of paid advertising. The first ad, by the way, purportedly offered a reward for the return of a dozen stolen horses.

By 1502, Germany could boast of publishing *Zeitung*, the continent's foundational newspaper and possibly the prototype of the genus to be issued anywhere.[4] *Trewe Encountre* is alleged to be the first English language news sheet, arriving in 1513. Not until 1609 was there a regularly published newsjournal in Europe, however; that was Germany's *Avisa Relation oder Zeitung*. And newspapers didn't surface in North America until 1690 when a Boston publisher circulated *Publick Occurrences Both Foreign and Domestick*.

Shortly thereafter the *Boston News-Letter* became the first recurring newsjournal in print in the American colonies, carrying ads by 1704. Early print ads during that period were especially helpful in promoting books, newspapers and patent medicines. The latter quantity was of increasing magnitude to those inhabitants residing in specific territories of disease-ravaged Europe. By 1729, Benjamin Franklin was making newspaper advertising more readable and thereby more appealing. He instituted larger-than-usual typefaces that traditional newsprint style had not previously borne.

In the American colonial period, meanwhile — those developments in the printing press notwithstanding — for the most part advertisements were still limited to signboards on inns, taverns, coffee houses and the like. Travelers needed information about inns but local denizens didn't require advertisements in order to locate the blacksmith's stall.

Following Gutenberg's momentous contribution, some three and a half centuries elapsed before another stunning upgrade in presses appeared on the scene. Although it didn't eclipse Gutenberg's breakthrough, it expanded the field into diversified contrivances. Lithography or litho printing was invented by Alois Senefelder (1771–1834) and patented in Germany in 1799 as chemical or stone copying. A native Czech, Senefelder developed and later refined a reverse-imaging process that vastly enhanced writing and art quality reproduction. With its inception, the illustrated poster became a reality. Lithography initially required limestone and correction fluid as its foundation, a technique Senefelder ultimately perfected. All of it was to have substantial impact on advertising in the centuries ahead. Germany, England, Austria, France and other European nations acquired lithographic presses before the first one appeared in the United States in 1819.

Such developments were symptomatic of a tidal wave of changes that were introduced by the Industrial Revolution in the decades falling more or less between 1760 and 1840. Most of those improvements began in the British Isles, thanks to advanced technology, state support and interlocking trading agreements. But they soon swept across Western Europe and North America and — in the first half of the nineteenth century — to Russia, Japan and other countries around the earth.

Technological, socioeconomic and cultural shifts occurred. Economies were almost exclusively dependent on manual labor for any advancement heretofore. That reliance in many systems, however, was replaced by power-driven machinery that significantly intensified commerce. The development was launched by mechanizing textile production and by deriving iron-making skills that wholly multiplied the ability to manufacture machinery. Trade expansion followed through the introduction of improved waterways, roads and railroads. Steam power and sophisticated equipment were responsible for spectacular growth in production capability.

In the middle of the nineteenth century, a Second Industrial Revolution commenced. Diffusion of steam power in the 1850s paved the way for a wave of industrial change in the 1870s and 1880s. Technological and economic progress gained phenomenal impetus with the development of steam-powered ships and the steam engine iron horse for extensive rail transport. The transcontinental railroad allowed relatively low-cost shipment of goods, making regional or national markets economically feasible. The internal combustion engine was invented. Electrical power could be generated and harnessed in incredible volume. By 1890, the American system of mass production characterized much of the national manufacturing scene.

The Second Industrial Revolution was marked, in fact, by a shift of technological leadership from Great Britain to the United States and Germany. U.S. Steel Corporation, General Electric Company and Bayer AG became behemoth industrial organizations with an enveloping global presence quite early. Amplified mechanization generated increased fixed costs. This provided an economic incentive to build bigger factories that could enjoy economies of scale in manufacture, yet were dependent on mass demand. Telegraph wires allowed low-cost and fast nationwide transmission of information.

The automotive industry was born, arriving on the heels of a surging escalation in chemicals production and petroleum refining and distribution. As America entered the twentieth century, Henry Ford, who would eventually be proclaimed the "father of the assembly line," declared a worthy ambition: "There is but one rule for the industrialist — to make the highest quality goods at the lowest cost and pay the highest wages possible."

These innovative modifications had all-encompassing effects on consumer goods and retail merchandising. Until late in the nineteenth century, only a few firms had been mass-producing branded consumer commodities, for instance. Patent medicine was the foremost exception. But by the 1880s — as a result of pioneering production know-how — standardized manufacturing of soap, canned food, cigarettes and other commodities targeted toward single buyers and their households started appearing in voluminous quantity. Purchasers became familiar with monikers identifying specific products. A housewife accustomed in the past to ordering a pound of generic baking powder began to rely only upon Royal baking powder, for example, for assurance in value and superiority. In the 1880s and early 1890s, similar national ad campaigns resulted, touting Babbitt's best soap, Corticelli Best Twist silk thread, Quaker Oats cereal and Procter & Gamble's Ivory bar, the latter by 1895 "99 and 44/100ths percent pure."

For the first time, consumers could link availability, dependability and respectability with explicit names. Brands increased the reputation and value of individual manufacturers: readily recognized nomenclature often translated into quality and safety in the buyer's mind, resulting in loyalty to particular trade names and suppliers, in many cases for the first time. As a result of these improvements, American consumers were exposed to an environment that had been heretofore unknown to most of those purchasers.

At the same time, retailers were relying on advertising to reach customers for the wares and services that the newer technology was delivering to their sales floors. At first, classified ads proliferated in newspapers. They were superseded by small and then larger space ads. Illustrious American dry goods emporiums appeared, appealing to their markets through newspapers, handbills, signage and other ink-based channels. Among an array of enduring general mercantile stores launched in the last half of the nineteenth century — together with their year of founding and original location — were:

> Macy's, 1858, New York City
> Marshall Field's, 1865, Chicago
> Rich's, 1867, Atlanta
> Bloomingdales, 1872, New York City
> Wanamaker's, 1876, Philadelphia
> Woolworth's, 1879, Lancaster, Pennsylvania
> Hudson's, 1881, Detroit
> Gimbels, 1887, Milwaukee
> Belk's, 1888, Charlotte
> Burdine's, 1898, Miami
> Foley's, 1900, Houston

Mail order establishments distributed vast numbers of catalogs to the hinterlands offering an endless assortment of goods that could be delivered directly to a patron's front door. Setting the pace were Montgomery Ward (1872) and Sears, Roebuck (1886), both to be headquartered in due course in Chicago. In the meantime, by one account, the nation's ad sales volume in the two score decades between 1880 and 1920 swelled from $200 million to $3 billion annually, an incredibley profuse escalation.

The industrial changes prompted awareness that — with so many favorable conditions netting new, cheaper and better goods produced quickly and in mammoth volume — persuasive techniques were needed to attract consumers to obtain those wares. A timeline[5] follows, highlighting some of the major innovations in American marketing techniques during the 85 years between 1835 and 1920.

In 1835, Jared Bell, a New York City printer, produced the first American outdoor poster exceeding 50 square feet. The large sign announced upcoming local circus performances. American roadside advertising, at its start, consisted of painted signs or glued posters on walls and fences. These were used to notify passersby that specific retailers to be encountered up the road had rheumatism pills, horse blankets and innumerable supplementary commodities for sale.

In 1837, *The New York Sun*, selling at a penny per copy since 1833, was — unofficially — the planet's biggest newspaper with a circulation of 30,000.

In 1843, Volney B. Palmer (1799–1864) opened the first American advertising agency in Philadelphia.[6]

In 1850, showman Phineas T. Barnum (1810–1891), a principal in the Ringling Brothers and Barnum and Bailey Circus, engaged singer Jenny Lind to perform in the United States. While her name was ambiguous to most Americans, Lind was widely acclaimed across Europe as a celebrated concert vocalist. For six months, Barnum (labeled by modern critics a "huckster" and "shameless promoter") plugged her appearances through newspaper ads, handbills and broadsides (large posters). On her arrival, 30,000 cheering New Yorkers met her at the boat docks, the culmination of Barnum's intensive sales campaign.

In 1850, exterior advertising was applied to streetcars for the first time, establishing a promotional venue (transit advertising) that was to persist to the modern age.

In 1851, the *New-York Daily Times*, forerunner of *The New York Times*, began publishing.

In the 1860s, advertising appeared in nationally distributed monthly magazines for the first time.

In 1864, the origins of the J. Walter Thompson Company, successive nomenclature of the oldest U.S. advertising agency in continuous service today, took root as William James Carlton started selling newspaper space ads. His business was soon renamed Carlton & Smith and, by 1867, he placed ads in religious publications. James Walter Thompson (1847 to 1928) was hired by Carlton in 1868 to keep books. Nevertheless, Thompson ultimately became a dynamic salesman, finding sales much more challenging and lucrative than accounting. In 1877, he bought out Carlton and his virtually silent partner Smith for $500 and paid them $800 for office furnishings. Thereupon, the agency was renamed the J. Walter Thompson Company. Thompson hired copywriters and artists, forming the first such creative unit, and was eventually cited as "the father of modern magazine advertising."

In 1868, Peck and Snyder, a New York sporting goods store, produced what was considered the first baseball trading cards. Bearing a well-known player's image on one side, the firm's athletic equipment was proffered on the opposite facing. It was a natural tie-in and spawned a glut of copiers who applied the concept to their own sundry merchandising interests. One of the most successful of the breed occurred in 1948 when Topps Gum Company packaged bubble gum with cards sought by traders and collectors. In the meantime, lithographer-printer Louis Prang accelerated the trade card explosion by mass-producing the inexpensive, modest-sized sales forms throughout the 1870s. The public was so struck by their novelty that the cards became objects of numerous collections, whether they featured baseball or other poignant passions.

In 1868, N. W. Ayer & Son opened in Philadelphia, the first full-service advertising agency to assume responsibility for ad content, and the first to charge a commission for its services, setting a precedent for most of its followers. Among Ayer's clients were Montgomery Ward, Pond's, Singer and Wanamaker's.

In 1869, the *People's Literary Companion* debuted, published by E. C. Allan of Augusta, Maine. It denoted the advent of the mail-order periodical.

In 1869, Boston advertising agency operator George P. Rowell launched annual publication of *The American Newspaper Directory* containing the first meaningful circulation figures for 5,000 journals in the U.S. and Canada. It became an indispensable tool to advertisers gauging the size of exposure for their newspaper space purchases.

In the 1870s, a few states banned advertising painting that was turning undisturbed scenic wonders into a proliferation of outdoor billboards via posters and signs inscribed on rocks, barns and assorted structures. Such actions fashioned an early antecedent of the Highway Beautification Act that Congress passed in 1965. That legislation was an attempt to remove unsightly advertising signage cluttering many of the nation's thoroughfares.

In 1870, the number of U.S. newspapers had increased by 612 percent in just 40 years, from 715 published in 1830 to 5,091 in 1870.

In 1871, Michigan established the first state bill posters' society, followed by Indiana, New York, Minnesota, Ohio and Wisconsin before a likeminded corps serving the nation and Canada was formed in 1891.

In 1871, the U.S. Patent Office had on file 121 registered brand names and trademarks; within four years, the number increased to 1,138 as manufacturers, retailers and the buying public became more discriminating and savvy in their purchasing habits.

In 1872, the Montgomery Ward Company, defunct today — a major retailer of consumer dry goods for personal and household use — issued its first mail order catalog. Within three decades, the initial sheet bearing 50 items increased to a 500-page book.

In 1873, American advertising agents across the nation convened in New York City for their first communal conference.

In 1876, the telephone was patented by Alexander Graham Bell. It became a device that was to have titanic implications in the years ahead for direct marketing to buyers of everything.

In 1877, selling for three cents a copy, *The Washington Post* premiered with an early readership of 10,000.

In 1882, with a commitment of $11,000, personal care and household wares manufacturer Procter & Gamble Company launched an unprecedented advertising campaign for its paramount Ivory soap. The formula for the floating solvent was discovered by chance by P&G in 1875 and dubbed Ivory in 1879.

In 1883, a couple of imposing periodicals with heavy advertising commitments published their inaugural issues — *Ladies' Home Journal* and *Life* magazines. Both relied upon advertising profoundly to underwrite much of their subscription soliciting, editorial, production and mailing expenses.

In 1884, the use of color in print was radically enhanced with the invention of the linotype machine.

In 1885, the number of subscription-based periodicals flourished as newly introduced postal rates trimmed the tariff for second-class mail to one cent per pound.

In 1886, an Atlanta druggist, Dr. John S. Pemberton, concocted the formula that became the world's best-known marketed beverage, Coca-Cola. Frank Robinson, Pemberton's bookkeeper, designed the flowing script identity familiar to more of earth's inhabitants than any other brand, instantly tagging the soft drink in ads, merchandising and the product itself. Coke was well on its way to universal acclaim in 1901, budgeting $100,000 for advertising that year.

In 1886, retail merchandiser Sears, Roebuck & Company originated in a small watch-selling business at North Redwood, Minnesota. In two years it was to launch mail-order commerce that was destined to set the standard for that segment of the retail promotion trade.

In 1887, the American Newspaper Publishers Association organized.

In 1888, George P. Rowell debuted what ultimately was recognized as not only the first but also the largest and most influential trade periodical for advertisers, copywriters and agencies — *Printer's Ink*.[7] Professionals were to affectionately know it as "the little schoolmaster in the art of advertising."

In the 1890s, advertising industry trade publications routinely proffered postal cards as an effective means of communicating with consumers at low cost.

In 1890, J. Walter Thompson became the first ad agency to bill $1 million annually.

In 1891, the International Bill Posters' Association of North America was formed in Chicago and later renamed the Poster Advertising Association. It merged with the Painted Outdoor Advertising Association in 1925, combining posters and bulletins to establish the Outdoor Advertising Association of America, still in service today. Those original bill-posters purposed to create awareness for posters as an ad medium, coordinate membership services and address ethical concerns of their trade.

In 1892, an innovative Sears, Roebuck & Company earned a phenomenal 25 percent mail response after sending 8,000 postal cards bearing a simulated handwritten sales message; the campaign netted 2,000 merchandise orders. Sears' mail order catalog, introduced a year later, was commonly branded America's "Wish Book" and the "Farmer's Bible."

In 1893, Joseph Pulitzer (1847 to 1911) purchased a four-color press to feature renderings of celebrated works of art in *The New York World* that he owned. Competitors duplicated Pulitzer's actions, as color illustrations, supplements and advertisements became an integral part of newsjournals. Printed color cartoons (consequently "the funnies") were ushered in via Pulitzer's paper in 1895.

In 1894 — focusing largely on the middle-Atlantic states — the nation's oldest continuous outdoor advertising firm opened for business: R. C. Maxwell Company. With the mass production of automobiles and an upgraded road system developing early in the next century, the value of billboards soon gained escalating visibility as permanent promotion venues.

In 1899, J. Walter Thompson opened an office in the United Kingdom, the first U.S. agency to jump the Atlantic with its business practice.

In 1900, a standardized billboard structure was adopted, ushering in a boom in national outdoor campaigns. Huge firms like Coca-Cola, Kellogg and Palmolive — for the first time confident that the same display would fit signage from Missoula to Miami — began mass-producing billboards for the national market.

In 1902, currently representing the oldest client relationship in advertising, European personal care and household commodities behemoth Unilever engaged J. Walter Thompson to push its Lifebuoy, Lux and other cleansing labels in America.

In 1903, only 12 minutes after he dispatched it around the globe, President Theodore Roosevelt (1858 to 1919, president from 1901 to 1909) received the message he sent signaling the inauguration of Pacific communications cables.

In 1908, to promote a Broadway theatrical production, airplane advertising was instituted as a permanent technique following its premier demonstration.

In 1908, the automobile age was ushered in to transport the masses as the Ford Motor Company displayed the Model T at a retail cost of $825. Ford introduced the moving assembly line in 1913 that rolled off a new Model T in three hours. By 1916, a half-million of that replica was being manufactured annually, selling for $360.

In the 1910s, mirroring the phenomenal growth in mass production, there was an unparalleled surge in retailing, too. To accelerate consumer buying, meanwhile, manufacturers and retailers invested millions of dollars in advertising and public relations.

In the 1910s, advertising was specifically pinpointed toward targeted buying groups after modern marketing research became developed.

In 1910, and over the next two decades, home appliances experienced diminishing costs as the nation's electric current was standardized.

In 1912, when the new electric billboard of *The New York Times* was unveiled, throngs swarmed Manhattan's Times Square to view World Series baseball scores.

In 1914, the Audit Bureau of Circulations was organized, unifying auditing measures and clarifying paid circulation.

In 1915, after the human voice was transmitted by radiotelephone from Arlington, Virginia, to the Eiffel Tower in Paris, the development of aural communications over long distances foreshadowed even greater things in the future, some visionaries proclaimed.

In 1917, the American Association of Advertising Agencies was formally launched with 111 charter-member outfits. The assemblage was to manifest extensive implications on its profession.

In 1917, Homer J. Buckley (1881 to 1953), founder of a Chicago letter-shop — a pioneer in using statement stuffers, also credited with coining the term "direct mail" — was elected first president of the Direct Mail Advertising Association (Direct Marketing Association since

1983). For the U.S. Tuberculosis Institute, Buckley was instrumental in pushing Christmas Seals (originating in Denmark in 1903) as a pervasive, enduring direct-response fund-raising mode.

In 1918, home delivery began for *The New York Times*, reaching a new pinnacle in availability and frequency for print advertising.

That brings the timeline under study to a conclusion.

Full-fledged advertising agencies proliferated in this era, meanwhile, particularly between 1890 and 1914. As a result, large-scale promotional campaigns were commonplace, linking newspaper and magazine advertisements with outdoor poster ads, handbills and shop-front exhibitions. Mass production netted mass consumption and a requisite for mass persuasion.

Lest their contributions be overlooked in the explosion of advancing technology and industrial achievements, in the meantime, those commercial criers of an earlier age can be referenced as a hardy species. In the twentieth century's teens and twenties, in fact, legions of independent criers surfaced, fanning out across America to push all manner of merchandise — including dry goods, hats, boots, clocks, firearms, furniture and patent medicines.

The patent medicine man often arrived in a village on a birch wagon drawn by a couple of sorrel horses. A Negro banjo-player might emerge from the covered wagon to strum while a second Negro danced and sang. After a crowd gathered, the salesman-showman commenced to sell bottles of a supernatural "surefire" fluid formula that could restore the blush of health to every cheek, or tender some other outrageous consequence.

"Few realize what strong precedents these hawkers had set," confirmed one wag. "The methods of the medicine man were the only known approaches to oral advertising." While these lively and often deceptive exhibitions were pulling in crowds at county fairs, meanwhile, in an isolated electronics lab, Dr. Lee de Forest (1873 to 1961) was perfecting the original designs of Nikola Telsa (1856 to 1943), Guglielmo Marconi (1874 to 1937) and others leading to broadcasting as we know it.

Some erudite academicians advocate that a German physics professor, Heinrich Hertz (1857–1894), conducted the first radio transmission in 1886. At the time, Hertz was attempting to prove some light and electrical wave theories of Scottish physicist James Clerk Maxwell (1831–1879). Yet, depending on one's definition of radio, Nathan B. Stubblefield (1860 to 1928), a Murray, Kentucky, melon farmer, educator and scientific wizard, seems a more worthy candidate. He may have achieved stature as the precursor of the field. In some rudimentary experiments, while applying an induction coil spreader he developed in 1885, Stubblefield initially transmitted the sound of a human voice without benefit of connecting cable.[8] Seven years beyond his exploits, in 1892 he broadcast the human voice by applying a wireless telephone linked to a land aerial, a more widely celebrated feat.

Although Stubblefield didn't patent his advancements in wireless telephony until 1908, he publicly demonstrated the experiments before some large crowds starting January 1, 1902, and for several months thereafter, using multiple receivers spaced as distant as a half-mile away. "While Marconi could barely send telegraphic 'dots and dash' signals with great difficulty through a static-filled medium," decreed one source, "Nathan Stubblefield had already transmitted the human voice with loud, velvet clarity."

His span was eclipsed on December 24, 1906, nonetheless, when Reginald Aubrey Fessenden (1866 to 1932) applied wireless telephony to transmit the human voice from Brant Rock, Massachusetts, to ships at sea hundreds of miles away.[9] Several of these fêted inventors, by the way — cited recently on an assortment of contemporary Web sites — have been dubbed "the father of radio" or "the father of broadcasting" by their modern exponents. There may be enough wealth there to encompass more than one for all of them indubitably seemed to be no less than joint patriarchs of the electronic age.

In the meantime, Marconi invented a wireless telegraph in 1897, initially incapable of transmitting beyond the Morse code.[10] Two years hence, nonetheless, his newly devised gizmo was instrumental in saving lives: it summoned help to a craft sinking off the coast of the British Isles, proving its practicality while doing so. Subsequently, in 1906, as both Stubblefield and Fessenden were continuing to make history by broadcasting the human voice, de Forest helped the process along by inserting a grid into a vacuum tube and then applying voltage to the grid. The American Telephone and Telegraph Company adopted his invention, called an audion, in 1913 to boost voice signals crisscrossing the continental United States. An audion was consequently adapted to radio set technology.

A wireless operator on board the SS *Avon* sailing on the Atlantic Ocean was totally dumbfounded when he plainly distinguished music pouring out of his headset on December 13, 1910. Sound on the airwaves was still in its infancy, of course, and hadn't become a novelty thus far; rather, such din was startling to the few who heard it. On that occasion, the seafarer was listening to the product of the pioneering Lee de Forest, who had placed microphones on the stage of the Metropolitan Opera House for the first time in that venue's illustrious history. Ricardo Martin, Enrico Caruso and Emmy Destinn were performing the operas *Cavalleria Rusticana* and *Pagliacci* on the premier ethereal exhibition. For the next decade, hobbyists would be duplicating such acts often as they played with their electrical toys in a quest to reach farther and farther while taking primitive steps in sound transmission.

On January 13, 1906, an educational magazine, *Scientific American*, published an advertisement on behalf of New York entrepreneur Hugo Gernsbeck, the commonly revered "father of science fiction." (Everybody, it seemed, was the father of *something*!) The print ad exhibited radio receivers selling at Gernsbeck's Electro Importing Company. At the low price of $7.50, they came with a "guaranteed reception" of about one mile. The future was evident to anybody observing very closely: a new wave of mass communications was rapidly gaining ground, and was just about to leap onto a stratospheric stage.

Advertising, a major beneficiary of all of this advancing technology, was to find itself playing in an altogether new-fangled arena relatively soon.

2

Commercializing the Ether

America was a land of changing landscapes as it entered the third decade of the twentieth century. Up until the 1920 census the nation had been predominantly rural. That watershed foreshadowed some hefty shifts. A postwar industrial explosion pointed the country in new directions, turning the economy from its weighty dependency upon agriculture to pervasive lifestyle changes influenced by education, electrification and manufacturing. For the first time, more than a million students practically doubled enrollment in schools of higher education. Sports, vaudeville, recreation and amusement parks, movies, circuses and other spare-time distractions vied for the discretionary hours of the populace.

Americans also found themselves in a buying frame of mind as the 1920s arrived. Commodities came on the market that made life simpler, more enjoyable, and required less effort in performing menial, repetitious tasks, even making some obsolete. Many people earning steady incomes were anxious to grab the brass ring. With newly available credit, they could afford to purchase goods that weren't available earlier or that previously were out of their reach.

At the turn of the century, manufacturers had primarily relied upon local distribution to accomplish the bulk of their trading. Newer production methods and automation improved America's ability to create more and better wares and to do so faster. By the twenties, consumer spending—fueled partially by increased availability of individual credit—paced a by and large prosperous economy as middle class purchasers sought automobiles, radios, household appliances and channeled their funds into leisure-time activities. These were luxuries they had never had access to en masse. With some assurance, it was indeed a heady epoch.

In the meantime, industrial wizards sought novel means of convincing consumers to buy their *particular* goods. Advertising became indispensable in promoting the diverse array of products and services available to them. The rise of mass circulation magazines, radio and—to a smaller extent—motion pictures, offered some novel means of reaching consumers with persuasive missives. Moreover, during this period advertising began to stress the ability of goods to meet emotional needs and—more to the point—took pains to create needs where none previously had been perceived.

Mass advertising not only increased demand but it allowed firms to sell their staples in widely scattered locales at the same time. Innovation in marketing had arrived at an auspicious peak. From 1900 to 1920, advertising volume increased at an annual rate of nearly 9 percent. In 1914, the annual volume of U.S. advertising reached $682 million. It more than doubled within five years, topping $1,409,000,000 by 1919. It more than doubled again by 1929, realizing $2,987,000,000 in revenues.[1] Advertising had proven its validity as a viable, constructive commercial trade.

Journalist-educator-broadcaster William Ackerman promoted a hypothesis that reflected mankind's commonality across the ages: "Somewhere back through the centuries a man was struck for the first time by a great thought: that he would rather try to persuade another man by talking to him than by writing him a letter."[2] Ackerman's notion substantiates the very core of the ether's ubiquitous appeal. The power of the human voice, properly applied, can be insuperable in inspiring its hearers to act. That premise underscores one of radio's most compelling reasons to exist. In less than a decade, the American system of broadcasting secured "the salesman [as] the trustee of the public interest with minimal supervision by a commission," a pundit noted suitably. The motivational influence of the human voice prompted the masses to respond. It had an extraordinary and unstoppable effect.

The concept of radio's dependency upon advertising to pay its bills gradually evolved into general acceptance. That isn't to say that it didn't meet with mocking disdain in some quarters. Nor did Congress formally adopt a broadcasting scheme that embraced the financing method that evolved. Viable options for underwriting such a mammoth undertaking were limited, however. To sustain the level of programming that most Americans anticipated, in due course it became clear that advertising extended the greatest promise of the available choices. Advertising, time would reveal, proffered novel ways to charm buyers with mammoth inferences.

In late February 1922, a groundbreaking radio conference in Washington, D. C., attended by a myriad of interested parties, produced an absorbing exchange on the topic of advertising. On that occasion, the participants commonly took a dim view of "ether advertising." Secretary of Commerce Herbert Hoover, appointed to his post by President Warren G. Harding a year earlier, expressed an official sounding tenor, decrying: "It is inconceivable that we should allow so great a possibility for service to be drowned in advertising chatter." Obviously he wasn't feeling his Cheerios that day, possessing little intuition for what wasn't all that far around the bend.

Hoover may have thawed a smidgen from his earlier stance over the next couple of years. He subsequently admitted to himself and to others "the hardest nut in the bowl" to crack was the solution to "the problem of remuneration for broadcasting stations." On reflection, it appeared that the door to selective possibilities was at least slightly ajar.

Hoover certainly wasn't alone in his convictions; some others sounded similar alarms. In a 1923 issue of *Radio News*, a writer disparaged: "If radio fans have to listen to an advertiser exploit his wares, they will very properly resent it, even though the talk may be delivered under the guise of public interest." Another labeled commercialization of the medium "outrageous rubbish" while demanding: "The use of the radio for advertising is wholly undesirable and should be prohibited by legislation if necessary."[3] U.S. Rep. Sol Bloom (D-N. Y.) followed that rebuke in 1925, calling for a law banning radio's promulgation of advertising. Still more in positions of authority and accountability lent their voices to the protest.

An initiative of *indirect* advertising alleviated some of the concerns of Secretary Hoover and others for a while in regard to plugging goods and services on the ether. Although nebulous to a degree, indirect advertising allowed airing an underwriter's appellation without selling to the public more emphatically. That practice generated skeptics, too. Writing in *The New York Times* on September 13, 1925, journalist R. D. Heinl pondered: "What is the distinction between announcing an orchestra under the name of a well-known brand of tea or coffee and actually talking about the tea or coffee?" In spite of questions like his, by the time of the Fourth National Radio Conference, Secretary Hoover had mellowed even more. For the first time, he openly advocated indirect advertising, apparently without hesitation. He was now convinced that it could bolster smaller stations without unduly vexing their audiences, or engaging the federal government or negatively affecting the big enterprises supporting radio.

Following the establishment of the Federal Radio Commission (FRC) in 1927, the tide of opposition to radio advertising commenced to weaken: the FRC commonly took the position that the method was a requisite support. "Any plan ... to eliminate the use of radio facilities for commercial advertising purposes, will if adopted, destroy the present system of broadcasting," the FRC told Congress following a six-month inquiry into broadcasting in which advertising attained special attention. Announcing this, the June 15, 1932, issue of the trade periodical *Broadcasting* further noted: "Advertising agencies ... say that any law limiting advertising on the air to announcement of sponsorship would cause most advertisers to cease their use of radio."

Incidentally, among radio commercials' most militant foes, as might be anticipated, were a couple of media quarters that were introduced in the previous chapter — magazines and newspapers. Meeting in annual session in April 1933, for example, the American Newspaper Publishers Association resolved that radio logs were advertising and should be published only if paid for. The self-serving opposition of the print media was purportedly out of a fundamental concern for the listeners themselves: the audience, said they, had few alternatives but to hear the promotional messages with which they were routinely inundated. The print media's concern for the public's welfare was far too munificent, of course, and could be dismissed by any perceptive intellectual. Furthermore, sponsors themselves wouldn't take long to realize that the major benefit of radio advertising over ink was just that — the aural medium could deliver an infinite captive audience.

While a New York City outlet — which will be explored in depth momentarily — is usually hyped for providing the earliest paid radio commercial, there is evidence that such a momentous occurrence was preceded by yet other marketers on the ether. Some seven years before the sterling signature incident occurred that has been cited by an impressive number of academicians, amateur radio operator Arthur B. Church of Lamoni, Iowa, delivered what is apparently thus far substantiated as the airwaves' very first commercial.[4] Speaking in 1915 over his experimental station 9WU, Church appealed directly to other unlicensed but equally committed ham operators.

On that occasion, he unabashedly publicized the supplies and parts he carried for sale in his own inventory for the apparatus used in transmitting ham radio. One reporter acknowledged that Church was "flooded" with responses and inquiries. In fact, his phenomenal success led him to open a direct-mail commerce that ultimately morphed into a wholesale and retail operation. Not bad for a purely amateur broadcaster and perhaps not lost on others with similar bents and resources.

Four years hence, Westinghouse engineer Dr. Frank Conrad registered yet another advertising standard.[5] Before examining that milestone, however, let it be noted that Conrad initially operated an experimental station, 8XK, a detail that is awesome in the annals of evolving radio development. His early test model was converted into Pittsburgh's KDKA in 1920. Soon afterward it became the infamous originator of the widely heralded Harding-Cox election returns broadcast on the evening of November 2, 1920. That singular episode has allowed nearly all radio historiographers to dub KDKA as the country's "pioneer station" and thereby certify the election night affair as "the beginning of radio." Conrad and his colleagues are due considerable acclaim for their contributions during broadcast radio's embryonic epoch, despite the fact that there were rivals who fancied themselves equal or superior to those Westinghouse conquests.[6]

More than a year before the momentous Harding-Cox event, on October 17, 1919, Conrad set yet another precedent — this one in advertising — which shouldn't be missed. While operating KDKA's forerunner station, 8XK, Conrad offered recorded music selections (thereby presumably becoming the world's first disc jockey) by placing a microphone before his gramophone. The attempt won considerable notoriety; mail responses indicated omnipresent reception and many called for specific records to be aired.

Unable to cope with his newfound escalating challenge, Conrad demurred. Instead of answering definite musical requests, he decided to "broadcast" (his designation) the records he had on hand for a couple of hours every Wednesday and Saturday night. After awhile he exhausted his supply of recordings. But the proprietor of Wilkinsburg's Hamilton Music Store, who was listening, agreed to furnish fresh vinyl discs to him if Conrad would announce that they were available for purchase from the retailer. What did he have to lose? In following suit, the engineer-showman instituted what is thought to be the first sponsor-broadcaster relationship. And so effective was his arrangement with the music seller, incidentally, that the records he spun became the merchandiser's top sellers. It was truly an early confirmation of radio's innate powers of persuasion to anybody who might be paying close attention.

Beyond all of this, there was still more unpaid self-promotion that occurred at least once on a non-experimental station before purchased radio time came into vogue. A short while prior to Christmas 1921, impresario Vincent Lopez engaged in some self-serving advertising over New York's station WJZ. Appealing to listeners from the Grill Room of the Hotel Pennsylvania, the maestro urged his unseen audience to call for reservations and "come on down" (an idiom that was to gain some traction on TV decades hence) to witness his band performing at that venue in person. "The flood of incoming telephone calls knocked out one of midtown Manhattan's major telephone exchanges," a reporter affirmed.[7] In the very first attempt at a remote band pickup, it was increasingly apparent that radio had the command to motivate many fans to do its bidding.

In this period, meanwhile, New York City generally became widely recognized as the center of the nation's major early broadcasting achievements. Two reasons can be highlighted for the development. The metropolitan complex unmistakably possessed the largest single pool of talent on the globe. And equally impressive is the fact that local station WEAF, owned by the American Telephone and Telegraph Company (AT&T) — in a seemingly unparalleled quest for broadcasting excellence — secured a stable, visionary managerial force to run its operation. AT&T established WBNY as a local outlet in 1921 and soon relocated it from atop a 21-story skyscraper, choosing a better site at the Western Electric building.[8] (Western Electric was an AT&T manufacturing subsidiary.) The call letters were also altered to WEAF.

With the improved transmission netting significantly greater reception capabilities, toll station WEAF was sent over existing telephone lines and became a favorite of those early listeners within its purview. (Toll broadcasting involved stations maintaining a curious policy of leasing out airtime to others for their own use.) Years of experimentation in the field began to pay off handsomely for AT&T, allowing it to equip its outlet with the most advanced gear and technology then available. This translated into a natural benefit for listeners, who were turning their dials in search of as near static-free listening posts as they could find.

WEAF could soon boast that it was the most frequently heard station within the environs of Gotham.

In the meantime, the imposing facility that in 1926 was to become the flagship outlet of the National Broadcasting Company's Red network is widely heralded by radio historiographers for putting the first paid sales pitch on the ether. In retrospect, of course, it appears that an asterisk might accompany that unmitigated declaration. While it may have been the first outlet to air promotional announcements for which cash physically changed hands in compensation for purchased airtime, properly noted nevertheless, WEAF was at least the fourth station (including no fewer than two documented experimental outlets) to transmit commercial pitches. In a sense, while the predecessor plugs may have been freebies, the sales of radio parts, phonograph recordings and nightclub seating were unquestionably their desired objectives. Taken in that light, all of those earlier announcements had strong commercial implications.

The foray into selling by WEAF transpired no less than a full quadrennium prior to the formation of NBC. The defining moment of the nascent industry is registered between 5:00 and 5:10 P.M. on Monday, August 28, 1922, and only a dozen days after WEAF officially went on the air (August 16) under its newly designated call letters. A shrouded voice identified only as "Mr. Blackwell" (H. M. Blackwell) was recognized that afternoon by WEAF announcer Vischer Randall. Blackwell delivered a 10-minute discourse about residential apartment living in Jackson Heights. That plug purportedly netted the station $50 for the use of its airwaves, paid for by the underwriting Queensboro Corporation. Looking back, however, due to its substantial length, the commercial seems more like it could be considered an infomercial today, a label that was still a few decades away. In a rambling exposition,[9] the firm's agent surmised:

> It is fifty-eight years since Nathaniel Hawthorne, the greatest of American fictionists, passed away. To honor his memory the Queensboro Corporation, creator and operator of the tenant-owned system of apartment homes at Jackson Heights, New York City, has named its latest group of high-grade dwellings "Hawthorne Court."
>
> I wish to thank those within sound of my voice for the broadcasting opportunity afforded me to urge this vast radio audience to seek the recreation and the daily comfort of the home removed from the congested part of the city, right at the boundaries of God's great outdoors, and within a few minutes by subway from the business section of Manhattan. This sort of residential environment strongly influenced Hawthorne.... He analyzed with charming keenness the social spirit of those who had thus happily selected their homes....
>
> There should be more Hawthorne sermons preached about the utter inadequacy and the general hopelessness of the congested city home. The cry of the heart is for more living room, more chance to unfold, more opportunity to get near the Mother Earth, to play, to romp, to plant and to dig.
>
> Let me enjoin upon you as you value your health and your hopes and your home happiness, get away from the solid masses of brick, where the meager opening admitting a slant of sunlight is mockingly called a light shaft, and where children grow up starved for a run over a patch of grass and the sight of a tree....
>
> Friends, you owe it to yourself and your family to leave the congested city and enjoy what nature intended you to enjoy. Visit our new apartment homes in Hawthorne Court, Jackson Heights, where you may enjoy life in a friendly environment.

There were four additional commercial messages for tenant-owned garden apartment living at the same cost-per-unit rate, plus a $100 evening treatise espousing a comparable theme.[10] The plugs proffered a rather dry delivery in somewhat less-than-urgent appeals for response.

Commenting on the outcome of Queensboro's groundbreaking efforts, a critic maintained: "The truth is that talk alone — unless it be on an absorbing subject — seldom does a good selling job."

At the same time, those landmark promotions established a pattern for more commercial messages that soon followed: branded "talks" by media observers, each one of those nascent pitches normally followed the 10-minute time formula established by Queensboro. Several underwriters followed suit. Jumping into the fray over WEAF were outfits like American Express Company; Gimbels, Hearn's and Macy's retail merchandising emporiums; Gillette Safety Razor Company; radio manufacturer A. H. Grebe; Haynes Motor Car Company; the William H. Rankin advertising agency; Shur-On Optical Company; the pharmaceutical firm of E. R. Squibb and Sons; Tidewater Oil Company; and the Young Men's Christian Association.

The sponsored infomercial also could be easily mistreated, a contemporary media authority ascertained.[11]

> Seed-producer Henry Field, for one, built a modest '20s empire with pitches on KFNF in Shenandoah, Iowa.... Field hawked "seeds, bacon, auto tires, pig meal, fresh hams, radio batteries, prunes, paint, tea, coffee, shirts, [and] shoes." Outright frauds — among them Milford, Kansas, huckster John Brinkley, who used his KFKB to market patent medicines and male virility restoration (with goat gland implants) — further discredited the genre, attracting federal regulatory attention.

Responding to public and government sentiment, WEAF officials cautiously navigated the waters of pioneer broadcast advertising. Policing its own commercial announcements by limiting them to an indirect approach which could be judged as only mildly persuasive, in April 1923 the station set down some regulatory guidelines. For several years, it methodically adhered to them in deciding whether to accept or reject commercial sponsorship.

In addition to forbidding pricing references in the commercials it carried, AT&T — WEAF's owner — also nixed package descriptions, sales arguments and offering the public product samples. Cigarettes and toothpaste were on a list of commodities that fixated broadcast officials due to their "personal or offensive nature." WEAF's earliest policies disallowed paid promotions on Sunday. (For a moment, dwell on the possibility of applying that rule to today's broadcast and cable networks, eliminating the stupendously lucrative revenues they derive on TV's most -watched night weekly.) Such banishments, which appeared to tarnish rather than brighten advertising's potential, undoubtedly found their way into the large successor radio chains that emerged not long after those warnings were written.

By the early 1930s, CBS banned all commercials for laxatives, depilatories and deodorants while censoring features depicting "unpleasant discussions of bodily functions, bodily symptoms or other matters which similarly infringe on good taste." The edicts coming from on high were handed down by no less an authority than William S. Paley, the net's new president. Curiously, the Paleys were initially attracted to radio because it offered a unique way to advertise the cigars the family manufactured. In the meantime, early in its existence NBC adhered to a list of 80 terms that were considered "no-nos" for acceptable advertising lingo. Among them: *stomach, pregnancy, blood, phlegm, hawk, infection, retch.*

Only a couple of months after WEAF became the first outlet to delve into whole programs that were backed by financial arrangements with marketers, an astute pundit — demonstrating remarkable topical savvy — responded to the question "Should Radio be Used for Advertising?" Writing in *Radio Broadcast* in November 1922, the outspoken naysayer pontificated:

Concerts are seasoned here and there with a dash of advertising paprika. You can't miss it; every little classic number has a slogan all its own, if it is only the mere mention of the name and the street address *and* the phone number of the music house which arranged the program. More of this sort of thing can be expected. And once the avalanche gets a good start, nothing short of an Act of Congress ... will suffice to stop it.

Perhaps fairly surprisingly, in the meantime, for quite a while several other major stations backed by a myriad of commercial enterprises failed to follow in the lecture-discourse advertising strain inaugurated by WEAF. Four key outlets owned by the Westinghouse Corporation, for instance, weren't selling time in those days and weren't planning to. Included were Pittsburgh's KDKA, New York's WJZ, Chicago's KYW and Springfield, Massachusetts' WBZ. Before 1926, appliance manufacturing tycoon Powel Crosley had no interest in attracting advertisers to his WLW in Cincinnati. Similar responses were posted by a handful of newspaper-owned stations like Detroit's WWJ, Chicago's WMAQ and Kansas City's WDAF.

Those broadcast enterprises weren't opposed to taking handouts for services rendered, however. For its publicity value, organizations were urged to underwrite specific programming, although time wasn't sold on those stations as such. As early as 1923, WLW's schedule was dotted with sponsorship of this nature. One source delineates the following types of features and their benefactors in parentheses: dance music (Hotel Sinton), stock quotations (Westheimer & Company), market reports (Henry Brow & Company), financial news (Fifth-Third National Bank), drama readings (Shuster-Marin School) and piano offerings (Baldwin Company). WJZ followed a similar pattern until 1926, augmenting listening habits with paid-for fare like the Rheingold Quartet, Schrafft's Tea Room Orchestra, Wanamaker Organ Concert, *Harper's Bazaar* fashion talks, *Harper's Magazine* book reviews and *Field and Stream* sports talks. Station WFAA in Dallas, pursuing another twist on terminology, distinguished its backers of remunerated offerings as *chaperones*, including local department stores, plus the Magnolia Petroleum Company Band, as opposed to *sponsors*.

The idea of commercial-free radio was broached by a number of intellectual types. Writing in the mid–1940s, one of the most respected mused[12]:

> For all the discontent with advertising ... it is questionable whether, even today, the average listener would be prepared to pay the modest price required to rid him of advertising altogether — an annual fee of approximately four dollars. For that is the estimated cost of all the programs that we hear. It includes capital outlay and depreciation costs for all the 900 and more stations on the air, their staffs, and program production costs. Jack Benny and Bob Hope, Fred Allen and Kate Smith, and all the rest of those who earn the astronomical fees paid for radio programs, could still be on the air and never a commercial from the beginning to the end, if every listener would subscribe.... But the lure of an illusory something for nothing is too much for most of us.

The pioneering WEAF linked with Boston's WNAC on January 4, 1923, to air a single program simultaneously, becoming what is believed to be the first network broadcast. That same year a quartet of outlets — WEAF, WNAC, Providence, Rhode Island's WJAR, and South Dartmouth, Massachusetts' WMAF — expanded the network concept by banding together to air specific features. Early in 1924, using its telephone lines to carry the shows, AT&T produced the first transcontinental network broadcast, adding San Francisco's KPO to the mix. That year the Republican National Convention at Cleveland and the Democratic National Convention at New York were broadcast coast to coast. That autumn (1924) a 23-member chain was patched together for a presidential address. Two years hence 26 affiliates extended the AT&T chain from Boston to Kansas City. All of it laid the groundwork for a debuting sponsored variety series, the medium's introductory smash hit, while making a powerfully convincing argument about radio's viability.

The Eveready Hour debuted on December 5, 1923, allowing people well beyond the confines of the Big Apple where it originated to simultaneously hear superb dance music by the Browning King Orchestra.[13] Browning King, incidentally, was a respected New York clothier. "Judged even by today's standards," claimed one reviewer, "it [the series] would not be found wanting." The premier included a concert orchestra, jazz band and *The Bungalow*, a one-act play starring Gene Lockhart, Eva Taylor and Lawrence Grattan as principals.

"Those who remember the first battery-powered tube receiving sets will remember ... the Eveready Hour, radio's first important commercial show, sponsored by the National Carbon Company," a critic recalled. "The direct sales objective of the program was to sell to radio set users the dry-cell Eveready batteries then necessary for power.... Company executives ... untied the purse strings and instructed its advertising agency to build a worth-while show." As a result, Irvin S. Cobb, John Drew, the Flonzaley String Quartet, George Gershwin, Julia Marlowe, Moran and Mack, Will Rogers, Weber and Fields and other big names of the era turned up regularly on *The Eveready Hour*.[14] The series was one of NBC's first, persisting to late 1930, providing a financial windfall to the National Carbon Company as well as to WEAF and NBC.

A couple of years afterward, on December 13, 1925, a second firm which was to heavily influence the direction of early radio advertising made its presence felt over WEAF. By then, however, there was a fledgling network to carry the show originating in New York to other markets, linked by telephone line hookup. The Clicquot Club Company, a Massachusetts-based ginger ale manufacturer, launched a musical series, *The Clicquot Club Eskimos*. It aired simultaneously in a dozen cities: New York, Boston, Providence, Washington, Philadelphia, Pittsburgh, Cincinnati, Buffalo, Detroit, Davenport, Minneapolis and St. Louis. The following year the firm became one of NBC's inaugural underwriters. The narrative behind that trailblazing series is fascinating reading in the annals of radio advertising history.[15]

> The brand's French name [Clicquot] was hard for Americans to pronounce and therefore to request.... Advertising textbooks maintained, radio had a special role to play in Clicquot Club advertising: "radio has taught listeners how to pronounce Clicquot," making "it easy to ask ... for the product." The announcer served as the teacher, "week in and week out," intoning that "Klee-ko is spelled C-L-I-C-Q-U-O-T." As brand names became increasingly important, radio made Clicquot Club part of everyday language.
>
> Clicquot Club also found itself in an expanding market during the 1920s. Demand increased for bottled soft drinks as alternatives to liquor banned during Prohibition and as mixers for bootleg liquor.... Tastes had changed and more people consumed cold drinks all year. Clicquot Club expanded with the demand, changing from a local bottler into a regional Northeast business.
>
> [Clicquot founder-president Earl] Kimball ... worked directly with ... WEAF representatives, [noting] "my advertising agency doesn't believe in radio, so we'll go ahead without consulting it." ... [WEAF] arranged an audition so Kimball could listen to a banjo orchestra led by Harry Reser and announced by Graham McNamee. Kimball loved the show and named the orchestra after his product's symbol, an Eskimo.
>
> The program ... became a prime model of the indirect advertising the radio industry then thought proper.... Frank Arnold [in *Broadcast Advertising*] portrayed the Clicquot Club Eskimos as "the ideal in the field of audible advertising" because "the program personifies the product." His textbook pointed out that the program produced "the effect of an effervescent beverage together with clinking ice in a crystal goblet," with the program's music chosen "to conform with this idea of personification until the Eskimos and their tinkling music program became synonymous with Clicquot Club Ginger Ale."

The series persisted to July 17, 1933, falling victim to the repeal of Prohibition and the Great Depression, both of which significantly decreased the sponsoring commodity's sales. Rising production and network time charges, meanwhile, contributed to the firm's decision to drop its well-established series.

While all of this was going on in the formative years, in addition to AT&T's broadcasting efforts, concurrently the Radio Corporation of America (RCA) was cultivating a network of its own. It purchased New York's WJZ in 1923 and then built WRC in Washington, D. C. AT&T, for obvious reasons meanwhile, wouldn't allow the competition to send programming along its telephone lines. RCA was forced to rely on the telegraph lines owned by the Western Union Company for its programming. This had diminishing effects, however; it wasn't nearly as static-free as telephone lines normally were in transmitting the human voice. Yet an AT&T monopoly also prevented RCA from selling airtime to sponsors, or even operating commercial (toll) outlets. According to one wag, an enterprising "RCA solved the problem in a time-honored American way: they bought the competition."

NBC, formed in the latter half of 1926,[16] became the undertaking of a trio of prominent communications rivals: Radio Corporation of America, purchasing 50 percent of the new web; General Electric Company, with 30 percent; and Westinghouse Corporation, 20 percent. The new enterprise reached an agreement with AT&T to buy WEAF for $1 million as a key originating station in its operation. AT&T went out of the program-generating business upon transfer of its title while retaining the lucrative fees for leasing its wires to carry the programming of the chains and local stations. That netted a win-win decision for all of the participants and certainly included the listening public.

NBC's time sales in its first 13 months of operations netted the firm $3,384,519 in revenue, a most promising start. Yet in the grand scheme of advertising evolution, that was chicken feed. By the close of 1930, just three years beyond, radio's gross billings combined stood at $40.5 million. At the close of 1931 they were $90 million. Indelible dye had been cast. Had there been any doubt about the potential of the new medium, even so, it should have been put to rest in 1928. Two months into a concerted radio advertising campaign for Lucky Strikes, the American Tobacco Company unequivocally proved radio's power as sales of its leading cigarette brand vaulted 47 percent!

The sale of time was negligibly mentioned in the Radio Act of 1927,[17] seemingly an afterthought. While those stations selling time were still in the minority, the tide was gradually turning although the office-holders gave only token notice. The taxonomy "advertising" was, thus far, ignored by lawmakers.

> Sec. 19. All matter broadcast by any radio station for which service, money, or any other valuable consideration is directly or indirectly paid, or promised to or charged or accepted by, the station so broadcasting, from any person, firm, company, or corporation, shall, at the time the same is so broadcast, be announced as paid for or furnished, as the case may be, by such person, firm, company, or corporation.

Within five years the Federal Radio Commission took note of paid advertising's mounting presence, nevertheless, observing that 33.8 percent of NBC's schedule and 21.94 percent of CBS's was underwritten. "The sponsored programs were getting the best hours and the main attention from radio columns and fan magazines," an observer fathomed. Advertising was depicted as "brief, circumspect, and extremely well-mannered." A high order of professionalism resulted. The paid agenda was in large measure bearing the cost to the networks of the vast amount of programming still sustained (carried by the chains without compensation). Noteworthy, by 1934, NBC was reimbursing its affiliates at $50 an hour for airing sponsored fare that was fed to them by the chain while charging those same stations $45 per hour for carrying its sustaining programs.

Rather than taking the approach that unsponsored time should be dealt with as easily and cheaply as possible, in radio's golden age (for our purposes, from the mid–1920s to the early 1960s) the four national webs frequently filled the unsold time at their disposal with programs of quality and even daring. During his declining days, one of the aural medium's most creative and talented geniuses, actor-director Orson Welles, insisted: "The reason that radio was often very good, and better than television is, is because there were many sustaining shows. That meant shows without sponsors, paid for by the networks, and given prime time. There is no such equivalent in television." In that arena, the theater of the mind ran rings around the one-eyed monster that encroached upon its turf and then devoured it.

Economics became a crucial element of radio programming. For instance, an hour in 1931 over NBC's nationwide hookup — including more than 50 outlets — garnered roughly $10,000 from a program's underwriter. For arranging the sale, an ad agency earned a 15 percent commission ($1,500), plus an added 15 percent based on its talent recruitment which might run as high as $6,000 for a primetime feature, netting another $900 in commissions to the agency. All of it was passed along to the sponsor, which could hypothetically cough up $390,000 to NBC and another $93,600 to the agency for a 39-week season. A tab for one program could thus approach a half-million dollars annually. Remarkable, considering that this was at the summit of the Great Depression when consumers had little discretionary funds for spending, even for the basics. Undoubtedly many firms were building name recognition for the eventual post–Depression era.

By 1930, 40 percent of American homes were equipped with a radio. A decade hence, the percentage had more than doubled. At first a novelty in many households, it became a virtual necessity to millions, proving to be a dependable source of inexpensive amusement, news and information for the masses. It was a comfort to families that huddled around it during an extended, nearly unrelenting hardship interval that combined a fight for economic survival and recovery with successive global war. Many more impressive figures could be cited as radio advanced through the 1930s and 1940s and into the early 1950s. Focusing on the postwar period, however, a few will suffice.

Taking 1948 as one of the aural medium's typically vibrant years, a single national advertiser — Procter & Gamble Company, a leading maker of household and personal care goods — purchased nearly 20,000 hours of broadcast time in a single year. Of the advertising business conducted by all broadcasters that year (including networks, their affiliates and independent commercial stations), 60 percent ($239 million) was with national or regional advertisers and 40 percent ($163 million) was with local concerns. Just six sponsors provided almost 36 percent of CBS's revenue in 1948, hinting at how dependent the chains were on a handful of subscribers.

No matter how promising this might all seem, there were media watchdogs who expressed more than casual concern about the stability of radio's livelihood. And with good reason, as it turned out. On the precipice of network radio's long slide toward oblivion, but slightly ahead of its ebbing days from glory, a leading exponent of the medium obsessed about radio's inability to control its financial future.[18]

> Radio in practice functions mainly as a middleman, subservient to the interests of advertisers; it is almost exclusively dependent on their patronage for its own revenue. Advertisers, in turn, are subservient to economic trends. When business is brisk, advertising expands. When times

are hard, there is a tendency to curtail advertising budgets.... Radio's financial rewards derive not ... directly from the quality of its product, but from ... the advertiser's *readiness* to buy time ... and the advertiser's *capacity* to do so....

There is little that it [radio] can do on its own account to maintain a stable, assured income. In a depression, the finest programs in the world will avail little, if at all, to attract advertisers. Thus radio's capacity to serve the public is limited by economic factors over which it has absolutely no control.

As it turned out, of course, radio not only couldn't control its financial fate, it lost the ability to control its own destiny.

Broadcast advertising, for all of its contributions, continued to draw outspoken detractors. Despite it, until the mid–1940s, protests against commercialized broadcasting were effectively quelled by the Communications Act of 1934. Ignoring advertising and the national chains, the legislation offered tacit sanction of the dominant model that had emerged for bankrolling radio's gargantuan price tag. In roughly 14 years, radio had transformed from amateur stations in garages airing phonograph recordings into sophisticated studios with well compensated celebrity talent, and from widespread rejection of commercialism to a structure financed altogether by direct advertising.

Opposition to commercialized broadcasting fleetingly resurfaced following the Second World War, nevertheless, fanned to a great extent by release of Frederic Wakeman's astoundingly acclaimed humorous narrative *The Hucksters* in 1946. The following year it was turned into a popular motion picture.

An assault in 1946 by the Federal Communications Commission (FCC), a successor to the earlier Federal Radio Commission, underscored that even the watchdogs were continually disturbed by paid advertising in radio. At the same time, the feds recommended no alternative measures to commercialization. A 10-point outline raised several issues that detractors had complained about before.

I. *Broadcasters are morally and intellectually negligent* in allowing commercials to intrude so jarringly upon the ears of the listening public.
II. *Commercials take too much time* from the entertainment part of programs, and seem to get longer every year.
III. *The vast majority of the listening public is thoroughly fed up with radio commercials*, as indicated by at least one survey and countless letters of protest.
IV. *Commercials falsify or misrepresent* in their zeal to sell their product.
V. *Radio is the black sheep among advertising media*, and is conducted on a much lower level than newspaper, magazine, and outdoor advertising.
VI. *Commercials appear to be conceived for listeners of below-average intelligence*, as indicated by tedious repetition, incredible exaggeration, silly jingles, and obnoxious references to physiological subjects.
VII. *Announcers frequently are repulsive in their delivery*, appearing either to coo, blat, or lull, or else to slap the listener with a mechanical-sounding hammer-and-tongs delivery.
VIII. *Entertainers, stars of a program, are obliged to yield their integrity* when sponsors require them to participate in commercials.
IX. *Radio sponsors and persons in the broadcasting industry are enjoying ill-earned incomes* through such questionable practices as cluttering up the air with blurbs that are spaced much too closely together.
X. *Advertisers and broadcasters are doing little if anything to improve the quality of radio advertising*, and appear thoroughly satisfied with the status quo.

Such resistance paled when pitted against the psychological and physical inducements of the networks themselves. The majority of the American people were satisfied with the status quo and the big chains were well aware of it. Whatever opposition had existed against broadcast advertising was virtually null and void, seldom able to muster more than a whimper in a clash that had been ultimately decided much earlier. Ironically and noteworthy, commercialization's antagonists were blinded by television's emergence, seemingly diverted by the fact that the method they decried in radio was infiltrating telecasting. When those outbursts against video ads became daunting several years afterward, advanced technology saw the invention of hand-held remote control devices with a mute button for silencing offensive material. If this had been available in radio's golden days, would the medium have gone out of business sooner?

Long before that, of course, radio advertisers had begun experimenting with methods that resulted in more effective commercials from the standpoint of the audience and advertiser alike. A couple of innovations established permanent results.

Until 1929, the single-voice pattern of promotional copy delivery was all that had been attempted. That changed as enterprising advertisers adapted the sketch format in pushing their wares. Two or more individuals conversed in plausible slice-of-life exchanges in which the sponsoring brand or organization was mentioned, greatly expanding the potential for creative development in the future.

At about the same time, the electrical transcription or recording emerged. That allowed the advertiser virtually total control over a commercial's airing even on remote stations that were considerable distances from carefully monitored production centers. It was an especially rewarding technique for national clients for it allowed higher quality standards; it encouraged repetitious messages that frequently reminded listeners of a brand, service or idea; and it often diminished production costs through increased efficiency.

Continuity and comedy writer Carroll Carroll, who is credited with many of the words that fell from Bing Crosby's lips during that radio singer's heyday, was also an eminent advertising executive. Carroll professed: "The real gut power of radio surfaced around 1931 when advertisers began to abandon such obvious broadcast nomenclature as the A&P Gypsies, Paul Oliver and Olive Palmer in the Palmolive Hour, the Gold Dust Twins, the Happiness Boys (later the Interwoven Pair — a sock act), the Clicquot Club Eskimos and [replace them] with the use of star talent."

Early on — for at least a trio of reasons — habitually, radio showmen were plucked from the recording industry: (1) they were already practiced before the microphone; (2) they were confident that broadcasting could expose their phonograph records to wider audiences; and, possibly the most important rationale, certainly so for those early radio sponsors, (3) they possessed anonymity. "The type of advertising used on radio called for performers who could submerge their own identities to promote a product," a critic asserted. The Goodrich Silver Masked Tenor, the Ipana Troubadours, the Gypsies, the Eskimos, the Twins and others of such nebulous nomenclature were carefully protected, their monikers held incognito by their clients. The reviewer persisted, "Advertisers in the 1920s and early 1930s wanted the emphasis placed on their brand names and looked to the performers not for prestige (as they would later), but for entertainment that would remind listeners of the product."[19]

As time advanced, clients favoring indirect appeals evaporated into thin air. The anonymous musicians playing nostalgic and semi-classical fare also disappeared. In their wake, radio's new performing acts became established vaudeville stars (Benny, Burns and Allen, Cantor, Vallee, Wynn).[20] That infusion persuaded many listeners that radio was an entertainment instead of an educational form and in that way could be commercialized. In the span of a few years, broadcast advertising became widely accepted, national audiences were available to hear it and small businesses—hit hard by the Great Depression—stopped advertising and were supplanted by large corporations and their advertising agencies.

At about the same time, an explosion in the number of advertising agencies handling radio accounts developed. The organizations proliferated between the late 1920s and late 1940s, becoming the middlemen of the air, acting as go-betweens for the major chains and their program underwriters. It was their task to sign advertising clients for the webs as well as to generate, produce and staff the shows that their clients sponsored. According to one eyewitness, the networks could "sit comfortably back at the receipt of custom, conceding slabs of time, and taking in return the increasingly large sums of money proffered by advertisers for time on the air."[21] The same source persisted, eloquently: "With the increasing prestige and initiative of radio advertising agencies and the increased demands for time on the air by advertisers, networks have largely abdicated to the interests and point of view of agencies and firms that have become more masters than clients. Yet the networks, not the advertising agencies or their clients—the commercial sponsors of radio programs—are the recipients of a public trust. They, not the advertising agencies or the commercial sponsors, are responsible for the balanced structure of programs, to which the public is entitled."[22]

That system continued until the networks at last rebelled, late in radio's halcyon era but only a short time before TV heavily eroded the aural medium of its audiences, advertisers, artists and agendas. By the time the webs achieved the upper hand in controlling their own schedules, the landscape had dramatically shifted, in fact. While the nets may have been in the driver's seat for a while, the vehicle they were steering was about to reach the end of the line.

By the fall of 1932, both national chains already in existence, NBC (founded in 1926) and CBS (1927), were allowing price mentions in their commercials, a defining moment in radio advertising. Afterward, such occurrences flourished. More innovations were on the way.

The first scrupulous sampling of radio audiences to determine who was listening to what, benefiting the advertisers and potential sponsors with indispensable information, was conducted by Archibald Crossley in 1929. Crossley's methods were expanded and refined by others, particularly including Clark-Hooper, Inc., in 1934 which refocused as C. E. Hooper, Inc., in 1938. Ultimately all of their precedent-setting exploits in the data-gathering field were overshadowed by the A. C. Nielsen Company beginning in 1943.

Despite later claims by others to the honor, the singing commercial was introduced in 1926. That year the Washburn Crosby Company, forerunner of General Mills, Inc., commissioned a barbershop quartet to plug one of its primary foodstuffs.[23] Sung a cappella to the tune of *Jazz Baby*, the lyrics became familiar to legions who heard them unremittingly over multiple decades.

> *Have you tried Wheaties?*
> *They're whole wheat with all of the bran.*
> *Won't you try Wheaties?*
> *For wheat is the best food of man.*

In 1937 the cooperative radio spot ad surfaced employing local station announcers to deliver the sales pitches during network programming. The form reached its zenith in golden age radio's last major feature, *Monitor* (1955 to 1975). *Monitor* was a weekend marathon series that blotted out years of red ink at NBC and, in doing so, pumped life back into a major chain for an extended period.

While at least some of this was transpiring, the major chains were appointing continuity acceptance departments to enforce their already inscribed commercial policies. Dedicated overseers meticulously scrutinized every piece of commercial copy before accepting it for airing. NBC opened its department in 1934. A year hence it reported that 560 prospective ads were found unacceptable. They included 164 that contained outlandish or inflated claims; another 88 were deemed "improper"; 87 incorporated disparaging statements about rival products and firms; 42 proffered "unfair competitive references"; and another 179 were banished for a myriad of miscellaneous explanations.

Advertising on radio flourished as the 1930s and 1940s sailed along. In the five-year period starting in 1940, gross revenues of the webs and their owned-and-operated outlets jumped by 79 percent, from $56.4 million in 1940 to $100.9 million in 1945. By 1943, radio had outstripped newspapers as the nation's most profitable advertising medium. Two years hence radio revenues earned more than 37 percent of the national (not local or regional) advertising dollars while magazines and newspapers trailed in that order.

Only 2 percent of all advertising expenditures in the United States were dedicated to radio in 1930, the first year for which total percentages were available.[24] The statistical ratio climbed steadily from there. Within four years it tripled; by 1940, it rose to 10 percent of advertising disbursements; it peaked in 1945 at 15 percent, netting $423.9 billion. Despite the fact that the percentages started to slide after that, in actual dollars radio persistently earned a greater influx of advertising revenues beyond its lofty percentage watermark. It took in $624.1 billion (9 percent) in 1952; $692.4 billion (6 percent) in 1960, the year many historians assign to the end of the golden age; and $735.8 billion (6 percent) in 1962 when a handful of surviving golden age features permanently left the airwaves.

These figures jointly represent network, national spot and local radio income. Of the aggregate, $210.6 billion was diverted to the radio chains in 1948. The year 1948 was that sector's zenith between 1930 and 1962 when 37.5 percent of the $561.6 billion radio collected was funneled into the national webs' coffers. Meanwhile, the nets — there were three of them at the time — took in 79 percent of radio's total advertising revenues in 1927, literally their ultimate year, in an era in which some unrealistic numbers favored the webs. By 1960, after abandoning most of their programming, the national hookups received $43.1 billion collectively, 6.2 percent of radio's total earnings. The tally shows a small dollar increase, to $45.8 billion in 1962, still just 6.2 percent of the total picture.

Across the years from 1930 to 1962, radio realized $13.11 trillion in advertising earnings of which almost $3.55 trillion was channeled to the networks (27.1 percent). Not to be overlooked, however, is the fact — while 85 percent to 94 percent of all advertising budgets in the country were focused on other media — large sums were continuing to have a strong effect on radio. An examination of how and why that capital was spent in a medium for which the images singularly existed in the minds of the recipients is where this volume is headed.

Thirteen sponsors paid CBS more than $1 million each for time purchased in 1945. Three of them — General Foods Corporation, Lever Brothers, Inc., and Procter & Gamble Company — spent in excess of $4 million each that year on CBS. Seven sponsors and six advertising agencies accounted for half of that network's billings in 1945. CBS's rivals also did really well. NBC sold $1 million in time to 11 underwriters while ABC earned $1 million from nine sponsors. And far smaller (in audiences reached) MBS charmed three $1 million buyers.[25]

Could anybody reasonably argue that the golden age hadn't laid a golden egg? But alas, the egg of radio's golden age was about to be plastered across the faces of those who stood steadfastly by it in the wake of impending doom. All of the aforementioned turned out to be a last hurrah. Within a short while, network radio was saying farewell to the mammoth prosperity it attracted in that spectacularly giddy era.

By the early 1950s — just as radio had done to vaudeville before it — television possessed a markedly devastating, cannibalistic effect on its own precursor. Although the transmission of pictures by wireless had originated in the late 1920s only a short time after radio got its foothold, it took two more decades to make TV viable. Technology had to be developed, radio had to earn the huge bucks required to support the spiraling costs of its development and the country had to be open to it. That propitious moment came during a booming postwar economy as the middle class was once again flush with steady jobs and dependable incomes.

As radio sponsors abandoned the hand that fed them — turning to the more stimulating prospects of video — mass communications' initial form of amusement and information was defenseless. Radio thereafter had to limp along without the big budgets of the advertisers, now focused on the tube. TV rapidly siphoned off audio's top talent, programs and audiences as well as its revenues, all of its lifelines to a profitable existence. It was too much. "In radio's last days," obsessed one wag, "some of its favorite shows suddenly found themselves sponsorless, padded with pallid public-service announcements that rubbed salt in an open wound."

A well-known media critic excoriated one network: "Unwilling to allow a half-hour drama to unfold uninterrupted, CBS insisted on at least one interruption in shows like *Gunsmoke, Suspense,* and *Have Gun, Will Travel,* then twiddled away the time with silly and often sanctimonious public service announcements: Mail early in the day for better postal service, Don't lose your head behind the wheel of a car, etc. It was almost enough to make a listener nostalgic for 'real' commercials!"[26]

Between 1945 and 1952, although radio advertising revenues rose, the networks' share of it, including the owned-and-operated stations, fell by more than half—from $23 million to a little past $11 million.[27] Networks repeatedly cut their time charges but to no avail. "Once network radio started to slip, it went fast," a source allowed. In 1952 the webs still took in 25 percent of radio advertising revenues. But as more independent outlets went on the ether and sponsor interest in radio networks eroded, that share plummeted to 6 percent in 1960.

One published report suggested that NBC felt the devastation much worse and much sooner than CBS, "partly because many NBC shows had lower ratings — a possible result of the 1948 CBS 'talent raid.'"[28] It had been CBS chairman William S. Paley's intent, when he ransacked his competition, to "save radio" rather than staff his newborn television network with talent. As it turned out, he may have ultimately accomplished both feats in his famous coup d'etat with its enduring repercussions.

"Without advertising, broadcasting, as we know it, would not exist," noted a foremost radio historiographer during the medium's golden age. "It is our radio's only source of revenue, accepted and acceptable in preference to any other known method of financing a very costly business. We cannot get something for nothing. A certain price has to be paid. The only question is how high a price makes for a fair exchange."[29] An application could be made to a modern advertising channel, the Internet. Millions complain about its potential for harassing patrons in a user-unfriendly barrage of unwanted sales promotion diatribes, or spam.

The next time you tune in a talk show or golden oldies showcase on your automated format radio station, punctuated by four to six commercial interruptions every hour, each typically extending three to six minutes, think about the advertising during radio's heyday. The greed of unmitigated excess so pervasive now would have been unimaginable then. Traditionally, the golden age commercials occupied about 12 minutes of network air per hour before evening arrived, and only six minutes during the primetime hours. Consider again: "The only question is how high a price makes for a fair exchange."

"And now, a word from our sponsor" all those years ago meant essentially that. By comparison, that would be welcome relief today. Those staunch detractors of radio commercials from the 1920s to the 1950s, if alive now would think they had been dabbling in mere child's play.

3

Ad Agencies: They Held the Whip Hand

An advertising agency could be simplistically defined as a "service business dedicated to creating, planning and handling advertising for its clients." It's more than just that, however; furthermore, it conducts overall marketing and branding strategies as well as sales promotions. Sometimes performing autonomously, an agency allegedly provides its patrons with an objective opinion on vending products and services. Conventional ad agency clients may be individuals, political campaigns, small- to medium-sized commercial ventures, behemoth corporations possibly of global stature, non-profit organizations and governmental entities.[1] An ad agency can be engaged to produce a sole announcement or a full-fledged campaign, identified by a recurring sequence of related marketing ballyhoo in one or more media — or perhaps something in between those extremes.

Previously we read that Volney B. Palmer of Philadelphia, in 1843, established himself as an advertising agent.[2] His business model not only became the forerunner of the advertising agency as a breed for profitable trade, he also fashioned its design for a few decades to follow. At that time, advertising agents were purely intermediaries in the propagational process: they purchased space from newspapers and resold it to a constituent wishing to advertise. The way Palmer and those who subsequently joined his ranks derived their livelihoods was by selling (renting) the space they bought at a higher rate than the advertising agent originally paid for it. They were, in every sense of the word, *middlemen*. It became advantageous to the agents — and the newspapers — to contract for large amounts of space at discounted pricing. The prospect of substantial profits was considerably inflated by doing so.

According to *Advertising Age*, a type of bible for the industry's commerce, in 1868 — a full quarter-century after Palmer launched the species — Francis Wayland Ayer, another Philadelphia advertising practitioner, paid Palmer $250 for his business. Ayer then re-established the agency as N. W. Ayer & Son, naming it for his dad. The enterprise he founded, dating its heritage with Volney Palmer, prided itself on being the most enduring continuous commercial advertising venture operating — at least, until it folded in 2002. While the J. Walter Thompson Company (JWT since 2005)[3] is now considered "the oldest U.S. advertising agency in continuous service today" with its genesis in 1864, Ayer — heir to Palmer's concept of the advertising agent — put down roots more than a couple of decades earlier. And although

Thompson rightly alleges to have formed the trade's first creative unit, and Thompson himself is dubbed by insiders as "the father of modern magazine advertising," Ayer was also responsible for some credible innovations.

Around 1880, for instance, his firm first offered clients an "open contract" designating Ayer as their exclusive advertising representative. For that, Ayer priced ad space at a cost-plus fixed-rate commission, an initiative that soon proliferated to rival agencies. Maintaining an agent of record, in fact, became basic to mainstream manufacturers wanting to advertise in print. The American Newspaper Publishers Association set a precedent in 1893 by cutting off discounts to firms buying advertising space without going through an ad agency. Eight years hence Curtis Publishing Company, on behalf of its *Ladies' Home Journal,* followed suit, blazing a trail that other major magazine publishers speedily adopted. By 1919, the publishing industry commonly embraced the cost-plus commission formula, standardizing the commission at 15 percent—paid to the agency by advertisers buying newspaper space.

Those advertisers were also responsible into the 1890s for conceptualizing and preparing their space advertising copy. As Ayer's plan caught on, however, ad agents could no longer compete with one another on mere price alone. They needed another method of separating their services from those of their competitors. The duties of *advertising agents,* whose businesses were soon re-labeled *advertising agencies,* expanded dramatically. Not only were they contracting for space, they were also writing copy, creating slogans, logos and trademarks and supervising the design of accompanying illustrations.

Ayer sculpted another prototype by hiring a full-time copywriter in 1892, a practice that was copied by the industry. Almost every agency employed one or more full-time copywriters and artists in its workforce by 1910; full service firms maintained staffs of multiple craftsmen in those disciplines. In its proud legacy, Ayer scribes coined familiar mottos like *When it rains, it pours* (Morton Salt, 1912); *I'd walk a mile for a Camel* (R. J. Reynolds, 1921); *A diamond is forever* (DeBeers, 1948); *Reach out and touch someone* (AT&T, 1979); and *Be all that you can be* (U.S. Army, 1981). Ayer relocated in 1973 from its Philadelphia origins to New York digs as the base of its operations. The firm subsequently experienced several mergers and acquisitions, in due course acquired by the Publicis Groupe, a transnational advertising enterprise rooted in Paris. Lamentably—from a historic standpoint—Publicis permanently shuttered Ayer's doors in 2002.

For all the panache that the addition of skilled artisans furnished the agencies, there was still an element of skepticism toward those who peddled goods and services of a third party for a living. "Advertising men were widely seen as no better than P. T. Barnum's sideshow barkers falsely hawking two-headed freaks," allowed one source, "rather than professionals presenting dignified, honest, and compelling images of bath soap."[4] Things improved considerably after the American Association of Advertising Agencies (AAAA) organized in 1917, which yielded commonly accepted principles of trade. The profession was afforded new respect. Because of advertising's ability to create mass demand, for instance, in a speech to the AAAA's 1926 convention, U.S. president Calvin Coolidge credited those advertising practitioners with commensurate success enjoyed by other branches of American industry.

Fortunately for the advertisers, the ability to reach a mass audience with radio intersected with the expansion of the national economy in the 1920s. The first president of the National Broadcasting Company, which was formed in 1926—Merlin H. Aylesworth—correctly assessed that radio was "an open gateway to national markets, to millions of consumers, and to thousands upon thousands of retailers." In later years, the Museum of Broadcast Communications acknowledged, "The vision of eager consumers gathered around this remarkable appliance was irresistible to potential sponsors." Some of the better established advertising agencies, including N. W. Ayer, J. Walter Thompson and more, accentuated their services with exclusively-focused broadcast departments. Buoyantly, they urged their clients to add the new medium sweeping the nation to their advertising portfolios.

Unquestionably the agencies had entered a new phase of their history. In relation to network radio, they were no longer sheer time brokers, wordsmiths and little else; they fashioned and formed whole programs instead, and — subject to mere token network review — determined the content. Of their service, venerated media pundit Erik Barnouw fittingly proclaimed: "They had in a few years come to control radio to an extent they would not have dared attempt with other media."[5] About one-third of all network time was sold for sponsored programming in 1934, occupying the choicest hours of the day and night, with more than half of those revenues derived by just 10 agencies.[6] In order of total volume, they were: Blackett-Sample-Hummert; Lord and Thomas; J. Walter Thompson; Benton & Bowles; Erwin Wasey; N. W. Ayer & Son; Young & Rubicam; Batten, Barton, Durstine & Osborn; Ruthrauff & Ryan; and Stack-Goble.

Blackett-Sample-Hummert (BSH), the leading advertising agency in total time purchases in 1934, continued to occupy that coveted spot four years later. By 1938, as the leading serials producer, the outfit was single-handedly responsible for no fewer than a dozen daytime dramas aired on the networks along with several weekly half-hour primetime features. Simultaneously, the fertile firm was testing several more shows on various stations for possible future network allocation. While a few more agencies were doing likewise, none was as successful to BSH's extent in that period.

The influence of the advertising agencies was pervasive. In its September 18, 1935, issue, *Variety* reported, "The talent agents give the ad agencies first call on all material." Earlier that year, on January 1, the trade paper declared: "Of 102 commercial shows now on the network or due to open by October 1, NBC wields staging and booking authority over only 12, or slightly more than 10 percent." The big chains' contributions to innovative series tapered off still more. A couple of years afterward, analyst Edgar A. Grunwald, writing in the *Variety Radio Directory, 1937 to 1938*, surveyed the landscape then: "Currently, network commercial program production stands virtually at zero — attesting to the profit derived from radio by the advertising agencies, and indirectly indicating no compliment to the networks for their style of programming." Was there any doubt about who held the reins on network transmissions at that juncture? It was apparent that the broadcasters were really in charge of possibly only a minuscule fraction of their own fate. Despite that, nobody directly affected by it seemed to have their noses out of joint over the arrangement.

Time sales brought the networks $56,192,396 in 1937. Affiliate stations and station-groups siphoned off $15,962,729 of that while the advertising agencies earned $8,428,860, leaving the networks with $31,800,807 for not doing a whole lot more than airing the shows. A tidy yield for everybody, it seemed. Federal Trade Commissioner George Henry Payne noted that the industry was raking in a 350 percent annual profit on its investment. Tens of millions of dollars in talent fees also pumped the surge. "The centerpieces ... were the commercials written by hundreds of writers at advertising agencies, at salaries well above those of sustaining dramatic writers," one wag pointed out. The ads supplied the oil that drove the machinery.

Let us take a moment to explain, parenthetically, that whenever it could get away with it, NBC exhibited a tendency to withhold statistics about its internal operations from public scrutiny, preferring to keep them close to its corporate bosom. Thus, even though NBC's competitors were disclosing relevant commercial data by 1944, the oldest chain remained aloof, reluctant to divulge similar reportage. It may have been wise. While the rivals were making a few admissions, their revelations prompted ire from some quarters. All of it pointed toward an inherent potential downside for this euphoria over radio and the advertising agencies.

For instance, 26 percent of CBS's business that year (1944) was derived from just four advertisers while 38 percent of the web's commerce was triggered by four advertising agencies. In the meantime, four advertisers were responsible for 25 percent of the Blue (soon to be ABC) network's business while four agencies controlled 37 percent of that web's trade the same year. At MBS, 23 percent of its programming was underwritten by four advertisers while four advertising agencies generated 31 percent of the chain's income-producing work.[7]

More than one media academician found revelations like these disturbing, to state circumstances bluntly. Gross billings of the combined networks in 1944 approached $190.7 billion (a growth rate exceeding 340 percent since 1937). Of that national radio advertising business, two merchandising disciplines — drugs and toilet articles (27.9 percent) and foods and food beverages (22.4 percent) — accounted for half of the year's enormous revenue. "Firms with coast-to-coast business are ... relatively few in number. Their monopoly of a high percentage of air time ... is therefore a foregone conclusion," allowed a critic. "The temptation for networks, admittedly, is very great. And it is intensified by one ominous aspect of the advertising picture. The bulk of networks' advertising revenue comes from a surprisingly small number of advertising clients, and a high percentage of their business is handled by a very small number of advertising agencies....

"When, as in the case of CBS, 38 percent of its business is handled by only four agencies and more than a quarter of its business comes from four advertisers, its independence is seriously affected. It would be only human nature if CBS executives, dealing with one of these eight giants, preferred compromise to principle rather than jeopardize or risk the loss of its business."[8]

The advertising agencies, as much as the advertisers themselves, were a fundamental part of the concern expressed about dominating the ether in those days, and perhaps rightly so. To a significant degree, their manipulative clout influenced what their advertising clients — the underwriters of radio and of the agencies themselves — put on the airwaves. Together they were, in effect, determining what Americans had access to on their radio sets. In reality, the reliance upon so few agencies and sponsors implied that the listening habits of the nation were spearheaded by an unbelievably narrow concentration. "A sponsor's word was law," media critic Leonard Maltin attested. "Smart sponsors put a lot of faith in their advertising agencies, and thus it was major firms like J. Walter Thompson, Young and Rubicam, BBD&O [Batten, Barton, Durstine & Osborn], McCann Erickson, and Foote Cone and Belding that really ruled the airwaves."[9]

The aforementioned Museum of Broadcast Communications delineates how business destined for the ether was transacted in those days, and how it shifted from its premiering stance.[10]

> Through the 1920s most commercial programming originated with networks and/or local stations, with the agency serving as broker, casting about for clients willing to purchase the rights to a broadcaster-produced show. By the early 1930s, however, the agencies had reversed the equation — they were developing shows in-house for clients, then purchasing air time from the broadcasters. The key function for the agency thus became to analyze a client's particular needs and design an entire program around it, an enormously complex and financially risky undertaking, yet one in which Madison Avenue [a synonym for advertising, signified by many large ad agencies headquartered on the infamous Gotham thoroughfare] was entirely successful.

By the end of the 1930s, agencies produced more than 80% of all network commercial programming.

With the advent of commercial television in 1946, ... most agencies accepted as an economic fact that they could no longer afford to create and produce their own shows as they had in radio.... Thus, agencies never assumed the kind of production control in television they enjoyed in radio; they could never put into play the same economies of scale as the networks and independent producers. The 15% commission that served as the source of agency revenue simply was not enough to cover the ever-increasing expenses associated with television production....

Today, the advertising agency is primarily responsible for the production of commercial spots as well as the purchasing of air time on behalf of clients.

Aside from the burgeoning expenses linked with deriving material for the voracious appetite of television — which the advertising agencies were unable to satisfy, causing them to alter their relationship with the big chains as video debuted on the scene — there was still another factor figuring into the equation that ultimately released the agencies' implicit stranglehold on the audio webs. Those nets had long wanted to wrest away the power over the programming they aired that had been almost totally vested in the agencies. With CBS chairman William S. Paley among powerful individuals leading the charge, the phenomenon that persisted for more than a decade and a half suddenly began to erode during the postwar years. Part of the lore of vintage radio that actually stemmed from reality evolved out of Paley's carefully devised plan to siphon off some of the rival chains' biggest name entertainers (e.g., *Amos 'n' Andy*, Jack Benny, Edgar Bergen and Charlie McCarthy, George Burns and Gracie Allen, Bing Crosby, Groucho Marx, Ozzie and Harriet Nelson, Harold Peary, Red Skelton, et al.) in 1948 and 1949.

A confirming byproduct of that extraordinary exploit was that Paley was able to loosen the ad agencies' inflexible grip on radio programming forever, making deals directly with the performers for the first time in a very long while. Theoretically, until then the various comedians, vocalists, instrumentalists, etc., had been *employees of the agencies themselves*. Those entertainers signed pacts directly with the advertising agencies that purchased the network time that was underwritten by the sponsors. In most cases, the sponsors also paid the agencies commission fees for the talent they recruited, on top of the 15 percent they received for producing and packaging the shows.

You will recall that originally advertising agents were literally the middlemen of the ether. As noted in a previous chapter, for a long while the big chains were content to recline "at the receipt of custom, conceding slabs of time, and taking in return the increasingly large sums of money proffered by advertisers." Those networks, an authority maintained, "largely abdicated to the interests and point of view of agencies and firms that have become more masters than clients." As time passed, and certainly after radio became entrenched, the professionals were light years removed from being mere intermediaries, however: in the opinion of many radio historians, they held the whip hand — in effect, an indispensable requisite for a heavyweight. Paley and his counterparts at the other coast-to-coast hookups, meanwhile, were gradually becoming anxious, even determined, to reacquire the absolute control of their webs' schedules that they had freely abandoned in the distant past of chain radio's earliest days.

Paley wasn't operating in a vacuum for sure. There were others in the industry that saw things as he did. NBC's champion in that respect was Sylvester L. "Pat" Weaver, who joined that chain as vice president in charge of television in 1949. An ingenious creative, Weaver was to heavily influence the programming of NBC Radio when he got hold of it four years hence after rising to the company's presidency. Despite the fact his early California radio career trailed off into advertising posts with Young & Rubicam and the American Tobacco Company, "Like a politician elevated to the Supreme Court, he showed signs of liberation from past pressures," noted one observer. "The network must regain control," Weaver emphatically pontificated. A few years earlier, Paley had already brought that notion to fruition at CBS. It occurred in a peculiar yet ingenious way.

During the Second World War, Paley fulfilled a largely ceremonial obligation to the U.S. Office of War Information. Beginning in 1943, he turned up in South America, Europe and wherever his presence might be considered advantageous to American party-line interests in time of conflict. A biographer filled in some details of the age of enlightenment that settled above and around the broadcasting guru.[11]

> As Paley neared the end of his wartime rite of passage, he resolved to change the way he worked and lived. He had a new appreciation of CBS as a worldwide communications medium. He had seen his network from a distance and through the eyes of others. He knew he had to recapture the power he had ceded to the advertising agencies before the war....
>
> In 1946, Paley introduced four CBS-produced half-hour radio shows. He put them on the air while he sought sponsorship. Instead of permitting advertisers to take over production, Paley offered only to sell the commercial time, theorizing that a successful CBS-owned show could serve as the anchor for an evening's schedule. Each show was supposed to deliver an audience big enough to keep the surrounding programs from defecting to NBC.
>
> Accustomed to calling all the shots, advertisers resisted Paley's plan. But he refused to budge, and in a matter of months they began to see that Paley's format could serve their interests as well. CBS-produced programs cost less and were also less risky for the advertising agencies. By the end of 1947 CBS was producing thirty-six of its own programs, fifteen of which had commercial sponsorship.

That's how such consequential features like *My Friend Irma, Life with Luigi, My Favorite Husband* and *Our Miss Brooks* originally took to the ether. All were huge successes, and all were in-house productions, most without sponsorship at their start. Out of that deal CBS was able to acquire the services of its biggest star of several decades, Lucille Ball, while transferring many of the series it originated as radio sustainers (sans underwriters) to television where they reaped vast audiences and generated titanic profits for the web.

In the early 1920s, before radio carried much advertising, the advertising agencies had considered all of the hoopla over the airwaves to be little more than "a fad."[12] During the 1920s, they resisted radio as an advertising method while broadcasters tended to view the agencies as competitors rather than potential allies. The agencies' entry into radio program production resulted from a combination of propaganda and profit maximization. "The advent of radio gave the agencies much trouble and expense, without any considerable amount of gain in revenue to offset the new burden," a scholar maintained.[13] Yet promoters of radio advertising believed that agencies and broadcasters could find working together profitable for both, chiefly because the agencies already wielded the power over most of the national advertising accounts.

Broadcast Advertising scribe Gordon Best, writing in July 1932, referred to the aural medium as a "lusty new member" of the professional trade, and urged the advertising agencies to accord it "recognition fully commensurate with its present importance and future potentialities." While radio stations had, out of necessity, originally been their own producers—conceiving of programs and procuring talent—promoters ascertained that programs designed by advertising agencies would be more effective as commercial vehicles than shows created by broadcasters.

The agencies provided package assistance to the networks and a few larger stations, usually situated in a handful of markets, as early as the 1931 to 1932 radio season. Their services included program selection, casting, direction and other strategic aspects of delivery, freeing the networks and outlets from those confining responsibilities. Yet, from the late 1940s onward, never again would the advertising agencies experience the almost unchallenged halcyon epoch they had enjoyed from the early 1930s. They had firmly held the reins for nearly two decades, sitting in the driver's seat of network programming and determining the listening habits of legions in immense nationwide audiences. While their output would continue to influence those who encountered their work — and still does so today — collectively, those firms wouldn't occupy positions of virtual hegemony of the day-to-day output of any media.

During the nearly two decades that the advertising agencies steered much of radio's direction, their responsibilities encompassed a diverse span of activities. In small agencies, one or two people could have worn several hats, performing multiple responsibilities. But in the bigger firms, tasks were spread across a range of assignments.

The core of an advertising agency, then as now, was the people who literally created the ads, frequently referred to as the creative department. They included copywriters, artists and other talented professionals. Another critical allocation was that of account services or the account management function. As the agency's sales reps, account executives met with clients to determine sales goals and establish creative strategies while coordinating the creative, media and production staffs behind a campaign. The creative services department of an agency, on the other hand, maintained contacts with media suppliers (print, outdoor, broadcast, direct mail and other forms). There were still more specialists on larger agencies' staffs working in production, research and support services, among a myriad of fields.

A succinct examination of the major steps involved when an advertising agency created a new program for a sponsor will supply some enlightening and possibly absorbing details into an agency's internal operations.

After the advertiser and the agency selected radio as their medium of choice, the agency created a program format or chose a show proffered by an independent package producer. Several possibilities might be presented to the advertiser, with whom the final determination rested on which program series would air. About that time, the agency sought a network and a time slot that could satisfy the sponsor's requirements sufficiently.

The chains themselves entered the picture at that juncture. The webs' research departments armed their network salesmen with audience and market-research data, optimistically hoping to persuade the advertiser to choose their net for its new series. Meeting with the radio department at the sponsor's agency, the radio salesmen lobbied hard. The advertiser pronounced the final verdict after hearing from the salesmen and in consultation with the agency's account executive. In the interim, before the formal contracts were signed, an exchange of letters between the agency and the network sufficed as a binding legal agreement.

In the meantime, the web would have already determined if the commodity or service to be advertised was acceptable for the ether. (For a while, laxatives, hard liquor, deodorants, toothpaste and a few other product lines were on an unapproved list.) Simultaneously, the chain's program department would have scrutinized the quality and suitability of the proposed feature to be sure that it met current levels of network stipulations of propriety. When those hurdles were satisfied, contracts — prepared by the network — were signed for specific calendar runs. Except in rare instances, they bore some variation of the traditional 13-week cycle unit, a third of the regular broadcast season. The ad agency's radio time-buyers initiated the details that were enumerated in the contract.

The next items on the agency's agenda called for contracting with the talent selected for the program followed by planning and writing the script for the opening program of the series. The agency's literary clearance staff approved handling of all quotations, dramas, books, parodies, lyrics, poems, impersonations, testimonial letters and fan mail called for in the script. The firm's music clearance panel sanctioned the melodies and authorized any composition royalty payments. At that point, the finished script had to gain approval of the network's sales service manager. After that was accomplished, the document was reproduced via mimeographing then rechecked by the agency's continuity acceptance department. At last, it was presented to the network and distributed to the show's participants — cast and crew — in time for rehearsals and broadcast.

In the meantime, the advertising agency had already picked two individuals from its staff, a producer and a director, who rode herd on the program from start to finish. Although they were in charge, they worked alongside a producer assigned by the network from its own staff. The studio engineers were supplied by the network's technical operations staff, among whose duties were to prepare both the studio and sound system. The network also furnished the sound effects technicians for each show.

To state that the advertising agency was in utter command of a scheduled program on a network in the 1930s and 1940s and leave it at that, of course, doesn't do justice to what actually transpired. Although in one sense the agencies out-and-out ran the show, the national chains maintained hundreds of staff aides who augmented all that the advertising agency did on behalf of the sponsor. Nearly a score of specialized staff department services existed at the big chains, charged with a multitude of duties. Almost all of them were connected in some way with virtually every program their web broadcast. Here's a list of the typical departments found at the network headquarters, along with their most conventional functions.[14]

General Sales— selling network time by lining up stations to air it
Research— gathering and analyzing audience measurement and marketing data
Continuity Acceptance— administering standards for program and commercial messages
Program— furnishing a surfeit of talent and program production personnel
Legal— preparing, approving, interpreting and administering contracts and official documents
Sales Promotion-Advertising— creating sales campaigns for network programming
Publicity— supplying news media with information on programs and artists
Photographic— preparing visuals to support the publicity function
Sales-Service— liaison between the client's agency and production staff, totally focused on the advertiser and the agency
Traffic— arranging program transmission, cut-ins, switches, reversals, station additions, and so on
Station Relations— acquiring and deleting affiliates and negotiating their contracts with the network
Mail-File-Mimeograph— sorting program fan mail and routing to agency account executive, reproducing and distributing press releases
Program Ticket— printing and dispatching tickets for audience shows
Page-Hostess-Guest Relations— the face of the sponsor at studio broadcasts, receiving, directing and informing eyewitnesses and network visitors
Program Development— crafting sustained programs, some of which become sponsored series

Script Library— maintaining a repository of permanent scripts aired, for legal, historical and promotional purposes
Sound Effects— providing specific noises called for in program scripts
News-Public Affairs— airing news, features and analyses, plus news inserts in non-news programming
Recording— taping programs for rebroadcast and general reference

By comparison with the vintage radio era, contemporary advertising agency revenues are staggering. Many of the larger firms, after several permutations, have been swallowed up by gargantuan holding conglomerates consisting of several of the planet's leading advertising agencies. Based on 2005 global revenues released by trade publication *Advertising Age*, the first place Omnicom Group headquartered in New York City generated billings in excess of $10,481,000,000 that year. Omnicom presently includes BBDO, DDB Worldwide, Goodby Silverstein & Partners, GSD&M, TBWA and the subgroup TBWA/Chiat/Day. The second place amalgamation, London-based WPP, spawned over $10 billion in business also. At this writing, WPP consists of Grey Global Group, JWT, Ogilvy & Mather and Young & Rubicam. Advertising is still handsomely rewarding those who can afford its services. Volney Palmer could hardly know how to respond to the mighty proliferation of his brainchild.

A contemporary ad agency operative flippantly recalls how things were in the trade when he entered it a few decades ago. They were pasting up ads then with X-acto knives and straight edges while pounding out copy on typewriters, making reproductions with carbon paper, physically cutting and splicing tape for radio and television commercials, mailing stuff or hand-delivering it because FedEx and fax machines "hadn't been invented" and researching at the library instead of online because that, too, was still down the line. But then the pensive historian turned solemn in his assessment — uncompromisingly so — while weighing modern ad agencies with those of their antecedents.[15]

> Another aspect of the advertising business that's undergone enormous change is the relationship between the agency and the advertiser. Agencies and their clients used to be a lot closer than they are today; the relationship was less adversarial and more collegial. What was once a true business partnership with real benefits on both sides has evolved into something that is often nothing more than a fairly casual buyer/supplier association.
>
> This is especially unfortunate, because the great creative work, the "big ideas," the savvy marketing advice is much more likely to come from an agency that feels it is part of the business of its client rather than a distant, outside vendor.
>
> When I first started in the advertising industry, ad agencies competed with other ad agencies for business. Today, we compete with our own clients. More and more of the work that was traditionally handed to professional communicators ... is now being handled "in-house".... Those companies that do go outside for marketing support services are often working with two or three different marketing communications firms, so no single one of them knows too much or has anything like control of the campaign....
>
> Let this be a plea for a return to the good old days, when advertisers took agencies into their confidence and made them full partners in the marketing process. Let's go back to a time when there was an honest commitment between agencies and clients.

It's a sensitive petition calling for a return to those thrilling days of yesteryear. A characteristic proffered by the golden days of radio was the harmonious relationship — a venerated respect, possibly — that existed between advertisers and their representatives in the ethereal age. For the client and the practitioner, it very likely was the best of both worlds.

4

Audience Measurement Services: Counting the House

> *"Is there anybody there?" said the Traveller,*
> *Knocking on the moonlit door; ...*
> *"Tell them that I came, and no one answered,*
> *That I kept my word," he said.*

Vintage radio was like Walter de la Mare's thwarted nocturnal journeyman in the poem "The Listeners": it was never absolutely certain who was there, who was tuning in. But that didn't stop radio — and a handful of enterprising capitalists — from giving the matter their very best shot at an educated guess.

"I would like research specialists to admit that a broadcast rating is merely an *indication* of an audience ... to begin to use some old-fashioned words like *approximately, possibly, perhaps,* and *maybe,*" asserted Jack Geller in *Broadcasting*. The vice president and media director of Weiss & Geller elucidated: "I would like them to be a little more humble."

"U.S. advertisers, who spend some $200,000,000 a year trying to persuade people to buy things," *Time* posited on January 4, 1943, "have never been quite sure what they were getting for their money, who was listening to their programs or for how long. Even replies to questions asked of radio listeners are not conclusive (few people watch their own radio habits like hawks)."

Early in broadcasting's life the need for audience measurement became clear. Simplistically speaking, reliable, accurate, objective statistics could assist in determining the size of the crowd hearing given programs. Networks and local stations could set their advertising rates thereby, based upon the projected numbers comprising their audiences. Network and station revenues were directly tied to ratings as a result. The information at that time was — as it is now for television programming — sold to sponsors, advertising agencies, networks, individual stations and other organizations that were and are vitally concerned with the relative standings of entertainers and their shows.

Separate rating service reports were readied for broadcast time buyers (advertisers and agencies) and sellers (networks and stations). While they were pricey — especially those prepared for sellers — the documents quickly gained status for their detail and precision. The initial raw quantitative data they furnished simply pacified most advertisers until the time qualitative reports surfaced down the road apiece. In regard to that information, program rating data could be deciphered then by income levels, geographic regions and other valuable statistical profiles, an innovation of sizeable merit to astute advertisers.

A few clarifications are probably in order before proceeding any further. At the outset, the word *rating* is sometimes confusing because it may be understood in both a distinct as well as a general context. Simplified, in a specific sense, ratings refer to the percentage of all the people or households in a signified locality who are tuned to a particular program. In contrasting broad-spectrum terms, however, the idiom suggests a process that seeks to establish the number and types of listeners (or today, TV viewers, although our applications hereafter will be limited to radio unless designated otherwise).

While making those distinctions, to avoid confusion within the mind of the novice whose background is acquainted with ratings in a limited or purely superficial context, let's distinguish between a *ratings point* and a *share* before proceeding. These are a couple of weighty expressions that characterize the province of audience measurement even more. While they are seemingly often publicized as crucial determinants, they remain vague and obscure to most of us without a working knowledge of the industry's internal structure. A single national *ratings point* represents 1 percent of the total estimated number of households equipped with radio receivers. A *share*, on the other hand, is the percentage of those sets currently in use and tuned to a definite (identifiable) program. Such numbers are usually reported as ratings points/ share.

As a model, consider that a ratings service may affirm that a current show received 8.8/13 during its broadcast. Interpreted, that means that an average 8.8 percent of the total radio-equipped households in the country were on at any given moment. Additionally, 13 percent of all radios in use at the time were airing the specific show. Ratings providers such as contemporary marketing research leader The Nielsen Company (formerly known as VNU) recalculate the number of American households at least annually in an effort to keep their projections current.

With that unadorned tutoring in basic vocabulary, before continuing, for a moment let's hearken back to a previous investigation (in Chapter 1): it will contribute some useful background for placing the history of broadcast audience measurement methods in its proper connotation.

> The development of radio advertising recapitulated aspects of the growth and professionalization of the larger advertising industry. The first national print advertisers had not known the circulations of the widely scattered newspapers in which they advertised. Daniel Pope noted that "until well into the new century, agents and advertisers bought literally billions of dollars of advertising space — worrying all the while — without a reliable idea of how many copies of the publications they were using actually were printed or reached customers." Uncertainty about the size and composition of the audience increased the participation of advertising agencies in the advertising process, as uneasy clients turned to professionals with specialized knowledge. The movement of advertising agencies from space brokers to advertisement producers to marketing advisers had been completed by the 1920s, when the process reoccurred in broadcast advertising. Early radio advertisers also lacked information about audience size and were therefore reluctant to use the medium. Contests and premiums designed to attract mail helped gauge the number of listeners. But the growing participation of advertising agencies in broadcasting also helped rationalize the process and calm the fears of advertisers.[1]

Until the arrival of professionals who scientifically gathered statistical data on radio listening habits, concerned parties had little choice but to depend on less exacting means of judging a show's acclaim. The most common system was to invite fans to request a complimentary — or at least nearly-gratis ("for just one thin dime and a box-top or product label") — premium (i.e., trinket, simulated jewelry, celebrity photograph, flower seeds or widget). When the sponsor knew how many gizmos had been shipped, he could guesstimate the size of the total audience. Virtually all of the episodic audio features utilized the premium ploy to skillful advantage, including the matinee soap operas, late-afternoon juvenile adventures and early evening serialized comedies and dramas.

While all of this primeval data-gathering was going on with network audiences, in the meantime, local outlets were being accosted by advertisers insisting on factual knowledge about their listeners as well before they purchased any time. Those enterprising broadcasters derived their audience figures by employing a myriad of tactics.

> Most stations were content to solicit reactions to programs and read incoming mail. Others, using FRC [Federal Radio Commission]-required engineering surveys of their coverage area, simply thought of the population residing within the coverage area as their audience. Under increasing sponsor pressure, they acknowledged that such figures did not reflect actual listenership, and turned to active methods of discovering audience loyalty and interest. Stations variously made free premium offers, to boost audiences and to gauge their size; analyzed set sales figures, to establish the size and approximate location of the potential audience; and mailed questionnaires that sought data on audience size, preferences, and basic demographic characteristics. A few larger stations sent out interviewers to collect the same data. Although costly, personal interviews avoided a sampling bias of telephone interviews: only about half the American homes had telephones in the early 1930s.[2]

Aside from such early and diverse conjecturing, nevertheless, the heritage of professional ratings gathering we are accustomed to today points back to a sacrosanct trio of entrepreneurial spirits and the firms they founded during radio's halcyon era. Their unforgettable surnames are Crossley, Hooper and Nielsen. All three carried big sticks in their industry. Almost all of the credit for the ground-breaking parameters of the business may, in fact, be attributed to this triumvirate. What they accomplished in audience measurement ultimately placed a crown on the heads of certain performers while symbolically quantifying others for deep six farewells. And as so much of the early information these pioneers collected was gathered via telephone, could any affirmation of them maybe be considered — just possibly, anyway — a "ringing endorsement"?

Despite the simultaneous donations of public opinion collectors Elmo Roper (1900 to 1971) and George Gallup (1901 to 1984) to the trade, the most impressive contributions to radio audience measurement's beginnings can be attributed to Archibald Maddock Crossley. Together Crossley, Gallup and Roper — who had earlier used simple straw polls to gain data, interviewing as many people as they could turn up — devised a foundational scheme applying a scientifically selected random sampling to proportionately represent the opinions of the entire population.

It was Crossley who pointedly focused the technique on the aural medium. Incidentally, he should not be confused with the enterprising automobile and appliance manufacturer and owner of WLW Radio in Cincinnati, industrialist Powel Crosley, Jr. (Note the surname spelling.) Instead, A. M. Crossley was born at Fieldsboro, New Jersey, on December 7, 1896, and pioneered in scientific polling techniques that heavily relied upon statistically representative population samples.

In 1926, he founded the New York market research firm Crossley, Inc., subsequently renamed Crossley Surveys. Three years hence Crossley became the first to direct his total attention to deciphering radio audiences. By 1936, he signed with the Hearst newspaper chain, writing a syndicated column appearing in more than 50 journals under his byline. In so doing, during the 1936 presidential campaign he competed directly with *Fortune* magazine's Roper Polls and Gallup's independent weekly reports. In the 1940s, Crossley became a prominent presidential election pollster, specializing in that arena until 1952. He retired from the business he had begun in 1962 and died May 1, 1985, at his Princeton, New Jersey home. He was 88.

In 1930, the Association of National Advertisers — a contingent of like-minded cohorts — launched a non-profit entity, the Cooperative Analysis of Broadcasting (C.A.B.). Organized by Archibald Crossley, it was the country's first national ratings service and its statistical nomenclature was soon popularly dubbed "the Crossleys." A short time prior to this, in May 1928, *Radio Broadcast* projected similar pursuits. The primitive trade periodical colorfully depicted the missions undertaken by Crossley and followers as "equivalent to determining the number of crickets chirping at any instant in a swamp on a foggy summer evening." Even Crossley himself is reported to have admonished, "A rating should always be considered as subject to some deviation, plus or minus." Just the same, the discoveries from ratings, according to one authoritative source, "almost at once became a factor in program decisions."[3] Many people, so it seemed, believed improved programming was an instinctive result.

Using random home telephone numbers from directories in 30 or more cities, Crossley's staff called individual homes to inquire about listening habits: specifically and initially, Crossley wanted to know what radio programs they had heard on the day before the call. The process was identified as the *recall method* because people were remembering what they had listened to on the previous day. The scheme was modified as competition arose, however, with subjects being telephoned four times daily to determine what they had been hearing in a recent two- to four-hour timeframe.

Because the calls cost about 40 cents each to make, the C.A.B. attempted to reduce its expenses by instituting a postal card application. The mail system was a dismal failure, regrettably; the response rate was never more than 5 percent and often as little as 3 percent.[4] So it was hastily discarded and the telephones began ringing again in randomly-selected homes. The C.A.B. made 3,000 calls daily nationwide and published the ratings information it derived every other week. Any single program's rating was based on no less than 1,500 calls across a two-week period. The prevailing Crossley technique was highlighted in a discourse appearing in *Time* on January 29, 1940:

> To lie-abeds or people in the shower, the chirrupy voice that sometimes phones at 8 A.M. to ask what radio programs you heard last night may seem a Galluping nuisance. But from radio's point of view, the early-bird checker for Crossley, Inc. is doing a mighty important job. She, and 50 other such investigators in 33 major network cities from coast to coast, are "counting the house," for in the radio business, "Crossley ratings" are the official box-office count. Crossley's boss is the Cooperative Analysis of Broadcasting, instituted eleven years ago by a fact-lacking group of advertisers and ad agencies, and now subscribed to, for from $40 to $300 a month, by 63 sponsors, agencies, broadcasters, etc.
>
> Last week, in the fortnightly trade journal Broadcasting-Broadcast Advertising, C.A.B.'s statisticky Manager Alcuin Williams Lehman reported on the Crossley ups & downs (i.e., audience preferences) for 1939.
>
> First in the hearts of radio listeners all year, with a Crossley rating over December of 40% or better of all radio homes sampled, was Chase and Sanborn's whittled imp, Charlie McCarthy. Second: Jack Benny. Third: Lux Radio Theatre. Next, in finishing order at year's end: Fibber McGee & Molly, Kraft Music Hall (Bing Crosby), Major Bowes, Bob Hope, Fitch

Band Wagon, Kate Smith, Pot o' Gold. Fred Allen, in the first ten since 1934, finished eleventh.

Humorist Allen, incidentally, was to have something to say — as he frequently did — about any perceived wrongs that needed righting. Speaking of the infamous "Hooperatings" in 1949, the successor to the Crossleys, the sardonic comic allowed: "[Hooper] calls up a few people ... and tells you how many listeners you have in the whole 48 states. It's like multiplying the bottom of a bird cage and telling you how many grains of sand there are in the Sahara Desert."

Since no one knew precisely how many radios were in operation altogether in the United States or were turned on at any specific moment, admittedly there could be no accurate ballpark figure for the total number of listeners to a show being aired. Nevertheless, the results of audience measurement testing were believed to be scientifically representative of the total number of households in a given geographical arena, and offered what was proffered as a plausibly reliable estimate of the crowd tuning in.

For its part, the C.A.B. divided the day into a quartet of time periods. The unit quickly discovered that the largest audiences were listening at night, something people of the modern age have known for decades but which was not readily established until that time. Half of the working radio sets were in use at 9 o'clock and 10 o'clock while a third were operating at 7 o'clock and 11 o'clock in the evening.[5] The premise of *primetime* hours was literally conceived during the vintage epoch and it remains with us now.

An inherent weakness in the Crossleys was that the person interviewed — often a housewife — could be speaking for several members of a family unit and would hardly remember every program heard by every individual. It put a strain on the respondent for yet another reason: sometimes memories play strange tricks in the matter of recalling what one believes to be fact.

After about 17 years as the dominant mode of collecting audience measurement data, in 1946 the Crossleys were finally outdistanced; the Hooperatings became the next dominant collection method. The transition came about as several for-profit commercial outfits began offering comparable services that surpassed the Crossleys in popular perception.

Claude Ernest Hooper, genially known as "Hoop" in radio circles, was born May 21, 1898, at Kingsville, Ohio. He was an alumnus of Amherst College (1921) and the Harvard School of Business Administration (1923). A colleague characterized him as possessing "a remarkable ability to cut through a maze of statistical detail to ultimate conclusions." He died at 56 on December 15, 1954, the victim of a freak boating accident on the Great Salt Lake at Salt Lake City, Utah.

In autumn 1934, Clark-Hooper, Inc., began selling audience research on magazines and radio to subscribing advertisers. "Clark" was Lloyd M. Clark, who — after four years of counting radio noses — left the business to become headmaster of a Pennsylvania prep school. That year, 1938, the radio enterprise was renamed C. E. Hooper, Inc. The new company's exclusive focus was on providing monthly ratings of network-sponsored — but not sustaining — programs.[6] The Hooper endeavor was, of course, in direct competition with Crossley's long-established C.A.B. service. When the radio networks began drifting into television, however, the Hooper firm refocused its attention to accommodate the growing TV audience, beginning in 1948.[7] The expanded dual-medium accent continued under the Hooper aegis only briefly on the other hand. In February 1950, the unit was sold to the A. C. Nielsen Company, yet another rival, with Hooper's assets swallowed by that escalating marketing organization.[8] Consequently, while the Hooper nomenclature is only nominally recalled today, in its heyday of about 1946 to 1949, "How's your Hooper?"—a reference to audience size of a series—was a familiar catchphrase.

Like Crossley before it, Hooper also employed the telephone as the key device in gathering audience measurement data. But unlike Crossley, which made inquiring calls the day *after* a program aired—or possibly a few hours after a show was heard (the *recall method*), Hooper's approach was to ask respondents what they were listening to *right then*. To obtain a rating, in 1942, for instance, 120 Hooper field workers (usually feminine ex-telephone company operators, former secretaries and teachers working from home) in 32 key cities made phone calls at a rate of 3,000 per hour during a broadcast under surveillance.[9] An inflexible configuration delineated in a 57-page manual given to "reporters" required them to make calls for 13 minutes and then rest for two minutes.[10] They posed a trio of basic questions to anyone answering a home telephone:

1. Were you listening to your radio just now?
2. To what program were you listening, please?
3. What station, please?

Listeners only—those who were asked questions 2 and 3—were then subjected to three more queries designed to elicit specific recall of what was heard plus concise statistical profile data. The supplementary quiz followed without regard to a given order:

4. What is advertised?
5. How many men, women and children are listening?
6. What is the occupation of the head of your household, please?

Households where there was no response were discounted as non-listeners. From the Hooperating, statisticians worked out an estimated audience for a given program. Season, network, geographical region, day of the week, time of day and other intangibles affected the outcomes, of course.

By the way, on one occasion, Hooper analysts took it upon themselves to trace the listening patterns of President Franklin D. Roosevelt's famous radio "fireside chats" to the nation.[11] Beginning with a low of 6.3 billion listeners (or a Hooperating of 9.7) on June 10, 1936, at their start, Roosevelt's track record wandered between extremes. Across his long tenure, he reached his peak with his war message of December 9, 1941, attracting an estimated audience of 62.1 billion for his highest Hooperating, 79.0. Although it isn't an established fact, it's possible the latter figure is the highest rating in radio's history.[12] It readily outperformed what ostensibly may be commercial radio's all-time high watermarks: a 53.4 C.A.B. (or Crossley) earned in early 1931 by a broadcast of *Amos 'n' Andy*, and a 58.4 C.A.B. in January 1933 by *The Chase & Sanborn Hour* starring Eddie Cantor.[13] FDR's impressive achievements to the contrary, the president who held radio near to his bosom had low moments on the ether, too. His Hooperating hit 19.0 in a nationwide speech before the International Student Assembly in early September 1942.

Returning to the subject at hand, the professionals labeled Hooper's technique the *coincidental method* of determining ratings data. That mode boasted a couple of clearly obvious advantages over the one espoused by Crossley: immediacy and greater accuracy. There was little memory loss among respondents with the Hooperatings, and the answers were swift and usually more reliable than attempting to remember what someone heard a few hours or a day earlier.

But there were also weaknesses with the Hooperatings, the chief one being its cost. The coincidental modus operandi required almost 10 times as many telephone calls as the recall method for it supplied data at quarter-hour intervals. And of course, both procedures experienced the complexities of telephoning in sparsely settled areas while discounting radio homes without telephones as well as those with unlisted numbers.

In the October 29, 1954, issue of *Collier's*, journalist Bill Davidson offered a potent exposition on the ratings game by hinting that "broadcasters rely on poll numbers they don't trust." Pensively, take a few moments to read the excerpt of what Davidson had to say and ponder it for a while. There will be a test.

> For years, C. E. Hooper was the kingpin of the radio ratings field. His so-called Hooperatings were based on samplings of listeners in 36 key American cities. Though Hooper never claimed he was producing accurate national ratings, most broadcasting bigwigs took it for granted that the 36 Hooper cities gave an exact picture of listening behavior all over the country.
>
> But then, in the late 1940s, came the mushrooming of television. As it turned out, nearly all of the new stations sprang up in Hooper's 36 cities, causing an inevitable decline in the radio ratings there. The advertising brass took one look at the plummeting ratings and rushed to get out of radio programming. The radio industry was dealt a blow from which it has never fully recovered. It just didn't occur to anyone that Hooper's city ratings bore no relation to what was going on in huge areas of the nation where television had not yet arrived.
>
> In sum, there can be little doubt that most of the damage done by the ratings, from the viewpoint of the audience, at least, results from misuse rather than from defects in the ratings themselves. Yet in some respects, the rating services do fail — just as in others they provide a useful tool for the industry.

Contemplate this for a while: is it conceivable — or possibly even likely — that the foremost audience measurement technique applied at the time figured (and prominently so) into the equation that resulted in the disaster that befell vintage radio in the 1950s? Coming off an inordinately strong 1940s (the quintessence of the "Golden Age," say some observers), did the Hooperatings contribute in any way to the collapse of network radio? Radio had, until then, been the almost universally dependent mass communications form in this country (the first of the breed) for amusement and enlightenment. Is it remotely possible that the ratings collectors played a part in its calamitous demise?

The thinking person would probably have to agree the answer is "yes," given the circumstances presented in Davidson's article. After all, the ratings-gathering operatives were a powerful force as they made headlines in the late 1940s, determining the future of many of the nation's entertainment pursuits. It would seem that they had a gigantic opportunity to influence the outcome of radio's — and television's — fortunes.

While most media historiographers haven't weighed in on that point, there is compelling evidence hinting that. It comes across as a kind of hidden factor in determining radio's fate. It can be added to a pool of dynamics that are typically more visible, and — therefore — projected more often. Among them: (1) television's arrival accompanied by euphoric fanfare among the audiences, artists, advertisers, agencies and affiliates; (2) demand by owners of local radio station affiliates for the release of more and more network time that could be sold more profitably closer to home; (3) shifting sociological patterns that were already beginning to impact long-held practices like families gathering around a living room radio (later, television) in the evenings, a shift that was to become even more pronounced in the late 1950s and 1960s.

As noted already, the firm that A. C. Nielsen founded superseded C. E. Hooper, Inc. Arthur Charles Nielsen, Sr. was born September 5, 1897, in Chicago. (An aside here: the trio of men who became the most influential and thereby the most powerful individuals in radio ratings — Crossley, Hooper and Nielsen — were born within an 18-month timeframe of one another, as the nineteenth century was wearing down. Talk about your coincidental numbers!) Educated at the University of Wisconsin's College of Engineering where Nielsen earned that school's highest scholastic average upon graduation in 1918, he was an ensign in the U.S. Navy during World War I. Following a year as an electrical engineer and three years in field research, in 1923, he founded the A. C. Nielsen Company. His death in Chicago on June 1, 1980, followed an extended illness.

The Nielsen firm's original purpose was to appraise the suitability of industrial machinery for manufacturers. During the epoch of the Great Depression, however, the concern enlarged its premise by tracking the retail sales of nationwide food, drug and liquor brands. According to A&E, the Nielsen Food and Drug Index became the enterprise's "largest operation." The firm expanded into branches located in England in 1939 and Canada in 1944.

By the late 1930s, the Nielsen enterprise entered the commercial segment for which it might be best known by more people in the world — that of measuring tuned-in broadcast audiences. Beginning with radio, the firm drifted into television in 1950, absorbing the trade's leader, C. E. Hooper, Inc., early that year.[14] Nielsen ratings, produced by international connections, subsequently helped the venture become the largest market-research company in the world, A&E reported.

After joining worldwide counterparts, for several years ACNielsen was renamed VNU and jointly based in New York City and Haarlem, The Netherlands. But early in 2007 the privately held global information and media behemoth renamed itself The Nielsen Company, recognizing its indelibly distinctive roots. Today it has more than 42,000 employees in offices in 100-plus countries, hardly imaginable when A. C. Nielsen launched it in 1923. The outfit now maintains leading market positions and recognized brands in marketing information (ACNielsen), media information (Nielsen Media Research), business publications (*Billboard*, *The Hollywood Reporter* and *Adweek*), plus trade shows.

In radio, Nielsen grabbed attention in the audience measurement trade by introducing the Audimeter. Developed at the Massachusetts Institute of Technology, the gizmo was acquired by Nielsen in 1936, *Broadcasting* reported. For four years, 1937 to 1941, the founder put it to use in field-testing audience size. In operation, the device was installed in radio sets and recorded a precise history of the radio's tuning mechanism. During the first year that Nielsen offered its applications commercially in 1942, seven major clients and their ad agencies paid for results from the Nielsen Radio Index findings determined by the gadget.

The Audimeter recorded every twist of the radio switch and dials with a stylus on a moving tape, no matter if a program was found by dial cruising, whether it remained on throughout a full period under study and no matter if it was tuned out at any point. One of the Audimeter's biggest advantages over its closest rivals, the Crossleys and the Hooperatings — aside from the obvious one of faithfully recording the dial twisting as it occurred — was its ability to tap into the preponderance of 1940s rural radio homes that had no telephone service, plus those people with unlisted telephone numbers. But as good an instrument as the Audimeter was, it failed on one major point: it couldn't establish whether anyone was actually listening to a turned-on radio. There were also the inevitable mechanical failures occasionally. Nielsen tended to keep its Audimeters in the same homes for long periods without altering the sample subjects, too, prompting objections in some industry quarters.

Nevertheless, the results of the four years of auditioning the Audimeter among a predetermined cross section of 200 households revealed several persuasive arguments prompting a few Nielsen clients to sign up for the service at $50,000 annually.[15] For instance, the trial effort confirmed that the sponsor's concluding commercial on one of radio's most popular nighttime features was missed by almost everybody who tuned in to the show. It seems that, because the program's host-star said "Goodnight" before the final advertising plug was scheduled, listeners fled. That situation, presumably, was remedied by the sponsor. Meanwhile, the pilot survey indicated that the majority of listeners turned their station dial at least once every quarter-hour. More people tuned in during February than any other month, a staggering 40 percent more than in July, traditionally the lowest listenership month. That was pretty strong proof that people generally stayed indoors during the colder months while many headed outside in the warmer months.

Parenthetically, today the principal radio audience measurement firm is Arbitron, begun in 1949 by Jim Seiler at American Research Bureau (later shortened to ARB, then renamed The Arbitron Company). Arbitron initially gathered TV viewing statistics in the 1950s but began collecting radio data in 1964, its chief focus since. The Arbitron mode requires participants to maintain written diaries in which they record the stations heard at various time periods. They also call for demographic information about age, gender, employment, income, marital status and so on. "Arbitron watches radio listeners," a contemporary institutional ad for the outfit allows. It currently surveys radio listeners in 300 local markets with more than 4,600 radio stations and 1,500 advertising agencies subscribing to its services. Nielsen, meanwhile, persists as the major television audience data-gathering venture.[16]

Bob Schulberg, a former ad agency executive who was eventually a CBS Radio marketing director for many years, simplified the ratings dilemma with this equation:

> Audience numbers determine ratings. Ratings are the basis of factors like cost per rating point, which are used by buyers to evaluate pricing. Sellers must similarly calculate the effect of ratings on their rates. Audience, ratings, and pricing are like horses on a carousel — they keep chasing each other's tails.[17]

In addition to the ratings, which provided estimates of audience size, the first serious research analyses of radio's effect on its audience began to appear. In 1934, Frederick Hillis Lumley's *Measurement in Radio* furnished comprehensive insights on the use of audience research. In 1935, the first report of in-depth audience research, Hadley Cantril and Gordon W. Allport's *The Psychology of Radio*, examined radio's intellectual environment — how listeners received specific programming components — and impending uses of this trial data.

A Rockefeller Foundation grant in 1937 awarded to Princeton University secured the opening of the Office of Radio Research. The unit shifted to Columbia University three years later. Paul F. Lazarsfeld was the inaugural director and was assisted by a couple of young researchers, Hadley Cantril and Frank Stanton. The latter, whose destiny included the presidency of CBS from 1946 to 1971, had been studying audiences for that chain since 1935. He earned a doctorate, incidentally, in part for an industrial psychology dissertation at Ohio State labeled "A Critique of Present Methods and a New Plan for Studying Radio Listening Behavior." The Office of Radio Research's first attention-grabbing exploit was a detailed description of audience ratings since that innovation was first practiced a decade earlier — and their implications upon the medium. Published in 1939 and authored by future NBC research director H. M. Beville, the work was titled *Social Stratification of the Radio Audience*.

In the meantime, Lazarsfeld and Stanton created an electromechanical audience analyzer. It had the capacity to acquire minute-by-minute reactions among a test audience of 30 to 100 people to radio series already on the air while projecting new ones. Participants equipped with separate hand-held gizmos herded together in one room reacted individually to what they heard as a light flashed. That indicated that a favorable or unfavorable response was due. Their reply, recorded graphically, told researchers at what precise points during commercials and programming those witnesses were either attracted or turned off by what they heard.

All of this influenced subsequent programming elements in an attempt to increase audience-holding appeal. The device helped in foretelling just how large an audience for a prospective program might be. While Stanton routinely downplayed the importance of their invention, some industry insiders credited it as the first qualitative measurement device. By the 1990s, the audience analyzer was still in service at CBS and was employed by other commercial interests as well, being particularly useful in gauging television's prospects. Multiple sources contend it maintained an accuracy rate of 85 percent.

So, what are the implications for advertisers and their agencies as a result of audience measurement findings?

In addition to providing the obvious information on how many were listening (as demographics were exploited) to a station, network or program — alluded to repeatedly in the foregoing — and who they were, the ratings data supplied something of additional (and possibly near-equal) importance to those underwriting the ethereal features: it told them how much they were spending to reach their show's fans in comparison to similar programming currently on the airwaves.

In its April 19, 1944, edition, for example, *Variety* released the following figures for a couple of dominant breeds of radio programming for the month of January 1944. Hopefully, the comparisons will be edifying.

Comedy-Variety Series	*Prod. Costs*	*Hooperating*	*Cost Per Point*
Bob Hope	$14,750	31.6	$467
Red Skelton	$ 8,000	31.4	$255
Bergen-McCarthy	$12,000	29.2	$411
Jack Benny	$22,500	27.2	$806
Abbott & Costello	$11,000	24.0	$458
Fred Allen	$14,000	19.8	$707
Situation Comedy	*Prod. Costs*	*Hooperating*	*Cost Per Point*
Fibber McGee & Molly	$10,000	31.9	$313
The Aldrich Family	$ 6,500	26.9	$242
Amos 'n' Andy	$ 9,000	17.1	$526
Blondie	$ 5,000	16.3	$307
The Great Gildersleeve	$ 5,000	16.0	$307
That Brewster Boy	$ 2,750	13.0	$212

By 1950, reported *Variety* in its February 8 issue, comedian Jack Benny's and singer Bing Crosby's weekly features required about $40,000 weekly to produce. At the same time, the typical crime-detective drama could be aired for something between $4,000 and $7,000 a week. While the latter sorting seldom reached the doormat of the Hooper and Nielsen higher echelons, cheaper production formats delivered more listeners per dollar than the prestigious comedy and variety acts. The usual evening mystery in 1950 yielded 267 households per dollar. At the same time, variety-musicals attracted 215 households; general drama, 187; variety-comedy, 163; and concert music, 123.[18]

In another ratings analysis conducted in early February 1946, observers learned that — of 16 programming categories under review — the top three spots among the Hooperatings were held by: A. variety shows headlined by acclaimed comics like Allen, Benny, Skelton (20.4

rating), B. variety shows topped by legendary singers like Como, Crosby, Shore (13.4), and C. situation comedies like *Our Miss Brooks* (12.8). Conversely, at the other end of the spectrum, the lowest three genres were: A. serious or classical concert music like *Metropolitan Opera* broadcasts (3.6), B. daytime audience participation shows like *Queen for a Day* (4.0), and C. daytime juvenile serials like *Jack Armstrong, the All-American Boy* (4.8).

Talent cost comparisons applied at the same time to the 16 program species under study presented an almost altogether opposite picture. The top three least costly categories to staff with performers were: A. women's daytime serials (at $2,211 weekly), B. daytime weekly dramas ($2,875), and C. daytime juvenile serials ($3,133). Meanwhile, the most costly shows in terms of artists permanently featured were: A. variety shows headed by venerated comics ($15,250), B. variety shows topped by popular singers ($13,417), and C. serious or classical concert music ($9,625).

Finally, in a comparison of weekly cost-per-point Hooperatings for the 16 breeds of programming investigated, the lowest three were: A. women's daytime serials ($361.99), B. mystery-detective-horror dramas ($397.21), and C. daytime weekly dramas ($401.84). The three types with highest cost-per-point were: A. serious or classical concert music ($3,156.43), B. semi-classical concert music ($1.070.43), and C. variety shows headlined by recognized singers ($1,019.63).

In the course of his extensive introspective into the wide-ranging spectrum of ratings, Charles Wolfe, who proved a leading advertising analyst of the 1940s, concluded[19]:

> Even though ratings are not infallible, and are frequently misinterpreted, they are the best gage [*sic*] yet devised of the week-by-week and month-by-month size of a program's audience, a point of importance to the advertiser wishing to reach the largest possible number of prospects. Hence ratings will continue, and sponsors, advertising agencies, and radio trade magazines will continue to compare programs ... on the basis of ratings.

Or, in the words of a trendy maxim: *If it ain't broke, don't fix it.*

5

Commercial Copywriters: Persuasive Penmanship

As the 1930s arrived and opportunities arose, an able radio practitioner recalled men with some years of experience in writing newspaper advertising who shifted their loyalties to radio commercials. Tongue-in-cheek, the astute observer depicted a scenario in which broadcast copy was "penned by the left hand of right-handed space writers." The results, he affirmed, were almost always "stiff and unconversational-sounding."[1] A college educator affirmed, "Broadcast advertising had adopted the language of 1920s print advertising."[2] Said another operative, who in 1934 was the first radio commercial wordsmith for an advertising agency: "Writing for the *eye* with illustrations and headlines and typesettings and visual tricks was entirely different from writing for the *ear*, where words, sound effects, and music had to do the job."[3]

Actually, nobody really understood how to tackle radio jargon for a while — not even those who hammered out the programs themselves. Ex-newspaperman Carlton E. Morse, who possessed one of the medium's most fertile pens (*One Man's Family, I Love a Mystery, His Honor — the Barber, The Woman in My House, I Love Adventure, Adventures by Morse, Family Skeleton*, et al.), admitted his frustration: "When I first started to write, which was back in 1929, nobody knew how to write for radio, for the air. They were taking old movies and old stage shows and trying to create something for the air, but it was never quite right. And so from 1929 to 1932, I was being paid to learn to write for radio."[4] But playwright Arch Oboler, who wrote a passel of that genre for the aural airwaves, gloated in the midst of whatever perceived handicaps existed: "Fortunately, radio's need of material is so great that even the good writer gets a chance once in a while."[5]

As the growth of the national chains persuaded the ad agencies that radio was a viable investment — and as local stations recognized that the agencies could generate more dollars for *their* pockets — the advertising professionals amplified their copywriting pursuits. To accomplish the feat, they added people (mostly males at the time) to their staffs with diverse copywriting talents. Almost invariably the earliest scribes proffered background concentrations in the print media. During that groundbreaking epoch, nonetheless, those hacks attempted to master a course in Elementary Copywriting for the Ear 101. There simply wasn't an abundance of skilled artisans who had written to sell to a listening body. Old habits die hard. Writing for a hearing audience instead of a seeing one was to become an acquired taste for the fledgling industry. Radio, and the agencies in particular, wouldn't have long to get it right.

With radio advertisers spending something beyond $400 billion in the late 1940s, an astute ad agency executive appropriately observed, "Every word in the sponsor's announcement assumes importance on a cost basis."[6] The expense of radio copy aired on a local 250-watt station at the time was projected at seven cents a word. During the same timeframe, the tally on the major hookups stretched to an incredible $70 a word! "Advertisers who realize how much attention their commercials deserve, try to maintain a balanced stand: they still keep a sharp eye on their programs, but they also hover over their sales messages with enlightened solicitude, and constantly improve their knowledge of commercial techniques," proclaimed Charles Wolfe, director of the radio and television testing bureau of Batten, Barton, Durstine & Osborn, Inc.[7]

Referring to the extraordinarily princely $56.2 billion the radio trade generated in 1937, media analyst Erik Barnouw cited nearly $8.5 billion of that sum commissionable to the ad agencies that year. Said Barnouw: "The centerpieces of the pageant were the commercials written by hundreds of writers at advertising agencies, at salaries well above those of sustaining dramatic writers."[8] In reality, those artisans that produced ear plugs had become valuable commodities, having perfected the diversification of merely selling to the sighted by encompassing the hearing as well. As one authority astutely recognized, "With radio, the production costs are no more for great words than they are for pedestrian words."[9]

Nevertheless, in recent decades, a sub-trade has ripened around autonomous radio production factories that write and produce radio commercials for ad agencies and their clients. Quite possibly because the money involved is dwarfed by that in television, numerous ad agency wordsmiths and creative directors scoff at radio commercial writing and production. Outsourcing, for them, is a welcome divergence as they concentrate their time and talents on meatier (e.g., more prosperous) tasks.

In the early 1980s, Judith Charles, president of her own retail advertising agency, averred: "A copywriter is a salesperson behind a typewriter."[10] The meaning lingers after updating "typewriter" with "personal computer" or "laptop" or "notebook computer." Freelance copywriter Luther Brock condensed *selling* into less than a score of words: "Placing 100 percent emphasis on how the reader will come out ahead by doing business with you."[11] And electronic keyboard artist Robert Bly insisted, "You must strive to make your copy relevant to the reader, understand what keeps him or her up at night, and address that need, desire, want, or fear."[12]

There are others in the business that underscore the necessity of tailoring the written copy insofar as possible to the specific individual who will be reading it on the air, whether live or via transcription. "Whatever is written for a commercial should not come from the writer's lips but from those of the announcer," a couple of broadcasters-turned-educators advocated. "You should write to fit your own personality when you are writing the commercial in addition to reading it." And when—as in most situations—someone pens the sales lines to be read by an ethereal hawker other than himself, "You must always remember to fit the announcer's personality."[13] That works when you *know who* will read it aloud; much of the time, of course, the writer doesn't.

"Before you begin to write," said a practiced radio scribe, "be aware that all the writing skills you have acquired privately or in a learning institution have been directed toward expressing your thoughts and ideas on paper, in written form. By definition, radio is the antithesis of the written word. The spoken word is governed by completely different rules."[14]

Instructing contemporary advertisers, a prominent retail consultant, Paco Underhill — in demand by consumer goods distributors from coast to coast — attests: "First you have to get your audience's attention. Once you've done that, you have to present your message in a clear, logical fashion — the beginning, then the middle, then the ending. You have to deliver the information the way people absorb it, a bit at a time, a layer at a time, and in proper sequence. If you don't get their attention first, nothing that follows will register. If you tell them too much too soon, you'll overload them and they'll give up. If you confuse them, they'll ignore the message altogether."[15] Underhill's admonitions, if stated four score years ago, could have been just as relevant. They still work today.

A radio writer could do worse, averred CBS marketing executive Bob Schulberg, than adopt Winston Churchill's five keystones of winning speeches: (1) Begin strongly, (2) Have one theme, (3) Use simple language, (4) Leave a picture in the listener's mind, and (5) End dramatically.[16]

Communications educator Robert Hilliard, who was subsequently an FCC staff executive, proffered five styles of commercials that appear to be as applicable now as they were in radio's golden age[17]:

Straight Sell — A straightforward statement about a product, service or seller that clearly communicates, possibly via a hard-sell slant without being antagonistic. An attention-grabber like emphasizing a commodity's unique feature is sometimes exploited.

Testimonial — A message may feature a celebrity endorsing a commodity, idea, etc., or an unknown individual who presumably solves issues similar to those experienced by real listeners while applying the product or service.

Humor — One-liner gags, parodies, subtle satire and other forms of gentle jesting add zip to commercials (depending on how it is used and, of course, what is being advertised).

Music — Messages in which melody is a prominent part are often remembered better than most other formats. About two-thirds of all radio spots used music by the mid–1970s.

Dramatization — Often employing music, testimonials and humor, this distinct category features a pithy narrative, creating suspense and netting a climax that reveals specific qualities of what's being advertised.

In his discourse *Modern Radio Advertising*, Charles Wolfe culled the commercial blueprints of professional media researchers Gordon W. Allport, Hadley Cantril, George Gallup, Paul F. Lazarsfeld, Horace Schwerin, Frank Stanton and more scholarly practitioners of the trade. In so doing, Wolfe offered commercial radio copywriters ideas toward more effective pitches. He focused on making commercials memorable, increasing understanding while attracting bigger audiences.

Maurice B. Mitchell — who became chancellor of the University of Denver in 1967 — was, in 1949, director of broadcast advertising for the National Association of Broadcasters. In that capacity, he set down some guidelines for improving audio copy, cutting awkward frivolity and going for the direct invitation. *Broadcasting* magazine was so impressed with Mitchell's remarks that it selected a portion of them for inclusion in its September 10, 1973, edition. Consider the following sample.

> One of the things we've never been able to understand is why an advertiser will put phrases in his advertising copy that people would never say aloud. Did you ever hear of a woman who called her husband on the phone and said..., "Would you mind stopping in at Jones's Department Store today and buying me a pair of slippers because, there, quality and variety go hand in hand?" ... Don't you think perhaps she might actually say, "I wish you'd buy me a pair of slippers at Jones' because their sale ends today and I can't get downtown"? She is telling her husband specifically what she wants, specifically why she wants it, and she makes a decision to buy for a specific reason....

The master showman of radio, Arthur Godfrey, turned out to be the medium's master salesman. Once he discovered he could sell more goods to more listeners by banishing the straitlaced formality that dominated the ether in its seminal epoch of mass persuasion, Godfrey triumphed as others failed. Talking one-on-one with his "customers," he introduced humor to his delivery, even sticking it to the sponsor, to the sheer delight of fans. His favorite female singer, Jan Davis, observes Godfrey eating a cracker on Nabisco's weekday segment of CBS's *Arthur Godfrey Time* as the studio audience is fed with various sponsors' wares.

While Mitchell's admonitions pertained to retail and service-oriented sellers, with slight adjustments, the proposals could be applied to a product or idea as well. And they seem to be as constructive for the twenty-first century as they were in the twentieth.

Radio commercials that sounded like people talked had (and still have) a lot going for them. The venerable radio showman Arthur Godfrey understood that principle as well as anyone and better than most. He became a harbinger for change in aural advertising, and as a result millions listened to him and bought the goods he recommended. But he wasn't all that successful before becoming convinced of the error of his ways.

It happened when Godfrey was laid up in a hospital bed for several months in 1931, the victim of a freak automobile accident that nearly took his life. Having little better to do, day after day he tuned in the programs reverberating from his bedside radio. Until then, he had been a typical radio announcer in a local market whose duty it was to deliver a never-ending barrage of commercials throughout the workday. Addressing no one in particular, he'd read copy penned in a stuffed-shirt manner, applying a broad-A British accent. The brogue was standard delivery among the early announcer-elocutionists and came naturally to Godfrey by way of his well-educated British father. The sales script frequently began, "Ladies and gentlemen," and proceeded from there. It was, in a word, dreadful.

While off work, Godfrey groused about it to himself so much that he determined he would implement a new style when he returned to the microphone. Instead of seeing a vast faceless audience from then on, he tailored his communications to a single listener as his primary challenge. His mission had become to convince that unseen individual to purchase the commodity he espoused. Godfrey chatted as if he was carrying on a conversation in a living room and not over the air. In so doing, he revolutionized commercial delivery as well as advertising copywriting for the air.

Although some in the industry were initially skeptical, his methods proved to be a stroke of genius. He sold unbelievable numbers of products: in his heyday in the late 1940s and early 1950s, Godfrey personally was responsible for generating 12 percent of CBS's annual revenues. On the air, he often claimed that he paid the network's expenses for the day before CBS chairman William S. Paley got out of bed for the day! Sponsors figuratively stood in line to get on Godfrey's programs, even when he took swipes at them, a departure the audiences loved which led to still more lucrative sales. While Godfrey was the front man, he was transforming copywriting all over America. As a result, he transitioned the industry to focus on what was important to the listener rather than the sponsor. It altered the auditory landscape permanently.

Godfrey got his jollies by poking fun at the commercials. Few, possibly with the exception of Henry Morgan, did it as well as he did. "Send in the boxtop from Post Bran Flakes for your free coupon," he told his audience on one occasion. "The Post folks [General Foods Corporation] need those boxtops. They ran out at the factory and if they don't get some tops for the boxes they'll have to send out their flakes loose. And you know those Bran Flakes people hate anything loose." The studio crowd responded with hearty guffaws.

One of his clients was Thomas J. Lipton Company which sponsored his longrunning *Talent Scouts* program on Monday nights plus a segment of his *Arthur Godfrey Time* variety show on weekday mornings to his final broadcast in 1972. He'd use those public airwaves platforms to crack up studio audiences as he stuck a needle in the sponsor and, by implication, the unseen copywriter that prepared those diatribes.

> I have here a piece of script from the client. Hey Arch [orchestra leader Archie Bleyer]—better give me some soft music. This is a poem ...
>
> In olden days each housewife had a pot ... [*Long pause, accompanied by gales of studio audience laughter*]
>
> Of soup ... upon the stove ... [*Reads rest of the poem*]
>
> I'll translate it. Lipton noodle soup and Lipton tomato vegetable soup is the doggedness' soup you ever had in your life. Ever see it in the box? Here, I'll put them up here ... This is the chicken noodle soup. [*Pause*] A chicken once sat in a nest near the pot. [*Pause*] It has a decided chickeny flavor. In fact, a delightful flavor. In fact, I think there's some chicken in it. [*Pause*] One moment. I will have a look. [*Opens the package, followed by long pause*] No chicken been in here! [*Uproarious laughter during pause*] But it's full of noodles....[18]

On occasions, Godfrey would pick up the commercial copy and hold it in the air for the fans to see. Then he'd toss it onto the floor or wad it into a ball and pitch it on the floor while ad-libbing for the sponsor, a visual and verbal demonstration of his "I-can-do-it-my-way-and-won't-be-bound-by-a-script" mindset. Of course, it irritated the advertising agency no end. Yet, he seldom made light of the commodities he championed—he got bigger laughs ridiculing those responsible for the formality he abhorred.

And his effectiveness was unquestioned. In a 1996 Arts & Entertainment cable network interview, CNN television personality Larry King recalled:

> I guess I was nine or ten years old. And I was home from school, sick. And Arthur Godfrey was doing a commercial for Peter Pan peanut butter. And he said, "I know you're not supposed to do this, but I'm gonna eat this peanut butter on the air." [*Pause*] He put it in his mouth, and naturally when you put peanut butter in your mouth, you can't talk very good, so he was saying [*King imitates Godfrey trying to speak with peanut butter in his mouth*], "Aw, this is good!" Well, I went nuts. I ran to the cupboard. We had no peanut butter. And with a fever I got dressed ... no one was home ... went to the store and bought a jar of Peter Pan peanut butter and brought it home. I could *taste* that peanut butter. I had to *have* that peanut butter. Arthur Godfrey *sold* me that peanut butter!

With all due respect, I ask you, could a scribe with three degrees in advertising and mass communications and years of on-the-job experience as a practiced artisan penning copy for the best agency in America have been more effective? We've probably come to the same conclusion.

Finally, a case study in commercialization that obviously sold and sold well (or else the format would not have persisted for so many years). These dual examples lend sparkle by replacing the oft-dreaded straightforward advertising plug: in both instances, the all-too-frequent droning solo salesman is missing, replaced by lighthearted dialogue between two familiar voices that instantly connect with the majority of (in this instance) homemaker-listeners. And by padding the mix with sound effects apropos to the milieu, the unnamed penmen and penwomen score a home run with their plugs virtually every time out. Working with considerable latitude and depth, they establish a running series of slice-of-life scenarios against a recognized, believable backdrop that exploits their sponsors' wares with attention-getting sequences. What they deliver is, in effect, a playlet within a play.

A couple of matinee misery mills ground out competing sales letters from their larders resulting in baking goods that sounded incredibly scrumptious and were made with espoused manufactured goods. The chefs applying them in their ethereal kitchens could produce a cake, pie, muffins, cornbread or dumplings in no time flat—about as fast as it took to extricate a greasy spot from a pantry shelf. Dwelling on the senses of smell, taste and sight, the agency copywriters had Aunt Jenny and Bess Pringle (*Young Doctor Malone*'s sporadic spokeswoman) whipping up tasty culinary treats in profusion, and the descriptive metaphors accompanying them were equally as tempting. Who, frankly, could resist?

For Lever Brothers, the makers of Spry shortening, announcer Dan Seymour popped into Aunt Jenny's sunlit kitchen every day. (Initially, Aunt Jenny was played by actress Edith Spencer, and later by Agnes Young. And as we discovered in a previous chapter, the airwaves personalities were really the employees of an advertising agency rather than of a network, in this case Ruthrauff and Ryan, the Lever Brothers advocate.)

The din of a boiling teakettle, frying skillet or a whistling canary (the latter provided by wildlife imitator Henry Boyd) turned Aunt Jenny's culinary oasis into an inviting sanctuary where she prepared her smorgasbord of delectable dining pleasures. Occasionally she might be whipping up a batch of fish fillets. Whatever it was, she was always anxious to share the secrets of her mouth-watering recipes with listeners. "To give your fish such a grand flavor," she allowed to Seymour and to us, "brush them with lemon juice ... then melted Spry ... and broil to a golden brown." (Never use that *other* all-vegetable shortening, of course!)

Seymour—she addressed him as "Danny"—was there to lend support to everything the gastronomic pacesetter vowed. In short order (no pun intended), he'd complete every sales plug with this rhyming invective: "For all you bake or fry, reply on Spry!" While his verse wasn't equal to, "Is it true blondes have more fun?" or "You're in good hands with Allstate," it was still memorable enough: liberally sprinkled throughout the dual commercial messages on Aunt Jenny's fleeting 15 minutes of fame, his singsong couplet reinforced the commercial pitch multiple times in that quadrant. In fact, its repetition must have gladdened the heart of the nameless hack that inspired it!

Ever the salesman, Seymour was the point man for things that might be much too ladylike for Aunt Jenny to discuss directly with her multitude of fans. During the Second World War, for instance, when supplies were sometimes scarce on market shelves, he reminded the ladies at home: "Both your grocer and the Spry folks have a world shortage to reckon with, as well as an ever-increasing demand for Spry. So if you can't get it the first time you ask, keep Spry on your marketing list until you *do* get it." As we learned earlier, calling for a direct response as Seymour did was a straight line to a bountiful harvest of increased sales.

When Fred, the mailman of fictitious Littleton, arrived in Aunt Jenny's kitchen on the broadcast of September 21, 1939, he was weighted down with a heavy load of letters from thousands of her admirers. That gave Aunt Jenny and Danny yet another opportunity to chat about a current premium offer that was about to expire. For one Spry disc off the can label and 10 cents in coin, Aunt Jenny would mail the sender her latest recipe book and six flavors of frosting tints. Danny proclaimed that the book included two-crust pies, one-crust pies, deep-dish pies, apple fritters, baked apple dumplings, Dutch apple cake and many more lip-smacking delicacies that listeners would relish serving their families and friends. It was a never-ending cornucopia of confectionary celebrations!

And the wordsmith behind their tête-à-tête made sure that postman Fred got a slice of apple crumb cake that Aunt Jenny had baked only that morning. If the listeners were keeping track, nevertheless, they surely must have wondered who on earth was eating all those foodstuffs she whipped up with Spry every weekday for more than 18 years (1937 to 1955). Aunt Jenny appeared to have no relatives nearby to share them with. After all, the parish bazaars could accommodate only so much, no matter how worthy and wonderful her palate-pleasing predilection!

In the meantime, just an hour later "over most of these same CBS stations," Bess Pringle was waving her pie server in the direction of son-in-law Tom Baugh. With uncanny precision, he stopped by his kin's home in fairy-tale Three Oaks, the setting of *Young Doctor Malone*, just as the elderly woman was pulling an apple pie or corn fritters from *her* oven. Hers were made with "the all-vegetable shortening," Crisco, a Procter & Gamble legacy. P&G carried the show in 1942 and again from 1945 to 1955. Compton Advertising had the Crisco account.

Although Baugh didn't turn up every day as announcer Dan Seymour did — Baugh's and Pringle's spot aired two or three times weekly — he was there often enough to make their exchanges predictable. For instance, nothing would ever do but that he must sample some of Bess's mouth-watering perfections. And he never found a delicacy he didn't like. It was like a replay of the previous sponsor's commercials, the shortening (which mammy's little baby loved) being the only substantive difference between the two.

On the *Malone* serial, the copywriter sustained a knockout punch with augmentation supplied by a Dixieland jazz band. Each day as the show arrived, this New Orleans-sounding deputation performed a rendition of a catchy refrain to the opening bars of "Muskrat Ramble."[19] That was instantly followed by a male vocalist belting out an appropriate prompt:

*They're ... cookin' with Crisco,
From New York to 'Frisco ...
Pies are so flaky, cakes are so light;
Fried foods digestible, with Crisco they're right ...
So-o-o-o, keep on cookin' ... with Crisco!*

Both shows presented a smorgasbord of gourmet gastronomy. And the lighthearted commercial dialogue that accompanied them — laden with savory statements about mouth-watering munchies — was dripping with allegorical imagery, thanks to the guys and gals who won the rights to script it. It was a feast for the nose, palate and eyes. And in those exhibitions, also for the ears.

To be totally fair, let us acknowledge that there were some observers who cast a wary eye toward persuasive-tilted wordsmiths. "Radio writing, as it is now developed, is simply an adjunct of advertising. The word is fitted to the product. The product is god. The word is the interval between the announcements of god."[20]

The advertising copywriters were generally unknown hacks who churned out reams of persuasive similes that paid the bills. One supplicant maintained that the programming was merely the filler material between the commercials. "Taking 100 per cent as the total radio value, we give 90 per cent to commercials, to what's said for the product, and we give 10 per cent to the show.... We are commercial and we cannot afford to be anything else. I don't have the right to spend the stockholders' money just to entertain the public."[21] Considered in that light, those normally reticent, nameless nerds with sharp eyes for convincing metaphors were, without reservation, hanging out at the top of the list of those who were unequivocally labeled indispensables on every show.

6

Commercial Spokesmen: They Delivered the Goods

Behind the scenes of a radio commercial there is usually a flurry of activity constantly transpiring. In previous chapters, we have examined some of the complex issues that impinge on the final outcome — the peculiar effects of broadcasting when it is included in a marketing plan; the nature of the commodity or service advertised; the audience; the timing and placement of a commercial; the specific purposes for advertising; the disparities in spot announcements and campaigns; the implications of agencies and ratings services; the impact of rival commodities, brands, firms, organizations and ideas; and so forth. In Appendix B, we consider sundry variables that contribute significantly to the structure of aural advertising.

Yet it seems that, once the broad panorama has been cast and the major determinants settled (including the decisions related to all of the above), we can at last concentrate on a two-part equation: *development* and *delivery*. The actual composition of the commercial — which usually begins with the writing and may be wholly vested in that pursuit, although not necessarily so (consider music and jingles, premiums and other interactive responses, sound and other special effects, for example) — was explored in an earlier chapter focused on copywriting. Admittedly that was not an in-depth investigation of a complicated, multidimensional province. Yet, given the scope, parameters and intent of the present volume, it was a sweeping endeavor to acquaint the novice not deeply involved in these matters with a critical building block of commercial construction.

If the formation of the commercial is — for our purposes — its most fundamental factor, lagging not far behind surely is the spokesman (or spokeswoman or, in some situations, spokespersons) who communicate its message to a group of witnesses (listeners, or viewers and listeners on TV, videos, films, Internet and other methods of electronic print communications). It is these two variables — the actual *dispatch* and the *dispatcher*— that become the nitty-gritty core of any commercial as it reaches a prospective audience. It doesn't really matter that it airs as part of a campaign or that a certain agency has negotiated it. The "hear and the now" is that people are tuning in to persuasive techniques pitched by one or more individuals who augment the underwriter's intent for buying the time and paying the associated production costs.

6. Commercial Spokesmen: They Delivered the Goods

A preponderance of those commercials in vintage radio days, and maybe so today, were and are delivered in a direct manner by a single voice. That individual can be classified under a myriad of designations (speaker, advertiser, narrator, host, interlocutor, salesperson, messenger, emcee, moderator, etc.), although we will refer to him or her as an announcer here. It's a designation that is perhaps as well understood now as then.

Radio historian Alfred Balk characterized the medium's earliest announcers in simple terms as the "nonengineering employees." They were charged, as Balk depicts them, "with everything from recruiting and greeting talent to sign-ons and sign-offs."[1] And, in time, when broadcasting acquired a little age, they were also accountable for selling everything that could be bought. Literally. For much of the time it was up to them to communicate the messages that paid the bills that kept the whole operation thriving and moving in the black. Unequivocally, theirs was one of those inescapably crucial posts.

Entertainer Arthur Godfrey maintained that there are only two essentials in motivating the listener, by the way: "Listen to what I'm saying and believe what I'm telling you."[2] Of course, it takes a respected, winsome personality to achieve those aims sometimes.

"Virtually everyone who became an announcer did so by accident, misdirection, or default," proclaimed media consultant Leonard Maltin. "And yet, those dulcet-voiced gentlemen established a presence as potent as that of any so-called stars. Indeed, many of the best announcers became well-recognized personalities, and active participants in the shows they announced."[3]

There were exceptions to Maltin's accident-misdirection-default theory, you may be sure. Jackson Beck was one. The actor-announcer decided to suppress his thespian ambitions and amplify the narrational-salesman bent that dwelled within him. "I found out that the character man comes and goes," said he, "but the announcer is there every day. And I figured, what am I fooling around with all this [acting] stuff?... I want to be there every damn day. It's a steady job, and I can get better money for that than I can for playing an Irish cop or a Spanish conquistador or whatever. I made the switch. I started insinuating myself into announcing situations and auditioning for them."[4] His professed intents to the contrary, of 58 radio series that have been documented for Beck, on all but a half-dozen, he acted. Maybe he was only playing around when he said he really wanted to announce.

The announcing profession developed a breed of entertainers that were sometimes as well known — at least by name — as the individuals and programs they introduced on the ether. While not all of those advertising salespersons could be instantly identified today by people who lived through that era, there is a handful whose names stand out even many decades since, whose responsibilities, prominence and all-encompassing influence impacted the airwaves well enough that they are remembered as sort of a universal presence. A couple of dozen are Jim Ameche, George Ansbro, Andre Baruch, Ford Bond, Norman Brokenshire, Ken Carpenter, Clayton "Bud" Collyer, Frank Gallop, Art Gilmore, Ben Grauer, Ed Herlihy, Durward Kirby, Tony Marvin, Marvin Miller, Ken Niles, Wendell Niles, Ron Rawson, Ken Roberts, Del Sharbutt, Warren Sweeney, Harry Von Zell, Jimmy Wallington, Harlow Wilcox and Don Wilson. Veritable legends, all.

Parenthetically, in 2007, McFarland & Company released a new volume by this author which profiles all of the above personalities in comprehensive detail, plus several hundred more announcers and added entertainers. It's the first text issued since the vintage years that focuses entirely on seven distinct genres of the aural broadcasting arena. The 360-page encyclopedic manual is titled *Radio Speakers: Narrators, News Junkies, Sports Jockeys, Tattletales, Tipsters, Toastmasters and Coffee Klatch Couples Who Verbalized the Jargon of the Aural Ether from the*

1920s to the 1980s—A Biographical Dictionary. It's filled with numerous references to the commercialization of radio and those who participated so pervasively in it.

The inaugural star announcer may have been a young red-hot initiate who set the pace for those succeeding in his train, a redoubtable Graham McNamee, an early WEAF personality in New York City. An ex-choral and stage singer, McNamee possessed a compelling inflection and striking panache complimented by a carefree manner. "With his cheery American manner, eye for color and detail, and dynamism, plus the vital ability to fill time during slow-moving games, McNamee fell naturally into sportscasting, which he soon ruled," recalled an admiring critic. He branched out from there, becoming Ed Wynn's announcer-straight man and commercial salesman.

McNamee's speaking style distanced him from the mellifluous sounds that subjugated the microphones of the 1920s, some of those voices affecting an ingratiating theatrical inflection. Some announcers resisted the stentorian delivery techniques that became commonplace in the profession in the decades of the 1920s and 1930s. It occurred during the inception of showman Arthur Godfrey's many years on the air. (For a more detailed review of Godfrey's reactions, see the previous chapter on copywriting.) Announcer Harry Von Zell, among those early commercial spokesmen, later summarized his own response: "An advertiser in radio would give me copy, orating and pounding and shouting the wares, and I simply couldn't do it. I said I will not holler at people in their own houses. You must speak to them as if you're sitting there with them in their home and appreciate [it] if they keep that dial tuned to where you are. You owe them a great debt of thanks for allowing you in and letting you stay. But they [the advertisers] never got it!"[5]

Ralph Edwards is best remembered as a master of ceremonies for exploitation vehicles (*Truth or Consequences, This Is Your Life* and several more that he produced). Yet he launched his network radio career as an industrious announcer, introducing as many as 45 shows a week in the late 1930s and early 1940s. Edwards shared some common interpretations with Godfrey and Von Zell, too. Media critic Leonard Maltin noted that Edwards "all but revolutionized" announcing in that period. The effusive host inserted "conversational punctuation" into scripted advertising copy, almost as if he was addressing each listener individually on a handful of soap operas that he narrated. One day Edwards ad-libbed this homily on the air.

> You know, when you listen to *Life Can Be Beautiful,* you get the feeling that Chi Chi and Papa David and all the others are sort of like old friends. Don't you think that's the way it is? Friends that you look forward to visiting with every day. Now, I never heard of anybody looking forward to dishwashing, but [*chortle*] just the same, I know a lot of you feel friendly to the soap that helps your hands look nice and gives you speedy suds at the same time. Yes, ma'am, I mean good old Ivory Flakes.

No one may have exceeded the languid-voiced Alan Kent, however, whose conversant style cast legions of women under his spell weekday afternoons between the mid–1940s and mid–1950s. The interlocutor of NBC's recurring *Pepper Young's Family* launched a memorable advertising jingle a few years earlier when he penned the lyrics of the Pepsi-Cola opus. Now he effortlessly combined vocabulary and harmony in pithy presentations to milady extolling the merits of Procter & Gamble's "soap of beautiful women." His technique was flawless.

> KENT: Say, do you know what I'm absolutely positive of? I know a lot of women are going to have younger, lovelier-looking complexions just because they heard this song....
> MUSIC: *Piano roll*

KENT: Listen....

MALE VOCALIST (*sings over piano accompaniment*)
    Did you know that just one cake of Camay...
    Can mean a smoother, softer skin?
    Say, did you know that just one cake of Camay...
    Is the way you should begin?
    You ought to try it now,
    You'd better start today;
    The Camay mild soap diet is the lovely woman's way...
    For a softer and more glamorous complexion...
    Camay ... Camay ... Camay!

KENT: Yes, you'll see a real improvement in your complexion if you'll change from incorrect skin care to regular, mild Camay care. Doctors' skin specialists tested Camay care. They had a whole group of women follow regular care with Camay. And those doctors reported ... definitely smoother, lovelier complexions for most of those women. So, follow the Camay mild soap diet. Directions are on the wrapper. And I promise ... with your very first cake of Camay ... you'll have a lovelier-looking skin ... yes, a softer, smoother complexion.

MALE VOCALIST (*sings over piano accompaniment*)
    Just one cake the Camay way ...
    Your very first cake and you will say ...
    Camay ... Camay ... Camay!

It was just what the housewives wanted to make them feel better about themselves. And the copy, the melody and the velvety-voiced delivery coalesced to sell billions of cleansing bars in the process.

Homer observed, "His speech flowed from his tongue sweeter than honey." The biblical author may have stated it even better in the celebration: "A word fitly spoken is like apples of gold in pictures of silver."[6]

In the 1940s CBS speech consultant Cabell Greet acknowledged that during a five-year period in which a staff committee auditioned about 1,000 men for announcing duties with that chain, it picked only 70 for positions with CBS. Greet lumped the 93 percent who were turned away into two categories he labeled as "pseudo-elegant" and "pounders."

The first, which he called "patronizers of God," spoke "Broadway British." He pontificated, "Their diction has a sort of eloquence which like the mule has neither pride of ancestry nor hope of progeny."[7] Greet branded as complex the imperative of making every syllable audible without obscuring, slurring or over-enunciating. He disdained the pseudo-British accent as "not good British speech" and cautioned that it wasn't being practiced in the United States. Only American English, he suggested, was acceptable.

In the other case — that of the pounders, who audibly emphasized everything they read, sometimes by liberally drumming the table with their fists — Greet acquiesced, "At least this group of men with excessive energy and desire to please are not as hard to change as the elegantees who listen to their dulcet tones, hand cupped to ear."[8] He called them "servants of Mammon" and said there was hope "they will change for gold." Referring to the pseudo-elegant again, Greet lamented, depicting them as "servants of their ideals and ... rather difficult to manage."

In their 1940s exposition which became the textbook for an introductory course in radio announcing at the University of Southern California, Art Gilmore and Glenn Y. Middleton — themselves active broadcast personalities — maintained: "The manner in which he delivers the commercial message is likely to be the foremost criterion by which the announcer is selected as the right man for the job; for, after all, the announcer's performance should represent the epitome of good salesmanship."[9] The authors acknowledge that both network staff and freelancing announcers were expected to read commercial copy. By the mid– to late 1940s, staff could anticipate a salary ranging between $30 and $100 or more each week for reading commercials as part of their normal daily duties. Gilmore and Middleton disclose, nonetheless, that spokesmen whose services were requested by specific sponsors could reap between $50 and $300 or more for reading the firm's plugs on a particular show. If the gods really smiled on such an announcer so he was engaged by multiple underwriters simultaneously, he could easily make $1,000 or more weekly. It didn't necessarily matter whether he was employed by a network as a permanent staffer or was out own his own as a freelancer, possibly hired by a advertising agency.

In an insightful memoir, NBC announcer George Ansbro revealed a great deal about salaries earned by inexhaustible network announcers in the 1930s.[10] By servicing lucrative local assignments, they could significantly boost their bottom lines as Ansbro did. Keep in mind that NBC was then comprised of two radio chains, the Red (with flagship station WEAF) and the Blue (with flagship station WJZ). Both operated out of the same headquarters facility.

> In the summer of 1938, Pat Kelly [chief of NBC announcers] notified me that beginning the following Monday I would be doing a new sustaining program called *Omar Herth, the Swingmaker* at 8 A.M. on WEAF and the Red network. For several months previously I had been the *Esso News*[11] reporter reading news at 7:55 on WJZ (without NBC's Blue Network), so I asked Kelly if I was being dropped from *Esso News*…. He said…, "You do the news for four and a half minutes, until 7:59:30, and during the next thirty seconds master control does the switching…." I heaved a sight of relief…. Since the very recent agreement with AFRA [American Federation of Radio Artists] the *Esso News*, being a commercial program, was now paying me a fee of $5…. I didn't want to lose it because I was the daytime *Esso News* reporter four times every day, five days a week…. My income had increased $100 a week over and above my base salary which, also because of AFRA, had jumped from $45 to $60….
>
> Pat Kelly called me in one day in mid–September [1938] to inform me that the Hummert office [Air Features, operated by infinite radio series producers Frank and Anne Hummert] had requested me to be their announcer on a new soap opera. It would begin Monday the 26th and would be on the air at 4:45 P.M. five days a week. I was to be in the studio for rehearsal at 4 o'clock. It was to be called *Young Widder Brown*…. He then congratulated me, not just for getting a new show without having to go through the audition process but because, thanks to AFRA, I would receive the minimum fee for such a program, $75 per week…. One other thing fate must have been aware of but, understandably, had no way of letting me know in advance was the fact that this "goody" would be part of my life, continuously, for the next eighteen years. The $75 fee was increased several times over those years in accordance with each new minimum scale negotiated by AFRA.

If you were keeping score there, the $235 Ansbro earned weekly from those programs ($100 from *Esso News*, $75 from *Young Widder Brown*, nothing extra from the sustaining feature *Omar Herth, the Swingmaker*, plus his base salary of $60) put him at $12,220 annually. Not bad for the post–Depression period. And that doesn't take into account additional commercial gigs with attached fees he may have acquired. Ansbro's gainful employment was typical of industrious spokespersons who earned their paychecks from multiple sources. Incidentally, to maintain the security of the increasing sum he was earning from the Hummert troupe on *Young Widder Brown*, Ansbro didn't request a vacation from it for six years, never missing a week in all that time! (His vacation request at the six-year mark was due to his upcoming wedding and honeymoon, otherwise, he might not have asked!)

In 1998, prolific radio announcer Ken Roberts (whose son is Hollywood actor Tony Roberts) and interviewer-author Chuck Schaden dialogued about the senior Roberts' profession during the early 1930s.[12] It was an epoch that transpired prior to many announcers leaving the security of their network folds to go out on their own as freelancers, where they were subsequently hired by the advertising agencies to appear on sundry shows. The exchange imparts some discerning clues about the working lifestyle of yet another busy network announcer in radio's early days.

> ROBERTS: I had not been there ... long when CBS landed its first big ... show ... for Chesterfield cigarettes [Liggett & Myers Tobacco Company].... To announce it, they held auditions.... I competed against ... Andre Baruch, David Ross, Frank Knight, Louis Dean and Harry Von Zell, who were all on staff with me, ... and I managed to win this program.... The more programs you did to the satisfaction of sponsors, the more certain was your job at CBS.... You wouldn't have been on staff very long if you didn't have your share of commercials.... It was six nights a week, 15 minutes a night ... with Andre Kostelanetz and his orchestra.... I did the Morton Downey program, too. That was for Camel cigarettes [R. J. Reynolds Tobacco Company].
> SCHADEN: Was this at the same time?
> ROBERTS: Oh, no, you couldn't do two cigarettes. Chesterfield was the first; then I went on after that to [the other].... I received a call one afternoon from the vice-president of CBS, ... Ed Klauber.... He said, "Chesterfield is very happy with your work and they would like to give you a fee for doing their program.... While we can't stop you from taking the fee, we would not smile happily upon it, since it is not our policy to allow our staff announcers to take fees. We would like you to continue working for us instead of for Chesterfield, ... [if you take the fee] that would be the end of your relationship with CBS.... [Otherwise] you would continue to work for us and Chesterfield, and we will give you an increase in salary."... I said, "I'll be happy to stay with CBS." So I got a $15 increase.... Chesterfield was prepared to pay me $200.
> SCHADEN: May I ask what your CBS salary was at that time?
> ROBERTS: I was making $55 a week.
> SCHADEN: But you didn't know how long the Chesterfield relationship would last.
> ROBERTS: That's right. Working with CBS became a permanent job.... Chesterfield decided to change announcers and I did lose the job, but my increase continued. [As] ... it might be uncomfortable for me to be relieved of my job from Chesterfield, [CBS] ... said, ... "You don't want to be here when the change is made. Why don't you go on a little vacation? We'll pay for it." ... [I went] to Atlantic City for two weeks, at their expense.... I had a marvelous career [with CBS] after that ... two or three soap operas a day.... *Joyce Jordan ... Life Can Be Beautiful ... This Is Nora Drake ... Easy Aces.*

Roberts later took two leaves of absence from CBS so he could be a freelancer, announcing shows on other chains during those interims. He never returned to the CBS staff following his second hiatus, but—in the Schaden interview—he professed only glowing acclaim for his former employer.

Roberts seemed to acquire a proclivity for working shows for cigarette manufacturers. Having earlier been the voice of Liggett & Myers and R. J. Reynolds, he subsequently became the virtually exclusive on-air presence of the Philip Morris Company, makers of Philip Morris and a few lesser-known brands. Thus, Roberts turned up on multiple networks on features like *Crime Doctor, It Pays to Be Ignorant, Philip Morris Playhouse, Take It or Leave It* and one or more musical series as he worked all the Philip Morris programs simultaneously on the air. Employed by the Beal Company advertising agency, he enjoyed serving not only the Philip Morris shows but those that Beal handled for Procter & Gamble, Eversharp and a few other underwriters.

In connection with all that cigarette advertising, there were some unusual situations (and stipulations) that occurred. Of course, they could have just as easily happened in another product dominion, but they occurred among the profusion of cigarette-backed programs.

> Mel Blanc remembered that when he was performing on three shows with three different cigarette sponsors [a condition that had been anathema to Ken Roberts' experience, you will recall], he had to be sure to smoke the correct brand for each job — Lucky Strike for the Jack Benny show, Chesterfield for Bing Crosby, and Camels for Abbott and Costello. It wasn't out of loyalty or tact; it was required. "Absurd, isn't it?" he recalled. "Especially since this was radio; who could tell which brand you were smoking? But the companies were so insistent that actors complied with inspectors, who carried out their duties with Gestapo-like zeal," said Blanc, who was once stopped by a cigarette cop for puffing Pall Malls on a Lucky Strike show, even though both brands were made by the same company. Mary Livingstone had it written into her contract that she could smoke Parliaments rather than Lucky Strikes.[13]

Could this be, perhaps, yet another incentive for abandoning smoking altogether? Just an errant thought.

Can you handle a couple more cigarette sagas? The tobacco firms were *huge* underwriters of radio in those halcyon days, in case you hadn't detected it already. While this next one isn't about an announcer, it illustrates the persnickety position that everybody on a show could find himself in at one time or another. In his exposition on radio sound effects, which is akin to the memoir of a guy who spent his professional life as a network sound technician, Bob Mott shares this first-person account.[14]

> I was scheduled to replace vacationing [soundman] Jack Amrhein on "Phillip [*sic*] Morris Playhouse" for a brilliant comedy, *Three Men on a Horse*. During the first reading, an actor read the line, "Gee, this has to be my lucky day!"
>
> The actor no sooner got the words out when an agency man interrupted the rehearsal to inform Charlie Martin, the director, that the word "lucky" was to be cut from the script. Lucky Strike cigarettes were one of Philip Morris' biggest rivals in the cigarette market, so on a program that was sponsored by Philip Morris, the best anyone could hope to be was "*fortunate*," never "lucky."...
>
> The problem was how to do a show like *Three Men on a Horse*, which involved a lot of talk about horse racing, without ever using the word lucky.
>
> Later, Charlie observed, "Thank God, we're not doing *Beau Geste*. How the hell could we get the people around the desert if there was no such thing as a camel?!"
>
> When it came time to let the audience in for the dress rehearsal, the same agency man came over and gave me a package of Philip Morris. I thanked him for his generosity but told him I used Chesterfields.... "You can smoke whatever you like, but the only cigarettes we'll ever see in this studio are the ones that pay the bills. And by the way, if you cough on the air, you're off the show."
>
> Next week, Amrhein was still on vacation and I was still on the show. Which indicates not how good I was but merely that when the show was on the air, I didn't cough.

There was another incident in connection with the *Philip Morris Playhouse* that Bob Mott remembered. Readers who lived through the epoch recall that Philip Morris produced a midget attired in the scarlet uniform of a hotel page-boy as its mascot and spokesman, Johnny Roventini, who had been a bellman at one time. He was widely recognized not only for his voice but because his picture was plastered everywhere Philip Morris cigarettes were sold, including at vendors, on product packaging, in advertising and promotions of every persuasion. At the *Philip Morris Playhouse* opening, meanwhile, the announcer would bark: "And here he is, stepping out of millions of store windows to say ..." as Johnny cried: "Callllllll for

Phil-lip Mor-r-r-r-a-i-s-s-s-s!" Four simple words — and Johnny was done. He was rewarded handsomely by Philip Morris to say them several times daily, like being richly compensated to say his own name. Mott picks up the story there, recalling an exchange he had with the infamous sales agent.[15]

> Evidently it [saying those four words] was more complicated than that, because that evening on air, Johnny not only stepped out of millions of store windows, but when he sang out "Call for Philip Morris," he read it from a *script*!
>
> After the show I asked him about it.... He smiled and said that the agency, rather than objecting, insisted on it. It seems that one night, he got up to the mike and when the cue came, he went completely blank. He remembered nothing! The announcer had to do his part in falsetto! Fortunately, his [Johnny's] face was so recognizable they couldn't fire him, but from that night on, he had to carry a script with him everywhere — just in case.

Make no mistake about it: "You had to please the sponsor first, and the audience second," Ken Roberts insisted. To illustrate his point, he told a story that happened to him while on the job.

> Roberts was designated as the exclusive commercial spokesman for Ex-Lax laxative. He paid a price for it. As part of his privileged contract he was required to visit the firm's Brooklyn factory on a weekly basis. There the company president handed him some commercial copy to be read on the air before ushering him into a small room with a microphone where Roberts read the copy aloud. The CEO, meanwhile — back in his office — heard the pitch through a loudspeaker. Subsequently, he coached the veteran announcer on what he perceived as proper voice inflection techniques. This persisted for many weeks. The president invariably attended the live presentations at the network studios, too. "He would grab me and say, 'Kenneth, that was *just* the way I wanted it. It was absolutely perfect,'" Roberts remembered. "Thank you, I appreciate that," the announcer responded.
>
> Nonetheless, the next morning Roberts perpetually received a telephone call from the Ex-Lax CEO asking him to come to the office that day. He would dutifully go out and the man always said something like this: "You know, there was one point in the commercial, where, I don't know, it just wasn't...." Roberts allowed those comments to continue for a while. Finally, he had had a bellyful and decided to challenge his accuser. On that occasion, he inquired of the top guy: "Sidney, what is happening here? You tell me how to do the commercial and I do it your way. I get off the air and you say it was wonderful, that it was perfect, exactly as you wanted. The next morning you're finding fault. I can't go on like this." The president acknowledged: "Well, I'll tell you the truth, Kenneth. I liked it very much, but when I get home my mother says, 'You know, Sidney, when you say Ex-Lax I believe you, but when that announcer says it, I don't believe him." Suddenly realizing he faced a winless situation — without mincing words or further deliberation — Roberts cut him off and canceled his select Ex-Lax contract on the spot. He figured some things simply weren't worth doing.[16]

Several other well known announcers gained traction as the spokesmen for a single advertising commodity or as a firm's exclusive representative. Ed Herlihy's friendly yet authoritative voice was — if not, according to one pundit, the unofficial Voice of Radio — the official voice of Kraft. For 42 years, Herlihy maintained a commercial relationship with the Kraft Foods Company as chief drumbeater on a variety of broadcast ventures in dual mediums. Until he left the business in 1953, meanwhile, Ford Bond held broadcasting's most durable sponsor-announcer connection as the prolific salesman of the Cities Service Oil Company. Bond also handled all of the daytime serials sponsored by B. T. Babbitt, a leading cleansing agent manufacturer. The Procter & Gamble Company, on the other hand, tapped manifold venerated representatives for some of its leading commodities: Clayton "Bud" Collyer, for

Duz detergent; Nelson Case, for Ivory soap; and Ron Rawson, as a utility man for nearly everything else. P&G spread its magnificent orators over a plethora of programs, just as several other broadcast underwriters did.

On many shows, those radio pitchmen cultivated an appetite for buddying up to the name stars of the shows on which they delivered commercial plugs at appropriate intervals. Earning sidekick roles, for example, were Ken Carpenter, the dependable mascot for singer Bing Crosby who — at the same time — could be a sales agent's nightmare to the masculine half of *Fibber McGee & Molly*; Frank Gallop, who possessed a deep, abundantly mocking inflection that sometimes cut comic Milton Berle to shreds; Harry Von Zell, the deadpan jester of the courts of George Burns and Gracie Allen as well as Eddie Cantor; and a jovial, rotund Don Wilson, the ever-faithful buttress to a much-maligned Jack Benny. There were many others, of course, who had similar responsibilities.

The point not to be missed is that relationships developed between those who were the series front men and those who read the commercials for them. Sometimes their feelings went very deep; a genuine rapport and respect for one another's capabilities ripened. For a while, Ernest Chappell introduced the most famous newscaster of radio broadcasting, Edward R. Murrow, while dispatching a sponsor's sales lines five nights weekly. When Chappell moved on to another opportunity, his mentor and friend — Murrow — took time out on Chappell's final night to share how he felt.[17] In doing so, he honored all the members of the announcing fraternity.

> I would like to talk about radio announcers, particularly those who announce news programs. Maybe many of you think they just announce commercials supplied by advertising agencies, but this is not the case. Often the announcer is the only tangible audience the commentator has, for he is the man across the mike, the only one you can see. You walk into the studio when the big red hand is sweeping the face of the clock for the last time. A good announcer is likely to say: "What have you got tonight?" and you reply: "It's a turkey, there is no news, and what there is has been written badly and the end result will probably be merely a contribution to confusion." And the announcer says: "It can't be that bad. Sit down and give it a reading," and while you read he listens and seems interested.
>
> When you fluff a line or get a backlash on a sentence and it begins to strangle you, he grins and shrugs his shoulders and says with his eyes: "Go on, let it alone. If you go back for a second try, it would be worse anyway and it wasn't as bad as you think." And occasionally, not too often, this good announcer, when the big hand has gone around the clock fifteen times and the program is off the air will turn to you and say: "You had a couple of minutes of good stuff in that show tonight." With a good announcer you always feel that if your throat closes up or you go crazy, you can throw him the copy and penciled notes and he will carry on and get you off on time. That's the kind of announcer Ernest Chappell is. After tonight, he will not be announcing this news broadcast and I wanted to take a minute of your time to say my thanks to him. Thanks, Chappie, carry on.

Radio historiographer Gerald Nachman observed, "Radio commercials [and, by inference, the announcers who read them] never seemed quite the noisy pests they are today — ingratiating allies of the show they sponsored rather than raucous interruptions to be zapped into silence."[18] He pointed out that, until the final years of old time radio, shows were usually sponsored by one organization which seemed "less strident" than those on the air today. "Some even had a sense of humor about themselves," Nachman reminded us. Those voices, it seems, have all been quelled in an effort to say more, say it faster and say it over and over on the ethereal and electronic mediums available to us now.

"We'll be right back after these words" didn't used to be a connotation that encouraged those tuned in to hit a button. The announcers, in many cases, were familiar friends with soothing voices that seemed to believe in what they sold and, in so doing, convinced us to buy it.

It hasn't been that way since vintage radio vanished, along with its salespeople extraordinaire. In this instance, the title and a prominent line of Pete Seeger's tune comes to mind: *Where have all the flowers gone?*

PART II

PATRONAGE OF AMERICAN NETWORK RADIO

American Home Products

History

American Home Products (AHP) dates to 1926 when a handful of enterprises in associated ventures combined their scientific expertise and manufacturing skills. As markets subsequently altered, the company abandoned its emphasis on lower-value commodities to concentrate on technologies offering higher potential returns. Following the Second World War, the firm targeted expansion of its high-tech prescription drug commerce. Yet it depended mostly on licensing as opposed to developing internal resources for innovations in medicine and marketing the results. AHP persistently posted huge profits on its low-tech over-the-counter items. Heavy reliance on advertising of its varied product lines increased the firm's revenues.

American Home Products' relationship with Wyeth pharmaceuticals is one bound so closely that the lines separating the two are invisible at points in their history. In the City of Brotherly Love, in 1860 siblings John (ca. 1835 to 1907) and Frank H. Wyeth (ca. 1837 to ?), graduates of Philadelphia College of Pharmacy in their native city, opened a drug store at 1410 Walnut Street. It included a small research lab and was initially identified as John Wyeth & Brother, Chemists.[1] The Wyeths' dad had been a journalist by trade and John Wyeth later purchased an interest in *The Philadelphia Record*. While "his [John's] activities did not extend to a participation in the conduct of that newspaper, ... he watched its policy closely."

In the meantime, as word of John and Frank's pharmaceutical exploits spread—and encouraged by the support of a few physicians—in 1862, the pair began manufacturing some medicines that were then in widespread demand. Within two years, as the Civil War raged on, the Wyeths filled larger prescription orders for the Union army. A decade beyond, in 1872, Wyeth technician Henry Bower invented a compressed rotary tablet device that accelerated their production incredibly while improving their precision at the same time. During the nation's Centennial Exhibition a quadrennial afterward, in fact, Wyeth was cited manifold times for this simple technical breakthrough. It helped put them on the patent medicine map.

A half-century later, American Home Products incorporated, on February 4, 1926. Its first headquarters was a structure in downtown Manhattan, New York, designated the Whitehall Building. (Whitehall Pharmacal Company was one of several divisional names under which AHP performed its work, seldom revealing its true identity to the public. Another leading branch, Boyle-Midway, Inc., exclusively favored household consumer products.) When Stuart Wyeth, company president and the son of founder John Wyeth, died in 1929, controlling interest was briefly transferred to Harvard University.

In the meantime, Wyeth's sales rose in the early decades of the twentieth century primarily due to the global acceptance of its Kolynos toothpaste. Yet, after Wyeth purchased pain reliever Anacin in 1930, at least one authority identified it as the company's "flagship product." (Note: You can read more about the origins of Anacin, and how it became a top seller on radio, under the "Exposition" section appearing later in this AHP article.) Over the years, the firm gained a reputation for acquiring numerous smaller business ventures that produced proprietary medicines. The first of those, in 1931, occurred when Harvard University sold John Wyeth & Brother, Inc., back to American Home Products for $2.9 million.

Between 1935 and 1950, AHP acquired 34 more enterprises, among them: Chef Boy-Ar-Dee and the S.M.A. Corporation, a pharmaceutical outfit specializing in infant formula advances; G. Washington Coffee Refining Company (1943)[2]; Ayerst, McKenna and Harrison, Ltd., of Canada (1943), maker of Premarin, the first conjugated estrogen tablets and still a major revenue producer (it became the number one seller among prescribed drugs in the U.S. in 1993); and Fort Dodge Serum Company (1945), helping AHP enter animal health care, an important segment of its business today. AHP's Whitehall Pharmacal Company unit became known as Whitehall Laboratories in 1957.

In the vintage radio era, meanwhile, American Home Products' vast arsenal of home, medical and food properties consisted of more than two dozen brand labels that were quite familiar to segments of the consumer-buying population, largely from the repetitious use of their names on broadcasts: Aerowax, Anacin, Aspertane, Benefax, BiSoDoL, Black Flag, Chef Boy-Ar-Dee, Dristan, Easy Off, FlyDed, Freezone, G. Washington, Heet, Hill's, Infrarub, Jiffy Pop, Kolynos, Kriptin, Melcalose, Neet, Old English, Preparation H, Primatene, Sani-Flush, Sleep-Eze, Wizard, and Woolite. In addition to its radio series (a list of which follow this history) — when television arrived — AHP was among the formative firms shaping daytime programming. From 1951 to the early 1970s, it underwrote *Love of Life*, and from 1954 to 1974, *The Secret Storm*, both widely recognized CBS-TV soap operas of the period.[3]

AHP's corporate headquarters were eventually shifted to Radnor, Pennsylvania, remaining there to 2003, after which they were transferred to Madison, New Jersey. "In the early 1980s," according to an assessment by Harvard Business School, "American Home Products decided to enlarge its higher-value-added healthcare business by attaching medical equipment to its portfolio and by divesting itself of the lower-margin non-healthcare divisions. In this restructuring, it benefited from the market for corporate control that in the 1980s was facilitating the selling of operating divisions and the acquiring of those of other companies." As a result, throughout the 1980s the firm cut whatever businesses were labeled non-core, including household commodities, food and confections.

AHP added Sherwood Medical (medical devices) in 1982. Two years later the company made medical history with the introduction of Advil, the first nonprescription ibuprofen medication in the U.S., as well as "the most famous prescription-to-OTC switch in history," an informant allowed. That same year (1984), it returned its gum business to creator William J. Wrigley. Two years hence it dispatched its Brach's candy business to a Swiss buyer. Also in 1986 AHP purchased Chesebrough-Pond's hospital supply products division to reinforce its earlier acquisition of Sherwood.[4] In 1987, the firm acquired Bristol-Myers' pet care sector and assimilated it into Fort Dodge Animal Health. AHP also bought A. H. Robins in 1988 with brand names ChapStick, Dimetapp, Robitussin and Dalkon Shield. AHP's household goods division was sold to British supplier Reckitt & Coleman in 1990 for $1.3 billion.

The company opened the industry's only pharmaceutical facility in 1993, solely pointed toward studies in female wellness. The Women's Health Research Institute runs tests pertaining to endometriosis, contraception, menopause and other female concerns. American Cyanamid and its auxiliary, Lederle Laboratories, were acquired in 1994, extending AHP's reach to the multivitamin Centrum.

The holding company experienced three consecutive years of bad luck when SmithKline Beecham vetoed a planned merger with AHP in 1998; a similar deal with Monsanto fell through in 1999; and AHP lost a friendly takeover bid for Warner-Lambert in 2000. Stung by all of this, American Home Products settled on Wyeth as its permanent corporate moniker in March 2002. Today it is one of the largest pharmaceutical manufacturers on the planet. Corporate headquarters remain at Madison, New Jersey, although the firm's pharmaceutical division—which generates the lion's share of Wyeth's revenues and profits—is situated in the Philadelphia suburb of Collegeville, Pennsylvania.

Today Wyeth's business is concentrated in a trio of components.

Wyeth Consumer Healthcare, which was formerly operated as Whitehall Robins Consumer Healthcare, produces goods under the trademarks Advil, Caltrate, Centrum, ChapStick, Dimetapp, Preparation H and Robitussin. Working in more than 65 nations, the sector realized sales of $2.5 billion in 2004. At that time, it was the fifth largest global over-the-counter health supplier.

Wyeth Pharmaceuticals, formerly Wyeth-Ayerst Laboratories, includes the labels Premarin, Effexor XR, Ativan, Protonix, Enbrel, Tygacil and Zosyn. This segment focuses on prescription drug research, development and marketing.

Fort Dodge Animal Health, founded in 1912 as Fort Dodge Serum Company, was established at Fort Dodge, Iowa, to produce hog cholera serum. It joined AHP in 1945, becoming a leading supplier of prescription and over-the-counter vaccines and pharmaceuticals for veterinary medicine plus livestock. Its headquarters are at Overland Park, Kansas. The unit produces dozens of wares in its disparate field.

Radio Series

Salty Sam, the Sailor, with Irving Kaufman—1931 to 1932, CBS (Kolynos)
Professor and the Major, with Bradford Browne and Al Llewelyn—1932, CBS (Kolynos)
Just Plain Bill—1933 to 1954, CBS, NBC, NBC Blue (Kolynos, Anacin, BiSoDoL, Freezone, Heet, Primatene, Infrarub, Hill's, FlyDed, Aerowax, Wizard)
Songs My Mother Used to Sing—1933 to 1934, CBS (Hill's)
Broadway Melodies, with Helen Morgan, Elizabeth Lennox, Victor Arden and His Orchestra, Willie and Eugene Howard, Fifi D'orsay—1933 to 1937, CBS (BiSoDoL)
Lazy Dan, the Minstrel Man, with Irving Kaufman—1933 to 1936, CBS (BiSoDoL, Old English)
Hammerstein Music Hall, with Ted Hammerstein—1934 to 1938, CBS, NBC (Hill's, Kolynos)
Easy Aces, with Goodman and Jane Ace—1935 to 1945, NBC, NBC Blue, CBS (Anacin, Old English)
The Romance of Helen Trent—1933 to 1955, CBS (Kolynos, Anacin, BiSoDoL, Kriptin, Freezone, Heet, Primatene, Infrarub, Hill's, FlyDed, Old English, Wizard, Benefax)

Mrs. Wiggs and the Cabbage Patch—1936 to 1938, NBC (BiSoDoL, Old English, Hill's)
Junior Nurse Corps—1936 to 1937, CBS (Anacin)
Mr. Keen, Tracer of Lost Persons—1937 to 1952, NBC Blue, CBS (Anacin, BiSoDoL, Kolynos, Kriptin, Hill's, Old English, FlyDed)
John's Other Wife—1936 to 1942, NBC, NBC Blue (Hill's, BiSoDoL, Old English, Kolynos, Anacin)
Our Gal Sunday—1937 to 1942, 1943 to 1950, 1951 to 1955, CBS (Kolynos, Anacin, BiSoDoL, Freezone, Heet, Primatene, Infrarub, Hill's, Black Flag, Old English, Wizard)
Front Page Farrell—1941 to 1954, MBS, NBC (Kolynos, Anacin, BiSoDoL, Kriptin, Freezone, Heet, Primatene, Infrarub, Hill's, Black Flag, Aerowax, Wizard, Melcalose)
News and Views by John B. Hughes—1942 to 1943, MBS (Anacin, Aspertane, Kolynos)
Friday on Broadway, with Jacques Renard and His Orchestra and Chorus—1943 to 1945, CBS
Boake Carter and the News—1943 to 1944, MBS (Chef Boy-Ar-Dee—multiple sponsorship)
What's Cooking? with Beulah Karney—1944 to 1945, NBC Blue (Chef Boy-Ar-Dee)
Real Stories from Real Life—1944 to 1947, MBS (Anacin)
The Adventures of Ellery Queen, with Lawrence Dobkin—1945 to 1947, CBS, NBC (Anacin, BiSoDoL, Hill's, Kolynos)
Give and Take, with John Reed King—1945 to 1946, CBS (Chef Boy-Ar-Dee)
The Bob Burns Show—1946 to 1947, NBC (Chef Boy-Ar-Dee, BiSoDoL, Hill's, Kolynos)
Surprise Party, with Stu Wilson—1946 to 1947, CBS (G. Washington)
Hollywood Jackpot, with Kenny Delmar—1946 to 1947, CBS (Anacin)
Hollywood Star Preview, aka *Hollywood Star Theater*—1947 to 1948, NBC (Anacin, BiSoDoL)
The Big Show, with Tallulah Bankhead, Meredith Willson and His Orchestra—1950 to 1952, NBC (Anacin—multiple participation)
The Man Called X, with Herbert Marshall—1950 to 1952, NBC (Anacin—multiple participation)
Duffy's Tavern, with Ed Gardner—1950 to 1951, NBC (Anacin—multiple participation)
Screen Director's Playhouse—1950 to 1951, NBC (Anacin—multiple participation)
The Magnificent Montague, with Monte Woolley—1950 to 1951, NBC (Anacin—multiple participation)
The Martin and Lewis Show, with Dean Martin and Jerry Lewis—1951 to 1952, NBC (Anacin—multiple participation)
Our Miss Brooks, with Eve Arden and Gale Gordon—1954 to 1956, 1957, CBS (Anacin and Old English—multiple participation)
Stop the Music!, with Bill Cullen—1954 to 1955, CBS (Anacin—multiple participation)
True Detective Mysteries—1955 to ca. 1959, MBS (BiSoDoL—multiple participation)

Exposition

According to the *International Directory of Company Histories*, American Home Products is sometimes referred to as "Anonymous Home Products" or the "withdrawn corporate giant." AHP's name never appeared on its commodity labels (e.g., Advil, Anacin, Anbesol, Centrum, ChapStick, Dimetapp, Dristan, Preparation H, Primatene, Robitussin). Writing in the years prior to the changeover to Wyeth as the firm's corporate moniker, the publication attested: "Public relations is considered such a low priority that until recently switchboard operators answered the phone with the company phone number instead of the company name."

Thus it probably comes as no surprise that during three decades of providing radio shows there was never any public revelation that AHP was the bankroller behind them. For many years, the commercials merely acknowledged that a particular program was being "brought to you by the makers of BiSoDoL analgesic tablets for upset stomach distress" or something similar. Listeners never really knew who those "makers" were. Down the road apiece, at last a flicker of light threw some illumination on the matter, albeit a flashlight instead of a spotlight.

The organization began announcing that "the Whitehall Pharmacal Company, the makers of Anacin and many other fine, dependable drug products" underwrote some of those series. Whitehall Pharmacal Company[5] — the name was later altered to Whitehall Laboratories, then Whitehall-Robins Healthcare, all tributaries of AHP — produced Kolynos toothpaste, BiSoDoL analgesic, Anacin pain reliever and scores of added remedies and consumer goods. Meanwhile, AHP's household products unit, Boyle-Midway, Inc., was responsible for product names like FlyDed, Black Flag, Aerowax, Old English and Wizard, among many. Finally, there was a foodstuffs division whose most prominent trademarks included Brach's, Chef Boy-Ar-Dee, Gulden's, Jiffy Pop, Mama Leone's and William J. Wrigley. But as a radio listener tuning in to vintage 1930s, 1940s and 1950s fare, one would be hard-pressed to have ever associated any of those with American Home Products, especially from a mere commercial. Whereas Colgate-Palmolive-Peet, General Mills and Procter & Gamble nearly shouted from the housetops on some series that they were paying the bills on shows they sponsored, there was dead silence from AHP about its ethereal involvement, an oddity never satisfactorily explained or acknowledged.

American Home Products' Anacin pain reliever brand quickly became one of the most profusely hawked medications on the air. Audiences were familiar with its name and spelling, its ingredients and presumed capabilities because of those commercials, which changed very little over the years. They were repeated on numerous programs several times weekly between the early 1930s and the middle of the 1950s. When television arrived, the ads persisted in great profusion.

The story of Anacin's development is a fascinating account in the annals of American packaged goods. The original formula was a mixture of four drugs widely consumed in the early twentieth century. The best known were caffeine and aspirin; quinine sulfate and acetanilide were the others.[6] In 1915 a Minneapolis pharmacist, William M. Knight, invented his own analgesic recipe that he dubbed *An-A-Cin*, a capsule combining the four ingredients. Three years hence he gained a trademark for the product under the modified spelling *Anacin*. Marketed by his Anacin Chemical Company, the capsules were initially dispensed to dentists for relieving pain and inflammation resulting from tooth extractions. The product was also pushed as a remedy for headaches and neuralgia.

Knight sold his Anacin brand in 1919 and it changed hands several times over the next few years. In 1926 Van Ess Laboratories, a Delaware corporation, purchased it. By then the American Dental Association was inquiring if Anacin's ingredient mixture was more effective than aspirin. Anacin makers capitalized on a popular notion that several components were "always better" than just one. This claim was to dominate much of the brand's advertising over the next half-century.

American Home Products bought Van Ess in 1930. Ironically, one of AHP's founders, Albert Diebold, also co-founded Sterling Products, Inc., the U.S. owner of Bayer aspirin since 1918, which was also destined to become one of radio's major sponsors.[7] In 1935, as Sterling spent more than $750,000 on Bayer advertising, American Home Products budgeted just $200,000 for its growing list of copious commodities. That wouldn't persist for long, however; in the next two years, Anacin's advertising budget increased fourfold and was heavily concentrated in radio. By 1941, Anacin outspent Bayer.

Anacin's commercials continued to emphasize the company's more-ingredients-are-better advertising strategy. "Anacin is a combination of medically proven and tested ingredients — not just one," said one radio spot. "Like a doctor's prescription," another emphasized. The ads were reinforced by varied marketing techniques. Anacin reps visited more than 500 doctors daily, while 65,000 samples were distributed monthly to physicians and dentists.

AHP purchased a plethora of aural series on which it repetitiously exhibited claims about Anacin's strengths. In addition to numerous pithy shows that lasted only a season or two, and a diverse range of multiple participation insertions, among AHP's most prominent and durable buys was the evening crime thriller *Mr. Keen, Tracer of Lost Persons*. It exclusively underwrote that drama from 1937 to 1951 (1,349 performances) plus it aired 51 more Anacin commercials in a subsequent participatory arrangement on that program, extending into 1952. There was also a bevy of longrunning daytime serials that began as early as 1933 and extended as late as 1955. Among their number were *Easy Aces, Front Page Farrell, John's Other Wife, Just Plain Bill, Our Gal Sunday* and *The Romance of Helen Trent*. In each of these, Anacin was consistently flaunted as Exhibit A. In all of them, Anacin's properties were spelled out in considerable detail so consumers could go to their druggists and other suppliers with the words of the Anacin commercials figuratively ringing in their ears. Their singsong approach became so familiar to regular listeners that many could recite their words right along with the announcer from broadcast to broadcast. This one was emblematic.[8]

Commercial

ANNOUNCER: The next time you're suffering from the pains of headache, neuritis or neuralgia, try Anacin. You'll bless the day you heard of this incredibly fast way to relieve these pains. Now the reason Anacin is so wonderfully fast acting and effective is this: Anacin is like a doctor's prescription. That is, Anacin contains not just one but a combination of medically proven active ingredients in easy-to-take tablet form. Thousands of people have received envelopes containing Anacin tablets from their own dentists or physicians and in this way have discovered the incredibly fast relief Anacin brings from pain of headache, neuritis or neuralgia. So next time such pain strikes, take Anacin. For most effective relief use only as directed. Your druggist has Anacin in handy boxes of 12 and 30, and economical family size bottles of 50 and 100. The name is Anacin. A-N-A-C-I-N.

American Tobacco Company

History

As forerunner and for many years the dominant player of its industry, the American Tobacco Company exhibited astoundingly pervasive and proficient marketing stimulus. This was especially true in radio broadcasting where, to some, for a while it very nearly appeared to be in control of the airwaves. Because the enterprise leads the alphabetical list of major players in its trade, the history of tobacco's rise to big business — common to all similar manufacturers — is explored here. Following an ephemeral introduction to the sector, this focus will be narrowed to this solitary behemoth.

There is obliging evidence that tobacco extends from plants grown in the western hemisphere — including North and South America — at least 6,000 years before Jesus Christ. Christopher Columbus intersected the weed in 1492 when gift-bearing Native Americans bestowed it on his exploratory party. So enamored were they that they carried some with them as they returned to their European homelands. Tobacco was swiftly transplanted; smoking was adopted in England, France, Spain, Italy, Holland and other voyage-dispersing empires. The practice eventually made its way back across the Atlantic to the colonists.

Native Americans, meanwhile — who were convinced that smoking leaves through a pipe resulted in supernatural powers — limited their use of tobacco, generally indulging only now and then. Their reliance was confined to medicinal functions and for ceremonial occasions. In the latter instance, they allocated sacred value to the substance. By contrast, the white man's encounters with it were purely for pleasure. In due course, the weed was the principal source of capital among the settlers of the earliest American colony, at Jamestown, Virginia, in 1612. While other cash crops were grown, tobacco outstripped all others in demand and value and became a prime factor in ensuring the permanency of the colonial establishment in the New World. It was the chief export of the Virginia, North Carolina and Maryland colonies.

A handful of the English settlers became instrumental in carrying the native commodity to its ultimate expression. Among them was Washington Duke, born in Durham County, North Carolina, December 18, 1820, a grain, vegetable and cotton farmer with 300-plus acres in the Piedmont central plains of the Tar Heel state. The enchanting history of the Duke clan and its pervasive influence across the geographical terrain is a transfixing tale of American ingenuity and free enterprise. Not only did it lead to the formation of the American Tobacco

Company, those exploits occurred largely in a day before machinery supplanted physical labor in manufacturing. Against great odds, Duke's achievements signaled the zeal of hardy early American entrepreneurs.

When his cotton crop failed in 1859, he turned to cultivating tobacco. By the end of 1863, Duke had converted all of his means to it. His efforts were coincidentally interrupted at the same juncture as he was conscripted by the Confederacy to fight in the Civil War. Leaving four offspring, his homestead and livelihood behind, the twice-widowed Duke went off to war. Captured by Union forces and imprisoned in Richmond, Virginia, for the duration of the conflict, he was eventually released and shipped to New Bern, North Carolina. Absent money and transit, in a colorful allegory, Duke returned to his homestead on foot, some 137 miles distant.

Regrouping, he and his children launched their tobacco operation anew in a small log structure. Although much of his stored leaf had been confiscated by the militia while he was away, the Dukes took the remnants of their once ample stash and crudely fashioned it by hand into smoking material. They promptly traded the product for supplies and cash.

In the meantime, a tobacco culture had developed in nearby Durham, a small village a few miles from the Duke family farm, as early as 1858. The most recognizable cigarette brand generated in what became a thriving tobacco production hub was Bull Durham (later a smoking tobacco). With the help of his dad, Brodie Leonidas Duke opened a tobacco factory in Durham. In 1869, Washington Duke consolidated the family's interests in a new Durham plant, having purchased two acres in town. After Sidney Duke (1844–1858), Washington Duke's eldest son, died, the surviving sons — Brodie (1846 to 1919), Benjamin (1855 to 1929) and James Buchanan "Buck" (1856 to 1925) — participated in the Durham operation while the patriarch concentrated on what was to become a company hallmark: the senior Duke trekked the nation promoting the firm's smoking tobacco. His marketing savoir-faire set a precedent that was to be a beacon to those coming along after him.

The firm was renamed W. Duke Sons and Company in 1878. It sold only smoking tobacco until stiff competition persuaded the Dukes to add cigarettes to their operation in 1881. Three years afterward, Buck Duke opened a branch in New York City, enabling the outfit to gain traction in the core of domestic and global commerce. That same year (1884), the Dukes installed a couple of cigarette-rolling machines developed by 18-year-old James A. Bonsack of Richmond, Virginia. While the devices weren't consistently reliable, when they worked they performed the labor of 96 hand rollers. For the first time, the process was automated, reducing manufacturing operating expense by 50 percent. A perceptive Buck Duke scored big time when he later signed an agreement with the Bonsack Machine Company guaranteeing to American Tobacco sole purchase of the contraptions. Still more machines were installed.

Rapidly becoming the nation's foremost cigarette producer, the firm's investment in large scale advertising helped it outsell its rivals. Having presumably picked up some marketing pizzazz from his father, Buck Duke — according to a journalist — "was always an aggressive advertiser, devising new and startling methods which dismayed his competitors and was always willing to spend in advertising a proportion of his profits which seemed appalling to some conservative manufacturers." Yet a biographer saw things somewhat differently: "Duke was considered a promotional genius by many. But he built on practices initiated by others, and later on was credited with advertising campaigns his staff had developed in his name.... Nor was Duke the father of the 'advertising blitz,' in which massive amounts of money were spent to saturate an area with slogans and premiums in order to destroy the opposition. This came out of the Bull Durham organization. What Duke did was to perfect what he found upon entering the field."[1] In reality, it appears that the chief promotional salesman he hired — Edward Featherstone Small — was not only "the right man" for the job, "Small was the innovator in advertising."[2]

Nevertheless, by the time Duke had reached his late twenties, the youngest offspring was certain a merger of all large-scale tobacco manufacturers would be a practical means for reducing selling and advertising expense while increasing efficiency. Five firms — including the Duke enterprise — divided most of the nation's cigarette trade. "Following a period of excessive spending on advertising," noted one reporter, "the large rival firms agreed that the Dukes' plan of merger was the most sensible proposal." That quintet of producers pooled their resources in 1890 to form the American Tobacco Company (ATC), a fusion widely identified as the "tobacco trust" due to its near-monopoly.

James Buchanan "Buck" Duke was the natural selection as president of the blended venture controlling the world's leading tobacco commerce. Upon reflection, a profiler intimated that the young Buck may have been "the most powerful businessman of his time." Over a period of two decades, he extended the influence of the American Tobacco Company through acquisitions, gaining control of 260 private ventures. Included in running the new enterprise, his sibling, Benjamin, was elected a director.

Not long after ATC's formal organization, Washington Duke — Buck's father and the man who launched the family's tobacco interests in 1858 — left it to his sons while concentrating on local projects. He persuaded Trinity College to relocate in Durham in 1892 and heavily endowed the small Methodist institution with capital. The school was renamed Duke University for its primary benefactor in 1924, nearly two decades beyond his death on May 8, 1905. Before he died, however, Washington Duke's philanthropic efforts extended to several other charitable enterprises. The Duke Endowment, established in 1924, perpetuated by his heirs, benefited the Dukes' native geographic territory as it funded schools, orphanages, hospitals and the Methodist Church in North and South Carolina. Despite those achievements, a source considered him little more than an independent, small time dirt farmer throughout most of his life. During his latter days, he was largely known as "Buck Duke's daddy," a folksy oddity visiting American Tobacco plants and chatting with workers while recalling the good old days in Durham. In actuality — with a handful of others — he spawned a global industry.

In the meantime, a compromise between rival manufacturers ATC and Great Britain's Imperial Tobacco Company Limited resulted in the creation of the British American Tobacco Company plc (BAT) in 1902. ATC owned two-thirds of BAT and Buck Duke was its founding chairman. The far-flung dual branches agreed to respect one another's domestic territories. Each company assigned brand rights to the other so consumers familiar with specific nomenclature weren't lost. Registered in London, the new enterprise acquired the recipes and trademarks of its instigators while obtaining the export business and overseas production of each company.

In 1907, the U.S. Justice Department filed antitrust charges against the American Tobacco Company.[3] The prevailing feeling among the public was that monopolies were harmful concentrations of power. Four years afterward — controlling 92 percent of the world's tobacco business — the leviathan operation was radically reduced after the Supreme Court ruled that much of the domestic tobacco industry was engaged in illegal practices in restraint of trade.

ATC's interests in BAT were divested but that was only the beginning. ATC was apportioned into four major U.S. tobacco-manufacturing units, each turning into an assertive contender for future sales with commensurate marketing operations, a great deal of it profoundly impacting the nation's airwaves. The ensuing tobacco challengers were identified by the monikers American, Liggett & Myers, P. Lorillard and R. J. Reynolds. All had previously functioned as independent tobacco processors.

Buck Duke had also been instrumental in incorporating the Continental Tobacco Company in 1898 and the Consolidated Tobacco Company in 1901. The latter entity took over the common stock of the American and Continental firms. Percival Smith Hill was among the directors of Consolidated. Born April 5, 1862, in Philadelphia, Hill launched a career as a carpet jobber before turning his focus to tobacco. He became sales manager of the Blackwell Durham Tobacco Company in 1892 and president in 1898. Hill's star rose like a comet. A year later, he was appointed sales manager of American Tobacco Company's Philadelphia district; in 1900, he moved to New York as ATC's vice president. He joined the board of British American Tobacco in 1901. When ATC was broken up in the antitrust action, in 1912 Buck Duke resigned the ATC presidency to concentrate on BAT as president. A biographer assessed the man and his career like this[4]:

> American Tobacco ... resembled a fruitcake, rich in nuts, dates, and fruits but rather weak in the binding.
>
> This resulted from Duke's drive to conquer not only plug but every other variety of tobacco product, and to control all operations from factory to retail outlet, controlling all suppliers along the way. Duke was not even content with this; he had to dominate the world market in tobacco, with his brands selling in every country in the world.
>
> But to what end? Power for its own sake? A drive to make cigarettes popular and oust plug is understandable, especially if you are a cigarette manufacturer. This was the goal of American Tobacco in its first incarnation, and Duke's initial dream. In its final form American Tobacco had no other goal but to survive, make profits, and, on occasion, serve as a vehicle for speculators.

Buck Duke's duties with BAT required little of his time. Consequently, seeking another conquest, he became interested in harnessing hydroelectric power. He was instrumental in establishing what was eventually known as Duke Power and Light Company, the Carolinas' leading utilities energy supplier.

Percival Hill succeeded Duke as ATC head. During his management, he was also chairman of the board of the subsidiary American Cigar Company, president of the Cuban Tobacco Company and he concurrently held several more imposing offices in the trade.

His son, George Washington Hill, who was born in Philadelphia on October 22, 1884, was named a director of American Tobacco in 1912 as his dad took the reins. The younger Hill had arrived at ATC as a youth of 19 in 1904; he was sales manager for its Pall Mall brand at 22. Pall Mall sales increased and he was appointed ATC's advertising director. That challenge was one he took quite seriously.

Next—upon the unexpected death of his father on December 7, 1925, after which he ascended to the firm's presidency—George W. Hill continued to personally call the shots for the tobacco leviathan's advertising program.[5] The flamboyant, innovative, eccentric leader employed some avant-garde methods that broached much of radio's golden age. He was seldom at a loss for micromanaging whatever he touched. Until death also claimed him unexpectedly on September 13, 1946, George W. Hill's omnipresence seemed to have permanent ramifications on the tobacco and broadcast industries, both of which he very nearly appeared to dominate at times. At his passing, *The New York Times* reported that ATC produced 80 billion cigarettes annually.

Network radio was less than a year old when the American Tobacco Company, convinced of the ether's potential for reaching untapped masses, purchased time on NBC for the first of numerous series, some of those quite durable. From the very start, ATC aggressively competed with five major U.S. tobacco manufacturers (Brown & Williamson, Liggett & Myers, P. Lorillard, Philip Morris and R. J. Reynolds) for the topmost split of the consumer market. For many years, ATC's Lucky Strike brand was the leader of the sector; much of the credit was attributed to ATC's unrelenting commitment to a diversified, innovative, hard-hitting advertising strategy. How did Lucky Strike achieve such an enviable status? The tale is absorbing.

It begins with a lesser known ATC brand, Blue Boar, and Lou Hartman, an affluent, ingenious New York advertising agent behind it. Among his novel ploys, Hartman persuaded ATC officials to reimburse retailers for the federal tax they paid on each pack of Blue Boar smoking tobacco. The father-and-son team of Percival and George Washington Hill were then president and advertising manager respectively at ATC. When Hartman carried the Blue Boar account to the New York office of Lord & Thomas, one of the world's most enveloping advertising agencies, magnate Albert D. Lasker — whom advertising guru David Ogilvy claimed "made more money and spent more money than anyone in the history of the business"— salivated over the possibility of acquiring the potentially far more lucrative Lucky Strike commerce.

Hartman invited Lasker, of Chicago, to meet the Hills over lunch at New York's newly opened Vanderbilt Hotel. Lasker biographer John Gunther allowed that the adman minced no words that day, telling father and son they "must stop frittering away their advertising on a variety of small accounts — all minor brands — and throw everything into one gigantic effort to build up Lucky Strikes. Otherwise," he maintained, "they would be drowned by [Liggett & Myers'] Chesterfield and [R. J. Reynolds'] Camel." Gunther succinctly summarized the outcome: "The Hills were much impressed by Lasker's line of thought, and before lunch was over proffered him the Lucky Strike account."[6]

Parenthetically, one of ATC's 1917 acquisitions was a small processor known as the Lucky Strike Company. ATC soon adopted that outfit's "toasted" tasting product, Lucky Strike cigarettes, as its paramount commodity, particularly in its fight for dominance against Reynolds' Camel — considered the first modern brand — introduced in 1913. The Lucky Strike moniker dated to a 1853 smoking mixture signifying the country's Gold Rush obsession. The name was reintroduced with a pipe tobacco in 1871 and as a cigarette in 1916.

It turned out to be propitious. A contemporary Web site recounting the legacy of Foote, Cone & Belding Worldwide, whose origins are rooted in Lord & Thomas from 1873, underscores: "In the 1930s and 1940s the most important accounts at Lord & Thomas were the American Tobacco Company and the Pepsodent division of Palmolive [the latter commodity sponsored radio's celebrated humorists *Amos 'n' Andy*]." The Web site notes that, ultimately, ATC's "principal product, Lucky Strike cigarettes, provided nearly one-fourth of Lord & Thomas' business."

In 1910, with American Tobacco controlling the commercial segment, the five sales-leading brands (all under ATC jurisdiction) were, in order: Pall Mall, Sweet Caporal, Piedmont, Helmar and Fatima. No cigarettes were selling coast to coast before 1917 when Lucky Strike, Camel and Chesterfield became available virtually everywhere. In 1930, the five sales leaders — all national brands — were, in order: Lucky Strike, Camel, Chesterfield, Old Gold and Raleigh.[7] A decade beyond, in 1940, the five ranking kingpins were the same, but four had shifted spots: Camel, Lucky Strike, Chesterfield, Raleigh and Old Gold.[8] The shakeout in 1950 read Camel, Lucky Strike, Chesterfield, Commander and Old Gold.

When the U.S. Surgeon General's report linking smoking with cancer was issued in 1964, the tobacco industry began a gradual but unmistakable downward spiral.[9] It resulted in health warnings on cigarette cartons and packages (1966), removing all broadcast tobacco commercials (1971) and many other sanctions against the industry resulting in financial payouts, downsizing, closing operations and redirecting much of the domestic efforts to third world nations.

At the same time, much of the tobacco business has consolidated, reducing it to a handful of major players on the global stage, all of which are widely diversified. American Tobacco Company, later renamed American Brands, resulted in a portfolio that included commodities and services beyond tobacco such as insurance (Franklin Life), alcohol (Jim Beam, Gilbey's, Lord Calvert, Old Grand Dad and others), toolboxes (Craftsman), staplers (Swingline), calendars (Pocket Day-Timer), faucets (Moen), cabinets (AristoKraft), pressure cookers (Prestige), locks (Dexter), microwave ovens (Kensington), golf clubs (Foot-Joy), golf balls (Titleist) and many additional wares. ATC had published the volume *Sold American: The First Fifty Years, 1904 to 1954* in the latter year. American Tobacco merged with FDS Holding Company of Springfield, Illinois, in 1979 (FDS was created in 1970 by Franklin Insurance Company).

American closed its Durham and Reidsville, North Carolina, factories in the late 1980s. Yet a postscript is worthy. In 2004, the previously abandoned American Tobacco site in Durham reopened as a complex of offices, retail shops and restaurants. Taking what appears an apposite turn, Capitol Broadcasting Company developed the project, a portion of which was still under construction in 2007. The endeavor was suitably dubbed the American Tobacco Historic District.

In an ironic twist of fate, BAT acquired its former parent, the American Tobacco Company, in 1994. This brought the Lucky Strike, Pall Mall, Herbert Tareyton, Sovereign, Hit Parade, Pro Bono Publico, Lord Salisbury, Sweet Caporal, Melachrino, Bull Durham, Cameo, Semper Idem, Duke of Durham, Pinhead, Cyclone, Cross Cut, Pedro, Town Talk and supplementary cigarette brands into BAT's collection. Joining them were plug tobaccos like Newsboy and Piper Heidsieck and smoking tobacco monikers like Bull Durham (which was also a cigarette), Half-and-Half, Blue Boar and Tuxedo. There were cigar appellations, too, including La Corona, Bock y Ca., Henry Clay, Cabanas and more. With assets in excess of a billion U.S. dollars, by the late 1990s BAT was cited as one of Britain's five largest commercial enterprises. It then controlled 15 percent of the market share and sold 300 trademarks in 180 nations.

There were further changes in store. Several leading American Tobacco labels, including Lucky Strike, Pall Mall and Tareyton, were assigned to a BAT auxiliary, Brown & Williamson Holdings, Inc. When that organization folded into a reorganized Reynolds American, Inc., on July 30, 2004, the ATC monikers became the property of RJR Tobacco, a wholly owned subsidiary of R. J. Reynolds Tobacco Holdings, Inc., under the auspices of Reynolds American. RJR proffered five of the sales leaders among cigarettes in the U.S. in 2005: Camel, Kool, Doral, Winston and Salem.

Doral and Pall Mall were discount brands while Lucky Strike — the one that ruled the industry for so many years and put ATC on the map — was relegated to a sideshow. A source noted that Lucky Strike was among a handful of once prestigious labels "no longer receiving significant marketing support."

If the indignity of passing into the hands of BAT — which ATC had launched many years earlier — had not been enough, the ATC status leaders next fell into the abyss of once rival Brown & Williamson. Subsequently, they were swallowed up by yet a second — and far more intimidating — competitor, R. J. Reynolds. The founding Reynolds and Buck Duke had never pretended to maintain cordial relations throughout their years of business dealings. Possibly suffering the greatest betrayal of all, the flagship brand was finally nearly snuffed out by its new owner. If it's feasible, Percival S. Hill and George Washington Hill could be turning over in their graves.

Radio Series

The Lucky Strike Dance Orchestra, aka *The Lucky Strike Dance Hour, The Lucky Strike Hour*, with B. A. Rolfe, Morton Gould, Jack Pearl, Paul Whiteman, Ted Weems, Vincent Lopez, Ferde Grofe —1928 to 1934, NBC (Lucky Strike)
The Lucky Strike Program, with Walter O'Keefe —1932 to 1933, NBC (Lucky Strike)
Metropolitan Opera —1933 to 1934, NBC Blue (Lucky Strike)
Red Trails —1935, NBC Blue (Lucky Strike)
Your Hit Parade —1935 to 1953, NBC, CBS, NBC Blue (Lucky Strike, Herbert Tareyton)
People in the News, with Dorothy Thompson —1937 to 1938, NBC (Pall Mall)
Hollywood Parade, with Dick Powell and Bob Hope —1937 to 1938, NBC (Lucky Strike)
Your News Parade, with Edwin C. Hill —1937 to 1938, CBS (Lucky Strike)
Melody Puzzles, with Fred Uttal —1937 to 1938, MBS NBC Blue (Lucky Strike)
Musical Mock Trial, with Ben Bernie —1938 to 1940, CBS (Lucky Strike)
The Eddy Duchin Show, with Eddy Duchin and His Orchestra —1938 to 1939, NBC (Pall Mall)
Kay Kyser's Kollege of Musical Knowledge —1938 to 1944, NBC (Lucky Strike)
Presenting Mark Warnow, with Mark Warnow and His Orchestra —1939, CBS (Lucky Strike)
Information Please —1940 to 1943, NBC (Lucky Strike)
All Time Hit Parade —1943 to 1944, NBC (Lucky Strike)
Believe it or Not, with Robert L. Ripley —1944, MBS (Pall Mall)
The Jack Benny Program —1944 to 1955, NBC (Lucky Strike, Herbert Tareyton)
The Wayne King Orchestra —1945, NBC (Lucky Strike)
The Fabulous Dr. Tweedy, with Frank Morgan —1946 to 1947, NBC (Lucky Strike, Pall Mall)
The Big Story —1947 to 1955, NBC (Pall Mall)
Light Up Time, with Frank Sinatra —1947 to 1949, NBC (Lucky Strike)
The Don Ameche Program —1948 to 1949, CBS (Lucky Strike)
Your Hit Parade on Parade —1949, 1955, CBS (Lucky Strike)
The FBI in Peace & War —1951 to 1958, CBS (Lucky Strike — multiple participation)
The Youth Opportunity Program, with Horace Heidt —1953, CBS (Lucky Strike)

Exposition

When George Washington Hill died, an obituary writer observed: "Credit for much of the increase in cigarette smoking in the last twenty years [1926 to 1946] went to Mr. Hill." Those weren't hollow words. His annual $20 million advertising budget was cited as "particularly lavish" in radio. (He canceled all print advertising to concentrate on the new medium for a time.) A biographer claimed he was obsessed with turning every non-smoker he could find into a smoker. Especially was he successful in converting the feminine gender.

Seeing a largely untapped market, he bore down in 1928. His "Reach for a Lucky Instead of a Sweet" campaign produced phenomenal results, turning millions of women and girls onto cigarettes and away from "overindulgence" in calorie-yielding confections. The same campaign was introduced a second time in 1936. Testimonials from distaff vocalists and movie legends personified Luckies' advertising. First-time feminine smokers tripled between 1925 and 1935; Lucky Strike captured 38 percent of the U.S. market in the decade.

A creative genius, Hill—who seemed to embody everything that the American Tobacco Company *was* during the peak of network radio's heyday—was a master in developing easily remembered and long-lasting catchphrases. Perhaps his most famous, following a few haunting keystrokes of a telegrapher, was: "LS/MFT ... LS/MFT ... Lucky Strike Means Fine Tobacco ... so round ... so firm ... so fully packed ... so free and easy on the draw ... With men who know tobacco best, it's Luckies — two to one...." Equally unforgettable is the tobacco auctioneer that Hill installed on the radio shows to deliver the lingering punch making the slogan so impressively stunning:

> Hey TWENTY NINE nine nine nine nine nine nine, roundem roundem roundem roundem roundem, am I right at thirty thirty thirty thirty thirty thirty thirty thirty thirty thirty thirty thirty THIRTY ONE thirty one thirty one one one one one one one one one one one one TWO thirty two two two two two two two two two two two two two two THREE thirty three three three three three three three FOUR thirty four four four four four come along come along long long long four four thirty four four four FIVE thirty five five five five grab it grab it grab it five thirty five thirty five thirty five five five am I right am I right am I right at thirty five five five SIX six thirty six six six six six six six six SEVEN seven seven seven thirty seven seven seven seven seven seven seven EIGHT eight eight eight thirty eight eight eight eight — sol-l-l-d A-merican!

Referred to by insiders as the "triphammer commercial," this memorable recitation was so unusual that it affected not only sales of Lucky Strikes but the methods by which commodities were advertised and sold in multiple industries. It began with Hill's simple observations at several tobacco warehouses across the South. He was intrigued by the rapid-fire delivery of the auctioneers and with the prospect of capturing that experience and pressing it into a useful merchandising tool. Hill solicited names of auctioneers who were quick on the trigger, enlisting L. A. "Speed" Riggs of Goldsboro, North Carolina, and F. E. Boone of Lexington, Kentucky. He paid them $25,000 annually and launched their chants on *The Jack Benny Program, Your Hit Parade* and other aural Lucky-backed series.

Those commercials' effectiveness drew heavily on replication, a Hill trademark. Once asked to identify the 10 most important principles of promotion, he offered his *Ten Commandments of Advertising*: 1. Repetition. 2. Repetition. 3. Repetition. 4. Repetition. 5. Repetition. 6. Repetition. 7. Repetition. 8. Repetition. 9. Repetition. 10. Repetition. Hill followed up by probing his inquisitors: "Did everybody get that? Anybody need it repeated?"

Hill got involved with his radio programs to the point of obsession, neurotically tinkering with each one. For the *Lucky Strike Dance Orchestra*, nothing escaped his notice: he personally approved the selection of every number beamed over the ether, the tempo at which it was played and the individuals who performed it, instrumentalists and vocalists alike. He supplied Dan Golenpaul, creator-owner-producer-director of *Information Please*, with a hand-picked catalog of celebrities, politicians and sports personalities who were *not* to be invited to sit on that venerated show's panel. (In a clash of wits, Golenpaul laughed in Hill's face.) There were sporadic hints that Hill's "scientific" determinants of chart-topping musical scores on *Your Hit Parade* might be partially man-made, given his incessant fidgeting with the process. He emphatically issued a directive to play up the melodies and keep the radio singers in virtual obscurity, nonetheless.[10] Throughout his dual decades as overbearing potentate, Hill clearly reserved for himself decisions that comparable industrialists would have delegated to far lower levels of management. It was unremitting evidence of his persistent peculiarities.

The American Tobacco Company was a tenacious, pervasive advertiser throughout radio's halcyon eon. Only a handful of firms underwrote the programming that made the mass form — particularly of network radio — viable to the extent that ATC did. With the charismatic drive of George W. Hill, ATC's innovations persuaded others to direct chunks of their advertising budgets to the neophyte medium. While those subscribers gained a return on the dollars they invested, simultaneously they secured a form of amusement and information that habitually satisfied the countrymen.

ATC also backed series that were genuinely admired by the listening public. A couple of its most durable entries earned imposing numbers: *Your Hit Parade* maintained a median 13.5 rating across its radio-only years (1935 to 1950); *The Jack Benny Program*, partially underwritten by ATC in 22 years of new shows (1933 to 1955), garnered an impressive median of 25.5, often ending a season in first place. ATC characteristically knew how to pick winners in more than one arena.

Commercial

1ST ANNOUNCER: (*cold*) *The Jack Benny Program*, presented by Lucky Strike.
AUCTIONEER: (*auction spiel, ending with*) ... sol-l-l-d A-merican!
1ST ANNOUNCER: Lucky Strike, and Lucky Strike alone, offers you important evidence — gathered in the tobacco country by the world-famous Crossley Poll. This evidence reveals the smoking preference of auctioneers, buyers and warehousemen ... the men who really know tobacco. Here's what the Crossley Poll found...
2ND ANNOUNCER: For their own personal smoking enjoyment, independent tobacco experts again name Lucky Strike first choice. Lucky Strike ... first choice ... over any other brand.
1ST ANNOUNCER: These experts know their business. Their overwhelming preference for Lucky Strike we believe has a direct relationship to the quality tobacco we purchase for Luckies ... and to the real, deep-down smoking enjoyment you may expect from fine tobacco. And when these veteran tobacco experts name Lucky Strike first choice for their own personal smoking enjoyment, then you'll know...
2ND ANNOUNCER: LS/MFT ... LS/MFT...
1ST ANNOUNCER: Lucky Strike means fine tobacco. And in a cigarette, it's the tobacco that counts. So smoke the smoke tobacco experts smoke ... Lucky Strike. Remember...
2ND ANNOUNCER: Independent tobacco experts again name Lucky Strike first choice ... Lucky Strike ... first choice ... over any other brand.
ORCHESTRA: (*plays opening bars of "I'm a Yankee Doodle Dandy" segueing into "Love in Bloom"*)
DON WILSON: (*theme under*) *The Lucky Strike Program* starring Jack Benny, with Mary Livingstone, Phil Harris, Rochester, Dennis Day and yours truly, Don Wilson...

An observation is reflective. Recall that George Washington Hill's *Ten Commandments of Advertising* called for applying a single idiom —*Repetition*—10 times. Note how many times this commercial from the Benny show's opening on April 25, 1948, mentioned *preference* (2), *smoking enjoyment* (3), *experts* (5) and *first choice* (5). Although the dialogue requires minimal imagination, it flawlessly illustrates the imperative of the tobacco tycoon that inspired it.

Andrew Jergens Company

History

Cincinnati had long been renowned as a soapmaking mecca when a couple of neighborhood pals began working alongside one another in that trade in 1880. Procter & Gamble, one of many such enterprises in the region, had established its business there more than four decades earlier. The laborers, meanwhile — Andrew N. Jergens, Sr. and Charles H. Geilfus — caught a glimpse of still greater possibilities for themselves in the same trade. Within a couple of years, they formed a partnership that led to a cosmetics giant bearing Jergens' moniker. In time, it produced the nation's best-selling hand lotion and one of its most celebrated facial cleansers.

A brief account of how they got to that point will be enlightening.

About a decade before Germany invaded southern Denmark, expanding its borders by annexing the Danish territory, Andrew Jergens was born in that portion of Denmark, in March 1852. Shortly before the arrival of the Germans, when young Andrew was seven, his parents took him and his brother to America to live. The family eventually migrated to Tell City, Indiana, an Ohio River port midway between Louisville, Kentucky, and Evansville, Indiana. Residing on a rented farm, Andrew Jergens matured.

When he was old enough to leave home, he sought solace at Cincinnati, about 100 miles northeast of Louisville, also on the Ohio River. At 20, in 1872, he found work as an apprentice in the wood-graining trade. But soapmaking, he soon discovered, held more promise; that was particularly true in that geographical area for it had a long established, prospering reputation there. He and Geilfus worked together in a small concern pursuing that line of work — one that eventually literally dried up (pun intended).

It was at that juncture that Geilfus urged Jergens to consider launching a venture with him that would compete with the big boys in the industry. Together, they might clean up (intentional pun again), he reasoned. There was just one catch: Geilfus had no money to start such an enterprise, although he knew that an industrious Jergens had $5,000 stashed in savings. Jergens had been raised in poverty, mind you, by first generation immigrants who taught him the value of putting something aside for a rainy day. It was a notion he never forgot. If that thrifty young man was willing to risk all of his capital, Geilfus was convinced they might have a fighting chance against those formidable established players in the business. But would he do so?

Seemingly throwing caution to the wind, in 1882 Jergens channeled every dime of what he had saved into starting up their new business, obviously believing the potential outweighed the risk. (To have come from where he did, incidentally, and have $5,000 to his name at 30 years of age in the nineteenth century was a sign that he possessed a strong work ethic and a head for business sense.) Simply because he provided the initial funding, their fledgling undertaking was named the Jergens Soap Company with Andrew Jergens as president.

They deliberately occupied a spot on Spring Grove Avenue near Cincinnati's foul-smelling slaughterhouses and meat-packing plants, an area known as Camp Washington in the modern age. Together, they reasoned that — without the lard by-products from those nearby stockyards — they couldn't net the pleasant fragrances that were to emanate from their own end products. Beginning with a single kettle, their soapworks hinged on stirring the pot in which their original commodity, coconut oil soap, was made, and subsequently selling it door-to-door out of a horse-drawn wagon. When one batch of soap was ready, the production halted until enough bars were sold to pay for a 1,000-pound pipe of coconut oil to follow.

W. L. Haworth joined in with Jergens and Geilfus in the earliest days of their endeavor, with the trio acquiring the raw ingredients as well as the manufacturing, packaging, selling, collecting and promotion of their wares. In assessing the threesome's humble beginnings more than a century hence, a *Cincinnati Post* reporter observed that the company was launched "at an opportune moment in American industrial and social history." It coincided with the Industrial Revolution, said the scribe, which was altering customs while at the same time "a growing middle-class was becoming more concerned with the refinements of life."[1]

Sometime during its first decade, the business moved to larger quarters on Spring Grove Avenue, a harbinger of its early success. By 1894, two of Andrew Jergens' siblings, Al and Herman Jergens, joined the growing undertaking. That year it was officially renamed Andrew Jergens and Company. Prospering, it became the first Cincinnati manufacturer to market its own French milling soap. As cosmetics for women became more common, the outfit expanded into creams, face powders and hand lotions, too.

Shortly after the turn of the century, in 1901, the enterprise incorporated as the Andrew Jergens Company, an appellation it would maintain for more than a century. That year it also significantly increased its capability by acquiring a couple of firms that decidedly raised its visibility in the decades ahead: the John H. Woodbury Company of New York City and the Robert Eastman Company of Philadelphia. Those acquisitions brought several enormously popular commodities under the Jergens umbrella. Woodbury Facial Soap was pitched as "a remedy for eczema, scaldhead, oily skin, pimples, flesh worms, ugly complexion, etc." The Woodbury outfit originated in Albany, New York, in 1870, begun by its namesake dermatologist.

According to Wikipedia — in the years from 1907 to 1910 — the Andrew Jergens Company, John H. Woodbury and the John H. Woodbury Dermatological Institute "were all involved in lawsuits against each other." The trio was unable to agree on which had rights to the Woodbury sobriquet. The Dermatological Institute was taken to court in 1908 for failure to hold a license in order to practice medicine. That group filed for bankruptcy protection in 1911. As a result, a precedent was set granting the state the authority to prevent corporations from practicing medicine, defeating the argument that no license was needed for a corporation as no individual was named.

In the meantime, a smooth white hand balm formula created by an Eastman chemist was to have still greater impact on increasing Jergens' image. That ware — originally known as Jergens Benzoin and Almond Lotion Compound — was later trimmed to Jergens Lotion.

The product and its manufacturer were eventually intertwined in the public's collective mind, thanks to Jergens' uncompromising marketing and advertising, truly making it the most widely known commodity of its kind in the U.S. To accomplish that, in 1904, Jergens began spending $70,000 annually on magazine and newspaper promotion.

From its earliest days, the wrapper for the Woodbury Facial Soap bar had borne creator John Woodbury's name and photo: According to one source, it was "an image reminiscent of an ape with a face cropped above the neck." While sales languished categorically behind the leading facial soap at first, in 1910, Jergens turned its Woodbury advertising over to the expertise of the J. Walter Thompson agency, long a contender for the nation's creative ad leader. For six months, the head of Thompson's women's editorial department, Helen Lansdowne, pondered that marketing dilemma.[2] Eventually she launched a series of innovative print ads that focused on reducing nose pores. While that approach may be unappealing and distasteful against today's marketing fads, it zeroed in on consumers' concerns of that day as opposed to mere manufacturer's qualities.

The real breakthrough for Woodbury came in 1911 when the soap began to proffer one of the most famous mottos in all of advertising history: "A Skin You Love to Touch." (The catchphrase was updated to the more familiar "The Skin You Love to Touch" in the 1920s.) The axiom was placed above gauzily romantic paintings of elegant young women, joyfully receiving the flattering concentrations of debonair young males. *Ladies' Home Journal* and many other mass circulation slicks carried those ads regularly. And as a result, for a decade, sales soared.

"Tame as it may now seem," a contemporary Web site noted, "several historians of advertising have called the 'Skin You Love to Touch' campaign the first to use sex appeal in modern advertising." Not only that, a quarter-century later (1936), Woodbury reportedly became the first commodity to invade its space ads with illustrations of nude females. "The women who saw the ads, paid attention to them, and then bought the soap could at least imagine themselves as the alluring objects of male attention," the site proclaimed. Was this possibly (and unintentionally) more oil to fan the flames of an approaching Women's Lib movement perhaps?

When chain radio came along, Jergens jumped in with both feet. By 1933, Woodbury was airing soon-to-be legendary singer Bing Crosby, and later soon-to-be celebrated comedian Bob Hope. *The Jergens Journal*, a headline-making newsjournal of the ether headlined by Walter Winchell, produced a gargantuan following every Sunday night throughout the 1930s and 1940s. Winchell's "with lotions of love" sign-off slogan became a radio classic. The firm was among the first using Hollywood star endorsements in its advertising, and further pioneered in selling through variety store chains, something untried heretofore.

Long after network radio passed, Jergens was involved in a unique marketing experiment. In the summer of 1992, the company announced that it would underwrite a six-month print advertising campaign, budgeting $25 million for it, all allocated to 19 popular magazines. *Cosmopolitan, People Weekly, Reader's Digest* and *Self* were among the 19 recipients. The target group was well-educated women in households with at least $30,000 incomes who were between the ages of 25 to 54. Until this experiment, Jergens committed about 75 percent of its ad budget to television. Ted Zimmerman, senior vice president at Jergens, reported that the company reached four out of five members of its target audience through the slicks. In *The Magazine for Magazine Management*, Zimmerman affirmed, "Magazines are the best source of beauty, grooming and skin tips."

Upon the death of Andrew N. Jergens, Sr., his only son, Andrew N. Jergens, Jr. (1881 to

1967) — who had worked at the Jergens factory as a youth to earn pocket money, then later became a full time assistant chemist in the perfume lab — succeeded to the presidency upon his dad's death in January 1929. The younger Andrews had saved the firm $200,000 at one juncture by creating synthetic aromatic chemicals. According to published reports, father and son weren't close: the father was a workaholic at the expense of his relationship with his son, and the son never shared the extreme frugality that characterized his elder in personal dealings.

During Junior's tenure at the helm, nevertheless, the firm solidified. Product lines expanded pervasively throughout the 1950s, 1960s and 1970s. Among the new goods was Dryad Roll-On antiperspirant and deodorant, Clear Complexion Bar, Jergens Nature Scents and Gentle Touch bubble bath additives. By 1980, the company launched the first liquid hand wash, enriched with Jergens lotion.

American Brands purchased the Andrew Jergens Company for $100 million in 1970. Eighteen years later, it was sold to the Kao [pronounced "Cow"] Corporation of Japan. (There will be more data about Kao presently.)

In 1997, the Biore product line premiered in the United States as Jergens acquired Bausch & Lomb's skin care business. The following year therapeutic skin moisturizing products and the Soft Sense brand of hand and body lotions joined Jergens' portfolio with the purchase of Curel. Ban deodorant and antiperspirant was added in 2000. The Andrew Jergens Company, still a wholly owned subsidiary of the Kao Corporation, moved into the hair care field in September 2002, buying the John Frieda Professional Hair Care businesses. Founded a dozen years earlier by the British hairdresser to the stars for whom it was named, the salon-based hair care firm was a market leader. To Jergens, it contributed trademarks like Brilliant Brunette, Frizz-Ease and Sheer Blonde.

In September 2004, the Andrew Jergens Company officially changed its name to Kao Brands Company. Kao's origins date to 1887 when it was organized as Kao Soap Company, Ltd. Now headquartered in Chuo-ku, Tokyo, Japan, Kao Corporation has about 7,000 employees worldwide. It has been labeled "the Procter & Gamble of Japan" and is one of that nation's leaders in personal care, cosmetic, laundry, cleaning, hygiene and bath additive products. Kao manufactures fatty chemicals, edible oils and specialty chemicals, too, and is one of the leading global suppliers of information technology products and services.

Kao's first commodity, a facial soap in 1890, bore the motto: "A Clean Nation Prospers." That year Kao brought out a crescent-moon logo, similar to one Procter & Gamble registered eight years before. That precipitated an enduring rivalry. By the end of the 1920s, Kao developed coconut alcohol-based synthetic detergents. Following the Second World War, it began manufacturing heavy-duty detergents.

Unlike its American counterparts, however, at least 25 percent of Kao's workers hold jobs in research and development. Early investigation into the properties of oils and fats, the basic elements in soap, have allowed Kao to expand its line of commodities rapidly to include finishing products, polishing agents, waxes, insecticides, antiseptics, fungicides and deodorants. The firm also maintains a unique network of proprietary wholesalers. In the early 1960s, it persuaded its wholesalers to establish jointly owned companies which distributed Kao goods exclusively.

Kao developed a highly absorbent polymer that reduced diaper rash in the 1980s. As a result, after 1983, its Merries brand of disposable diapers far outsold the multiple brands proffered by Procter & Gamble in Japan. Four years later, Kao began selling Attack concentrated laundry detergent, one of its most salient introductions. Within six months, Attack commanded nearly 50 percent of the Japanese detergent market. By 1990, Kao was the Japanese market leader in eight of its 10 main product categories, holding more than half the market in these five: laundry detergents, fabric softeners, bleaches, skin cleansers, household cleaners.

After Kao acquired the Andrew Jergens Company in 1988, Jergens was placed within the firm's U.S. subsidiary, Kao Corporation of America. High Point [North Carolina] Chemical Corporation, a specialty chemical enterprise acquired in 1987, supplies the raw materials for the Jergens toiletry and skin-care products, still manufactured in Cincinnati. A move into Germany was completed in 1989 when Kao purchased 75 percent of Goldwell GmbH, a manufacturer of hair-care and beauty products through global professional hairdressers.

"Our underlying values and goals," a Kao Brands Company Web site certifies, "are to continue to be an innovator of premium beauty products that enhance the appearance, health, and general well-being of women around the world." KBC has worldwide operations in North America, Europe, the Middle East and Australia, presently serving 54 markets nationally and internationally.

Radio Series

The Morton Downey Show, with Leon Belasco and His Orchestra, Paul Whiteman and His Orchestra — 1932 to 1933, 1934, 1935 to 1936, NBC Blue, CBS (Woodbury)
The Jergens Journal, aka *The Woodbury Journal,* with Walter Winchell — 1932 to 1948, NBC Blue, Blue, ABC (Jergens, Woodbury)
The Bing Crosby Show, with The Mills Brothers, The Boswell Sisters, Georgie Stoll and His Orchestra — 1933 to 1935, CBS (Woodbury)
Dangerous Paradise, with Nick Dawson and Elsie Hitz — 1933 to 1935, NBC Blue (Woodbury)
The Rippling Rhythm Revue, with Shep Fields and His Orchestra, Frank Parker, Bob Hope — 1936 to 1937, NBC Blue (Woodbury)
Follow the Moon, with Nick Dawson and Elsie Hitz — 1937, NBC (Jergens)
Hollywood Playhouse, aka *Promoting Priscilla,* with Harry Sosnik and His Orchestra — 1937 to 1940, NBC Blue, CBS (Woodbury)
The Parker Family, with Leon Janney — 1939 to 1943, NBC Blue, CBS (Woodbury)
The Tony Martin Show, with David Rose and His Orchestra — 1941, NBC (Woodbury)
How Did You Meet? — 1941, NBC (Woodbury)
The Adventures of the Thin Man, with Les Damon — 1941 to 1942, NBC (Woodbury)
Mr. and Mrs. North, with Joseph Curtin and Alice Frost — 1942 to 1946, NBC (Woodbury)
The Chamber Music Society of Lower Basin Street — 1943 to 1944, NBC Blue, Blue (Woodbury)
The Hollywood Mystery Theater, with Earle Stanley Gardner — 1944 to 1945, Blue (Woodbury)
Louella Parsons, aka *Inside Hollywood,* aka *The Woodbury Hollywood News* — 1944 to 1951, 1952 to 1954, Blue, ABC, CBS (Jergens, Woodbury)
Romance, aka *Jergens Hollywood Playhouse,* aka *Playhouse of Romance* — 1952 to 1953, CBS (Jergens)
Time for Love, with Marlene Dietrich, Robert Readick — 1953 to 1954, CBS (Jergens)

Exposition

"At the same time that Woodbury's ads are documents about gender relations and sexuality in early twentieth-century America [see text under "History" above], they are also evidence of the marketing situation of American consumer goods manufacturers.... Soap and cosmetic advertising helped to shift 'beauty culture' from small-scale production, often by women entrepreneurs, to an industry based on the sale of mass-produced commodities. Woodbury's also reflected a transition from nineteenth-century advertising's emphasis on product-centered appeals to depictions of those who use the product. Probably the most successful American soap campaign prior to 'A Skin You Love to Touch' was Procter & Gamble's advertising of Ivory Soap, beginning around 1882. Ivory was 'Ninety-nine and 44/100 Percent Pure,' it proclaimed. 'It floats,' initially a secondary appeal, soon became Ivory's primary slogan. The soap bar itself was at the center of illustrations. Here, the physical characteristics of the product — only tenuously related to its use or its users — bore the task of selling the soap. In the Woodbury advertisements of the 1910s, the bar itself appeared only as a reminder in the lower corner of the page, a throwback to product-centered advertising of earlier decades. The promise of the ad was in the social interactions it would inspire."[3] And of course, its benefit to the user was what the radio commercials — which arrived later but built upon a print heritage — were all about. Woodbury and Jergens, in that regard, seemed to be among the leaders of the pack.

Andrew Jergens demonstrated an affinity for Sunday night radio on the NBC Blue-Blue-ABC chain (the web went by multiple monikers as the years advanced). Not only did Jergens underwrite a quarter-hour for Walter Winchell there over a 16-year period, it did likewise for Louella Parsons for seven years and *The Parker Family* for three-and-a-half years. In addition, it sponsored briefer runs of *The Chamber Music Society of Lower Basin Street*, *Hollywood Playhouse* and *The Rippling Rhythm Revue* (with Bob Hope, Frank Parker and Shep Fields) in that time zone. Jergens virtually bought out ABC's nine o'clock half-hour on Sunday evenings, running a couple of 15-minute back-to-back series from the early 1930s to the early 1950s. Few advertisers made that kind of commitment to prime time programming, particularly for anything less than single continuing features of at least a half-hour's duration.

Commercial

Enterprising radio commodity pluggers sought creative methods of selling their wares, frequently including endorsements by celebrities and ordinary citizens in their spiels. In the following commercial, typical of a surfeit of audio pitches, a spokeswoman was hired to impersonate a purchaser of the sponsor's soap. Having liked its benefits, she apparently studied up on the cleanser and became an informed advocate. Or so it must have seemed to listeners of *The Woodbury Journal* with Louella Parsons on September 6, 1948.

MARVIN MILLER: Girls, if you want to stand out and be someone he wants to know better, well, it's wonderful how Woodbury lovely skin can catch and hold his eyes. Take tonight's romance: At a Georgia Tech fraternity dance, football star Paul Duke danced with Woodbury deb Jean Frazer. Danced once, danced twice, and couldn't take his eyes off the Woodbury smooth sparkle. Yes, for the come-hither romance appeal of her skin, Jean tosses a big bouquet to Woodbury. In her words ...

JEAN FRAZER: I do thank Woodbury ... beauty care that's truly mild.

MILLER: Ah, Woodbury is extra mild.

FRAZER: It's creamy rich lather.

MILLER: A rich beauty cream ingredient goes into Woodbury, actually a skin-smoothing ingredient ...

FRAZER: To keep skin smooth, fascinating, try this rich Woodbury cocktail: first, apply a lather massage, then rinse it.

MILLER: The beauty reward?

FRAZER: Skin that glows ... looks romantic.

MILLER: Only Woodbury of all popular facial soaps contains this beauty-cream ingredient. That's why Woodbury is *really* different — a true beauty soap, to coax your skin to its softest, freshest beauty. Remember ... Woodbury facial soap ... for the skin you'll love to touch!

Bristol-Myers Company

History

A couple of ex-fraternity brothers at Hamilton College, Clinton, New York, took a big risk in 1887 when they each sunk $5,000 collateral into a failing drug manufacturer. The new owners took over Clinton Pharmaceutical Company on December 13 of that year. The reconstituted enterprise was carried on by William McLaren Bristol (1861 to 1935) as president and his partner and vice president, John Ripley Myers (ca. 1866 to 1899). Bristol graduated from Hamilton in 1882 while Myers finished in 1887.

Their small operation dispensed medical preparations to physicians and dentists in and around Clinton. Its original distribution system consisted of a horse-drawn buggy. Unfamiliarity with remedies and a lack of capital hindered the duo from the start. Distribution significantly improved, however, when — in 1889 — they relocated the business to Syracuse, New York. A decade later (1899), the enterprise moved again, to Brooklyn, New York, where it gained access to a wider base of purchasers, especially residents throughout New England and Pennsylvania.

Some tweaking of the outfit's name occurred during the period. Still known as Clinton Pharmaceutical Company in 1898, the firm's moniker was changed that year to Bristol, Myers Company. Following the death of John Myers, nevertheless, the business was incorporated in 1900 and the moniker altered again. That year the comma was replaced with a hyphen between the surnames. Bristol-Myers was to remain undisturbed until another partner was added to the mix nine decades beyond.

By the turn of the century, Bristol-Myers appreciably beefed up its small sales force, focusing on wholesale and retail druggists. Increasingly it turned its marketing strategies away from individual doctors and dental practitioners, favoring a wider audience in their stead. Earning its first profit in 1900, the firm began developing specialty goods. By then it had created a couple that hadn't yet acquired much notice, although they would eventually put the company on the map.

In 1895, chemist J. Leroy Webber developed a laxative mineral salt which — when dissolved in water — reproduced the taste and effects of natural Bohemian mineral waters. Webber labeled it "a poor man's spa" and Bristol-Myers christened it Sal Hepatica. The company developed toothpaste about the same time, with a disinfectant base that targeted bleeding gums. Ipana was a departure from everything else on the market. And by 1903, the two commodities took off, creating demand that literally transformed the supplier from a little-known regional manufacturer to a widely recognized national and international personal care goods supplier. Sal Hepatica and Ipana turned into instant cash crops. The flagship products put Bristol-Myers on consumers' radar screens for the first time.

Gross profits topped $1 million in 1924. With its goods sold in 26 nations by then, the company opened an export department to process the growing global demand. A new manufacturing plant was added at Hillside, New Jersey. In the meantime, John Myers' heirs eventually sold their shares in the company and the Bristol family solidified its control. In 1915, William's oldest son, Henry Platt Bristol (born ca. 1889), became the firm's general manager. After acceding to the presidency in 1949, he became chairman. Henry's siblings, Lee Hastings Bristol (1892 to 1962) and William McLaren Bristol, Jr. (born 1896), respectively took over the advertising and manufacturing departments in 1928.

Lee, who later became board chairman like his brother, was a promotional wizard. Instead of going after the medical community that Bristol-Myers had almost exclusively proffered its wares to in the past, he decided to advertise directly to the end-use consumer market. Not only did he put his firm's jingles on radio in the 1920s, underwriting multiple network features in the 1930s, he insisted on socking 26 percent of the company's sales revenues into advertising. Those efforts resulted in turning an essentially obscure drug-maker into an established $160-million-a-year pharmaceutical house.

The outfit discontinued manufacturing prescription drugs in the wake of a recession that hit the country following World War I. It concentrated on specialty goods like Sal Hepatica and Ipana instead, plus about a dozen more commodities ranging from toiletries and antiseptics to cough syrups. It was a smart decision: picking a few winners paid off handsomely in establishing public confidence while steadily contributing to the firm's bottom line. A few years hence, during the Great Depression epoch, Bristol-Myers relocated its headquarters to 345 Park Avenue in Manhattan, the prestigious address it still occupies today.

But while that was going on, from 1928 to 1933, the drug supplier became part of a holding company: Drug, Inc., produced proprietary medicines while operating a major retail chain. Bristol-Myers continued to develop and advertise more and more products at the same time. William L. Bristol, Sr. was Bristol-Myers' chairman in that period, eldest son Henry was president, middle son Lee was vice president and youngest son William, Jr. was secretary. To claim that the Bristols were running the business would be an understatement.

Bristol-Myers again made ethical (prescription) drugs during World War II, mass producing penicillin for Allied forces through a subsidiary, Bristol Laboratories. In 1943, Bristol-Myers acquired Cheplin Laboratories of Syracuse, New York. The name was subsequently changed to Bristol. In the postwar era, that strategic lab turned to antibiotic production for consumer use.

Investing heavily in TV promotion by then, Bristol-Myers continued its growth, turning to acquisitions for some of its increases. It diversified into hair coloring in 1959 by purchasing Clairol, Inc. In 1965, it acquired household products manufacturer Drackett. Two years later, it expanded into infant formula and vitamins for juveniles by adding Mead Johnson. A research facility was opened at Wallingford, Connecticut, in 1984. In 1989, the firm merged with ER Squibb Corporation, becoming known as Bristol-Myers Squibb Company (BMS).

Begun by Edward Robinson Squibb (1819 to 1900) in 1858, that pharmaceutical lab was established in Brooklyn, New York, predating William Bristol and John Myers' entry into the field by three decades. When the founder transferred day-to-day operations to his progeny, Charles and Edward, in 1895, it was renamed E. R. Squibb & Sons (later commonly ER Squibb). The heirs sold it five years after their dad's death. While still bearing the Squibb nomenclature, the company passed from the founding family's hands in 1905.

Land for a production plant was purchased that year at New Brunswick, New Jersey, by Squibb's new owners. During the Second World War, the site housed the largest penicillin factory on the planet. ER Squibb expanded manufacturing into Mexico, Italy and Argentina in the postwar years, significantly increasing its global presence. A new headquarters facility was completed at Princeton, New Jersey, in 1971. When Squibb merged with Bristol-Myers in 1989, it created what was then the world's second-largest pharmaceutical operation.

With a mission "to extend and enhance human life," the combined firm has remained on the cutting edge of drug breakthroughs. Company publicists acknowledge that Bristol-Myers Squibb chemists are participating in advancements for the treatment of cancer, cardiovascular and metabolic diseases, hepatitis, HIV/AIDS, psychiatric disorders, rheumatoid arthritis and other grave illnesses. BMS continues to pursue personal care commodities in addition to health care quests. Its major goods include cholesterol reducer Pravachol, anti–blood clotting agent Plavix and chemotherapy drug Taxol. In addition to prescription preparations, the firm manufactures over-the-counter painkiller Excedrin. Its ConvaTec auxiliary sells medical supplies like ostomy bags and wound dressings. Another subsidiary, Mead Johnson, produces Enfamil baby formula and Boost nutritional supplements. Yet another division concentrates on medical imaging.

The company reported assets of $27.22 billion in 2006 with profits of $2.22 billion that year. It also maintained a global workforce of 43,000. Early in this century its principal competitors were Aventis S. A., Glaxo Wellcome and Merck & Company, Inc.

Radio Series

The Ipana Troubadours, with instrumentalists Sam Lanin, Red Nichols, Joe Tarto, Harry Horlick, Benny Goodman, Jimmy Dorsey, Tommy Dorsey, Jack Teagarden, and vocalists Billy Jones, Irving Kaufman, Scrappy Lambert, the Singing Sophomores, and more — 1926 to 1934, NBC, NBC Blue (Ipana)
The Sal Hepatica Revue, aka *The Hour of Smiles*, aka *Town Hall Tonight*, aka *The Fred Allen Show* — 1934 to 1940, NBC (Sal Hepatica, Ipana, Minit-Rub)
Through the Looking Glass, with Frances Ingram — 1930 to 1932, NBC Blue (Ingram's)
Ingram Shavers' Orchestra — ca. early 1930s, NBC (Ingram's)
Town Hall Big Game Hunt, with Norman Frescott — 1938, NBC (Ipana, Sal Hepatica)
Town Hall Varieties, with F. Chase Taylor — 1938, NBC (Ipana, Sal Hepatica)
For Men Only, aka *The George Jessel Jamboree*, aka *George Jessel's Celebrity Program*, with Fred Uttal, George Jessel and Mary Small — 1938 to 1940, NBC (Vitalis, Ipana, Sal Hepatica)
Don Winslow of the Navy — 1939, NBC Blue (Ipana)
The Life of Mary Sothern (transcribed repeats) — 1939 to 1943, Syndication (Ipana)
Time to Smile, aka *The Eddie Cantor Show* — 1940 to 1946, NBC (Sal Hepatica, Ipana, Trushay, Minit-Rub)
Mr. District Attorney, with Jay Jostyn — 1940 to 1952, NBC, ABC (Vitalis, Ipana, Sal Hepatica, Ingram's)
Quizzer Baseball, with Budd Hulick and Harry Von Zell — 1941, NBC (Ipana, Sal Hepatica)

Songs by Dinah Shore, aka *In Person, Dinah Shore*—1941 to 1943, NBC Blue (Sal Hepatica, Minit-Rub)
Those We Love—1942, NBC (Ipana, Sal Hepatica)
Duffy's Tavern, with Ed Gardner—1942 to 1949, NBC Blue, NBC (Ipana, Trushay, Sal Hepatica, Minit-Rub, Ingram's)
Noah Webster Says, with Haven MacQuarrie—1943, NBC Blue (Ipana, Sal Hepatica)
A Date with Judy, with Louise Erickson—1943, NBC (Sal Hepatica, Ipana)
The Parker Family, with Leon Janney—1943 to 1944, Blue (Ipana)
Nitwit Court, with Ransom Sherman—1944, Blue (Ipana, Sal Hepatica)
The Alan Young Show—1944 to 1947, ABC, NBC (Ipana, Sal Hepatica)
The Gracie Fields Show—1944 to 1945, Blue (Ipana)
Correction Please, with J. C. Flippen—1945, NBC (Ipana, Sal Hepatica)
Break the Bank, with Bert Parks—1946 to 1951, ABC, NBC (Vitalis, Trushay, Sal Hepatica, Resistab, Bufferin, Mum)
Hi Jinx, with Tex McCreary and Jinx Falkenberg—1947, 1948, NBC (Ipana)
This Is Nora Drake—1953 to 1954, 1955 to 1956, CBS (Sal Hepatica, Ipana)
Yours Truly, Johnny Dollar—1950s, CBS (Ipana—multiple participation)
Gunsmoke, with William Conrad—ca. 1957 to ca. 1961, CBS (Trig)

Exposition

When Lee Hastings Bristol, middle son of one of the founders of the company, was put in charge of the firm's advertising strategies in the 1920s, the timing could hardly have been better: Bristol-Myers made a colossal shift in its promotional philosophy at the time. It was turning away from spotlighting the medical professionals almost exclusively to targeting the end-users of its products, the retail consumer market. That decision occurred at just about the point in time that radio was arriving on the horizon. Within a few years, the airwaves became a powerful marketing medium that reached zillions of listeners simultaneously.

The Ipana Troubadours (sometimes spelled *Troubadors*) were among the pioneer entertainers wafting onto the ether, appearing as early as 1923 over New York's premier WEAF. Exposing listeners to that cluster's namesake Ipana toothpaste in a period when product names were included in a show's title and commercials were literally prohibited, the *Troubadours* were responsible for converting scads of the previously uninformed. They were "a remarkable group of early radio and recording artists," one reviewer observed. "The fare was a mix of novelty tunes and hot swing." Several notable musicians of the future (the Dorseys, Benny Goodman, Billy Jones, Jack Teagarden) emerged from *Troubadour* apprenticeships, underscoring another byproduct of those performances.

Soon the catchphrase "Ipana for the Smile of Beauty—Sal Hepatica for the Smile of Health" became an identifying symbol for Bristol-Myers' dual flagship products, instantly recognized by remedy and personal care buyers across the land. In the 1930s, over a period of a half-dozen years, *The Fred Allen Show* (which often aired under sundry sponsor titles) was emblazoned with that unforgettable tagline. As one of NBC's most acclaimed weekly features, the comedian's sarcastic wit drew millions to the Bristol-Myers moneymakers.

In addition to underwriting a stable of pithy fill-in series for regulars on summer hiatus, plus a handful of single-season features, in practice Bristol-Myers concentrated the bulk of its radio budget on a half-dozen programs that obviously met with gratifying receptions.

In addition to *The Ipana Troubadours* (on the network ether for eight years and still longer on its New York originating station), there were separate comedy-variety series headlined by Fred Allen and Eddie Cantor (whom Bristol-Myers carried for six years each). Then there was a seven-year run for the sitcom *Duffy's Tavern* and five more years for the quiz show *Break the Bank*. The firm really went all out for the crime drama *Mr. District Attorney*, paying its bills for a dozen years. It even sent series star Jay Jostyn to a full season on ABC-TV in the key role (1951 to 1952).

All of Bristol-Myers' radio business except for three series at the end of the era was sent to NBC, NBC Blue or MBS. If there's a theory why CBS got the drippings as radio's golden age lay on its deathbed, it hasn't surfaced. Was Lee Bristol playing footsy with the other chains? Did CBS simply not impress him, at least not until the rates tanked? Perhaps only his hairdresser (who certainly applied Vitalis) knew.

In the 1940s and 1950s, radio shows exhibited incessant mentions of their sponsors' goods, going far beyond the zones designated for commercials. Instead, they unabashedly and unapologetically seized every opportunity to mention a subscriber's commodities. On *Break the Bank*, for instance, time after time emcee Bert Parks dutifully updated fans with precisely how much dough was stashed in "the Vitalis-Trushay bank," a figure that fluctuated as the game proceeded. When a reference to one of the sponsor's wares could be inserted into any neighborly repartee between the show's principals, it was. There may never have been a five-minute lapse in any *Break the Bank* broadcast when the radio listeners weren't reminded who was underwriting it. It was the nature of the beast; several protégé series paid for by others were doing likewise.

Commercial

Repetitiously, radio made use of dialoguing in plugging its wares. Overhearing conversations of two or more individuals may have made a more potent impact on the listeners. It certainly removed the risk of turning an audience off by using the sometimes offensive, nauseating monotone of a solitary voice, a method applied by the majority of audio advertisers. During a sponsor's spot in between contestants on the primetime edition of *Break the Bank* on February 1, 1950, master of ceremonies Bert Parks relinquished the microphone to "host" Bud Collyer (who was actually the show's announcer) and "our paying teller" Janice (her only identification). Those two exchanged wordplay about one of Bristol-Myers' handful of consumer products.

BUD COLLYER: Say, Jan, explain yourself ... What do you mean you lead a "double life"?
JANICE: Well, most women lead double lives, Bud ... at least our hands do. We keep a shining clean house.
BUD COLLYER: Which I suppose means lots of soap-and-water chores? Not good for hands.
JANICE: Unh-uhh. And then the glamorous side of living ... parties, dancing, entertaining.
BUD COLLYER: But, what about those hands?
JANICE: Bud ... did you forget about Trushay?
BUD COLLYER (*laughs*): I was leading you on! Everybody should know about Trushay, the beforehand lotion. Trushay helps keep hands at work lovely for play.
JANICE: Trushay is an entirely different idea in hand care ... a lotion so soothing and oily-rich we use it beforehand to ward off chapping, drying, soap-and-water damage, even when we use hot soapy water.

BUD COLLYER: And Trushay leads a double life, too ... you use Trushay not only beforehand, but any time, whenever you need a soothing lotion.

JANICE: So ... one bottle of Trushay in your kitchen ... another on your dressing table ... is a good idea, girls.

BUD COLLYER: For keeping busy hands lovely, too, begin today to use Trushay, the beforehand lotion.

Brown & Williamson Tobacco Company

History

The early beginnings of tobacco growth and commerce are documented in the *American Tobacco Company* article in this section.

The Brown & Williamson firm resulted in 1894 when Robert Lynn Williamson and his brother-in-law, George T. Brown, bought out Williamson's father, with whom the latter had partnered in tobacco commerce. T. F. Williamson and Company had operated in the little hamlet of Winston, North Carolina, since the elder (known by intimates as "Captain Tom") moved his clan there in 1880. (The town later incorporated the nearby village of Salem and was thereafter known as Winston-Salem.)

Thomas Farish Williamson was born February 10, 1836, in Caswell County, North Carolina. His father was a wealthy planter and merchant. He died when Tom was only 12, leaving a wife and seven children to run extensive property holdings and business interests. Young Tom matured with the intent of growing and improving tobacco, a pursuit he was good at. He became a prosperous planter, manufacturer and devout Presbyterian layman. In the early 1870s, he launched a plug and smoking tobacco operation, marketing Red Juice and Red Crow chewing tobaccos and Golden Grain granulated smoking tobacco. Those brands were continued by his successors at Brown & Williamson. The patriarch maintained his earliest factory in Caswell County while opening a second plant in Reidsville, North Carolina, in 1878. He closed the Reidsville operation two years afterward and reopened at Winston while maintaining the original site in Caswell County. By 1900, Captain Tom had moved to Leaksville (now Eden) where he operated a general mercantile store and served on the town council.

George Brown, meanwhile, had also emerged from a tobacco producing family. Brown Brothers Tobacco Manufacturing Company at Mocksville, not far from Winston, co-managed by George and his sibling Rufus, was the largest tobacco business in that town. Their father was also a successful tobacco merchant. George Brown and Robert Williamson formed their new partnership in 1893. In February 1894, the company known as Brown & Williamson (B&W) leased a small Winston factory, hired 30 hands and began operations. It incorporated as Brown & Williamson Tobacco Company in 1906. During its early years it concentrated on chewing tobaccos with monikers like Bloodhound, Brown & Williamson's Sun Cured and Red Juice.

After gaining momentum, B&W purchased the J. G. Flynt Tobacco Company and its trademarks in 1925. That automatically gave them the already locally popular Sir Walter Raleigh smoking tobacco label, one Flynt had marketed regionally since 1884. B&W began to advertise and distribute it nationally. Sir Walter Raleigh became a hallmark appellation clearly identified with the firm, proving a savvy move. With that slice of the business under its belt, in 1926 the firm ventured into manufacturing cigarettes. That year it bought the R. P. Richardson Company. Until the turn of the century, the cigarette market had been relatively weak, well behind cigars, plug, twist and pipe tobacco. But once cigarettes were issued to U.S. soldiers in World War I, demand escalated rapidly. B&W initiated an aggressive drive and significant profit growth resulted. Now B&W's foundation was securely established in several lucrative sectors.

The firm's solid achievements and budding promise made it especially attractive to outside investors seeking to expand their trade holdings. B&W's success didn't escape notice by the London-based British American Tobacco plc (see the American Tobacco Company article), a global conglomerate serving expansive commercial tobacco interests. BAT purchased B&W in 1927 as a subsidiary, altered its moniker to Brown & Williamson Tobacco Corporation, and added extensive manufacturing plants at Louisville, Kentucky, the following two years. By 1929, it opened a many-storied tower in downtown Louisville, shifting its headquarters operations from Winston-Salem. For the first time, B&W was able to significantly increase production output and expand distribution beyond the southeastern United States.

In 1928, the firm launched its first national brand, Raleigh, a premium cigarette. Five years later, it introduced the first menthol cigarette to achieve national distribution, Kool. By 1936, it was manufacturing the industry's first filter cigarette with a cork tip, Viceroy. Those brands — along with Sir Walter Raleigh smoking tobacco — gave B&W impetus as a significant player in the trade. To achieve even greater market share, it advertised its hallmark brands vigorously both in print and — more and more — on radio. While B&W would not become one of the top three in its industry until many years after radio's golden age passed, it was much more than an also ran factor in the burgeoning tobacco market and economy.

In 1929, B&W introduced the first economy priced cigarette, Wings, which sold for a dime a pack as opposed to the 15-cent brands that predominated. Wings became a big seller in Depression-laden America. It was also the first to wrap its contents in a moisture-proof cellophane package, blazing an innovative trail for almost all others.[1] B&W soon followed its value-priced entry with yet another, Avalon, which sold even better than Wings. In the mid–1930s, B&W purchased Bugler and Kite cigarette brands from their manufacturers. The company further pioneered in yet another area, bringing out the first U.S.-made roll-your-own package, the Bugler Thrift Kit.

In the twilight of radio's halcyon era, B&W introduced an alternative national menthol cigarette, Belair, in 1960. Two decades beyond, it brought out an ultra-low tar cigarette, Barclay, supplied with an Actron filter. B&W acquired the marketing rights for the discount-priced cigarette GPC in 1984. It established the superslim cigarette category in 1987 with the introduction of Capri, a stylish cigarette with a 17-millimeter circumference.

After the middle of the twentieth century, Kool was clearly B&W's most popular brand. Heavily favored by the African American market, about 70 percent of black smokers were puffing menthol cigarettes. Kool dominated all menthol brands then sold, accounting for 10 percent of U.S. cigarette sales by the early 1970s. In the middle of that decade, B&W controlled 17 percent of American cigarette sales. Led by Kool, its bottom line was boosted by Kool Milds, Viceroy Extra Milds and Raleigh Extra Milds. Nevertheless, in 1975 Kool steadily began to decline, losing market share to Salem and Newport menthol smokes. By 1985, Kool's share had plunged 3.4 percent, to about 6.9 percent. By 1984, the company was investing heavily in the value-oriented brands of Viceroy, GPC Approved, Raleigh Extra and Richland.[2] B&W also moved aggressively into cigarette markets in Africa, Asia, Europe, Japan, the Middle East, Puerto Rico and South America.

After British American Tobacco plc acquired control of the assets and operations of American Brands, formerly the American Tobacco Company, B&W's inventory increased to include such well-known sobriquets as Lucky Strike, Pall Mall, Tareyton and Carlton.

In the late 1990s, B&W was the focus of an intensive inquiry into whether it knowingly manipulated the content of cigarettes. The CBS-TV series *60 Minutes* became involved. Whistleblower Jeffrey Wigand, a former B&W vice-president of research and development, starred in a fictionalized account that was turned into an award-winning cinematic production, *The Insider*, released late in 1999. Wigand's part was portrayed by actor Russell Crowe. In real life, Wigand insisted that B&W introduced chemicals into its products to increase habit-forming nicotine dependency.[3] None of it bodes well for a troubled tobacco trade, which faced a lack of public confidence since the U.S. Surgeon General issued his opinion in 1964 that "smoking may be detrimental to your health."

The second (R. J. Reynolds) and third (B&W) largest U.S. tobacco producers were combined under one umbrella when British American Tobacco plc and R. J. Reynolds Tobacco Holdings, Inc., signed a 2003 pact. Reynolds American, Inc., a newly-created moniker, became the parent company on July 30, 2004. B&W's assets, liabilities and operations were folded into RJR Tobacco, a wholly owned subsidiary. Operations in Louisville were suspended; Winston-Salem, B&W's original home town, became its controlling center again.

Radio Series

The Raleigh-Kool Cigarette Program, with Tommy Dorsey and His Orchestra, Jack Pearl, Jack Leonard and Morton Bowe, Jo Stafford—1936 to 1939, NBC, NBC Blue (Raleigh, Kool)
Avalon Variety Time, with Red Foley, Red Skelton, Curt Massey, Cliff Arquette—1938, 1939, 1940 to 1941, NBC (Avalon)
Home Town Dramas—1939 to 1940, NBC (Raleigh)
Showboat, aka *Home Town Unincorporated*, with Cliff Soubier, Dick Todd, Virginia Verrill, Marlin Hurt—1939 to 1940, NBC, NBC Blue (Avalon)
Paul Sullivan Reviews the News—1939 to 1941, CBS (Raleigh)
Raleigh's Radio Rally—ca. late 1930s, NBC (Raleigh)
Uncle Walter's Doghouse, with Tom Wallace—1939 to 1940, 1941 to 1942, NBC (Raleigh)
Wings of Destiny—1940 to 1942, NBC (Wings)
The Raleigh Cigarette Program, aka The *Red Skelton Show*—1941 to 1944, 1945 to 1949, NBC (Raleigh)
Captain Flagg and Sergeant Quirt, with Victor McLaglen and Edmund Lowe—1942, NBC (Wings)
Tommy Dorsey's Variety Show, with Tommy Dorsey and His Orchestra and Jo Stafford—1942 to 1943, NBC (Raleigh, Sir Walter Raleigh)

The Raleigh Serenade—1942 to 1943, NBC (Raleigh)
People Are Funny, with Art Linkletter—1942 to 1951, NBC (Wings, Raleigh)
Beat the Band, with the incomparable Hildegarde—1943 to 1944, NBC (Raleigh)
Carton of Cheer, with Henny Youngman—1944 to 1945, NBC (Raleigh)
The Raleigh Room, with the incomparable Hildegarde—1944 to 1946, NBC (Raleigh)
The Gay Mrs. Featherstone, aka *The Billie Burke Show*—1945, NBC (Raleigh)
An Evening with Romberg—1945, 1946, 1947, 1948, NBC (Raleigh)
The Penguin Room, with the incomparable Hildegarde—1946, NBC (Kool)
A Life in Your Hands—1949, 1950, NBC (Raleigh)

Exposition

Like some other radio sponsors, Brown & Williamson concentrated the series it underwrote in a handful of entertainers. However, because it placed no higher than fourth or fifth in its industry during radio's golden age, B&W tailored its advertising to just a minuscule handful of headliners even though most were very big names. Much of its work went to Tommy Dorsey, Hildegarde, Art Linkletter and Red Skelton. B&W remained faithful to all of them for years, aiding their celebrity careers while profiting through enduring pitches.

The firm's ad agency created a catchy refrain for Kool cigarettes. In thousands of radio recitals, an unidentified—although quite recognizable—male vocalist ended the familiar piano-backed ditty cajoling: "Switch ... from hots ... to ... Kools!" An animated penguin in print ads (and later on TV commercials) turned in an effective performance that buttressed the musical sound-bite.

Commercial

When the studio audience applauds the commercial, something unexpected is going on. While Brown & Williamson's ad agency wasn't doing anything that hadn't been thought of by somebody else, the novelty of its plugs for Avalon cigarettes on *Avalon Time* was unusual, even with delivery by a single voice. The variety series was headlined by comedian Red Skelton, who was then just getting established as a national entertainer. He was supported by country singer Red Foley, The Avalon Chorus, Bob Strong and His Orchestra and a few added regulars.

The broadcast of June 3, 1939, was typical. During the show's opening, the chorus presented a short jingle for the sponsor, announcer Del King introduced himself and welcomed the radio audience. He identified the show's cast before proclaiming: "The orchestra opens with 'Step Up and Shake My Hand!'" At once, the instrumentalists swung into a fast-paced rhythm. But they had hardly begun when their volume went down and gradually the music disappeared altogether. Here's what happened next:

MUSIC: *Plays for 25 seconds*
DEL KING: (Music fades) Friends, when you find a product with just one distinct advantage
    that makes it superior to all others ... well ... you'll gladly give it a try, won't you? Well,
    Avalon cigarettes have two all-important advantages ... highest quality ... exceptional
    economy ... points of marked superiority that have made them the outstanding

cigarette buy of today. Avalons are union-made from an unsurpassed blend of the world's finest Turkish and domestic tobaccos. Millions of smokers say: "You couldn't get finer quality cigarettes *regardless* of price ... regardless of brand." That's why you'd never guess that Avalon costs you less. Only 10 cents for a full pack of 20. Yes, only 10 cents, plus any city or state tax. Highest quality cigarettes at a worthwhile savings. Avalons certainly deserve a trial. Why not get a pack tonight?
MUSIC: *Resumes full volume for 22 seconds to finish*
Applause

While it may not have been unique, the tactic still had the innovation of catching listeners by surprise. With little warning, Brown & Williamson played "Gotcha!" For fans who tuned in for the music, distractions that kept their attention from the commercials probably diminished compared with times when listeners *knew* a paid pitch was in the offing.

Campbell Soup Company

History

Imagine if you can, making *every single can* of Campbell soup *by hand*—not the soup, the *can*! Impossible, you say? There were few alternatives when the operation began about 14 decades ago. And that's precisely how it was done—*one can at a time*—after fruit merchant Joseph Campbell (1817 to 1900) and tin icebox manufacturer Abraham Anderson (1835 to ca. 1905) shook hands in 1869 in Camden, New Jersey.[1] Forming the Joseph A. Campbell Preserve Company, the two men's primitive labors resulted in a multinational adventure in innovative dining that, in 1922, was renamed the Campbell Soup Company. The newer and more applicable appellation has been instantly recognized around the globe by billions in successive generations.

At its start, the business generated a variety of farm products for the dinner table, never overemphasizing any single one. They included canned tomatoes, vegetables, jellies, soups, condiments and mincemeat. While Abraham Anderson rolled out the packaging a tin can at a time (as the original tin man?), Joseph Campbell, at 52 as they began, planted the seeds, harvested the crops and turned the fruits of his labors into tasty edibles capable of supplying much of the local populace with portions of their diet. In addition, he handled promotion, collections and distribution, the latter from a horse-drawn wagon as he plied the streets of Camden hawking his goods. Be it ever so humble, the beginnings were a far cry from the far-flung global enterprise we know as Campbell today.

At America's Centennial Exposition just seven years hence (1876), the Joseph A. Campbell Preserve Company received a medal (probably not made of tin) for quality, an early harbinger of its widespread public acceptance. Not quite everything was working favorably, however. That same year Campbell and Anderson reached an impasse over how the business was to grow. Campbell lobbied for brisk product development while Anderson recommended caution; the latter sought to escalate their wares at a more leisurely pace. The two men were unable to resolve their differences. They decided to dissolve their business relationship as a result. Remaining friends afterward, Campbell bought out Anderson to form a new partnership with an affluent flour and timber merchant, Arthur Dorrance (1849 to 1922). Make note of the surname: it was to prevail for a very long time. At that juncture, the firm was renamed Joseph Campbell & Company.

The handle changed again in 1891 to Joseph Campbell Preserve Company. While the designation *preserve* returned to the nomenclature originally selected, Campbell was responsible for preserving a whole lot more than mere jams and jellies. Its "Beefstake Ketchup," for instance, was its most widely recognized commodity then. Unlike anything we can link to the ketchup in use today, the flavored sauce — a culinary staple of the time — contained just about everything but the kitchen sink: cinnamon, mace, cloves, black pepper, mustard and vinegar, and was made with an assortment of bases that incorporated walnut, mushroom, anchovy, lobster, soy and oyster. An oddity to most contemporary tastes to be sure, and certainly no condiment for today's French fries!

Six years before his death in 1900, Joseph Campbell retired, ending the Campbell clan's relationship with the firm it established a quarter-century before. Arthur Dorrance took the reins as president that year (1894). Within a few months, the Joseph Campbell Preserve Company began a sustained promotional program. Appointing an internal advertising committee, the firm erected 100 large identity signs (forerunners of billboards) in New York City, Philadelphia and St. Louis. It was an early indication that Campbell understood the adage "you have to spend money to make money," one it has liberally pursued since.

In 1895, ready-to-serve beefsteak tomato soup joined a growing list of commodities offered by Campbell to America's cooks. Yet it was two years later, in 1897, tomato soup — possibly perceived since as the firm's most durable product — was introduced without the addition of beef, vegetables or another substance. Could too many ingredients spoil the broth? According to current Campbell publicists, "Tomato still ranks as one of the top ten selling dry grocery items in U.S. supermarkets today."

That same year (1897) was a pivotal one for the Joseph Campbell Preserve Company. A gargantuan portion of its fortunes were to turn on what transpired during the year, in fact. All of the web sites checked (and there was a myriad of them) invariably inserted the idiom *reluctantly* in every reference reporting that CEO Arthur Dorrance agreed to hire his well-educated and trained nephew, Dr. John Thompson Dorrance (1873 to 1930), 23, that year as a Campbell chemist.[2] In no case did those sources noting his hire suggest *why* Arthur Dorrance was so reluctant. Nepotism? Another personal family explanation? A trait he found hard to abide? We are left to speculate.

Apparently to discourage the young man, his uncle agreed to pay him just $7.50 weekly.[3] Dr. Dorrance also had to provide his own personal lab equipment in order to perform his experiments. If that was dispiriting, however, there appears to be little record of it. Instead, the chemist comes across as an eager, ambitious and willing fellow; might he not have been predisposed to accepting the job without any compensation? Ponder that momentarily. At any rate, the senior Dorrance made sure his protégé was kept humble (in more ways than one), as we shall observe shortly.

In his very first year with the company, John Dorrance contributed enough to benefit the firm so phenomenally — an outfit that had been skeptical about him — that his early efforts seemed to make him worth whatever they paid him in successive years, *right then*. What did he do? He was the first in the industry to develop a formula for commercially condensed soups. By removing the water from the canned product, volume of the can was reduced from 32 to 10 ounces. Weight was costly in delivery of canned goods. The production, storage and distribution savings allowed Campbell to drop the price of its canned soups from 34 to 10 cents, a godsend to the American homemaker seeking easy-to-prepare dishes on minuscule budgets. Five varieties of Campbell condensed soups went on grocers' shelves in 1897: tomato, consommé, vegetable, chicken, and oxtail.

A Campbell historian reports: "Dr. Dorrance finds he must induce the public to eat soup and convince buyers that his inexpensive, condensed soup is also high quality, so he takes to the road offering tastes [of the product]. The soups are an almost instant success.... Dorrance undertakes the difficult task of convincing housewives to buy canned soup instead of making their own at home by showing them that Campbell's soups are terrific, inexpensive, and incredibly time-saving."

If the matter of condensing the soup made 1897 a banner year for Campbell, an incident in the following year would have remarkable, consequential, pervasive and permanent effects on everything Campbell did thereafter. It resulted from, of all things, a Cornell-Penn State football game attended by Campbell executive Herberton Williams. So striking to him were the new red-and-white uniforms worn by the Cornell players, on returning to work, Williams was unable to shake the image from his mind. His suggestion prevailed that the design scheme for the Campbell can labels in use then be replaced with red-and-white. It was, the company allows, "the single most successful promotional decision Campbell has ever made."

That year (1898), with John Dorrance's push for condensed soups appearing in bright new red-and-white cans, Campbell became profitable for the first time in many years. For John's discovery, his uncle saw to it that his nephew was rewarded: John found the proverbial "little something extra" in his weekly pay envelope. To his surprise, he was no longer making $7.50 a week — he was given a 20 percent raise, upped to $9.00 weekly! His condensation recipe was paying off handsomely (but seemingly, not all that well for him at the time).[4]

John Dorrance placed the very first advertising to appear on New York City streetcars, in 1899, on behalf of his employer. Big Apple purchases of Campbell wares doubled. (Did Dorrance's talent — and value — know no bounds?) Those ads were comprised of a promotional jingle and a huge graphic of a red-and-white can of soup. As for Dorrance, his star was at last beginning to rise: the following year (1900), he was elected a director and vice president of the Joseph Campbell Preserve Company. When Campbell's soups won the Gold Medallion for excellence during the Paris Exposition that year, the medallion was added to the soup can labels where it persisted more than a century later.

By 1902, Campbell had achieved national recognition and trust. It expanded its product line to include 21 varieties of soup, a figure that remained constant for the next three decades. Citing a "huge problem" that existed in the soup industry by 1904, a Campbell biographer allowed: "The long duration required for soup stock simmering leaves the workers with nothing to do during the day, so in order to combat this lack of productivity, John Dorrance adds a new product to be manufactured during these time lapses: Pork and Beans. It becomes a very profitable sideline."

Also that year the Campbell Kids were born when Philadelphia illustrator Grace Wiederseim Drayton sketched the figures for a series of streetcar promotions. Eventually reproduced as post cards, lapel buttons and a variety of other merchandise, these familiar animated characters grew up right before Americans' eyes. Originally conceived as little children playing games, the Campbell Kids eventually matured and became adults, performing adult-oriented tasks. By 1910, Campbell Kids dolls were offered as promotional premiums and became an overnight hit. Those dolls have since become popular collectors' items. Although the Kids remained silent from 1958 to 1990, in the latter year, they resurfaced in a TV commercial singing a rap song about the benefits of soup.

As the sales of soup rose, Campbell stopped producing preserves, jellies, jams and fruit butter in 1905. A new name, Joseph Campbell Company, was adopted to reflect that historic turn of events. An initial *Good Housekeeping* display ad observed: "21 Kinds of Campbell's Soup — 16 million cans sold in 1904." By 1907, Campbell narrowed its focus still further. Abandoning the production of mincemeat, another of its original staples, the firm concentrated virtually all of its energies (beyond pork and beans, of course) on its single most profitable and best-selling commodity — condensed soups in 21 varieties.

That year, a source remarked, "A master marketer, John Dorrance effects a huge change in American eating habits by publishing a number of cookbooks and meal planners and creating a nation of canned soup eaters." For many, it was a "new fad" that Campbell was persuading them to try. Dorrance expanded the possibilities still further a decade down the road when the company released *Helps for the Hostess* (1916). That recipe manual demonstrated how easily homemakers could cook with condensed soup, significantly expanding the possibilities for variety in meals created at home. Campbell published many similar expositions in later years. The company's first full-length cookbook, *Easy Ways to Good Meals*, was issued in 1941.

In 1910, John Dorrance became the firm's general manager. Four years hence, he succeeded his allegedly once-skeptical uncle (by then, hopefully convinced) as president. A year later (1915), John Dorrance bought out his aging relative and became the sole owner of the Joseph Campbell Company. The man who had begun his career there almost two decades earlier as little more than a $7.50-per-week flunky was eventually not only running the show but owning it as well! What a difference 18 years makes!

His presidency is defined by several noteworthy achievements.

The younger Dorrance continued to be an innovator in the field of marketing, particularly in magazine advertising. He left an imprint there that reverberated throughout the industry, one copied by many other contemporary advertisers. Known as "the Campbell's soup position," Dorrance's mock-up insisted that all Campbell ads appear as "the first advertisement following ... text, on a right hand page facing a full page of text." In the century since, that model has been scrutinized by legions of students formally training for journalism and advertising careers. By 1926, meanwhile, Campbell also added color to its display ads in multiple leading women's magazines.

One of Campbell's most pervasive acquisitions occurred on John Dorrance's watch. He oversaw the purchase of the gourmet cuisine-specializing Franco-American Food Company in 1915. The Franco-American line of spaghetti, sauces and a plethora of added pasta products became an integral part of an expanding storehouse of Campbell culinary wares.

Dorrance was there when the Joseph Campbell Company was formally disbanded in 1921 and sold for a dollar to a successor venture — the one familiar to a great deal of the world's inhabitants since — the Campbell Soup Company. That moniker evolved through several permutations to amplify Campbell's most recognized and profitable commodity, then and now. Just two years later, in 1923, a subsidiary — Campbell Sales Company — was launched, reflecting its leadership's profound interest in marketing, promotion and advertising. It bode well for the network broadcasting mediums looming just over the horizon.

When chemist-marketer-director-vice president-president-owner Dr. John Thompson Dorrance died in 1930, Arthur Calbraith Dorrance (1893 to 1946), his junior brother by two decades, succeeded him in running the company, only its fourth president in 61 years. Thus, dual Arthur Dorrances — uncle and sibling — bracketed John's term of service, whose impact is still felt.

The radio advertising that eluded John Dorrance but which he would undoubtedly have been committed to — based on his enveloping exhibitions into all things marketing — began to emerge for Campbell Soup Company within a year of his death. In 1931, under the watchful eye of Arthur C. Dorrance, Campbell started underwriting numerous national features on the air. Before long, America had a new catchphrase on its lips as the recurring *M'm! M'm! Good!* jingle reverberated from millions of radio receivers, complete with its *That's what Campbell's soups are...* denouement. With that ditty ringing in their ears as they approached the store shelves in the decades afterward, American consumers hardly needed another reminder to rely on a single brand of soup, no matter what the variety.

Hoover's attests that Campbell's is "the world's biggest soup maker; its almost 70% share in the US is led by Campbell's chicken noodle, tomato and cream of mushroom soups." It also reveals, "Descendants of John Dorrance, who invented condensed soup, own approximately 43% of Campbell." Hoover identifies General Mills, Inc., H. J. Heinz Company and Kraft Foods, Inc., as Campbell's three primary rivals currently.

Radio Series

The Campbell Orchestra, with Robert Simmons, Howard Lanin and His Orchestra — 1931 to 1932, NBC (Campbell)
The Lanny Ross Program — 1932 to 1933, NBC (Campbell)
Hollywood Hotel, with Dick Powell — 1934 to 1938, CBS (Campbell)
The Campbell's Tomato Juice Program, aka *The George Burns and Gracie Allen Show* — 1935 to 1937, CBS (Campbell)
Amos 'n' Andy, with Freeman Gosden and Charles Correll — 1938 to 1943, NBC, CBS (Campbell)
First Person Singular, aka *The Mercury Theater*, with Orson Welles — 1938, CBS (Campbell)
The Human Side of the News, with Edwin C. Hill — 1938 to 1939, NBC (Campbell)
The Campbell Playhouse, with Orson Welles — 1938 to 1941, CBS (Campbell)
The Lanny Ross Program — 1939 to 1942, CBS (Franco-American, Campbell)
Brenda Curtis — 1939 to 1940, CBS (Campbell)
Campbell's Short, Short Story, with George Putnam — 1940 to 1941, CBS (Campbell)
Charlie and Jessie, with Donald and Florence Cook — 1940 to 1941, CBS (Campbell)
Life Begins, aka *Martha Webster* — 1940 to 1941, CBS (Campbell)
Fletcher Wiley — 1940 to 1942, CBS (Campbell)
You're the Expert, with Fred Uttal — 1941, CBS (Campbell)
The Man I Married — 1941 to 1942, CBS (Campbell)
The Arkansas Traveler, with Bob Burns — 1941 to 1942, CBS (Campbell)
Radio Reader's Digest — 1942 to 1945, CBS (Campbell)
The Jack Carson Show, with Arthur Treacher — 1943 to 1947, CBS (Campbell)
Request Performance — 1945 to 1946, CBS (Campbell)
Meet Corliss Archer — 1946, 1947 to 1948, CBS (Campbell)
The Incomparable Hildegarde — 1946 to 1947, CBS (Campbell)
Robert Trout and the News — 1946 to 1947, CBS (Campbell)
Club 15, with Bob Crosby and the Bobcats, The Andrews Sisters, Jo Stafford, Dick Haymes — 1947 to 1953, CBS (Franco-American, Campbell, V8)
Edward R. Murrow and the News — 1947 to 1950, CBS (Campbell)
Double or Nothing, with Walter O'Keefe — 1947 to 1954, CBS, NBC, ABC (Campbell, Franco-American, V8)
Grand Central Station — 1954, ABC (Campbell)

Exposition

A slip of the tongue one night in 1934 on radio's *Amos 'n'Andy* significantly altered the popularity of one of Campbell's mainline soups, introduced that year as "Chicken with Noodles." But on the particular broadcast, as actor Freeman Gosden (playing the part of Amos Jones) read his lines of commercial copy, instead of calling the new soup by its rightful name, he managed to say "Chicken Noodle" soup. Uncorrected it stood and when the Campbell Soup Company began receiving hundreds of requests for the new soup — infusing a moderate seller with sudden zest — the firm banished the original moniker and stayed with the one Amos Jones mispronounced on the air. The soup became so popular with consumers that today the company claims it adds nearly a million miles of noodles to that mix now to fulfill orders. Not bad for an unintended slip of the tongue.

There was another more infamous slip of the tongue on another Campbell-backed radio series in the late 1940s that very nearly cost the sponsor and network a program and toastmaster Walter O'Keefe (1900 to 1983) a job. It occurred on a live broadcast on October 15, 1948. That afternoon on the quiz *Double or Nothing* O'Keefe was interviewing a guest from the studio audience before she answered a series of questions for cash prizes. The contestant, a young lady who earned her livelihood as a waitress, told O'Keefe she had a male friend she was troubled over who had colossal emotional problems. What prompted mention of him in her earthy monologue is anybody's guess. After reciting a few of the man's disturbing issues, she remarked that a feminine confidante had suggested that she simply advise him he could get out of his melancholy state if he would merely "get a good-looking girl and take her home and just have a big old screwing party!"

The flushed emcee, knowing the NBC censors could pull the plug and leave the chain with dead air in an instant, reacted at once. O'Keefe recovered by amending the topic and accelerating the young lady through the contest. While some people in the studio audience quite obviously missed what the guest said, it didn't fall on deaf ears among those tuning in at home. The NBC switchboard lit up like a Christmas tree as irate callers vented their fury in no uncertain terms.

The program had not yet aired on the West Coast — it occurred in the era in which pre-recorded shows had only recently been approved, eliminating the necessity for a second live performance for the most distant listeners. Local stations in the far West transcribed the live show for playback at a later hour. But on that day NBC officials ordered their affiliates that had not yet aired *Double or Nothing* to destroy those tapes, canceling the show for that one day only. Obviously, at least one such transcription survived, and duplicate copies of the X-rated episode have become a collector's item across the years.

The incident was so shocking by mid–twentieth century standards that, years later — when writer Shirley Gordon recalled it in a piece submitted to *Radio Life* magazine — she never revealed precisely what transpired. Writing in *Quiz Craze: America's Infatuation with Game Shows*, media historian Tom DeLong surmised: "After a dozen years of audience-participation programs, this was reputedly the first blatantly suggestive episode to hit the airwaves."

Occasionally, a radio underwriter discovered an announcer whose voice inflections were so recognizably distinctive that he was tapped as an unofficial company spokesman. Del Sharbutt (1912 to 2002) became the darling of the Campbell Soup Company and his resonant basso profundo delivered pitches for Campbell soups and juices and Franco-American pastas and sauces for years. In fact, he turned up regularly on no fewer than 10 of the manufacturer's audio features: *Amos 'n' Andy, The Campbell Playhouse, Club 15, The Jack Carson Show,*

The Lanny Ross Show, Life Begins, The Man I Married, Meet Corliss Archer, Request Performance and *You're the Expert*. Few interlocutors were awarded that many opportunities to proffer a single firm's commodities. When Sharbutt said *uuummmm ... uuummmm ... ggoood!* nonetheless, it persuaded even the most satiated listener to quell his next hunger pangs with the most widely acclaimed broth on the planet.

The Campbell Soup Company showed partiality not only for an authoritative voice to deliver its messages but in demonstrating resilience for placing most of its programming at a single address, CBS. Of 27 shows documented above — in the timeframe that they were underwritten by Campbell — 21 aired exclusively over CBS. Two more appeared on CBS during part of their runs for Campbell. What was the reason? We can conjecture from this distance. CBS was one of the major chains and drew huge audiences for much of its fare. There may also have been interconnecting relationships between executives of the broadcaster and the soup-maker which could have influenced the outcome. The true explanation apparently has been left unwritten.

Commercial

The popular and talented Andrew Sisters were so much a part of the commercials on Campbell's enduring *Club 15* nightly on CBS (1947 to 1953) that the plugs were actually easy to listen to. Almost invariably, the trio sang once, twice or three times per show on behalf of the sponsor, often with original lyrics about one of the soups. While that wasn't always the case, they performed a lilting version of the familiar tune that was widely linked with the firm behind it as in this pitch airing October 18, 1950.

DEL SHARBUTT: Just plain wonderful for school-day lunches ... that's Campbell's Vegetable Beef Soup. It makes a fine dish to serve along with sandwiches and milk ... easy to fix, yet filled with the hearty nourishment youngsters need. Campbell's Vegetable Beef Soup is real old-fashioned vegetable beef soup with tenderest pieces of lean beef mingled all through it. And along with those tender pieces of beef, the rich beef stock is filled with luscious vegetables. Uuummmm ... ggoood! For marvelous school-day lunches, serve Campbell's Vegetable Beef Soup.

ORCHESTRA: *Sliding scale down*

ANDREW SISTERS (*singing*) Uuummmm ... good! Uuummmm ... good! That's what Campbell's soups are ... Uuummmm ... good!

Coca-Cola Company

History

The jug that Dr. John Stith Pemberton (1831 to 1888) hauled down an Atlanta street to Jacobs Pharmacy on May 8, 1886, from his home laboratory contained an elixir like none the world had ever tasted — although most of its inhabitants in succeeding generations eventually would. While he didn't have a name for the sweet-savored syrup in his flagon, Pemberton found a ready reception for it at Jacobs anyway. There his mixture was purposely or perhaps inadvertently combined with carbonated water (the stories vary) and offered for five cents a glass to fountain counter patrons by soda jerk Willis Venable, citing it as a "delicious and refreshing" drink. Sales averaged a modest nine drinks daily during its first year, but enough for some entrepreneurial types to begin to stir a little.

Bookkeeper Frank M. Robinson proffered the name that is still more widely recognized by earth's denizens than that of any other single brand: Coca-Cola. He had a flair for ingenuity and visualized the matching C's at the start of the dual words working together in whatever promotion followed. In a flourish of calligraphy, he penned the acclaimed trademark "Coca-Cola" that has been an instant symbol of the product for almost a century and a quarter. In its first year, Pemberton peddled Coke syrup in bright red wooden kegs that held 25 gallons. Red has been a distinctive hue linked with the soft drink ever since.

The Atlanta Journal published the first Coke ad on May 29, 1886, inviting thirsty citizens to try "the new and popular soda fountain drink." Meanwhile, hand-painted oilcloth signs reading "Coca-Cola" pitched the unique beverage on storefront awnings. Linked with the urgent-sounding "Drink," that suggestion encouraged passersby to stop and enjoy a glass at the soda fountain within.

Pemberton's legendary conception wasn't his first attempt at quenching Atlantans' thirst, however. Behind that venerated concoction was another he developed a couple of years earlier that turned some of the locals into sporadic sippers — and possibly into inveterate imbibers. The original brew, popularly known as Pemberton's French Wine Cola, actually contained real wine plus some extract from the leaf of the Peruvian coca plant supplemented by the kola nut.[1] In addition to its satisfying properties, Pemberton allowed to an *Atlanta Journal* reporter in 1885: "It is the most excellent of all tonics, assisting digestion, imparting energy to the organs of respiration, and strengthening the muscular and nervous systems." It was advertised, in fact, as an "intellectual beverage" and an "invigorator of the brain." A Coca-Cola label from 1887 noted that the drink "makes not only a delicious ... and invigorating beverage ... but a valuable Brain Tonic and a cure for all nervous affections."

The druggist subsequently confessed that his formula was patterned after one by Parisian bottler Vin Mariani that had been circulating at least since 1863. No matter who invented it, his potion caught on in Atlanta and fared well until city forefathers passed a prohibition ordinance taking effect in 1886. Forbidden to lace his French Wine Coca with true wine any longer, Pemberton tinkered with the recipe with hopes of maintaining escalating momentum. Substituting sugar syrup for the wine, he also discarded the moniker applied to it. That's when he mixed a batch in a three-legged kettle in his backyard and put the results in a jug and headed down to Jacobs with his then unnamed tonic in tow.

"We'll return to our story in a moment," as scores of radio announcers used to say. But first, some biographical background to fill in the gaps about the famous Dr. Pemberton seems worthy. This will enlighten our understanding and appreciation of the man and his most noteworthy bequest to the world's population. Born at tiny Knoxville, Georgia on January 8, 1831, he attended the schools of nearby Rome before leaving home to study medicine and pharmacy at Macon's Reform Medical College of Georgia. Subsequently earning a medical degree (although the precise institution hasn't been confirmed), he returned to Rome to practice medicine and surgery.

Moving to Columbus, Georgia, in 1855, Pemberton launched a wholesale-retail drug enterprise, J. S. Pemberton and Company, specializing in *materia medica*, or in essence, manufacturing ingredients that comprised medical remedies. Prior to the Civil War (1861 to 1865) in which he served as a lieutenant colonel with the Georgia Cavalry, Pemberton received a graduate degree in pharmacy although the exact date and institution are also unsubstantiated.

He became the principal partner in the firm of Pemberton, Wilson, Taylor and Company in 1869, moving with it to Atlanta the following year. Pemberton joined the Atlanta Medical College board of trustees in 1872, forerunner of the School of Medicine at Emory University. In the meantime, after viewing the equipment Pemberton brought with him from Columbus for his Atlanta-based business, a reporter for *The Atlanta Constitution* gushed that it was "one of the most splendid Chemical Laboratories that there is in the country," dubbing the operation "a magnificent establishment." Within a short while, Pemberton opened a second facility in Philadelphia where his pharmaceuticals were mass-produced in large quantities. Simultaneously, from 1881 to 1887, he served on the first Georgia examining board licensing state pharmacists.

Pemberton biographer Monroe Martin King, who devoted 21 years of his life to researching his subject, is genuinely miffed at Coca-Cola historians that characterize Pemberton as "'a local pharmacist' who concocted the world's most craved soft-drink syrup in a three-legged brass pot in his backyard" and then dismiss the inventor with little else. "Coca-Cola was not the creation of an inept, small-time corner druggist," King insists. "He's occasionally portrayed as a wandering medicine man. But Dr. Pemberton worked in a fully outfitted laboratory and claimed to manufacture every chemical and pharmaceutical preparation used in the arts and sciences." In addition to his most famous beverage, he also invented several other commodities like Indian Queen hair dye, Gingerine and Triplex liver pills.

While he became "a most respected member of the state's medical establishment" proclaimed yet another source, Pemberton's "gift was for medical chemistry rather than regular medicine." Active throughout his professional life in medical reform, "His most enduring accomplishments involve his laboratories, which are still in operation ... as part of the Georgia Department of Agriculture."

Pemberton's analytical lab, King attests, became "the first state-run facility to conduct tests of soil and crop chemicals." In addition to Coca-Cola, the enterprising Pemberton began 17 more business ventures in the 18 years he lived in Atlanta. Such acknowledgements are frequently overlooked in the rush to cite his "sterling achievement" as if it was singular, and often as if it was his good fortune to have stumbled onto it by accident. King agrees with Coca-Cola cataloguers today who intimate "Dr. Pemberton never fully realized the potential of the beverage he created." In fact, he maintains, "Pemberton actually remained more interested in expanding the market for French Wine Cola" after prohibition was lifted in Atlanta in 1887. At that juncture, the doctor turned over production of Coca-Cola to his son, Charles, while he resumed making and marketing his earlier seller.

Gradually, Dr. Pemberton sold portions of his Coca-Cola enterprise to others who apparently saw more to his latest creation than he. While several reporters claim he was in failing health and in debt, too, prompting his need for a quick buck, this isn't confirmed by any means. He spent $77 in Coke's first year to produce and promote it, yet his "profits" that year were only a measly $50, leaving him in the hole. Shortly before Pemberton's death on August 16, 1888 — when the Atlanta newspapers depicted him as "the oldest druggist of Atlanta and one of her best known citizens"[2] (Note: Atlanta pharmacists must have died quite young in those days; Pemberton, "the oldest," was 57) — he sold whatever interest he had left in the beverage to a prosperous Atlanta banker and patent medicine manufacturer, Asa Griggs Candler (1851 to 1929) for the princely sum of $2,300. Actually, in Candler's early twenties, 14 years before this (1872), Pemberton had hired Candler as an employee. So they knew one another quite a while. It wasn't long before a now entrepreneurial Candler convinced others who had previously purchased shares in Coca-Cola to relinquish them to him. Soon Candler owned it all. What might he do with it?

One of the first things he did was to alter Pemberton's original Coca-Cola recipe. Hiring the inventor's bookkeeper, Frank M. Robinson, who gave the product both its name and its flowing typeface, Candler and the calligrapher collaborated on a modified mixture of ingredients. According to Charles Candler, the entrepreneur's son, his dad and Robinson "perfected the formula."[3] It was patented on January 31, 1893. The technique wasn't changed again until 1985. The imbroglio that ensued then as a result — to be considered in some detail later — appears, in retrospect, hardly of value to anybody.

The mixture modified by Candler and Robinson is one of the great mysteries of merchandising. That proprietary trade secret bears the code name "Merchandise 7X." It is today as difficult to acquire as the blend of herbs and spices in Colonel Sanders' Kentucky Fried Chicken recipe held by YUM Brands in Louisville, Kentucky; it might be easier to gather the well-guarded gold at nearby Fort Knox! Coke's furtive formula has been stashed in a vault of the Trust Company of Georgia bank (now SunTrust Bank) since 1919, when that institution came to the aid of Coke. Only a minuscule handful of individuals purportedly know the contents of the recipe. All are required to sign non-disclosure statements. To further preserve the secret, it's also alleged that they are never permitted to travel together.

Dallas became the site of Coke's second syrup plant, opened in 1894. The first factories outside the United States — in Cuba and Panama — both opened in 1906.

What else did Candler do with Coca-Cola? Not a whole lot beyond pushing it relentlessly and aggressively wherever there was a fountain counter in America that wasn't dispensing it. He pushed it in newspapers and on billboards. In the former, he included coupons for free Cokes at any fountain. Beyond that, for about a decade it appeared as if others had the inspirations while Candler hardly took notice. In 1894, for example, Joseph A. Biedenharn — proprietor of a Vicksburg, Mississippi, confectionary emporium — began filling Hutchinson glass bottles (undistinguished from most other containers of the day) with Coca-Cola so his clientele could enjoy the beverage at home. One of Candler's nephews had already proposed to Candler that the commodity be bottled; that netted an immediate brush-off by his uncle. And when Biedenharn shipped a complimentary case of bottled Coca-Cola to Candler, the brand's owner remained unmoved. After thanking his benefactor, he resolved once more that fountain sales offered the greatest promise for his ware.

It took Candler five more years to relent. Whether he had an actual transformation about it or was possibly worn down by persistent would-be bottlers, the fact that he sold those rights for a dollar bill in 1899 prompts fascinating guesswork. The winners of the bottling rights were a couple of Chattanooga, Tennessee, lawyers — Benjamin F. Thomas and Joseph B. Whitehead, soon joined by a third Rock City barrister, John T. Lupton. Virtually the whole country was theirs to market to with sales of Coca-Cola in glass bottles. (They had it all except for the Magnolia State — Mississippi — which Candler had already given to Biedenharn.) These young entrepreneurs were establishing the prototype of the largest, most widespread production and distribution network on the globe. Their system is still practiced today, not only by Coca-Cola but also by virtually every other supplier of soft drinks in the U.S.

What a windfall for them! And what a missed opportunity for Candler, who was expanding *some* of the business's potential while allowing stunning chances to pass through others' hands before they reached his own! Hello! Is there something wrong with this picture? Candler was occasionally labeled an eccentric. If there's truth to that, this may be Example A. Despite the skepticism, let's give credit where it is due, nonetheless: in the decade of the 1890s, syrup sales increased by more than 4,000 percent! Asa Candler's unremitting drive to place it everywhere there was a fountain counter in America is responsible for most of that boon.

The trio of pioneering bottlers divided the nation geographically and sold rights to local entrepreneurs. Within a decade, almost 400 Coca-Cola bottling plants were running; most of them were family-owned enterprises. Coca-Cola started selling syrup to independent bottling companies licensed to sell the beverage.

Those bottlers, however, complained that Coca-Cola's straight-sided container was often confused with an influx of imitators that tried to copy the drink. The company solicited new designs from glass manufacturers that could distinguish its contents from the competition. The final selection, in 1916, was a contoured bottle submitted by the Root Glass Company of Terre Haute, Indiana, and its staff designer Earl R. Dean. Like the script type years before, the shape became an identifying symbol for Coca-Cola. It is one of few packages granted trademark status by the U.S. Patent Office (in 1977) and has become one of the most readily identifiable icons on the planet — even so in darkness!

Asa Candler eventually left Coca-Cola to run for mayor of Atlanta. He won that post handily and served with distinction. He was community-minded and gave millions to a wide variety of benevolent causes. A devout Methodist, Candler funneled a large portion of his gifts to charities supported by his faith, although there were plenty of civic and private enterprises, too.[4] His successor at Coca-Cola, Robert Winship Woodruff (1889 to 1985), performed likewise and was often referred to as "Mr. Anonymous" in his attempts to keep his identity hidden surrounding his good deeds. The two men are respectfully remembered by Atlantans for their particular devotion to their city. Their generosity through diversified philanthropic pursuits benefited education, health and private enterprise. In addition, the Web site geocities.com underscores that the firm itself has been beneficial to its community: "One great earmark that the Coca-Cola Company has is helping the people of Atlanta. They accomplish this through scholarships, hotlines, donations and contributions."

Woodruff took control of Coca-Cola at 33 in 1923 after his wealthy father, Ernest Woodruff, and a few more investors purchased it from Candler's children for $25 million. The senior Woodruff's son was installed as president. Surely no one could have predicted that Robert Woodruff's tenure would persist into parts of seven decades. But indeed it did. He ran the company until 1981, four years before his death at 95. During his time at the helm, Coca-Cola rose from national to international dominance of the soft drink market.

By 1923, six-bottle cartons were a popular method of carrying Coke home. Five years hence, bottled sales eclipsed fountain sales. Coca-Cola introduced metal open-top coolers a year beyond (1929). Automatic fountain dispensers premiered during the Chicago World's Fair in 1933, a boon to Coke and other soft-drink varieties. By the start of the Second World War (1941), Coca-Cola was routinely dispensed in 44 nations.

Coca-Cola began to advertise on radio in 1927. Slogans became a big part of its aura and lore from the Woodruff epoch forward. America knew each of these well: *The Pause That Refreshes* (1929), *I'd Like to Buy the World a Coke* (1971), *Have a Coke and a Smile* (1979), *Always Coca-Cola* (1993). *I'd Like to Buy the World a Coke* became such a memorable hit that it was released as a single recording for purchase by adoring fans. In 1934, Olympic champion swimmer Johnny Weissmuller and motion picture actress Maureen O'Sullivan appeared together on a metal serving tray for Coca-Cola. They set a precedent for tens of thousands of trinkets to follow, often adorned by well-known icons of the entertainment and sports professions. Among those merchandising promotions were souvenir fans, calendars with robust young women, clocks, stained-glass lampshades, signs, tickets, souvenir programs and anything else on which the words "Coca-Cola" could be stamped. Those early advertising strategies inaugurated the most extensive promotional campaign for a single product in history.

The D'Arcy agency received Coke's advertising business in the first decade of the twentieth century and maintained it for a half-century. In 1956, the Coke account was transferred to McCann-Erickson agency. Back in the early days, incidentally, all claims for medicinal properties of Coca-Cola were quietly abandoned in the drink's promotions. Coke allocated $1 million to advertising in 1911, an early indication that it intended to capture market share and retain it.

Until the 1960s, carbonated beverages were enjoyed by hamlet and metropolis dwellers at soda fountains in drug stores and ice cream parlors. That setting supplied a venue at which people of all ages gathered. Frequently, this was combined with luncheon counters. After commercial ice cream, bottled soft drinks and fast food establishments began to pick up steam, however, the soda counters began to diminish everywhere.

Robert Woodruff was president when the 12-ounce Coke can debuted in 1960. He was also there when the two-liter plastic bottle emerged in 1978. Coke reportedly was the first manufacturer to make and use recycled plastic bottling. It was also on Woodruff's watch that a new corporate headquarters was opened on Atlanta's North Avenue in 1979, known locally as "The Tower." In 1982, Coca-Cola broadened its portfolio by buying Columbia Pictures. While a few films were produced in which subtle publicity resulted with Cokes placed in strategic footage, Columbia under-performed and was sold in 1989.

Starting in 1960, meanwhile, Coke had launched an intensive program of diversification by acquiring other brands and creating new ones of its own. It bought the fruit juice and

Hi-C beverage-maker Minute Maid Corporation (1960), Duncan Foods Corporation (1964), natural and processed water producer Belmont Springs Water Company, Inc. (1969), desalting machinery manufacturer Aqua-Chem, Inc. (1970), and Taylor Wines Company and added wineries (1977). Aqua-Chem and Taylor were eventually divested. Several new beverages also began to appear on the market in the 1960s: Sprite (1961), Tab (1963), Fresca (1966), and diet versions of all of these.

Robert W. Woodruff, who ran Coca-Cola for more than six decades, stated emphatically that he would never change the formula of the company's flagship product. While he didn't, within weeks of his death at 95 on March 7, 1985, his hand-picked successor, CEO Robert Goizueta, did precisely what Woodruff said he never would: on April 23, 1985, a little more than six weeks following Woodruff's passing, the formula was altered. And therein lies one of the greatest blunders — and recoveries — in the history of merchandise marketing. It came about after Coke sales fell sharply (by one estimate, $500 million) as chief rival Pepsi-Cola gained unparalleled market share. In blind taste tests, ordinary citizens were asked to pick which drink they liked best, not knowing which was Coke and which was Pepsi. Overwhelmingly, those samplers picked Pepsi, which had higher sugar content and — some in the trade alleged — most people's preferences tend to gravitate naturally toward sweetness instead of a more subdued tartness tang. That was all the confirmation anybody seeking to alter the 99-year-old "secret formula" of Coca-Cola needed. (Four million dollars' research had gone into that study, and maybe it seemed useful to act on it.)

But aha! The alteration created a totally unexpected backlash with an incensed public crying, "Give us back our Coke!" Coke's 800-telephone number was jammed with 6,000 callers daily, most of them enraged over the change. The company received over 40,000 letters of protest. One said Coke had "betrayed a national trust." A historian observed, "Some compared changing the Coke formula to rewriting the American Constitution." Those who spoke were almost altogether irate. Nobody, apparently, at Coca-Cola had planned for such an eventuality. Having done the wrong thing, somebody within the Coke Tower came to a brilliant decision: they would give the masses what they asked for, in effect having *two* formulas — New Coke, and returning the old formula (under the revised trademark Coca-Cola Classic) to the supermarket shelves, vending machines and other dispensaries.

Eighty-seven days following the heralded introduction of New Coke, on July 10, 1985, the company restocked retailers' shelves with the original formula. Eighteen thousand callers to the 800 line expressed a collective sigh of relief. The comeback drove Coke stock prices to their highest levels in a dozen years. But some outside the Coke compound claimed it was all part of a well-orchestrated plot to raise Coke's market share. The firm's president, Donald Keough, responded brilliantly to cynics: "Some critics will say Coca-Cola made a marketing mistake. Some cynics will say that we planned the whole thing. The truth is, we are not that dumb and we are not that smart." CEO Robert Goizueta assured: "We have heard you." It was a classic marketing retreat. To supply any other solution would not have produced the same outcome. They really weren't dumb.

Market share for New Coke dwindled to only three percent the following year. It was renamed Coke II in 1992, not to be confused with Coke C2, a reduced-sugar cola launched by Coke in 2004. By 1998, it was sold in only a few places in the Midwestern U.S. Meanwhile, in January 2007, the word Classic was removed from the original brand, as it was no longer needed for identification. The formula remains as it was in 1891.

In 1990, the Coca-Cola Company opened a multistoried museum-like structure in downtown Atlanta designed to tell the story of Coke's evolution over the previous century-plus. It featured many of the original ads and merchandise premiums that became so familiar to generations of Coke lovers. It also included numerous unusual concoctions that the firm supplies around the globe to whet the tastes of diversified cultures with unique preferences. The World of Coca-Cola was so acclaimed by hundreds of thousands of people who viewed it and participated in its interactive exhibits that — on May 24, 2007 — an even more sophisticated facility, The New World of Coca-Cola, replaced it. It is also situated near several leading tourist attractions in downtown Atlanta; its initial entrance fee was advertised at $15 a pop (no pun intended) for adults.

In 1917, Coca-Cola became "the world's most recognized trademark," an identification it has never relinquished. Today, 94 percent of earth's inhabitants instantly know what it represents when they see it. The company owns four of the five top soft-drink brands: Coca-Cola is first; Diet Coke, Fanta and Sprite are third, fourth and fifth, respectively. Pepsi, produced by PepsiCo, Coke's largest competitor, is un-owned by Coke within those top five. As the world's leader, the Coca-Cola Company currently serves 1.3 billion beverages daily. Just 30 percent of its sales are generated in North America. Coke's principal rivals in the beverage industry are presently PepsiCo, Inc.; Nestle A. A.; Cadbury Schweppes plc; Groupe Danone; and Kraft Foods, Inc.

Radio Series

The Coca-Cola Hour, aka *The Coca-Cola Top Notchers*, with Gus Haenschen and His Orchestra, Graham McNamee, Grantland Rice — 1930 to 1932, NBC (Coca-Cola)
The Pause That Refreshes, with Frank Black and His Orchestra — 1934 to 1935, NBC (Coca-Cola)
Refreshment Time, with Ray Noble and His Orchestra, Connee [sic] Boswell, Don McNeill, Walter Blaufuss and His Orchestra — 1935 to 1937, CBS, Syndicated (Coca-Cola)
Song Shop, with Frank Crummit and His Orchestra — 1937 to 1938, CBS (Coca-Cola)
The Coca-Cola Hour, aka *The Pause That Refreshes*, with Percy Faith and His Orchestra — 1938 to 1940, 1948 to 1949, MBS, CBS (Coca-Cola)
The Pause That Refreshes, aka *The Coca-Cola Hour*, with Andre Kostelanetz and His Orchestra — 1940 to 1944, 1947 to 1949, 1950, CBS (Coca-Cola)
Spotlight Bands — 1941 to 1946, MBS, NBC Blue, Blue, ABC (Coca-Cola)
The Coke Club, with Morton Downey — 1943 to 1944, 1945 to 1947, 1950 to 1951, Blue, MBS, CBS (Coca-Cola)
The Spotlight Revue, with Spike Jones and His Orchestra — 1947 to 1949, CBS (Coca-Cola)
The Coca-Cola Summer Show, with Roger Pryor — 1948, CBS (Coca-Cola)
The Edgar Bergen and Charlie McCarthy Show — 1949 to 1952, CBS (Coca-Cola)
Coke Time, with Mario Lanza — 1951 to 1952, CBS, NBC (Coca-Cola)
Coke Time, with Eddie Fisher — 1952 to 1953, 1954 to 1955, CBS, NBC, MBS (Coca-Cola)

Exposition

Virtually all of this sponsor's programming referenced its flagship product in the titles of its radio series, some repetitious as first one and then another performer transferred in as headliner for a while (*The Coca-Cola Hour, The Coke Club, Coke Time, The Pause That*

Refreshes, Refreshment Time). Coca-Cola advertising never spotlighted the world's troubles. Only the good, cheerful, positive situations were featured. A marketing textbook allows that the only ethereal format Coke consistently refused to underwrite was news. "Our product is associated with happy times," a company spokesman averred. "Too often the news brings us gloomy messages."

Across the years, Coke sponsored numerous musical entries that seemed to be a more middle-of-the-road choice. Music traditionally appealed to varied tastes without offending large segments of the audience. Coke never sponsored anything on radio that didn't include music as part or all of its substance, including a trio of seasons with one of the medium's most popular comedy-variety amusements, *The Edgar Bergen and Charlie McCarthy Show*, as it coasted toward its finale while still drawing huge numbers. Coke also had the good fortune of signing a handful of first-rate maestros and singers whose credentials were previously established, among them: Morton Downey, Percy Faith, Eddie Fisher, Andre Kostelanetz, Mario Lanza and Ray Noble.

Commercial

Coca-Cola, like other sponsors, made extended use of its series stars by putting them to work in endorsement dialogue with a resident announcer, as in this July 5, 1954, aircast of *Coke Time* with Eddie Fisher and spokesman Fred Robbins.

FRED ROBBINS: Say Eddie, I was just wondering.... How many people listen to us on portable radios?
EDDIE FISHER: That would be hard to tell, Fred. It's too bad they don't have portable telephones so that we could call 'em and find out.
FRED ROBBINS: Oh, it sure is. You know, this is the time that people are going on vacations. And if you happen to be up in the north woods or out at a beach resort, your radio is just about your only link with your life the rest of the year.
EDDIE FISHER: It's not the *only* link, Fred. Wherever you go you're bound to see that familiar sight ... the bright red cooler that serves you frosty bottles of Coca-Cola. A bottle of Coke really makes you feel at home.
FRED ROBBINS: You've got something there, Eddie. Ice cold Coke is available just around the corner from anywhere. Everyone goes for the *matchless* flavor of Coca-Cola. In fact, it's the most popular soft drink in all the world. Coke is delicious and refreshing. And mighty welcome, whether you've been fishing in a mountain stream or basking on a sunny beach. When you're on your vacation, keep an eye out for the familiar red cooler for Coca-Cola. That's where you know you'll get *complete* refreshment, with a frosty bottle of delicious Coke.

Colgate-Palmolive-Peet Company

History

Colgate-Palmolive-Peet Company's growth from a minor candle and soap processor to one of the most powerful consumer products giants on the planet is the result of aggressive acquisition of other firms, persistent attempts to overtake its foremost U.S. rivals and — decades ago — an intensive effort to secure an overseas presence where little competition existed. It paid off. Today the enterprise operates within more than 200 nations while only 30 percent of its revenues are derived in its home country, the United States. Contemplate the answer to this burning question before proceeding: whatever happened to Peet? To quench an insatiable curiosity, keep reading.

The origins of the commercial leviathan that was to spring up as Colgate-Palmolive-Peet (CP) can be traced to 1806, more than three decades before William Procter and James Gamble launched its most formidable competitor hard by the banks of the Ohio River in Cincinnati. Colgate was also at work about eight decades prior to the launch of a similar manufacturing operation in London fostered by William and James Lever. Their firm would present a strong challenger in the race to capture global personal care and household packaged goods trade. In fact, Procter & Gamble, Lever Brothers and CP would persist permanently in direct competition with one another, fiercely contending for improved market share.

In 1806, a 23-year-old English immigrant to America, William Colgate (1783 to 1857), was one of the earliest of the breed. At New York City's Dutch and John streets, he launched a tiny manufacturing facility and retail shop making and selling starch, soap and candles. The following year, Francis Smith joined him in business and the little facility was renamed Smith and Colgate, nomenclature retained for five years. That ended when Colgate bought out Smith's share in 1812 and formed a new partnership with his sibling, Bowles Colgate. At that juncture, the enterprise was renamed William Colgate and Company.

By 1817, Colgate was running ads in a New York newspaper for "Soap, Mould & Dipt Candles." Three years hence, the physical operations were transferred to nearby Paulus Hook (Jersey City), New Jersey, deemed by some to be "Colgate's Folly." There Colgate's dominant wares of the period, Windsor toilet soaps and Pearl starch, were manufactured. John Gilbert, Colgate's brother-in-law, joined him in building the starch factory. The following decade — in the 1830s — the firm began selling individual soap bars in uniform weights, a novel innovation. The company opened an eight-story Jersey City factory in 1906; four years later, its headquarters operations left their original buildings in New York and relocated in Jersey City.

On the roof of one of the Jersey City factories, meanwhile, in 1908 Colgate installed a phenomenal octagon-shaped clock measuring 37.5 feet in diameter and covering 1,104 square feet, equipped with hands of 20.5 and 16 feet respectively. It was a dynamic addition to the New Jersey waterfront. That clock, larger than London's Big Ben, was shipped to a new Colgate plant at Jeffersonville, Indiana (on the opposite bank of the Ohio River from Louisville, Kentucky), in 1924. It was replaced in Jersey City by an even larger timepiece measuring 1,963.5 square feet, boasting a 25-foot 10-inch minute hand and a 20-foot hour hand. The Colgate clocks have been signature company icons in the communities they served.

The sign over the front door was altered to a simplified Colgate and Company after the death of founder William Colgate in 1857. His son, Samuel, subsequently took over the business and ran it for four decades. During that period, Colgate's product assortment expanded to include fragrances of many types, among them scented soap. Cashmere Bouquet, the first milled perfumed toilet bar, was trademarked in 1872. When a fire in 1866 destroyed the Jersey City factory in which the firm's starch was made, that line was discontinued. So was candle-making after the electric light bulb became a staple in American homes and public gathering places.

Not until 1873 did the company begin to manufacture the commodity for which it was to be forever recognized thereafter: that year, CP started dispensing an aromatic dental cream in glass jars. And 23 years more elapsed before it introduced the collapsible toothpaste tube (1896)—a container still in common use—for its Colgate Ribbon Dental Cream. This made teeth brushing much more convenient and was readily adopted by the masses. By 1906, celebrating its centennial, Colgate's product line exceeded 800 commodities. In addition to 625 perfumes and 160 varieties of toilet soap, the firm manufactured laundry detergent and dental care goods. Five years afterward (1911), the outfit distributed free toothbrushes and toothpaste and provided oral hygienists to exhibit proper teeth-brushing in a pervasive health education initiative that was aimed at youngsters.

Colgate established a Canadian subsidiary in 1914, its first outside U.S. borders. The subsequent decade of the 1920s was one characterized by diverse and widespread expansion. More manufacturing operations were launched in France, Australia, the United Kingdom, Germany, Mexico, the Philippines, Brazil, Argentina and South Africa. India was added in 1937 by the successor firm and—by the close of the 1940s—CP was operating in nearly every South American nation.

While all of this was transpiring with Colgate, meanwhile, there were some developments going on farther in the American interior that were to have a profound impact on Colgate's East Coast operations. The namesake founder (1824 to 1901) of the B. J. Johnson Soap Company launched his endeavor to make cleaning agents in Milwaukee in 1864. Johnson's most notable commodity was a palm- and olive-based cleanser, introduced in 1898, one that—according to a historian—"was about to change its [the maker's] destiny."

By 1902, the year following the founding father's demise, "stylish" advertising for the brand was launched, highlighting purity of ingredients and key benefits derived from its use. An advertised attribute was that the soap floated. (Procter & Gamble had promoted the same quality in its Ivory bar since 1879, a discovery that it stumbled upon purely by accident, legend has it. See the separate *Procter & Gamble* article.) The cleansing block drew such rave reviews from consumers that, in 1916, the outfit making it was renamed the Palmolive Company for what was "the best-selling soap in the world" bar none (pun intended). Today, 54 varieties of Palmolive are sold in nearly 90 nations.

While all of this was going on, since 1872 Kansas City, Kansas siblings Robert (1846 to ?) and William (1847 to 1934) Peet were selling similar wares from their Peet Brothers Soap Company. The enterprising pair, English immigrants who resided in Cleveland, Ohio, before proceeding farther westward, were among the pioneers also pursuing the acquisition route. They took over the Standard Soap Company of Ocean View, California, in 1916. Standard had been established in San Francisco in the early 1870s by Captain R. P. Thomas, a wealthy Berkeley Hills businessman.

Reportedly, the Peet Brothers enterprise grew to be the largest soap factory beyond the Mississippi River. According to *The New York Times*, by 1918 theirs was "the second largest manufacturer of soap and glycerine [sic] in the United States." Glycerin, incidentally, was used in high explosives, putting Peet Brothers in the enviable spot of being heavily relied upon by the U.S. government as "essential to the conduct of the [First World] war." As a result, sales jumped from $5.6 million in 1915 to $24 million three years hence. Colgate-Palmolive, which eventually acquired the Peets' 1872 soap-making plant, continued using it for that purpose until late 2006 when the historic facility was phased out and 250 jobs were eliminated at that site.

Undoubtedly seeing greater advantages for themselves — and acting only a moment before the nation was mired in economic upheaval, a result of the 1929 stock market crash that created the Great Depression — in 1927, the Peets of Kansas City, Kansas, and the Johnsons of Milwaukee joined their units into one under the new name Palmolive Peet Company.[1] That wouldn't last long, however; the following year (1928), the outfit — sensing still greater opportunities — added Colgate to its mix: the result was the Colgate-Palmolive-Peet Company, headquartered in a magnificent 37-story art deco high-rise tower in a neutral city. The Palmolive Building opened on Chicago's business-friendly Michigan Avenue in 1929. The imposing structure was to be the nerve center for the multinational's far-flung operations for about five years, until April 1934, when the headquarters was established at Jersey City, New Jersey. In 1956, the company command took up residence at yet another prestigious address, 300 Park Avenue in Manhattan.

But we are getting ahead of our story: immediately following the merger, Palmolive Peet's managerial staff took control of the amalgamated conglomerate. Had it not been for the stock market crash, there would have been yet further additions to the consolidated venture. Just four days before the bottom fell out, documents were signed — on October 25, 1929 — that were to extend the fusion even further, embracing the Kraft Phenix Cheese Corporation of Chicago, forerunner of the Kraft Foods Company, and the Hershey Chocolate Company of Hershey, Pennsylvania. While the trio of manufacturers was to operate independently, they were all to be subsidiaries of a holding firm, International Quality Products Corporation. But that plan was scuttled after the market imploded. That economic disaster precipitated the ascendancy of Bayard Colgate as president of Colgate-Palmolive-Peet in 1933. The shift of power effectively ended the brief driver's seat tenure of the Johnsons and Peets, who would nevermore occupy any of the firm's upper echelon posts.

Not long after the 1828 merger, Colgate-Palmolive-Peet brought out a new soap bar, Octagon. By the 1940s and 1950s, it turned to acquisitions as a principal method of growing its business, along with a few new product innovations. Purchasing a number of small consumer product outfits, CP introduced consumers to some newly created wares like Fab detergent and Ajax cleanser (both 1947) and Vel dishwashing liquid (late 1940s). A historian admits:

"These acquisitions and new products, however, did little to close the gap between Colgate and its arch-rival, the Procter & Gamble Company, a firm that ... had by now assumed a commanding lead over Colgate in selling detergent products in the United States."

The "Peet" appellation was abandoned in the company's title without much explanation in 1953.[2] The originators of Peet Brothers in Kansas City, Kansas in 1872 were all dead then, of course, and there was never a commodity named for them. The Palmolive nomenclature was retained, possibly because there was Palmolive soap and Palmolive brushless shaving cream (and, in 1966, Palmolive dishwashing liquid) — all readily identified as some of the firm's biggest moneymakers that weren't going away any time soon. So Peet was history; from 1953 until the present age, the outfit would be known as Colgate-Palmolive Company.

As television emerged in the late 1940s and early 1950s, CP hoped to effectively compete with Procter & Gamble as a sponsor of daytime serials. While it partially underwrote many soap operas, the company sponsored only one by itself, NBC's *The Doctors* (1963 to 1982). It was far more successful with *The Colgate Comedy Hour* (1950 to 1955), a glitzy, live, hour-long primetime feature that NBC-TV threw against Ed Sullivan's *Toast of the Town* on CBS. The guest-hosted hour with some of entertainment's most venerated stars kept audiences coming back for more. Although it cost the sponsor $3 million annually for time, talent and production, it exposed legions of eyewitnesses to CP's ample product line.

In the meantime, Colgate Chlorophyll toothpaste was launched in 1952 "at a time," according to company historians, "when the public were intrigued by anything chlorophyll." Even the green bar of Palmolive soap drew attention to the fact "nature's chlorophyll is in every tablet." By 1956, Colgate-Palmolive's share of similar brands in the U.S. consumer market reached 23 percent, an increase of 14 percent in nine years. CP opened a research facility in Piscataway, New Jersey, in 1962. Sales reached $1 billion for the first time in 1967. The following year, Colgate Dental Cream was reformulated to include fluoride while Ultra Brite toothpaste was brought to market for the first time.

Cold Power laundry detergent also emerged in the 1960s. A new antiperspirant, Soft & Gentle aerosol, arrived in 1976. The same year the company acquired a major revenue generator when it purchased Hill's Pet Products. A business observer dubbed it the "hidden jewel within the Colgate empire." In 1986, Colgate Junior and Colgate Tartar Control toothpastes made their way to market. The firm bought the Softsoap liquid label in 1987 along with a few more from the Minnetonka Corporation. In 1991, CP purchased the Murphy-Phoenix Company, bolstering its household care division with Murphy Oil Soap, a leading U.S. wood-cleaning agent.

Its "most dramatic" buy, however, occurred in 1992 when it acquired the Mennen Company for $670 million. Gerhard Mennen had opened a Newark, New Jersey, pharmacy in 1879; over time it grew into the diversified Mennen Company. CP's acquisition added the top-rated U.S. deodorant brand, Mennen Speed Stick, to its personal care lineup along with the second biggest seller in infant care labels, Baby Magic. In addition, Colgate gained footholds in skin-care and hair care products, while the Mennen brands gained the power of Colgate's global distribution network and extensive marketing reach.

Furthermore, CP became the worldwide leader in liquid soap when, in 1993, it purchased the European and South Pacific liquid hand and body soap brands manufactured by S. C. Johnson & Son. Colgate acquired the Latin American firm Kolynos Oral Care from American Home Products in 1995, raising its share in the hemisphere's Hispanic oral-care market from 54 percent to 79 percent.

At the same time that Colgate-Palmolive was making several smart business decisions, hindsight indicates it was also making some that were less sensible. CP acquired cosmetics manufacturer Helena Rubinstein in 1973. After persisting against rivals' trend of distributing through high volume drug stores — proffering Rubenstein wares via an ineffective department store system — Colgate finally gave up and sold the money-losing venture in 1980. Possibly to pacify a then-executive leader, CP bought Ram Golf Corporation and Bancroft Racket Company in 1974 and golf and tennis shoe manufacturer Charles A. Easton Company in 1976. It also purchased the Mission Hills Country Club in Palm Springs, California, so the CEO (David Foster) could personally supervise greens maintenance for the women's professional golf tournament known as the Colgate-Dinah Shore Winner's Circle. None of those acquisitions was particularly profitable; by the early 1980s, most were divested by Foster's successor. That included most of the business acquired in 1976 with the purchase of Riviana Foods (Texas long-grain rice, pet food, kosher hot dogs and candy). Only the pet food — Hill's Pet Products, ultimately to turn out to be a huge revenue-producer — was kept. In the meantime, "Thus while Procter & Gamble's sales and margins were increasing, Colgate's were on the decline," a source noted.

Despite all the bad news, there was one innovation in the 1990s that appeared to strategically make up for the shortcomings of two decades earlier. In the late 1980s, Colgate began developing a toothpaste that contained a gingivitis-fighting antimicrobial agent, triclosan. Researchers discovered a method for applying polymers to bind triclosan to teeth up to 14 hours, permitting users to incessantly fight bleeding gums and bad breath with only two brushings daily. The firm began marketing it overseas in 1992 under the brand name Total, eventually reaching 100 countries. It was an incredible winner. Its introduction in the U.S. was delayed for five years by the Food and Drug Administration (FDA). But when it arrived in late 1997, accompanied by a $100 million marketing blitz, the response far outweighed Colgate's anticipation. Suddenly, for the first time in 35 years, CP took the lead away from Procter & Gamble in the American toothpaste market. P&G was helpless in mounting a quick response, thanks to a lengthy FDA approval process, even though it was selling triclosan-based toothpaste in Canada already.

Colgate continued to introduce new products as a new century dawned. In 2000, it brought out the Colgate Actibrush battery-powered toothbrush followed by new wares in the burgeoning at-home tooth-whitening sector (Simply White gel, Total Plus Whitening toothpaste, etc.), plus — in 2002 — a new line of premium dog and cat food made with natural ingredients, Hill's Science Diet Nature's Best. The company announced its intent to acquire Tom's of Maine in 2006, a leading maker of natural toothpaste, founded by Tom Chappell in 1970.

Since the early 1970s, a non-profit track meet open to women of all ages, the Colgate Women's Games, has been underwritten by Colgate-Palmolive. Held at Brooklyn's Pratt Institute with finals at New York's Madison Square Garden, the annual event provides trophies and educational grants-in-aid to winners. A Baptist seminary established in 1819 in New York attracted William Colgate when it was shifted to Hamilton, New York, in 1823. There it was renamed Hamilton Literary and Theological Institution. The appellation was altered again to Madison University in 1846. And after seven decades of Colgate family involvement, Madison University changed its name once more, to Colgate University, in 1890. Colgate's theological side merged with Rochester Theological Seminary in 1928, becoming Colgate Rochester Divinity School, leaving Colgate to become a coeducational nondenominational university.

Colgate-Palmolive employed 36,000 individuals in 2004 while racking up sales of $10.58 billion. To remain competitive, it announced that same year that by 2008 it would close 26 of its 78 factories and cut 4,400 jobs, about 12 percent of its global workforce. "Colgate continued to deemphasize its detergent business," an assessor maintained. "It seemed likely to seek buyers for its Fab and Ajax brands."

CP's principal competitors are presently Procter & Gamble, Unilever (formerly Lever Brothers), the Clorox Company, S. C. Johnson & Son, Inc., Johnson & Johnson, Alberto-Culver Company, Reckitt Benckiser plc, Sara Lee Corporation, Church & Dwight Company, Inc., and the Dial Corporation. Today CP focuses on a quartet of core businesses: oral care, personal care, home care and pet nutrition. As of 2006, it sold brands in 222 countries and territories.

As this is written, among its most recognizable trademarks are Afta, Ajax, Axion, Colgate, Crystal White Octagon, Dynamo, Fab, Hill's Science Diet, Hill's Prescription Diet, Irish Spring, Kolynos, Mennen, Murphy Oil Soap, Palmolive, Softsoap, Speed Stick and Tom's of Maine.

Radio Series

The Palmolive Hour, with Paul Oliver and Olive Palmer — 1927 to 1931, NBC (Palmolive)
Clara, Lu 'n' Em — 1931 to 1935, NBC Blue, NBC (Super Suds, Colgate, Palmolive)
Fashions in Loveliness, with Myndall Cain — 1931 to 1932, NBC Blue — Midwest region (Palmolive)
Floyd Gibbons' True Stories — ca. early 1930s, CBS (Colgate)
Colgate House Party, with Joe Cook, Al Goodman and His Orchestra — 1934 to 1935, NBC (Colgate)
The Palmolive Beauty Box Theater, with Nat Shilkret and His Orchestra, Al Goodman and His Orchestra, and Jessica Dragonette — 1934 to 1937, NBC, NBC Blue, CBS (Palmolive)
The House of Glass, with Gertrude Berg — 1935 to 1936, NBC (Palmolive, Super Suds)
The Ziegfeld Follies of the Air, with Fanny Brice, Patti Chapin — 1936, CBS (Palmolive)
Goose Creek Parson — 1936 to 1937, CBS (Super Suds)
Gangbusters — 1936 to 1939, CBS (Palmolive)
Come On, Let's Sing!, with Jack Arthur — 1936 to 1937, CBS (Palmolive)
Hilltop House — 1937 to 1938, CBS, MBS; 1938 to 1941, CBS (Palmolive)
Kay Fairchild, Stepmother — 1937 to 1942, CBS (Colgate)
Ask-It Basket — 1938 to 1941, CBS (Colgate)
Myrt and Marge — 1938 to 1942, CBS (Super Suds, Halo)
This Was Our Love — ca. late 1930s, MBS (Palmolive)
Strange as it Seems — 1939 to 1940, CBS (Palmolive)
Wayne King and His Orchestra — 1939 to 1941, CBS (Halo, Cashmere Bouquet)
Colgate Sports Newsreel, with Bill Stern — 1939 to 1951, NBC Blue, NBC (Colgate)
The Story of Ellen Randolph — 1939 to 1941, NBC (Super Suds)
City Desk — 1940 to 1941, CBS (Palmolive)
The Story of Bess Johnson — 1941, NBC (Palmolive, Halo, Super Suds)
Colgate Spotlight, with Ed East — 1941, CBS (Colgate)
Guy Lombardo and His Orchestra — 1941 to 1942, CBS (Colgate, Halo)
Hobby Lobby, with Dave Elman — 1941 to 1942, CBS (Colgate, Palmolive)
Bachelor's Children — 1941 to 1942, NBC (Colgate, Palmolive)
Woman of Courage — 1941 to 1942, CBS (Octagon)

The Al Jolson Colgate Program—1942 to 1943, CBS (Colgate)
Can You Top This?—1942 to 1948, NBC (Colgate, Lustre-Crème)
The Judy Canova Show, aka *Rancho Canova*—1943 to 1944, 1945 to 1951, CBS, NBC (Colgate, Halo, Palmolive, Super Suds)
Million Dollar Band, aka *Palmolive Party*, aka *The Barry Wood-Patsy Kelly Show*—1943 to 1945, NBC (Palmolive)
Inner Sanctum Mysteries—1943 to 1944, CBS (Colgate, Palmolive)
Kay Kyser's Kollege of Musical Knowledge—1944 to 1948, NBC (Colgate, Lustre-Crème, Palmolive)
Theater of Romance—1944 to 1946, CBS (Colgate, Halo)
Blondie, with Arthur Lake and Penny Singleton—1944 to 1949, CBS (Super Suds, Lustre-Crème)
Daily Dilemmas, with Jack Barry—1946 to 1948, MBS (Super Suds and Veto—multiple participation)
A Day in the Life of Dennis Day, aka *The Dennis Day Show*—1946 to 1951, NBC (Colgate, Cashmere Bouquet, Lustre-Crème, Palmolive)
Mr. Blanc's Fix-It Shop, aka *The Mel Blanc Show*—1946 to 1947, CBS (Colgate, Cashmere Bouquet, Halo)
Mr. and Mrs. North, with Joseph Curtin and Alice Frost—1947 to 1954, CBS (Halo, Colgate, Palmolive, Cashmere Bouquet, Lustre-Crème)
Our Miss Brooks, with Eve Arden and Gale Gordon—1948 to 1954, CBS (Colgate, Lustre-Crème, Palmolive, Vel)
Second Honeymoon, with Bert Parks—1949 to 1950, MBS (Lustre-Crème)
The Steve Allen Show—1950, CBS (Lustre-Crème, Cashmere Bouquet, Palmolive, Halo, Colgate)
Satan's Waiting, with Frank Graham—1950, CBS (Colgate, Palmolive, Halo, Lustre-Crème, Cashmere Bouquet)
Strike It Rich, with Warren Hull—1950 to 1957, CBS, NBC (Vel, Fab, Palmolive, Colgate, Lustre-Crème, Halo)
King's Row—1951 to 1952, NBC (Colgate)
Brooding with Brady—ca. early 1950s, CBS—West Coast region (Vel)
The Bob and Ray Show, with Bob Elliott and Ray Goulding—1952 to 1953, NBC (Colgate)
Lorenzo Jones—1952 to 1955, NBC (Colgate)
Louella Parsons—1953 to 1954, CBS (Colgate, Lustre-Crème, Palmolive)
The Phrase That Pays, with Red Benson—1953 to 1955, NBC (Colgate)
The Couple Next Door—ca. 1958, CBS (Brisk)

Exposition

From its earliest days as an aural advertiser, Colgate-Palmolive-Peet—whose breakthrough on the ether effectively dates to network radio's beginnings—aired some of the most charismatic tunes in audio commercials. CP's plethora of bouncy jingles wasn't only beguiling but prolific. By the 1940s and 1950s, those strains emanated from several spots on the dial every week as the manufacturer's glut of situation comedies, audience participation series and mystery dramas essentially replaced most of its earlier surfeit of soap operas, variety shows and musical features.

Who could forget, for instance, the memorable melody that accompanied this refrain? *Halo, everybody, Halo! Halo is the shampoo that glorifies your hair, so Halo, everybody, Halo!* Or this ditty? *Lustre-Crème is Hollywood's fav'rite, Lustre-Crème shampoo ... It never dries ... It beautifies ...* et al. Or this? *Brush your teeth with Colgate, Colgate Dental Cream, It cleans your breath ... what a toothpaste ... while it cleans your teeth....* And one of the exhortations etched in the minds of listeners earlier in the period: *Super Suds, Super Suds, Lots more suds with Super Suds!*

Colgate-Palmolive-Peet was one of the firms that left America singing. And its effective use of repetitive, playful numbers with easy-to-remember lyrics translated frequently into cash registers ringing. And that had to be a nice tune in any advertiser's ear.

Commercial

Colgate-Palmolive-Peet capitalized on the interplay between program hosts and chief announcers on some of its durable radio series. This commercial, aired on *Strike It Rich* on May 22, 1950, appeared at a time before commercial dishwashers were in widespread use in American homes — and that less-than-glorious job was still done by hand. CP introduced a new product that MC Warren Hull and interlocutor Ralph Paul extolled. Particularly notice the references applied to a largely distaff audience.

WARREN HULL: Vel cuts dishwashing time in half.
RALPH PAUL: I'll say that's good sense, girls. Save half of your dishwashing time with Vel ... V-E-L ... made by Colgate-Palmolive-Peet. Vel leaves no soap scum or streaky film to polish away so dishes and glassware gleam without wiping. Just wash with Vel, rinse, and ... yes ... even glassware dries sparkling clear.
WARREN HULL: And here's still more sense, girls ... clean your pots and pans with Vel. Vel gets 'em shiny clean without hard scouring. You soak your pots and pans with Vel suds while you do the rest of the dishes 'cause by that time, Vel removes grease so fast and completely you can wash even the greasiest roaster so clean it shines.
RALPH PAUL: And girls ... get this ... Vel's amazingly mild to hands ... Know why? Well, because Vel's completely neutral, contains no alkali. Your hands will *love* Vel's mildness. So ask for Vel next time you're marketing.
WARREN HULL: Get Vel, the great new soapless suds that actually cleans dishes *cleaner* than soap and actually saves up to *half* your dishwashing time.

Ford Motor Company

History

Henry Ford was born into a prosperous Dearborn, Michigan, farming clan on July 30, 1863. In adolescence, he performed the menial agricultural and livestock chores required of him in the hours he wasn't attending a one-room school. Yet as time moved along it was obvious to anybody closely observing him that young Ford was gaining an overriding bias for mechanics and not the family business as his life's work. He took apart everything he got his hands on and earned a reputation in his community for repairing watches that had quit working. Ultimately he was to put his stamp on a new family enterprise, one that would signify the Ford moniker almost everywhere, making it instantly recognizable to a predominance of the world's inhabitants. But until the age of 16, when he went off to Detroit to learn a new trade, Henry Ford carried out the expected responsibilities of a dutiful son.

Arriving in nearby Detroit in 1879, he found work as a machinist's apprentice and, over the next three years, moved from job to job. Not only did he earn experience, he also confirmed any lingering doubts that he was cut out for an industrialized occupation as opposed to one growing grains and raising cattle. In the years immediately following that epoch, Ford split his time between repairing steam engines, securing temporary work in Detroit factories and overhauling his daddy's farm implements. For a while, he worked part time at the Westinghouse Engine Company in Dearborn. In his spare time, meanwhile, he tinkered with his own experiments in a homemade machine shop that he put together on the family spread. By 1890, he constructed a gas engine; while it had nothing to power it, it was evident that the young man wasn't destined to spend his life exclusively in agricultural quests.

After he married in 1888, Ford ran a sawmill, needing the security of a regular paycheck. But by 1891, he returned to Detroit to focus his skills at the Edison Illuminating Company. "This event," noted one reporter, "signified a conscious decision on Ford's part to dedicate his life to industrial pursuits." And when, in 1893, he advanced to chief engineer of his company, he acquired the time and capital needed to concentrate his off-hours to a growing love of internal combustion engines, an arena in which he incessantly experimented.

Henry Ford finished his first self-propelled "horseless carriage," branded a "quadricycle," in 1896.[1] Built on a buggy frame and boasting a gas-powered engine, it moved on four heavy, oversized wire bicycle-looking wheels. Steered like a boat by a tiller, it had two forward speeds and no reverse. The contraption led to a larger vision of producing motor cars for a traveling public. Ford would not be the inventor of the form: indeed, no single individual was, and several others were already doing what he was experimenting with. When he began, in fact, there were 15 automobile manufacturers in Michigan alone and 88 altogether across the United States! Yet he would make a profound and lasting impact on an industry then pervasively being established.

Twice he tried unsuccessfully to establish a vehicle manufacturing operation. The third time, proverbially, was the charm. With the assistance of 11 investors and pooled resources amounting to $28,000, the Ford Motor Company was launched on Detroit's Mack Avenue in a former covered wagon plant on June 16, 1903. Ford was vice president and chief engineer in its earliest days. Among the original investors were two brothers, Horace Elgin Dodge and John Francis Dodge, who were to be Ford competitors when they went into a similar venture under the Dodge Brothers Motor Vehicle Company flag.

On July 20, 1903, barely a month into Ford's existence as an entity, the fledgling firm delivered its inaugural vehicle to a Detroit physician. In those days, groups of two or three men assembled a single vehicle, drawing upon made-to-order components provided by a diverse array of suppliers. According to one source, in that early epoch, only three cars a day were produced. The founder insisted that the future of their business rested in the production of affordable cars for a mass market. This led to increasing friction between Ford and his business partners. Some pulled their money out and Ford bought their shares, increasing his holdings to 58.5 percent. By 1906, John S. Gray, the company's founding president, was history, and Henry Ford occupied his chair. He would hold a strategic place in the firm's management and decision-making for the remainder of his life. The following year (1907), the Ford oval trademark was introduced, although the familiar script type didn't appear until 1928.

In 1908, the Model T Ford was developed. Between then and 1927, some 15 million Model T's rolled from Ford plants. By the end of 1919, Ford produced half of all the cars made in U.S. assembly plants. More than half of all U.S. automobiles were Model T's by 1923. Concentrating the firm's energies on a single form in black only (a shade that purportedly dried rapidly), production levels were strikingly improved; thus, workers and machinery turned out the same car over and over again. Not until rival carmaker General Motors began satisfying the masses with more powerful and stylish Chevrolets available in a myriad of hues did Ford depart from its accustomed practice. After experimenting with a six-cylinder Model A, Ford shut down all of its U.S. plants on May 31, 1926, for retooling the assembly lines. When they reopened six months later, the firm mass-produced the Model A. In a quadrennium (1927 to 1931), 4.5 million of the new Fords were sold.

Opening a new manufacturing facility at Highland Park, Michigan, Ford paved the way for what was to become — according to contemporary Ford publicists — the company's "greatest contribution to automotive manufacturing": the moving assembly line. Henry Ford reasoned that allowing individual workers to stay in one place and perform the same task on every vehicle passing by them could prove incredibly efficient. Introducing the world's first moving production line in 1913 reduced chassis assembly from 12 hours 30 minutes to 2 hours 40 minutes. Delivery of parts by conveyor belt to the workers was carefully timed to keep the assembly line moving smoothly and efficiently. Not only did the change assist the company in surpassing the fabrication levels of rival firms, it cut their costs and therefore made their products more affordable to purchasers. The factory was able to turn out a car in 93 minutes as opposed to earlier quotas, resulting in about a million vehicles annually or one every 24 seconds.

The changeover, however, didn't translate into a user-friendly workspace. In fact, it had the opposite effect, resulting in higher turnover rates as slower employees dropped the ball while many became disenchanted with performing repetitious tasks. At first, that netted higher costs in training more and more workers. To counteract the effect, Ford more than doubled the compensation that automobile assemblymen were getting, from $2.34 to $5 daily (figured at $103 daily in 2006 terms), in effect buying back the allegiance of his employees while improving productivity. According to one assessment, "Wall Street ... disagreed with Ford's generous labor practices when he began paying workers enough to buy the products they made." Parenthetically, 15,000 job-seekers applied for 3,000 positions at Highland Park. A combination of highly efficient factories, well-paid workers and low prices revolutionized the industry and was characterized by the term "Fordism" in 1914.[2]

At the same time, Henry Ford reduced the number of shift hours from nine to eight. A new standard was set for American businesses — a 40-hour workweek. Ford also instituted the triple daily shift, allowing the assembly lines to run continuously around the clock. Productivity soared, turnover plunged and cost per vehicle plummeted. Ford reduced the retail selling prices of cars multiple times while establishing a system of franchised dealers loyal to its brand name, another first in the industry. Ford branched into producing trucks and tractors in 1917.

A conflict with stockholders two years later over millions of dollars to be spent on a mammoth manufacturing complex complete with a steel mill of substantial proportions, glass factory and vehicle assembly line resulted in Henry Ford and his son, Edsel, gaining the upper hand. The proposed size of the new plant alongside the Rouge River in Dearborn scared the others off. Henry and Edsel bought them out and in doing so owned the entire company. At River Rouge, iron ore and coal were brought in on Great Lakes steamers and by rail freight car, making iron and steel. Rolling mills, forges and assembly shops transformed the steel into springs, axles and vehicle bodies. Foundries converted iron into engine blocks and cylinder heads that were assembled with other components into engines. By September 1927, all the steps required in manufacturing from refining raw materials to final assembly of an automobile occurred at the vast Rouge plant, symbolizing Henry Ford's long-held concept of mass production. At its peak, 1930, the one factory employed 81,000 workers.

Ford acquired a financially troubled Lincoln Motor Company for $8 million on February 4, 1922, expanding into the luxury car market for the first time. Sixteen years later, in 1938, Ford Motor Company added the Mercury division to reach a midprice-oriented auto market. The two separate divisions, Lincoln and Mercury, were merged in 1945.

In the meantime, Henry resigned the presidency in 1919, turning the reins over to his progeny, who remained the titular head at least until his death from cancer in May 1943. "But, in fact," noted one chronicler, "Henry continued to direct the company strategy and spent much of his time developing a farm tractor called the Fordson. He also published a conservative weekly journal, the *Dearborn Independent*." Another biographer was less charitable: "Henry Ford was often criticized for repeatedly undermining his son's efforts to improve the company, and the managerial crisis which occurred after Edsel's death is directly attributable to Henry Ford's persistent failure to prepare capable managers for future leadership of the company."

As a result, Henry Ford temporarily resumed the presidency. But two years later, he stepped down again, handing control to his grandson, Henry Ford II, 28, who ran the outfit from 1945 to 1960. The latter was chief executive officer from 1945 to 1979, chairman of the board of directors from 1960 to 1980 and chairman of the finance committee from 1980 until his death in 1987. Henry Ford, who remained as chairman beginning in 1945, met his own death on April 7, 1947, at 83.

Henry Ford had been an outspoken pacifist during both the First and Second World Wars. He had even gone to Europe on a peace mission in 1915, joining others hoping to halt the first war. Subsequently, he went on to support that effort with the Model T becoming the underpinnings for allied military vehicles. Nevertheless, Ford viewed war as a waste and publicly expressed that he didn't wish to profit from it. Yet, during the second war, Ford's Willow Run plant was converted from a car-making factory into one turning out B-24 bombers for the allied defense. Mass production of those planes began in August 1943. Not only did Ford Motor Company play a pivotal role in the conflagration that the founder at least outwardly opposed, his personal stock and reputation and earnings skyrocketed from its participation.

According to one historian's interpretation, "[Henry] Ford had a complex, conflicting and strongly opinionated personality. Most of the company's struggles were linked to his stubborn management style. He refused to unionize with the United Automobile Workers, and to prevent his employees from doing so he hired spies and company police to check in on his workers." Still, others apply some of his philosophical theories in conducting business. Among them:

"There is one rule for the industrialist and that is: Make the best quality of goods possible at the lowest cost possible, paying the highest wages possible."

"I do not believe a man can ever leave his business. He ought to think of it by day and dream of it by night."

"It has been my observation that most people get ahead during the time that others waste."

"The competitor to be feared is one who never bothers about you at all, but goes on making his own business better all the time."

"A business absolutely devoted to service will have only one worry about profits. They will be embarrassingly large."

Ford regained its place as America's second leading carmaker in 1950, overtaking Chrysler Corporation, which had supplanted it in the early 1930s. The company continued to profit as it adjusted to changes in the consumer environment and as newer technologies and other innovations arrived. The Thunderbird appeared in the 1950s and also a chance to own a part of Ford Motor Company. The family-owned firm was shared with about 350,000 stockholders after it went public on February 24, 1956. Ford of Europe was established in 1967. Four years later American, Canadian and Mexican ventures were combined into North American Automotive Operations, ahead of the North American Free Trade Agreement by more than two decades.

Ford created a bombshell in autumn 1957 with the premier of the Edsel, a car few wanted. With unsold vehicles on its hands, the line was discontinued two years later. The Merkur met a similar fate in 1989, although it persisted for four years. The company unveiled one of its most popular vehicles in 1964 with the Mustang, which promptly convinced a half-million buyers in its initial 18 months on the market. The Ford Pinto, however, arriving in 1971, was marred by some gas tank explosions that occurred in rear-end collisions, resulting in several deaths and incalculable negative publicity. After acquiring a 25 percent stake in Mazda in 1979, Ford increased its holdings with controlling interest in 1996. In 1989 Ford purchased Jaguar, a British vehicle trademark. Within five years, it bought Hertz Rent-A-Car Company; in five more years (1999), it owned Volvo. A year later, Ford owned Land Rover from British carmaker BMW.

Henry Ford and Harvey S. Firestone had signed a working agreement in 1904 that persisted for nearly a century in which Firestone supplied tires for many of Ford's vehicles. But in August 2000, Bridgestone-Firestone recalled 6.5 million tires following 271 rollover deaths in Ford Explorers, according to a contemporary website. Ford unilaterally recalled 13 million more tires. The longstanding partnership between the two firms ended abruptly with Bridgestone-Firestone paying Ford $240 million toward tire losses amounting to $2 billion.

While a booming American economy, soaring stock market and low fuel costs translated into huge vehicle sales in the mid– to late 1990s, Ford was mired in a slump in the early years of the twenty-first century blamed on multiple uncontrollable factors: legacy healthcare outlays, higher fuel prices and a faltering economy, netting depressed market shares, fewer sales and diminished profit margins. Introducing the hybrid-electric Ford Escape and Mercury Mariner in 2005 and 2006 respectively, innovative Ford technicians achieved significant progress in improving fuel efficiency.

Presently, Ford Motor Company is a family of automotive, truck and farm machinery brands embracing Ford, Lincoln, Mercury, Mazda, Jaguar, Land Rover and Volvo. Although it has steadily lost market share since 1995, Ford was the No. 3 automaker on the planet — behind General Motors and Toyota — in 2006, based on worldwide vehicle sales. Ford manufactured 6.6 million vehicles that year while employing 280,000 individuals in approximately 100 global operations facilities. Some 60,000 suppliers produce the goods and services Ford Motor Company currently requires to manufacture its vehicles. With 17.5 percent of U.S. market share, Ford was second in sales in this country in 2006, ranking seventh among 2007 Fortune 500 enterprises with American bases.

Despite the optimism, however, realistically — following a net loss of $12.7 billion in 2006 — the firm revealed that it won't return to profitability before 2009. To counteract the distressing downturn, in late 2005 Ford announced a resizing plan that includes deleting some unprofitable and inefficient models from inventory, consolidating production lines, closing 14 factories and scrubbing 30,000 jobs. Its wholly owned subsidiary, Hertz Rent-a-Car, was sold in 2005 to a private equity group for $15 billion cash and debt acquisition. None of it was good news for a company that had traditionally been one of the world's 10 leading revenue-earners as well as one of the most profitable global business ventures.

Radio Series

Ford Sunday Evening Hour, aka *Ford Summer Hour*, with the Detroit Symphony, John Charles Thomas, Gladys Swarthout, Helen Jepson, Lawrence Tibbett, Jane Pickens, James Melton and Francia White and orchestras conducted by John Barbirolli, Fritz Reiner, Donald Voorhees and Meredith Willson —1934 to 1942, CBS; 1945 to 1946, ABC (Ford)
The Fred Waring Orchestra and Chorus—1934 to 1936, CBS, NBC Blue (Ford)
Ford V8 Revue, with Bob Crosby, Fred Grofe —1936, CBS (Ford)
Universal Rhythm, with Raymond Chandler and His Orchestra —1936 to 1937, NBC Blue (Ford)
Watch the Fun Go By, with Al Pearce and Arlene Harris —1937 to 1938, CBS (Ford)
Watch the World Go By, with Earl Godwin —1942 to 1944, ABC (Ford)
Early American Dance Music—1943 to 1945, ABC (Ford)
The Greenfield Chapel Choir—1943 to 1945, ABC (Ford)
Stars of the Future—1944 to 1945, ABC (Ford)

Bob Crosby and the Bobcats—1945 to 1946, CBS (Ford)
The Ford Festival of American Music, with Alfred Drake and Leigh Harline and His Orchestra—1946, ABC
The Ford Show, with Dinah Shore—1946 to 1947, NBC (Ford)
Ford Showroom, with Meredith Willson and His Orchestra—1947, CBS (Ford)
The Fred Allen Program, with Al Goodman and His Orchestra—1947 to 1949, NBC (Ford)
The Ford Theater—1947 to 1949, NBC, CBS (Ford)
Can You Top This?—1949 to 1950, MBS (Ford)
Escape—1949 to 1950, CBS (Ford)
The Saint—1949 to 1950, MBS (Ford)
Robert Trout and Cedric Adams and the News—1952 to 1953, CBS (Ford)
The Tennessee Ernie Ford Show—1958, CBS (Ford)

Exposition

The Ford Sunday Evening Hour, a longstanding tradition in many American homes in the 1930s and 1940s, appealed to the sense of "wanting to feel cultured without really being so," claimed its producer, William Reddick. It accomplished that by furnishing listeners with a cross-section of ballads, classics, operatic music and sacred song. Taking a personal interest in the program's development, Henry Ford sought to "please the public" with a powerfully symbolic replica of a major American firm that accepted responsibility for giving the customers what they expected. Commercials were sparse, almost as if the show was too important to be interrupted with secular matters. The series became one of the exalted features of the air, speaking volumes about its sponsor sometimes by hardly doing so.

While the company subscribed a score of additional aural series, none carried the weight of the original. Unlike some other firms that successfully underwrote several stars over extended periods, except for brief respites with Fred Waring, Bob Crosby, Dinah Shore, Fred Allen and Tennessee Ernie Ford—none of which persisted beyond two years, some for only two months—Ford didn't pick venerated, established superstars to headline its radio glories for long. By the late 1940s, the firm seemed to have thrown caution to the wind, dropping dollars here and there in a crazy-quilt pattern that appeared to have little cohesive forethought. At mid-century, Ford removed itself almost entirely from network radio concentration, preferring to invest unreservedly in television.

Commercial

On a *Ford Theater* presentation on January 4, 1948, Kenneth Banghart offered this homily-sounding essay in keeping with the prestigious tradition of the acclaimed series and its earlier counterpart, *The Ford Sunday Evening Hour*.

ANNOUNCER: Among the hardest working and most respected people in our nation are the country doctors ... the men and women who bring healing knowledge and skills to even the most remote farms and homes. Day after day in all kinds of weather they make their rounds through forests and mountains and deserts, going wherever they're needed. And because their work is so important and their travel is frequently difficult, the Ford Motor Company is proud that so many doctors prefer to drive Ford cars. One of these is Dr. H. F. Lawson of Crossville, Tennessee. The people who live and work in the hills around Crossville know Dr. Lawson very well. Summer or winter ... dust or snow or mud ... over the roughest roads and steepest hills ... Dr. Lawson gets there when he's needed. Recently, Dr. Lawson wrote the Ford Motor Company to say why he prefers to drive a Ford. He said he can always start his Ford in any kind of weather ... that it rides comfortably ... that his Ford always takes him where he wants to go, no matter how bad the driving conditions. "My Ford has never failed to come through," he wrote. "As a rural doctor, I am qualified to say that no other car can beat a Ford for all-around performance under all conditions." That's the kind of service and dependability that millions of Americans have learned to expect from Ford products. That's the kind of performance *you* can expect from any product made by Ford.

General Foods Corporation

History

After another generation passes, there will be only a handful of earth's inhabitants still living who recall the General Foods Corporation. But in its heyday, that ubiquitous entity was one of the most powerfully and pervasively influential food and beverage processors impacting the lives of nearly all Americans. Almost every household in the U.S., it can be speculated, could have exhibited one or more General Foods' breakfast, dessert, baking, condiment or liquid goods at a given moment. And not only in its homeland for the multinational's outreach encircled the globe, figuring solidly in the culinary judgments made in kitchens overseas as well as in America.

For so vast an enterprise whose corporate moniker and symbolism no longer exist, except for the wares still manufactured and distributed under its familiar trade names, General Foods was a giant in American business.[1] With few exceptions, the brands it proffered originated within our borders. The success it enjoyed for multiple decades is a tribute to the innovation, genius and perseverance of a group of entrepreneurs who cast their lots together during the 1920s in a commercial quest that mushroomed into a formidable competitive venture.

General Foods' origins date to 1895 when Charles William Post (1854 to 1914), the first of the capitalists to merge his resources three decades hence, organized the C. W. Post Company at Battle Creek, Michigan. He had been a resident of that fair burg since 1891. Post was duly impressed by the values, therapy and diet afforded him during a time he was a patient at a holistic health resort operated by Dr. John Harvey Kellogg.[2] Although he arrived there in a wheelchair, by the time Post left the Battle Creek Sanitarium he claimed to be cured of his ailments.

And while he was getting well, the enterprising industrialist was taking notes on an equally fascinating activity that was going on about him: Kellogg and his younger brother, Will Keith Kellogg, were simultaneously experimenting in the infirmary kitchen with flaked wheat which was also being served to a receptive constituency at breakfast, the health spa's clients. In fact, after their dismissal, some of those ex-patients requested that shipments of the stuff be sent to their homes. Of course, the surname of the Kellogg siblings hints that the two were in the formative stages of creating the acclaimed Kellogg Company, another global food processor. None of this was lost on C. W. Post, meanwhile. Upon his release, energized anticipation coupled with physical rejuvenation led him to see what he, too, might be able to do with a dry corn flake.

His first commodity, in 1895, wasn't a cereal, surprisingly. Instead, in a little white barn at Battle Creek, he stirred up a batch of a cereal-based drink that could be substituted for coffee, an absolute "no-no" at the sanitarium. Calling it Postum, the principal composition of the caffeine-free beverage was wheat grain, bran and molasses. While it was initially brewed like coffee, by 1911 Post had remixed and remastered the powdered formula, Postum Instant Cereal Beverage. The commodity is still being made in Battle Creek.

His second foray into the field was to be — at least, down the road apiece — still more rewarding. Two years after Postum premiered, Post bought the rights to a crunchy blend of wheat and barley that another small manufacturer created. In 1897, he dubbed the ready-to-eat cold breakfast food "Elijah's Manna." For an unknown reason, it took him a decade — to 1907 — to alter his labeling to Grape-Nuts. This was after he had long before found potential customers were put off by the biblical inference associated with its original trade name, yet he delayed his compliance with reality for a long spell.

By then calling his outfit the Postum Cereal Company, in 1905 Post had more than $10 million in capital and was channeling $400,000 annually into peddling his wares. That he could do so to that extent was an incredible feat in that epoch. His trendsetting marketing pizzazz, now widely accepted as basic industry practice, included couponing, offering free samples, product demonstrations, plant tours and recipe booklets. It's claimed he invented the cents-off coupon.

As the years rolled by, his health began to deteriorate, meanwhile. Post, living with incessant depression as well as challenging physical maladies — ended his life in 1914 with a self-inflicted gunshot. He had nevertheless groomed someone to take over his work which was already a $20 million enterprise. His 28-year-old daughter, Marjorie Merriweather [sic] Post, inherited his wealth *and* his business. She ran the latter for eight years (1914 to 1922), until her second husband — one of Wall Street's principal activists, E. F. Hutton, whom she wed in 1920 — assumed chairmanship of the Postum Cereal Company.[3] He turned it into a corporate giant that shaped the eating habits of people living all over the world.

The upgrade began with a series of strategic acquisitions that proved to be perceptively shrewd. Over a quadrennium, between 1925 and 1929, the organization's portfolio was tactically diversified as various wares were added to its mix that proffered high visibility for the manufacturer. First up was the purchase of the Jell-O Company, a small, highly industrialized plant situated in the hamlet of LeRoy, New York. It produced powdered blends resulting in unique dessert complements.

Jell-O's history is a compelling review of simple American entrepreneurship in the foods industry. Its concept can be traced to 1845 when industrialist-inventor Peter Cooper dabbled in his home kitchen with a primitive forerunner of commercial gelatin. Although he experimented with it for some time, even obtaining a patent that covered his process, Cooper never carried it very far beyond his own domicile. While others may have heard the story of Cooper's tests, more than a half-century elapsed before anybody successfully went any further. It was a LeRoy craftsman, Pearle B. Wait, a carpenter by trade, who took Cooper's original inspiration to the next level. At home one day in 1897, Wait was putting up a cough remedy and laxative tea when he, too, began mixing up a fruit-flavored gelatin formula. His wife, May, named the thus-far-unidentified stuff Jell-O. But without sufficient funds and skills that could help him make and market his new-found substance, in 1899 Wait transferred ownership of the "invention" to an entrepreneurial townsman, Orator Frank Woodward, for $450.

Already prospering as a manufacturer of proprietary medicines, Woodward had been a resident of LeRoy since 1860, four years following his birth. In 1897, he incorporated his endeavor as Genesee Pure Food Company. The year before, he began marketing a roasted cereal coffee labeled Grain-O "for those who can't drink tea and coffee." Woodward's accomplishment there allowed him to persist with Jell-O until it ultimately exceeded Grain-O in sales. Although the gelatin-based dessert was slow to take off, in 1900, Woodward started peddling it under the Jell-O moniker. Over the years, Jell-O changed from a hand-packaged business to a highly mechanized factory.

Hiring an advertising agency, the Genesee Pure Food Company launched a tenacious promotional campaign. By 1902, Woodward and others were exceedingly well satisfied: Jell-O sales reached $250,000. Two years beyond, the firm began distributing product samples and recipes. Genesee spent $366 for an initial space ad in *The Ladies' Home Journal*, a sizable sum at the time, which proved space ads that were strategically placed worked. Meanwhile, recipe pamphlets illustrated by Rose O'Neill, Maxfield Parrish, Coles Phillips, Norman Rockwell, Linn Ball and Angus MacDonald turned Jell-O into a household word well beyond the local confines. As many as 15 million such leaflets were produced annually, in fact.

So popular was the new quest that, in 1923, Genesee Pure Foods Company altered its own name to Jell-O Company, Inc., in an effort to protect the value of its trade appellation by closely linking it to the venture. That same year the firm started marketing a sugar-free gelatin, D-Zerta, plus a powdered mix for at-home ice cream-making.

Such a prize was one that E. F. Hutton believed could acutely enhance the bottom line of the Postum Cereal Company. On December 31, 1925, Jell-O was the first acquisition of more than a dozen subsidiaries it added in rapid succession, expanding Postum's product line to more than 60 commodities. Parenthetically, as a throwback to an absorbing past, local LeRoy interests today operate a Jell-O Museum at 23 East Main Street. There is a Web site for it, too: http://www.jellomuseum.com/.

Following Jell-O into the fold at Postum, in 1926 the latter bought Igleheart Brothers, Inc., of Evansville, Indiana, a milling operation that had existed for seven decades, since 1856. Its most promising commodity was Swans Down cake flour. The Iglehearts, too, had long been in the recipe-distribution business. Around the turn of the twentieth century, they were producing a continuous supply of printed leaflets pertaining to innovative ideas in homestyle cakemaking. As time progressed, the promotions became even more sophisticated. By 1929, as a new subsidiary of Postum, Igleheart dispatched this typically titled booklet: *Make Them Better Than Ever Before Pies, Waffles, Muffins, Biscuits, Cookies with Swans Down*. While the Swans Down sobriquet was clearly identified with cakes in the minds of most homemakers familiar with its name, expanding literature showed the kitchen artisans of that day that they could have their cake and eat it (the brand) in several other forms, too.

Earlier, in 1894, Susan Stavers, a Bostonian, created a dessert concoction when she churned tapioca flakes through a coffee grinder. Yet, like Pearle Wait, who experimented about then with Jell-O—he didn't have the wherewithal to mass produce and sell it, you recall—Susan Stavers knew she had something but she was unable to carry it any further. That year (1894) she sold the rights to her process to an enterprising John Whitman of nearby Orange, Massachusetts. He took her recipe for "Tapioca Superlative" (her designation) and renamed it Minute Tapioca. Whitman had such good luck with it that in 1908 he revised the name of his business to amplify the product's branding, just as the Jell-O folks eventually did with their foremost ware. And in 1926, Whitman sold Minute Tapioca to the Postum Cereal Company, which—with its collection of ventures recently added—posted phenomenal revenues that year of about $47 million.

Next in the acquisition line was a couple of similarly named confectioners, both purchased in 1927. One was chocolate manufacturer Walter Baker & Company, Ltd., of Dorchester, Massachusetts, whose venture began in 1765.[4] The other was coconut producer Franklin Baker Company, with sweets dating to 1895 and its origins rooted as a flour milling concern earlier in the century. In 1921, the founding Baker and his son, Franklin Baker, Jr., launched a production facility at Santa Mesa, Manila, Philippines. That plant was closed after Postum bought it and opened a new one, nearer the coconut plantations, at San Pablo, Laguna, Philippines. Still another plant was added in 1968 at Davao, Philippines.

In short order, Postum bought Towle Maple Syrup Company of St. Paul, Minnesota, the manufacturer of Log Cabin syrup. It began in 1887 after St. Paul grocer P. J. Towle took an aversion to the syrups then available to him to dispense to his patrons. Instead, he developed his own maple-flavored blend. In an April 1917 *Ladies' Home Journal* advertisement, Towle sold one-pound syrup tins for a quarter, two-pound tins for a half-dollar and five-pound tins for a dollar. Until the late 1940s, when glass bottles came into vogue extensively, Log Cabin syrup was sold in metal containers shaped like log cabins.

Still another major acquisition in 1927 was a business that Richard Hellmann established in 1913, producing Blue Ribbon mayonnaise and salad dressings, named after him. Five years afterward, Richard Hellmann, Inc., then a division of its new owner, and Best Foods, a California unit of the Gold Dust Corporation that also made salad dressings and mayonnaise, combined under the moniker Best Foods, Inc. At the time, Hellmann operated six plants and Best Foods five, with all 11 continuing production. As the largest manufacturer of those edibles in the U.S., the new enterprise was jointly owned by Gold Dust and General Foods and no stock was issued for sale to the public.

Meanwhile, in 1906 a native German, Dr. Ludwig Roselius (1874 to 1943), invented a decaffeination process. Subsequently, working under sundry trade names, he retailed coffee sans caffeine throughout Europe. His brew at last hit American store shelves in 1923, labeled Sanka in this country. Sanka became attractive to the Postum Cereal Company, too, for the firm had never introduced a coffee product. Officials there bought Roselius's operation, Kaffee HAG; it may have been the first coffee in the Postum portfolio but by no means would it be the last.

The following year (1928), Postum acquired the Cheek-Neel Coffee Company of Nashville, Tennessee. The firm's flagship beverage was named for a renowned, majestic old hotel in downtown Nashville where a piping hot brew was served in a stately dining room signified by striking accouterments. The coffee was dubbed Maxwell House for its hotelier origins. The application of that sobriquet began in 1892. While the U.S. coffee market was splintered with multiple trademarks — with no single brand claiming anything approaching dominance — that was about to change. Given the advantage of an infusion of heavy promotion following its purchase, Maxwell House — with the memorable advertising slogan "Good to the Last Drop" — grabbed first place among U.S. coffee-drinkers and held it into the 1980s. It is still a major contender today.

Satina starch and La France Bluing Flakes became part of Postum's mix (and the first non-edibles in its collection) in 1928 when La France Manufacturing Company joined the burgeoning conglomerate. Calumet Baking Powder Company was also added the same year. That commodity originated in 1889 when a Chicago salesman formulated a "better quality" double-acting baking powder than that he was then selling. He named it after the nearby hamlet of Calumet City, Illinois.

Among Postum's most impressive acquisitions during the era was one that occurred near the end of the rapid expansion period. In 1929, it purchased the frozen-foods firm of Clarence

With point of purchase advertising like this — for the product *and* the radio series it underwrote — how much better could it get for General Foods? In this co-op venture in 1938, an enterprising rep for the behemoth food-and-beverage maker placed a poster in the window of a coffee shop facing a New York City street. General Foods acquired the brand a decade earlier from a Nashville distributor. To establish name recognition in New York in such a brief time (in an industry where there was no clear winner before) was a credible hint in how far Maxwell House had come. Fifteen cents for coffee and doughnuts wasn't a bad deal either.

Birdseye (1886 to 1956). In fact, that move prompted Postum Cereal Company to alter its own nomenclature, becoming General Foods Corporation — signifying the unquestioned halcyon days for the international operation — for over a half-century.

Birdseye, in the meantime, is a fascinating study in creative ingenuity by himself. Born in Brooklyn, New York, the naturalist-businessman-inventor, lacking funds to complete his studies at Amherst College, went into fur-trading as a line of work. From 1912 to 1917, he lived on the Canadian peninsula of Labrador. While there, Birdseye made a simple discovery that revolutionized the frozen food industry: poultry, seafood and other meat frozen in the bitter cold of an arctic winter tasted better than similar foods frozen in the milder temperatures of spring and fall. Quick freezing was the term applied by the Eskimos to the technique — freezing so quickly that only small ice crystals had time to form. Cell walls weren't damaged and when the frozen fish and meat was thawed and cooked months after being stored in barrels of sea water, maximum color, texture and flavor were preserved.

After Birdseye returned to America, in 1923 — with an investment of $7 for an electric fan, buckets of brine and cakes of ice — he invented and perfected a system of packing fresh food into waxed cardboard boxes and flash-freezing them under high pressure. Two years hence, in 1925, Birdseye developed an apparatus which he branded a quick-freeze machine. Despite his intense lobbying to sell the device, however, customers weren't standing in line to buy: their distrust of frozen foods from bad experiences using less modern methods of preservation made them suspicious of any so-called advanced design. Nor was the appliance cheap to produce and maintain. Yet the "father of frozen food" didn't give up easily.

After Birdseye's General Seafoods Company of Gloucester, Massachusetts, was sold to Postum for $22 million, along with its patented quick-freeze methods, the inventor became president of two more outfits — Birdseye Electric Company and Birds Eye Frosted Foods (by then his surname had been divided). Turning his attention to grocery stores, in 1934 he found a more accessible market for still another process, manufacturing freezing units capable of holding fresh frozen food until their purchase, a virtual impossibility previously. Patrons were delighted with the freshness of those goods and so were store owners. Birdseye's accomplishments had yet another profound effect, according to one authority: "The space and power requirements for the burgeoning frozen-food section was one factor which led to the rapid development of larger self-service supermarkets beginning in the late 1930s." Across his lifetime, Birdseye held almost 300 patents and brought out a line of about 100 frozen vegetables, fruits and meats that turned his moniker into a household word. The birth of retail frozen foods is thus credited to him.

In the meantime, the new General Foods Corporation wasted little time in vigorously promoting its growing arsenal of culinary delights. Not only did it rely heavily on women's magazines, newspapers, billboards, transit advertising, product literature and packaging, special events, premiums and promotions of many types, by 1926 network radio was bidding for advertising attention. General Foods heard and answered the call, vociferously, repeatedly and prolifically. *The Maxwell House Concert*, featuring Donald Voorhees conducting an orchestra, was there as NBC premiered the first of its dual nationwide hookups in late 1926. An independent investigation revealed that General Foods ultimately aired more radio broadcasts (actual series seasons) over the next three decades than any other commercial sponsor except Procter & Gamble. Perhaps that adds something to the somewhat startling implausibility that, as a separate corporate identity, General Foods no longer exists — and hasn't, in nearly a quarter-century!

From time to time, General Foods added more brands to its assortment of goods, the result of its own research and product development as well as continuing to make strategic acquisitions. In 1953, for example, it bought Perkins Products Company, gaining the multi-flavored powdered Kool-Aid beverage mixes. In 1920, Edwin Perkins, son of a southwest Nebraska general store proprietor, started selling a concentrated drink mix he invented that he dubbed Fruit Smack. Seven years later, the young entrepreneur figured out a way to remove the liquid from his product, allowing him to package it in envelopes for easier handling and distribution. He renamed it Kool-Ade, then Kool-Aid. Food brokers disseminated it to grocery stores, candy shops and other similar vendors. Reaction was so favorable that, by 1931, Perkins was concentrating solely on Kool-Aid. For more efficiency in dispersal, that year he moved the operation to Chicago. In 1950, 300 production workers were turning out about a million packets of Kool-Aid daily. Buying Perkins out three years hence was, to a diversifying General Foods, a colossal addition.

Other major General Foods internal creations: Jell-O pudding and pie fillings (1936),

Maxwell House Instant Coffee (1945), Tang flavor crystals (1957), Dream Whip topping mix (1957), Maxim freeze-dried coffee (1964) and Cool Whip whipped topping (1966). In 1981, General Foods purchased Oscar Mayer & Company, introducing the food processor to processed meat packing for the first time. Still more acquisitions broadened the product line, among them: Gaines pet food (1943), Burger Chef fast food chain (1967), Rax roast beef restaurants (1968), Burpee seeds (1970) and Entenmann's bakery goods (1982).

Despite its stupendous accomplishments (or possibly because of them), in 1985 General Foods Corporation was bought by Philip Morris Companies, Inc., for $5.6 billion, the largest non-oil acquisition in U.S. history. Three years later Philip Morris bought Kraft, Inc., for $12.9 billion. In early 1989, the dual formidable food giant subsidiaries were combined, thereafter known as Kraft General Foods, Inc. It became the largest food processing firm in America.

Subsequently, as of January 1995, Philip Morris obliterated the General Foods nomenclature altogether; from that time forward, its edibles division was identified only as Kraft Foods, Inc. even though Jell-O, Maxwell House, Baker's, Kool-Aid, Cool Whip, Tang, Log Cabin and many other trademarked goods produced by General Foods persisted. Philip Morris added Nabisco Holdings (National Biscuit Company) to its Kraft mix in 2000; many more well known trademark appellations were integrated into the existing unit.

In 2002, the parent firm, Philip Morris, changed its own name to Altria Group, Inc. On January 31, 2007, the Altria board of directors voted to authorize the spinoff of Kraft Foods, Inc. And on March 30, 2007, Altria distributed approximately 88.9 percent of the outstanding Kraft shares owned by Altria to Altria's shareholders. It was a new day for some past rivals as they continued to work in tandem, this time being (at least, presumptively) their own boss again.

Radio Series

The Maxwell House Concert, with Donald Voorhees and His Orchestra—1926 to 1932, NBC, NBC Blue (Maxwell House)
The La France Orchestra— ca. 1928 to ca. 1929, NBC (La France, Satina)
Maxwell House Melodies—1929 to 1930, NBC Blue (Maxwell House)
The National Home Hour—1930 to 1931, NBC (General Foods)
Baker's Chocolate Broadcast—1930, network unsubstantiated (Baker's)
The Boswell Sisters—1931 to 1932, CBS (Baker's chocolate)
The Maxwell House Tune Blenders, with Lanny Ross, Donald Voorhees and His Orchestra— 1932, CBS (Maxwell House)
The Maxwell House Show Boat, with Lanny Ross—1932 to 1937, NBC (Maxwell House)
The Adventures of Admiral Byrd, aka *Byrd Expedition Broadcasts*—1933 to 1935, CBS (Grape-Nuts)
The Wizard of Oz, with Nancy Kelly—1933 to 1934, NBC (Jell-O)
Frances Lee Barton, aka *Kitchen Party*—1932 to 1935, NBC (Calumet, Swans Down)
The Jell-O Program, aka *The Grape-Nuts Program*, with Jack Benny—1934 to 1944, NBC (Jell-O, Grape-Nuts)
The Helen Hayes Theater—1935 to 1937, NBC Blue (Sanka)
The Jell-O Summer Program, aka Tim and Irene—1936, NBC Blue (Jell-O)
We, the People, with Gabriel Heatter—1936 to 1942, NBC Blue, CBS (Jell-O, Calumet, Sanka, Swans Down)

The George Burns and Gracie Allen Show—1937 to 1938, NBC (Grape-Nuts, La France, Satina)
Baby Snooks, aka *Good News*, aka *Maxwell House Coffee Time*, aka *Post Toasties Time*, with Fanny Brice, Frank Morgan, Hanley Stafford—1937 to 1948, NBC, CBS (Maxwell House, Post Toasties, Sanka, Jell-O, La France, Post-Tens, Satina)
Log Cabin Jamboree, aka *The Jack Haley Show*—1937 to 1938, NBC (Log Cabin)
The Kate Smith Show, aka *Kate Smith Sings*, aka *The Kate Smith Variety Show*, with Glenn Miller and His Orchestra—1937 to 1947, CBS (Calumet, Swans Down, Grape-Nuts, Jell-O, Sanka, Postum)
Kate Smith Speaks, aka *Kate Smith Chats*—1939 to 1947, CBS (Maxwell House, Grape-Nuts, Jell-O, Swans Down, Baker's chocolate and coconut, Gaines, Calumet)
Believe It or Not, with Robert L. Ripley—1937 to 1938, NBC Blue, NBC (Post Bran Flakes)
Al Pearce and His Gang—1938 to 1939, NBC (Grape-Nuts)
The Joe E. Brown Show, with Harry Sosnik and His Orchestra—1938 to 1939, CBS (Post Toasties)
Lum and Abner, with Chester Lauck and Norris Goff—1938 to 1940, CBS (Postum)
Mary Margaret McBride—1937 to 1939, CBS (Minute Tapioca, La France, Satina)
The Aldrich Family, with Ezra Stone, Dickie Jones, Norman Tokar, Raymond Ives—1939 to 1951, NBC, CBS (Jell-O, Grape-Nuts, Postum)
Joyce Jordan, Girl Interne [sic], aka *Joyce Jordan, M.D.*—1939 to 1942, CBS (La France, Satina, Minute Tapioca)
My Son and I—1939 to 1941, CBS (Swans Down, Calumet)
Young Doctor Malone—1939 to 1945, NBC Blue, CBS (Post 40% Bran Flakes, Post Toasties, Post Grape-Nuts, Post Raisin Bran)
Kate Hopkins, Angel of Mercy—1940 to 1942, CBS (Maxwell House)
Home of the Brave, with Tom Tully, Richard Widmark—1941, CBS, NBC (Swans Down, Calumet)
Portia Faces Life—1940 to 1951, CBS, NBC (Post Raisin Bran, Post 40% Bran Flakes, Post-Tens, Gaines, Jell-O, Maxwell House, Satina, La France)
William L. Shirer and the News—1941 to 1945, CBS (Sanka)
When a Girl Marries—1941 to 1952, NBC, ABC (Calumet, Baker's chocolate and coconut, Swans Down, Sur-Jell, Maxwell House, La France, Satina)
Post Toasties Time—1942, NBC (Post Toasties, Maxwell House)
Those We Love—1942 to 1944, CBS, NBC (Grape-Nuts, Maxwell House, Sanka)
We Love and Learn—1942 to 1944, CBS (Gaines)
Birdseye Open House, aka *The Dinah Shore Show*—1943 to 1944, CBS (Birdseye, Gaines, La France, Satina)
The Adventures of the Thin Man, with Les Damon, Les Tremayne, David Gothard—1943 to 1947, CBS, NBC (Post Toasties, Sanka)
The Charlie Ruggles Show, with Mary Astor—1944, CBS (Sanka)
Hop Harrigan—1944 to 1946, Blue, ABC (Grape-Nuts)
Two on a Clue—1944 to 1946, CBS (Satina, La France)
Maxwell House Coffee Time, with George Burns and Gracie Allen, Meredith Willson and His Orchestra—1945 to 1949, NBC (Maxwell House)
The House of Mystery, with John Griggs—1945 to 1949, MBS (General Foods)
The Second Mrs. Burton—1946 to 1954, CBS (Satina, La France, Calumet, Swans Down)
Juvenile Jury, with Jack Barry—1946 to 1951, MBS (Gaines)
McGarry and His Mouse—1947, MBS (General Foods)

Buck Rogers in the Twenty-Fifth Century, with John Larkin—1946 to 1947, MBS (General Foods)
Wendy Warren and the News—1947 to 1954, CBS (Maxwell House, Gaines, Baker's coconut)
The Danny Thomas Show—1948, CBS (General Foods)
Maxwell House Summer Show, aka *Meredith Willson and His Orchestra*—1948 to 1949, ABC, NBC (Maxwell House)
My Favorite Husband, with Lucille Ball—1948 to 1951, CBS (Jell-O, Sanka, La France, Satina)
Gangbusters—1949 to 1954, CBS (Grape-Nuts)
Father Knows Best, with Robert Young—1949 to 1954, NBC (Maxwell House, Postum, Post 40% Bran Flakes, Post Toasties)
The Goldbergs—1949 to 1950, CBS (General Foods)
Hopalong Cassidy, with William Boyd, Andy Clyde, Joe Duval—1950 to 1952, MBS, CBS (General Foods)
Renfro Valley Sunday Morning Gatherin,' with John Lair—1950 to 1955, CBS (Calumet)
Renfro Valley Country Store, with John Lair—1951, CBS (General Foods)
The Roy Rogers Show, with Pat Buttram, Dale Evans—1951 to 1953, NBC (Post)
Sanka Salutes, with Win Elliott—1952 to 1954, CBS (Sanka)
The Bob Hope Show—1952 to 1954, NBC (Jell-O)
The Falcon—1953, MBS (multiple participation)
The Crime Files of Flamond, with Everett Clarke—1953, MBS (General Foods)
The Grady Cole Show—1951 to 1953, CBS (General Foods)
Beulah—1953 to 1954, CBS (multiple participation)
The Brighter Day—1955 to 1956, CBS (Swans Down—multiple participation)

Exposition

General Foods provided American radio listeners and magazine readers with some of the most imaginative and memorable mottoes they encountered. All are familiar with what is possibly its best line of all, Maxwell House coffee's "Good to the Last Drop," initially applied in 1915, well before that brand joined Postum Cereal Company's by-then bulging briefcase. So well recognized is that catchphrase, in fact, that *Advertising Age* magazine—something akin to the bible in its industry—picked the famous watchword as sixth on the *Top 10 Slogans of the Century*. (If you're curious, number one is DeBeers' "Diamonds are Forever.")

And speaking of diamonds, there were plenty more jewels among General Foods' stash of one-liners, among them: "Fill It to the Rim with Brim" (coffee), "Bring Out the Hellmann's and Bring Out the Best" (mayonnaise and salad dressings), "Your Best Bet is Calumet" (baking powder), "It's Everything You Love About Coffee without the Caffeine" (Sanka), "It's a Kick in the Glass" (Tang), "Celebrate the Moments of Your Life" (General Foods International Coffees) and "Oh, Yeah!" (Kool-Aid).

And if you heard Henry Aldrich and cohort Homer Brown launch into a rip-roaring chorus of, "Oh, the big red letters stand for the Jell-O family!" at the start of weekly installments of NBC Radio's *The Aldrich Family* for a dozen years (1939 to 1951), it's likely still with you. Jell-O was a big radio commodity back then. When Jack Benny was sponsored by those "six delicious flavors—strawberry, raspberry, cherry, orange, lemon and lime" (1934 to 1942), the comedian came on the air each week with the greeting: "Jell-O again!" As Jimmy Durante incessantly allowed, "Everybody wants to get into the act!"

Commercial

Hugh James (1915–2001) was gifted with one of the most distinctive voices among network announcers. His basal tones eloquently enunciated many a sponsor's message in the glory days. Not only did he introduce the arias and artists every Monday night for a tiremaker, eventually including the live simulcast (radio-TV) on *The Voice of Firestone*, he won many more auditions. James became something of a commercial spokesman for General Foods Corporation, introducing soap operas on its behalf for years at noon (*Wendy Warren and the News*), 2 o'clock (*The Second Mrs. Burton*) and 5 o'clock (*When a Girl Marries*) weekday afternoons. During the same era, he worked for Procter & Gamble narrating *The Right to Happiness* at 3:45. A right busy fellow, Hugh James!

On occasion, to avoid an on-air conflict between sponsors proffering the same types of wares, an announcer or actor altered his name on one or more series to remain employed. Hugh James applied that premise while he was the interlocutor for *Wendy Warren and the News*. He was referred to as Bill Flood there although anyone routinely hearing him on his other radio commitments could easily figure it out. Here's a typical commercial from the midday *Warren* aircast of April 15, 1949.

Bill Flood: You know we Americans take a special interest in success stories. Yes, we like to know the *hows* and *whys* of any special achievement ... so, let's take a look at the outstanding success of Maxwell House, the coffee that's *bought* and *enjoyed* by more people than any other brand in the world. What accounts for the tremendous popularity of Maxwell House? Famous "good to the last drop" flavor tells *this* success story, a *superb* flavor that results from the careful selection of premium highland-grown coffees from Latin America ... *fine* coffees chosen for their mellowness, richness, vigor and *full* body. Then these fine coffees are blended with *masterful* skills ... and *radiant* roasting, a process developed *by* Maxwell House brings out the *full* flavor perfection of every bean. Finally, there's vacuum packing to bring you Maxwell House that is *always* fresh, not just days fresh but *roaster* fresh. Yet with *all* these *extra* dividends in flavor, Maxwell House costs you but a fraction of a penny more per cup than the lowest priced coffees sold. So today when you're shopping, ask for Maxwell House. Pay your family and guests the compliment of serving coffee that's *always* "good to the last drop!"

General Mills, Inc.

History

It began as "Washburn's Folly." People sneered, snickered and some even laughed right out loud as Cadwallader Colden Washburn (1818 to 1882) completed his first grain refinery on the banks of the Mississippi River. In 1866, he situated it near the Falls of St. Anthony, not far outside the borders of Minneapolis, Minnesota. In the meantime, onlookers were absolutely convinced that the demand for flour from Midwestern spring wheat could never grow to match the projected capability of an enterprise so large. A visionary Washburn persevered, nevertheless; and while he lived only long enough to see the skimpy formation of his hypothesis beginning to seriously take shape, he realized enough from it to know he had proven the skeptics wrong.

What he began there would eventually turn into what is now acknowledged as the world's fifth largest food-processing enterprise. Furthermore, it is the third such largest firm in America, and also the largest cereal manufacturer in the United States.[1] The resulting conglomerate ranked fifty-third on a list of global advertisers by expenditures in a recent year while proffering more than 100 trademarked brands of pre-packaged goods, most of them baking supplies and edibles. In fiscal 2006, the operation Washburn launched earned revenues of $11.6 billion while generating a net income of $1.09 billion from the contributions of more than 28,000 employees. With these numbers available, in hindsight, to intimate that Cadwallader C. Washburn was out of touch with reality was a bit of a stretch.

For a decade, beginning in 1856, Washburn — a future Wisconsin governor (1872 to 1874) — acting under his corporate designate, the Minneapolis Milling Company, gained control of and leased the power rights to the water flowing over the St. Anthony Falls to nearby mill operators.[2] In 1866, the entrepreneur built his own incredibly large mill (officially dubbed the Washburn "B" Mill), fully persuaded that he could turn a profit there. Not only was he able to do so, but eight years hence, he also erected a second, still larger Washburn "A" Mill not very distant.

One of Washburn's local competitors in the flour milling business was Charles A. Pillsbury.[3] Seeing some advantages for both of them, in 1869 the two investors jointly formed the Minneapolis Millers Association. One of their purposes was to seek methods of turning Midwestern winter wheat into improved grades of flour. With the assistance of a French engineer, Washburn not only discovered a means to do so but eventually began manufacturing and distributing what one source cited as "the best flour available in the United States." After Pillsbury adopted Washburn's technique, Minneapolis unofficially became the center of the nation's flour-milling commerce. According to local historians, Minneapolis dominated the globe in flour production from 1882 to 1930. And while Pillsbury impacts Washburn's operation only marginally at this juncture in the nineteenth century, the firm itself will return to the account and have a profound effect on it in the twenty-first century. In due course, the legacies left by the founders of both wheat-processing endeavors will be significantly affected by one another.

Three years after the Washburn "A" Mill was established, in 1877, C. C. Washburn formed a partnership with businessman-investor John Crosby. The original venture's sobriquet was altered to the Washburn Crosby Company, a name under which it was to operate for a half-century. In 1878, the Minneapolis Millers Association was reorganized to appease the farmers who felt its practices were unfair to them. That same year the "A" mill was demolished, resulting from a tragic internal explosion. The lives of 17 employees were lost while several adjacent facilities were also destroyed. The structure was rebuilt and enlarged, however, and the firm continued production on that site for nearly nine decades.

Participating in the first International Millers' Exhibition held at Cincinnati, Ohio, in 1880, Washburn Crosby went home with signal honors. The firm's entries were judged winners of the event's bronze, silver and gold citations for third, second and best flours submitted. Not long afterward, the company altered the nomenclature of its first-place flour, marketing it as Gold Medal, a designation that persists to the modern era.

Parenthetically, in a 1922 expansion move, Washburn Crosby purchased the Star & Crescent Milling Company flour mill in south Chicago. Enlarging still further, in August 1923 Washburn Crosby opened a newly constructed seven-story cereal mill near the Star & Crescent facility. Together, they constituted the newly named Gold Medal Products Company. Another subsidiary, Star Grain Company, debuted that same year in south Chicago, too, storing wheat and supplying grain for the Chicago milling operations. The trio of plants continued in production until May 1, 1995, when they were finally shuttered.

Washburn died in 1882. Seven years later James S. Bell ascended to the presidency of the firm (1889), having persevered past Washburn's heirs. It was to be Bell's son, however — James Ford Bell — and James S. Bell's successor, who was to facilitate and preside over the most extensive increase in the enterprise yet. We'll get to that matter momentarily. But first....

In the early 1920s, Washburn Crosby came to the rescue of a failing Twin Cities radio outlet that was clearly on the ropes. Whether the Bells viewed it as a mere novelty (as most radio was perceived in those early days), whether they were simply compassionate fellows, whether they saw some grandiose potential for the company they represented by being on the ground floor of a budding industry, or perhaps for some other reason, or possibly all of the above — those visionaries (if they may be supposed as such) bought the faulty station outright. Altering its call letters to WCCO (for Washburn Crosby Company), they began broadcasting as a sideline venture. And thereby hangs a tale that is clearly intertwined with their core business.

At about the same time, in 1921 the moniker Betty Crocker was selected as a pen name for the company to use in responding to cooking-related inquiries from patrons who bought and utilized Washburn Crosby's expanding lines of culinary wares. Of course, as we know now, the advertising icon Betty Crocker that developed as that mythical, yet knowledgeable authority was appreciably enhanced over time. In due course, the nomenclature became one of the most recognizable imprints on packaging to occupy grocers' shelves.

The notoriety associated with the appellation extended with the company's purchase of the little Minneapolis radio station that was about to go off the air. In 1924, the *Betty Crocker Cooking School of the Air* premiered over WCCO, a feature that was to have enveloping impact on the national airwaves in the decades ahead. It's believed that an unidentified Betty Bucholz may have been the first actress (for that's what she was) to speak for the company as its original advertising mascot. We know that when Washburn Crosby broadened its promotion to encompass network radio as that form debuted in 1926 Bucholz was the lady playing the role of the well-rehearsed chef-in-residence, Betty Crocker.[4] Her audio series extended to late 1953, airing multiple times per week, intermittently over NBC and CBS. It was a fabulous method of creating customers: simply name the program and the imposing figure presiding over it for some of the products being pitched, have her tell how to use them and wait for the cash register to ring (the lapse wasn't very long).

While on the subject of Betty Crocker, CBS and later NBC Radio featured a daily women's series headlined by and named for Adelaide Hawley (1905 to 1998) that aired from 1939 to 1946. Her feature was sponsored by various underwriters, some in direct competition with Betty Crocker. As television arrived, Crocker expounded on her goods through live and filmed commercials in which she demonstrated her proficiency in the kitchen with her sponsor's wares. Hawley was tapped as the physical incarnation of the mystery woman whose appearances had heretofore been limited almost altogether to package illustrations, magazine advertising, billboards, newspapers and product literature. From 1949 until she was dropped in 1964 for an updated, more sophisticated replacement, Hawley reveled as Betty Crocker.

When she was no longer needed there, she returned to school; at 62 in 1967, she graduated from New York University with a doctorate in speech communications. So stupendous was Hawley's run as Betty Crocker, however, that — in the 1950s — she was proclaimed the nation's "second most recognizable woman, next to Eleanor Roosevelt." A TV critic cited her as "the most famous woman created through advertising in the twentieth century." Hawley taught English to international students until a few days before her death at 93.

A series of printed guides known as the *Betty Crocker Cookbook*, introduced in the postwar era of the 1940s, became widely acclaimed among gourmet cooks — and those that aspired to be — everywhere. And all of this Crocker business took off after the Washburn Crosby Company bought a little hometown radio station in dire financial straits. It was an early indication of the value that present and future leadership was to maintain on marketing the firm's wares, increasingly doing so on the ether as the years progressed.

In addition to those humble beginnings with Betty Crocker, 1924 was to be a defining year for yet another weighty Washburn Crosby product development, this one initiated literally by accident. A Minneapolis health clinician spilled some bran gruel on a hot stove one day. The mixture crackled and sizzled into a crisp wheat flake that was incredibly palate pleasing. The clinician took a few samples to George Cormack, the head miller at Washburn Crosby Company. An idea for a whole-grain cereal was born using the tasty flakes as its nucleus.

Cormack perfected a process to mass produce the flakes. By November 1924, Gold Medal Whole Wheat Flakes, a new ready-to-eat cereal, was headed for market. Meanwhile, a contest was conducted among Washburn Crosby insiders to alter the cumbersome label initially assigned to the commodity. A company executive's spouse, Jane Bausman, won the competition for her submission of *Wheaties*. The brand was to become one of the most powerful sellers in the organization's bulging portfolio.

Of course, Wheaties' association with the sports world, and particularly baseball, is widely proclaimed. That link was inaugurated less than a decade later, in 1933, when an advertising sign was installed on the left field wall at Nicollet Park in south Minneapolis. A broadcast deal between the manufacturer and the minor league Minneapolis Millers to air games over its radio station, WCCO, included the large signboard. Wheaties adapted it to its use, introducing its new catchphrase there.

Knox Reeves, head of the Minneapolis-based advertising agency bearing his name, was asked what to print on the signboard for his client. Taking out a pad and pencil, he sketched a Wheaties package, thought momentarily, and scribbled "Wheaties — The Breakfast of Champions" alongside it.[5] From that modest start, Wheaties' storied sports heritage with its familiar motto has embraced many of the great athletes of all time with scores of those personalities gracing the fronts of Wheaties boxes. Radio broadcasts of baseball games sponsored by Wheaties are far too numerous to count. The product rivals beer in its adherence to sportscasting promotions. The cereal underwrote the very first commercial sportscast on television. It was a baseball match-up between the Brooklyn Dodgers and the Cincinnati Reds on August 29, 1939, with the play-by-play provided by Red Barber over a fledgling NBC-TV.

By the late 1920s, James Ford Bell (1879 to 1961) was president of the Washburn Crosby Company. There were 5,800 employees in 1928 and annual sales reached $123 million that year. Washburn Crosby's three best sellers were Gold Medal flour (established in 1880), Softasilk cake flour (introduced in 1923) and Wheaties (in 1924). While the horizon looked promising, the competition looked formidable. Bell, by nature an entrepreneur, seized upon the opportunity to consolidate Washburn Crosby's operations with those of its leading competitors. More than any other individual, he was instrumental in combining 27 such firms, often signing one mill at a time. On June 24, 1928, a consortium known from then on as General Mills, Inc., was created. The assemblage was comprised of all the mills constructed or purchased by Washburn Crosby since 1866 plus the Red Star Milling Company of Kansas and three Montana firms: Kalispell Flour Mills Company, Rocky Mountain Elevator Company and Royal Milling Company.

As a part of General Mills, these operations maintained their separateness while assigning product development and advertising to company headquarters. The consolidation was well timed, meanwhile, providing strength to survive and even prosper through the Great Depression, when earnings grew steadily and stock in the outfit was stable. In 1931, General Mills introduced the first baking mix, Bisquick; it was followed in 1937 with its first ready-to-eat puffed cereal, Kix; and, in 1941, yet another ready-to-eat cereal, Cheerioats and renamed Cheerios in 1946, arrived, eventually becoming the number one selling cereal in America. Betty Crocker cake mixes premiered in 1947 and the presweetened cereal Trix followed in 1954. Hamburger Helper didn't come along until 1970 and Pop Secret microwave popcorn not until 1985. Other strategic developments or acquisitions included Fruit Roll-Ups fruit-flavored snacks, Chex cereals and Chex Mix snacks, Nature Valley granola bars, Bugles corn snacks, Yoplait and Go-GURT and Colombo yogurts, Nouriche smoothies, Progresso soups, Old El Paso Mexican foods, and Cascadian Farm and Muir Glen organic foods.

During the Second World War, the firm's factories were realigned to produce vital machinery for the U.S. Navy, plus medicinal alcohol, containers for sandbag usage and dehydrated foods. An animal feed industry that had developed following the First World War was turned into a permanent chemical division. In 1958, Charles H. Bell — yet another in the line of famous Bells who ran General Mills and its chief predecessor moved the headquarters of the operation from downtown Minneapolis to suburban Golden Valley, Minnesota, where it remains today.

Pillsbury was one of chain radio's active flour millers. It bought quarter-hour segments in daytime features aimed at milady tuning in to Art Linkletter's *House Party*. As producer John Guedel (left) approves, the lady — selected from the studio audience — warbles with singer Vic Damone (facing her) as Linkletter studies his script. He's awaiting the next Pillsbury commercial. When Pillsbury merged with its old rival General Mills in 2001, it was just enough to push it ahead of Kellogg, reportedly becoming first for the first time in cereal sales.

By the early 1960s, General Mills was into food service products for restaurants and hotels. Numerous acquisitions followed. It entered the domain of snack foods by purchasing Morton Foods, Inc., in 1964; added the Tom Huston Peanut Company two years hence; and began buying snack food companies overseas in 1968 in England, Belgium, France, Latin America and Japan. Other noteworthy acquisitions included Gorton's, a frozen fish company (dispensed with in 1995), plus an aggressive push into the toy and game industry, buying Rainbow Crafts (Play-Doh), Kenner and Parker Brothers, all in 1968. With $482.3 million in sales of toys internationally by 1978, a third of General Mills' revenues, playtime was providing a very good time for the parent corporation.

Although General Mills missed the growth of fast food chains, it launched its own restaurant division in 1970 with the purchase of five existing Red Lobster restaurants. By the time it divested them in 1995, that chain had gone nationwide with no fewer than 657 restaurants. The restaurant group was, for awhile, General Mills' second largest division, particularly after it launched the Olive Garden Italian chain in 1983. By the 1995 divestiture, there were at least 429 Olive Gardens in operation. The firm also owned nine China Coast Restaurant units in three American cities — Fort Worth, Indianapolis and Orlando — which it also dispensed with.

The multinational conglomerate made the first of many buys in clothing manufacturers and distributors in 1969 when it acquired David Crystal, Inc. (Izod Lacoste), followed by Monet Jewelry the same year (introducing General Mills to specialty retailing); then it added Eddie Bauer, Inc., in 1971 and Talbot's two years beyond. There were many more similar purchases. Yet, by 1985, the world's largest toymaker divested everything in its portfolio that represented more than 25 percent of its sales, including toys, fashion and non-apparel retailing. Retained were a furniture group (Kittinger, Pennsylvania House) and Eddie Bauer and Talbot's. All were divested at last in 1989 when General Mills left retailing altogether.

Also in 1989 the firm began tenacious efforts to expand internationally, a sector that archrival Kellogg had exploited for decades. Together with the Swiss-based food products giant Nestlé S.A., General Mills formed Cereal Partners Worldwide, intending to reduce Kellogg's stranglehold on the European cereal market. As the partnership advanced, Mexico was added to those efforts in 1991. The following year, with PepsiCo, Inc., a North American-based competitor, General Mills formed a second partnership, Snack Ventures Europe, intending to gain greater market share in snack foods on the continent.

By 1999, General Mills was running neck and neck with Kellogg in the U.S. cereal sector, claiming 31.6 percent of sales to Kellogg's 31.7 percent. Do you remember the operation bearing the surname of Charles A. Pillsbury at about the time Cadwallader Washburn was launching his first mill? The two formed a professional relationship, Minneapolis Millers Association, in 1869. The Pillsbury Company was founded that year in Minneapolis and eventually became one of the best-known monikers in American food retailing. It, too, had an icon like Betty Crocker: Ann Pillsbury.[6] Two more of its mascots are widely recognized — the Pillsbury Doughboy and the Jolly Green Giant. Among its most famous brands are Häagen-Dasz premium ice creams and Totino's frozen pizza and snacks.

One of the firms's better remembered byproducts, the Pillsbury Bake-Off Contest — producing prize-winning recipes that have become national classics — originated in 1949. That year Pillsbury Mills, Inc., held a Grand National Recipe and Baking Contest to mark its eightieth birthday. Subsequent events stirred imaginative culinary efforts and received phenomenal recognition in the media, supplying gargantuan public relations infusion.

Whatever happened to the Pillsbury Company, one of General Mills' chief rivals through the years? In 1989, Pillsbury was purchased by London-based Grand Metropolitan plc which altered the parent firm's sobriquet to Diageo plc in 1997. But three years hence, still poised to overtake its major archrival Kellogg, General Mills learned of an opportunity to buy its old competitor, Pillsbury. In doing so in 2001, it instantly surpassed Kellogg as the nation's foremost cereal-maker, a goal it had never previously realized.

Late in 2004, General Mills transitioned its entire breakfast cereal line (known as Big G cereals) into whole grains. The health of consumers was to be positively impacted, said a scientific study. General Mills' principal competitors today include Groupe Danone, Kellogg Company and Kraft, Inc.

Radio Series

Betty Crocker, with Betty Bucholz—1926 to 1953, NBC, CBS (Betty Crocker)
The National Home Hour—1928 to 1930, NBC (Betty Crocker, Gold Medal, Softasilk, Wheaties)
The Wheaties Quartet—1929 to 1930, CBS (Wheaties)
Gold Medal Fast Freight—1929 to 1932, CBS (Gold Medal, Wheaties)
Gold Medal Express, with Vic Arden and Phil Ohman—1931 to 1932, NBC Blue (Gold Medal)
Skippy, with Franklin Adams, Jr.—1932 to 1933, NBC, CBS (Wheaties)
Paul Wing, the Story Man—1932 to 1933, NBC (Post Toasties)
Betty and Bob—1932 to 1940, NBC Blue, CBS, NBC, Syndicated (Bisquick, Gold Medal)
Jack Armstrong, the All-American Boy, aka *Armstrong of the SBI*—1933 to 1951, CBS, NBC, MBS, NBC Blue, Blue, ABC (Wheaties)
Hymns of All Churches, with Joe Emerson—1936 to 1947, CBS, NBC, ABC (Betty Crocker, Bisquick, Gold Medal, Kix, Softasilk, Wheaties)
Love Song—1936 to 1937, MBS (Gold Medal)
Modern Cinderella—1936 to 1937, CBS (Gold Medal)
Who's Who in the News, with John R. Watkins—1936 to 1937, CBS (General Mills)
Hollywood News—1937 to 1938, CBS (Betty Crocker, Bisquick, Gold Medal, Softasilk)
Curtain Time—1938 to 1939, MBS (Kix)
Arnold Grimm's Daughter—1937 to 1942, CBS, NBC (Softasilk, Kix)
Those Happy Gilmans, with Bill Bouchey—1938 to 1939, NBC, NBC Blue (Kix)
Valiant Lady—1938 to 1946, CBS, NBC (Bisquick, Cherrioats, Gold Medal, Wheaties)
The Grouch Club, with Jack Lescoulie—1939 to 1940, NBC (Kix)
Billy and Betty, with Jimmy McCallion and Audrey Egan—1938, 1939 to 1940, NBC, CBS (Wheaties, Kix)
Caroline's Golden Store—1939 to 1940, NBC, CBS (General Mills)
By Kathleen Norris—1939 to 1941, CBS (Wheaties)
Beyond These Valleys—1940, CBS (General Mills)
Beat the Band, with Ted Weems and His Orchestra—1940 to 1941, NBC (Kix)
The Light of the World, with Bret Morrison—1940 to 1950, NBC, CBS (Bisquick, Gold Medal, Softasilk)
The Mystery Man—1941 to 1942, NBC (Betty Crocker, Wheaties)
Stories America Loves—1941 to 1942, CBS (Wheaties)
Harvey and Dell, aka *Thus We Live*—1942, CBS (General Mills)
Lonely Women—1942 to 1943, NBC (General Mills)
The Lone Ranger—1942 to 1956, ABC, NBC (Cheerioats/Cheerios)

The Guiding Light—1942 to 1946, NBC (Bisquick, Cheerioats, Gold Medal, Softasilk, Wheaties)
Kitty Foyle—1942 to 1944, CBS (General Mills)
Joyce Jordan, M.D.—1942 to 1945, CBS (General Mills)
John Gunther, News and Comment—1943 to 1944, NBC Blue (General Mills)
Melodies of Home, with Burl Ives—1943 to 1944, CBS (General Mills)
This Life is Mine—ca. 1943 to ca. 1945, CBS (General Mills)
Today's Children—1943 to 1950, NBC (Betty Crocker, Bisquick, Gold Medal)
Woman in White—1944 to 1948, NBC (Betty Crocker)
Masquerade—1946 to 1947, NBC (General Mills)
Famous Jury Trials, with Maurice Franklin—1947 to 1948, ABC (General Mills)
The Green Hornet—1948, ABC (Cheerios, Kix, Wheaties)
The Story of Holly Sloan—1947 to 1948, NBC (General Mills)
Nightbeat, with Frank Lovejoy—1950, NBC (Betty Crocker, Wheaties)
Dangerous Assignment, with Brian Donlevy—1950, NBC (Betty Crocker)
Live Like a Millionaire, with Jack McCoy—1950 to 1952, NBC (General Mills)
The Silver Eagle, with Jim Ameche—1951 to 1953, 1954 to 1955, ABC (General Mills)
Joe Emerson's Hymn Time—1951 to 1954, ABC (General Mills)
Whispering Streets—1952 to 1954, ABC (General Mills)
Movie Quiz—1952 to 1953, MBS (General Mills)
The Bill Ring Trio—1952 to 1954, ABC (General Mills)
The Falcon—1953 to 1954, MBS (multiple participation)
The Crime Files of Flamond, with Everett Clarke—1953, MBS (General Mills)
General Mills Radio Adventure Theater, with Tom Bosley—1977, CBS (General Mills)

Exposition

Prolific drama mama Irna Phillips (1901 to 1973)—whose inexhaustible mental and physical agility allowed her to impact radio and television soap operas pervasively, establishing a repertoire of nearly a score of narratives—was behind an innovative daytime programming exercise that focused on General Mills. The powerful wordsmith, who penned the first matinee serial in 1930, was instrumental in lining up three of her episodic sagas—*The Guiding Light*, *Today's Children* and *Woman in White*—in back-to-back quarter-hours on NBC Radio in 1943. Because each washboard weeper, plus a fourth produced by Frank and Anne Hummert—*The Light of the World*, based on biblical accounts—was underwritten by General Mills between two and three o'clock Eastern Time on weekday afternoons, the experiment was dubbed *The Gold Medal Hour*. Perhaps because that nomenclature locked in what could be advertised, the appellation was soon altered to a broader *The General Mills Hour*. That expanded the commercials to such wares as Betty Crocker, Bisquick, Cheerios, Kix, Softasilk, Wheaties and other labels.

To add to the cohesion of *her* 45-minute timeframe, Irna Phillips went a few steps further. Ever the innovator, she picked a single voice—actor Ed Prentiss, who portrayed a major character (Ned Holden) in *The Guiding Light*—as the announcer for all three serials under her auspices. To further signal unification, she ran those three quarter-hour dramas in odd lengths: one might fill 12 minutes one day, another 19 minutes and the third 14 minutes. Going a step farther—in a test that would be repeated several times in other broadcasting ventures but would never work again quite as well — Phillips inserted a "crossover effect." Her figures moved freely back-and-forth between the trilogy of serials. Dr. Jonathan McNeill, for instance, a character in *The Guiding Light*, wandered through *Woman in White*'s Municipal Hospital while visiting some of his patients. Later, he consulted with Dr. Paul Burton on *Today's Children* about another case involving both medics. All the while, commercials for sundry General Mills kitchen commodities were pitched at odd times between stretches of dialogue. While the stories may have sounded familiar, the format was totally different from anything else — and definitely not your mother's soap opera!

Aside from Procter & Gamble, General Mills invested more interest in daytime dramas than any other firm, incidentally. The food manufacturer underwrote more than a score of them. General Mills left other impressions from its audio gigs: a trio of its series manifested religious themes (*Hymns of All Churches, The Light of the World, Joe Emerson's Hymn Time*). The fact that collectively they aired for two dozen years indicates a strong commitment to such fare, possibly the most unshakable devotion for a commercial firm in broadcast history before or since.

And while General Mills proffered more than 50 aural series — a host of which weren't sponsored by the food processor after a few months — by the same token, its list of enduring shows is notable. Features aired by General Mills for five years or longer included *Betty Crocker* (27), *Jack Armstrong* (18), *The Lone Ranger* (14), *Hymns of All Churches* (11), *The Light of the World* (10), *Betty and Bob* (8), *Valiant Lady* (8), *Today's Children* (7) and *Arnold Grimm's Daughter* (5). That's 108 years of broadcasting just nine series — a dozen years each — and superior to the typical record of most firms underwriting that many shows.

Commercial

In addition to the narrator-announcer many dramas provided for their radio series, early network sponsors offered a separate voice as a commercial spokesman. This is demonstrated by Art Millet on a May 16, 1939, broadcast of *Valiant Lady*. The commercial copy would never pass muster today, regrettably: while the sales message might have been compelling then, today's sophisticated audiences and the reason given for making the purchase would hardly be considered by the modern homemaker (who wouldn't be hearing it anyway — she'd be at work). Notice the repetition here; three sentences begin with *Well* (ho-hum) and four more start with *Now* (pointless). But perhaps then, with little vying for milady's listenership elsewhere, it worked.

ART MILLET: You know, when a man's working in an office or almost anywhere else, he can't stop and get himself a bite to eat about eleven in the morning if he feels empty and sort of run-down all of a sudden. Probably you've heard your husband say he needs a breakfast that will stay by. Well that's certainly important, because no man wants to be caught at a disadvantage when the big boss or an important client shows up an hour or so before lunch. Well, if it's a full morning supply of nourishment you want your husband to get, I'm recommending a big bowlful of Wheaties ... with milk or cream, of course, and some fruit. *There's* a breakfast that will do a *real* job of helping to see your husband through until lunch time. Now it may be that you're thinking that cereal flakes might not be so very substantial. Well, of course, it's not the *form* of a food that counts for nourishment. It's the food itself. And Wheaties are whole wheat, which speaks *volumes* for food value. Those crisp, crunchy Wheaties flakes are whole wheat with a bang-up supply of good, honest food energy. Now that, as you know, is the fuel that any man or grownup or child burns up as he works or plays. Now you know the other ingredients that are provided by whole wheat ... good proteins, also the minerals, phosphorous and iron and vitamin B. All this kind of valuable nourishment ... comes in Wheaties. Now perhaps your husband has been complaining about that "eleven o'clock slump." Well, do try giving him Wheaties. They're extra nourishing, and I'm sure he'll enjoy the crisp, refreshing quality of these golden brown toasted flakes. Wheaties taste something grand! You'll like Wheaties yourself. And oh, will that youngster of yours! So, why don't you ask your grocer for a package or two of Wheaties ... today?

General Motors Company

History

The earliest detectable traces of the behemoth that was to become General Motors can be found as far back as 1892. That year Ransom E. Olds withdrew his life's savings and put it into transforming his dad's naval and industrial engine factory into one that could build horseless carriages. Despite the outcome, Olds didn't meet with overnight success. It took him three years to move from simple experiments to realities. In 1895, he produced a four-seat model with five horsepower that could travel a distance of 18.6 miles an hour.

The resulting Olds Motor Vehicle Company, Inc., which he organized in 1897 with capital of $50,000—including 5,000 shares of stock at $10 per share—was one of the first identifiable trademarks to be fused into the multiple-brand General Motors shortly after the start of the twentieth century. Olds' first real car, in 1897, was a luxury prototype priced at $1,200. Learning from it, Olds subsequently produced a scaled-down version of his Oldsmobile (the trademark nomenclature applied) for $650.

In 1899, on Detroit's Jefferson Avenue East, Olds built the first U.S. facility fashioned solely for designing and producing gas-powered automobiles. By 1900, he had made and sold at least 1,400 vehicles, a number that zoomed to 4,000 replicas annually within only a couple of years.

In the meantime, many other innovators were at work in and around Detroit in similar pursuits. Multiple entrepreneurs attempted to bring out gas-powered buggies of their own, some seeking to transcend Olds' success. Among them was Henry M. Leland, who labored as a protégé under Ransom Olds' tutelage before opening a precision automotive component manufacturing plant. Later, in 1902, he established the Cadillac Automobile Company.

The initial Cadillac, prominent by its opulence, was available that same year. Within a year, Leland set a new trend by banishing the boat-like tiller used to guide the car with an easier-to-use steering wheel. Others adopted his lead. Setting the pace for rivals, Cadillac, in 1910, became the first U.S. car manufacturer offering closed bodies as standard fare. That revolutionized motoring convenience and provided all-weather comfort and cleanliness.

Another of the early capitalists who met with success was David Dunbar Buick, who incorporated a car-manufacturing facility to which he gave his surname in Detroit in May 1903. Buick Motor Company transferred operations to Flint, Michigan, that September.

With so many manufacturers competing against one another at that juncture—augmented by depressing market instability—the weaker firms vanished while the remainder tended to combine. An enterprising director of the fledgling Buick Motor Company, William Crapo "Billy" Durant (1861 to 1947)—co-founder of the Durant-Dort Carriage Company of Coldwater, Michigan, a self-made millionaire and grandson of a Michigan governor (H. H. Crapo, 1865 to 1869)—saw an opportunity to capitalize on circumstances. His grasp was possibly exceeded only by his own ego, in fact. His obituary appearing in *The New York Times* nearly four decades hence allowed: "Mr. Durant envisioned control of the entire motor car business of the United States." To state simply that he was ambitious would be underestimating his intents. He was an astute businessman as well. According to another source, "Durant believed that the only way for the automobile companies to operate at a profit was to avoid the duplication that occurred when many firms manufactured the same product."

With that shrewd acumen, he was able to corral several automotive ventures exhibiting promise into a consortium that he headed. Taking control of Buick on November 1, 1904, Durant was subsequently instrumental in establishing General Motors (GM) Company on September 16, 1908. To it he added Oldsmobile as his next quarry on November 12, 1908.

He acquired half-interest in the Oakland Motor Car Company on January 20, 1909, which was established at Pontiac, Michigan, by Edward M. Murphy in 1907. When Murphy died a half-year later, GM suddenly controlled all of it. The Oakland nomenclature was replaced with Pontiac in 1932. By July 29, 1909, GM was also overseeing Cadillac, although founder Henry Leland and his son Wilfred continued operating Cadillac until they left GM to form Lincoln Motor Company in 1917.

The public's take on all of this maneuvering, newspapers reported, was to label it "Durant's Folly."[1] Not one to be dissuaded easily, nonetheless, the entrepreneur pressed on in his quest to build an empire. He faced a major setback in 1909, however, when some prosperous pals who had helped him with loans and investments to get where he was absolutely refused to put up another $8 million in capital so he could buy out Henry Ford. Ford, a major competitor, wanted $2 million up front with the rest over time. Durant's extravagant designs, for once, were thwarted. It wouldn't be the last time.

He was still able to add several other members to the GM collective, a fact that is long forgotten by all but the most avid automobile historians. Prominent among them were Cartercart, Elmore, Ewing, Marquette, Northway, Rainer, Randolph, Scripps-Booth, Sheridan, Welch and Welch-Detroit cars. GM also bought Rapid Motor Vehicle Company of Pontiac, Michigan, and Reliance Motor Truck Company of Owosso, Michigan. Out of the latter two emerged the GMC Truck Division. By 1920, GM integrated more than 30 competitors into its burgeoning conglomerate by some type of affiliation, usually involving the purchase of whole companies although sometimes only portions of their stock.

Long before this, however, William Durant's seemingly insatiable appetite for expansion and acquisition plus other costly moves put General Motors on extremely shaky financial footing. In exchange for some loans to avoid total collapse, in 1910, Durant was removed from GM management by the firm's bankers. At the time, GM's acquisitions had pushed its indebtedness to a million dollars, significant by 1910 standards.

Parenthetically but quite related, Chevrolet Motor Company of Michigan was incorporated in Detroit in November 1911 by a trio of investors: Edson Campbell, William Durant's son-in-law; Louis Chevrolet, French racing car enthusiast; and William Little. The 1910 census revealed, incidentally, that Durant had divorced his second wife, whom he married in 1908, and was living at the residence of his daughter Margery and her husband, Edson Campbell, along with their two children.[2] By September 13, 1915, Durant himself—who had been putting together still more auto firms after leaving GM—formed a holding outfit, Chevrolet Motor Company of Delaware, that included the original Chevrolet venture.

During all of this time, he had been acquiring more stock in GM, having retained that which he owned when he was running the company. By November 16, 1915, he owned enough to land a position of strength among the stockholders. In a short while, he announced that Chevrolet owned 54.5 percent of GM's outstanding shares, allowing him to wrest the presidency from Charles W. Nash (who occupied that office from 1912 to 1916). For a second time, Durant acceded to the throne.

For a moment, please allow an interruption in the flow surrounding Durant to consider a second GM official of that epoch, Pierre Samuel du Pont (1870 to 1954). He was elected chairman at the same stockholders' meeting of November 16, 1915, during which Durant resurfaced. Du Pont is a fascinating figure in the annals of American enterprise. A descendant of one of the nation's early industrial entrepreneurs, he was born into a U.S. clan emerging from an assiduous French political refugee. A century before, E. I. du Pont de Nemours arrived in America to launch a commercial enterprise in Wilmington, Delaware, that was based on producing chemical powder suitable for explosives for a variety of uses. Around the turn of the century, when the factory he built was about to fall into other hands, an enterprising Pierre du Pont and two cousins—exhibiting the entrepreneurial spirit of their forefather—stepped in. Together, they jointly purchased the business in 1902.

Ultimately, Pierre du Pont succeeded his cousin T. Coleman du Pont in running the operation. The uncanny thing not to be missed is that in 1915—the year in which he was elected chairman of GM in Michigan—he had just assumed the presidency of the firm named for his ancestor in Delaware. Thus, the industrial magnate by heritage and experience became one of the few Americans of his day to run two major organizations, and to do so simultaneously. His presidency at du Pont extended only four years (1915 to 1919), after which he served it as chairman (1919 to 1940) and honorary chairman (1940 to 1954).

Despite the reality that du Pont was GM chairman, nonetheless, it seemed clear to many—figuratively and literally—that William Durant was securely in the driver's seat once more. With du Pont dividing his time between Wilmington and Detroit and two very different commercial pursuits at the same time, upon reflection, this may have worked to Durant's advantage. It certainly could have freed his hand to operate in his earlier autocratic style. Although it doesn't appear in official GM documentation we have read, there is a contemporary Web site hinting—for whatever the reason—that du Pont may have helped Durant return to the company presidency. That is speculative, of course.

A detail most sources have overlooked, nevertheless, clarifies that Durant's return to power was prompted by a hoax. "It was revealed that Mr. Durant had perpetuated an amazing bluff," said *The New York Times*. "The pile of papers he had dumped on the mahogany board table represented only 40 per cent of the stock. His bluff worked." Recall that he had claimed Chevrolet owned 54.5 percent of GM's outstanding shares. Clearly, he was so well entrenched in the job the second time around that—upon the discovery of his ruse—he wasn't removed even for the most obvious reasons.

Not to be overlooked in the firm's political maneuverings, not long afterward (in May 1918) GM purchased the operating assets of Chevrolet Motor Company. Over the long haul, that was to be a far more imposing development for GM than any backstage shenanigans between passionate egos. Construction of the General Motors headquarters, Renaissance Center, in Detroit began in 1919. That same year General Motors Acceptance Corporation was established to finance the sale of GM cars and trucks.

Also in 1919 GM acquired total shares of Frigidaire Corporation, another buy strongly influenced by William Durant. He had sunk personal funds into Guardian Frigerator [sic] Company, Frigidaire's predecessor sobriquet, the previous year. Guardian was attempting to produce a relatively new product at the time, an electric ice box. Frigidaire was to remain an important commodity in the GM portfolio until it was spun off late in the century.

It now seems clear that — by whatever methods he employed to reacquire the company's presidency in 1915 — William Durant's second departure from the GM throne in 1920 came *with* the sanction of Pierre S. du Pont. The industrial tycoon was still chairman of the board. Stockholders were angry. A postwar depression sent GM stock tumbling from a high of $400 to $12 per share. Durant cast $12 million of a personal fortune into the mix to shore up the decline but it was still not enough to save his job. Somebody's head had to roll and once again, it was his.

Du Pont, in fact, was then elected to succeed Durant as president of the powerful American automotive enterprise. A historian, assessing those days, characterized GM as "thrown together by William Durant and held in place by Pierre DuPont." Accordingly, "DuPont's balance of engineers and financial people was designed to prevent the riches-to-ruins swinging caused by Durant's mix of genius and over-reaching." Various du Pont interests would continue to hold "large or controlling share holdings" at GM until the middle of the twentieth century.

And what of Durant? After his second inglorious retreat from GM, he went on to establish Durant Motors four months after his ouster "which very nearly repeated his success with Chevrolet," an observer allowed. Having at one point commanded a fortune worth $120 million, following the stock market crash of 1929, as he filed a petition for bankruptcy in 1936, Durant listed his assets as $250 in clothing (the proverbial clothes on his back) and debts of $814,000. Yet, at the time of Durant's death in 1947 at 85, he was reportedly operating a bowling alley. Ever the dreamer with grandiose plans, he nonetheless expected to establish a nationwide string of bowling alleys. Considering his potential and ambition, his life, so it seemed, was one of rags-to-riches-to-rags.

There were other acquisitions and expansions of considerable magnitude at General Motors. Champion Ignition Company, whose name was later changed to AC Spark Plug, joined GM in 1909. In 1923, GM opened a European assembly plant at Copenhagen, Denmark, under the appellation General Motors International A/S. It was the first of many to be established on overseas soil. It wasn't the first foreign operation set in motion by GM, however: that occurred when McLaughlin Motor Car Company, Ltd., and Chevrolet Motor Company of Canada, Ltd., merged in 1918 to form General Motors of Canada, Ltd.

With its diverse spread across much of U.S. automobile manufacturing, General Motors fostered an internal notion — whether ever expressed publicly — that it led the American car buyer through a series of upwardly mobile steps in making purchases. Creating loyalty with a first vehicle, the basic lower-priced Chevrolet, the idea was to push the buyer along through a maze of progressive steps that led higher. As many consumers presumably gained greater discretionary spending power, they would ascend a rising scale at GM, carrying them from the basic rung through Pontiac, Oldsmobile, Buick and — for some — to Cadillac, the pinnacle of GM production wares. The various GM divisions weren't in the business of competing with one another; instead, they were passing along the consumers who hopefully would always purchase GM vehicles.

The postwar automobile industry, meanwhile, became enamored with the perception of "planned obsolescence" based on a three-year technical and styling innovation cycle. As a result, a basic new body shell was introduced one year and modified in the succeeding two with minimal alterations. The proviso was shared by GM, Ford and Chrysler. But by 1958, the divisional distinctions at GM began to blur as high-performance engines in Chevrolets and Pontiacs emerged. Bringing higher trim models like the Chevrolet Impala and Pontiac Bonneville onto the market that were similarly priced to certain Olds and Buicks baffled customers. When Pontiac, Oldsmobile and Buick introduced correspondingly styled and priced compact models in 1961, the old "step-up" structure between divisions not only eroded but was headed for extinction.

In the 1960s, compact and intermediate classes of cars were developed. By the middle of that decade, most GM vehicles were constructed on common platforms that maintained few differences beyond internal and external trim. In a sense, the mass-produced vehicle became more massive. In the 1980s, GM rebadged a division's successful vehicle into multiple models across other divisions, all positioned close to one another. A new GM model's main competition, in those cases, could be another model spawned from the same platform. This led to market cannibalization with the various GM divisions devoting increasing efforts at stealing sales from one another under the GM umbrella. Traditional GM loyalty among consumers tapered off. Under burgeoning debt, the firm steadily lost ground while Ford, Chrysler and Asian carmakers made hay at GM's expense.

It didn't matter that General Motors had been the longtime leader of the U.S. automotive industry. Going back to 1929 when it took first place from formidable competitor Ford Motor Company, GM was able to hang on to that coveted spot into 2007. By then, Toyota rose up to overtake it as the world's leading car seller. A durable epoch in first place had finally met its match.

Earlier, in 1941, GM accounted for 44 percent of U.S. automobile sales compared with 12 percent in 1921. Production was disrupted from 1942 to 1945 as the company manufactured defense material for the nation valued at $12.3 billion. Non-military work was halted. GM's contribution during the Second World War ran the gamut from minuscule ball bearings to behemoth tanks, naval ships, fighter planes, bombers, guns, cannons and projectiles. During that concentration, the firm turned out 13,000 planes and a fourth of all U.S. aircraft engines. Following the war, it resumed its strategic place in meeting the demands of domestic transportation. The firm continued to grow, selling nearly nine million vehicles in 2004.

Innovators at GM produced the Saturn in 1984 to compete with the growing presence of Japanese automobiles in the United States. In 2000, GM became the sole owner of Saab Automobile AB.

As this is prepared in 2007, General Motors owns some of Fiat, Alfa Romeo, Lancia, Subaru (with Fuji), Isuzu, Suzuki, Maruti and Daewoo-SsangYong. This is in addition to Chevrolet, Corvette (Europe and Japan), Buick, Opel (Vauxhall in the United Kingdom), Holden (Australia and New Zealand), Pontiac, Cadillac, GMC, Saturn, Saab and Hummer. It also owns the Oldsmobile nameplate, one of its first two brands, which was withdrawn from the market in 2004 to the dismay of hordes of proud and apparently loyal owners. GM also sold stakes in Fiat and Fuji Heavy Industries (Subaru) that year as well as a locomotive manufacturing enterprise.

Other prominent GM nameplates of the past include Elmore, LaSalle, Marquette, Oakland and Viking. Surprisingly, only GMC and Saturn among about a score of present trademarks were created by GM. The others were bought or are the result of mergers.

For the first time in more than three decades, Chevrolet brand vehicles outsold domestic competitor Ford brand vehicles in 2005, an indicator that many Americans still appreciate GM craftsmanship. The firm also owns a number of subsidiaries, among them Fisher Body, General Motors Acceptance Corporation, OnStar (a vehicle safety, security and information service) and GM in various nations and geographical regions of the world.

Early in the twenty-first century GM, like its competitor Ford, struggled under the weight of escalating health care and pension cuts for workers. For some relief, the company sought to shed some of its less profitable ventures. While the firm has been losing money and is faced with multiple complex issues, acarplace.com believes GM "*can* be turned around." The Web site theorizes: "The size of the company is such that it could survive for quite a long time on sales of its investments in other companies, not to mention its brands in other nations." After the U.S., GM's largest national markets are presently China, Canada, the United Kingdom and Germany. GM sold more vehicles outside the United States than inside it in 2004.

In fiscal 2006, GM had global revenues of $207,349 billion, earned net income of $529 million and maintained operations employing 327,000 workers. Its principal competitors included AmeriCredit Corporation, Bayerische Motoren Werke AG, Credit Acceptance Corporation, DaimlerChrysler AG, Ford Motor Company, General Electric Capital Corporation, General Electric Company, Honda Motor Company Ltd., Hyundai Motor Company, Mazda Motor Corporation, Mitsubishi Motors Corporation, Nissan Motor Company Ltd., PSA Peugeot Citron S.A., Renault S.A., Suzuki Motor Corporation, Toyota Motor Corporation and Volkswagen AG.

Radio Series

The Champion Spark Plug Hour, with Gus Haenschen and His Orchestra—1926 to 1929, NBC Blue (AC)
General Motors Concerts, aka *General Motors Family Party*, with Nat Shilkret and His Orchestra, Frank Black and His Orchestra, Leopold Stokowski and His Orchestra, Erno Rapee and His Orchestra—1927 to 1931, 1934 to 1937, NBC, NBC Blue (Chevrolet, Oakland-Pontiac, Oldsmobile, Buick, LaSalle, Cadillac, GMC)
Parade of the States—1931 to 1933, NBC, NBC Blue
The Buick Revelers, with James Melton, Olga Albani, Phil Dewey—1931 to 1932, NBC (Buick)
Stoopnagle and Budd, with F. Chase Taylor and Budd Hulick, Andre Kostelanetz and His Orchestra, Jacques Renard and His Orchestra—1932 to 1934, CBS (Pontiac)
Paul Whiteman and His Orchestra—1932 to 1933, NBC Blue, NBC (Pontiac, Buick)
The Oldsmobile Program, with George Olsen, Ethel Shutta, Gus Van, Ruth Etting, Johnny Green—1933, NBC; 1934, CBS (Oldsmobile)
The Chevrolet Program, with Jack Benny—1933 to 1934, NBC (Chevrolet)
The Buick Program, aka *Buick Presents*, with Robert Benchley and Andre Kostelanetz and His Orchestra—1933 to 1934, CBS (Buick)
The Cadillac Symphony Orchestra, with Bruno Walter—1933 to 1935, NBC Blue (Cadillac)
The Pontiac Surprise Party—1934, CBS (Pontiac)
The Pontiac Program, with Jane Froman, Frank Black and His Orchestra—1934 to 1935, NBC (Pontiac)
Isham Jones and His Orchestra, with Tito Guizar—1934 to 1935, CBS (Chevrolet)

The Chevrolet Show, aka *Chevrolet Musical Moments,* with Dave Rubinoff and Hugh Conrad—1935 to 1937, NBC, CBS (Chevrolet)
Oldsmobile Headlines, with Ed Smalle—ca. 1936, network unsubstantiated (Oldsmobile)
Paducah Plantation, aka *Plantation Party,* with Irvin S. Cobb and Whitey Ford—1936 to 1937, NBC (Oldsmobile)
The LaSalle Style Show, with Eddy Duchin and His Orchestra—1936 to 1937, NBC (LaSalle)
The Pontiac Varsity Show, with John Held Jr., Paul Dumont—1937, NBC, NBC Blue (Pontiac)
The NBC Symphony Orchestra, aka *General Motors Symphony of the Air,* with Arturo Toscanini, conducting—1943 to 1946, NBC (Chevrolet, Pontiac, Oldsmobile, Buick, Cadillac, GMC)
John W. Vandercook and the News—1945 to 1946, NBC (Oldsmobile)
Your Land and Mine, with Henry J. Taylor—1945 to 1956, MBS, ABC, NBC
The Mindy Carson Show—1952 to 1953, CBS (Buick)
Café Istanbul, with Marlene Dietrich—1952, ABC (Buick)
The Dinah Shore Show—1953 to 1955, NBC (Chevrolet)
Lowell Thomas and the News—1954 to 1956, CBS (Oldsmobile)
Chevrolet Spotlights the News, with Allan Jackson, Larry Lesueur, Robert Trout—1954-ca. 1958, CBS (Chevrolet)

Exposition

If some imagery may be permitted, General Motors' aural marketing efforts frequently took the high road (translation: highbrow) with programming selections as opposed to other formats. Although it did underwrite comics *Stoopnagle and Budd* and the cornpone humor of "the Duke of Paducah" (Whitey Ford), GM nevertheless put most of its money into refinement and culture. It showed a conspicuous favoritism for classical, semi-classical and pop instrumentalists and vocalists for the bulk of its audio-only ventures gauged by the number of symphonies, orchestras, bands and singers it presented. It even went so far as to name a musical series after each of its major vehicles!

Did that mean that consumers with other tastes couldn't be persuaded to purchase GM products? Certainly not. GM, like competitor Ford—who put great emphasis on its popular *Ford Sunday Evening Hour* which aired for nine seasons and was pleasing to the uppercrust as well as the commoner—seemed to foster an image that was a little beyond average. It worked. Roughly half of GM's offerings were of that persuasion, intimating that it found a formula it was comfortable with and the listeners were, too.

For a half-dozen years (1937 to 1943), GM was noticeably absent from the network airwaves. The Second World War accounted for some of that lapse when GM operations were focused on national defense rather than domestic car-making. Yet it doesn't explain why — with the kind of assets GM controlled and the image-building it was committed to, for present and future years—the firm withdrew entirely from nationwide radio during the heyday of its golden age.

Soon after GM returned to the aural ether, it selected a new course for its leading emphasis: while its programming was more diversified than before, it concentrated most of its radio dollars on a handful of prominent newscasters who kept the names of GM brands before the public daily, nightly, weekly and throughout weekends. Simultaneously, GM was underwriting the first nightly network news program on TV with Douglas Edwards reporting for

Oldsmobile. This news-oriented stress may have been attributable in part to the Second World War and the Korean Conflict which turned many Americans' attention spans outward and to the world of international affairs.

Commercial

The idea of gathering sanction for a product or service from satisfied customers for use in radio advertising wasn't solely limited to the medium's waning days although it was prevalent there. This commercial, aired during a 1935 broadcast of *Chevrolet Musical Moments*, is a typical exhibition in applying the method. At the same time, it demonstrates that not all the vehicles General Motors (and its competitors) were plugging had just rolled from the assembly lines. In a particular acknowledgement to its dealers, GM often included such pitches as this one, especially after the national economic downturn of the Great Depression and in the recovery epoch.

ANNOUNCER: The persistent power of nationwide endorsements is sending 7,000 people every day to buy their used cars from Chevrolet dealers. Listen ... hear what people everywhere are saying about the dependability and value of guaranteed OK'd Used Cars. Chicago ... Bernard S. Weinshenker, past president, Chicago Retail Druggists Association, says....

WEINSHENKER: About a year ago I purchased one of your red tag used automobiles. Up to the present, I haven't spent anything for repairs. I shall be pleased to recommend the quality of your OK'd Used Cars.

ANNOUNCER: New York City ... Harry Mooney, manager, Daniel Reeves Store, says....

MOONEY: I've had perfect satisfaction with the guaranteed OK Used Car purchased from you, and take pleasure in sending my friends to you.

ANNOUNCER: Kansas City, Missouri ... C. B. Beckwith says....

BECKWITH: A year of service without a cent of expense is my record with an OK'd Used Car.

ANNOUNCER: San Francisco, California ... Chester Iverson says....

IVERSON: A few months ago I purchased an OK Used Car. I haven't spent a penny for repairs, and its economy over my previous car has paid me for the car. I wouldn't hesitate in buying another OK Used Car.

ANNOUNCER: Doesn't that sound convincing? Visit your Chevrolet dealer. Take the guaranteed OK way to used car satisfaction and value.

Kellogg Company

History

Shortly after the close of the Civil War, as the reconstruction aftermath of that American bloodbath was about to begin, a small, yet transfixing religious sect—the Seventh-day Adventists—established the Western Health Reform Institute. The church-sponsored agency focused on improving one's lifestyle to achieve optimum wellbeing. It opened September 5, 1866, in the obscure little burg of Battle Creek, Michigan, 112 miles from Detroit and 162 miles from Chicago. Yet its influence was to be powerful, ultimately extending far beyond its corporal confines and the most unimaginable dreams of its founding fathers. Eventually it would perpetuate a legacy that reached global proportions.

The fledgling enterprise favored proper nutrition as a principal means of improving an individual's physical state. In the course of their explorations, the practitioners within its confines intensely focused on grains—members of the grass family—with starchy seeds that were capable of supplying a basic edible ingredient. Surprisingly, those hardy scientists are now identified as the originators of the first modern commercial cereal foods made of wheat, rice, rye, oats, barley, corn and sorghum.

Their product, cereal, was to put Battle Creek on the map, figuratively speaking, a hamlet that previously was hardly recognized by anybody living any distance from it. With but 3,000 inhabitants in 1855, a phenomenal acceleration of the populace occurred over the next half-century. Eventually, more than 40 plants that manufactured cereal augmented the local workforce, steadily infusing it with increased numbers of newcomers to the area. The institute that spawned the revolution not only figured prominently in developing a health foods industry but also became a leading advocate of a movement cultivating vegetarianism while proffering temperance as yet another healthy ideal. The society strongly espoused a diet that eliminated caffeine, meat and alcohol and discarded tobacco from an individual's lifestyle. While the institute was to become, in time, a playground for the very rich—where those who could afford its healthful services found solace of mind and body in a respite removed from the stresses of everyday living—it would also be remembered as the mother of invention.

All of the facility's early practices were preliminary to still more weighty matters that occurred in subsequent decades. A young Battle Creek surgeon, John Harvey Kellogg (1852 to 1943), a Michigan State Normal School alumnus (now Eastern Michigan University) who earned an M.D. degree from New York City's Bellevue Hospital Medical College (1875), was appointed the institute's medical director a year later. By 1877, he saw the healthcare facility's moniker altered to Battle Creek Sanitarium. That sobriquet was soon shortened by many of its clients to a mere "san." According to one source, from the 1880s, the san was considered "the most famous health institution in the country, a reputation it held until World War II."[1]

Dr. John Harvey Kellogg was elevated to the post of superintendent of the Battle Creek Sanitarium. He espoused a mixture of health-related treatments that could easily classify him as an oddball today. A couple will suffice.

Advocating a "squeaky clean intestine," Kellogg made a daily colon clean-out mandatory for every san patient, railing against "too-slow breakdown of food in the intestines and colon. In a matter of seconds, a rapidly-acting enema apparatus forced 15 gallons of water through a recipient's "unfortunate bowel," an assessment allowed. This was followed by a pint of yogurt — half ingested by the patient through the mouth, the other half injected by enema, "thus planting the protective germs where they are most needed and may render most effective service." Convinced that most disease is alleviated by a change in intestinal flora, Kellogg argued that yogurt replaced harmful bacteria residing in the colon.

Another peculiarity associated with John Harvey Kellogg was his relentless and fanatical remonstrations against masturbation, dubbing it "self-abuse" as opposed to more familiar jargon. According to the physician, who performed more than 22,000 surgeries of many types during his career, and penned a volume released in 1888 titled *Treatment for Self-Abuse and Its Effects, Plain Facts for Old and Young*: "Neither the plague, nor war, nor small-pox, nor similar diseases, have produced results so disastrous to humanity as the pernicious habit of onanism [self-gratification]." Such behavior, claimed Kellogg, led to cancer, urinary disease, impotence, epilepsy and insanity among its sundry scourges. To ward off its allure, he recommended circumcision without any anesthetic for boys and pure carbolic acid directed to the clitoris in girls.

Among the famous names that availed themselves of the upscale services of the Battle Creek spa treatment center were C. W. Barron, Sarah Bernhardt, Richard Byrd, Amelia Earhart, Thomas A. Edison, Harvey S. Firestone, Henry Ford, S. S. Kresge, J. C. Penney, Charles W. Post, John D. Rockefeller and William Howard Taft. Its cost was effectively prohibitive for the typical common man.

As the doctor was formulating his principles of healthful living, meanwhile, a younger sibling — Will Keith Kellogg (1860 to 1951) — joined the san's staff. At his start there, Will performed the menial chores of a clerk as he handled stock. A little earlier, in his teens, he had assisted their father as a traveling salesman, representing the patriarch's broom-making endeavor. Demonstrating considerable aptitude, he was later appointed business manager at the san. As a sideline, both brothers tinkered with some of the pioneering concepts at the institution, implementing innovations that were to permanently revolutionize the eating habits of the world. Some historians have additionally credited John Kellogg with originating the electric blanket as well as a menthol nasal inhaler and peanut butter in a diverse line of medical and dietary breakthroughs.

"For years he [Will] assisted his brother [John] in research aimed at improving the vegetarian diet of the San's patients, especially the search for a digestible bread-substitute by the process of boiling wheat," noted one scholar. "They never achieved their basic purpose, but stumbled on a major dividend."

According to lore, after cooking some wheat one day in 1894, the pair was unavoidably detained from their timely culinary pursuits. Returning to the kitchen later, they noticed that the wheat had become stale. They decided to force the tempered grain through a rolling processor which they used anyway. It normally turned their experiments into long sheets of dough. To their amazement, it didn't work out the way they expected that time, however. The wheat berries were flattened and molded into thin flakes. Subsequently baking the flakes, the men discovered a tasty new edible creation. They had no way of knowing then, of course, that they had stumbled onto an entirely new food business, a cold cereal made from coarse cornmeal that was to be adopted by the kitchens of the world. They served it to their clientele and it became an on-the-spot favorite.

In less than a half-dozen years, Will Keith Kellogg — exhibiting an entrepreneurial trait that was to characterize his life — put corn flakes on the market for widespread consumption. Under the appellation Sanitas Food Company, their original mail-order business began operating in 1900. Among the first customers were former patients of the san. Having enjoyed the breakfast food there, they dispatched staggering numbers of requests for the pre-packaged goods following their stays. As word of mouth circulated, the commodity became even more popular. The nomenclature shifted and Battle Creek Toasted Corn Flakes Company was born a half-dozen years after that. It was touted as "the world's first ready-to-eat cereal company."

While his sibling showed little interest, Will managed a burgeoning packaged food venture. Applying economics, marketing skill and possessing a resilient perseverance, he steadily increased production and distribution, relying heavily upon innovative advertising and sales techniques. A few years after going commercial, in 1909, he offered the very first cereal premium, a Funny Jungleland Moving Pictures Booklet, given to anybody buying two packages of the stuff. That promotion continued to 1932, giving rise to the eventual marketing on cereal boxes and the airwaves and in print ads and other sales promotion methods still in use today. The tradition had to begin somewhere; W. K. Kellogg borrowed some of it from successful vendors in other industries and adapted it to his.

Kellogg introduced Rice Krispies cereal to the marketplace in 1929. Its venerated Snap! Crackle! Pop! cartoon models have been familiar characters virtually from the commodity's inception, becoming instantly identifiable figures on product packaging and advertising. Those sound figures were particularly adaptable to radio commercials and arrived just as the new medium was taking off.

It took Will Kellogg three decades from the discovery of corn flakes to expand production to Australia (1924) and another 14 years (1938) to reach England. Latin American and Asian plants were added in the 1950s. Becoming an animated icon in American advertising culture, meanwhile, Tony the Tiger emerged in 1958 as a spokesman for Kellogg's Frosted Flakes ("They're G-r-r-r-r-eat!"). More product innovations were on the horizon, including breakfast convenience foods like Pop-Tarts toaster pastries, Eggo frozen waffles and Nutri-Grain bars. There were also health-friendly cereals flooding the market like Special K, All-Bran and Product 19 cereals. Kellogg's bought the vegetarian-based Worthington Foods in 1999 and the organic-based Kashi Company a year later. A year beyond that (2001), it acquired Keebler Foods Company.

The entrepreneurial spirit of Will Kellogg, meanwhile, was caught by *his* son, John. He pioneered the use of waxed paper in 1915, an innovation called "WaxTite" that consumers made into an overnight sensation. John's progeny, Keith Kellogg, Jr., bought the Kellogg packaging company (now General Packaging Products) and applied the hands-on commonsense techniques espoused by his grandpa. *His* son, meanwhile, William Keith Kellogg, III, is president of the wrapping firm today.

With revenues surpassing $10 billion in 2005, the Kellogg Company — still independently operated in 2007 as opposed to having been purchased by a larger concern as was most of its competition — employed 25,000 in its 2005 workforce at 17 global manufacturing plants. That year it marketed cereals and convenience edibles in more than 180 nations. According to corporate publicists, Kellogg's is now "the world's largest breakfast producer and leading provider of convenience foods." The latter food group is made up of cookies, crackers, toaster pastries, cereal bars, frozen waffles and meat alternatives. Trademarks include Kellogg's, Keebler, Pop-Tarts, Eggo, Cheez-It, Club, Nutri-Grain, Rice Krispies, All-Bran, Special K, Mini-Wheats, Chips Deluxe, Sandies, Morningstar Farms, Famous Amos and Kashi.

Will Keith Kellogg was 46 when he founded the firm in 1906. Himself a product of a devout Seventh-day Adventist home, he practiced the faith's precepts in his own life. He was never comfortable with affluence, for example.[2] Said one biographer[3]:

> In the 1920s, when many captains of industry were building castle-sized summer "cottages" with 4-car garages, Kellogg lived a comparatively modest life. Even as a millionaire, he resided for years in a two-story stucco house....
>
> As a father, he feared the pitfalls of unearned wealth. None of his children would ever become rich through inherited money. Explaining his tight rein on the family purse, Kellogg once wrote, "I want that my sons develop into conscientious and truthful men." ...
>
> Over the years, his support of charitable causes was enormous and varied. He became convinced that the most good could be accomplished by helping young people. So in 1925, he established the Fellowship Corporation [which] ... helped to build an agricultural school and a bird sanctuary, and to establish an experimental farm and a reforestation project. Kellogg also donated nearly $3 million to hometown causes, such as the Ann J. Kellogg School for handicapped children, a civic auditorium, a junior high school, and a youth recreation center. [He also provided the city's first airport.}
>
> President Herbert Hoover named him a delegate at a White House Conference on Child Health and Protection. He returned from the conference determined to help. As a result, in June 1930, the W. K. Kellogg Child Welfare Foundation was born. A few months later, he broadened the focus of the charter, and named it the W. K. Kellogg Foundation [initially endowing it with $66 million in company stock]....
>
> Kellogg demonstrated great compassion and caring and acted on his belief that the most good came from helping people to help themselves.

One of the most practical ideas he implemented to benefit the common man occurred when, in 1930, Kellogg went to a six-hour workday at his manufacturing plants, giving more people work during the nation's Great Depression.[4] His intent was to restore a measure of stability and dignity to people's lives in the midst of sudden, excruciating hardship. It involved altering the normal eight-hour tri-shift work pattern to employ more individuals in four daily six-hour shifts. At the same time, he gave his workforce a generous increase in compensation to allow for the reduced number of hours. "In a downsized world we live in," assessed one scribe, "it is hard to conceive of a CEO who would add a shift in order to employ people laid off by other plants and raise the six-hour shift workers' wages more than 12% to make up for the loss of two work hours per day."

Kellogg had another motive, too: "The other half of his plan was to increase people's involvement in their community and their families' lives. Kellogg workers, especially the women, managed to find things to do with their extra time until World War II; after the war, workers, particularly men, seemed less able to find ways to fill their unstructured time." The plan became so universally acclaimed by employees at its start, in fact, that the temporary experiment persisted for 55 years until 1985! It was an idea born in the hearts of futurists in the middle of the nineteenth century that was frequently shunned by U.S. labor.

Finally, in a blaze of disenchantment, the six-hour workday expired not from lack of productivity but because employees demanded more hours so they could consume more, a reporter said. A published summary indicts those working-class laborers for valuing income above leisure time. Following interviews with many who served under Kellogg's six-hour workday, an investigator "paints a sad picture of a society where people prefer buying things to socializing, a world where a shorter work day is no longer desirable because few know what to do with their spare time." As it turned out, only females protested when the abbreviated schedule bit the dust. "Most men had succumbed to the belief that working longer was more manly and that going home after six hours to be with the family was not really the thing to do.... It could serve as a wake-up call for a nation in big trouble if the jobless future comes to pass."[5]

In an evaluation of *The Kellogg Brothers*, now available on DVD but originally appearing as a televised History Channel biography, viewers learn: "One was an eccentric crusader for health. The other was a sober businessman who turned their humble invention the corn flake into the cornerstone of one of the most successful companies in the nation." The film highlights "one of the most dramatic and bitter family feuds in American history," in which the two brothers who had two decades earlier been partners were driven apart. W. K. wanted to develop a large-scale advertising campaign to compete with ex-San patient Charles W. Post, who had created successful rival breakfast foods like Post Toasties and was winning converts handily with heavy marketing emphases.[6] W. K. began to seek methods of taking control of their joint enterprise after his insistently frugal sibling refused to spend the money to promote.

The frugality on John's part was ill-fated: he had gotten employees at the san to accept low pay supplemented by stock in the cereal firm. W. K. secured financing from a St. Louis insurance broker and quietly began buying the employees' shares. By 1906, he was in the driver's seat, and court battles and hard feelings characterized the pair for the rest of their lives. W. K. put his own signature on the box—he included the slogan "The Genuine Bears This Signature—W. K. Kellogg"—and added sugar to the recipe to increase sales. The breakfast food became a hit with almost everyone after it was no longer utterly focused as a nutritional dietary supplement for the ill and afflicted.

Will Keith Kellogg formed "the world's most successful cereal company" resulting in a decade-long legal battle over the family nomenclature. "For years," insisted one source, "the brothers never spoke to each other." PR wordsmiths cite the filmed documentary about their lives as "the tumultuous story of the star-crossed fortunes of the Kellogg brothers" in a depiction of the celluloid contents. While Will established the W. K. Kellogg Company to manufacture dry breakfast cereals, John founded the Battle Creek Food Company, producing coffee substitutes and soymilk. John also edited the *Good Health Magazine* promoting vegetarianism and espousing his utterly radical health notions.

By 1906, the sponsoring Seventh-day Adventist church had become disenchanted with their great physician and excommunicated him. Ultimately, the sect separated itself from the sanitarium he headed. He faced still greater obstacles during the Great Depression when the bulk of that facility's formerly well-heeled patrons fell away. The san limped along to 1938, then $3 million in debt. Its doors closed that year and, four years hence (1942)—a year before John's death—it was sold to the U.S. government as a military hospital.

A couple of footnotes indicate how pervasive the Kellogg influence has been. The Kellogg School of Management opened its doors at Chicago's Northwestern University in 1908. The school prepares executive leadership for American and international service in multiple degree endeavors. Today, also, Kellogg's Cereal City USA in Battle Creek is a themed family attraction that celebrates the cereal-making industry. It offers educational, historical and entertaining exhibits. Patrons may even buy Kellogg's Corn Flakes boxes with their own pictures on them.

Radio Series

Kellogg's Slumber Hour—1930 to 1931, NBC Blue (Pep)
The Singing Lady, with Ireene [sic] Wicker—1931 to 1938, NBC Blue
Buck Rogers in the Twenty-Fifth Century—1932 to 1933, CBS
Painted Dreams—1933 to 1934, CBS
College Prom, with Red Nichols and His Orchestra—1935 to 1936, NBC Blue
Girl Alone—1936 to 1938, NBC
The Quality Twins, with Ed East and Ralph Dumke—1937 to 1938, CBS
Howie Wing—1938 to 1939, Don Lee, CBS
Don Winslow of the Navy—1938 to 1939, NBC Blue
Tom Mix—1939 to 1940, NBC Blue
Jack Berch and His Boys—1943 to 1944, MBS (Krumbles)
The Adventures of Superman—1943 to 1945, MBS (Pep)
Gilbert Martyn and the News—1943 to 1947, NBC Blue, Blue, ABC
Breakfast in Hollywood, aka *Breakfast at Sardi's*, with Tom Breneman—1944 to 1945, Blue/ABC (Krumbles, Pep)
Galen Drake—1945 to 1948, ABC
Hollywood Story, with Charles Paul—1946 to 1947, ABC
The Breakfast Club, with Don McNeill—NBC Blue-Blue-ABC, ca. 1950s (Pep—multiple participation)
The Clyde Beatty Show—1950 to 1952, MBS
Mark Trail—1950 to 1951, MBS
Tom Corbett, Space Cadet—1951 to 1952, ABC (Pep)
Wild Bill Hickok—1951 to 1954, MBS (Sugar Corn Pops)
Ma Perkins—1960, CBS (multiple participation)

Exposition

Of more than a score of documented radio series underwritten by the Kellogg Company, about half were targeted at adolescents who—Kellogg research indicated—consumed large portions of their products. Another thread manifest throughout the firm's aural promotional model points toward series running multiple times weekly, often in quarter-hour strips that aired on five weekday afternoons. Kellogg unapologetically went after a juvenile crowd, correctly figuring that they heavily influenced the people who actually paid for their wares. The prevailing theory seemed to be: win them over and you win at the supermarket; and furthermore, as they grow up, supply them with tasty, nutritional adult-preference foods. By then, they are already familiar with the brand and trust it for reliable staples on their home pantry shelves. The object is to transfer that longstanding loyalty to the new households they create after they mature and leave the care of formative ties.

Kellogg didn't just rely on kids alone in pushing its edible commodities, however. Most of the remaining 50 percent of the company's radio programming was directed at the housewives, the stay-at-home moms of those pubescent youngsters. Throughout the day the ladies tuned into variety and music series as well as soap operas and informational features. Primarily, the shows aimed at them were also cast in repetitive five-day-a-week slots that proved regular reminders in prompting the purchase of expanding lines of breakfast foods.

Although Kellogg didn't buy as much radio time as some of its competitors, it concentrated heavily in the dual segments where it counted — moms and kids — and thereby established a presence in people's lives that became virtually synonymous with starting the day in millions of American domiciles.

And if you're keeping score... this is a company, unlike most other enveloping radio advertisers, that went again and again to the little guys on the ether. Specifically, half of the shows sponsored by Kellogg originated on the chain that was known as NBC Blue-Blue-ABC at varying times. Another quarter went to MBS while yet another quarter graced CBS. Only a single feature for which documentation has surfaced was sold to NBC (Red). This is generally the opposite of the pattern most other underwriters pursued when distributing their advertising.

Why the fondness for the little guys? The most obvious is, the time charges were considerably less at ABC and MBS than at CBS and NBC. There was a price to pay for that, too: the minor webs generally drew smaller audiences as a result of less favorable, usually less powerful affiliates in the markets where they competed with bigger rivals. Nevertheless, once Kellogg assigned a program to a specific web — once again unlike many others buying radio time in myriad industries — they left their money there, seldom switching a series to another network in an effort to improve position.

Kellogg could be isolated in more ways than one.

Commercial

The authority figure in this commercial was Dr. Joan Dale, one of the physicists at the laboratory currently featured in the *Tom Corbett, Space Cadet* storyline (ca. 1951 to 1952). Integrating one of the leading personalities from the narrative into the sponsor's pitches had hypnotic powers on the series' youthful fans. The announcer is Jackson Beck.

JACKSON BECK: Here's the tele-recorder. Dr. Dale recorded a message to be played to all boys and girls in all planet colonies. I'll play it for you.
SFX: *Switch being turned on*
DR. JOAN DALE: Here's an important reminder to all spacemen and space girls, too. Be sure you're getting enough vitamins. Eat the right foods that give you those vitamins. At breakfast, you can get a whole day's supply of vitamin D and a valuable amount of vitamin B1 by eating Kellogg's Pep. And when you eat Pep, you're getting the kind of food value that helps you do things better ... that goes for play, school, work and sports. So remember ... for a really good supply of important vitamins ... and a really enjoyable way to start the day ... help yourself to Kellogg's Pep ... End transmission.
SFX: *Switch being turned off*
JACKSON BECK: Well, spacemen, you learned two important things today. You learned about communications ... and you heard about the best breakfast cereal in the universe. So, don't forget now ... ask mom for Kellogg's Pep. P-E-P. Pep.

Kraft Foods Company

History

James Lewis Kraft was born of Mennonite parentage near Stevensville, Ontario, Canada, in 1874. His daddy was a farmer. In his youth, J. L. Kraft clerked in a grocery store near his home and in doing so made a simple but profound discovery that was to have an effect on the rest of his life. Kraft realized that cheese, while popular, was an unstable, highly perishable product. After he moved to Chicago in 1903, he was transfixed by that perplexing dilemma. In time, he found an opportunity that would create a niche and ultimately prove lucrative for him.

Due to the short shelf life of cheese and its unpredictability, Windy City grocers had to visit a central warehouse — primarily the South Water Street wholesale market in downtown Chicago — every day to purchase their wheels of cheese. Hauling them back to their retail operations, they cut sections from those wheels at their customers' requests. During the pre-refrigeration epoch, the cheese spoiled quickly after it was cut open. Kraft understood that he could save the grocers one daily time-consuming headache by picking up the cheese for them and delivering it every morning to their stores. Renting a horse-drawn wagon (with a horse named Paddy, no less!), he began earning a small livelihood for himself.

To get the best available cheese, Kraft made sure he was the first in line every morning at the South Water Street Market. Nevertheless, at least one source claims that — in his earliest days in business for himself — Kraft's venture was dismal. In fact, he lost $3,000 and his horse during the first year. But things eventually began to improve. Once his notion caught on with several grocers, he began turning a profit. Before long, Kraft had visions of still greater grandeur: he would wrap the cheese he peddled, and then he'd place his own name on the packaging before he delivered it. He was one of the first entrepreneurs to take cheese from a commodity to a branded product. By 1909, Kraft's four siblings — Charles, Fred, John and Norman — joined him in his budding enterprise. The name was changed over the doorway to J. L. Kraft & Bros. Company.

Within two years, Kraft was into advertising big time, mailing circulars to retail grocers while promoting their products to end users through elevated train signage and billboard advertising. So sold was he on spreading the word far and wide that, by 1919, he bought space in national magazines and ran color ads, being among the first to do so. In the meantime,

Kraft inaugurated a makeshift lab to experiment with blending sundry types of cheese, cooking temperatures and mixing methods. The object was to produce higher quality wares with longer shelf lives. In 1911, it was one of the first test kitchens. Three years hence, the Kraft firm opened its own cheese processing plant at Stockton, Illinois.

In 1915, Kraft discovered that heating and continuously stirring the cheese and placing it in a sterile container allowed it to regain its solid state once the cheese cooled. The process cheese created such demand that he was forced to add more plants. Soon the firm was dispatching 31 varieties of cheese throughout the nation. It was sold in tins weighing 3½ ounces and 7¾ ounces. Kraft gained a U.S. patent for his processed cheese in 1916 and the following year supplied the U.S. armed forces during the First World War. The firm's reputation was being made a tin at a time. From 1918 to 1945, Americans consumed 50 percent more cheese than they had in previous years, thanks in large measure to its availability and the innovations of J. L. Kraft. Employing 10,000 people by 1928, his company was then selling a million pounds of cheese daily.

Acquiring or introducing many added foods followed developing acclaim. With the firm's name altered to Kraft Cheese Company in 1924, that year it opened a sales office in London, added Hamburg in 1927 and soon followed it with many more facilities around the globe. Kraft Foods Australia resulted in 1926 when Kraft and Fred Walker of Australia, that nation's leading cheese-maker, formed a partnership. Kraft Cheese Company merged with the Phenix Cheese Corporation — maker of Philadelphia brand cream cheese — in 1928. That product originated in 1880, incidentally, when Kraft was only six. By 1930, Kraft-Phenix Cheese Corporation captured 40 percent of the national cheese market. National Dairy Products Corporation acquired Kraft-Phenix on May 12, 1930, yet Kraft functioned independently from New York–based National Dairy, which acted as a holding company.[1]

In the meantime, Velveeta pasteurized process cheese spread appeared in 1928. In 1933, Miracle Whip salad dressing debuted. Kraft Macaroni and Cheese Dinner came on the market in 1937. Appearing for the first time in 1940 was Parkay margarine. Innovative radio advertising encouraged quick public acceptance of the new wares. *The Kraft Musical Revue*, a two-hour musical variety feature, debuted in 1933, followed by the hour-long *Kraft Music Hall* headlined by crooner Bing Crosby in its heyday.

During the Second World War, Kraft was a leading food supplier. By the close of 1941, for instance, the firm shipped four million pounds of cheese weekly to Great Britain. The nomenclature was altered in 1945 to Kraft Foods Company. The business underwrote the *Kraft Television Theater*, the first commercial network television program. When James L. Kraft, who had been the company's president since 1909, passed in 1953, the Kraft family's leadership died with him. Kraft became an autonomous subsidiary of National Dairy Corporation, still operating as a single company in 1956 to 1957. National Dairy changed its name to Kraftco in 1969 and to Kraft, Inc. in 1976.

In the meantime, in 1950, Kraft introduced the first commercially packaged sliced process cheese in the U.S., Kraft Deluxe. Cracker Barrel natural cheese came along in 1954. The following year, Kraft tomato ketchup premiered in Germany; in 1960, Kraft peanut butter surfaced in Canada. The company brought out jellies and preserves (1956); jet-puffed marshmallows (1959); barbecue sauce (1960); individually wrapped cheese slices (1965); Light n' Lively yogurt and ice milk (1969); squeezable Parkay margarine (1973); and Breyers yogurt (1977).

Philip Morris Companies, Inc., purchased Kraft, Inc. in 1988 for $12.9 billion. The following year the food products divisions of Philip Morris, General Foods and Kraft were merged into Kraft General Foods and Kraft General Foods International. The firm was reorganized as Kraft Foods, Inc., in the 1990s. In 2000, Philip Morris bought Nabsico Holdings and folded those numerous brands into the Kraft business worldwide.[2] It was a year in which Kraft, with 117,000 employees, sold $34.7 billion in goods. By then, Kraft was second only to Nestlé S. A. at the forefront of global food and beverage sales. On January 27, 2003, Philip Morris changed the title of the parent company to Altria Group, Inc.

With two principal operating units — Kraft Foods North America (KFNA) and Kraft Foods International (KFI) — in a recent year, 73 percent of the firm's revenues were generated by KFNA. Brands were divided into five categories: snacks, beverages, cheese, grocery, convenient meals. Seven Kraft brands were billion-dollar sellers: Jacobs, Kraft, Maxwell House, Nabisco, Oscar Mayer, Philadelphia, Post. Meanwhile, more than 60 Kraft brands are $100 million sellers, among them: A-1, Altoids, Balance, Cheez Whiz, Cool Whip, DiGiorno, Freia, Gevalia, Jell-O, Kool-Aid, Life Savers, Miracle Whip, Oreo, Planters, Premium, Ritz, Stove Top, Tang, Toblerone. Other major trademarks: Baker's, Country Time, Crystal Light, Handi-Snacks, Minute Rice. The company holds the top global position in 11 product species: coffee, cookies, crackers, cream cheese, dessert mixes, dry packaged dinners, lunch combinations, powdered soft drinks, process cheese, salad dressings, snack nuts. Kraft operates in excess of 220 manufacturing plants with sales in more than 140 nations. Its core businesses are in beverage, cheese and dairy, snack foods and confectionery, convenience foods, and cereals.

Kraft's major rivals are currently identified as Nestlé S. A., Unilever, ConAgra Foods, Inc., Groupe Danone, H. J. Heinz Company, Sara Lee Corporation, General Mills, Inc., Campbell Soup Company, Kellogg Company, Quaker Oats Company, Dean Foods Company and Frito-Lay Company.

According to a contemporary Web site, "The tobacco business, and its associated litigation, has long cast a shadow over Kraft's development. Altria floated part of Kraft Foods in 2001, but for many years was adamant that it had no plans to fully demerge its food operations. In 2004, however, the group acknowledged that it might now consider spinning out Kraft as an independent entity, and that process was completed at the end of March 2007." On February 1, 2007, the company announced its intent to spin-off Kraft Foods, Inc. The stake of the firm in the food-processing giant was distributed to its shareholders. Altria no longer holds any interest in Kraft, the latter headquartered in the Chicago suburb of Northfield, Illinois.

Radio Series

Kraft Music Hall, with Paul Whiteman and His Orchestra and Al Jolson —1933 to 1935, NBC (Kraft, Miracle Whip, Parkay, Philadelphia)
Kraft Music Hall, with Bing Crosby, John Scott Trotter and His Orchestra, Bob Burns, Don Ameche —1935 to 1946, NBC (Kraft, Miracle Whip, Parkay, Philadelphia)
The Great Gildersleeve, with Harold Peary and Willard Waterman —1941 to 1954, NBC (Kraft, Miracle Whip, Parkay, Philadelphia)
Kraft Music Hall, with Eddie Foy, Eddy Duchin, Edward Everett Horton, Frank Morgan, Al Jolson, Nelson Eddy, Dorothy Kirsten —1946 to 1949, NBC (Kraft, Miracle Whip, Parkay, Philadelphia)
Marriage for Two—1949 to 1950, NBC (Kraft, Miracle Whip, Parkay, Philadelphia)

The Falcon, with Michael Waring—1950 to 1951, NBC (Kraft, Miracle Whip, Parkay, Philadelphia)

Bobby Benson and the B-Bar-B Riders—1951, 1953 to 1954, MBS (Kraft)

The Edgar Bergen and Charlie McCarthy Show—1954 to 1955, CBS (Cracker Barrel, Kraft, Miracle Whip, Parkay, Philadelphia)

Kraft Music Hall, with Rudy Vallee—1955, CBS (Cracker Barrel, Kraft, Miracle Whip, Parkay, Philadelphia)

Exposition

You've heard about putting all your eggs in the proverbial single basket. Kraft came close. Not only did it concentrate on NBC for more than 95 percent of its airtime (its features elsewhere usually ran shortened seasons); it put almost all of its cheese, margarine, marshmallows, mayonnaise, salad dressing and other advertised edibles in a single package. Certainly so in *two* packages—and little else.

The first was *Kraft Music Hall* and for 14 years (1935 to 1949) that premier aural feature did for Kraft what the prestigious *Lux Radio Theater* did for a soap sponsor. Each week *Kraft* offered a legendary headliner (for most of the run it was crooner Bing Crosby) who drew the crowds and possibly earned the extraordinary (bizarre, perhaps?) salaries Kraft forked over to keep those audiences coming back for more. A second radio entry, *The Great Gildersleeve*, proved one of the medium's favorite weekly sitcoms. Kraft underwrote it for 13 consecutive seasons (1941 to 1954) at a fraction of what *Kraft Music Hall* was appropriating from its advertising budget.

When the latter passed and as vacancies occurred as other sponsors pulled out of radio, Kraft divided its audio commercials among a handful of fleeting ventures: a soap opera (*Marriage for Two*), a detective-mystery drama (*The Falcon*), a juvenile adventure (*Bobby Benson and the B-Bar-B Riders*), a comedy-variety series (*The Edgar Bergen and Charlie McCarthy Show*) and a comeback try for the venerable *Kraft Music Hall*, this time headlined by a celebrated superstar of the 1920s and 1930s, Rudy Vallee. Kraft had transferred most of its investment to television by then, of course. In their day, however, the *Music Hall* and *Gildersleeve* were among the top tier programs competing in different genres. Together, they helped turn a cheese factory into a household name.

As for Crosby and Kraft, the two were interlaced, seemingly inseparable. Despite the on-the-surface pleasantries, however, an insatiable ego fortified by a defiant demeanor portended trouble as the iconic Crosby began to show signs of wear under Kraft instruction. It would eventually burst from behind the curtains and onto the stage.

Crosby chafed when asked to give product endorsements on behalf of the sponsor. His insistence against allowing an audience to view the live studio performances nearly torpedoed his deal with Kraft. He protested vehemently when a script called for him to have very many lines. "I'm a singer—let somebody else do the talking," he admonished. Crosby repented later, softening his resistance in being told what to do on those matters. But it took awhile for the chill to thaw.

"It was the Kraft Music Hall that cemented Bing's relationship with his public," biographer Michael Freedland validated, despite the vocalist's troublesome manner backstage. "To millions, it was the only thing on the radio that they wanted to hear. When Crosby was on the air, young couples stayed home instead of going to the movies. Older people cancelled visits to restaurants. If they were visiting, they made sure they could sit in front of their hosts' radio sets." Radio historiographer John Dunning affirmed: "In the decade that Crosby remained with Kraft, he became the best-loved star on the American scene." A 1939 poll of American newspaper editors picked series fronted by Jack Benny, Edgar Bergen and Bing Crosby as "the best shows in radio."

Nevertheless, after a few years, his tenure with the Kraft Foods Company arrived at an impasse and ended with an ignoble conclusion. The official line given reporters was that Crosby and his employers (Kraft, through its advertising agency) couldn't reach a satisfactory financial compromise. But for some time the independent-minded Crosby had implored both Kraft and NBC to allow him to record his programs in advance of airdates. That would let him tape several shows at once, giving him more time to golf, trout fish in Canada and relax at his Idaho ranch.

In addition, the star's own sideline production firm was beginning to improve and market recording equipment which some speculated he hoped to exhibit on the air, netting a lucrative return for himself in increased sales. He resonated with the ability to edit out sections of shows he didn't like. Even better, perhaps, was the chance to dispense with the rebroadcast of live performances for the West Coast audience, providing still more free time to Crosby.

But the major networks, including NBC, had handed down edicts years before preventing prerecorded programming from airing on their wavelengths. No compromise was possible. Unfortunately for Kraft and NBC, Crosby pulled a stunt that he had used when he became unhappy with his treatment at the Cocoanut Grove 14 years earlier (in June 1931). When things didn't go to his satisfaction, he quit. In June 1945, he picked up his marbles and went home — again. He intended to find somebody who *would* transcribe his show and air it.

Kraft and NBC retained high-priced attorneys. Neither was about to let Crosby off the hook because he didn't want to play ball. Crosby had earlier signed a binding contract for five more seasons. He countered Kraft's position by claiming that — under California law — personal contracts couldn't continue more than seven years. The warring factions quibbled for months. The 1945 to 1946 radio season kicked off without him, headlined by several lesser stars. The legal melee was at last resolved in early 1946 when Crosby agreed to return to *Kraft Music Hall* to finish the season. At the end of it, he was relieved of duty; Kraft and NBC were satisfied that he had fulfilled his contractual obligations.

Following that inglorious end to what had been one of the radio fans' most stimulating associations, Crosby found a new network (ABC) and sponsor (Philco) that — somewhat nervously — allowed him to transcribe his show and play it back later. In so doing, new ground was broken by a major chain; before long, Groucho Marx got a similar deal; and a majority of web-based programming went speedily to transcriptions. The parting of Crosby and Kraft set a broadcast precedent that lingers in memories to the present age.

Commercial

In contrast to many radio commercials — and unlike those Kraft delivered on television in which every step of a recipe including a Kraft commodity was painstakingly exhibited in precise detail — the sponsor sometimes offered pithy nods toward its products on the aural ether. Often they filled segments of just 30 seconds. Here's the opening plug from the December 22, 1948, installment of *The Great Gildersleeve* demonstrating how Kraft sold cooking fats with few words. The announcer is John Wald.

JOHN WALD: Millions of women ... all over America ... serve Parkay because it ... tastes *so* good! Why, Parkay tastes like it should cost twice as much.
ENSEMBLE: (*sings*) To market, to market, to get some Parkay!
        Home again! Home again! Try it today!
        You'll like it! You'll love it! Like millions who say ...
        The flavor of margarine ... means ...
ANNOUNCER: P-A-R-K-A-Y! Parkay margarine ... made by Kraft.

Lever Brothers Company

History

Lever Brothers Company, a consumer package goods enterprise, was a wholly owned subsidiary of Unilever United States, Inc., during the network radio years and for three decades thereafter. Today the American segment is headquartered in Englewood Cliffs, New Jersey. In the 1990s, it adopted the Unilever moniker applied since the 1920s by dual European parent organizations operating as a single unit. Both produced goods made of oils and fats, principally soap and margarine. Both needed coconut, palm, cottonseed, soybean and whale oil, plus animal fats. The ingredients in the dual lines could be imported more cheaply in larger quantities, of course. The history of their alignment is a captivating tale of cohesive survival in international commerce born of necessity.

Unilever's earliest beginnings date to 1872 when a couple of Netherlands margarine producers, Jurgens and Van den Bergh, joined forces in a collaborative arrangement. They named their outfit Margarine Unie. A dozen years afterward — and unrelated to their joint venture at that time — an entrepreneurial William Hesketh Lever (1851 to 1925) left the security of his father's wholesale grocery business in London, England, to attempt something more adventurous. As a sideline, the family was already marketing Lever's Pure Honey, a soap made especially for them. Young William — who was to become the first viscount Lord Leverhulme in 1822 — was a salesman in James Lever's (his daddy's) business pursuits. Against some well-intentioned advice from his elder, he decided to expand into manufacturing in addition to marketing and distribution. A Unilever historian characterized him as possessing "a personality that combined the rationality of the businessman with the restless ambitions of the explorer."

As a child, William's first job in his papa's grocery store had been to cut and wrap soap. He also knew the value of a brand name that could be registered for exclusive applications. Having already identified an essential non-cyclical commodity in common demand, William Lever opened a soap factory at Warrington, England, in 1885 as an adjunct to the grocery operation. He chose the name Sunlight for a new line of soaps, initially contracting with various manufacturers to produce it. Lever packaged and marketed his products himself. He is, incidentally, credited as the first soap manufacturer to imprint a brand name on a bar of soap (Sunlight) and to wrap it for sale, a practice carried over from his childhood.

According to Unilever spokesmen, Lever's Sunlight "helped popularize cleanliness and hygiene in Victorian England." Lever set down his ideas for the commodity before it emerged. It was "to make cleanliness commonplace; to lessen work for women; to foster health and contribute to personal attractiveness, that life may be more enjoyable and rewarding for the people who use our products." While this was decades before a corporate mission statement was envisioned, Unilever now maintains "these ideas have stayed at the heart of our business.... We've created products that help people get more out of life—cutting the time spent on household chores, improving nutrition, enabling people to enjoy food and take care of their homes, their clothes and themselves."

Raw materials were inexpensive and workers were readily available at that intersect in English history. Before long, Lever determined to open his own soapmaking factory. Together with his brother James, William Lever arranged a loan; in January 1886, production began. James Lever, incidentally, never actively ran the business, making the Lever Brothers designation incongruous. William Lever's biographer, Adam MacQueen, speculates that James suffered from mental instability aggravated by a traffic mishap in his youth. James also suffered from diabetes. Another supposition posits that his symptoms—prior to the discovery of insulin and effective treatment—were simply mistaken for cerebral unsteadiness.

Initially the Lever plant generated 20 tons of soap (an English style of measurement) weekly using a recipe derived from oils rather than tallow that other industrialists traditionally applied. The Levers inaugurated a practice that would be pursued well into the twentieth century: they produced all of the raw components required for their cleansing agents, margarine and other wares, a custom not in widespread use previously.

At the beginning, meanwhile, they sold their products locally; but before long, they were extending their trade to Scotland, Holland, Belgium, South Africa and Canada. So popular was their Sunlight brand some distance from them that—within two years—William was able to purchase property on the banks of the Mersey River to locate the operation on a permanent site (they had been leasing space heretofore). The location near Liverpool was dubbed Port Sunlight and—with adjacent territory to be purchased later—consisted of 330 acres for their manufacturing facility. It was a model of community housing and supported Lever Brothers' workers, who enjoyed generous wages and innovative benefits. A source expounded: "Lever's philanthropy had definite paternalistic overtones, and life in Port Sunlight included intrusive rules and implied mandatory participation in activities. With accommodation tied to employment, a worker losing his or her job could be almost simultaneously evicted. Nonetheless, conditions, pay, hours, and benefits far exceeded those prevailing in similar industries."

William Lever increased his product line with a second sustaining commodity in 1894, Lifebuoy soap, a household bar with carbolic acid as a disinfectant. Five years later, Lever added a third permanent commodity to the growing mix: Lux soap flakes. There is an absorbing tale behind the latter's development. Until the start of the twentieth century, washing clothes for most women at home entailed a repetitive, monotonous task of generating sudsy water by slicing chips off large slabs of laundry soap. That is—until a Lever technician in Great Britain found a method of producing an incredibly thin sheet of soap that could be cut into flakes. First marketed in England in 1899 under the label Sunlight Flakes, the moniker was altered to Lux the following year. As a trade name, Lux proffered multiple advantages: it was short and easy to recall; in Latin Lux referred to light and was thereby related to Sunlight; and it suggested a luxurious connotation.

Registered as a U.S. trademark in 1906, Lux flakes began rolling from the Cambridge,

Massachusetts, plant in 1907. While its initial sales were modest, several measures turned Lux into a major cleanser used in home laundries: American women began wearing more silks and other fine fabrics; U.S. factory capacity was greatly increased in 1915; and the J. Walter Thompson agency repositioned the product that year from one that advertised it "won't shrink woolens" to one whose safety was guaranteed in washing "all fine fabrics." By 1918, three years later, Lux annual sales soared from 10,000 cases to more than a million. While Lever originally focused on newspaper ads to market the "wonderful new product," it soon branched into color illustrations in widely circulated magazines like *Ladies' Home Journal*. A frequent tagline read "the pure essence of soap in flakes." The ads even provided directions to consumers on how to use the flakes.

By 1922, some of the ads also promoted Lux flakes for washing dishes. When Lever Brothers officials asked women to submit testimonial letters about their diversified uses of Lux in a 1924 competition, to their amazement 53,000 replied. Among the discoveries, women were extending Lux to the general realm of toilet soap, applying the flake form to hands, bath, babies and shampooing. The data collected convinced Lever's brass to create a soap bar. Initially christened Lux Toilet Form, it was quickly re-dubbed Lux Toilet Soap and became highly successful as hand soap over the next three decades.

In 1895, the firm opened a small office in New York City to process sales of Sunlight and Lifebuoy to American buyers. Lever acquired a small factory in Cambridge, Massachusetts, three years hence (1898) and began manufacturing its wares in the United States. A few years beyond, it bought a second factory at Philadelphia. The Cambridge plant produced goods bound for New England while the Philly operation distributed to the rest of the nation.

Individually wrapped Sunlight soap was produced in tablet size, a dimension that pleased purchasers in Europe, Australia, Canada and South Africa. American consumers thought it poor value for the money, however; they were accustomed to buying larger bars of soap and thus Sunlight never did well in the U.S. and it was finally phased out here. After a slow start, Lifebuoy began to catch on, along with another Lever soap bar brand, Welcome, both marketed in larger sizes than Sunlight. But it was Lux flakes that proved the most popular commodity of all. With Lux repositioned as high quality soap suitable for even the most delicate material, by 1919 Lever sold 1.5 million cases; it had sold only 3,000 cases in 1913.

In this same epoch, Lever introduced Rinso soap powder which became a success story, too. While consumers bought 64,000 cases in 1919, by 1923 they purchased 800,000 cases. And in the decade between 1913 and 1923, sales of Lifebuoy jumped from 84,000 cases annually to 550,000. Beginning in 1925, Lever brought Lux Toilet Soap to market. For all of these reasons, by 1929 Lever Brothers was the third largest soap and glycerin manufacturer in America, behind Procter & Gamble and Colgate-Palmolive-Peet.

While all of this was transpiring, for some years the parent firm back in England had been in negotiations with Margarine Unie of the Netherlands — the other major European producer of similar goods. Margarine Unie grew through mergers with other margarine producers in the 1920s. Beginning in 1917, Lever Brothers began to diversify into foods, acquiring fish, ice cream and canned goods. Together, the competing firms maintained operations in more than 40 nations. The behemoths finally agreed to discontinue waging an aggressive rivalry resulting in a costly drain on the resources of each firm. An alliance, said they, "wasted less of everybody's substance than hostility." They formalized a new partnership using the nomenclature Unilever while continuing to operate like separate enterprises. Unilever plc (public limited company) is based in London while Unilever NV (Naamloze Vennootschap, meaning limited-liability company) is based in Rotterdam. While they are legally distinct entities and transact their business with dual sets of shareholders, they are managed by a single board of directors. The fusion officially began on September 2, 1929.

Lever Brothers of America, an appendage of Unilever, continued to be innovative and brought new products to market. One of those commodities, in 1936, was Spry shortening. Within three years, following a massive roll-out advertising campaign, 50,000 tons of Spry was sold annually. That was about 75 percent of the sales of market leader Crisco, Procter & Gamble's all-vegetable shortening, which had been around for a quarter-century (since 1911).

America's Great Depression didn't have a particularly negative effect on sales of Lever Brothers commodities, unlike some other industry manufacturers experienced (automobiles, major appliances, housing, leisure pursuits, etc.). One source speculated about Lever's good fortune in that epoch: "This may have been due to Americans' high regard for cleanliness, making soap a necessity rather than a luxury." In the decade from 1929 to 1939, Lever's U.S. revenues rose 134 percent, from $39 million to $91 million. Profits more than doubled, from $3 million to $7 million.

While Unilever continually tested new formulas for projected innovations in its various product lines, it also augmented its commodity lineup through numerous acquisitions, including Thomas J. Lipton Company (1937); The Pepsodent Company (1944); John F. Jelke Company (1948); portions of Monsanto Chemical Company (1957); Good Humor Company (1961); Shedd's Food Products Company (1984); Fabergé and Elizabeth Arden cosmetics lines (1984); J. H. Filbert Company (1986); Chesebrough-Pond's (1986); Helene Curtis Industries, Inc. (1996); and Best Foods (2000).

Advertising dollars spelled the difference between competing products that could be fundamentally distinguished by traits such as scent, shape or color. "Procter & Gamble spent massive amounts of money on advertising and promotion and controlled 45 percent to 50 percent of the household products market," said one observer. Lever Brothers' competition, on the other hand, was weak until at least the 1980s. Interviewed by *Fortune* magazine in 1986, the chairman of Unilever's North American operations, Michael Angus, claimed Lever Brothers was "in a vicious cycle caused by low profitability." He explained: "Low profits caused managers to cut costs, such as advertising, which produced lower market shares, lower volumes, and higher production costs. In addition, research and development resources had been reduced as management tried desperately to stay profitable." Despite all of this, there were encouraging signs. Beyond U.S. borders, for instance, Unilever was the world's leading manufacturer of both detergents and margarine.

The innovative products kept coming. They included the 1950s heavy-duty liquid laundry detergent Wisk, the 1980s Sunlight automatic dishwashing detergent and Snuggle fabric softener, and the "all-in-one" deodorant and moisturizing soap for the whole family, Lever 2000, in 1990. Lever Brothers pulled ahead of Procter & Gamble in the toilet soap category in 1991, thanks to Lever 2000. It was the first time the firm overtook P&G in any product category. Lever spent more than $25 million to advertise that year. Its winning in the toilet soap market "convinced the company that it could dominate other market segments too," a confidence it may not have outwardly expressed before.

In the late 1990s, Unilever sharpened its focus on fewer product categories, cutting its brands from 1600 to 400 as its core business. The 400 comprised about 90 percent of the firm's 1998 revenue. This affected packaging, distribution and promotion in addition to the goods themselves. Identified as its strongest core areas were ice cream, margarines, tea-based beverages, detergents, personal soaps, skin care products and prestige fragrances. Several more were named as developing core areas: frozen foods, culinary products (sauces, side dishes), hair care, oral care, deodorants, household care and industrial cleansing commodities. Businesses outside these areas were candidates for immediate disposal.

With 206,000-plus on its payroll, the Anglo-Dutch conglomerate had revenues exceeding $50 billion in 2005. At that time, Unilever's major rivals were Procter & Gamble, Nestlé, Mars and Reckitt Benckiser. Facing stiff competitive pressure, particularly from P&G, a report noted: "Unilever was clearly no longer the risk-averse, staid organization of the past." The firm has been criticized for environmental pollution, testing products on animals and employing child labor, among other censures.

In food and beverages, some of Lever's most prominent goods today are marketed under the brand names: Ben and Jerry's, Best Foods, Breyers, Country Crock, Fudgsicle, Good Humor, Hellmann's, I Can't Believe It's Not Butter, Imperial, Knorr, Lawry's, Lipton, Popsicle, Promise, Ragú, Skippy and Slim Fast. Unilever is now the world's largest ice cream manufacturer. Among the most identifiable home and personal care brands Unilever markets are All, Brut, Caress, Close-Up, Degree, Dove, Lever 2000, Lifebuoy, Lux, Pepsodent, Pond's, Q-Tips, Rinso, Suave, Sunlight, Sure, Surf, Vaseline and Wisk.

Radio Series

Rinso Talkie Time, aka *Talkie Picture Time*—1930 to 1931, NBC (Rinso)
Lux Radio Theater—1934 to 1955, NBC, CBS (Lux, Spry, Vimms)
The Lifebuoy Program, aka *The Rinso Program*, aka *Tuesday Night Party*, with Al Jolson, Dick Powell, Walter O'Keefe—1936 to 1939, CBS (Lifebuoy, Rinso)
The Lifebuoy Program, with Ken Murray—1936, CBS (Lifebuoy, Rinso)
Big Sister—1936 to 1946, CBS (Rinso, Lifebuoy)
Aunt Jenny's Real Life Stories, aka *Aunt Jenny's True Life Stories*—1937 to 1956, CBS (Spry, Silver Dust)
Big Town—1937 to 1942, 1948 to 1952, CBS, NBC (Rinso, Lifebuoy)
Beatrice Fairfax—1937 to 1938, MBS (Silver Dust)
The Answer Man, with Albert Mitchell—ca. 1937 to ca. 1956, Syndication (Rayve)
The Life and Love of Dr. Susan—1939, CBS (Lux)
Here's Morgan, aka *The Henry Morgan Show*—1940 to ca. 1943, MBS (Rinso, Vimms and Rayve—multiple participation)
Uncle Jim's Question Bee, with Jim McWilliams—1940, CBS (Spry)
Grand Central Station—1940 to 1942, NBC Blue, CBS, NBC (Rinso)
Meet Mr. Meek—1940 to 1942, CBS (Lifebuoy)
The Helen Hayes Theater—1940 to 1942, CBS (Lipton)
Hollywood Premiere, with Louella Parsons—1941, CBS (Lifebuoy)
The George Burns and Gracie Allen Show—1941 to 1945, CBS (Swan, Vimms)
Bright Horizon—1941 to 1945, CBS (Swan, Vimms)
Victory Theater—1942, CBS (Lux)
Bob Burns, the Arkansas Traveler—1942 to 1946, NBC (Lifebuoy, Rinso, Vimms)
Tommy Riggs and Betty Lou, with Johnny Cash—1942 to 1943, CBS, NBC (Swan)
Mayor of the Town, with Lionel Barrymore—1942 to 1943, CBS, NBC (Rinso, Lifebuoy, Swan, Vimms)
Broadway Bandbox, with Frank Sinatra—1943, CBS (Lux, Vimms)
That's Life, aka *The Fred Brady Show*—1943, NBC (Lifebuoy, Rinso)

The Amos 'n' Andy Show—1943 to 1950, NBC, CBS (Rinso, Lifebuoy, Swan, Vimms)
Boston Blackie, with Chester Morris—1944, NBC (Rinso)
The Jack Pepper Show—1944, CBS (Swan)
The Adventures of Charlie Chan, with Ed Begley—1944, NBC (Lifebuoy, Rinso)
The Bob Hope Show—1944 to 1948, NBC (Pepsodent); 1948 to 1950, NBC (Swan, Lux, Spry, Rayve)
Inner Sanctum Mysteries—1944 to 1946, CBS (Lipton)
Easy Aces—1945 to 1946 (repeats), MBS (Rinso)
Joanie's Tea Room, with Joan Davis—1945 to 1947, CBS (Swan)
Philo Vance, with José Ferrer—1945, NBC (Lifebuoy)
A Woman's Life—1945, CBS (Swan)
Dunninger, the Mentalist, with Joseph Dunninger—1945, 1946, NBC (Rinso)
The Jack Kirkwood Show—1946, CBS (Lux)
Vox Pop, with Parks Johnson and Warren Hull—1946 to 1947, CBS (Lipton)
Grand Marquee, with Jim Ameche and Olan Soule—1946 to 1947, NBC (Rayve)
Call the Police—1947, 1948, 1949, NBC, CBS (Rinso)
Arthur Godfrey's Talent Scouts—1947 to 1956, CBS (Lipton)
My Friend Irma, with Marie Wilson—1947 to 1951, CBS (Pepsodent, Lifebuoy, Swan, Spry)
Junior Miss—1948 to 1950, CBS (Rayve)
Arthur Godfrey Time, with all the Little Godfreys—ca. late 1940s, early 1950s, CBS (Spry, Rinso)
Hit the Jackpot, with Bill Cullen—1950, CBS (Rinso)
Broadway is My Beat, with Larry Thor—1950, CBS (Lipton, Lux)
Joyce Jordan, M.D.—1951 to 1952, ABC
Lone Journey—1951 to 1952, ABC
Romance—1952, CBS (Lux)
Art Linkletter's House Party—1952 to 1956, CBS (multiple participation)

Exposition

The greatest exponent of Lux toilet soap — and of the Lux sobriquet itself— was unequivocally a radio series that came to be synonymously known simply as *Lux* although its full title was *Lux Radio Theater*. Airing from 1934 to 1955, the big-budget, spectacular showcase originally offered snippets of Broadway dramas. But the series achieved even more commanding success when it switched in 1935 to adaptations of first-run Hollywood films. Those attractions were augmented by silver screen idols who recreated their original roles in pithy reproductions before live studio audiences. Soon every star on the West Coast knew about *Lux* and being on that show was considered one of the desirable attributes in marketing careers of cinematic legends. Meanwhile, many of the Hollywood starlets appearing on those glamorous occasions reported how Lux beauty treatments had, in effect, saved their skin for the cameras. It didn't get any better than that for Lever Brothers; those first-person testimonials from celebrated beauty queens sold billions of bars of Lux. For the sponsor, agency, network and stars, it was cash they could take to the bank.

Aside from *Lux Radio Theater* which aired for 21 years, Lever Brothers underwrote a minuscule handful of additional formidable and enduring features. Foremost was the closed-ended daytime serial with a fresh drama weekly, *Aunt Jenny's Real Life Stories*, which ran 19 years. *Big Town* and *Arthur Godfrey's Talent Scouts* (the latter for Thomas J. Lipton, an acquisition) were heard nine seasons each. *Amos 'n' Andy* was on for Lever products for seven years; *Bob Hope*, six years (four of which were for Pepsodent, another acquisition); and *Burns and Allen* and *My Friend Irma*, four years each. To maintain its timeslots while the regular fare was on summer hiatus, Lever provided many entertainment fillers that supplanted long-playing series. Quite a few of these replacement shows were heard for only a few weeks, although some returned multiple summers.

Possibly the most relaxed salesman on network radio, Arthur Godfrey — whose weekday morning segments sometimes plugged Spry and Rinso — purposely mispronounced his words to get a laugh. He'd substitute "Oh-ho-ho" for "Ohio," for instance, while twisting other expressions if he saw an opportunity. He'd allow that "Glass Wax," for example, "cleans *thutty* kinds of dirt in *thutty* seconds." When Godfrey mentioned the makers of Rinso and Spry by name, he labeled them "the Lover Brothers," invariably precipitating a ripple of giggles among the studio audience. And for Lipton tea — a commodity then owned by Lever — while perhaps not goofing it up, he never seemed to tire of reminding listeners: "It's the cheapest thing you can drink next to water."

Commercial

It wasn't just the print ads that relied on Lux recipes. The *Lux Radio Theater* frequently made use of that format in commercializing, too. Here's one from December 20, 1948, on a night when *Miracle on Thirty-Fourth Street* featured original stars Maureen O'Hara, John Payne and Edmund Gwenn.

ANNOUNCER: Before our stars return for their curtain call, Libby Collins wants to tell you about the wonderful way to decorate your Christmas tree, as we promised at the opening of the show.
LIBBY COLLINS: You can give your tree that fresh-from-the-woods look by covering it with real-looking snow you make yourself ... from a box of Lux flakes.
ANNOUNCER: So many people have asked for the Lux recipe for Christmas snow that we gave last week, we'll repeat it tonight. Listen carefully.
LIBBY COLLINS: Take a large box of Lux flakes. Gradually add two cups of lukewarm water ... and beat with an egg-beater until it has the consistency of thick, whipped cream. Then, with your fingers, spread the mixture over the branches of your tree. And that's all.
ANNOUNCER: This snowy covering dries quickly ... it won't melt ... and lasts as long as the tree. Ask your dealer for a copy of this Christmas snow recipe.
LIBBY COLLINS: I don't know of any other decoration that costs so little yet does so much for your tree. It looks lovely used just with tree lights ... or, you can use your usual ornaments if you prefer.
ANNOUNCER: Try it on your mantle decorations and table arrangements, too. It gives them a very professional look.
LIBBY COLLINS: And makes the whole house look more Christmasy ... Now, I'll repeat that recipe. Take a large box of Lux flakes ... gradually add about two cups of lukewarm water ... and beat with an egg-beater. While moist, spread the mixture along the branches. If you want some extra glitter, shake on some shiny, artificial snow before the mixture dries. Let the children help ... they'll *love* doing it ... and *love* the snowy tree.

Liggett & Myers Tobacco Company

History

The early beginnings of tobacco growth and commerce are documented in the *American Tobacco Company* article in this section.

Of the familiar monikers to emerge from United States tobacco history, Liggett & Myers — as far as the public is concerned — no longer exists, not with that nomenclature anyhow. While its origins predate the War of 1812, its myriad ownerships make it one of the most colorful components in the chronicles of U.S. tobacco history. The firm was emblazoned in the nation's collective mind by its hallmark Chesterfield brand that entertainer Arthur Godfrey and other icons of the airwaves hawked repeatedly in "those days." Yet it may be recalled even more because the two letters fronting its appellation were applied to a popular filter-tipped cigarette appearing in the 1950s — L&M. Today anyone would be hard-pressed to find profuse, lingering references to Liggett & Myers Tobacco Company. It's one of several processors whose identities were almost totally snuffed out in the shifting tide of consolidating upheaval. This was particularly true as the twentieth century neared its end. But we are getting ahead of our story.

The beginnings of Liggett & Myers (which will be distinguished as L&M) history can be traced to tobacco farmer-industrialist Christopher Foulks. He was born of German parentage in Philadelphia in 1771. Early in the nineteenth century, Foulks earned his livelihood operating a snuff mill in the little burg of New Egypt, New Jersey. Some time after his property was seized and razed by British militia during the War of 1812, Foulks packed up his family and goods and migrated west. Resettling at Belleview, Illinois, in 1822, he opened a new snuff factory. But he literally closed up shop more than a decade hence to relocate his tobacco mercantile trade in the thriving commercial metropolis of St. Louis, Missouri, where he set up shop in 1833.

At about 18 (ca. 1844), Foulks' young grandson, John Edmund Liggett (1826 to 1897), quit school and entered the tobacco manufacturing venture of Foulks and Shaw. Foulks was Liggett's maternal grandfather and Herman Shaw was his stepdad. Upon Foulks' retirement from the business in 1847, the 21-year-old Liggett became a partner with his stepfather in a newly named Hiram Shaw and Company. Eighteen months down the line, in 1849, Liggett's younger sibling — William C. L. Liggett, born in 1828 — purchased Shaw's interest. The enterprise was renamed J. E. Liggett and Brother. By 1855, "Brother" had sold his participation to a native German, Henry Dausman. For nearly two decades, the establishment operated as Liggett & Dausman.

When the latter sold his share to Missourian George Smith Myers in 1873, the outfit was re-labeled Liggett & Myers, its most memorable and enduring moniker. That imposing nameplate was to persist for more than a century — until 1976, when the Myers portion of the sobriquet was deleted. From that time on, Liggett — applied in various combinations, sometimes alongside other monikers — formed the entity's enduring handle. Nevertheless, even that one was often submerged under corporate identities.

Liggett & Myers was selling L&M plug chewing tobacco by 1876 and in less than a decade it achieved widespread notoriety as "the world's largest manufacturer" of the product. In that epoch, it also expanded into cigarettes, a segment in which the firm was to typically perform better than elsewhere in the diverse tobacco market. The outfit incorporated as Liggett & Myers Company in 1878, the same year it introduced Crimps cigarettes. L&M boasted in print ads, "The laps [papers] on Crimps Cigarettes are secured by crimping. There is no paste or glue on them." Sweet Moments, meanwhile, became L&M's sales leader in those days, while Book, Good Form, Long Voyage, Music, Sledge and Tent smoking brands were marketed simultaneously.

During this pioneering epoch, a St. Louis rival plug manufacturer, Drummond Tobacco Company, fostered by James T. Drummond (1834 to 1897), was to have a profound effect on Liggett & Myers — more than once. Possibly as early as 1869, Drummond manufactured a cigarette brand known as Chesterfield.[1] While geographically distant from that weed's namesake source — Chesterfield County, Virginia — the product very possibly culled some of its ingredients there. It was a blend of Turkish and Virginia tobaccos that derived its earliest popularity among regional smokers. Hold that thought in abeyance for the moment; we shall return to it shortly.

During 1897 and 1898, the Drummond and L&M outfits combined forces to rail against the monopoly run by James B. Duke and the substantial forces of his rising behemoth at the American Tobacco Company (ATC). Although the Missourians fought tenaciously, they lost. Duke bought Drummond's company in October 1898 and L&M the following year, folding both into the burgeoning tobacco trust that ATC spearheaded. (See the article on American Tobacco Company for background.) It was not a happy response in St. Louis.

In the interim, L&M founder John E. Liggett died in 1897. George S. Myers, his surviving partner who had worked alongside Liggett for two dozen years, didn't live to see the dissolution of the trust in 1911; he died in 1910. With each of the major tobacco manufacturers going their separate ways following the breakup of the trust, L&M was reborn, although not in St. Louis. Ties to North Carolina's bright leaf tobacco-growing and producing economy were entrenched after more than a decade spent under the American Tobacco Company umbrella.

With the founding fathers of the business all dead, their successors implemented a shift in location. Leaving a pipe tobacco plant in St. Louis, they consolidated L&M's headquarters offices and cigarette-making operations at Durham, North Carolina, a city that American Tobacco had long dominated. Eventually L&M added cigarette plants at Richmond, Virginia, and San Francisco, California. The firm also consolidated its plug chewing tobacco production at Toledo, Ohio, under the name Pinkerton Tobacco Company.

In the years ahead, L&M marketed plug tobacco labels like Every Day Smoke, Granger Twist, Horse Shoe, Tinsley's Thick Natural Leaf and W. N. Tinsley's, along with Velvet pipe tobacco. But these wouldn't be the wares that defined the company in the annals of tobacco heritage. In the dissolution process — the Drummond founder also dead — L&M was awarded the Chesterfield brand that Drummond instigated four decades earlier. Chesterfield underpinned the company throughout its heyday, for several decades certified as its legacy trademark. The blend of Turkish and Virginia tobaccos was reintroduced in 1912, the year following the separation from the trust. Three years hence, burley and Maryland tobaccos were added to its mixture. A source claims that Chesterfield was the first brand, in 1916, providing a moisture-proof, overall cover to the paper and foil pack. This seems speculative; the same claim is made by historians for Brown & Williamson's Wings cigarettes in 1929.

Nevertheless, after R. J. Reynolds' Camel variety was introduced in 1913 ("the first modern brand") and shortly thereafter became a national commodity advertised coast to coast, Chesterfield followed suit. The two obtained widespread recognition before American's Lucky Strike did likewise and went national. This was to be particularly advantageous, of course, when network radio became available only a decade or so later. Chesterfield's early ads carried the tagline "They *do* satisfy!" It was later altered to "They satisfy!" a phrase that radio and ultimately television audiences would habitually hear, repeated thousands of times. The idiom was reinforced on highway billboards and in magazine and newspaper print ads. Often the slogan was accompanied by the photograph of an entertainment or sports icon smoking a Chesterfield.

Chesterfield and Fatima were L&M's sales leaders in 1918. While its Piedmont cigarette label was promoted in newspaper ads and on trolley car signage, L&M was then concentrating on newspaper space to push its Favorite, Home Run, Perfection, Richmond Straight Cut and Virginia Bright trademarks. By 1952, Chesterfield diversified into king size and regular selections.

The firm's name was altered in 1968 to Liggett & Myers, Inc. In this same period — as other labels brought out extra-long 100-millimeter cigarettes — Chesterfield went one better, naming its 101. That was derived from a length of 101 millimeters; advertising touted it as "a silly millimeter longer." A catchy singing jingle based on the melody of Ritchie Valens' *La Bamba* was effective. In 1970, a new cigarette, Eve, was launched in regular and menthol varieties.

Another name change occurred in 1976, to Liggett Group, Inc., with Liggett & Myers Tobacco Company merely as a division. Under that stance, tobacco provided some but not all of the firm's revenues; the corporate parent had diversified into wine, spirits and pet foods. Liggett bought or developed labels in the liquor market such as Wild Turkey, an upscale bourbon distributed by its subsidiary Austin, Nichols & Company. ANC imported table wines and liqueurs, Italy's Campari aperitif being a prime example. The Paddington Corporation ancillary, meanwhile, imported J & B Scotch. Liggett also produced and sold Alpo, the U.S. market leader in canned dog food. Alpo rapidly became one of the conglomerate's biggest profit makers.

The international cigarette business of Liggett Group, Inc., was sold to Philip Morris Companies, Inc., in 1978.[2] Over vehement protests, again Liggett's operation was acquired by yet another owner, this one London-based. In 1980, British liquor and entertainment multinational Grand Metropolitan plc was the victor in a hostile takeover. Three years beyond, its U.S. operation was renamed GrandMet USA with the tobacco unit identified as Liggett Group, Inc. In the early 1980s — well before the competition followed suit — Liggett launched a line of generic cigarette brands under an ancillary, Gary Tobacco Company. The Liggett trademark was reapplied in 1992.

In the meantime, sales and profits plummeted; in 1986, some U.S. investors took Liggett off Grand Met's hands at a basement bargain price ($137 million — Grand Met had purchased it six years earlier for $575 million). Liggett became an auxiliary of holding company Brooke Group Ltd. Its cache of cigarette labels included Decade, Dorado, Duke of Durham, Eagle, Pyramid and Stride. Brooke failed in an attempt to take over the much larger R. J. Reynolds Tobacco Company in 1995 and 1996. However, the Liggett Group became the first tobacco manufacturer to settle smoking-related litigation brought by the attorneys general of a multiplicity of states in 1996 and 1997.

In 1999, holding company Vector Group Ltd. of Miami, Florida, took over the Liggett unit, making Eve, Grand Prix and Liggett Select cigarettes, along with a profusion of generic lines. That same year it sold its legacy brand Chesterfield (still popular in Europe), Lark and L&M to Philip Morris Companies Inc. (renamed Altria Group). In 2003, the Liggett unit released a Quest strain of genetically engineered low-nicotine and nicotine-free cigarettes.

Liggett was, in the early twenty-first century, the fifth largest manufacturer of cigarettes in the United States. Through its subsidiary Liggett-Ducat Ltd., it manufactures and markets cigarettes in Russia. Through Vector's majority-owned unit New Valley Corporation, the multinational controls investment banking and brokerage business deals in the U.S., real estate development in Russia and scattered Internet and software-related enterprises.

Liggett Vector Brands is, at this writing, the exclusive sales, marketing and distribution agent of Liggett Group, Inc. and Vector Tobacco, Inc. Liggett Vector Brands maintains corporate offices at Research Triangle Park, North Carolina. Its production operations were transferred from Durham — where it was headquartered for most of the twentieth century — to a state-of-the-art manufacturing structure at Mebane, North Carolina.

Radio Series

The Chesterfield Quarter-Hour, with the Boswell Sisters (Martha, Helvetia, Connee) — 1931 to 1932, CBS (Chesterfield)
Music That Satisfies, with Nathaniel Shilkret and His Orchestra, Alexander Gray, Arthur Tracy, Bing Crosby, Ruth Etting, Lennie Hayton and His Orchestra, Tom Howard and George Shelton, Jane Froman — 1931 to 1933, CBS (Chesterfield)
The Philadelphia Symphony Orchestra — 1933 to 1934, CBS (Chesterfield)
The Chesterfield Show, aka *Chesterfield Presents*, with Andre Kostelanetz and His Orchestra, Lawrence Tibbett — 1934 to 1938, CBS (Chesterfield)
Chesterfield Time, aka *Music from Hollywood*, with Hal Kemp and His Orchestra, the Kay Thompson Singers and Alice Faye — 1937, CBS (Chesterfield)
Chesterfield Presents, with Paul Whiteman and His Orchestra and Clark Dennis — 1937 to 1939, CBS (Chesterfield)
The Chesterfield Sports Show, with Paul Douglas — 1937 to 1938, NBC (Chesterfield)
The George Burns and Gracie Allen Show — 1938 to 1939, CBS (Chesterfield)
Chesterfield Time, aka *Pleasure Time*, aka *Victory Tunes*, with Fred Waring and His Orchestra — 1939 to 1944, NBC (Chesterfield)
Chesterfield Time, with Glenn Miller and His Orchestra — 1939, 1940 to 1942, CBS (Chesterfield)

Chesterfield Time, aka *Music That Satisfies*, with Harry James and His Orchestra—1943 to 1945, CBS (Chesterfield)

The Chesterfield Music Shop, with Johnny Mercer and His Orchestra and Jo Stafford—1944, NBC (Chesterfield)

The Chesterfield Supper Club, with Perry Como, Jo Stafford, Bill Lawrence, Johnny Johnston, Sammy Kaye, Mitchell Ayers, Peggy Lee—1944 to 1950, 1954 to 1955, NBC (Chesterfield, Fatima)

Arthur Godfrey Time—1946 to 1953, CBS (Chesterfield)

Tales of Fatima, with Basil Rathbone—1948 to 1949, CBS (Fatima)

Dragnet, with Jack Webb—1949 to 1951, 1952 to 1955, NBC (Fatima, Chesterfield, L&M)

The Bing Crosby Chesterfield Show—1949 to 1952, CBS (Chesterfield, Fatima)

The ABCs of Music, with Robert Q. Lewis—1950, CBS (Chesterfield)

The Bob Hope Show—1950 to 1952, NBC (Chesterfield)

Mr. Keen, Tracer of Lost Persons—1951 to 1952, NBC (Chesterfield—multiple participation)

The Dean Martin and Jerry Lewis Show—1952 to 1953, NBC (Chesterfield)

The Perry Como Show—1953 to 1955, MBS, CBS (Chesterfield, L&M)

Gunsmoke, with William Conrad—1954 to 1957, CBS (Chesterfield, L&M)

Exposition

In an early chapter, the topic of naming a radio series after a sponsor's product was considered. This was a popular and prevalent means of keeping the advertiser's moniker before the audience, particularly so in that period when commercial radio was not yet fully accepted. Most sponsors outgrew that notion as they matured. Liggett & Myers was one of a handful of exceptions. The company attempted to attach *Chesterfield* to everything it could. While it wasn't the only underwriter doing so (Reynolds did it with a multiplicity of *Camel Caravan* outings, for instance), it did so with such a flourish and profusion of radio artists that there was little mistaking the trend.

Listeners heard *The Bing Crosby Chesterfield Show* instead of *The Bing Crosby Show*. There were so many subspecies of *Chesterfield Time* and *The Chesterfield Supper Club* (sundry singers and instrumentalists) and—not far removed—*Music That Satisfies*, a throwback to the smoke's celebrated motto. It was George Washington Hill, king-marketer for competing American Tobacco Company, who pushed his Lucky Strikes down people's throats (figuratively, if not literally). Hill's *Ten Commandments of Advertising* consisted of the single word repetition—10 times yet. What was good for the goose worked just as well for added tobacco partisans.

For many years, a trio of broadcasting superstars was identified with Chesterfield cigarettes. A couple of them were legendary vocalists, Perry Como and Bing Crosby. Yet unambiguously the most unforgettable of the trio was master showman Arthur Godfrey. That triad appeared together for the first time on the same dais in Chicago in April 1950 when Liggett & Myers paraded them before the National Association of Tobacco Distributors. Doting spectators reveled in their jocular exchanges highlighted by a sketch, "Mr. and Mrs. Chesterfield and Their Son, Ash Tray."

In so many ways, Godfrey was the most emblematic, readily discernable spokesman for the brand, if for no other reason than that he was *there* confronting Americans switching on their radios and TVs up to six days a week. In his prime, Godfrey controlled 14 hours weekly of CBS Radio and Television airtime, with nearly 40 percent of that underwritten by Liggett & Myers for Chesterfields. Five years following his death in 1983, Godfrey became a featured player in an early lawsuit brought against a tobacco manufacturer by an individual who was seeking damages for misleading advertising. Godfrey's claims from various broadcasts were played for the jury. One from September 24, 1952, was particularly damaging, in which he read from a Chesterfield ad appearing in a newspaper.

"You hear stuff all the time about 'cigarettes are harmful to you'.... If you smoke it will make you feel better, really...." He read the ad copy: "Nose, throat, and accessory organs not adversely affected by smoking Chesterfield. This is the first such report ever published about any cigarette." A group of smokers from various walks of life were recruited to smoke only Chesterfields for six months and then were given extensive medical examinations. "Now here's the important thing," and he went on to read how the medical specialist had found no ill affects. "Now that ought to make you feel better if you've had any worries at all about it. I never did and I smoke two or three packs of these things every day. I feel pretty good. I never did believe they did you any harm and now we've got the proof."

"Arthur Godfrey was incredibly trusted," noted Richard A. Daynard, Professor of Law at Northeastern University in Boston, who heads up the Tobacco Control Resource Center there. Based partly on this testimony, the plaintiff was awarded damages.

Less than a year later, when Godfrey emerged from hip surgery and discovered that cigarette smoking now made him nauseous, he gave up cigarettes — and Chesterfield's sponsorship as well....

When Godfrey stopped smoking in 1953, he told his long-time sponsor, the Chesterfield people, "I can't sell your product when I don't believe in smoking any more. I think it's a terrible thing." Millions of dollars left CBS' balance sheet that day. But Godfrey had to be true to himself and his credibility. "He did a very brave thing," believes Andy Rooney. "He had espoused their cause for so long. He was very much associated with Chesterfield Cigarettes. He realized he had been wrong ... and he didn't want any more part of them."

But at the time he, like most Americans, saw no connection between smoking and lung cancer.

It was only his personal ordeal with the disease in 1959 that gave Godfrey first-hand experience with the connection. He was devastated, knowing he had influenced the purchases by millions of people who now might be as vulnerable as he was to the effects of tobacco. And in later years he would often speak of smoking as a dirty habit and encourage anyone he met who did to stop, though there was no effective way to correct the damage he had done.[3]

Liggett & Myers' most memorable radio jingle featured two of its foremost advocates, comedian Bob Hope and crooner Bing Crosby, who were pals. The duo frequently appeared on each other's shows while starring together in box office hits on the silver screen. Stemming from an era of military history, Americans began to sing and stomp their feet right along with them to a battle brigade chant: "Sound off! Sound off! Sound off for Chesterfields!"

Commercial

DICK STARK: The mask is off ... The mask is off in cigarette advertising. Chesterfield is first to name all of its ingredients because you should know what gives you the best possible smoke ... The right combination of the world's best tobaccos ... pre-tested by laboratory instruments for the most desirable smoking qualities ... and kept tasty and fresh with tried and tested moistening agents ... pure, natural sugars ... chemically pure, harmless, far more costly glycerol ... nothing else. Only these are entirely safe for use in the mouth, as proved by over 40 years of continuous use in tobacco products. And remember ... your Chesterfields are wrapped in cigarette paper of the highest purity ... the best that money can buy. We name our ingredients because every smoker should know what makes Chesterfield the best possible smoke ... much milder, with an extraordinarily good taste and ... most important ... no unpleasant aftertaste. Ask your dealer for Chesterfields. Sound off for Chesterfields and do it today.

This commercial — delivered by the recorded voice of Dick Stark on an NBC broadcast of *Mr. Keen, Tracer of Lost Persons* on April 3, 1952 — engenders visions of Stark puffing a cigarette against a forebodingly black background as he hosted CBS-TV's *Danger* during the same era (1950 to 1955). (The TV series was underwritten by Block Drug Company for Ammi-dent toothpaste and tooth powder, by the way.) As smoke rings encircled the set, the cigarette became a device of superior proportions on a black-and-white screen that was virtually empty besides the narrator. The smoke had a fairly mesmerizing effect on the viewers, meanwhile. Now that we've been exposed to Stark's Chesterfield radio commercial, it's natural to ponder: What brand was *he* smoking during those five years on *Danger*?

The radio commercial — which referred to Chesterfield's components — broadly hints at the very thing that eventually led to public outcry: "Only these are entirely safe for use in the mouth, as proved by over 40 years of continuous use in tobacco products." (What does that tell listeners in practical terms?) While this predates the U.S. Surgeon General's fears by a dozen years (1964), it's obvious that the radar of the typical adult was already up over the potential risks of health hazards. Yet it seems strange that Liggett & Myers and its rivals go there intentionally. Perhaps it was more of an issue than we suspected — or maybe more than government suspicions were willing to yet admit.

In the unrelated, protracted show opening (from October 8, 1948) that follows, it appears as if Liggett & Myers has invested in a cowcatcher commercial, except there is but one product plugged throughout this Godfrey segment. Repeated five days a week, it has a powerful impact on the legions tuning in.

NETWORK CUE: (*bong*)
TONY MARVIN: A ... B ... C ... Always Buy Chesterfields, a better cigarette because it's milder ... the best cigarette for you to smoke.
JANETTE DAVIS: (*music underneath*) A ...
THE MARINERS: (*sing*) Always milder ...
JANETTE DAVIS: (*music underneath*) B ...
THE MARINERS: (*sing*) Better tasting ...
JANETTE DAVIS: (*music underneath*) C ...
THE MARINERS: (*sing*) Cooler smoking ...
JANETTE DAVIS: A ... B ... C ...
ARTHUR GODFREY: Always Buy Chesterfields ... they satisfy!
THE MARINERS: (*sing*) Smoke dreams ... from smoke rings ...
JANETTE DAVIS: (*sing*) While a Chesterfield burns ...
MUSIC: Segues into orchestral theme *Seems Like Old Times* as Godfrey whistles the tune
TONY MARVIN: (*music underneath*) Chesterfield presents ... Arthur Godfrey Time ... Yes, it's Arthur Godfrey and all the Little Godfreys ... Janette Davis, The Mariners, Bill Lawrence, Archie Bleyer and His Orchestra. And now, here's that man himself ... Arthur "buy 'em by the carton" Godfrey!

In addition to the band, it took seven other performers to open that segment of the Godfrey marathon. If Liggett & Myers was shelling out a fee to each artist for his or her participation, it was costing a bundle just to get the show on the air! Yet its effectiveness couldn't be counted in cash for the group participation intimated that *everybody* was on Chesterfield's bandwagon. Not surprisingly, until Godfrey pulled the plug and said "no more," Chesterfield was his most enduring and potent underwriter.

P. Lorillard, Inc.

History

The early beginnings of tobacco growth and commerce are documented in the *American Tobacco Company* article in this section.

P. Lorillard, Inc. is the oldest tobacco processor in the United States. It was established in 1760 when a French Huguenot who had immigrated to the United States — Pierre Lorillard — opened a snuff-making "manufactory." It was initially located in the Bronx borough of New York City. Strikingly, a "P. Lorillard" was to preside over this firm into the twentieth century as no fewer than five successive generations by that moniker assumed the helm.

Eventually, the plant produced cigars, pipe tobacco and plug chewing tobacco in addition to snuff. These were the most requested commodities by users in that early epoch. A century after its launch, the Lorillard firm added roll-your-own cigarettes to its product mix (1860). And as the demand for cigarettes mounted, by the 1880s, the enterprise was manufacturing them, too. Cigarettes would ultimately define the manufacturer's significance in the industry, in fact. But it would do so with only a couple of trademarks out of more than 160 labels it produced. Sales exceeded $10 million annually by 1883. At the same time, production surpassed 25 million pounds of tobacco goods. The Lorillard workforce stood at 3,500 with a weekly payroll of $35,000 (an average of $10 weekly — many of those were youngsters attending Lorillard's free evening school). By the 1890s, the firm produced Beech-Nut chewing tobacco, which captured a substantial share of that segment.

Lorillard unsuccessfully targeted women with its Helmar and Murad cigarette brands. Then it hit pay dirt. Within four years after the firm introduced Old Gold cigarettes in 1926, the firm took a 7 percent share of the market for that one brand; in 1930, its sales hit 8.5 billion. While Old Gold was far behind the leaders — Lucky Strike, Camel and Chesterfields — it stood way out in front of fifth-place Raleigh. Lorillard paid big bucks to win those smokers, too, incorporating flappers, pretty girls and comic-strip illustrations into its innovative marketing stash. One of Old Gold's memorable campaign themes obviously resonated with retail buyers: "Not a Cough in a Carload."

Like some of its counterparts, Lorillard became an effective master at advertising. Paying farmers to allow hand-painted signs on the sides of their barns,[1] the firm's marketing savvy included trading cards placed within product packaging and creating a plethora of premiums. Lorillard may have been responsible for originating the concept of the cigar store Indian, too, that was linked with tobacco as early as 1789.

As time elapsed, Lorillard did not escape the health imbroglio that enveloped all of the tobacco manufacturers. In 1946, a Lorillard chemist sent a memo to the firm's manufacturing committee in which he said: "Certain scientists and medical authorities have claimed for many years that the use of tobacco contributes to cancer development in susceptible people. Just enough evidence has been presented to justify the possibility of such a presumption."[2] What did he suspect that the rest of the country would wake up to in time?

As the cigarette scare picked up steam, manufacturers — generally operating independently of one another at the time — began to address the issue with answers of their own. In 1987, *Los Angeles Times* reporter Myron Levin gave an assessment after Lorillard's advertising hailed the Micronite filter attached to its new Kent cigarettes some 35 years earlier.[3]

Kent was launched in 1952 by P. Lorillard Co. and named for its president, Herbert A. Kent. Something of a maverick among the cigarette makers, Lorillard came closest to admitting that cigarettes were harmful. It promoted Kent as the brand for "the 1 out of every 3 smokers who is unusually sensitive to tobacco tars and nicotine." It said Kent offered them "the greatest health protection in cigarette history."

In double page magazine ads that played on the public's gee-whiz faith in science and technology, Lorillard said its quest for the new filter "ended in an atomic energy plant, where the makers of KENT found a material being used to filter air of microscopic impurities."

"What is 'Micronite'?" another ad asked. "It's a pure, dust-free, completely harmless material that is so safe, so effective, it actually is used to help filter the air in hospital operating rooms."

In reality, the Micronite filter — whose actual composition the ads never revealed — contained a particularly dangerous form of asbestos. It was dust from this "dust-free, completely harmless material" that killed ... more than a score ... who made filter material for Lorillard.

There was asbestos in the filter from 1952 at least until 1957. During this time, according to sales figures, Americans puffed their way through over 13 billion Kents.

Another source allowed, "Asbestos was a popular material in the 1950s.... In those days, the discovery of a new asbestos mine was announced in the newspapers and celebrated.... [Kent] was promoted as the first sanitary cigarette. 'Do you like a good smoke but not what smoking does to you?' Kent's adverts inquired."[4] Pondered today, it is a chilling thought.

Headquartered in New York, P. Lorillard Company was acquired by Loews Corporation in 1968, becoming a wholly owned auxiliary under the sobriquet Lorillard, Inc. Lorillard Tobacco Company is a subsidiary of Lorillard, Inc. Beginning in the mid–1990s, Loews Corporation was comprised of five key ancillary units: Bulova Corporation, CNA Financial Corporation, Diamond M-Odeco Drilling, Inc., Loews Hotels Holding Corporation and Lorillard, Inc. The latter's cigarette inventory included the Kent, MaxSatin, Newport, Old Gold, Golden Light, Spring, Style, Triumph and True trademarks. Of the 20 top cigarette brands in America in 1979, Lorillard claimed four rungs of that prestigious ladder although all of its steps were far from the top, a telling sign that the halcyon days had passed: Kent (10th place, 19.3 billion sold), Golden Lights (12th, 13.2 billion), True (15th, 11.5 billion) and Newport (18th, 9.8 billion). The top five sellers were, in order: Marlboro (103.6 billion, from Philip Morris), Winston (81.0 billion, R. J. Reynolds), Kool (56.7 billion, Brown & Williamson), Salem (53.2 billion, R. J. Reynolds) and Pall Mall (33.9 billion, American).

Lorillard's manufacturing arena was relocated from the Bronx to Jersey City, New Jersey, in the 1870s. The enterprise incorporated in 1891 and joined the tobacco trust with several other competing makers in the 1890s. (See the article on the American Tobacco Company for extensive detail.) When that amalgamation disbanded in 1911, the larger members again went their separate ways as independent tobacco processors. Lorillard persisted in operating cigar and plug factories in Jersey City, vacating and releasing its principal facility to rival R. J. Reynolds in 1928, which made Camel cigarettes. Today a block-long warehouse at 111 First Street is part of a district relegated to arts development. While a sign still identifies it as "P. Lorillard Company," the facility's interior accommodates commercial galleries and rental studios for artists.

Early in the twentieth century, Lorillard opened a second factory site in the heart of burley tobacco country at Louisville, Kentucky. Rival tobacco manufacturer Brown & Williamson established its headquarters in Louisville in 1928 and a third competitor, Philip Morris, opened a large plant in Louisville, too. Lorillard's operations were phased out in Louisville in 1986. The unit's headquarters staff transitioned from Jersey City to a new consolidated home base and manufacturing center at Greensboro, North Carolina. Greensboro is situated in the heart of bright leaf tobacco country, in close proximity to R. J. Reynolds (Winston-Salem) and former headquarters sites of American and Liggett & Myers (Durham).

Radio Series

The Old Gold Hour, with Bing Crosby, Paul Whiteman and His Orchestra — 1929 to 1930, CBS (Old Gold) Note — This musical variety hour with Paul Whiteman sponsored by Old Gold debuted over New York's WEAF (the flagship station of the NBC Red chain) on January 4, 1928; it was heard locally until the Columbia network beamed it to a wider audience starting February 5, 1929
The Fred Waring Orchestra and Chorus — 1933 to 1934, CBS (Old Gold)
The Old Gold Program, with Dick Powell and Ted Fio Rito and His Orchestra — 1934, CBS (Old Gold)
Charles McCall, Hollywood Gossip — 1937 to 1938, CBS (Old Gold)
Melody and Madness, aka *The Old Gold Program*, with Robert Benchley, Artie Shaw and His Orchestra, Jimmy Durante — 1938 to 1939, CBS (Old Gold)
Barry Winton and His Orchestra — 1939 to 1940, NBC (Old Gold)
What's New, with Benny Goodman and His Orchestra — 1941, NBC Blue (Old Gold)
The Old Gold Program — 1941 to 1942, NBC Blue (Old Gold)
The Nelson Eddy Program — 1942 to 1943, CBS (Old Gold)
The Bob Crosby Show, with Bob Crosby and the Bobcats and Jo Stafford — 1943 to 1944, NBC (Old Gold)
The New Old Gold Show, with Monty Woolley and Sammy Kaye and His Orchestra — 1943 to 1944, CBS (Old Gold)
The Old Gold Show, with Woody Herman and His Orchestra — 1944, CBS (Old Gold)
Which is Which, with Ken Murray — 1944 to 1945, CBS (Old Gold)
The Old Gold Comedy Theater, with Harold Lloyd — 1944 to 1945, NBC (Old Gold)
Meet Me at Parky's, with Harry Einstein and Peggy Lee — 1945 to 1947, NBC (Old Gold)
Songs by Sinatra, with Frank Sinatra and the Pied Pipers — 1945 to 1947, CBS (Old Gold)
Rhapsody in Rhythm, with Jan Savitt and Connie Haines — 1946, NBC (Old Gold)
The Bickersons, aka *The Old Gold Show*, aka *The Don Ameche Show*, with Don Ameche, Frances Langford and Frank Morgan — 1947, 1948, CBS (Old Gold)
Ted Mack's Original Amateur Hour — 1948 to 1952, ABC (Old Gold)

Dr. I. Q., the Mental Banker—1950, ABC (Embassy)
Queen for a Day, with Jack Bailey—1950 to 1951, MBS (Old Gold)
Stop the Music!, with Bert Parks—1951 to 1952, ABC (Old Gold)
Two for the Money, with Herb Shriner—1952 to 1956, NBC, CBS (Old Gold)
Monday Morning Headlines, with Don Gardiner—1952 to 1954, ABC (Old Gold, Kent)
Taylor Grant and the News—1952 to 1954, ABC (Old Gold)

Exposition

P. Lorillard tended to put its advertising eggs into solitary baskets. It did so twice.

Compared with some of the other tobacco marketers that comprehensively plugged myriad wares on the air — doing so in a colossal fashion on NBC (including NBC Red *and* NBC when there was no longer a Blue web), to the near-exclusion of chief competitor CBS — Lorillard appeared to follow that procedure in reverse. For most of the company's aural-only years, CBS was the unmistakable winner in acquiring Lorillard-backed series with NBC acquiring little more than leftovers. For nearly two decades, in fact, Lorillard shared far more of its advertising revenue with CBS than with any other coast-to-coast hookup. Not until the underwriter began to concentrate on competitive audience participation shows and newscasters did it commit much of its radio budget someplace else. And in the waning days of the golden age, it turned out to be ABC — not NBC — that substantially profited from Lorillard's generosity. Was there an advertising manager at Lorillard who, perhaps, was an alumnus of CBS or ABC, or who had an axe to grind with NBC? The answer isn't clear but the pattern is difficult to miss.

Secondly, with few documented exceptions — unlike its counterparts in the tobacco business — at least until the 1950s, when Kent arrived, Lorillard focused almost all of its commercial broadcast messages on a single label, Old Gold, while some others pitched manifold commodities. This seems to be true despite American's nearly unyielding bent for Lucky Strike and R. J. Reynolds' strong preference for Camel until mid-century. Unfortunately for Lorillard, it didn't overcome its competition. The reasons are potentially many: the product itself, its distribution system, the shows on which Old Gold advertised, their airtimes and network placement (including the competition for listeners thrown against them), the commercial messages and their delivery. In the heyday of network radio, while Old Gold achieved fourth place among sellers at the start of the 1930s, at the start of both the 1940s and the 1950s, it could do no better than rank in fifth spot.

Commercial

The following commercial is from a *Songs by Sinatra* show (ca. 1945). The feature was performed live before a studio audience that inexorably embraced hordes of screaming teenyboppers. Notice the interplay between the star and announcer, a common practice in hawking commodities during the epoch. Most plugs in these exchanges, as in this case, quickly lost the banter between host and interlocutor to give the latter opportunity to emphatically make his points about the sponsor's product. The star's presence was usually little more than a lead-in to transacting the business at hand.

BILL LAZAR: The other day a friend of mine asked me: "What do you mean with the slogan, 'Why be irritated? Light an Old Gold.' Why an Old Gold?"

FRANK SINATRA: I trust that you had a very ready answer, William?

BILL LAZAR: Yes indeed, Frank. I told him, to get extra smoking comfort when you need it the Old Gold folks go to extreme lengths to give you a superior cigarette ... to the last detail. Only the finest is good enough.

FRANK SINATRA: Good, good, good. Fine, fine, fine. That's Old Gold, hey! (*audience laughter*)

BILL LAZAR: P. Lorillard had a passion for detail. In every detail of the products he sold, he gave more than the smoker expected. And Old Gold keeps faith with this honored Lorillard quality code. It isn't content with the world's choicest tobaccos. It adds another detail ... another refinement. It isn't satisfied with ordinary moistening agents. It adds a special ingredient — apple honey — another refinement to make Old Gold your comforting friend. So ... when we say, "Don't let little annoyances get you down," we mean just that. For real smoking relaxation, try a pack of Old Golds today.

Miles Laboratories, Inc.

History

If there never had been a Miles Nervine, the hoopla that eventually translated into Miles Laboratories, Inc., might never have occurred. But a patent medicine tonic for treating anxiety developed by Dr. Franklin L. Miles (1845 to 1929) of Elkhart, Indiana, turned a small-time operation into a global supplier of curative goods. Furthermore, his firm found its own relief in the competitive industrial wars by becoming the object of a takeover bid by another of the world's major drug manufacturers. That was far into the future, of course, long after Miles' burgeoning product line came to be widely recognized and respected for its ability to treat common maladies with over-the-counter preparations.

Its wares (Alka-Seltzer, Bactine, Miles Nervine, One-A-Day, Tabcin, etc.) were familiar in U.S. households throughout the golden age of radio, the result of a relentless and massive advertising program. Miles gained a strong foothold with American consumers by adopting the airwaves as a promotional tool. That coincided with its commodities arriving in profusion on local store shelves. It was just about that time that radio was becoming a new medium of choice in persuading potential purchasers. As one of its heavy hitters, Miles underwrote daytime and primetime broadcast fare in dual media. Its investments then are still paying off now as its convincing arguments, taglines and jingles remind buyers of an earlier day when they bought those brand names with confidence.

The namesake founder of all this activity, Franklin Miles, branded by one source a "country doctor," returned to Elkhart at age 30 in 1875.[1] The physician's early concentration was in treating eye and ear disorders. While he focused on a patient's total wellbeing, Miles specialized, too, linking the nervous system with the general physical condition of his clients. Nine years hence he established Dr. Miles Medical Company — incorporated in 1885 — and dedicated to his fairly unique interests in medical practice for the period.

A pithy examination of a fragment of Miles' early life and training will probably impart an appreciation for the kind of individual capable of launching one of the world's foremost patent medicine enterprises. The man who focused much of his career on nervous disorders may have come by his predilection naturally: while he was still young, during a widespread outbreak of disease, his mom and sister succumbed. His father, meanwhile, was a fortune hunter. Fairly estranged from his family during most of Franklin Miles' adolescence, he usually resided in far away California and Hawaii. The youth's nurturing, therefore, fell to some Elkhart kin.

The lad was no dummy, however. Industriously, he applied himself in whatever circumstances he encountered. He became an enthusiastic learner. And when his dad died, he took a $5,000 inheritance and funded an intensive course of advanced academics for himself. For a dozen years, he intermittently progressed through diverse pursuits in Eastern and Midwestern schools. He was certified in twin disciplines, attaining the doctor of medicine and bachelor of laws degrees.[2] He also wrote extensively, penning expositions in a variety of subjects signifying a high degree of competence in areas of his medical concentration.[3] According to *The Milwaukee Journal*, which surveyed his accomplishments in 1894, Miles was by then "one of the best known specialists in the U.S. in diseases of the brain, heart and nerves."

Upon establishing a medical practice in Elkhart, not long afterward the physician was producing a home remedy dubbed Dr. Miles Restorative Nervine. It was proffered for treating uneasiness or related symptoms in a spate of weakened circumstances, depicted as "nervousness or nervous exhaustion, sleeplessness, hysteria, headache, neuralgia, backache, pain, epilepsy, spasms, fits and St. Vitus' dance." Another source added dizziness to the mix. While "not a cure-all," Miles' wonder drug nevertheless "soothes, quiets and restores the nerves and their centers to their normal condition," a report obsessed. Any remedy that could satisfy all those conditions had to be good.

To advertise his bromide sedative syrup — a precursor to modern tranquilizers — Miles circulated a lightly camouflaged marketing tool that he published regularly — *Medical News*. When word spread concerning his redemptive formula, he went into the manufacturing business. That initial commodity opened the door for a variety of supplementary tonics, blood purifiers and liver pills. The following year Miles added a couple of dry goods vendors as partners — Norris Felt and Hugh McLachlan. Until local businessmen George E. Compton, a miller who had already invested in Miles' scheme, and druggist A. R. Burns bought Felt's and McLachlan's shares in 1887, the fledgling enterprise showed lackluster execution, nevertheless.

That was about to change.

In 1889 Albert Raper Beardsley, scion of Elkhart's founding family and a leading local businessman [a starch manufacturing executive], bought into the company as well. Beardsley became general manager and eventually treasurer; Compton became vice president. In 1890 Albert Beardsley's nephew, Andrew Hubble "Hub" Beardsley, began working at the Dr. Miles Medical Company; he eventually became secretary of the company and played a leading role in its development. He was the company's first chairman in 1925 and, with Miles's death in 1929, became its first president. All told, five Beardsleys served as president of the company between 1929 and 1964. It was Miles's new partners who made the company a success. They convinced him to cede day-to-day control of the business to professional managers, and they aggressively marketed and promoted his medicines. It was marketing that was the basis of the success of the Dr. Miles Medical Company.[4]

Acquiring space vacated by *The Elkhart Independent* at 110 High Street in 1888, Miles' exposure to journalism's hallowed halls might have been a catalyst prompting heavy investment in printed advertising material on its own presses. The equipment was presumably left behind by the previous occupants. In 1893, Dr. Miles Medical Company earmarked no less than $100,000 for advertising, a huge chunk of cash by any stretch of the imagination in that age. Miles printed a wide variety of colorful almanacs that it mailed to rural patrons (producing 20 million annually by the 1940s); there were calendars dispatched to retail druggists for handing to their customers; and a "Little Book" series on health and housekeeping matters was issued, which pooled helpful information and product promotion. The use of print media set a pattern that would be exploited with the discovery of radio a few decades later.

In 1890, Miles supplied the first mail order requests for the health-giving Nervine tonic, pitched as a "calmative" aid. By then, the firm was turning a profit for the first time. Dr. Miles Restorative Nervine was responsible for a major share of the outfit's sales into the mid–1930s. The commodity was to persist as a packaged medication into the late 1960s, in fact, re-labeled Miles Nervine some years earlier. While that sedative became the foundation of a soon-to-be proliferating product line, by no means could it be considered the unambiguous and unchallenged leader of an array of medications touted by Miles. That honor indisputably belongs to Alka-Seltzer, which came on the market a quadrennial before the firm's most recognizable appellation, Miles Laboratories, Inc., was adopted in 1935. Dr. Miles Medical Company had been reduced to a more simplistic Dr. Miles Laboratories in 1932 before attaining its most famous moniker.

Alka-Seltzer resulted after Hub Beardsley, nephew of founding associate Albert Beardsley, rose through the ranks of his uncle's business from clerk (1890) to chairman of the board (1925). He engaged one of the outfit's chemists, Mikey Wiseman, in transforming Nervine into an innovative combination that could be housed in an effervescent capsule. But before Wiseman's work had gone very far, Beardsley learned that, by merely consuming a liquid blend of bicarbonate of soda and aspirin, some journalists at *The Elkhart Truth* staved off all signs of colds. What if, he thought to himself, we could derive an effervescent aspirin-bicarbonate of soda dosage in something like a pill?

After combining acetylsalicylic acid (aspirin), sodium bicarbonate (baking soda) and citric acid, Wiseman and his associates created some large effervescent tablets. Mixed with water, they produced carbon dioxide gas (seltzer) as the acid and bicarbonate reacted robustly while dissolving. The ingested solution offered users a quick remedy for headache, heartburn and hangovers by treating their pain while it neutralized excess stomach acid.

After conducting many tests, Miles' Alka-Seltzer went on the market in 1931. The product's "immediate and increasing success had much to do with the repeal of prohibition," noted one corporate authority. "As the incidence of hangovers increased, so did consumption of Alka-Seltzer. Even today Alka-Seltzer remains the world's number one cure for the hangover."

Miles turned its new discovery into a gold mine by plugging it in multiple advertising media, including printed tracts and all the added promotional tools that rolled from its presses. Within a few months, nevertheless, advertising guru Charles Beardsley — yet another descendant of one of the company's early fathers, a man whose destiny would also include the firm's presidency — led Miles into an early radio buy. The syndicated *Alka-Seltzer Comedy Stars of Hollywood* in spring 1932 and the *National Barn Dance* emanating from Chicago on NBC Blue in autumn 1933 were the first of numerous sponsorships for Alka-Seltzer, "first aid for acid indigestion," in what would become a pervasive aural presence.

Miles began tinkering substantially with the focus of its product line in the 1960s through new product development, acquisitions and divestitures. Pursuing a new strategy in health care, it purchased Worthington Foods Company, a pioneer in developing vegetable protein substitutes, especially soybeans. In the late 1960s and early 1970s, the firm introduced a wide range of supplementary vitamins, including some for juveniles (Bugs Bunny, Chocks and Flintstones brands), to One-A-Day brand with minerals and iron, on the market without the extras since 1943.

A fifth of Miles' sales and a still higher percentage of earnings were derived by the firm's professional product group. That included diagnostic agents and ethical drugs for treating allergies and skin conditions plus lab supplies and electronic instruments. In the five-year period beginning in 1972, Miles' fortunes fell as consumer product sales faltered, accounting for less than half the company's sales (they had been responsible for 75 percent of sales in 1961). It was a difficult reality with Miles' flagship Alka-Seltzer trademark suddenly underperforming expectations. There were reasons for this: (a) increasing medical awareness of the general public, who realized it wasn't in their interest to ingest a multi-symptom remedy without having all of the symptoms it treated (like a headache *and* an upset stomach); (b) a growing trend away from aspirin-based cures to acetaminophen- and ibuprofen-based pain relievers; (c) a disturbingly noticeable lackluster, dry, dusty savor.

As sales of Alka-Seltzer in its original form diminished, Bayer HealthCare (the former name of Miles Laboratories, Inc.) applied the instantly identifiable sobriquet to newly-created preparations, like the common cold line of medications dubbed Alka-Seltzer Plus. Some of the creations no longer carry aspirin as part of their ingredients, nor are they any longer effervescent. "This is because the billions of dollars building the brand through advertising are still yielding benefits," claimed one source.

By the late 1970s, Miles' ethical drug sector, Dome Laboratories, introduced new wares for treating allergies, skin disorders and mental illness. In the meantime, although the founders' heirs continued to populate the company's board, beginning in 1977, outsiders assumed much more profound participation in running the drug-maker. According to one historian: "In the 1970s the leadership of Miles Laboratories, led by chairman Walter Ames Compton and president Rowland G. Rose, concluded that the corporation lacked adequate assets for growth, and they explored opportunities for joint ventures and mergers."[5] Out of the blue, Miles was abruptly faced with the prospect of a takeover by the much larger Bayer AG of West Germany, fourth largest chemical manufacturer on the planet.

Bayer's original North American commerce, situated in the United States and Canada, was seized as enemy assets near the end of the First World War. Bayer AG's original possessions here were long gone, having been confiscated and dispatched as adversarial substance by the U.S. government decades before. But in 1978, the Leverkusen, Germany-based multinational was prepared to start over. It purchased Miles Laboratories, Inc., and its auxiliary unit, Miles Canada, plus Cutter Biologicals, yet another Miles accessory that produced insect repellent and Factor VIII, a synthetic human clotting solution for hemophiliacs. In acquiring Miles, Bayer AG reestablished its presence in this hemisphere. Bayer ultimately paid almost $254 million for Miles, the costliest purchase involving a U.S. firm by an international pharmaceutical outfit to that date.

"Analysts now agree that the Bayer takeover was simply the most dramatic occurrence in a growing industry trend of established European companies entering the U.S. market by acquiring medium-sized American companies," declared one business observer. "Rather than build their own distribution systems, foreign companies save a great deal of trouble and money by buying American firms in the same business that have already developed successful operations. While maintaining its identity, Miles Laboratories in Elkhart effectively became Bayer's headquarters for its U.S. pharmaceutical operations."

Beginning in 1985, Miles' health care commodities rose to the forefront, dominating all the subsidiary's other wares. By then, Bayer AG had acquired a half-dozen additional American firms with competing product lines. Yet it was Miles Labs that unambiguously "remains the most prized of Bayer's acquisitions" wrote one reporter. Noting that a third of Miles' profits were derived from international markets, the scribe added: "Its sales have grown impressively since the takeover." Miles was also strategically placed to market an extensive line of Bayer derivatives. "For now, at least, neither management nor investors can quarrel with Miles' impressive performance and Bayer's very satisfying profit margins," another assessment read.

The holding firm transferred its American headquarters to Pittsburgh, Pennsylvania, in 1992, when it merged Miles with a half-dozen other U.S. interests acquired by Bayer. The new name was Miles, Inc., but it, too, was living on borrowed time. In 1995, the Miles nomenclature was totally abolished from all commodities, physical plants and other markings. Bayer AG had acquired Sterling Winthrop in 1994, manufacturing Bayer aspirin in North America. It thereby reclaimed the rights to its own name and trademarks as well as to Bayer aspirin.

Radio Series

Alka-Seltzer Comedy Stars of Hollywood, with Franklin Brown, Kay LaValle, The King's Men—1932 to 1934, Syndication (Alka-Seltzer)
National Barn Dance, with Joe Kelly—1933 to 1946, NBC Blue, NBC (Alka-Seltzer)
Uncle Ezra's Radio Station, aka *Sunday Afternoon in Rosedale*, with Pat Barrett—1934 to 1939, NBC (Alka-Seltzer)
Alec Templeton Time—1939 to 1941, NBC (Alka-Seltzer)
The Quiz Kids, with Joe Kelly—1940 to 1951, NBC Blue, NBC, Blue, ABC (Alka-Seltzer)
Lum and Abner, with Chester Lauck and Norris Goff—1941 to 1948, NBC Blue, Blue, ABC, CBS (Alka-Seltzer, Miles Nervine, Bactine, One-A-Day, Tabcin)
News of the World, with John W. Vandercook—1941 to 1946, NBC (Alka-Seltzer)
The Roy Rogers Show, with Pat Buttram and Dale Evans—1946 to 1947, NBC (Alka-Seltzer)
Queen for a Day, with Jack Bailey—1946 to 1950, MBS (Alka-Seltzer)
News of the World, with Morgan Beatty—1946-ca. 1958, NBC (Alka-Seltzer)
Ladies Be Seated, with Johnny Olsen—1947 to 1949, ABC (Alka-Seltzer and Tabcin—multiple participation)
Alka-Seltzer Time, with Herb Shriner and the Raymond Scott Quintet—1948 to 1949, CBS (Alka-Seltzer)
Hilltop House—1948 to 1954, CBS (Alka-Seltzer, Bactine, Miles Nervine, One-A-Day, Tabcin)
The Curt Massey-Martha Tilton Show—1949 to 1954, CBS, MBS (Alka-Seltzer)
One Man's Family—1950 to 1954, NBC (Alka-Seltzer, Tabcin, Bactine, One-A-Day, Miles Nervine)
Break the Bank, with Clayton "Bud" Collyer—1953 to 1955, NBC, MBS (Alka-Seltzer)
Just Plain Bill—1954 to 1955, NBC (Alka-Seltzer)
Fibber McGee & Molly, with Jim and Marian Jordan—1955 to 1956, NBC (Alka-Seltzer, Tabcin)
The Woman in My House—1955 to 1957, NBC (Alka-Seltzer, Tabcin, One-A-Day, Miles Nervine, Bactine)

Exposition

Miles Laboratories, Inc., applied a pervasive formula to its radio advertising, much as it did in the patent medicines it manufactured. All of its shows touted Alka-Seltzer in at least one commercial and often in multiple pitches. But before most of the firm's series left the air each day or week, in a closing plug — commonly branded by broadcasting as a hitchhike commercial — Miles rotated in one of its other "fine, dependable products": Bactine antiseptic, Miles Nervine anxiety calmative, One-A-Day multiple vitamins or Tabcin antihistamine cold tablets were the most common in these concluding spots.

"The common denominator of both the company's radio and subsequent television commercials has been humor — memorable and amusing jingles for radio, exaggerated and often hilarious depictions of the 'before and after' Alka-Seltzer patient for television," wrote one reviewer. As has been noted, Miles Laboratories wasn't hesitant about spending money to increase its presence on the ether, having done so from the early 1930s to the latter days of its enveloping impact as Miles' reputation as a drug manufacturer increased. Its innovations in broadcast advertising, particularly for Alka-Seltzer, created these unforgettable taglines to all who saw or heard them in repeated airings:

I can't believe I ate the whole thing!

Mama mia, that's some spicy meatball!

Try it, you'll like it!

Plop, plop ... fizz, fizz ... oh, what a relief it is!

Each expression was summarily adopted by American radio listeners and TV viewers and added to the nation's omnipresent everyday vernacular. Subsequently, Alka-Seltzer celebrated its 75th anniversary on March 28, 2006, with a record-setting buffet featuring more than 500 dishes. The event was staged at the Hilton Hotel in Las Vegas and infused the product with some needed promotion reminiscent of its earlier years.

One of the most imaginative creations of Miles' numerous forays into ad campaigns resulted when commercial artist Bob Watkins and advertising account executive Chuck Tennant, of the Miles business at Chicago's Wade Advertising, combined their ideas. The pair had been buddies during the Second World War. When they coalesced, the result (which reportedly took only three hours to produce) was a caricature figure that was to sell billions of boxes and bottles of the bicarbonate preparation that had already made Miles renowned and prosperous in previous decades. Speedy Alka-Seltzer, exhibiting a tablet-emblem body complete with hat and effervescent wand, initially turned up in the slick women's magazines during the spring of 1952. While he sang his little heart out on radio commercials — actually, it was pint-sized actor Dick Beals speaking; Beals had launched his career on radio's *The Lone Ranger* a few years earlier — possibly not until the character appeared on scads of TV commercials did mainstream Americans begin to seriously interact with him. In a decade, 1954 to 1964, the little animated fellow adorned 212 commercials, making more than 20 debuts a year.

When Alka-Seltzer began to fall out of favor with the younger drug buyers as the 1960s wore on, some imaginative thinking was elicited to reverse the ebbing fortunes of a brand that had "become the symbol of people who drank too much and ate too much." Employing (Jack) Tinker & Partners advertising think tank, Miles underwrote a new campaign offering reasons for people to use Alka-Seltzer. To get that across, the firm exhibited some amusing new commercials.

For one thing, at Tinkers' suggestion, sales of the product increased sharply when users were instructed to drop *two* tablets in a glass of water. While revenues didn't double, there was a dramatic shift of fortune attributable to that hint. The emphasis was fortified with the catchy, enduring jingle *Plop, plop ... fizz, fizz ... oh, what a relief it is!* If audiences hadn't gotten the message before, the thought that anyone had ever used anything less than *two* Alka-Seltzer tablets at one time was now anathema — erased from public consciousness by the sound and sight of dual tablets hitting the water. It worked on radio about as effectively as it did on TV for you could *hear* the twin substances striking the H_2O before the fizz began.

In another dimension, the popular *One Man's Family* (1932 to 1959) radio series — which originated as a weekly primetime drama and finished its ethereal career as a daytime serial — proffered numerous premium hooks over its lifetime. Offers were frequently mentioned on the air for cookbooks, flower seed packets, photographs, diaries, sheet music, record albums and scrapbook recollections of the infamous Barbour family's past. Listeners could receive "one of these cherished mementoes for your very own" by dispatching a label from one of the underwriter's advertised commodities accompanied by a dime or a quarter (as inflation struck). More than a half-million requests poured in for copies of *Teddy's Diary*, reportedly in her own handwriting, in 1937, underscoring the value of such promotions in getting people to tune in and, more importantly, buy the advertised product. *Jack's Camera Scrapbook* was another popular premium.

Such enthusiasm for a trinket representing a favorite audio series didn't abate with the passage of time, surprisingly. Miles Laboratories, Inc., which paid the bills for a quadrennium (1950 to 1954), experienced its endgame full force, too. When Father Barbour's printed legacy to each member of his family, *This I Give*, was pitched on the broadcast of March 23, 1953, and for several installments thereafter — after the series had been airing for more than two decades — tens of thousands of Bactine boxtops accompanied by quarters arrived at the Elkhart offices of Miles Labs. There was little doubt that *One Man's Family* was still riding the crest of enormous fan loyalty, no matter that radio's lifeblood was draining away freely in some jurisdictions. Miles had a particular knack for picking features that the listeners adored. And the sponsor liberally exploited them until the wheels of network radio figuratively fell off the track.

Commercial

For more than 13 years (1947 to 1960), radio actor Sandy Becker was the authoritative voice of CBS Radio's *Young Doctor Malone*. As the calm, reassuring medical practitioner, he appeared to dispense psychological advice more often than he did prescriptions on that enduring daytime serial. By the early 1950s, nonetheless, the versatile Becker also added hawking Alka-Seltzer "and other fine, dependable products made by Miles Laboratories" to his resume. On that occasion, he returned to the CBS microphones weekday afternoons as the interlocutor for the longrunning *Hilltop House* underwritten by Miles.

There, perhaps ironically, the same fellow who had been playing doctor 90 minutes before was meting out advice about calming stomach indigestion and other maladies for the leviathan drug-maker. It must have seemed a tad bizarre to anyone realizing it was the same guy. Did the Miles marketers think Becker's superior credentials as a respected "physician" added impetus to his ability for them? That may be too much a stretch although it could actually be true. Here's one of those *Hilltop House* openings, from the broadcast of July 16, 1953.

NETWORK CUE: (*bong*)
SANDY BECKER: Alka-Seltzer ... first aid for the relief of headaches, acid indigestion, and muscular aches and pains ...

INTERLUDE: (*a few bright organ notes ascending the scale*)
SANDY BECKER: (*music under*) Alka-Seltzer ... brings you ... Hilltop House.
THEME: "Lullaby" by Brahms, on organ and xylophone
SANDY BECKER: This is Sandy Becker, reminding you that warm weather menus may change from heavy pot roasts to light tossed salads ... from freshly baked pies to chilled melons. Yet ... hot weather can still tempt you into eating unwisely ... and the result can be ... acid indigestion. So how's your Alka-Seltzer supply, ladies? Remember, speedy Alka-Seltzer for relief when acid indigestion comes along. Let Alka-Seltzer help you feel better ... fast. Alka-Seltzer has instant alkalizing action ... to reduce excess acidity in the stomach in a hurry ... and to ease that uncomfortable feeling. And Alka-Seltzer is soothing and settling to an acid upset stomach. It works with *gentle* action. So next time you're uncomfortable with after-meal acid indigestion, try a glass of sparkling, tangy Alka-Seltzer for *fast* relief. One or two tablets dissolve in a glass of water to make a refreshing effervescent solution. It's pleasant to take, too ... really refreshing. So, get a package of Alka-Seltzer from your druggist. And then ... when unwise eating causes acid indigestion ... be wise ... alkalize ... with Alka-Seltzer.
INTERLUDE: (*a few bright organ notes ascending the scale*)
SANDY BECKER: (*music under*) And now ... Hilltop House.
Bridge Music

Philip Morris Company

History

The Englishman Philip Morris made his livelihood out of tobacco. Unlike other major names in the industry who initially grew and harvested it before turning to producing it to meet the growing demands of an insatiable public, Morris concentrated on importing cigars and operating a little mercantile shop on London's Bond Street. He opened for business in 1847 where he hawked tobacco and ready-made cigarettes. His name is better known in the commercial tobacco trade than that of just about anyone else, with the possible exception of R. J. Reynolds, whose company was also named after him.

The moniker of Philip Morris is certainly more widely recognized than the surnames of founders of other tobacco enterprises such as Brown, Duke, Liggett, Lorillard, Myers and Williamson. The reason, of course, is that the commodities labeled after a few of them never received the worldwide marketing focus enjoyed by the Philip Morris cigarette. Had he lived to see any of that, the London shopkeeper would have been astounded by the application of his nomenclature in the turn of events.

After the mercantilist died in 1873, Morris's wife, Margaret, and his brother, Leopold Morris, continued operating the little emporium that Philip Morris launched a quarter-century earlier. In 1880, Margaret sold her shares to Joseph Grunebaum. Leopold Morris and Grunebaum formed a new partnership and, in 1881, the business persisted as Philip Morris & Company and Grunebaum, Ltd. Within a quadrennium the partnership dissolved, however; the firm did business as Philip Morris & Co., Ltd. thereafter. At last, in 1894, it passed from the founding Morris family's hands some 47 years after Philip Morris inaugurated it.

At that juncture, creditors inherited it. Majority control was assumed by William Curtis Thompson and his relatives, who oversaw the day-to-day operations. Subsequently, in 1901, in a stroke of good fortune, by royal warrant Philip Morris & Company was appointed tobacconist for King Edward VII; the following year, the business was incorporated by Gustav Eckmeyer in lower Manhattan on Broad Street in New York City. Ownership was split equally between the British parent and its U.S. partners. Eckmeyer had been Philip Morris's solitary agent in America since 1872, importing and selling English-made cigarettes in this country. He was soon distributing brands with the names Blues, Cambridge, Derby, Marlborough and Philip Morris.

After American women began to dance in public, and women's suffrage gave them the vote, some of those expressive free-spirited, hell-bent, freedom-chasers were determined to smoke in public, too. Their outspoken desire issued a clarion call to the tobacco manufacturers.[1]

> The firm of Philip Morris, which had moved across the Atlantic and was now a New York niche manufacturer, was first into the market. It revived one of its English trademarks, named after the Duke of Marlborough, which it abbreviated to "Marlboro." The new brand — slogan: "Mild as May" (1924) — began life as one for the ladies, targeting "decent, respectable" women. Initial advertising copy adopted a softly softly approach — as if there was still a need to justify women smoking: "Has smoking any more to do with a woman's morals than has the color of her hair? ... Women — when they smoke at all — quickly develop discerning taste. That is why Marlboros now ride in so many limousines, attend so many bridge parties, and repose in so many handbags." Marlboros were not only branded but engineered for women, incorporating an ivory tip of greaseproof paper to prevent them adhering to lipstick. Marlboro's lead was followed by other manufacturers.

Can you believe that the effeminate Marlboro was repositioned and reintroduced to a male audience three decades later, in 1954, with the most virile imagery possible? Credit Chicago adman Leo Burnett for selecting a cowboy as "the most generally accepted symbol of masculinity in America" to project the revamping. Propelled to fame by an enormous advertising budget, the cigarette's initial campaign, "Delivers the Goods on Flavor," was a splendid start. An unidentified radio songstress, singing a catchy tune, belted out over the airwaves: "You can't say no ... you can't say no ... no you can't say no ... to a Marlboro ... New, long-sized, filterized Marlboro." A decade hence, in 1964, the Marlboro Man was riding tall in the saddle and across American TV screens nightly as viewers were urged to "Come to where the flavor is. Come to Marlboro Country." Sales grew 10 percent annually for several years thereafter.[2]

> He lived in a giant, scenic landscape named "Marlboro Country".... Marlboro Man did not look like he would succumb to lung cancer. The associations were all wrong. Marlboro Man breathed clean air. His diet and lifestyle were simple and healthy. He was never shown whipping slaves or reliving equivocal parts of America's heritage. Who would you rather trust? Someone you had never heard of in a white coat who spent their life wandering around hospital wards counting dying people, or Marlboro Man?

Philip Morris knew how to pick a winner. In 1975, Marlboro overtook R. J. Reynolds' Winston cigarette as the number one seller in the nation. It's now in a fourth decade on that lofty perch. Furthermore, the Philip Morris Company itself overtook Reynolds in 1983 to become the number one tobacco producer in U.S. sales. Distaff dalliances, indeed.

But we are getting ahead of our story. As time proceeded, the little New York Philip Morris business flourished. In 1929, the firm purchased a cigarette manufacturing facility in Richmond, Virginia, and began making its own cigarettes. Fifteen years later, in 1944, it bought an existing plant in Louisville, Kentucky; in 1952, it opened a second factory in Louisville.

By the mid–1950s, the company was thriving in American culture. In 1955, it launched an international division to manufacture and market goods globally. Philip Morris USA was born in 1968. The outfit acquired Miller Brewing Company the following year and the Seven-Up Bottling Company in 1978, along with the international cigarette business of the Liggett Group, Inc., in 1978. In 1985, it took control of General Foods, Inc., for $5.6 billion, the largest non-oil acquisition in U.S. history. The Kraft Foods Company was added to its fold in 1988 for $12.9 billion, a new record for the nation's largest non-oil acquisition. Those latest additions combined as Kraft General Foods in 1989, becoming the largest food processing firm on U.S. soil. In 2000, Philip Morris Companies acquired Nabisco Holdings and the Nabisco brands were integrated into the Kraft Foods worldwide business.

The firm sold all but 36 percent of Miller Brewing Company to a South African brewery in 2002. The following year, the parent was dubbed Altria Group, Inc., with subsidiaries Kraft Foods, Philip Morris USA, Philip Morris International and Philip Morris Capital Corporation. Early in 2007, Altria announced the spin-off of Kraft Foods in order to focus on its tobacco activity in the future.

By 2004, Philip Morris USA brands included all of these: Accord, Alpine, Basic, Benson & Hedges, Bristol, Bucks, Cambridge, Chesterfield, Collector's Choice, Commander, Daves, English Ovals, L&M, Lark, Marlboro, Merit, Parliament, Players, Saratoga and Virginia Slims. The latter brand, incidentally—introduced in an effective 1968 campaign with the catchphrase, "You've come a long way, baby"—was Philip Morris's successful attempt to do something for the ladies that it had first tried in 1924. They had come a long way, and waited a long while for attention in the interim.

Radio Series

Leo Reisman and His Orchestra, aka *Johnny Presents*—1934 to 1937, NBC (Philip Morris)
The Ferde Grofé Show—ca. 1932 to 1934, NBC (Philip Morris)
Eddie Dooley and Sports—ca. 1935 to 1936, MBS (Philip Morris)
Russ Morgan and His Orchestra, aka *Johnny Presents*, with Jack Smith—1937 to 1939, CBS, NBC (Philip Morris)
What's My Name?—1938 to 1939, MBS (Philip Morris)
Who Are We?—ca. late 1930s, MBS (Philip Morris)
Guess Where, with Budd Hulick and June Walker—1939, MBS (Philip Morris)
Johnny Presents Dramatized Short Stories—1939, CBS (Philip Morris)
Breezing Along, aka *In the Modern Manner*, aka *Johnny Green and His Orchestra*, with Jack Smith—1939 to 1940, MBS, NBC Blue (Philip Morris)
Johnny Presents, with Barry Wood—1939 to 1942, 1944 to 1946, NBC (Philip Morris)
Name Three Quiz—1939 to 1940, MBS (Philip Morris)
The Philip Morris Playhouse—1939 to 1944, 1948 to 1949, 1951 to 1953, CBS, NBC (Philip Morris)
Crime Doctor—1940 to 1947, CBS (Philip Morris)
Great Moments from Great Plays, with Ray Bloch and His Orchestra—1941, CBS (Philip Morris)
City Desk—1941, CBS (Philip Morris)
The Ginny Simms Show, aka *The Purple Heart*—1942 to 1945, NBC (Philip Morris)
Author's Playhouse—1942 to 1943, CBS (Philip Morris)
It Pays to Be Ignorant, with Tom Howard—1944 to 1948, CBS (Philip Morris)
Johnny Desmond Follies-Margaret Whiting Follies—1946, NBC (Philip Morris)
The Rudy Vallee Show—1946 to 1947, NBC (Philip Morris)
Heart's Desire, with Ben Alexander—1946 to 1948, MBS (Philip Morris)
The Milton Berle Show 1947 to 1948, NBC (Philip Morris)
The Horace Heidt Talent Hunt, aka *The Youth Opportunity Program*, aka *Philip Morris Night with Horace Heidt*—1947 to 1951, NBC, CBS (Philip Morris)

When Johnny Roventini spoke, America listened. The diminutive mascot in the red, black and gold bellman's uniform was not only a talking symbol of the cigarette brand he espoused (at least a million times, so he believed) but a poster boy, too. He turned up in store windows (which — radio announcers assured — he stepped out of) and public places where his signs were welcome. Backed with familiar "On the Trail" music, Philip Morris created an ingenious cultural icon, recognized over four decades for the company and brand he proffered.

Call for Music, with Dinah Shore, Harry James, Johnny Mercer—1948, CBS, NBC (Philip Morris)
Everybody Wins, with Phil Baker—1948, CBS (Philip Morris)
The New Mel Torme Show—1948, NBC (Philip Morris)
This Is Your Life, with Ralph Edwards—1948 to 1950, NBC (Philip Morris)
Kate Smith Sings—1948 to 1949, MBS (Philip Morris)
Hogan's Daughter, with Shirley Booth—1949, NBC (Philip Morris)
Casey, Crime Photographer—1949 to 1950, CBS (Philip Morris)
Ladies Be Seated—1949 to 1950, ABC (Philip Morris)
One Man's Opinion, with Walter Kiernan—1949 to 1951, ABC (Philip Morris)
Candid Microphone, with Allen Funt—1950, CBS (Philip Morris)
Johnny Olsen's Luncheon Club—ca. 1950 to 1951, ABC (Philip Morris)
Truth or Consequences, with Ralph Edwards—1950 to 1951, CBS (Philip Morris)
Queen for a Day, with Jack Bailey—ca. 1950 to 1957, MBS (Philip Morris)
The Bickersons, with Lew Parker and Frances Langford—1951, CBS (Philip Morris)
The Eddie Cantor Show, aka *Show Business Old and New*—1951 to 1952, NBC (Philip Morris)
Against the Storm—1951 to 1952, ABC (Philip Morris)
The Strange Romance of Evelyn Winters—1951 to 1952, ABC (Philip Morris)
Break the Bank—1951 to 1953, ABC (Philip Morris—multiple participation)
What's My Line?—1952, NBC, CBS (Philip Morris)
My Little Margie—1952 to 1955, CBS, MBS (Philip Morris)
Sports Ten—1953 to 1954, MBS (Philip Morris)
The Tennessee Ernie Ford Show—ca. 1954 to 1955, CBS (Philip Morris)
The New Edgar Bergen and Charlie McCarthy Hour—ca. 1955 to 1956, CBS (Philip Morris—multiple participation)
The Story of Ruby Valentine—1955 to 1956, National Negro Network (Philip Morris—multiple participation)

Exposition

Philip Morris achieved phenomenal success with its seemingly ubiquitous small-fry spokesman, Johnny Roventini (1910 to 1998), its original company mascot who kept turning up everywhere. Before his voice changed, a pituitary gland gone awry halted his development, leaving him with a 12-year-old body the rest of his life. At his diminutive peak, the 59-pound hawker stood three feet, nine inches. A convivial persona impressed legions of vocalists, comedians and other entertainers whom he introduced to ethereal audiences. Appearing at ribbon-cuttings, grand openings and staged events—as well as on billboards, in magazines and newspapers and on radio and television—Roventini became one of American advertising's most recognizable symbols. Invariably he was attired in a signature red usher's jacket with gold trim, striped trousers, black pillbox hat and white gloves. The uniform was inspired by a 1919 poster of a bellboy; his outfit has since been exhibited by the American Ad Museum in Portland, Oregon.

A print journalist recalled the spellbinding tale of his magnificent call to splendor.[3]

> Born to Italian immigrant parents, Roventini got a job as a bellboy at the Hotel New Yorker and earned minor fame when the hotel put his picture on postcards. He was identified as "the smallest bellboy in the world."

When advertising agency president Milton Biow came up with the idea of having his cigarette paged as if it were a man, he stopped by New York's Commodore Hotel and asked for the best bellhop in town. He was sent to the Hotel New Yorker and spied Johnny.

Biow gave him a dollar and told the naïve youth to page Mr. Philip Morris.

"I went around the lobby yelling my head off, but Philip Morris didn't answer my call," Roventini would tell people for years afterward.

It was 1932 at the onset of the Depression, and Biow offered the bellboy $100 a commercial.

"I have to ask my mother," said Roventini, who was then 22 years old.

Adeline Roventini said fine. Roventini made his radio debut accompanied by "On the Trail" from Ferde Grofé's "Grand Canyon Suite." The music, like the uniform, became linked to the living trademark.

For $20,000 a year, Johnny promised never to appear in public without a bodyguard and never to ride the subway during rush hour. When his salary rose to $50,000, Philip Morris insured Johnny's voice, with its perfect B-flat call, for that amount.

By the 1950s, Philip Morris began replacing Johnny in its advertising with dancing cigarette packages.

In the meantime, it was a stroke of pure genius that led creative marketer Biow — whose agency packaged all of Morris's broadcasting wares in the 1930s — to pick Roventini as a permanent icon for Philip Morris. And it was Roventini's good fortune to catch a break in the midst of bad times. Over his extensive career — which concluded with his 1974 retirement more than four decades later — Roventini believed he had called out the slogan more than a million times while shaking the hands of more than a million people. Radio announcers introduced the larger-than-life figure with an unforgettable line: "And here comes Johnny now, stepping out of thousands of store windows to greet you!" Audiences of countless aural shows heard him deliver a beacon that became part of the American lexicon: "Callllllllll for Philllllip Morrraisssss!" It was a brilliant inspiration, capturing the fancy of a large segment of the smoking population.

When the load of personal and radio appearances became too heavy for Roventini, a second pint-sized pitchman was plucked from obscurity. Albert Altieri (1915 to 2002) was engaged by Philip Morris two years after Roventini. Altieri stood two inches shorter than his predecessor. Favoring the already established Roventini, he was dubbed "Johnny Morris, Jr." and dispatched to events the original model simply couldn't make. The pair sold war bonds while turning up as goodwill ambassadors at Army camps, naval stations and hospitals during the Second World War. At other times, they were parade grand marshals, appeared at state fairs and lots of other places where they handed out free samples of the sponsor's product.

Yet it was on the air that both men, appearing separately, caught the imaginations of American listeners. Few advertising inspirations rivaled that of the Philip Morris bellhop. It left a memorable impression on the ear and eye that was seldom equaled in its epoch. "His [the spokesman's] voice was so familiar," assessed one reviewer, "that when Philip Morris decided to sponsor a radio variety show in 1939, the company named it 'Johnny Presents,' for the pitchman instead of the product." When Altieri died, a newspaper observed that he had "shared with Roventini a piece of Americana." It was a sobering reflection.

Commercial

Sometimes advertisers made use of special devices to assist in pushing their wares on radio. In the broadcast of the *Philip Morris Playhouse* on May 13, 1949 in which screen icon Howard

Duff starred in the play "Four Hours to Kill," an echo chamber helped an unidentified messenger plug the namesake commodity. Note the persuasive, authentic-sounding sanction of health care professionals for the product, also.

ANNOUNCER: When your cigarette leaves a stale, musty, smoke-foul taste in your mouth ...
ECHO CHAMBER: That's cigarette hangover.
ANNOUNCER: When your cigarette leaves your throat tight, dry, uncomfortable ...
ECHO CHAMBER: That's cigarette hangover.
ANNOUNCER: Yes, *that's* what takes the joy out of smoking. And when that happens to *you*, it's time to *change* to Philip Morris. *Remember* ... Philip Morris is the *one* ... the *only* cigarette proved definitely less irritating ... definitely milder ... than *any other* leading brand. That fact is recognized by eminent medical authorities: *No other cigarette* can make that statement. Remember ... top-ranking doctors ... eminent nose and throat specialists ... actually suggest Philip Morris in cases of irritation due to smoking. That's why we say, "If you're tired of cigarette hangover, join the millions and *change* to Philip Morris." You, too, will discover in Philip Morris a *milder* smoke, a fresher, cleaner smoke than you've ever known before. Yes, you'll be glad tomorrow you smoked Philip Morris today. Philip Morris ... America's finest cigarette.

Procter & Gamble Company

History

When the Englishman William Procter (1801 to 1884) and Irishman James Gamble (1803 to 1891), both immigrants to this country in the early nineteenth century, stopped over in Cincinnati, neither man planned a long respite. Both were headed west, determined to settle in a new, undisturbed land that held promise for their futures. But their futures got no farther than the "Queen City of the West" hard by the banks of the Ohio River. As fate turned out, Procter's wife, Martha, took ill. He cared for her at Cincinnati, until her unexpected death a short time following their arrival. Gamble, meanwhile, experienced medical problems himself, and sought professional assistance there.

As a consequence, both men put down roots: Procter was a candlemaker, a thriving occupational pursuit in the pre-electric light era; and Gamble apprenticed as a soapmaker. (The candlemaking extended to the 1920s and was then phased out due to electricity's all-encompassing dependency.) Had the two ultimately not wed sisters — Olivia and Elizabeth Norris — they might never have met. The girls' father, Alexander Norris, persuaded his new sons-in-law to combine their careers under one roof. The pair became working partners. As a result, an intrepid new venture was established. On April 12, 1837, William Procter and James Gamble started making and selling their soap and candles out of the same shop, with a formal partnership agreement signed on October 31, 1937. Neither could have envisioned the far-flung multibillion-dollar enterprise that their simple handshake would ultimately realize. Neither could have imagined how far and how wide their names would be projected, presumably encircling the globe for centuries into the future. Theirs was but one of a dozen or more candle- and soap-making entities in Cincinnati at that very moment. But it was theirs that was to have profound influence on the buying habits of billions of consumers in many lands across multiple generations.

In the 1850s, the moon and stars first appeared as an unofficial trademark for Procter & Gamble. Within a decade, it was an identifying symbol of the company's goods, correspondence and signage, one of the earliest logos applied in American commerce. The company grew rapidly; by 1859, just 22 years after its birth, it sold a million dollars' worth of goods manufactured by a workforce of 80. During the American Civil War, P&G won contracts to supply the Union army with soap and candles. In addition to increased profits, of even greater importance was the war's assistance in signifying P&G's capabilities. In a period before national newspapers existed — when there were few widespread magazines, no radio or highway billboards to advertise on — those military contracts introduced soldiers from all over the country to the wares of Procter & Gamble. After the war ended and the men returned home, they bought the firm's commodities at retail establishments or by mail order. P&G was one of a handful of manufacturers that took advantage of its good fortune during the wartime, building its reputation for quality and dependability.

A couple of decades later, one of the outfit's great milestones occurred. According to lore, one day in 1879 a P&G employee — on his way to lunch — forgot to turn off a soap mixer. A batch of "White Soap," a pure white cleansing bar that the firm was selling by that simple name, received an added infusion of air. Fearing the consequences of his oversight on discovering it, the employee kept silent about his mistake. Instead of discarding the batch due to his small error, he poured the soap into frames, it hardened, was cut, packaged and shipped. Within a few weeks, P&G began receiving requests from some purchasers for more of the "soap that floats." When officials learned what had occurred, a new cleansing strain was created.

The workman's mistake that resulted in the firm's famous economical white bar that was equal to quality imported castile soap has been attributed by one reporter to chemist James Norris Gamble, son of one of the founders. Whether it was Gamble or some other dubiously unheralded inventor, Harley T. Procter — the other founder's son — is credited with the soap's memorable appellation. At church one Sunday, Procter read the biblical words "out of the ivory palaces." He felt "ivory" depicted the white soap's purity, mildness and durability. Three years later Procter convinced the partners to spend $11,000 to advertise Ivory soap nationally. Word of the product's floating capabilities first reached subscribers to *The Independent*, a weekly newspaper, in 1882.

Harley Procter totaled the components that didn't fall into the category of pure soap, incidentally, and they equaled 56/100 percent. He subtracted from 100, and wrote the slogan "99 44/100% Pure — It Floats." It became a pledge of quality to Ivory consumers. The phrase is so identified with Ivory in fact it is registered as a trademark. "It Floats" was added to Ivory's motto in 1891.

Ivory's immediate success led the company to brand much of whatever else it produced with that identifying moniker. By 1886, P&G manufacturing was being carried out in the Ivorydale factory. It replaced another facility on Central Avenue that burned in 1884. The firm's twin office spires in downtown Cincinnati, completed in 1985, have been dubbed by locals "the Ivory towers." In the meantime, the name has been carried by extension to every commodity where P&G could reasonably apply it. In addition to the longstanding Ivory white soap in bar form, there is Ivory body wash, Ivory dishwashing liquid, Ivory liquid detergent, Ivory Snow detergent, and — during the network radio years — Ivory Flakes detergent. Millions of people around the world have purchased the brands that resulted from Harley Procter's church-going experience on a Sunday in 1879.

Ivory is but one of P&G's soap labels, however; by 1890, it proffered more than 30 such wares. Not long afterward, its flagship Ivory soap was the focus of an initial color print ad in *Cosmopolitan* magazine. The "Ivory Lady" appeared in 1896. Fifteen years hence, in 1911, P&G introduced a breakthrough in culinary artistry — an all-vegetable shortening that offered a healthier alternative to cooking with animal fats and was more economical than butter. The firm named it Crisco and it joined a growing stable of household and personal care products on which P&G was building its enviable reputation.

P&G was instrumental in altering the way America's grocers operated when, in 1919, it began to sell directly to retailers. The change stabilized production at the Ivorydale plant and reduced employee layoffs that had resulted by selling to wholesalers. The company hired 450 salesmen to facilitate the changeover. Within five years, P&G established a market research department to study consumer preferences and buying habits, one of the first such entities in American business. Two years later, in 1926, a growing preference for perfumed beauty soaps led it to produce Camay, "the soap of beautiful women."

There were scores of other innovations coming through the pipeline. A few, and their introductory dates follow:

- Dreft, the first synthetic detergent for household use (1933)
- Drene, the first detergent-based shampoo (1934)
- Tide, the "washday miracle," providing cleaning performance superior to other marketed brands (1946); within four years it was the number one seller, and still is
- Prell, a shampoo that established a cornerstone in the health and personal care segment (1946)
- Crest, the first toothpaste incorporating cavity-fighting fluoride (1955)
- Downy, P&G's first liquid fabric softener (1960)
- Pampers, becoming the preferred method to diaper babies (1961)
- Bounce, aiding in dryer-softening of clothes (1972)
- Liquid Tide (1984)
- Pert Plus–Rejoice, shampoo combining washing and conditioning (1986)
- ThermaCare, air-activated heat-wraps (2002)

In the meantime, over the latter half of the twentieth century, Procter & Gamble purposefully bought other companies that could diversify its product line and significantly increase its bottom line profits. Some of the major acquisitions:

- Charmin Paper Mills, including napkins, toilet tissue and towels (1957)
- Folger's Coffee Company, its entry into the coffee business (1963)
- Norwich Eaton Pharmaceuticals, increasing P&G's prescription and over-the-counter health care industry (1982)
- Richardson-Vicks Corporation, including Vicks respiratory care and Oil of Olay product lines (1985)
- Noxell Corporation, including CoverGirl, Noxzema and Clarion cosmetics and fragrances, a new category to P&G (1989)
- Shulton Corporation, maker of men's Old Spice personal goods (1990)
- Max Factor and Betrix, makers of cosmetics and fragrances (1991)
- Giorgio Beverly Hills, another fragrance line (1994)
- Tambrands Corporation, with the global leading Tampax tampon (1997)
- Iams Company, a leader in premium pet foods (1999)
- Recovery Engineering, Inc., with PUR home water filtration systems (1999)
- Clairol, the Bristol-Myers Squibb Company hair color–care segment (2001)
- Gillette Corporation, including Gillette and Braun shaving and grooming commodities, Oral-B dental care line and Duracell batteries (2005)

The latter acquisition, incidentally, completed on October 1, 2005 — the largest in the company's history — pushed Procter & Gamble ahead of rival packaged goods manufacturer Unilever, an Anglo-Dutch enterprise. P&G is currently the world's biggest producer of consumer commodities. Its corporate strategists deal with the possibilities that one or more of their own products could cannibalize the sales of another, a fact that occurs in the very real world of manufacturing competing goods.

While all of the development and acquisitions have been occurring, P&G has consistently expanded its presence around the globe. It sells wares under its American brand names as well as under labels produced locally in various parts of the world. Through sales and acquisitions, long ago it became a multinational force in consumer packaged goods beyond United States borders. By 1993, sales topped $30 billion; for the first time, more than half of that was generated outside America.

The company has not been spared controversy. Animal rights groups decry P&G's animal testing in connection with sundry products, most notably the Iams pet food line. In the 1980s, there was a concerted effort to depict the company's logo as a satanic symbol, based on a misunderstood biblical passage. In the midst of glaring and undesirable publicity, the corporate giant engaged in lawsuits against those who spread the rumors, and the logo was replaced to quell the crowd. In 1980, the Centers for Disease Control linked the Rely tampon produced by P&G and toxic shock syndrome. Although reluctant to do so, the firm withdrew the brand voluntarily.

An unauthorized P&G history offers a perceptive inquisition into the controversies: Alecia Swasy's *Soap Opera: The Inside Story of Procter & Gamble* (Times Books, 1993) shatters the ethical image consumers have traditionally held of the household goods manufacturer. Calling it an "explosive exposé," a reviewer says Swasy "tells the chilling story of life within P&G," depicting it as "a sobering look at the price of success in American business." More company histories include: *Eyes on Tomorrow: The Evolution of Procter & Gamble* (Doubleday, 1981), by Oscar Schisgall; *Procter & Gamble: The House That Ivory Built* (NTC Business Books, 1988), by the editors of *Advertising Age*; and *Rising Tide: Lessons from 165 Years of Brand Building at Procter & Gamble* (Harvard Business School Press, 2004), by Davis Dyer, Frederick Dalzell and Rowena Olegario.

According to Hoovers, Inc., Procter & Gamble finished 2006 with 138,000 employees and a workforce growth of 25.5 percent over 2005. In that same one-year period, its worldwide sales increased 20.2 percent, exceeding $68.2 billion for the year, with net income almost $8.7 billion, 19.7 percent above the previous year's posting. More than a score of P&G brands were selling at least a billion dollars' worth of goods annually. Among the better known are Actonel, Always-Whisper, Bounty, Charmin, Crest, Downy-Lenor, Folgers, Iams, Olay, Pampers, Pantene, Pringles, Tide and Wella. Hoovers identified Johnson & Johnson, Kimberly-Clark and Unilever as P&G's leading competitors in 2007.

Some other well-known P&G brand names currently manufactured include Boss, Braun, Camay, Cascade, Cheer, Dawn, Dreft, Duracell, Era, Febreze, Fixodent, Gain, Gillette, Gleem, Head & Shoulders, Ivory, Joy, LaCoste, Luvs, Metamucil, Millstone, Mr. Clean, Noxzema, Old Spice, Oral-B, Pepto-Bismol, Prilosec OTC, Puffs, Safeguard, Scope, Secret, Swiffer, Vicks and Zest. A few prominent names have been sold or are no longer produced (the latter indicated by asterisks) including Banner*, Biz, Bold*, Chloraseptic, Cinch, Citrus Hill*, Clearasil, Coast, Comet, Crisco, Dash*, Jif, Duncan Hines, Hawaiian Punch, High Point*, Lava, Lilt, Monchelle*, Oxydol, Pace*, Pert, Prell, Puritan*, Salvo*, Self*, Spic 'n Span, Sunny Delight, Sure, Thrill*, Top Job, White Cloud* and Wondra*.

Radio Series

George, the Lava Man 1930 to 1931, NBC Blue (Lava)
East and Dumke, aka *Sisters of the Skillet*, aka *The Quality Twins*, with Ed East and Ralph Dumke — 1931 to 1932, NBC Blue (Crisco)

The Ivory Program, with B. A. Rolfe and His Orchestra—1932, NBC Blue (Ivory)
The Mills Brothers—1932 to 1933, CBS (Crisco, Chipso)
Ma Perkins—1933 to 1956, NBC, CBS (Oxydol)
The Gibson Family—1934 to 1935, NBC
Dreams Come True, with baritone Barry McKinley—1934 to 1935, NBC
Vic and Sade—1934 to 1944, NBC, NBC Blue, CBS (Crisco)
Captain Tim Healy, aka *Ivory Stamp Club*, aka *Captain Tim's Adventures*—1934 to 1937, NBC, NBC Blue (Ivory, Chipso)
Cooking Travelogue, with Winifred S. Carter—ca. mid- to late 1930s, NBC Blue, NBC, CBS (P&G White Naphtha)
Home Sweet Home—1935 to 1936, NBC (Chipso)
The O'Neills—1935 to 1942, NBC, NBC Blue, CBS (Ivory)
The Ivory Reporter—1936, NBC Blue (Ivory)
The Magic Voice—1936, NBC Blue (Chipso)
Edward McHugh, the Gospel Singer—1936 to 1939, NBC Blue, NBC (Ivory Flakes)
Five Star Jones—1936 to 1937, NBC Blue (Oxydol)
Personal Column of the Air—1936 to 1937, NBC Blue (Chipso)
Barry Wood—1936 to 1937, NBC, NBC Blue (Drene)
Pepper Young's Family—1936 to 1957, NBC, NBC Blue (P&G White Naphtha, Duz, Camay, Fluffo, Joy, Tide)
The Couple Next Door—1937, MBS (Oxydol)
Jimmy Fidler in Hollywood—1937 to 1940, NBC, NBC Blue, CBS (Drene)
The Goldbergs—1937 to 1945, CBS (Oxydol, Duz)
The Guiding Light—1937 to 1941, NBC (P&G White Naphtha); 1947 to 1956, CBS (Duz)
The Story of Mary Marlin—1937 to 1943, NBC, NBC Blue, CBS (Ivory Flakes, Ivory)
The Road of Life—1937 to 1955, CBS, NBC (Chipso, Duz, Ivory, Crisco)
Central City—1938 to 1939, NBC (Oxydol)
Houseboat Hannah—1938 to 1941, NBC Blue, NBC (Lava)
Life Can Be Beautiful—1938 to 1954, CBS, NBC (Ivory, Camay, Spic 'n' Span, Crisco, Ivory Flakes, Ivory Snow, Tide)
This Day Is Ours—1938 to 1940, CBS (Crisco)
Professor Quiz—1939 to 1940, CBS (Teel)
What's My Name?—1939 to 1940, NBC (Oxydol)
Against the Storm—1939 to 1942, NBC (Ivory)
Kitty Keene, Incorporated—1939 to 1941, MBS, NBC (Dreft)
The Man I Married—1939 to 1941, NBC (Oxydol)
Manhattan Mother—1939 to 1940, CBS (Chipso)
Midstream—1939 to 1940, NBC, NBC Blue (Teel)
The Right to Happiness—1939 to 1956, NBC Blue, CBS, NBC (P&G White Naphtha, Duz, Crisco, Ivory, Cheer, Spic 'n' Span)
Painted Dreams—1940, NBC Blue (Chipso)
Lone Journey—1940 to 1943, NBC (Dreft)
This Small Town—1940 to 1941, NBC (Duz)
Those We Love—1940 to 1941, CBS (Teel)
Everyman's Theater—1940 to 1941, NBC (Oxydol)
Woman in White—1940 to 1942, CBS (Camay, Oxydol)
Truth or Consequences, with Ralph Edwards—1940 to 1950, CBS, NBC (Ivory, Duz)

Knickerbocker Playhouse—1940 to 1942, NBC (Drene)
The Bartons—1941 to 1942, NBC (Duz)
Keeping Up with Rosemary—1942, NBC (Drene)
Abie's Irish Rose—1942 to 1944, NBC (Drene, Ivory Flakes)
Snow Village Sketches—1942 to 1943, NBC (P&G White Laundry)
Charles Dant and His Orchestra—1943, NBC (Drene)
I Love a Mystery—1943 to 1944, CBS (Oxydol)
Dreft Star Playhouse, aka *Hollywood Theater of the Air*—1943 to 1945, NBC (Dreft)
Brave Tomorrow—1943 to 1944, NBC (Ivory Flakes)
Breakfast in Hollywood, aka *Breakfast with Breneman*, aka *Welcome to Hollywood*, with Tom Breneman—1943 to 1945, Blue/ABC (Ivory Flakes—multiple participation)
Perry Mason—1943 to 1955, CBS (Camay, Tide)
A Woman of America—1943 to 1946, NBC (Ivory Snow)
Crisco Radio News, with Bernadine Flynn—1943 to 1945, CBS (Crisco)
Let's Listen to Spencer, with Bob Sweeney and Hal March—1944, NBC (Oxydol, Ivory)
The Rudy Vallee Show, aka *Villa Vallee*—1944 to 1946, NBC (Drene)
The Gay Nineties Revue, aka *Gaslight Gaieties*—1944 to 1945, NBC
The Jack Kirkwood Show—1944 to 1946, CBS (Oxydol)
The FBI in Peace and War—1944 to 1950, CBS (Lava, Duz)
Glamour Manor, aka *The Kenny Baker Show*—1944 to 1947, ABC (Ivory)
Rosemary—1944 to 1955, NBC, CBS (Ivory Snow, Dash, Tide, Camay, Prell)
Teel Variety Hall—1945, NBC (Teel)
The Oxydol Show, aka *The Tide Show*, with Jack Smith—1945 to 1952 (Oxydol, Tide)
Mommie and the Men—1945 to 1946, CBS
Meet Margaret MacDonald—1945 to 1946, CBS (Ivory Flakes)
The Life of Riley, with William Bendix—1945 to 1950, NBC (Teel, Dreft, Prell)
Joyce Jordan, M.D.—1945 to 1948, NBC (Dreft)
Young Doctor Malone—1945 to 1955, CBS (Crisco, Joy)
The Lanny Ross Show, with Lanny Ross and Evelyn Knight—1946, CBS (Oxydol)
The Bickersons, aka *Drene Time*, with Don Ameche and Frances Langford—1946 to 1947, NBC (Drene)
This Is Hollywood, with Hedda Hopper—1946 to 1947, CBS
Mystery of the Week—1946 to 1947, CBS (Ivory, Dreft)
Big Sister—1946 to 1952, CBS (Ivory, Dreft, Joy, Spic 'n' Span)
The Frank Parker Show—1947, NBC (Drene)
Beulah, with Hattie McDaniel, Lillian Randolph and Amanda Randolph—1947 to 1953, CBS (Tide)
Lowell Thomas and the News—1947 to 1953, CBS
What Makes You Tick?—1948 to 1949, ABC, CBS (Ivory Flakes)
The Brighter Day—1948 to 1955, NBC, CBS (Cheer)
The Red Skelton Show—1949 to 1950, CBS (Tide)
Welcome Travelers—1949 to 1954, NBC
Lorenzo Jones—1949 to 1952, NBC (Dreft)
Our Gal Sunday—1950 to 1951, CBS
Backstage Wife 1951 to 1955, NBC (Cheer, Spic 'n' Span)
Mr. Keen, Tracer of Lost Persons—1953 to 1954, CBS (multiple participation)

Exposition

The story of P&G's practice of spending money to make money, principally through advertising, is one of the most fascinating in the annals of marketing consumer packaged goods. In the early years of the twentieth century, P&G spent vast sums to keep its wares before American buyers. By the start of the Depression era it concluded that it must shell out even more to retain and increase market share. But before doing so, the firm conducted an extensive program of market research.

Survey results told P&G that American women doing household chores at home during daylight hours wanted to be entertained by radio, not instructed as many series were then doing. Typical programs of the period (including some local or regional) included *Crisco Cooking Talks*, *Emily Post's* etiquette chats, Helen Chase's *Beauty Forum*, *Washing Talks* and *Sisters of the Skillet*. P&G, performing independently of other firms, was on to something big. In 1932, it decided to experiment with dramatic programming aired in the daytime and targeting the distaff audience.

To test its theory, P&G turned to its local Cincinnati clear-channel powerhouse, WLW, with 50,000 watts of broadcasting range. (Some actors appearing on the station claimed the call letters WLW stood for "World's Lowest Wages.") For its Oxydol granulated brand of laundry detergent, P&G's advertising agency purchased a serialized domestic comedy, *The Puddle Family*, akin to a comic-strip story. It aired on WLW starting in late 1932 and was far less than an instant success.

But early in 1933 the Oxydol trade was transferred to a different agency. An account executive, Larry Milligan, readily suggested a continuing narrative that would revolve around a "helping hand" character. He proposed the tale of a self-reliant widow whose family and friends leaned heavily upon her—*Ma Perkins* it would be called. Oxydol's *own* Ma Perkins. The idea clicked with agency directors and P&G officials.

At the time all of this was going on, a lovely young blonde actress, Virginia Payne, then 23, was portraying the title role in a WLW drama about a southern diva, *Honey Adams*. Jane Froman, who was destined to become one of the nation's most popular vocalists a few years later, supplied the singing on the drama.

Unlike the homespun character for whom she would be recalled for the rest of her days, Payne was a highly cultured young woman. The daughter of a local physician, she was well educated, holding two master's degrees (one in literature, the other in music) from the University of Cincinnati. A devout Roman Catholic, she held high principles that personified the everyday trust in human nature that Ma Perkins would embrace.

Payne was obviously in the right place at the right time. Despite her youth, a certain tremolo in her versatile voice could make her sound as if she was considerably older. Thus, she was tapped for the role of Ma, never dreaming how far it would take her in years, miles and association.

A 16-week trial run was launched on WLW on August 14, 1933. Unlike its predecessor, *The Puddle Family*, the series was quickly adopted by its Cincinnati audience. P&G noted too that grocers in the area were asking wholesale distributors for many more boxes of Oxydol than before, as listeners responded positively to the program's commercials. It was obvious that P&G's market research was correct: women wanted radio entertainment while working in the home.

With that kind of success in a local market, P&G was ready to send its fledgling feature to a national audience. Under the soapmaker's watchful eye, the serial was entrusted to Frank

Hummert and his assistant Anne Ashenhurst (the future Mrs. Hummert) of Chicago's Blackett-Sample-Hummert advertising agency. Those innovators had already met with some success in *Judy and Jane*; *Betty and Bob*; *Marie, the Little French Princess*; *Easy Aces*; *Just Plain Bill*; and *The Romance of Helen Trent*. On December 4, 1933, at three o'clock Eastern Time, *Ma Perkins* debuted over the NBC network coast to coast. A new form of daytime programming was permanently established, one that was to persist until the last vestiges of chaos wore out their final threats to beleaguered heroines during network radio's ebbing days. *Ma Perkins* would be among the last quartet of continuing tales to be cancelled on "the day radio drama died," November 25, 1960. And until only four years earlier, it would be responsible for selling billions of boxes of Procter & Gamble's Oxydol, just as the same sponsor marketed other commodities over the decades on dozens of additional daytime serials. Without any stretch of the imagination, Procter & Gamble made soap opera everything that it came to be. Through Procter & Gamble Productions, its pervasive influence still impacts the form today.

Of no fewer than 87 radio series (that have been documented thus far) presented by Procter & Gamble, at least half (44) were drawn from the genre of the daytime serials. This underscores the unmistakable reality that P&G almost single-handedly put soap operas on the ethereal map. Nobody made the commitment to the recurring narrative in dollars or time that P&G did. While it underwrote *Ma Perkins* for 23 years, it prolonged a handful of other radio dramas for a decade or more: *Pepper Young's Family* (20 years), *The Road of Life* (18), *The Right to Happiness* (17), *Life Can Be Beautiful* (16), *The Guiding Light* (13), *Perry Mason* (12), *Vic and Sade* (10), *Young Doctor Malone* (10). That kind of involvement broadly suggests that P&G was a driving force in keeping the washboard weepers alive well beyond the time the slippage began toward television.

Beyond that model, however, P&G brought many other forms of amusement and information to America's ears. It is typically recalled for a number of series with a commanding and enduring airwaves presence, among them *Truth or Consequences*, *The FBI in Peace and War*, *The Life of Riley*, *The Jack Smith Show*, *Beulah*, *Lowell Thomas* and *Welcome Travelers*. Procter & Gamble was utterly committed to radio; for more than a quarter-century, it paid the bills of legions of performers and the series that broadcast them. No other company appeared to believe in radio to that extent. None ever really came close to matching its feat. Those who reveled in vintage radio may owe the company a boatload of gratitude for such enveloping dedication to the nation's entertainment.

Commercial

MALE VOICEOVER: The following program is transcribed.
DAN DONALDSON: For a wash that's deep clean ... sparkling clean ... use deep cleaning Oxydol.
MALE VOICEOVER: Oxydol is deep cleaning ... deep cleaning ... deep cleaning.
THEME: Variation of "My Old Kentucky Home," original tune by Larry Larson and Don Marcotte
DAN DONALDSON: (*music under*) Oxydol's ... own ... Ma Perkins. (*as theme ends*) All over America, the news is out, and everywhere there's a tremendous amount of talk and excitement about deep cleaning Oxydol. Women are getting washes so wonderfully clean and white they can hardly believe it. They're discovering that deep cleaning Oxydol reaches deep down into fabrics and gets out the grey dirt left in clothes by the leading washday suds ... the leading short-cut suds. Now this fact was demonstrated to

women recently, and ... I'd like you to hear from Mrs. John Rising of St. Bernard, Ohio, who attended the demonstration. Here's what she saw....

MRS. RISING: In this washing demonstration they used *my* clean clothes ... well, at least, I thought they were clean, because I had just washed them with the leading suds, the way you're told to. Then, they washed those clothes over again — this time with deep cleaning Oxydol. You should have seen the dirty wash water come out of those clothes I thought were clean. That dirty wash water showed me ... Oxydol really can get out the grey dirt left in clothes by those leading short-cut suds.

DAN DONALDSON: Thanks, Mrs. Rising ... And ladies, here's something we'd like you to try. Next washday, use deep cleaning Oxydol and see for yourself how much dirt Oxydol can get out of *your* clothes. And even more surprising ... look at the clothes themselves. When you use deep cleaning Oxydol, your clothes look sparkling white and bright ... your clothes feel soft and fluffy. Your clothes smell sweet, too. Yes, your clothes look clean ... feel clean ... smell clean ... because they *are* clean with deep cleaning Oxydol. Yet, Oxydol is really safe ... deep clean clothes stay brighter ... new looking longer. So don't wash clothes with suds that leave dirt in. Get clothes deep clean ... sparkling clean ... with deep cleaning Oxydol.

MALE VOICEOVER: Oxydol is deep cleaning ... deep cleaning ... deep cleaning.

DAN DONALDSON: Ask your dealer for Oxydol ... today.

BRIDGE MUSIC: (*segue into narrative*)

If you had any doubts about the intensity with which radio advertising copywriters applied the rule of repetition (encountered several times already in this text), put it to rest. Announcer Dan Donaldson's expressions "deep clean" and "deep cleaning" (and those of a voiceover speaker) are used no fewer than 16 times at the opening of this *Ma Perkins* chapter on August 23, 1950. Was it that noticeable to listeners? Probably not. Those insertions — twice per episode — were scheduled five days a week for perhaps a couple of years. The fans who were regular devotees must have heard it hundreds, maybe thousands of times. It had the desired effect for P&G sold millions of boxes of the stuff from the one "deep cleaning" campaign.

Quaker Oats Company

History

The official line of the Quaker Oats Company in regard to its early history intimates that there was little beyond the merger of a trio of competing oat-producing manufacturers preceding the establishment of the century-old breakfast-food giant that is recognized by generations of Americans. But as is so often the case, there was a whole lot more going on behind the scenes among those early rivals. Much of it was unfriendly, in fact, at times downright cutthroat as the threesome attempted to occupy the catbird seat. A succinct analysis of that epoch will provide food for thought as its revelations offer mesmerizing effects.

The earliest vestiges of what were to become the Quaker Oats Company are documented as far back as 1856. Ferdinand Schumacher (1822 to 1908), who emigrated from Germany to Akron, Ohio, in 1851, opened a small grocery store there. Among the products he marketed were oats. But to his surprise, most locals considered oats unfit for human consumption; oats qualified as livestock feed and little else. Because meat prices were exorbitant by many European immigrants' budget standards and as many of them traditionally ate oats in their native homelands, Schumacher found a ready-made consumer contingent that was an easy sell. He began to package his oats in one-ounce square blocks, a size particularly amenable to homemakers. Slowly, opinions started to shift among the diehards who were unaccustomed to oats for human consumption, and the notion gradually began to catch on.

In 1856, Schumacher purchased a mill and launched a second business with greater potential than the grocery, the German Mills American Oatmeal Factory. His preoccupation with it eventually branded him "The Oatmeal King." Coincidentally, in the early 1860s, the Civil War was a shot of adrenalin for his venture: the government found oats to be relatively inexpensive, accessible and nourishing, and ordered hundreds of barrels from him to fortify the Union troops. When the war ceased in 1865, oats were becoming an increasingly familiar commodity on American breakfast tables. Oat milling was a low-cost operation and soon Schumacher found himself in the midst of a great quantity of competition. As oats caught on with the general populace, rival producers sprang up to replicate his dietary innovation.

Schumacher's Empire Barley Mill opened in Akron in 1863 and became the town's largest employer. Everything was rocking along fine, despite the mounting competition, until fire razed the facility in 1886, having a devastating effect upon Schumacher's enterprise and Akron's economy. The owner had resisted buying insurance on his property, believing God would protect him. In regrouping, he proposed a merger with the Akron Milling Company. Because of the quality of his product as well as his sterling reputation, his offer was accepted. The combined endeavor proceeded as the F. Schumacher Milling Company.

While all of this was transpiring, in Ravenna, Ohio, a hamlet none-too-distant from Akron, William Heston and Henry D. Seymour established one of those rivals that made headway against the Schumacher operation. Exhibiting a flair for marketing genius, the pair selected Quaker Mill Company as the name of their business with doors opening in 1877. They also registered the now famous trademark long associated with their most visible early products.

Before going further, a point worth noting is that there isn't a link between the oats and the Quaker sect, also known as the Religious Society of Friends. Wikipedia clarifies: "The company chose its name because Quakers are reputed for honesty in their dealings. The antiquated image used by Quaker Oats looks nothing like a modern Quaker as that form of dress has been abandoned by the religious movement for quite some time." The article continues: "Many members of the Religious Society of Friends do not approve of the name usage by the company as the company was not founded by Quakers and does not follow the same codes of behavior Quakers follow. They believe the company's use of their name is dishonest behavior and, at best, causes public confusion, even to the point that many people assume they are similar to the Amish in their customs and beliefs."

Not long afterward, Heston and Seymour sold their oat-making venture to an entrepreneur and philanthropist, Henry Parsons Crowell (1855 to 1943), who took their product and built on it. Wrapping his oats in tidy, hygienic two-pound paper packages that included cooking directions, Crowell won quick acceptance in the marketplace. Most of his competition was selling their oats in 180-pound barrels, a form not so desirable to the homemaker preparing breakfast for a hungry clan. It was soon obvious that Crowell, instead, was feeling *his* oats: he advertised in newspapers with circulations to German, Irish and Scottish readers — people whose backgrounds included familiarity with oats as a dietary staple. The resulting success quickly impinged on Schumacher's turf; urban patrons were expressly requesting Quaker oats by brand name, a fact Schumacher could hardly ignore.

Oat production and its consumption as a breakfast cereal wasn't limited to Ohio, of course. Over in Cedar Rapids, Iowa, in 1873 John and Robert Stuart, father and son Canadian emigrants, opened what Cedar Rapids publicists still claim today was and is "the world's largest cereal manufacturing facility." At the time, it went under the name North Star Oatmeal Mills. A year later, Robert Stuart (1852 to 1926), a native of Ingersoll, Ontario, who was to prominently influence the production of oat-based cereals in this country, struck up a partnership with successful railroad builder George Bruce Douglas, Sr. (1817 to 1884). After Douglas's death, Stuart acquired a second mill in Chicago in 1888. The two mills marketed oats for American homes throughout the Midwest, particularly in Chicago, Detroit and Milwaukee. In pursuit of new business, North Star was nonetheless careful to shun regions previously staked out by Schumacher and Crowell.

Within a few months, it was clear to both Crowell and Stuart that if their respective enterprises were to continue to grow, new strategies were inevitable. Together, eyeing Schumacher as their chief opposition, the two men agreed to pursue a price war against his far larger enterprise. An industry-wide Oatmeal Millers Association failed to get off the ground when Schumacher refused to join that year. But after the latter's plant burned in 1886, Crowell raised his prices and the three agreed to launch the jointly operated Consolidated Oatmeal

Company. Officers included Crowell, president; Stuart, vice president; and Schumacher, treasurer. Their arrangement was tenuous from the start.

Actually, only about half the oatmeal trade in the U.S. was produced by Consolidated. The many millers making up the other half trained their guns on it in an effort to end it. According to one source, "Competitors built mills they did not want, knowing Consolidated would purchase them simply to keep them out of production." With an estimated half of Consolidated's revenues earmarked for superfluous mills, the financial and legal weight was more than Consolidated could bear. The firm failed in 1888.

But there was triumph that year in a subsequent attempt to fuse the stronger millers into a single consortium. Seven large oat-based operations united under the banner American Cereal Company. Gaining controlling interest, Schumacher became president and Crowell general manager with Stuart secretary-treasurer. After combining all of their work into just two mills — at Akron and Cedar Rapids — the new venture doubled the seven firms' previous production in only two years. Crowell vigorously promoted Quaker Oats while Schumacher — relying on his own commodity — plugged F. S. Brand alongside Quaker, blunting the success of the better-known, better-selling Quaker.

Things weren't working very well in the background, either. In 1897, Stuart defied Schumacher by buying a couple of food companies at bargain rates while also investing in equipment for the Cedar Rapids mill. In the exchange that followed, Schumacher got rid of Stuart. The following year he pushed Crowell out, too.

The political shenanigans had only just begun. Stuart and Crowell together owned 24 percent of American Cereal Company. Quietly, they began to purchase available shares. In 1899, following a proxy fight, they wrested control from Schumacher. The latter was removed from the scene by angry investors who simply couldn't tolerate the animosity he stirred up any longer. From being the most powerful member of the trade for most of the nineteenth century, he had at last fallen from grace permanently. In less than a decade, Schumacher would be dead (1908). He had been the pioneer commandant of an industry, wielding pervasive power and influence. In the end, he was virtually ignored by it altogether.

Meanwhile, it was now Stuart and Crowell's turn to occupy the fabled catbird seat. Stuart rapidly built more mills and diversified the product line (to wheat cereal, farina, hominy, corn meal, baby food and livestock feed) while Crowell substantially increased the marketing. American Cereal Company was renamed the Quaker Oats Company in 1901, taking advantage of its flagship product's sobriquet. It enjoyed sales of $16 million that year. Headquartered in Akron, the firm remained there until 1970 when it ceased production locally and moved the nerve center to Chicago.

Two decades of growth succeeded the firm's formal opening in 1901, including a wartime peak of $123 million in 1918. In the decades to follow, a son, grandson and more ancestors of Robert Stuart occupied the seat of controlling power. With the exception of one stretch (1953 to 1966), Quaker was a family-run business through 1979, a total of 65 years in Stuart hands. John Stuart, eldest son of Robert Stuart, succeeded his father in guiding the company for 31 years (1922 to 1953).

Having been tutored by Henry P. Crowell in the art of marketing, R. Douglas Stuart, younger sibling of CEO John Stuart, followed in Crowell's footsteps as advertising guru. He adopted the radical (for its time) policy of employing multiple advertising agencies in the years after the Second World War. Guessing correctly that pet foods, convenience products and ready-to-eat cereals would proliferate in the grocery trade in the years ahead, the Stuart brothers matched the firm's product line and promotions with their convictions.

Their years of service largely coincided with radio's golden age. Although they flourished in print advertising and product promotions, a cursory glance at their programming collection suggests that they lagged behind several rival cereal makers in establishing a serious presence on the air. (This topic is examined a little more under "Exposition" below.)

Over Quaker's long history, the ride sometimes has been smooth while at other times quite bumpy as it experimented with new product development, largely for the breakfast table, while acquiring and divesting all sorts of outside ventures. Most additions and subtractions were in the food and beverage industry but several didn't conform at all to what was seemingly the core business. Among the more notable exchanges across Quaker's history:

1911: Quaker buys Mother's Oats Company, giving Quaker half of all milling operations east of the Rocky Mountains.

1926: Quaker buys Aunt Jemima Mills Company and spends $100,000 on national advertising for that brand of pancake flour and syrup.

1942: Quaker enters the pet food industry by buying Ken-L-Ration; it follows with Puss 'n Boots cat food in 1950 and Anderson Clayton & Company (Gaines) in 1986; Quaker gets out of the pet food business entirely in 1995 when it sells both its American and European operations.

1963: Quaker introduces a new product, Cap'n Crunch cereal, diverting $5 million to make the public aware of it.

1969: Quaker buys Fisher-Price Toy Company; by 1979, it accounts for a quarter of Quaker's total sales, although it is spun off in 1991.

1970: Quaker buys Magic Pan restaurants, which it sells in the early 1980s, along with its chemical division, Mexican toy operations, Needlecraft and cookie-maker Burry.

1972: Quaker buys Louis Marx Toy Company.

Early 1980s: Quaker buys Jos. A. Bank Clothiers, mail-order firm Brookstone, and Eye-Lab; all are divested in 1986.

1983: Quaker buys Stokley-Van Camp, gaining not only pork and beans and similar food lines but — even more promising — Gatorade sports drink; its confidence works out this time — by 1987, Gatorade is deriving more revenue than any other Quaker-owned commodity; the bean and chili portions of that buy are dispatched in 1995.

1986: Quaker buys Golden Grain Macaroni Company, maker of Rice-A-Roni packaged dinners.

1994: Quaker buys Snapple Beverage Corporation — maker of juice and tea beverages — unknowingly at the peak of its performance, for $1.7 billion; it sells it three years later for $300 million, seeing a net loss of $931 million that year (1997).

When Robert S. Morrison, a former head of Kraft Foods' North American operations, became CEO of Quaker Oats Company in late 1997, there were strong indications from industry analysts that "Morrison was getting Quaker Oats in shape for a sale." While this didn't occur immediately, it turned out that those prognosticators were right on the money. Having pared the company down with a 10 percent workforce reduction, restructuring management, combining some operations and focusing on the core business, Quaker was ripe for picking.

The outfit that landed the prize in 2001 was PepsiCo, a worldwide name in convenient foods and beverages, with 168,000 employees in 2006 and $35 billion in revenues that year. That parent firm currently (as this is written in 2007) consists of four divisions: Frito-Lay North America, PepsiCo Beverages North America, PepsiCo International, and Quaker Foods North America. While PepsiCo's operations are controlled from Purchase, New York, less than an hour from New York City, the Quaker Oats Company remains headquartered in Chicago.

Quaker's current inventory includes brand names Cap'n Crunch, Life, Quisp, Quaker (in dozens of varieties), Kretschmer, Aunt Jemima, Granola, Rice-A-Roni, Pasta Roni, Near East and more.

Radio Series

Aunt Jemima, aka *Aunt Jemima Man*, aka *Cabin at the Crossroads*, aka *Aunt Jemima Home Folks*, with Harriette Widmer, Tess Gardella—1929 to 1930, 1937 to 1938, 1943 to 1945, 1952 to 1953, CBS, NBC Blue (Aunt Jemima)
Phil Cook, the Quaker Man—1930 to 1932, NBC Blue (Quaker)
Gene and Glenn—1930 to 1932, NBC (Quaker)
Lum and Abner, with Chester Lauck and Norris Goff—1931, NBC (Quaker)
Kaltenmeyer's Kindergarten, with Bruce Kamman—1935 to 1937, NBC (Quaker)
Dick Tracy—1938 to 1939, NBC (Quaker)
Margo of Castlewood—1937 to 1938, NBC Blue (Quaker)
Quaker Party, aka *The Quaker Variety Show*, with Tommy Riggs and Betty Lou—1938 to 1940, NBC (Quaker)
Girl Alone—1938 to 1941, NBC (Quaker)
Stop Me If You've Heard This One, with Milton Berle—1939 to 1940, NBC (Quaker)
Your Dream Has Come True, with Ian Keith—1940 to 1941, NBC (Quaker)
That Brewster Boy—1941 to 1945, NBC, CBS (Quaker)
Those Websters, with Willard Waterman—1945 to 1948, CBS, MBS (Quaker)
Terry and the Pirates—1943 to 1948, Blue, ABC (Quaker)
Ladies Be Seated, with Johnny Olsen—1945 to 1947, ABC (Quaker)
The Roy Rogers Show, with Pat Buttram, Dale Evans—1948 to 1951, MBS (Quaker)
The Challenge of the Yukon, aka *Sergeant Preston of the Yukon*—1947 to 1955, ABC, MBS (Quaker)
Man on the Farm Quiz—1949 to 1954, MBS (Quaker)
Quick as a Flash—1949 to 1950, ABC (Quaker)
The Gabby Hayes Show—1951 to 1952, MBS (Quaker)
Hotel for Pets, with Charlotte Manson—1954 to 1956, NBC (Ken-L-Ration, Puss 'n Boots)

Exposition

For all of the Stuart brothers' demonstrated marketing pizzazz, political savvy and savoir-faire in running and expanding a firm and promoting its products, their grip on network radio—at least until the early 1940s—was spotty. While there were attempts at a perpetual presence there, Quaker tended to leap from one format to another with succinct programming snippets lasting only a few months to a couple of seasons. Thus, in sustained recognition on the air, it underperformed some of its rival food manufacturers. Quaker leaped from a handful of song-and-patter offerings in chain radio's early days to a multiplicity of genres—soap operas, juvenile adventure serials, sitcoms, audience participation shows—ending with a quirky blend of serialized narratives plus animal preservation tips under the banner *Hotel for Pets*, a not-so-subtle means of plugging its pet foods.

Its most noteworthy feature, *The Challenge of the Yukon*, aka *Sergeant Preston of the Yukon*, ran eight years. Runners-up for continuous longevity included *Man on the Farm Quiz* and *Terry and the Pirates* (five years each), *That Brewster Boy* (four years) and *Girl Alone, The Roy Rogers Show* and *Those Websters* (three years each). Yet there were some years during the halcyon days that finding Quaker on national radio hookups would have been difficult, an oddity for a firm building market share and having already exhibited enhanced marketing skills.

Quaker appeared smitten with underdogs, or possibly doing things the way the competition didn't. Throughout the final decade of its aural airtime life — instead of concentrating on the powerhouse webs (CBS, NBC) that delivered vast, although dwindling, audiences — Quaker put most of its money into the chains that proffered the smallest numbers of listeners (ABC, MBS). Of nine series it aired between 1946 and 1956, eight were on ABC or MBS. While those webs broadcast more features in that era that appealed to the small fry (a target of Quaker advertising), the firm missed the exposure of generous numbers that the other networks could have provided through a more diverse allocation of its programming resources.

According to the contemporary Web site operated by Collectibles.com, the most popular of a vast array of radio premiums offered by the Quaker Oats Company was a 1950s' *Sergeant Preston of the Yukon* promotion to young listeners with free deeds for single square inches of land in Yukon territory. There were also cookie jars, Aunt Jemima memorabilia in many forms, plastic mugs of Roy Rogers and the Quaker Man, puzzles, trading cards and a wide assortment of added collectibles offered by Quaker. Many were proffered by salivating network radio announcers appearing on a handful of late afternoon adventure serials for the juvenile set.

Commercial

The commercial pattern aired on a December 1942 installment of *That Brewster Boy*, a teen-focused family comedy-drama, appears in contrast to the format adopted by most other primetime sponsors in food processing and other lines. To begin with, immediately following the theme song, there was a pithy — *very* pithy — plug for the practicality of the flagship commodity.

ANNOUNCER: Did you have your Quaker Oats today? It's an economical breakfast ... it still costs less than half-a-cent a serving. Serve your family delicious, healthful Quaker Oats, America's super breakfast ... regularly.

The brief announcement, delivered cold, was so fleeting that — had it preceded the theme music — it might have been considered a cowcatcher commercial, a condensed pitch for an underwriter's wares at the top of a show. Most opening deliveries on primetime series were considerably longer than that used by Quaker in this sample.

A third of the way through the program, meanwhile, there was a discourse on the benefits of whole grain foods that nearly turned into a dissertation. An "authority," whose credentials were never clearly identified, endorsed the manufacturer by offering a lecture-style address on the topic. Coupled with the introduction by the announcer, the commercial ran two and a half minutes, a little long for radio listeners to be asked to swallow as they waited for the interrupted storyline to resume.

ANNOUNCER: I would like to call your attention to a statement of great importance. Recently, our Dr. Frank L. Gunderson, eminent biochemist and one of the nation's leading authorities on nutrition, said ...

GUNDERSON: The United States government, doing all it can to improve the nation's health, has through its national nutritional program, urged all of us to eat more whole grain foods. Certainly it is very important that all of us include plenty of whole grain foods in our diet. I'd like to point out that one of the most economical ... one of the most accessible of whole grain foods ... is whole grain oatmeal. It may never have occurred to you ... you may even be surprised to learn that one of the finest whole grain foods is oatmeal. Oatmeal as used in Quaker Oats is strictly a whole grain food. Probably because the bran in oatmeal is so bland, so soft, so palatable, you've never thought of oatmeal as a whole grain food ... but, that's just what it is. As a matter of fact, it is a delicious form of whole grain foods. Oatmeal as used in Quaker Oats contains all the whole grain goodness as well as the whole grain benefit. You mothers can be sure that oatmeal is one form in which your family will welcome a whole grain food. Oatmeal as used in Quaker Oats is an ideal way for you mothers to make *sure* that your family gets the whole grain food it *needs*. Whole grain oatmeal is a rich source of Vitamin B-1, the great anti-fatigue vitamin, the morale vitamin that is so widely deficient in American foods. And that vitamin is of prime importance if there are youngsters in your family. Vitamin B-1 is an absolute necessity for the normal growth of children. Now, whole grain oatmeal contains phosphorous and iron for rich, red blood. Whole grain oatmeal leads all other whole grain cereals in protein needed to help build muscle and prepare for the daily wear and tear on body tissues. Whole grain oatmeal is one of the richest sources of food energy or body fuel for the day's work. This combination of important food elements makes whole grain oatmeal as used in Quaker Oats one of the most healthful foods you can eat. If every mother in America served whole grain oatmeal regularly, I believe we should have healthier individuals, healthier families and a healthier nation.

R. J. Reynolds Tobacco Company

History

Richard Joshua Reynolds, the son of a tobacco farmer, was born in Patrick County, Virginia, situated hard against the North Carolina line, in 1850. At 24, he sold his share of the family business and trekked the 50 miles southeast to the little community of Winston, North Carolina. (Winston would later unite with the neighboring hamlet of Salem and consolidate as the city of Winston-Salem.)

Although Winston could boast only a few hundred residents and not a paved road, a discerningly shrewd, entrepreneurially-minded Reynolds saw it as a place with budding promise. Not only was it a manufacturing base for flue-cured tobacco leaf, it had the good fortune of sitting on a new rail line. Reynolds determined to cast his luck there.

In 1875, he opened a small chewing tobacco factory. In ensuing years, he was responsible for flooding the market with a variety of plug brands — Brown's Mule, Dixie's Delight, Golden Rain, Purity and Yellow Rose. By 1899, he incorporated his business as R. J. Reynolds Tobacco Company, the first of several monikers. And by putting down roots in the community, he set forth a Reynolds presence that was to infiltrate much of it and extend to the present era. In truth, the Reynolds name and culture was to be inextricably linked with the progress of Winston-Salem all the way to today. Reynolds was active in building roads, launching a savings bank, he was a city commissioner, buttressed numerous educational and human-service incentives, and so on.

He was also a hands-on manager, personally choosing the recipes and wrappings for his firm's commodities. Reynolds knew almost everybody who worked for him, even after the company grew to sizeable proportions. In 1912, deliberately protecting his workers, he provided an employee stock plan. Using a profit-sharing formula that paid shareholders an extra dividend, Reynolds made many of those hands very comfortable in their latter years.

Before any of that transpired, however, there was the matter of the tobacco trust. Controlled by James B. Duke, president of the American Tobacco Company, it had a profound effect upon the operations and management of all the major trade houses. (For more on the trust, see details in the article on the American Tobacco Company.) While Reynolds would have little eventual choice but to bow down to Duke — caving in reluctantly to the trust in 1900 — there was no love lost between the two men; their relationship was more contentious than that of most players, and remained strained.

Duke's perception of Reynolds was that he was "a man he disliked and who despised him.... [Duke] had almost no control over Richard J. Reynolds, whose firm was under the American Tobacco flag, but who had undisguised contempt for Duke as a man and manager.... Richard Reynolds refused to follow corporation strategy, taking an independent line whenever it suited him, undercutting other trust brands and conducting pointless price wars. Duke wasn't able to control him."[1]

Commenting on what occurred thereafter, the source added: "After the divestiture Reynolds took over at his own company once more [in 1911], and soon after [Percival S.] Hill became president of American Tobacco, still the largest firm in the industry. During the next ten years Reynolds made his company a major factor in the field, while Hill, heading the old Duke 'team,' consistently lost ground. Whatever virtues Duke had as a manager, creating an efficient and effective staff was not one of them."[2] This assessment underscores Reynolds' already highlighted talent as a manger.

Good fortune was to smile on the Reynolds firm when it introduced Prince Albert pipe tobacco in 1906 and proffered it to a nationwide market a couple of years afterward, pitching it as "the joy smoke." It would become a strong leader in that quarter of the tobacco trade. The image added of Chief Joseph of the Nez Perce Indian tribe gave impetus to the product and its print promotion by 1913, an effective means of turning it into a readily recognized commodity.

Yet, the fact that — after a decade of virtual subjugation — Reynolds was able to turn his firm into a leading industry contender is probably justly tied to his decision to concentrate an overwhelming focus on a solitary cigarette brand. He selected a combination of ingredients that resonated with smokers and backed it with capital for an effective advertising strategy. The brand was Camel, introduced in 1913 as the industry's first modern cigarette. With the promotion tagline, "A pleasure to burn," Camel combined flue-cured, burley and Turkish tobaccos. By 1915, it had become the first cigarette to transcend its regional status, appealing to a national smoking contingent. It set a pattern that Liggett & Myers was quick to follow with Chesterfields and American Tobacco was forced to play catch-up to with Lucky Strikes as the trio of manufacturers sought the same consumers coast-to-coast.

All of this bode well for the firm's future, despite the death of founder Reynolds in 1918 at age 68. By 1921, the business was spending $8 million on advertising, almost totally for Camels, when it launched its famous, "I'd walk a mile for a Camel" catchphrase — one that would pour out of radios and televisions as well as from print advertising pages, billboards and transit signage for many years into the future. It was a memorable symbol and soon joined the American vernacular. Within a year, thanks to Camel, Reynolds captured first place in the cigarette race with an astounding 45 percent of market share. While that coveted honor would, for years, jockey back and forth between Luckies and Camels, it was an enviable spot to be in.

According to one source, Reynolds' innovations set in motion "virtually every packaging standard in the U.S. cigarette industry." The firm is credited with the 20-cigarette package (1913), the single-piece 10-pack carton (1915) and with being the first to package its cigarettes in "a moisture-proof, sealed cellophane outerwrap to preserve freshness." While no evidence to refute the first two claims appears to have surfaced, both Liggett & Myers' Chesterfields (1916) and Brown & Williamson's Wings (1929) make similar assertions about originating protective wrapping.

Camels set off an industry price war in the depths of America's Great Depression by raising the cost of its cigarettes a penny a package (1931). Until then, containers of 20 cigarettes were selling for 14 cents or two for 27 cents. Camel's action prompted its rivals to follow suit. At the same time, it unleashed a glut of discounted knock-offs available at a dime a pack, taking a fifth of the majors' collective market share by 1932. The majors were forced to rescind the extra penny charge in 1933, yet the discounts retained 11 percent of the cigarette trade for the remainder of the decade.

In 1954, with its focus strictly on taste (and not health), Reynolds brought Winston to market, a filter-tipped cigarette that quickly became a habit-forming favorite of legions of smokers. With its catchy radio and TV jingle, "Winston tastes good, like a cigarette should!" Winston dominated the U.S. market from 1966 to 1976. A second innovation in the same epoch caught on pervasively, too, but with a different consumer segment. Salem, a menthol filter-tipped cigarette, appearing in 1956, eventually dominated its category.

A 20-story office tower, the Reynolds Building, occupying some prime real estate in downtown Winston-Salem, opened in 1929 near several Reynolds factories. An adjacent office structure, RJR Plaza, was completed in 1982 and is connected to the first skyscraper. In 1961, the firm occupied a million-square-foot manufacturing facility, Whitaker Park, only a few miles distant. A quarter-century beyond (1986), Reynolds opened a two million-square-foot plant at Tobaccoville, North Carolina, in close proximity to Winston-Salem. Other facilities are situated at Winston-Salem (research and development, and tobacco sheet manufacturing); Chester, Virginia (tobacco sheet manufacturing); Wilson, North Carolina (leaf operations); Blacksburg, South Carolina, and Richmond, Virginia (tobacco storage); and the British Virgin Islands (foreign sales).

The company itself, meanwhile, was the nation's leading cigarette manufacturer for a quarter-century, 1958 to 1983. Possibly responding to the handwriting on the wall, in the 1960s, Reynolds began buying non-tobacco enterprises, diversifying into food and other forms. R. J. Reynolds Industries, Inc., was created as the parent firm with R. J. Reynolds Tobacco Company as one of its auxiliaries (1970). The shift in nomenclature seemed to be hinting at growing concerns about health. That same year (1970) the Mouse House Massacre occurred as an internal research project studying emphysema and smoking was dismantled. In a deposition, ex-scientist Joseph E. Bumgarner reported that he and 25 more Reynolds biological researchers were ordered to relinquish their records to the firm's legal department and then fired — more casualties of the well-being issues stemming from tobacco use. In 1987, the company resurrected a mascot for Camels — a caricature of a smoking Joe Camel — which got into trouble with the American Medical Association for unwittingly influencing juveniles as young as five about the pleasures of smoking. Reynolds maintained the figure was never meant that way; its appeal was focused toward adults instead. The controversy gave the character considerable publicity and — in the process — Reynolds' smoking goods, too.

Reynolds Industries acquired Nabisco Brands in 1985, renaming the parent firm RJR Nabisco, Inc., in 1986. Kraft General Foods acquired Nabisco cold cereals in 1993; in 2000, Philip Morris Companies, Inc., bought Nabisco and merged it with Kraft Foods, Inc. Meanwhile, R. J. Reynolds Holdings, Inc., became an independent, publicly-traded company on June 15, 1999, with R. J. Reynolds Tobacco Company as a wholly owned subsidiary. In 2003, following a pact-signing with British American Tobacco plc, Reynolds American, Inc., was born. It assumed control of BAT's U.S. manufacturer — Brown & Williamson Tobacco Corporation of Louisville, Kentucky, the nation's third largest producer of tobacco products. Effective July 30, 2004, both operations were consolidated under the Reynolds American,

Inc., flag. In 2007, Reynolds employment was nearly 7,000. It is the second largest tobacco producer in the U.S., after Altria (ex–Philip Morris U.S.A.), controlling a fifth of the American tobacco market.

On a Web site in 2007, Reynolds brands included five of the top 10 selling trademarks — Camel, Winston, Kool, Salem and Doral. Other cigarettes in Reynolds' assortment include Barclay, Belair, Capri, Carlton, Eclipse, GPC, Lucky Strike, Misty, Monarch, More, Now, Pall Mall, Tareyton, Vantage, Viceroy and a host of private labels. In addition, the firm manufactures roll-your-own tobacco products; premium cigarettes; little cigars; cigars; pipe tobaccos; pipes; and related paraphernalia (filters, cleaners, holders, hand-rolling machines, cigarette tubes and papers).

Radio Series

Camel Pleasure Hour—1930 to 1931, NBC Blue (Camel)
Alice Joy, with the Van Loan Orchestra—1931 to 1932, NBC (Prince Albert)
The Camel Quarter-Hour, with Morton Downey and Tony Wons—1931 to 1932, CBS (Camel)
Camel Caravan, with Glen Gray and His Orchestra, Connee Boswell, Walter O'Keefe—1933 to 1936, CBS (Camel)
Benny Goodman's Swing School, aka *Camel Caravan*, with Benny Goodman and His Orchestra—1936 to 1939, CBS (Camel)
Jack Oakie's College, aka *Camel Caravan*, with Jimmy Durante—1936 to 1937, CBS (Camel)
The Eddie Cantor Program, aka *Camel Caravan*, with Edgar "Cookie" Fairchild and His Orchestra—1938 to 1939, CBS (Camel)
Camel Caravan, with Bob Crosby and the Bobcats—1939, 1940 to 1941, CBS, NBC, NBC Blue (Camel)
Blondie—1939 to 1943, CBS (Camel)
Al Pearce and His Gang—1940 to 1942, CBS (Camel)
Uncle Ezra's Radio Station—1940 to 1941, NBC (Camel)
Luncheon at the Waldorf—1940 to 1941, NBC Blue (Camel)
Penthouse Party, with Vaughn Monroe and His Orchestra—1941, CBS, NBC Blue (Camel)
Grand Ole Opry—1941 to 1957, NBC (Prince Albert)
The Cugat Rumba Revue, with Xavier Cugat and His Orchestra—1941 to 1942, NBC, NBC Blue (Camel)
How'm I Doin'?—1942, CBS (Camel)
Camel Caravan, with Connee Boswell, Lanny Ross, Herb Shriner, Xavier Cugat and His Orchestra—1942 to 1943, CBS (Camel)
The Abbott and Costello Show, with Bud Abbott and Lou Costello—1942 to 1947, NBC (Camel)
The Camel Comedy Caravan, with Ginny Simms—1942 to 1945, CBS (Camel)
The Jimmy Durante-Garry Moore Show—1943 to 1945, CBS (Camel)
The Bob Hawk Show, aka *Thanks to the Yanks*, with Bob Hawk—1943 to 1953, CBS, NBC (Camel)
Camel Caravan, with Vaughn Monroe and His Orchestra—1946 to 1954, NBC, CBS (Camel)
The Jimmy Durante Show 1948 to 1950, NBC (Camel)
The Screen Guild Players—1948 to 1950, NBC (Camel)
The Bob Hope Show—1950 to 1951, NBC (Camel)

The Bing Crosby Show—1950 to 1951, CBS (Camel)
Richard Diamond, Private Detective—1950 to 1952, ABC (Camel)
Walk a Mile—1952 to 1954, NBC (Camel)
My Friend Irma, with Marie Wilson —1952 to 1953, CBS (Camel)

Exposition

Similar to other tobacco processors, R. J. Reynolds invested heavily in musical artists, singers and instrumentalists to plug its masterwork Camels. Yet Reynolds also spread its mix — perhaps more completely than other prominent cigarette makers. For instance, it presented amusement drawn from no less than a half-dozen aural entertainment species: comedy, drama, music, mystery, quiz, and variety. Others in its industry, by and large, tended to cluster their messages into music and possibly one or two more programming breeds. Reynolds acknowledged the diversity among American listeners' tastes and sought to reach a wider audience camped on the dial. Of course, having a strong revenue-streaming ware like Camel in its arsenal made it inordinately easier for the firm to underwrite more and better programming and thereby appeal to a bigger segment of consumers.

While Camel was heavily favored in Reynolds' marketing efforts, let it not be missed that — for more than 16 consecutive years, extending almost to the end of radio's golden age — for 52 weeks a year, Reynolds underwrote the half-hour portion of the *Grand Ole Opry* that was beamed to the nation. The commodity it advertised exclusively was Prince Albert smoking tobacco. Reynolds found a good fit between an appreciative audience and its leading loose tobacco in a can. Not even the infamous *Camel Caravan* with its multiplied renderings headlined by a surfeit of entertainers boasted the consistency of Reynolds' allegiance to the *Opry*. While some NBC affiliates were hesitant to carry the Nashville shindig at first, most came aboard early and soon it was emanating from radio sets across the land. That includes most of the nation's largest metropolitan centers. As a byproduct, Reynolds' enduring commitment went a long way to energize and establish country music nationally, adding respectability for it in quarters of America not accustomed to a Saturday night hoedown. The sponsorship generated an acceptance for the music and artists that, to some extent, prevails today.

Commercial

On some shows, sponsors incorporated verbal exchanges between two or more subjects in their commercial pitches. Sometimes they employed jingles, sound effects and miscellaneous devices in their efforts to grab and hold the audience's attention and underscore salient points. In the exhibition herewith from the October 31, 1938, *Camel Caravan* variety series starring Eddie Cantor, announcer Walter King got a little assistance from the show's resident musicians.

WALTER KING: When you hear the orchestra hit a discord like this ...
CHORUS: Hold a note off key three or four seconds
WALTER KING: ... it's just their way of demonstrating musically that nerves *can* get out
    of tune. You see, sometimes they're beautifully in tune ... and then again ... well, you
    know how it is when you have one of those tiring, nerve-wracking days. That's when

your nerves *need* a rest. There *is* a truly pleasant way to sidestep nerve strain and tension: Just let up ... and light up a Camel. Smoking Camels is a grand way to rest your nerves ... and, it's a treat for the taste, too. So ease up ever so often and enjoy a Camel cigarette. Camel pays millions more for finer tobaccos. And smokers find that Camel's costlier tobaccos *are* soothing to the nerves.

Standard Brands, Inc.

History

Amalgamation is possibly the most descriptive term we can think of in assessing the chronicle of Standard Brands, Inc. That encompasses its 52-year run as an independent concern (1929 to 1981), its 66 years of preceding storyline dating from the beginnings of a trio of firms that eventually commingled their assets in Standard Brands (1863 to 1929), and years of additional mergers and acquisitions that have elapsed since Standard Brands lost its solitary identity in 1981. In other words, here's an enterprise now bearing down on its sesquicentennial, some of its roots extending back no fewer than 145 years on American soil in 2008. And there are vestiges of what it generated in its heyday that are still evident today.

Standard Brands itself resulted in June 1929 — just four months shy of the nation's worst stock market debacle in history — when Chase & Sanborn, Inc., coffee importers controlled by Royal Baking Company, and Fleischmann & Company merged their diverse food and beverage business interests. The resulting blend, according to William Safire writing in *The New York Times* in 2005, was created "in hopes that *brand names* would produce *brand loyalty*." There is evidence that their intentions were satisfied.

On that occasion, Chase & Sanborn was reorganized as a wholly-owned subsidiary by the Fleischmann-Royal combo, which was formally dubbed Standard Brands, Inc. The beverage-leaning auxiliary began operating as a merchandising company, importing such commodities as coffee, tea, spices, food sauces and similar specialties. According to *Time* magazine, at that intersect "the Standard Brands management also spent a busy week denying persistent rumors that Pet Milk was next on the list of foods to be swallowed up." While its denials proved correct, there were enough further acquisitions in Standard Brands' future to keep the rumor mills operating at an accelerated pace.

As pointed out already, the history of Standard Brands includes a handful of successful prior business ventures. Two in an elongated line of progression date to 1863 when some Hoosier druggists collaborated to make baking powder while a couple of Boston importers pooled their wherewithal to jointly sell tea and coffee.

Siblings Cornelius and Joseph Hoagland, who operated a small pharmacy at the corner of Calhoun and Columbia streets in Fort Wayne, plus a subordinate, possibly Thomas Biddle — he was there at about that time — initiated the notion of premixing baking soda and cream of tartar so homemakers could dodge that menial but necessary chore. They called the substance Royal Baking Powder. A decade later, they incorporated their operation (1873).

There was a fascinating sidebar in the early decades of this firm, reported by *The New York Times* in its edition of June 2, 1888. By then William Ziegler had become a stockholder in the baking venture. He sued to stop three members of the founding Hoagland family from taking exorbitant salaries, winning before a Supreme Court judge in Brooklyn. The arbiter ruled against $50,000 in compensation for President J. C. Hoagland, reducing it to $15,000; he cut Vice President C. N. Hoagland's pay from $30,000 to $10,000; and he downsized Treasurer Raymond Hoagland's wages from $6,000 to $4,000. The jurist allowed that the Hoaglands "raised their own salaries, not as reasonable compensation for labors performed, but to force a stockholder to sell out." (Parenthetically, where are those judges with the authority to set limits on a CEO's pay today? If there were any blessings bestowed upon a working class toiling in a primitive American corporate culture in the nineteenth century, in retrospect, surely this could be considered one of them.)

The business had been relocated in New York City by this time. According to a contemporary Web site, by 1893 Royal Baking Company was "the biggest advertiser in the world." Whether true or not, it was a sign of the convincing authority borne by this segment of the future conglomerate. The founding fathers' successors persisted in experimentation and innovation, at last diversifying their product line in 1925 with Royal gelatin desserts, with puddings soon following and tapioca by the late 1940s.

Likewise, mercantilists Caleb Chase and James Sanborn, pursuing similar interests, decided to go into business together in 1863, the same year the Hoagland boys were starting to make baking powder. As their new venture proliferated, Chase and Sanborn, too, innovated. Within 15 years, they had become the first in the industry to pack and ship roasted coffee in sealed tin cans (1878).

Then, finally, in 1868—only five years after this bunch launched their respective enterprises—a couple of siblings, who had left their native homeland in Austria-Hungary to settle in America, formed a partnership with entrepreneur James Gaff. With financing by the latter, the brothers, Charles and Maximilian Fleischmann, opened a Cincinnati, Ohio, plant manufacturing compressed yeast cakes. It was the first commercially produced yeast product in the U.S. Charles Fleischmann had previously managed an Austrian distillery making spirits and yeast. Having arrived in America in 1865, he was disappointed in the quality of local bread-making.

Through its modernization, Gaff, Fleischmann & Company literally revolutionized home and commercial baking. Introducing their yeast to bakers, they were inundated by orders, having set a new standard in the baking industry. By 1900, they were operating a plant with a state-of-the-art research lab at Peekskill, New York. Following Gaff's death in 1905, the Fleischmanns re-titled their shop Fleischmann & Company.

This trio of entrepreneurial commercial endeavors formed the nucleus of Standard Brands, Inc., in June 1929. But after a few decades there was to be much more included in that fusion. Within two months afterward, in fact, the Canadian branches of the parent companies, including E. W. Gillett, officially joined up, too, expanding the firm's nomenclature to Standard Brands Limited.

At a Century of Progress exposition in Chicago in 1934, Standard Brands bankrolled an exhibit for the baking industry on behalf of Fleishmann's yeast. Five years later, the corporate parent operated its own pavilion during the New York World's Fair. Subsequently, in the 1940s, Fleischmann introduced a preferred blended whisky and purchased Indianapolis' Standard Margarine Company (1942) and Daviess County (Kentucky) Distilling Company,

Owensboro. In 1947, Standard Brands International was established as a wholly-owned subsidiary, marketing the firm's goods around the globe.

Among several newer commodities, the outfit introduced vacuum-packed Chase & Sanborn coffee and instant tea in 1947; instant Tenderleaf tea, the first water-soluble tea shortly thereafter; it expanded the varieties of Royal pudding and custard desserts; and, in 1948, brought to market a fast-rising dry yeast from Fleischmann. In 1956, the firm purchased Clinton (Iowa) Corn Processing Company and carried Fleischmann Vodka to market. Five years hence, it bought Planters Nut and Chocolate Company of Wilkes-Barre, Pennsylvania (1961). And three years after that, it acquired Chicago's Curtiss Candy Company, maker of Baby Ruth, Butterfinger and other prominent confectionary bars, extending from a heritage that originated in 1916.

In the meantime, operating independently of all of this was the National Biscuit Company (N.B.C.) with headquarters in New York City, which was to merge with Standard Brands, Inc. in 1981 to form Nabisco Brands, Inc.[1] The "biscuit" in the original moniker, incidentally, is a Brit English and early American English idiom meaning "cracker products." National Biscuit's history, too, is rich in American ingenuity and entrepreneurial savvy. Launched in 1898, it was the result of a merger of a trio of enterprises: the American Biscuit Company, itself the result of the collaboration of 40 Midwestern bakeries dating to 1830, at least 33 years before the precursors of Standard Brands; the New York Biscuit Company, which was developed from eight bakeries; and the United States Baking Company.[2]

Recognizing the need to hawk its wares, N.B.C. spared little expense in doing so, becoming a U.S. marketing pacesetter. During its first decade of existence, the firm spent an unprecedented $7 million in advertising and sales promotion. By 1981, this amalgamated leviathan held a virtual monopoly on American cookie and cracker processing, having folded 114 privately operated bakeries into its mix with assets of $55 million. Yet, according to one source, "the inflation and mounting energy costs of the 1970s led Nabisco to consider the possibility of a merger with another large food concern." In early 1981, Standard Brands chairman F. Ross Johnson and Nabisco chairman Robert Schaeberle announced plans to combine the two foodstuff operations.

Within a year after the formation of Nabisco Brands, Inc., the firm jettisoned Chase & Sanborn. The coffee wound up with Nestlé USA, which in 2000 dispatched it to Sara Lee Corporation. In the meantime, four years after Nabisco Brands, Inc., was established, R. J. Reynolds Industries, Inc., bought it for $4.9 billion. In one of the largest acquisitions in U.S. business history, the 1985 takeover netted the country's largest consumer products entity with annual sales exceeding $19 billion. Nabisco Brands reportedly sought the merger to avoid any potential hostile takeover bids while Reynolds wanted it to diversify from its heavy emphasis on tobacco. Later that year the corporate sobriquet was altered to RJR Nabisco, Inc. F. Ross Johnson, who had headed Standard Brands, then Nabisco Brands, became president of RJR Nabisco.

In 1985, with mergers and acquisitions still the name of the game, Philip Morris took control of General Foods, Inc., for $5.6 billion, the largest non-oil acquisition in U.S. history. The Kraft Foods Company was added to Morris's fold in 1988 for $12.9 billion, a new record. Those latest additions combined into Morris's Kraft General Foods unit in 1989, becoming the largest food processing firm on U.S. soil. In 2000, Philip Morris Companies acquired Nabisco Holdings and its trademarks. Some of the familiar names from Standard Brands were integrated into the Kraft Foods worldwide business. Early in 2007, Altria announced it intended to spin off Kraft Foods to focus on tobacco interests.

Radio Series

The Chase & Sanborn Choral Orchestra—1929 to 1931, NBC (Chase & Sanborn)
The Fleischmann Hour, aka *The Sunshine Hour*, with Rudy Vallee—1929 to 1936, NBC (Fleischmann)
The Chase & Sanborn Hour, with Eddie Cantor and David Rubinoff and His Orchestra—1931 to 1934, NBC (Chase & Sanborn)
The Royal Vagabonds, with Ward Wilson, Ken Murray, Fanny Brice—1932, 1933, NBC Blue, NBC (Royal)
The Chase & Sanborn Tea Program, with Georgie Price—1932, CBS (Chase & Sanborn)
Great Moments in History—1932 to 1933, NBC Blue (Fleischmann)
The Jack Pearl Show—1934, NBC (Royal)
The Baker's Broadcast, aka *The Joe Penner Show*, with Ozzie Nelson and His Orchestra—1933 to 1935, NBC Blue (Fleischmann)
The Opera Guild, with Deems Taylor—1934 to 1935, NBC (Chase & Sanborn)
Mary Pickford Dramas, aka *Parties at Pickford*—1934 to 1935, NBC (Royal)
One Man's Family—1935 to 1936, NBC (Royal); 1936 to 1949, NBC (Tenderleaf)
The Royal Gelatin Hour, with Rudy Vallee—1936 to 1939, NBC (Royal)
Believe It or Not, aka *Baker's Broadcast*, with Robert L. Ripley, Ozzie Nelson and Harriet Hilliard—1935 to 1937, NBC Blue (Fleischman)
Do You Want to Be an Actor?, with Haven MacQuarrie—1937, NBC (Chase & Sanborn)
The Chase & Sanborn Hour, aka *The Chase & Sanborn Show*, aka *The Charlie McCarthy Show*, with Edgar Bergen, Don Ameche, Mortimer Snerd and Effie Clinker—1937 to 1948, NBC (Chase & Sanborn)
Ozzie Nelson and His Orchestra, with Harriet Hilliard—1937 to 1938, NBC Blue (Fleischmann)
Those We Love—1939 to 1940, NBC (Royal)
I Love a Mystery—1939 to 1942, NBC, NBC Blue (Fleischmann)
What's My Name?, with John Reed King—1941, 1942, NBC, MBS (Chase & Sanborn, Fleischmann)
The O'Neills—1942 to 1943, NBC
The Story of Mary Marlin—1943 to 1945, CBS (Tenderleaf)
The Open Door—1944, CBS
The Spike Jones Show, with Frances Langford—1945, NBC (Chase & Sanborn)
The Fred Allen Show—1945 to 1947, NBC (Tenderleaf)

Exposition

Several things stand out about this company and its radio advertising strategies.

First, Standard Brands was quick to market its goods, beating virtually everybody else to the airwaves — no matter what industry others were in — with lightning speed. The company was formed in the summer of 1929. With the opening of that fall's radio season, Standard Brands was airing not just *one* but *two* network programs, including one that was to be among the medium's longstanding traditions, the legendary Rudy Vallee. From the earliest days, unequivocally, Standard Brands took to radio like a duck takes to water.

Second, Standard Brands either chose its programming well, got lucky, or both. By the 1933 to 1934 season for example, it had bought series headlined by four venerated entertainers: Eddie Cantor, Jack Pearl, Joe Penner and Rudy Vallee. Most Americans turning on a radio for amusement during the primetime hours in the 1930s and 1940s eventually heard one or more of Standard Brands' celebrated icons. Many became loyal fans, remaining steadfast to those veteran performers for years and, presumably, to the products that brought them to the ether.

Third, Standard Brands persisted with a minuscule handful of winners for many years. It paid the bills of a trio for a decade or longer: Rudy Vallee (10 years), Edgar Bergen and Charlie McCarthy (11 years) and *One Man's Family* (14 years).

Fourth, inconsistently and surprisingly, Standard Brands was one of the first radio clients to pull the plug on the medium. While there may have been undocumented commercial insertions in multiple participation programming in the 1950s, it appears that — with the episode of *One Man's Family* broadcast on September 25, 1949 — Standard Brands permanently departed the network radio business, at least as far as subscribing complete shows was concerned. It should be further noted that with only two more exceptions — Fred Allen, whose sponsorship was withdrawn in 1947; and Edgar Bergen and Charlie McCarthy, experiencing the same fate in 1948 — in the years after 1945, Standard Brands didn't budget for any more radio series, period.

Although it poured money into television as did scores of competing radio solicitors, unlike most that did — before the 1940s were history — it simply abandoned a sweeping, unified aural-oriented advertising approach. Most other firms continued a while longer, many to the mid–1950s or beyond. We can only conjecture, of course, but wonder how Standard Brands executives arrived at their 1949 decision to withdraw the little capital they were still earmarking to network radio sponsorship. After all, it was a viable medium then; and across two decades, it had made them exceedingly wealthy.

If the reader will indulge me, I'd like to add a personal word. In the 1940s, my father was a sales representative for Standard Brands, Inc. I clearly recall my mother's loyalty to Tenderleaf tea, Chase & Sanborn coffee, Blue Bonnet margarine, Fleischmann's yeast, Royal gelatin and puddings, et al., even in the years after my dad accepted employment for somebody else.

To the point: Sunday evenings in our home in that decade were spent around the living room radio, just as they were (I would later learn) in legions of other American domiciles. Somehow I got the impression it was important to my dad's job for us to tune in a spate of features appearing from week to week in the fall, winter and spring months that were underwritten by Standard Brands. Indeed, while I didn't understand what I was hearing in that preschool epoch, I took my cues from my parents, who were enthralled by the continuing narrative of *One Man's Family*. In addition, I observed them nearly falling out of their chairs in laughter over the quips of Senator Claghorn, Titus Moody and Mrs. Nussbaum, residents of Allen's Alley, on *The Fred Allen Show*; plus the retorts of the irascible marionette Charlie McCarthy to his master, Edgar Bergen.

Standard Brands offered all three programs to NBC listeners every week. It's the first memory I have of radio and one that has persisted for a literal lifetime. I owe the firm a debt of gratitude. Even though I didn't understand the plots or the jokes, by watching at home, I fell in love with the little electric box containing so many diverse sounds that possessed such incredible sway over those who heard its words.

Commercial

Have you ever had rancid-tasting coffee? Standard Brands' ad agency thought it was an angle worth mentioning to listeners when this commercial aired on *The Edgar Bergen and*

Charlie McCarthy Show on December 12, 1937. Notice the clever premium offer included, "premium" perhaps being an operative word for characterizing coffee.

Don Ameche: America has gone wild over Charlie McCarthy! Everybody's sending for Charlie's marvelous likeness that we're giving away free. Day and night we're mailing out these wonderful presents to homes everywhere. And you'll love Charlie, too. He's over 20 inches tall, made of strong cardboard, and printed in full color. He sits on your knee, and you can make his mouth move and his eyes roll. And here's how you get him free ... simply mail us four bag fronts cut from four one-pound bags of Chase & Sanborn dated coffee and we'll Charlie promptly and postpaid. This offer will last long enough so that you can buy your dated coffee as you need it ... never more than one pound at a time ... then you're *sure* your coffee's fresh, never stale and rancid-tasting ... a blend free from the harmful effects stale coffee may have on your system. For Chase & Sanborn dated coffee is guaranteed fresh by our unique dating and rapid delivery system. It's rushed to your grocer fresh from roasting with the delivery date clearly marked on the money-saving dated bag. You can't buy it stale. Try dated coffee ... buy only one pound at a time, and when you save four bag fronts, mail them to us for the big action-likeness of Charlie McCarthy. Take down our address ... Chase & Sanborn ... 420 Lexington Avenue ... 4-2-0 Lexington Avenue ... New York City. Start getting Charlie now. Buy Chase & Sanborn dated coffee from your grocer tomorrow.

Sterling Drug, Inc.

History

With only about 35,000 inhabitants at the time, Wheeling, West Virginia seems like an illogical spot on the map to launch the headquarters of the nation's largest patent medicine enterprise. So when the Neuralgyline Company opened its doors there in 1901, the prospects weren't particularly imposing. It would be a few years, in fact, before the business grew into incredible, nearly invincible proportions, finally becoming a competitive multinational health and personal care goods manufacturer bearing far flung interests. It performed steadily however, moving at amazing speed as it hurtled toward its ultimate destiny.

The endeavor was the instigation of a couple of high school alumni, Albert Henry Diebold (1872 to 1964) and William Erhard Weiss (1879 to 1942). Both were born and raised in Canton, Ohio. In 1900, Diebold started a career as a small-town druggist at Sistersville, West Virginia. Weiss was drawn in a similar direction, acquiring a Ph.G (graduate pharmacist) degree at the Philadelphia College of Pharmacy (1896). After working a spell in retail pharmaceuticals, Weiss and Diebold crossed paths again and renewed their friendship of a few years earlier. In 1901, the two formed a partnership peddling patent medicines. Launching it with $1,000, they named their business Neuralgyline Company after their very first commodity, a pain reliever dubbed Neuralgine. Three days a week the duo made their analgesic in a Wheeling plant on Ninety-Second Street. Three other days each week they were, for a while, Neuralgine's sole distributors: they took their wares door to door, traveling by rented horse-drawn buggies, a method familiar to many salesmen, manufacturers and distributors until motorized vehicles came into vogue.

Canvassing the hilly Mountain State countryside, a persistent Diebold and Weiss not only recouped their initial investment in their first year of operations but earned an additional $9,000. They helped themselves tremendously by posting the merits of their pain reliever on fenceposts and tree signs along roadways, beginning what would signify the business as an aggressive marketer. The pair plowed every dollar of their first year's profits back into the future, too, skipping the usual route selected by many.

Instead of purchasing any physical assets or saving it, the proprietors funneled their net proceeds into advertising, mostly in a couple of Pittsburgh newspapers. Pittsburgh, with a population of nearly a quarter-million, was the next major town. And Diebold and Weiss's promotional instincts proved solid. By 1906, their small upfront investment of five years before rewarded them with an enterprise worth $500,000! Along with it, they earned a substantial reputation in the burgeoning trade they had joined.

There are conflicting reports, nonetheless, about whose hand was actually on the wheel guiding the Neuralgyline ship safely through potentially tempest seas a few years into their voyage. Multiple informants credit Weiss and Diebold by name and no one else. At least one cites Weiss as singly occupying the driver's seat, unequivocally "the firm's primary leader" during its earliest years.[1] An obituary published in *The New York Times* at Weiss's death from a 1942 vehicle accident notes that he was the former chairman of the board of Sterling Products, Inc., of New York. Contrast this with *Time*, a reference unaccustomed to making grievous errors of extensive proportions. Upon the passing of Diebold in 1964, the newsweekly noted that his "brilliant marketing" plus "an unerring eye for mergers parlayed Neuralgine ... into a $250 million-a-year business." *Time* observed that Diebold was "a founder in 1901 and president until 1941 of Sterling Drug, Inc." So who was running the show? Either founder or was it both together? (The latter, a real possibility.) Could it perhaps have been someone else? The name of H. Fred Behrens (1870 to 1935) comes to mind.

A couple of witnesses identify Wheeling businessman Behrens—a director of two local banks—as president of remedy-maker Neuralgyline.[2] In that model, Diebold was the secretary-treasurer; Weiss ran the operation as general manager; and four more businessmen—none overtly related to the others—were board members (directors). A board meeting was occasionally called to deal with issues like the practicality of buying a safe, installing a telephone and securing a stenographer at $5 weekly—concerns, according to a theorist, that were obviously near the start of their entrepreneurial enterprise.

Despite such trivial-sounding pursuits during the early years—and regardless of who was *really* in charge—if the acquisition records are any gauge, these men were phenomenally successful in plotting their course. Parenthetically, so successful was Diebold that, in 1926, he was instrumental in establishing one of the firm's most formidable and durable competitors, American Home Products (see separate heading). He remained a director there until the year before his death, succeeded in that capacity by his son. In the first decade of Neuralgyline's existence, meanwhile, Diebold and Weiss purchased several rival patent medicine outfits including the Pape and the Pape-Thompson companies of Cincinnati and four more in Wheeling: Drake, J. W. James, Knowlton Danderine and Sterling Remedy companies.

A Wheeling biographer, assessing their accomplishments in 1912, gushed: "The management of the various companies controlled by the Neuralgyline Company includes men of long experience in the patent medicine business.... The persistent demand reinforced by worldwide advertising is indicated in the fact that a million boxes of cascarets [a medicinal ware] are sold each month to the druggists of the United States. The trademarks are copyrighted everywhere, and millions of dollars are spent in advertising." By that time, the business was worth $4 million, having achieved status as "the country's foremost patent medicine conglomerate," according to industry historians.

Neuralgyline merged with still another small unidentified outfit in 1917 and at that time renamed its business Sterling Products (cited in some records by the longer sobriquet Sterling Patent Medicine Company). A year later, the entrepreneurs were fixed well enough to ante up $5.3 million to buy the American assets of a German chemical and pharmaceutical enterprise, Bayer. That firm had invented aspirin, initially appearing on the market in 1899.[3] (A contemporary Bayer Web site immodestly flaunts aspirin as "the drug of the century.") According to some modern analysts, "Bayer had developed aspirin into one of the most successful medical products of its time (and, indeed, of the entire twentieth century). Protecting its sales from counterfeiters and preparing for aspirin's patent expiration, Bayer had invested significantly in branding its medication. As a result, the Bayer cross was a widely recognized icon in North and South America as well as Europe."

Bayer's U.S. assets were seized by our government during the First World War. After that conflict drew to a close, in 1919, they were auctioned off to the highest bidder (Sterling) by the U.S. Office of the Alien Property Custodian.[4] In hindsight, knowing Bayer's incalculable influence on the world as a palliative in the decades since, including its commanding and divergent presence on druggists' shelves today, how phenomenally successful were those Sterling medicine men!

Along the way, Sterling purchased a 50 percent interest in pharmaceutical manufacturer-distributor Winthrop Chemical Company. It completed that deal in 1945 when it bought the other half. At the time, Atabrine, penicillin, sulfa drugs and critical war drugs predominated on Winthrop's assembly line. The unit persisted thereafter as the Winthrop-Stearns subsidiary of Sterling Drug, Inc. Meanwhile, at the close of 1942, Sterling absorbed 16 more wholly owned domestic auxiliaries into its operations, the result of extensive purchases among smaller competing rivals.

As the years rolled along, Sterling Products, which became Sterling Drug, Inc., in 1942, developed or acquired many other commodities for its health goods inventory. At the same time, it expanded into fields relatively distant from medicinal lines. It became, according to one authority, "the most diversified member of the pharmaceutical industry." Its consumer product assemblage ranged from cosmetics to Beacon Wax, fragrances to d-Con insecticides, and chemicals to animal health care wares.

Among its storehouse of better recalled properties are Astring-O-Sol mouthwash, Bayer aspirin palliative, Cal-Aspirin palliative, Campho-Phenique canker sore medication, Double Danderine shampoo, Energine cleaning fluid and Energine Shoe-White polish, Fletcher's Castoria laxative, Haley's M-O mineral emulsion oil laxative, Ironized Yeast vitamin supplement, Lyon's toothpaste and Dr. Lyon's Tooth Powder, Mollé shave cream, Mulsified Coconut Oil shampoo, Phillips' Milk of Magnesia laxative (and also antacid, toothpaste, tooth powder, skin and cleansing creams), and ZBT baby powder. (There was never a readily available explanation for the peculiar dissimilarity involving the monikers Lyons toothpaste and Dr. Lyons tooth powder. Both were usually advertised in tandem, especially on the air — in the same programs, with separate commercials. It must have left millions pondering the difference beyond paste and powder with the same spelling of Lyons embracing both.)

In 1960, with scores of health and beauty wares in a bulging portfolio, Sterling's profits achieved $19 million on sales soaring past $200 million. The company had long abandoned its roots in Wheeling, however, moving its headquarters and other operations to New York City under the corporate banner of Sterling Drug. A historian's scrutiny resulted in this opinion.[5]

> Wheeling's small size and relatively rural surroundings led it to have both a lesser ability to supply research-driven drugs and a lower demand for them. Wheeling lacked both a major medical research facility and a public health system that was organized to develop innovative medicines. Because frontier-level medical research knowledge diffuses slowly across distances and often requires the large-scale medical research facilities or local expert researchers, the costs of the leading-edge knowledge required for a research-driven approach to drug-making was relatively higher in Wheeling, WV than in locations rich in such resources. At the same time, because of Wheeling's relatively low population (and, more importantly, population density),

the demand for medications to treat bacteriological illness, which were the few illnesses for which leading-edge science was developing cures, was lower than in cities with high population densities.

Although the costs and benefits research-driven drug-making may have been higher in urban areas, this was not the case for advertising- and marketing-driven patent medicines. Patent remedies had historically high demand in rural areas, and their appeal was facilitated by emerging advertising opportunities in newspapers and other print media. Thus, the local Wheeling environment contained the key resources Sterling required to organize itself around the production and distribution of patent-medicines, but lacked the resources most essential to a research-driven approach to making drugs.

Despite all its good fortune and promising future, after experiencing a marvelous first half of the twentieth century, at times Sterling found itself in a heap of trouble in the second half.

A merger with Lehn & Fink (Hinds, Lysol) in 1969 resulted in a suit by the Federal Trade Commission (FTC) citing a reduction in competition among packaged goods advertisers. While Lehn & Fink was allowed to persist as a Sterling subsidiary, the government's attorneys argued that control of health care, beauty and home products resided in the hands of a reduced number of players. Consumers were denied a fair review of commodities due to Sterling's heavy and disproportionate spending in advertising, the FTC maintained, compared to revenues generated from sales (a throwback to Sterling's predecessor days).

Then, in 1971, Sterling crossed swords with the U.S. Food and Drug Administration. Concerned about potentially adverse effects of hexachlorophene, the agency ordered products including this chemical in their composition to be sold by prescription only. Sales of Sterling's over-the-counter pHisoHex, which contained hexachlorophene and had become the largest-selling antibacterial cleanser, were severely and adversely affected by the ruling, putting a dent in Sterling's bottom line.

The "hardest blow," according to one chronicler, that Sterling faced in the era occurred when competitors finally found a way to take vast sums of Sterling's Bayer business away by creating improved alternatives. The new wave of marketable breakthroughs signaled that they had overcome the occasional side effects of upset stomachs sometimes associated with aspirin's use. That coupled with faster relief and higher potency allowed newly-introduced non-aspirin formulas like Tylenol, Bufferin, Excedrin Extra-Strength and more analgesic compounds to give Bayer a run for its money from 1971 forward. Twelve years later (1983), having fully controlled at least half of the aspirin market in its past, Bayer was reduced to a mere 10 percent share of $1.3 billion in annual aspirin sales.

As if that fiasco wasn't bad enough, Sterling created its own acetaminophen (aspirin substitute), Panadol, hoping to reclaim a colossal segment of the business it had lost. But shortly before Panadol was ready to market, in 1982, Tylenol was yanked from druggists' shelves following tragic cyanide poisonings that left seven people dead, a result of package tampering. Had Panadol been ready, it might have stepped into the void and scooped up the suddenly disenfranchised Tylenol buyers. But the timing had a negative effect: when Panadol got to the stores in 1983, Tylenol had already returned (in tamper-proof packaging) and quickly recaptured 80 percent of its old market. It left Sterling officials wringing their hands in frustration, thinking about what might have been.

In the meantime, the Food and Drug Administration clamped down on Sterling again, in 1978, over perceived distortions in advertising related to pain-killer safety. Sterling withdrew offending ads. And in 1981, a Federal Trade Commission administrative law judge ordered

Sterling to "refrain from making claims about its nonprescription drug products' efficacy or superiority unless those claims are based on competent and reliable scientific evidence."

Between governmental watchdogs, energized and innovative competitors and missed opportunities, Sterling simply wasn't enjoying the party nearly as much as it used to — or as much as some of the other guests. In 1988, Eastman Kodak acquired Sterling Drug for $5.1 billion. The ride was brief and somewhat bumpy. "Kodak had never really figured out how to fix an ailing and underfunded Sterling Drug," surmised one observer.

Sterling partnered with French drug-maker Elf Sanofi (now Sanofi Aventis) in 1993. That firm acquired the prescription drug operations of Sterling-Winthrop in 1994 from Kodak for $1.675 billion. That left Kodak owning the over-the-counter drug business, including Bayer aspirin and the U.S. rights to the Bayer name and trademarks. That year (1994) Kodak sold those rights to SmithKline Beecham for $1 billion, which immediately sold the rights back to Bayer AG for $1 billion. Sterling Drug, Inc., is publicly traded today and recently posted almost $2 billion in sales with a workforce exceeding 27,000.

Radio Series

Rock-a-Bye Lady—1927 to 1928, NBC Blue (Fletcher's Castoria)

The American Album of Familiar Music, with Frank Munn, Frank Parker, Gustav Haenschen and His Orchestra, Abe Lyman and His Orchestra—1931 to 1931 to 1951, NBC, ABC (Bayer, Dr. Lyons)

The Manhattan Merry-Go-Round, with Richard Carlay, Thomas L. Thomas, Victor Arden and His Orchestra, Andy Sannella and His Orchestra—1932 to 1949, NBC Blue, NBC (Dr. Lyons)

The Mollé Minstrels— ca. early 1930s, NBC (Mollé)

Skippy, with Franklin Adams, Jr.—1933 to 1935, CBS (Phillips Milk of Magnesia and Tooth Powder)

The Castoria Program, with Albert Spalding, Conrad Thibault—1933 to 1934, CBS (Fletcher's Castoria)

The Shirley Howard Show, with The Jesters—1933 to 1934, NBC (Mollé)

Waltz Time, with Abe Lyman and His Orchestra—1933 to 1948, NBC (Phillips Milk of Magnesia)

Whispering Jack Smith—1934 to 1935, CBS, NBC (Ironized Yeast)

Roxy Revue, aka *Roxy's Gang*—1934 to 1935, CBS (Fletcher's Castoria)

Mollé Minstrels—1934 to 1935, NBC (Mollé)

Lavender and Old Lace, with Frank Munn, Lucy Monroe, Fritzi Scheff—1934 to 1936, CBS (Bayer)

Melodiana, with Abe Lyman and His Orchestra—1934 to 1936, CBS, NBC Blue (Phillips Milk of Magnesia and Tooth Powder)

Painted Dreams—1935 to 1936, MBS (Cal-Aspirin)

Vox Pop, aka *Sidewalk Interviews*, with Parks Johnson, Jerry Belcher, Wally Butterworth — 1935 to 1938, NBC (Mollé)

Backstage Wife—1935 to 1951, MBS, NBC Blue, NBC (Dr. Lyons, Lyons, Energine, Mulsified Coconut Oil)

How to be Charming, with Beatrice de Sylvara—1936 to 1938, NBC (Phillips Milk of Magnesia, Dr. Lyons, Phillips Skin/Cleansing Cream)

Broadway Merry-Go-Round, aka *Folies Bergere of the Air*, aka *Folies de Paree*, aka *Revue de Paree*, with Fanny Brice, Beatrice Little—1936 to 1937, NBC Blue (Dr. Lyons)
Sweetest Love Songs, with Frank Munn—1937, NBC Blue (Phillips Milk of Magnesia)
Radio Newsreel, with Wally Butterworth and Parks Johnson—1937 to 1938, NBC (Energine)
Second Husband, aka *Ethel Barrymore Theater*—1936 to 1946, NBC Blue, NBC, CBS (Bayer, Dr. Lyons, Energine)
Lorenzo Jones—1937 to 1949, NBC (Phillips Milk of Magnesia Tooth Powder/Skin Cream/Cleansing Cream, Bayer, Dr. Lyons, Ironized Yeast)
Spy Secrets—1938, NBC (Energine)
Battle of the Sexes, with Frank Crumit and Julia Sanderson, Jay C. Flippen, Walter O'Keefe—1938 to 1944, NBC, NBC Blue (Mollé, Energine)
The Goodwill Hour, with John J. Anthony—1938 to 1943, 1951 to 1953, MBS, NBC Blue (Ironized Yeast, Mollé)
Alias Jimmy Valentine—1938 to 1939, NBC Blue (Dr. Lyons)
Stella Dallas—1938 to 1954, NBC (Phillips Milk of Magnesia/Skin Cream/Cleansing Cream/Tooth Powder, Haley's M-O, Ironized Yeast, ZBT)
Young Widder Brown—1938 to 1956, NBC (Cal-Aspirin, Bayer, Phillips Tooth Paste/Tooth Powder/Skin Cream/Cleansing Cream, Haley's M-O, Dr. Lyons, Energine)
Spelling Bee, with Paul Wing—1938 to 1940, NBC (Energine)
The Court of Missing Heirs, aka *Are You a Missing Heir?*, with Jim Waters—1939 to 1942, CBS (Ironized Yeast)
Orphans of Divorce—1939 to 1942, NBC Blue (Dr. Lyons)
What Would You Have Done?, with Ben Grauer—1940, NBC Blue (Energine)
Here's Morgan, aka *The Henry Morgan Show*—ca. 1940 to 1941, MBS (Ironized Yeast)
Manhattan at Midnight—1940 to 1943, NBC Blue (Energine, Mollé)
Amanda of Honeymoon Hill—1940 to 1946, NBC Blue, CBS (Cal-Aspirin, Haley's M-O, Phillips Milk of Magnesia, Ironized Yeast)
Monday Merry-Go-Round, with Victor Arden and His Orchestra, Bea Wain, Phil Duey—1941 to 1942, NBC Blue (Dr. Lyons, Mulsified Coconut Oil)
A Helping Hand, with John J. Anthony—1941 to 1942, CBS (Ironized Yeast)
American Melody Hour, with Frank Munn, Vivian Della Chiesa, Victor Arden and His Orchestra, Frank Black and His Orchestra—1941 to 1948, NBC Blue, CBS (Bayer)
Lights Out—1942 to 1943, CBS (Ironized Yeast, Energine, Mollé)
Big Town, with Edward Pawley—1943 to 1948, CBS (Ironized Yeast, Bayer)
Mollé Mystery Theater, aka *Mystery Theater*, aka *Hearthstone of the Death Squad*, aka *Mark Sabre*—1943 to 1954, NBC, CBS, ABC (Mollé, Dr. Lyons, Ironized Yeast)
My Best Girls—1944 to 1945, Blue (Energine)
Bride and Groom, with John Nelson—1945 to 1950, ABC (Energine, Dr. Lyons, Mulsified Coconut Oil)
Zeke Manners—1947, ABC (Mollé, Phillips Milk of Magnesia Tooth Powder)
Mr. Chameleon, with Karl Swenson—1948 to 1951, CBS (Bayer, Dr. Lyons)
National Barn Dance—1949 to 1950, ABC (Phillips Milk of Magnesia)
My True Story—1949 to 1956, ABC (Sterling Drug—multiple participation from 1949 to 1952)
Pursuit, with Ben Wright 1951 to 1952, CBS (Mollé, Dr. Lyons, Energine, Ironized Yeast)
Ladies Fair, with Tom Moore—1951 to 1954, MBS (Sterling Drug)

Exposition

Pityrosporum ovale was a condition that most people had no idea they could catch. Such a pity! Thankfully, in the late 1940s and early 1950s, there were well-intentioned men with commanding voices like Ford Bond and Howard Claney who were obliged to warn them against that possibility. They did so eloquently on daily broadcasts of the serials *Backstage Wife* and *Stella Dallas*. *Pityrosporum ovale* was an application that Sterling Drug gave to the malady pityriasis, a skin anomaly marked by dry scaling or scurfy patches. It could be prevented — according to Messrs. Bond, Claney and others of their ilk — by Double Danderine. Never identified by the term "shampoo" on the air although that's what it was, the product was absolutely the best way to inhibit the possibility of scaling, at least, to hear them tell it.

Bond and Claney were two of a half-dozen interlocutors who spent much of their professional lives hawking wares of rival health care and consumer goods manufacturers Sterling Drug, Inc., and American Home Products. The good fortune of those commercial spokesmen was linked to the interests of inexhaustible radio producers Frank and Anne Hummert. The famous couple lucked upon those two clients and sewed up their broadcasting business for a couple of decades. The Hummerts are credited with maintaining a hand in no fewer than 125 audio series. Most of those they inspired, wrote, staffed, produced and sold to sponsors and networks in packages, using assembly line techniques and hundreds of minions to carry out their directives.

Among their underlings was a cadre of authoritative-sounding fellows whose voices were quite familiar to radio listeners in the 1940s and 1950s. Others who proffered there included George Ansbro, Andre Baruch, Frank Gallop and Roger Krupp. Each plugged the same commodities repetitiously, ad infinitum. Frequently they pursued a Hummert hallmark: a cowcatcher commercial at the start of a show delivered cold followed by theme and introduction, a regular (longer) commercial, program installment content (music or drama), another regular commercial, and ending with a brief hitchhike pitch. The Hummert system usually assigned one man as a program's announcer who handled narration or introductory duties plus delivering the regular plugs (virtually never accompanied by a jingle, another Hummert distinctive). There would be one or more other Hummert men supplying the cowcatcher and hitchhike. In so doing, four of Sterling's commodities, for example, could be advertised on quarter-hour or half-hour shows, some of it with fresh voices. Thus you might have Double Danderine, Phillips Milk of Magnesia, Ironized Yeast and Energine cleaning fluid (recall the motto that was run into the ground — "Keep it clean with Energine!") hawked in a single feature.

In the case of *Backstage Wife* and *Stella Dallas*, dramas that aired back to back for most of their ethereal years, Howard Claney (*Stella's* announcer) stepped across the 30-second station ID line to deliver pithy messages on *Backstage Wife*; Ford Bond (*Wife's* announcer) reciprocated on *Stella Dallas*. Keeping it in the family helped the Hummerts craft an empire virtually on the backs of the two firms. The evening musical shows in their arsenal, plus a few audience participation series, juvenile adventures, an occasional mystery and dozens of daytime serials made them a wealthy pair, thanks to Sterling and American Home Products.

Incidentally, mention is made elsewhere about *The General Mills Hour*, an experiment that competitor soap opera producer Irna Phillips achieved. Starting at 2 o'clock weekday afternoons in the Eastern Time zone in the mid–1940s over NBC, Phillips launched 45 minutes' worth of washboard weepers with the Hummerts contributing another quarter-hour for the same sponsor. While there never was a *Sterling Hour* identified by that sobriquet, it existed nonetheless. From the late 1930s to the early 1950s, four Sterling serials aired back to back weekday afternoons on NBC beginning at 4 o'clock: *Backstage Wife, Stella Dallas, Lorenzo Jones* and *Young Widder Brown*. As daytime dramas began to ebb, and indeed as radio did, Sterling concentrated its efforts in that format at NBC. Earlier, however, Sterling shared the wealth, scattering its advertising budget across the four national hookups. A biographer of William S. Paley, CBS chairman, in the meantime, indicated that the Hummerts were so powerful that *they*—and not the major chains—picked the webs carrying most of their shows. It was, to be sure, an intimate circle in which the Sterling radio marketers worked.

Commercial

The opening of the June 2, 1948, aircast of *Backstage Wife* illustrates an example mentioned under "Exposition" above, employing the services of dual announcers to deliver the cowcatcher and primary pitches.

SYSTEM CUE
BRIDGE MUSIC: A few bright notes on the organ
H. CLANEY: (*cold*) Ladies, check up on your hair ... Keep it as fresh and cleanly fragrant as it *could* be. Shampoo your hair regularly with Mulsified Coconut Oil shampoo. Its creamy lather leaves no after-film to become unpleasant, and Mulsified is *so mild— so gentle*—you can use it as often as you like. So for gleaming, *always* cleanly fragrant hair, remember ... Mulsified Coconut Oil shampoo.
THEME: *The Rose of Tralee*
FORD BOND: (*theme under*) Now we present, once again, *Backstage Wife* ... the story of Mary Noble, a little Iowa girl who married one of America's most handsome actors, Larry Noble, matinee idol of a million other women ... the story of what it *means* to be the wife of a famous star.
(*following theme*) No matter what claims you may hear about others, remember that the best toothpaste you can buy today is new Lyons toothpaste. For new Lyons toothpaste is better ... better *by far* than any toothpaste on the market—*bar none*—for brightening teeth. The evidence is found in *thousands* of laboratory tests on *scores* of individual teeth ... tests which prove beyond *all* challenge ... that Lyons toothpaste actually gets teeth brighter ... two-and-a-half to five-and-a-half *times* brighter ... than *any* of the five leading brands. In fact, it gets them brighter *by far* than any leading toothpaste you've ever heard about, bought or used. Yes, new Lyons toothpaste *does* what no other toothpaste can do. And the reason is that it's not just another *old* toothpaste with an added ingredient, but is *completely* new and *radically* different in formula. New Lyons toothpaste *actually* cleans *without* soap and polishes *without* chalk. It cleans beautifully because of its patented cleansing agent ... polishes brilliantly because of its *exclusive* polishing agent. And because new Lyons toothpaste *is* made *without* soap, it actually *tastes* better, too ... has a pleasanter, cleaner, *more* refreshing flavor that even your children will like ... a *wonderful* new taste in toothpastes. So for an *utterly* new, *radically* different toothpaste that gets teeth *far* brighter than any other, try new Lyons toothpaste.

Appendix A: 100 More Advertisers in Radio's Golden Age

Be aware that—through exits, mergers, acquisitions, alliances and divestitures in the years since— some of these enterprises no longer survive, and certainly may not under the identifications accredited to them here, their nomenclature during part or all of the halcyon days of network radio. Also, in all cases, the dates shown are for the period of time a specific advertiser subscribed to a given radio series. Some of those features were also on the air in different seasons for other organizations.

1. Allis-Chalmers Company
Sector: Farm machinery, more heavy duty equipment and energy systems
Brand: Allis-Chalmers
Radio: For three years, broadcasts of the *Boston Symphony Orchestra* (1943 to 1946)—dating its network radio life from the very start of the medium—were picked up by Allis-Chalmers. A key building block in the firm's promotional arsenal was *The National Farm and Home Hour* (1945 to 1958, NBC). That "farmer's bulletin board" conducted by Everett Mitchell offered news, political opinion, music, farming advice and live coverage of "the most spectacular happenings in agricultural America." By the time the epic series left the air, Allis-Chalmers was already underwriting stable segments of the long-playing weekend magazine marathon *Monitor* (1955 to 1975, NBC).

2. Anchor Hocking Glass Corporation
Sector: Glassware
Brand: Anchor Hocking
Radio: For 20 months, Anchor Hocking signed for the sitcom *Meet Corliss Archer* (1944 to 1945, CBS), complete with all the foibles and fallacies of turbulent teendom. The firm is likely better recalled, however, for *Casey, Crime Photographer* (1946 to 1948, CBS) and the bass accents of announcer Tony Marvin for Anchor Hocking. Marvin was the familiar voice that daily proclaimed: "It's *Arthur Godfrey Time!*"

3. Armour and Company
Sector: Meat processing and canning
Brand: Armour Star

Radio: *The Armour Star Jester* with Phil Baker (1933 to 1935, NBC Blue) was an impressive mix of comedy, music and variety. Amour sallied forth to subscribe *Hedda Hopper's Hollywood* (1944 to 1946, CBS, ABC) during the heyday of the gossipmonger's startling revelations from behind the silver screen. For more than two years, Armour presented the daily *Hint Hunt* (1947 to 1949, CBS). Next, it picked up the Saturday matinee anthology *Stars Over Hollywood* (1948 to 1951, CBS) with some of Tinseltown's celebrated denizens. At a time when Dave Garroway hosted the premiering *Today* on NBC-TV, a daily quarter-hour of *The Dave Garroway Show* (1950 to 1953, NBC) aired for Armour on radio. And after General Foods bowed out, Armour bought *The Second Mrs. Burton* (1954 to 1955, CBS) for eight months, until the daytime serial went to multiple sponsorship.

4. The Association of American Railroads
Sector: Freight services and passenger transportation
Brand: All rail common carriers
Radio: Despite the fact that the fraternity of rail carriers in the United States provided only a solo audio series, its effort — *The Railroad Hour* (1948 to 1954, ABC, NBC) — left a huge impact. Beyond its entertainment value, the show supplied a political platform for the industry. Threatened by potentially harmful interests, including truck freight lines and growing highway and air competition, a three-minute segment at the show's midpoint was adapted to convey trade opinions. Announcer Marvin Miller prudently explained the federation's legislative stances, interrupting the lighthearted operettas, narratives and musical treats awaiting the fans' return. Singer Gordon MacRae presided and starred in often first-rate productions alongside some of the icons of performing arts (e.g., William Bendix, Eddie Cantor, Jeff Chandler, Nadine Conner, Gene Kelly, Jeanette MacDonald, Patrice Munsel, Jane Powell, Dinah Shore, Rudy Vallee, Margaret Whiting and more).

5. The Atlantic & Pacific Tea Company
Sector: Retail grocer with in-store brands (jam, jelly, vegetables, coffee, tea, bread, cake, pie, ice cream, etc.)
Brand: Atlantic & Pacific (A&P), Ann Page, Bokar, Eight O'Clock, Jane Parker, Red Circle
Radio: Preceding the inception of web radio, at the dawn of broadcasting over New York's WEAF (1923 to 1927) *The A&P Gypsies* offered "exotic music with a nomadic motif" (1927 to 1936, NBC and NBC Blue). A&P's celebrated feature — launched with a six-piece ensemble and expanded to a 25-piece entourage — was headed by maestro Harry Horlick along with singing guests Frank Munn, Jessica Dragonette and several more of their ilk, careers ascending. A&P inserted a couple of short-lived junkets into the radio schedule, too, though they weren't especially promising: *Our Daily Food* (1930 to 1932, 1933, NBC, NBC Blue), a homemaking tips show with George Rector; and *Maude and Cousin Bill* (1932, 1933, NBC Blue), a comedy with Vivian Block and Andy Donnelly. There were no superior additions to A&P's arsenal until the grocer jumped aboard the *Kate Smith A&P Bandwagon*, launched as *Kate Smith Coffee Time* (1935 to 1937, CBS). Smith — a marquee attraction already — proffered the retailer's Bokar, Eight O'Clock and Red Circle coffee labels in that venue.

6. Atwater Kent Manufacturing Company
Sector: Electronics, including radios, other small electric devices and automobile components
Brand: Atwater Kent
Radio: A concert music series, *The Atwater Kent Hour* (1926 to 1931, 1934, NBC, CBS) set a model for the era's programming types. A symphony orchestra conducted by Josef Pasternack accompanied performances by Metropolitan Opera singers. The hypothesis had proven worthy in an 11-station hookup beginning in 1925 — months before there was NBC — and originating over New York's WEAF.

7. B. T. Babbitt Company
Sector: Consumer goods for home and farm

Brand: Bab-O cleanser, Babbitt's Best soap, Glim liquid detergent, Lycons laundry detergent flakes (consumer-activated commodity)

Radio: Babbitt was an aggressive advertiser that capitalized on scores of premiums offered to the fans of its trio of daytime serials: *David Harum* (1936 to 1951, NBC Blue, NBC, CBS, MBS), *Lora Lawton* (1943 to 1950, NBC), and *Nona from Nowhere* (1950 to 1951, CBS). The well-recognized staccato delivery of interlocutor Ford Bond — applied to all three dramas along with some repetitious commercials — paid off handsomely. Listeners were constantly reminded of *Beeeeee-ayyyyyy-beeeeee ... ohhhhhh* and urged to "buy two cans ... one for the kitchen ... one for the bathroom." Bab-O languished in seventh place among household cleansers when *David Harum* started, Babbitt's most durable program. The firm's fortunes steadily rose until it became the leader of the pack, a fact primarily attributed to the power of *Harum* and supporting print advertising.

8. Barbasol Company

Sector: Men's shaving cream and accessories
Brand: Barbasol
Radio: The firm's most acclaimed series, *Singin' Sam, the Barbasol Man* (1930 to 1933, 1935 to 1937, 1943, CBS, MBS, NBC Blue), featured ex-vaudevillian and minstrel performer Harry Frankel. He was also doing a second show simultaneously while still in his more famous gig: *The Old Singing Master* (1932, NBC Blue), also for Barbasol, where he warbled to the accompaniment of William Stickles and His Orchestra. Frankel, a Hoosier native, got into radio at Cincinnati's WLW in the 1920s. When a Barbasol rep heard him as *Singin' Sam, the Lawn Mower Man*, he was signed — given network status — and the balladeer went to work trilling the very same tune with different lyrics: *Bahrrr-baa-sawl ... Bahrrr-baa-sawl ... no brush, no lather, no rub in ... wet your razor ... then begin!* Finally, Barbasol demonstrated it could feature somebody other than Frankel. It carried popular newsman *Gabriel Heatter* (1941 to 1946, MBS) through the Second World War and in the early postwar era.

9. Bell Telephone Company

Sector: Nationwide telephone communications and related services
Brand: Bell telephone system (with regional names)
Radio: The firm's signature *Bell Telephone Hour* (1940 to 1958, NBC) was a cornerstone of NBC's enduring "Monday Nights with Music" as four half-hours were devoted to melody (others: *The Railroad Hour, Voice of Firestone, Cities Service Band of America*). Donald Voorhees conducted the Bell Telephone Orchestra while enchanting artists like Nelson Eddy, Jascha Heifetz, Grace Moore and Ezio Pinza graced its stage. After radio, the music persisted on NBC-TV through 1968, followed by radio repeats on *Encores from the Bell Telephone Hour* (1968 to 1969, NBC). Altogether, the series was one of broadcasting's hardiest efforts, lasting a cumulative 29 years.

10. Borden Company

Sector: Dairy foods and beverages
Brand: Borden
Radio: *The Ginny Simms Show* (1945 to 1947, CBS) starring the pop songstress was but one of a number of pithy features Borden underwrote. But after jumping from one ephemeral audio project to another, Borden seemed to find its niche with *County Fair* (1945 to 1950, ABC, CBS), a glitzy audience participation show couched as a contest that also included celebrity guests. It was set against the backdrop of a fair midway with diverse distractions. Originally, Jack Bailey emceed followed by Peter Donald and then a more stable Win Elliot — putting Elliot on the fast track to expansive airtime adventures.

11. Bowery's, Inc.

Sector: Dairy foods and beverages
Brand: Dari-Rich

Radio: Bowery's paid the bills for the full sponsored run of *While the City Sleeps* (1936 to 1937, NBC), though it was brief. Its next investment focused on a juvenile audience with the adventure serial *Terry and the Pirates* (1938 to 1939, NBC, NBC Blue). By the following decade, Bowery became a seasoned radio advertising buyer. It purchased a weekly Saturday matinee dramatic anthology that presented some of the silver screen's most venerated icons: *Stars Over Hollywood* (1941 to 1948, CBS), aimed at a more mature audience than the one it left behind chasing pirates and other assorted bad guys.

12. Brown Shoe Company
Sector: Shoes
Brand: Buster Brown
Radio: The most pervasively recalled link to this youngsters' apparel segment was the radio series *Smilin' Ed and His Buster Brown Gang* (1944 to 1953, NBC) starring Ed McConnell. Characters like Squeakie the Mouse, Midnight the Cat and Froggie the Gremlin were always present. A host of weekly visitors arrived whom Froggie tied in contortions to the raucous delight of a live pre-teen studio audience. Brown's aural success allowed the show to jump to NBC-TV in the 1950s. In an atypical commercial style, McConnell accompanied himself on the piano as he spoke, dramatically stressing points with sharp cords, a trademark of the show throughout its lengthy run.

13. Carnation Company
Sector: Dairy foods and beverages
Brand: Carnation evaporated milk
Radio: For two full decades, the *Carnation Contented Hour* (1932 to 1951, NBC Blue, NBC, CBS) was an impressive showcase. Music conducted by impresarios Frank Black, Josef Pasternack, Percy Faith and Victor Young included vocalists Gladys Swarthout, Josephine Antoine, Reinhold Schmidt, Buddy Clark, Tony Martin, Jo Stafford and Dick Haymes. For a trio of seasons, Carnation was attracted to the luminaries populating *Stars Over Hollywood* (1951 to 1954, CBS), a Saturday drama anthology. For 15 months, the firm was also the final sponsor to buy the total property of the longrunning daytime serial *When a Girl Marries* (1954 to 1955, ABC).

14. Carter Products
Sector: Over-the-counter remedies, pharmaceuticals and consumer goods
Brand: Carter's Little Liver Pills constipation reducer, Arrid deodorant
Radio: In the 1940s and 1950s, as web radio was making a final sweep of the ether in a fast-paced clip toward an exit, Carter turned up often. It filled gaps left by departing advertisers and aired new series — buying whole shows and, more often, appearing in segments of others. Carter's mixture included Hollywood gossipmonger *Jimmy Fidler* (1942 to 1950, NBC Blue, Blue, ABC, MBS); singer Dorothy Kirsten in *Keepsakes* (1943 to 1944, Blue); crime series *Police Woman* (1946 to 1947, ABC) with Betty Garde as heroine; dramatic anthology *City Hospital* (1951 to 1954, CBS), Santos Ortega as the chief physician; and controversial commentator *Drew Pearson* (1952 to 1953, ABC).

15. Chanel SA
Sector: Cosmetics and fragrances
Brand: Bourjois, Chanel No. 5
Radio: There's nothing to equal naming a show for a sponsor's product and that's what happened on this firm's initial air date. Frank Parker, Agnes Moorehead, Elsie Hitz, Patricia Barlow and Odette Myrtil were celebs touting the scent while singing or acting on *Evening in Paris* (1928 to 1934, 1935 to 1936, NBC, CBS, NBC Blue). The product, Evening in Paris, was lauded as singer Buddy Clark headlined a later variety series, *Here's to Romance* (1943 to 1945, CBS). Returning to the sponsor's wares, *Powder Box Theater* (1945 to 1946, CBS) was a natural for Bourjois. It offered Ray Bloch and His Orchestra flanked by vocalists Evelyn Knight and Danny O'Neil.

16. P. M. Chappel Company
Sector: Pet foods
Brand: Ken-L-Ration
Radio: Appearing on the cusp of an industry set to blossom in America, Chappel provided listeners a natural tie-in with the trade: *Rin-Tin-Tin* (1930 to 1934, NBC Blue, CBS). Chappel never said it was going to the dogs to stuff its cans with the carcasses of deceased horses — animals raised for that purpose. The dogs, of course, swallowed it whole, but it stirred ire among some who learned the firm's secret.

17. Chesebrough Manufacturing Company
Sector: Oil-based commodities
Brand: Vaseline Petroleum Jelly
Radio: Chesebrough underwrote many audio entries (false starts?) before finding a permanent niche. With a kindly old country physician as a pivotal figure, the firm aired warmhearted *Dr. Christian* (1937 to 1954, CBS) dramas with Jean Hersholt in the lead. The feature was an institution in creative melodrama ("the only show in radio where the audience writes the scripts") and had a lock on CBS's Wednesday-at-8:30 half-hour during its last 14 years.

18. Chrysler Corporation
Sector: Vehicles, parts, accessories and service
Brand: Chrysler, DeSoto, Dodge, Plymouth
Radio: For three months one spring, Chrysler sponsored the *Ziegfeld Follies of the Air* (1932, CBS) musical variety series with Al Goodman and His Orchestra. A few years hence it subscribed nearly the complete run of *Major Bowes' Original Amateur Hour* (1936 to 1945, CBS), a talent competition hovered over by Edward Bowes. When Bowes became too ill to continue, Chrysler hung in there for another seven months. It filled the void with *Shower of Stars* (1945, CBS) featuring impresarios Morton Gould and Donald Voorhees and guest artists. For a season, the firm set its sights on Andre Kostelanetz and His Orchestra's weekly workout, *Music Millions Love* (1945 to 1946, CBS). And in another year, it paid the bills for *Christopher Wells* (1947 to 1948, CBS). Searching for the right vehicle (no pun intended) in game shows — an attractive form for listeners and sponsors in the 1940s — Chrysler bought *Hit the Jackpot* (1948 to 1949, CBS) for its DeSoto-Plymouth brands. Although a convivial Bill Cullen was master of ceremonies, Chrysler moved on within 18 months. The corporation's broadcast ties are still better recalled today for a singular series pitching DeSoto and Plymouth; neither of those makes is still around any longer. The comedy quiz *You Bet Your Life* (1950 to 1956, CBS, NBC) swept irascible host Groucho Marx onto NBC-TV, preserving the show's life for its auto dealers for several more years (1950 to 1961), giving the sponsor high visibility in dual mediums. During a couple of summers, on the other hand, Chrysler filled some vacant radio timeslots with the comedy quiz *It Pays to be Ignorant* (1950, 1951, CBS, NBC) emceed by Tom Howard. And in an unconscionable twist of fate, the automotive giant subscribed *The Roy Rogers Show* (1954 to 1955, NBC) for its Dodge cars and trucks. Horseback, buggies and rail were the transport methods of the old West. In that year, nevertheless — Rogers' last on radio — Trigger, his golden palomino, seemed to be headed to pasture. Finally, in the era of proliferating multiple participation series on CBS, Chrysler bought a few scattered segments on the one chain: *The Lineup* (1952); *Escape* (early 1950s to ca. 1954); *The Amos 'n' Andy Music Hall* (ca. 1954 to ca. 1960); *Suspense* (ca. 1956 to 1960, 1961 to 1962); *Gunsmoke* (ca. 1957 to ca. 1961); *Frontier Gentleman* (1958); and *Arthur Godfrey Time* (ca. late 1950s to ca. 1972).

19. Cities Service Petroleum Company
Sector: Petroleum and other vehicle products and services
Brand: Cities Service
Radio: While everything else that this firm aired on radio is forgotten, one series won't be by anyone who heard it: *The Cities Service Concerts,* sometimes appearing as *Highways in Melody* and —

more familiarly — *The Cities Service Band of America* (1927 to 1949, NBC), continuing to 1956 without Cities Service in name or sponsor. Maestros Edwin Franko Goldman, Rosario Bourdon, Frank Black and Paul Lavalle did the honors with vocalists Jessica Dragonette, Ross Graham, Lucille Manners, Frank Parker and Robert Simmons.

20. Clicquot Club Company
Sector: Soft drinks, with special emphasis on ginger ale
Brand: Clicquot Club (pronounced "Klee-Ko")
Radio: In the national hookups' initial decade, *The Clicquot Club Eskimos* (1926 to 1933, 1935 to 1936, NBC, NBC Blue, CBS) was an accepted "establishment." Appearing on the air initially before commercials were permitted, the unit was conducted by versatile artist Harry Reser who may have played every instrument but concentrated on the banjo. In fact, his ensemble included six individuals who strummed a banjo — simultaneously. The group pioneered still further, applying sound effects to its broadcasts. The ensemble proffered its wares silently by simply naming itself for the sponsor as so many more did in that era until the advertising ban was lifted. The series became airborne on December 13, 1925, in the pre–NBC days, concurrently appearing in a dozen cities via telephone line: New York, Boston, Providence, Washington, Philadelphia, Pittsburgh, Cincinnati, Buffalo, Detroit, Davenport, Minneapolis and St. Louis.

21. Columbia Broadcasting System
Sector: Network broadcasting, manufacturing, phonographs, recordings
Brand: Columbia Broadcasting System (CBS), Columbia
Radio: CBS provided a few celebrated series appealing to sophisticated tastes including *The Columbia Phonograph Hour* (1927 to 1938), *The Columbia Workshop* (1936 to 1942, 1944, 1945, 1946 to 1947) and *Columbia Presents Corwin* (1941, 1944, 1945). They were image-building PR vehicles, perhaps more that than directly proffering goods.

22. Consolidated Cigar Corporation
Sector: Cigars
Brand: Dutch Masters, El Producto
Radio: In radio's second (and first full) season, Consolidated reverted to an earlier American entertainment form by introducing the *Dutch Masters Minstrels* (1928 to 1930, NBC Blue) which highlighted rural comedy and song. The firm replaced it with an eight-month series titled *Dutch Masters* (1931, CBS). Keep in mind that in this era banning direct appeals from sponsors, it was common practice to rely on a product's name in the show's title to plug some wares.

23. Corn Products Refining Company
Sector: Corn products milling
Brand: Linit Bath Salts
Radio: Christening him "The Knight of Bath," *The Linit Bath Club Revue* (1932 to 1933, CBS) projected resident comic Fred Allen to radio stardom. Corn Products presented multiple series, though none equaling the brilliance of Allen. Included in its bag of tricks were *The Linit Orchestra* (1931, CBS), *Midday Bath Club* (1932, CBS), *Seven Star Revue* (1933 to 1934, CBS), *The Hour of Charm* (1935, CBS), *Five Star Revue* (1936 to 1937, CBS, partial participation), *Society Girl* (1939 to 1940, partial participation) and, finally, *Sunshine Sue* (1953 to 1954, 1956, CBS). The latter was a five-minute version of a country music shindig emanating from Richmond, Virginia's WRVA. Again, after Allen — soon to be among radio's most venerated performers — everything else could probably have been considered suspect.

24. Crazy Water Crystals Company
Sector: Mineral laxative
Brand: Crazy Water Crystals

Radio: Was Crazy Water Crystals but a flash in radio's advertising pan? So it seems. It's remembered today for a solo ethereal feature, a vaudeville-styled musical variety exhibition, *Carefree Carnival* (1933 to 1935, NBC, NBC Blue). In addition to emcee Ray Tollinger, who often portrayed a stooge, there was The Commodores Quartet; Meredith Willson and His Orchestra; the comedy of Tim and Irene (Tim Ryan, Irene Noblette, the latter to be Granny on *The Beverly Hillbillies* decades afterward); Pinky Lee (another future TV icon); and more cornpone characters. And in its day, it held the crowd.

25. Cream of Wheat Corporation
Sector: Food processing
Brand: Cream of Wheat
Radio: Cream of Wheat's ethereal ties are to a single show in some minds, *Let's Pretend* (1943 to 1952, CBS). The make-believe fantasy in fairyland drew legions of Cream of Wheat eaters, precocious, pubescent kids who turned heaping bowlfuls into ringing cash registers. The pretenders sang of the hot cereal that's "so good to eat ... we have it every day" ending with "for all the family's breakfast, you can't beat Cream of Wheat." Meanwhile, with Armstrong Cork's departure following 12 years there, Cream of Wheat subscribed at least one more radio feature, *Theater of Today* (1953 to 1954, CBS), for its final Saturday matinee season.

26. Cudahy Packing Company
Sector: Household cleaning agents
Brand: Old Dutch Cleanser
Radio: In a run that was frequently interrupted, Old Dutch sponsored the daytime serial *Bachelor's Children* (1936 to 1938, 1940 to 1941, MBS). Short runs typified much of Cudahy's early airtime presence, including the soaps *Helpmate* (1941 to 1944, NBC) and *Tena and Tim* (1944 to 1946, CBS). Finally, after years as a sustainer and perhaps facing extinction, *Nick Carter, Master Detective* (1946 to 1952, MBS) was picked up by Cudahy. Its six years there proved the sponsor could find something of endurance to spend its money on.

27. R. B. Davis Company
Sector: Food and beverage
Brand: Cocomalt
Radio: Davis presented a trio of aural features: *Mr. Coco and Mr. Malt* (1931 to 1932, NBC Blue Midwest hookup) with Al Cameron and Pete Bontsema; *Buck Rogers in the Twenty-Fifth Century* (1933 to 1935, CBS) with Matt Crowley in the title role; and *The Park Avenue Penners* (1936 to 1938, CBS) with Joe Penner, who had previously established his radio entertainment credentials.

28. E. I. du Pont de Nemours and Company
Sector: Industrial products
Brand: Du Pont
Radio: Rather than pushing specific wares, Du Pont offered mostly image-making plugs on one of radio's premier historical dramatic anthologies, *The Cavalcade of America* (1935 to 1939, 1940 to 1953, CBS, NBC Blue, NBC). A historian cited the early shows as "sanitized." Du Pont gained vast sums by making gunpowder for World War I and was labeled by some "merchants of death." The aural series improved, nevertheless, after playwright Arthur Miller and poet-novelist Carl Sandburg, among "name" contributors, got hold of it.

29. The Electric Auto-Lite Company
Sector: Vehicle parts, equipment and accessories
Brand: Alemite, Auto-Lite
Radio: Starting the year it bought Alemite Die-Casting and Manufacturing Company, Auto-Lite presented *The Horace Heidt Show* (1935, 1936 to 1938, CBS, NBC), a musical variety series known

for most of that time as *The Alemite Half-Hour*. Auto-Lite itself is better remembered for backing those gripping anthology dramas of *Suspense* (1948 to 1954, CBS). Salesman Harlow Wilcox plied listeners with spark plugs, horns, generators, batteries, lamps, wiring and so on.

30. Emerson Drug Company
Sector: Over-the-counter drugs
Brand: Bromo-Seltzer headache remedy
Radio: With its impressionable chug-chug-chug commercials reminiscent of a train pulling out of a station and delivered by a raspy-voiced vendor ("Fight headaches three waaaaayyys ... Bromo-Seltzer ... Bromo-Seltzer ... Bromo-Seltzer...."), Emerson Drug introduced multiple favorites in diverse genres to waiting ears: *NTG and His Girls* (1935 to 1936, NBC) with Nils Thor Granlund; *Hollywood News* (1938, NBC Blue) with gossip columnist Harriet Parsons, soon to be renamed Louella Parsons; *Vox Pop* (1941 to 1946, CBS, NBC Blue), a sidewalk interview feature with Parks Johnson and Wally Butterworth; and *The Saint* (1945, NBC) with Edgar Barrier as an urbane private eye. Emerson Drug subsequently signed for *Inner Sanctum Mysteries* (1946 to 1950, CBS). Those misadventures in the macabre were chilling, including a squeaking door and Raymond, its eerie host (Paul McGrath, House Jameson). Splendidly, it all complemented those unique sound plugs for Bromo-Seltzer.

31. Eveready Battery Company
Sector: Batteries of many types
Brand: Eveready
Radio: Eveready underwrote one of the medium's very first variety revues, *The Eveready Hour* (1926 to 1930, NBC), a show preceding chain radio by three years on New York City's WEAF. Its viable format for early audiences was copied by scores of successors.

32. Eversharp Pen Company
Sector: Writing instruments
Brand: Eversharp
Radio: With consecutive quizmasters Bob Hawk, Phil Baker, Garry Moore, Eddie Cantor and Jack Parr, how could a game show like *Take It or Leave It* (1940 to 1950, CBS, NBC) fail to tantalize? Another key Eversharp building block, *Let Yourself Go* (1944 to 1945, CBS), starred comic Milton Berle. He was soon to scale legendary heights in TV. *Maisie* (1945 to 1947, CBS) followed, a comedy in which Ann Sothern played secretary Maisie Revere. In the same era, Eversharp underwrote the petulant wit *Henry Morgan* (1946 to 1947, ABC).

33. Firestone Tire and Rubber Company
Sector: Tires, inner tubes, other vehicle parts, accessories and services
Brand: Firestone
Radio: The firm's signature series, *The Voice of Firestone* (1928 to 1957, NBC, ABC) was a highbrow musical experience blending opera and classics for more than three decades on radio and TV. The show maintained a lock on the 8:30 P.M. half-hour on Mondays. Hugo Mariani, William Daley, Alfred Wallenstein, Howard Barlow and Wilfred Pelletier were the concert maestros; some artists appeared weekly until the series settled on a rotating crop of professionals.

34. F. W. Fitch Company
Sector: Hair care preparations
Brand: Fitch
Radio: "Laugh awhile, let a song be your smile, use Fitch shampoo" a chorus sang weekly on *The Fitch Bandwagon* (1938 to 1948, NBC) in web radio's heyday. It began with several bands and finally concentrated on the music of Cass Daley, then Phil Harris and Alice Faye. While this was Fitch's most impressionable entry in chain radio, the firm underwrote a handful of added series

in whole or in part. Some were forgettable: *The Fitch Professor* (1932 to 1933, CBS), *Sunset Dreams*, aka *The Morin Sisters* (1935 to 1937, CBS), *Interesting Neighbors* (1937 to 1938, NBC), and *Happy Jack Turner* (1941, NBC). Others had exciting premises like *Rogue's Gallery* (1945 to 1946, 1947, 1950 to 1951, MBS, NBC, ABC) and *Vic and Sade* (1946, MBS). There was also a trio of CBS dramas after multiple-participation kicked in: *Yours Truly, Johnny Dollar* (ca. 1955 to ca. 1960), *Suspense* (ca. 1956 to 1960, 1961 to ca. 1962) and *Have Gun, Will Travel* (1958 to 1960).

35. General Cigar Company, Inc.
Sector: Cigars
Brands: Robert Burns, Van Dyck, White Owl, William Penn
Radio: General Cigar produced a number of programs for the airwaves in network radio's formative years. On its very first show, *The Robert Burns Panatella Program* (1927 to 1933, CBS), Guy Lombardo and His Royal Canadians were the featured act — at least, until the sponsor signed a couple of ex-vaudevillians for comedy relief in early 1932. Their addition was credited with more than doubling the show's ratings within a year, to the extent that General Cigar bade farewell to Lombardo and company but retained Burns and Allen in their own successive features: *The White Owl Program* (1933 to 1934, CBS) and *The Adventures of Gracie* (1934 to 1935, CBS). The couple hadn't yet hit upon the idea of turning Gracie into a zany airhead; in those days, the two were featured as unmarried singles, with George in constant pursuit, unlike the premise now widely remembered.

36. General Electric Company
Sector: Large and small household and commercial appliances, not limited to but including radios and phonographs
Brand: General Electric (GE)
Radio: For a full decade, Phil Spitalny and His Orchestra backed musical guests turning up on *The Hour of Charm* (1936 to 1946, CBS, NBC) that GE applied for its key radio voice in that era. Overlapping its latter days, GE offered a new interactive feature, the daily *House Party* (1945 to 1949, CBS, ABC) hosted by a gregarious Art Linkletter, whose destiny was only just beginning. Opening his show cold, he'd ask: "Ladies, who sponsors the next program?" To which he got the expected thunderous response from a primed and exuberant studio audience: "General Electric!" It was, in a sense, electrifying.

37. The Gillette Company
Sector: Safety razors and shaving accessories for men and women
Brand: Gillette
Radio: The Gillette sobriquet and sports broadcasting are synonymous in radio and television. While the firm underwrote a few other series like *Community Sing* (1936 to 1937, CBS), it is profusely identified with athletics, particularly baseball, though other sports, too. One of its most durable series, officially listed *Madison Square Garden Boxing* (1941 to ca. 1959, MBS, ABC, NBC) but more commonly labeled the "Friday Night Fights," gave visibility to an arena that possibly had not been as widely recognized until Gillette entered its domain.

38. BFGoodrich
Sector: Tires, inner tubes, other vehicle parts, accessories and services
Brand: Goodrich
Radio: Three days following the inception of network radio, *The Goodrich Silvertown Orchestra* (1926 to 1928, 1933 to 1934, NBC) debuted under the baton of B. A. Rolfe. The troupe had appeared as early as February 12, 1925, on New York's WEAF, flagship outlet of the newly formed NBC Red chain launched on November 15, 1926. The local series persisted for its sponsor on WEAF through January 11, 1926 (mentioning little more than the product's name, as commercial pitches were unacceptable at that time, a good reason for naming a series for its benefactor). The NBC show

included a banjo ensemble dubbing itself The Goodrich Zippers, yet another reminder of who paid the bills. With the exception of *Uncle Abe and David* (1930 to 1931, NBC) with Parker Fennelly and Arthur Allen in key roles, Goodrich was hardly heard from again until the mid–1940s; it had seemingly made its most impressive contributions to radio with its first series. Goodrich attempted a comeback with *Detect and Collect* (1945 to 1946, ABC), a quiz changing horses in midstream. With Wendy Barrie as emcee, studio contestants tried to guess what was hidden behind a curtain on stage (did anybody say "forerunner of *Let's Make a Deal*"?— not a fabulous model for a radio audience). Revising the formula, replacing Barrie with Vincent Lopez, in a second incarnation listeners counted how many times a precise tune was repeated as multiple selections were played. That pandemonium wasn't all that effective, either, and the show was quickly pulled. Goodrich's day had passed.

39. Goodyear Tire and Rubber Company

Sector: Tires, inner tubes, other vehicle parts, accessories and services
Brand: Goodyear
Radio: Goodyear turned up all over radio's landscape, underwriting popular music, reports from rural America and past life on the plains. *The Goodyear Program* (1931 to 1932, NBC) featured singer Grace Moore and the Revelers Quartet. Veteran newsman Don Goddard delivered *Goodyear Farm Radio News* (1938 to 1939, NBC, NBC Blue). And if you think Goodyear's backing *The Roy Rogers Show* (1944 to 1945, MBS) unusual, be aware that the cowboy was presented by Alka-Seltzer and Dodge, too, neither linked with the nation's frontier, nor with the kids that dominated his audience. And for a full decade, Goodyear presented a religious narrative, *The Greatest Story Ever Told* (1947 to 1956, ABC), on Sunday evenings

40. Grove Laboratories, Inc.

Sector: Pharmaceuticals and over-the-counter drugs
Brand: Bromo Quinine laxative (also bearing the Grove label)
Radio: For five months Grove underwrote *The Fred Waring Show* (1938 to 1939, NBC), including orchestra, chorus and guest artists. The firm may have found so large an entourage too much for its blood; it soon bought *The Adventures of Sherlock Holmes* (1939 to 1942, NBC Blue, NBC) co-starring Basil Rathbone and Nigel Bruce. Bromo Quinine underwrote a season of *The Shadow* (1949 to 1950, MBS) with Bret Morrison. Then there was multiple participation with *X-Minus 1* (1955 to 1958, NBC). Several other Grove-backed shows included familiar names as well as obscure appellations: *Pat Kennedy* (1934 to 1935, CBS); *General Hugh Johnson* (1937 to 1938, NBC Blue); *The Lynn Cole Orchestra* (1938 to 1939, MBS); *Troman Harper, Rumor Detective* (1942 to 1943, MBS); *Gabriel Heatter* (ca. 1942 to ca. 1959, MBS, multiple participation); *Ray Dady* (1943 to 1945, NBC, MBS); *Lanny and Ginger* (1944 to 1945, MBS); *Cliff Edwards* (1945, MBS); and *David Harding, Counterspy* (ca. 1954 to ca. 1957, MBS, multiple participation).

41. Gulf Oil Corporation

Sector: Petroleum and other vehicle accessories and services
Brand: Gulf
Radio: After presenting *The Phil Baker Show* (1935 to 1938, CBS), Gulf Oil made a lasting impression on radio listeners by subscribing the venerated human interest series *We, the People* (1942 to 1951). Commoners and celebrants brought unique tales of personal experience before the microphone. Hosted by names like Gabriel Heatter, Dwight Weist, Dan Seymour and Burgess Meredith, the show's commercials were forgettable. Yet its signature musical sequence at their finish — spoken by an announcer accompanied by Oscar Bradley and His Orchestra — left a memorable impression: "For the life of your car ... go Gulf!"

42. Hall Brothers Company

Sector: Greeting cards for all occasions

Brand: Hallmark

Radio: In Hall's initial ethereal exposure, *Tony Wons' Radio Scrapbook* (1940 to 1942, NBC), its host shared sentiments from its greeting cards and urged listeners to "Look on the back for an identifying mark ... a Hallmark card." It was a first for trade manufacturers; heretofore, they never so identified their wares. But it worked. People sought the name as a symbol of quality. The greeting card company subscribed *Meet Your Navy* (1942 to 1944, NBC Blue, Blue) next followed by the narrative anthology *Radio Reader's Digest* (1946 to 1948, CBS). The latter feature led Hallmark (as the firm was re-branded in 1954) directly into a couple of prestigious back-to-back drama series under its own appellation: *Hallmark Playhouse* (1948 to 1953, CBS), an omnibus of plays narrated by James Hilton, followed by *Hallmark Hall of Fame* (1953 to 1955, CBS), another collection. That latter title, incidentally, persists to the present age, embracing a sporadic series of narratives currently telecast on cable TV.

43. Health Products Corporation

Sector: Over-the-counter health care remedies

Brand: Feenamint laxative, Chooz breath mints and antacid medication

Radio: One of Feenamint's prevailing efforts was a primetime quiz that later transferred to daytime for Campbell Soup: *Double or Nothing* (1940 to 1947, MBS). Exchanges between successive emcees Walter Compton, John Reed King and Todd Russell and their game-playing guests kept the show lively. During the 1947 to 1948 radio season Health Products underwrote a quartet of features, all on the Mutual network: *The Adventures of Charlie Chan* (1947 to 1948, MBS) with Santos Ortega in the namesake role; *Official Detective* (1947 to 1948, MBS); *The Jim Backus Vaudeville Show* (1947 to 1948, MBS); and *Song of the Stranger* (1947 to 1948, MBS) with Bret Morrison as a French undercover patriot. As web-based radio wound down, Feenamint and Chooz were also winding up, participating in a plethora of features, among them the daytime serials *Hilltop House* (1955 to 1957, NBC) and *The Romance of Helen Trent* (1955 to 1960, CBS).

44. Healthaids, Inc.

Sector: Pharmaceuticals and over-the-counter health care goods

Brand: Geritol energy booster, Serutan laxative, Sominex sleep aid

Radio: During the Second World War, Healthaids underwrote the commentary of Drew Pearson and Robert Allen, at times titled *News for the Americas* (1941 to 1945, NBC Blue). The programs often included famous predictions about the future, many of which came true. They appeared for Serutan laxative ("Remember, Serutan is natures spelled backwards"). Developing a proclivity for newscasters, Serutan next picked up Don Gardiner's *Monday Morning Headlines* (1944 to 1946, ABC). During the postwar era, the firm aired newscaster *William L. Shirer* (1945 to 1947, CBS). Shirer had been CBS chief reporter Ed Murrow's first hire when, in 1937, he staffed the European theater to cover war preparations. Newscasters *Gabriel Heatter* (1942–ca. 1959, MBS, multiple participation) and *John B. Kennedy* (1950 to 1951, ABC) were added by Serutan, too, as was Richard Maxwell's daily *Hymns You Love* (1945 to 1946, MBS). Finally, the health and diet advice of *Victor Lindlahr* (1944 to 1953, MBS) was adopted by Serutan, a "natural" for such a conduit.

45. H. J. Heinz Company

Sector: Foods and condiments

Brand: Heinz (purveyed as 57 varieties)

Radio: In an experiment combining serial narrative and variety with an orchestra conducted by B. A. Rolfe and Mark Warnow, the underwriter offered an innovative *Heinz Magazine of the Air* (1936 to 1938, CBS). For two full years, Heinz bought *Information Please* (1943 to 1945, NBC), a panel show moderated by Clifton Fadiman. The firm also subscribed *The Adventures of Ozzie and Harriet* (1949 to 1952, ABC) with Ozzie, Harriet, David and Ricky Nelson as themselves; *The Adventures of the Thin Man* (1950, ABC) with Joseph Curtin and Claudia Morgan in key roles; and *A Life in Your Hands* (1951, ABC) with actor Lee Bowman as a friend of the court.

46. George A. Hormel & Company
Sector: Meat processing and canning
Brand: Hormel
Radio: Network radio had been underway a decade when Hormel bought in. Its premier entry, *Swing with the Strings* (1936 to 1937, CBS) lasted six months to the day. Two years elapsed before Hormel dipped its toe into the water again, that time with *It Happened in Hollywood* (1939 to 1940, CBS) with John Conte and Martha Mears. The series persisted 15 months. One season before *The George Burns and Gracie Allen Show* (1940 to 1941, NBC) turned the pair from unwed pals to a wedded duo working in broadcasting, thereby incredibly reviving then-flagging fortunes — including adding a third more listeners — Hormel bought in. Regrettably, the firm pulled out just as the big transformation was about to occur. Hormel could be jinxed in radio, it seemed, at least until it took one more stab. It presented the sounds of the *Hormel All-Girl Band* (1949 to 1954, ABC, CBS, NBC), a novelty then. In chain radio's ebbing days, the unique blend resonated with weekend listeners, thereby saving Hormel's bacon.

47. Lewis Howe Company
Sector: Over-the-counter drug remedies
Brand: Tums heartburn reliever
Radio: Musician Horace Heidt enjoyed a radio run in part thanks to Lewis Howe which brought a mixed bag of treats under Heidt's moniker and others: *Tums Treasure Chest, Musical Treasure Chest* and *Pot o' Gold* (1939 to 1944, NBC). Tums' interests turned to *Correction Please* (1943 to 1944, CBS) with quizmasters Jack Shilkret and J. C. Flippen. More noticeably, it provided *A Date with Judy* (1944 to 1949, NBC), a sitcom starring Louise Erickson in the namesake role (Judy Foster). She was a teen beset by boyfriend, parent, peer, study and money pressures — stuff of which radio adolescents despaired. *Bulldog Drummond* (1945 to 1946, MBS) spent time in Howe's portfolio. In its final two seasons, ending with the unexpected demise of star Fanny Brice, Tums presented the antics of *Baby Snooks* (1949 to 1951, NBC).

48. International Silver Company
Sector: Sterling silver tableware, serving utensils and similar goods
Brand: 1847 Rogers pattern
Radio: International Silver brought two sterling (ahem!) long-playing series to waiting ears, one of drama, the other comedy. *The Silver Theater* (1937, 1938 to 1942, 1943 to 1944, 1945, 1946, 1947, CBS) was a dramatic anthology offering plays in a disjointed, broken pattern of installments. International Silver is perhaps best recalled for its 1847 Rogers Brothers silver place settings proffered by *The Adventures of Ozzie and Harriet* (1944 to 1949, CBS, NBC). The Nelsons (Ozzie, Harriet, David, Ricky) lived at 1847 Rogers Road which, not coincidentally, coincided with the sponsor's leading commodity. The focus on the family ultimately jumped to TV for a pooled 24 years in dual mediums, an unblemished record for such fare.

49. Iodent Chemical Company
Sector: Personal care commodities (toothpaste, baby shampoo, lotions, powders, aerosols)
Brand: Iodent
Radio: One of web radio's original advertisers — debuting during an era in which commercials couldn't be read on the air — the firm dubbed its inaugural series for itself: *The Iodent Program* (1927, NBC Blue). It reminded those tuning in of its toothpaste brand. While no other data has surfaced about this musical variety entry, in the 1930s Iodent added a trio of similar series to its programming storehouse. By then, it could speak of its wares with descriptive joy. Fans also know the artists there: *Iodent Club of the Air* (1930 to 1932, NBC) with Joe Rines and His Orchestra; *The Iodent Program* (1932 to 1933, NBC) with singer Jane Froman accompanied by Roy Shields and His Orchestra; and *The Iodent Dress Rehearsal* (1936 to 1937, NBC Blue) starring Joe Rines and Mabel Albertson. Notice that the business and its flagship product are named in all of these pioneer features, a perennial pattern for numerous sponsors in that epoch.

50. S. C. Johnson & Son
Sector: Household, commercial and vehicle cleaning compounds
Brand: Johnson's Wax
Radio: The sponsor is unequivocally recalled for one aural series though it supported others. Tuesday nights in the halcyon era announcer Harlow Wilcox opened it like so: "The Johnson Wax program, with *Fibber McGee & Molly*" (1935 to 1950, NBC). Weekly visits to 39 Wistful Vista included stops by several of the mythical hamlet's denizens including Wilcox, whose commercials for Glo-Coat or other commodities inexorably sparked the ire of the homeowner. McGee drew laughs by branding Wilcox as "Waxy." Some more Johnson properties, all of which were NBC replacements for *Fibber McGee & Molly* during their summertime sabbaticals: *Alec Templeton Time* (1939); *Words at War* (1944); *The Victor Borge Show* (1945); and *King for a Night*, aka *The King's Men* (1949).

51. Kimberly-Clark Corporation
Sector: Paper products for home and commercial use
Brand: Kleenex
Radio: Kimberly-Clark underwrote a trio of network radio series, all of them soap operas: *The Story of Mary Marlin* (1934 to 1943, NBC); *Her Honor, Nancy James* (1938 to 1939, CBS); and *The Story of Bess Johnson* (1941 to 1942, CBS, NBC).

52. Charles B. Knox Gelatine Company
Sector: Foods processing
Brand: Knox gelatine
Radio: Knox brought *Jack Berch and His Boys* (1936 to 1937, MBS) to national visibility, a gregarious persona who entertained the ladies for two decades. Congruently, Knox offered "Quality Twins" Ed East and Ralph Dumke in a kitchen-themed bit with the unusual title *Sisters of the Skillet* (1936 to 1937, CBS). In still another venue, it turned to a musical quiz, *What's the Name of That Song?* (1944 to 1945, MBS). Dud Williamson called for the identifications. While the show persisted three more years after Knox's succinct contribution, it never touched the glory of Bert Parks' *Stop the Music!* (1948 to 1952) or *Name That Tune* (1952), both in like vein. In yet another arena, *Murder is My Hobby* (1945 to 1946, MBS), Knox spotlighted actor Glenn Langan.

53. Lady Esther Cosmetics Company
Sector: Cosmetics
Brand: Lady Esther
Radio: This firm's relationship with a handful of popular orchestras boded well. Its most durable tie was to Wayne King where overlapping editions of *Lady Esther Serenade* (1931 to 1938, NBC, CBS) often played on dual chains. Entourages headed by Guy Lombardo (1938 to 1940, NBC) and Freddy Martin (1942, CBS) followed, plus *The Lady Esther Screen Guild Theater* (1942 to 1947, CBS) with impresario Wilbur Hatch. Initially, Lady Esther paid King $500 weekly; phenomenal sales soon upped him to $15,000. "King helped establish this struggling cosmetics company and made it one of radio's most potent advertisers," a media historiographer reflected.

54. Lambert Pharmacal Company
Sector: Over-the-counter remedies, personal goods and pharmaceuticals
Brand: Listerine antiseptic mouthwash
Radio: For a season, Lambert dipped its feet into radio's waters with the serialized narrative *Country Doctor* (1932 to 1933, NBC Blue). For three months, it supported the *Metropolitan Opera* (1934 to 1935, NBC). Long-term success seemed elusive then but better days lay ahead. In the formative years of yet another important drama anthology, *Grand Central Station* (1937 to 1940, CBS), Listerine signed on for a while. For three more years, it provided the comedy feature *Fashions in Rations*, aka *The Billie Burke Show* (1943 to 1946, CBS). And as the network ship began to genuinely list, Lambert agreed to underwrite *The Adventures of Ozzie and Harriet* (1952 to 1954, ABC)—by then abandoned by longtime sponsors International Silver and Heinz. In a joint link

with General Electric, Lambert and GE devoted alternate weeks plugging their wares with the Nelson clan, a foretaste of more innovative efforts in web-based radio advertising in the few remaining years before the ship sank.

55. Lehn & Fink Products
Sector: Personal care and household goods
Brand: Hinds Honey and Almond Cream cosmetics, Lysol disinfectant, Nivea toothpaste, Pebeco toothpaste
Radio: Lehn & Fink subscribed a handful of audio treats for its Hinds and Lysol labels: *Hinds Romance Exchange* (1932, NBC Blue) with Ray Heatherton and Beatrice Fairfax; *Hinds Hall of Fame* (1934, NBC); *Club Romance* (1935, CBS) with Conrad Thibault and Lois Bennett; *The Life of Mary Sothern* (1935 to 1938, MBS, CBS); *The Gumps* (1936 to 1937, CBS) with Wilmer Walter and Agnes Moorehead; *The George Burns and Gracie Allen Show* (1939 to 1940, CBS); and *Blind Date* (1943 to 1946, ABC) with toastmistress Arlene Francis. Meanwhile, as the American manufacturer and distributor of Pebeco toothpaste — a dentifrice Lehn & Fink (L&F) advertised as the most expensive in the world to make, yet "costs no more" than rival brands — L&F invariably found itself swimming upstream in competitive waters. Pebeco languished on several short-term ethereal entries in the thirties. The product offered listeners a piano trio, *The Pebeco Playboys* (1932, CBS); *Stories of the Living Great* (1932, CBS) with Ida Bailey Allen, followed by *Today's Pioneer Women* (1932, CBS) also with Allen headlining; *The Gumps* (1934 to 1935, CBS) with Wilmer Walter and Agnes Moorehead; *The Eddie Cantor Show* (1935 to 1936, CBS); and *Follow the Moon* (1937 to 1938, CBS), a daytime serial. Pebeco, which originated in Germany, never made a huge splash in the U.S. radio market — or even in its marketplace. Within a few years, it literally disappeared from the shelves.

56. Libby, McNeil and Libby
Sector: Canned fruits and vegetables
Brand: Libby
Radio: In the third season of network radio, Libby instituted a musical travelogue, *Around the World* (1929 to 1930, NBC Blue). While it didn't last, it gave the Chicago canner some valuable exposure to the medium and its audience to Libby. While the firm was to invest sparingly in radio advertising, it would do so carefully. It's probably best recalled for a protracted run of *My True Story* (1944 to 1949, ABC). The weekday morning narrative anthology was complemented by announcer Glenn Riggs' authoritative-sounding, mouth-watering commercials for an assortment of Libby goods.

57. Luden's, Inc.
Sector: Confectionery and over-the-counter remedies
Brand: Luden's cough drops
Radio: Although it was never a big spender in radio, Luden was among the first to try it — and to do so twice. Dan Rybb and Conrad Thibault were regulars on *Luden's Novelty Orchestra* (1931 to 1932, CBS) while *Luden's Music Revue* (1934 to 1935, CBS) featured Robert Armbruster and His Orchestra. After a decade in absentia, Luden reentered the marketplace, underwriting a quarter-hour Sunday afternoon entry with composer *Hoagy Carmichael* (1946 to 1947, CBS). Then it subscribed the human interest audience participation feature *Strike It Rich* (1947 to 1949, CBS) in its pre–Colgate era. There the unfortunate, poverty-stricken and destitute told tales of woe and tried to win cash — and maybe even draw upon the generosity of listeners. In the Luden days, Todd Russell preceded a better remembered Warren Hull as emcee. The show soon went to TV.

58. Manhattan Soap Company
Sector: Laundry and personal care cleansing agents
Brand: Blu-White Flakes detergent, Sweetheart soap

Radio: Manhattan was a serials-backer that amassed a stockpile of daytime dramas in the 1940s and 1950s: *Barry Cameron, Family Skeleton, Katie's Daughter, One Man's Family, Rose of My Dreams, The Strange Romance of Evelyn Winters, We Love and Learn, The Woman in My House.* Though most weren't incredibly durable, Manhattan subscribed a couple of them for a quadrennium, *Winters* (1944 to 1948, CBS) and *Woman* (1951 to 1955, NBC). Don't overlook this fact: here was a *soap-maker* (exclusively, unlike some rivals) that aired *soap opera*, and had the good fortune of picking a few respected dramas.

59. Mennen Company
Sector: Personal care goods and over-the-counter remedies
Brand: Mennen
Radio: Mennen unequivocally filled its quiver with radio properties sporting brief runs of mostly no better than second-tier series, often persisting for one season or less: *Famous Jury Trials* (1936 to 1937, MBS); *The People's Rally* (1938 to 1939, MBS), a public affairs audience participation feature with John B. Kennedy and Bob Hawk; *Quixie-Doodles* (1939 to 1941, MBS, CBS) with F. Chase Taylor as Colonel Lemuel Q. Stoopnagle; and *Ed Sullivan Entertains* (1943 to 1944, CBS).

60. Nash-Kelvinator Corporation
Sector: Automobiles, home appliances, heating and cooling equipment
Brand: Nash, Kelvinator
Radio: Nash and Kelvinator, which united under a single banner on January 4, 1937, were jointly proffered, albeit briefly, on *Professor Quiz* (1937 to 1938, CBS). Craig Earl was quizmaster. The firm reappeared a few years hence when it underwrote the *Andrew Sisters Revue* (1944 to 1946, ABC) with Patty, Maxine and Laverne, one of the most popular singing trios in broadcasting history.

61. National Biscuit Company
Sector: Snack foods
Brand: Nabisco
Radio: Nabisco gave maestro Benny Goodman his first national venue by putting *Let's Dance* (1934 to 1935, NBC) on the air. A few months hence, Goodman led America into the era of big band sounds. By the late 1940s and early 1950s, Nabisco underwrote a segment of *Arthur Godfrey Time* daily on CBS, a provocative, amusing showcase of recurring talent. For young ears, the firm introduced Howard Culver in the juvenile adventure of a Comanche impersonating a white man who wore Indian regalia as he crusaded for justice in the old West: *Straight Arrow* (1948 to 1951, MBS). Familiarity with the hero's background helped adolescent fans sort it all out.

62. National Dairy Products Corporation
Sector: Dairy foods and beverages
Brand: Sealtest
Radio: For a half year, Sealtest put an unimpressive *Rising Musical Stars* (1937 to 1938, NBC) on the air with Alexander Smallens and His Orchestra. Next came *Your Family and Mine* (1938 to 1939, NBC, CBS), also ending rather abruptly. Sealtest shifted its money from soaps back to musical variety then, a venue in which it had infinitely better luck. Following a gratifying *Vallee Varieties* (1940 to 1943, NBC) starring the legendary artist Rudy Vallee, it purchased an even more enduring *Sealtest Village Store* (1943 to 1948, NBC). There Joan Davis, Jack Haley, Eve Arden and Jack Carson performed as steadies. Advice columnist *Dorothy Dix* (1949 to 1950, ABC), occupying a daily quarter-hour, filled the last of National Dairy Products' network time buys.

63. Norwich Pharmacal Company
Sector: Over-the-counter health care remedies and pharmaceuticals
Brand: Pepto-Bismol stomach distress reliever, Unguentine skin burn ointment

Radio: With J. Scott Smart appearing as the plump private detective Brad Runyon, *The Fat Man* (1946 to 1950, ABC) spent almost all its run under Norwich auspices. Next, the sponsor briefly invested in the daytime closed-end drama *Modern Romances* (1950 to 1951, ABC).

64. Pacific Borax Company
Sector: Mining operations, household commodities
Brand: Twenty Mule Team Borax mined in Death Valley, California
Radio: Death Valley Days (1930 to 1945, NBC, NBC Blue, CBS), which jumped to TV later, and the sponsor's ware were so intertwined that the show and the underwriter were permanently connected by most Americans of that vintage — not a bad position at all for a marketer.

65. Pepsi-Cola Company
Sector: Soft drink beverages
Brand: Pepsi-Cola
Radio: Pepsi-Cola simply never exhibited the kind of audio advertising prowess that its chief rival, Coca-Cola, demonstrated. Numerous broadcast features flowed from Coke. Although Pepsi hit the spot with its "12 ounce bottle, that's a lot" commercial jingle (the familiar lyrics of which were penned in 1941 by future *Pepper Young's Family* announcer Alan Kent), the cola firm appears to have maintained only one network show, and that one for only a season: *David Harding, Counterspy* (1949 to 1950, ABC). Don MacLaughlin was the chief espionage agent of the federal government.

66. The Pepsodent Company
Sector: Oral dentifrice care commodities
Brand: Pepsodent toothpaste and tooth powder
Radio: Pepsodent bankrolled two strategic longrunning comedy series. *Amos 'n' Andy* (1929 to 1937, NBC) was first. Freeman Gosden and Charles Correll, white actors with a penchant for imitating hilarious blacks in the big city — introduced nationally by Pepsodent — ruled the airwaves for three decades. *The Bob Hope Show* (1938 to 1948, NBC) featured the stand-up comic provoking gales of laughter in pithy vignettes with weekly guest luminaries. (*Note:* In 1944, Lever Brothers Company bought Pepsodent.)

67. Pet Milk Company
Sector: Dairy foods and beverages
Brand: Pet evaporated milk
Radio: One of the more enduring mythical homemakers-in-residence to grace the airwaves in radio's halcyon days, *Mary Lee Taylor* (1933 to 1954, CBS, NBC) — acting under the guise of supplying household tips and Pet recipes — unremittingly pitched the evaporated milk in perpetual tête-à-têtes with milady. Showing a proclivity for long-winded series, Pet underwrote the musical variety show *Saturday Night Serenade* (1936 to 1948, CBS) with Mary Eastman (to 1941) and Jessica Dragonette as resident vocalists. *The Pet Milk Show* (1948 to 1950, NBC) brought singers Vic Damone and Kay Armen to the microphone, backed by Bob Crosby and the Bobcats. When Johnson Wax finally threw in the towel after a 15-year tie-up, Pet picked up the slack on *Fibber McGee & Molly* (1950 to 1952, NBC), extending one of America's most beloved ethereal couples in comedic fiascoes. For a change, hawker Harlow Wilcox, formerly "Waxy," was labeled "Milky." Pet turned next to Ralph Edwards' raucous stunt show *Truth or Consequences* (1952 to 1954, NBC).

68. Philco Radio Corporation
Sector: Radios, TVs and small appliances
Brand: Philco
Radio: One of the medium's first symphony concert series, *Philco Radio Hour* (1927 to 1931, NBC Blue, CBS), offered a form soon adopted by others. The firm underwrote newscaster *Boake Carter* (1933 to 1938, CBS) in his longest airwaves' run. There was the *Radio Hall of Fame* (1943 to 1946,

Blue, ABC) with impresario Paul Whiteman. Philco next rescued singer Bing Crosby after he fell out with longtime sponsor Kraft, setting a precedent for future aural series — by transcription. Crosby's *Philco Radio Time* (1946 to 1949, ABC) broke a ban on prerecorded shows. After years as a sustainer, *Burl Ives* (1946 to 1948, MBS) drew Philco to pay his bills. And the firm's last gasp — one of the medium's final breaths, too — was *Philco Radio Playhouse* (1953 to 1954, ABC), a drama anthology. With a break in continuity, it lasted just six months; the handwriting on the wall was by then becoming pretty legible.

69. The Pillsbury Company
Sector: Milling and food processing (flour, cornmeal, baking goods)
Brand: Pillsbury
Radio: Like similar firms in early radio, Pillsbury derived mythical homemaker authorities to answer listeners' requests while hawking its wares. *Mary Ellis Ames* (1933 to 1936, CBS) — never recalled as well as her successor, Ann Pillsbury, Josephine Gibson (H. J. Heinz) and an infinitely better known Betty Crocker (General Mills) — joined a profuse breed of spokeswomen freely sharing culinary expertise.

70. Pond's Extract Company
Sector: Cosmetics
Brand: Pond's
Radio: Few radio sponsors underwrote series featuring the spouse of a soon-to-be-sitting president. For three months in late 1932 and early 1933, *Pond's Program* (1931 to 1934, NBC) allowed the country to hear from Mrs. Eleanor Roosevelt. While first ladies may be old hat in current media, that wasn't the case then. They were seldom heard until Roosevelt and Pond's changed the landscape, in fact.

71. Prudential Insurance Company
Sector: Individual, home and commercial insurance
Brand: Prudential
Radio: Not a lot of insurers chose radio as a means of communicating with prospective buyers but this one did so, prolifically by comparison. It pushed its wares on the daytime serial *When a Girl Marries* (1939 to 1941, CBS) until it established serious traction with audiences via a ritzy showcase of classical and operatic standards on *The Prudential Family Hour* (1941 to 1948, CBS). What began as a 45-minute vehicle was compacted to a half-hour in 1945 but its iconic names prevailed including Eileen Farrell, Ross Graham, Sterling Holloway, Patrice Munsel, Jack Smith, Risë Stevens, Gladys Swarthout and more. Deems Taylor offered their observations and the outings presented pithy narrative sketches about the composition of various works, highlighting the lives of Beethoven, Schubert and others of the strain. When public interest waned, the modus operandi was revised. Without missing a beat, the sponsor marched forth with *The Prudential Family Hour of Stars* (1948 to 1950, CBS) on the same evening as its previous entry. There a half-dozen silver screen legends (Humphrey Bogart, Bette Davis, Gregory Peck, Ginger Rogers, Barbara Stanwyck, Robert Taylor) appeared in freshly penned dramatic fare. According to a critic, however, "This had much the same sound as half a dozen 'Hollywood glitter' shows then on the air.... The sound was the same, due to the glut of such programming on CBS and the other networks." Prudential redeemed itself, nonetheless, when — for nearly a decade — it underwrote an effervescent entertainer and staff, *Jack Berch and His Boys* (1945 to 1954, ABC, NBC). It was a giddy daytime quarter-hour that non-professional singers could affirm; surely many of them belted out the familiar novelty tunes with Berch and lively bunch.

72. Pure Oil Company
Sector: Petroleum and other vehicle products, accessories and services
Brand: Pure

Radio: After trying some attempts in radio that didn't last, Pure Oil Company hit its stride by securing newscaster *H. V. Kaltenborn* (1940 to 1955, NBC). The colorful commentator of German vintage developed a clipped speech pattern, a staccato style that resonated with listeners. Kaltenborn gained momentum with the public as a CBS newsman (1927 to 1940) and was well-versed in world affairs. His announcer's incessant reminder "Be sure ... with Pure" was yet another identifying symbol of his durable series. When, at age 70, Kaltenborn cut back to three nights weekly, Pure hung on to his accustomed 7:45 P.M. ET slot, substituting respected journalist *Richard Harkness* (1948 to 1953, NBC). Could lightning strike twice?

73. Radio Corporation of America
Sector: Radios, records, phonographs
Brand: RCA Victor
Radio: As the parent firm of the National Broadcasting Company, RCA had a vested interest in radio where it plugged its wares on a myriad of musical treats. One of its most impressive and durable was *The National Symphony Orchestra* (1927 to ca. 1939, NBC, NBC Blue) with Walter Damrosch as the maestro. Furthermore, RCA brands were often interjected into aural series aired by NBC Radio when a program was sponsorless or had commercial time to fill as in the case of partial or multiple participation. For example, during the single season (of an 18-year run) that the venerable old private eye *Mr. Keen, Tracer of Lost Persons* aired on NBC (1951 to 1952), most weeks RCA occupied a one-minute slot as other underwriters did. The other spots alternated among American Home Products (Anacin), Liggett & Myers (Chesterfields) and American Chicle (Dentyne). The solution helped NBC and parent firm RCA in two ways: increased sales and filling slots that might go to repetitious unpaid messages about fire, water or driving safety, a profusion of which flooded the airwaves in the 1950s after sponsors pulled out.

74. Ralston Purina Company
Sector: Foods processing for humans and animals
Brand: Ralston cereals, Purina pet food
Radio: While it subscribed multiple radio series, Ralston Purina is duly remembered for just one, *Tom Mix* (1933 to 1940, 1941 to 1942, 1944 to 1950, 1951, NBC, NBC Blue, MBS), and the cowboy star who sang its jingle: "Shredded Ralston for your breakfast starts your day off shining bright...." The buckaroos could recite it and hardly resist the "bite size and ready-to-eat" treat he proffered. Another major Ralston radio contribution was *Checkerboard Jamboree* (1946 to 1950, MBS), a daytime quarter-hour most of the run with country singer Eddy Arnold yodeling to the ranch hands. Continuing its focus on kids, Ralston underwrote *Space Patrol* (1951 to 1954, ABC) with Ed Kemmer as terrestrial protector-commander Buzz Corey.

75. Rexall Drug Company
Sector: Retail pharmacies
Brand: Rexall
Radio: A trio of name brand aural powerhouses — *The Jimmy Durante-Garry Moore Show* (1945 to 1948, CBS, NBC), *The Phil Harris-Alice Faye Show* (1948 to 1950, NBC) and *Amos 'n' Andy* (1951 to 1954, CBS) — gave Rexall superlative exposure, indelibly marking the chain as a key player among retail pharmacies.

76. Shell Oil Company
Sector: Petroleum and other vehicle products, accessories and services
Brand: Shell
Radio: Its most prestigious series, *Shell Chateau* (1935 to 1937, NBC), a flashy Saturday night musical comedy hour, was developed for superstar Al Jolson. After a year, Jolson turned his attentions elsewhere and a couple of unknowns (Smith Ballew, Joe Cook) replaced him as host. As a result, the whole thing fell off the track; it lost 40 percent of its audience when Jolson departed and was a goner at season's end.

77. Sherwin-Williams Company
Sector: Paint and accessories
Brand: Sherwin-Williams
Radio: For one season, Sherwin-Williams tried out radio in the medium's early epoch with *Keeping up with Daughter* (1931 to 1932, NBC), dramatic fare with recurring actress Nan Dorland. That venture failed but Sherwin-William's next attempt was a roaring success. For a decade, the firm underwrote half of the popular Milton Cross-hosted *Metropolitan Opera Auditions* (1935 to 1945, NBC, NBC Blue). The series was an offshoot of the acclaimed Saturday afternoon Metropolitan Opera broadcasts that Cross also hovered over, offering serious traction for this one from the very beginning.

78. Sinclair Oil Corporation
Sector: Petroleum and other vehicle products, accessories and services
Brand: Sinclair
Radio: An early radio series named for its sponsor, *The Sinclair Wiener Minstrels* (1932 to 1937, NBC Blue), linked interlocutor Gene Arnold with a trio, quartet and Malcolm Claire as Negro impersonator "Spare Ribs." It was a throwback to an earlier age. Sinclair signed up a couple of also ran newscasters, too: Arthur Hale, whose *Confidentially Yours* (1939 to 1947, MBS) persisted beyond most not-well-knowns, and the better recalled Frank Singiser, touted as the *Sinclair Headliner* (1943 to 1947, MBS).

79. Smith Brothers Cough Drop Company
Sector: Over-the-counter cough remedies
Brand: Smith Brothers
Radio: Much has been written about the monikers that actors Billy Hillpot and Scrappy Lambert were known by on *Trade and Mark, the Smith Brothers Program* (1926 to 1934, NBC Blue, CBS, NBC). To keep druggists from selling generic lozenges, the company had, in 1872, identified the two men's illustrations on cough drop packaging as "Trade" and "Mark," popular appellations that persisted for years. Its transferal to an aural medium was easily accomplished and reinforced what had long been on the product packaging.

80. Socony Oil Company (Standard Oil of New York)
Sector: Petroleum and other vehicle products, accessories and services
Brand: Socony
Radio: Actors Parker Fennelly and Arthur Allen were village rubes in the *Soconyland Sketches* (1928 to 1935, NBC, CBS) that evolved into a better recalled *Snow Village Sketches*. They persisted under that banner for other firms at intervals to 1946. Fennelly and Allen turned their characterizations into careers, meanwhile, appearing in five similar incarnations inspired by the Socony show. When a few more oil firms set a new focus, Socony signed newscaster *Raymond Graham Swing* (1942 to 1944, NBC Blue). Socony amused again, proffering *The Victor Borge Show* (1946 to 1947, NBC) backed by Benny Goodman's musical troupe. One of its final network gigs was the *New York Philharmonic Orchestra* (1948 to 1949, CBS), yet another dimension.

81. E. R. Squibb & Sons
Sector: Over-the-counter health care remedies and pharmaceuticals
Brand: Squibb
Radio: Squibb's handful of radio series was as undistinguished as it was fleeting. Somehow the firm got hold of third-tier properties, all of which bore its name, like *The Squibb Program* (1932 to 1933, NBC) with The Revelers and Frank Black and His Orchestra, *Squibb Golden Treasury of Song* (1940 to 1942, CBS) that initially spotlighted vocalist Jan Peerce who was followed by Frank Parker, and *The Squibb Show*, aka *To Your Good Health* (1943 to 1945, CBS) with Lyn Murray. Regrettably, there were no strong ratings-builders there.

82. Staley Corporation
Sector: Household laundry supplies
Brand: Sta-Puf
Radio: There is documentation that Staley underwrote only a single radio series by itself, the daytime serial *Sweet River* (1943 to 1944, Blue). While network airtime spiraled toward its final fling with destiny during the latter half of the 1950s and the year 1960, meanwhile, Staley intermittently participated in buying commercial time on the very last vestiges of soap opera, all on CBS: *Backstage Wife, Ma Perkins, Our Gal Sunday, The Right to Happiness, Road of Life, The Second Mrs. Burton, This Is Nora Drake, Young Doctor Malone.*

83. Standard Oil Company of New Jersey
Sector: Petroleum and other vehicle products, accessories and services
Brand: Esso
Radio: Esso gave the Marx Brothers their initial national exposure beyond the silver screen on *Flywheel, Shyster and Flywheel* (1932 to 1933, NBC Blue). During the first half of the 1930s, Standard Oil of New Jersey invested heavily in radio, only to see every one of more than a half-dozen series withdrawn within a few months. (Presumably, this was the sponsor's decision much of the time.) In addition to the Marxes, the company subscribed all of these: *The Esso Hour*, aka *Believe It or Not* (1931 to 1932, NBC Blue); *The Adventures of Charlie Chan* (1932 to 1933, NBC Blue); *Esso Theater* (1932 to 1933, NBC Blue) *Tabloid Operetta* (1932 to 1933, CBS); *The O'Flynns* (1934 to 1935, CBS); and *Guy Lombardo and His Royal Canadians* (1935 to 1936, CBS). Was Esso testing the water or did it, possibly, take calculated risks that ended in humorless blunders? That's for conjecture. While withdrawing almost altogether from the national broadcast arena following the early trial period (or period of trials?), the oil firm hit on a gusher: it would channel advertising funds into a robust effort of news capsules in multiple insertions daily in local markets. The five-minute insertions labeled *Your Esso Reporter* featured staff newsmen (with an established presence and distinctive voice on those stations) reading headline bulletins — local, regional, national and international. A few seconds of identifiable tones signified the start and finish of the fleeting newsbriefs interjected into the day's programming at scheduled hours. Often the reports appeared on the outlet considered most powerful (in wattage and prestige) in a given geographic territory. While *Your Esso Reporter* prevailed in some places earlier or later, its peak came in the 1940s and early 1950s. Most cities selected for it featured it an average of four times daily. Standard Oil of New Jersey rejoined the national radio trade with a season's sponsorship of *The New York Philharmonic Symphony* (1948 to 1949, CBS). Its petroleum brand may not have been available across America, thus its alternative marketing plan, pursued vigorously, proved a rewarding method of reaching its audience.

84. Studebaker Manufacturing Company
Sector: Automobiles
Brand: Studebaker
Radio: In a decade after the inception of national hookups, *The Studebaker Champions* (1929 to 1931, 1934 to 1937, NBC, CBS) was a namesake variety series. It projected the product in an era when, at first, commercials weren't allowed. Richard Himber, Jean Goldkette and more impresarios conducted; Dick Powell was frequently featured. Staying out of the audio marketplace for two decades, late in the network era the car-maker jumped back in with scattered commercials in a couple of Western-themed adventures: *Gunsmoke* (1957 to ca. 1959, CBS) with William Conrad in the starring role, and *Frontier Gentleman* (1958, CBS) with John Dehner in the lead. By then, the sponsor was combining its operations with one of its rivals to form Studebaker-Packard Corporation. In 1960, those innovative marketers not only adopted *Mr. Ed*, a proposed CBS-TV property, but Studebaker dealerships bought time from their local CBS affiliates to air the show. In so doing, the Studebaker champs took the ad industry on a wild ride (imagine that today!) to say nothing of bullet-nosed vehicles with front-and-back resemblances!

85. Swift & Company
Sector: Meat processing and canning
Brand: Swift
Radio: In the medium's early days, Swift leaned heavily into musical fare, offering lesser known ensembles and humorists backed by full orchestras. Later, it underwrote the teenage sitcom *Archie Andrews* (1947 to 1948, NBC) for one season ("Tender beef ... juicy pork ... known from the West Coast to New York ... Swift's premium franks"). Yet its strongest presence was likely Don McNeill's *Breakfast Club* on ABC. In the 1940s and 1950s, Swift bought not one but *two* quarter-hour segments to tout its Brookfield sausage and other edibles.

86. Sylvania Electric Products, Inc.
Sector: Lighting fixtures and accessories and small appliances
Brand: Sylvania
Radio: Another couple of early radio entourages named for the sponsor while appearing in a period that banned authentic commercials, *The Sylvania Foresters Quartet* (1927 to 1928, NBC Blue) and *The Sylvanians* (1931 to 1932, CBS) amplified the sponsor without ever going very far. Think how many references could be squeezed into a half-hour segment by a convivial announcer's soothing-toned reminders: "And now, ladies and gentlemen, the Sylvania Foresters Quartet brings to our microphone a happy rendition of a brand new tune, 'Ain't She Sweet?'" For the sponsor, it was.

87. The Texas Company
Sector: Petroleum and more vehicle products and services
Brand: Texaco
Radio: Opera lovers are indebted to this firm forever for filling the ether with the music they loved. Under successive names, Texaco aired the *Metropolitan Opera* (1940–2004, NBC Blue, Blue, ABC, CBS, and a dedicated hookup) worldwide, a broadcaster-sponsor tie perhaps exceeding all others in endurance and reach to multiple outlets. Meanwhile, on *Texaco Town* (1936 to 1938, CBS), entertainer Eddie Cantor hosted a variety show that lasted in effect from 1931 to 1954. *Texaco Star Theater* (1938 to 1946, 1947 to 1949, CBS, NBC), still another variety feature, offered a plethora of big name emcees — Adolphe Menjou, John Barrymore, Fred Allen, James Melton, Tony Martin, Gordon MacRae and Milton Berle — and star-studded guests, too.

88. The Toni Company
Sector: Hair care preparations for women and girls
Brand: Toni
Radio: In the late 1940s, Toni burst onto the radio scene out of nowhere, filling a void left by sundry departing sponsors and becoming a major presence in the succeeding decade. Toni's slots included the game show *Give and Take* (1947 to 1951, CBS) with quizmaster John Reed King interrogating contestants. The same year, *This Is Nora Drake* (1947 to 1952, CBS) debuted for it, one of the last hardy daytime serials. The following year the firm picked up *Casey, Crime Photographer* (1948 to 1949, CBS) with Staats Cotsworth as a sleuthing newspaper shutterbug. For a full year, Toni subscribed the Saturday matinee anthology *Grand Central Station* (1951 to 1952, CBS). In the four months *A Crime Letter from Dan Dodge* (1952 to 1953, ABC) aired with Myron McCormick as the failed private eye, Toni signed on. The brand also underwrote a handful of other shows: *Fun for All* (1952 to 1953, CBS, ABC) hosted by Bill Cullen and Arlene Francis, *One Man's Family* (1954 to 1955, NBC), *Young Widder Brown* (1954 to ca. 1956, multiple participation), *Our Miss Brooks* (1954 to 1956, CBS, half sponsorship) starring Eve Arden, Arthur Godfrey's *Talent Scouts* (1955 to 1956, CBS), and *Young Doctor Malone* (1955 to ca. 1958, CBS, multiple sponsorship).

89. United States Steel Corporation
Sector: Steel
Brand: U.S. Steel

Radio: With a sound like none other, *Theater Guild on the Air*, later dubbed *The United States Steel Hour* (1943 to 1944, 1945 to 1953, CBS, ABC, NBC), brought "legitimate theater that at its best forged a near-perfect alliance with radio," a critic said. Its Broadway productions easily surpassed *First Nighter* and let *Steel* seamlessly transfer into a TV series for another decade (1953 to 1963), awarding it dual decades.

90. Vick Chemical Company
Sector: Over-the-counter health care remedies
Brand: Vicks
Radio: In its search for glory, Vick made a couple of pithy stops: *Matinee Theater* (1944 to 1945, CBS) with Victor Jory presenting but 25 weekly dramas; and six months of kicking off what would pay off for others big time in a streak of *Break the Bank* (1945 to 1946, MBC), a captivating quiz hosted by Bert Parks and later by Bud Collyer.

91. The Wanderer Company
Sector: Dairy foods and beverages
Brand: Ovaltine
Radio: A couple of lengthy connects with juvenile adventures typified Ovaltine's long association with radio. The first included the comic strip character *Little Orphan Annie* (1931 to 1940, NBC Blue, NBC, MBS). Annie dispatched decoders and shake-up mugs galore for a dime and an aluminum strip seal inside Ovaltine containers. When Wanderer milked that as much as it profitably could, it shifted its funds to *Captain Midnight* (1940 to 1949, MBS, Blue) where the premium giveaways and club memberships proliferated.

92. G. Washington Coffee Company
Sector: Coffee processing and packing
Brand: G. Washington
Radio: Named after founder George Constant Louis Washington (1871 to 1946), the firm had a pervasive influence in U.S. radio for a few years starting with *The Adventures of Sherlock Holmes* (1930 to 1933, 1934 to 1935, NBC, NBC Blue). William Gillette, Clive Brook, Richard Gordon and Louis Hector held the namesake part in Washington's era. On the verge of spinning another crime tale, Holmes' sidekick, Dr. Watson (actor Leigh Lovel), invariably found a hot cup of G. Washington coffee to be a satisfying indulgence, particularly on bitterly cold nights. In its way, those commercials were integrated into the content of the show. Washington signed for *Uncle Jim's Question Bee* (1936 to 1939, NBC Blue) with quizmaster Jim McWilliams. A trio of added features completed the firm's chain radio repertoire: *O'Henry Stories* (1932, NBC Blue), *Professor Quiz* (1936, CBS) and *Surprise Party* (1946 to 1947, CBS).

93. Welch Foods Company
Sector: Food and beverages
Brand: Welch's
Radio: For 11 years, Welch's underwrote the anthological narrative fare that was labeled *Irene Rich Dramas* (1933 to 1944, NBC Blue, CBS).

94. Wesson Oil and Snowdrift Company
Sector: Cooking additives
Brand: Wesson Oil, Snowdrift shortening
Radio: Preceding her eminently better remembered daytime quiz *Grand Slam* (1946 to 1953, CBS), *Irene Beasley Songs* (1943 to 1945, CBS) had its namesake host doing what she did well for Wesson and Snowdrift. For a season, the sponsor picked up Edwin C. Hill's commentary, *The Human Side of the News* (1946 to 1947, ABC). Late in chain radio's history, Wesson-Snowdrift offered housewives a new daytime serial, *Dr. Paul* (1951 to 1953, NBC). The drama was about a self-effacing

rural physician (Russell Thorson) although it was as much about his unhappy spouse (Peggy Webber). She ignored the thrill of serving humanity while incessantly dwelling on relocating in New York, which would allow them to join society's upper crust.

95. Westinghouse Corporation
Sector: Household and commercial appliances
Brand: Westinghouse
Radio: The Westinghouse Program (1943 to 1946, NBC) was sometimes labeled after its singing star, baritone John Charles Thomas. A habitual audio presence, Thomas seemed as comfortable performing at the Met as he did on the *Bell Telephone Hour*, another frequent venue. Westinghouse, which would purchase CBS in 1995, subscribed only two more coast-to-coast radio series. One was a renewal of a popular 1930s feature in the last half of the 1940s, Ted Malone's poetry and conversation show, *Between the Bookends* (1945 to 1949, ABC), offered in both daily and Saturday segments. The firm's last effort in aural broadcasting turned out to be a loser: *Pick the Winner* (1952, CBS) persisted just 13 weeks that fall. By then, Westinghouse — and many others — were shifting their eyes and fortunes (budgets) to TV, and few of them were looking back.

96. Wheatena Corporation
Sector: Milling and food processing
Brand: Wheatena cereal
Radio: In the 1930s, Wheatena was all over the dial. None of its programs, however, might be branded smashing successes. A few focused on adolescent listeners: *Raising Junior* (1930 to 1932, NBC Blue) with Peter Dixon and Aline Berry; *Wheatenaville Sketches* (1932 to 1933, NBC) with Raymond Knight and Alice Davenport; *The Happy Minstrels* (1933 to 1934, CBS); *Bill Bachelor Sketches* (1933 to 1935, NBC); *Popeye, the Sailor* (1935 to 1937, NBC, CBS) with Detmar Poppen and Floyd Buckley in the lead; *The Children's Corner* (1936 to 1938, CBS) with Dorothy Gordon spinning yarns; and *Wheatena Playhouse* (1940 to 1941, NBC), an anthology with changing casts. Wheatena may have received poor media advice; short runs and low numbers indicate it seldom competed with the programs of industry giants General Foods (Post), General Mills, Kellogg, Quaker and Ralston.

97. Wildroot Cream Oil Company
Sector: Men's hair care preparations
Brand: Wildroot
Radio: "Get Wildroot Cream Oil, Charlie ... you will have a tough time, Charlie ... keepin' all those gals away!" The idioms of a jingle zillions sang with a chorus are remembered now from features like *Woody Herman and His Orchestra* (1945 to 1946, ABC), *The King Cole Trio* (1946 to 1948, NBC) with Nat King Cole, and *The Adventures of Sam Spade* (1946 to 1950, CBS, NBC) with Howard Duff as the private eye. The wheels came off in the latter show, unfortunately. Spurred by allegations that Duff was a Communist sympathizer in an epoch of blacklisting public figures, Wildroot replaced him and then replaced its hit series altogether. *Charlie Wild, Private Detective* (1950, NBC) starring George Petrie followed but it didn't succeed; Wildroot pulled its money in just eight weeks. By the start of the new year, the firm was one of multiple sponsors assisting agent Adam Sheppard (actor Martin Blaine) and the rest of his brigade on *The FBI in Peace & War* (1951 to 1958, CBS), capturing big-time hoods on the prowl. Furthermore, Wildroot single-handedly supported *The Shadow* (1951 to 1953, MBS) in *his* quests, with Bret Morrison portraying the infamous invisible sleuth (Lamont Cranston). For a fleeting spell, the sponsor added a game show, *Twenty Questions* (1952 to 1953, MBS), with panel moderator Bill Slater.

98. William R. Warner & Company, Inc.
Sector: Personal consumer goods and over-the-counter pharmaceuticals
Brand: Sloan's Liniment muscle-relaxing agent, Richard Hudnut cosmetics, fragrances and hair care preparations

Radio: Under a myriad of titles, most often *Twenty Thousand Years in Sing Sing* (1933 to 1939, NBC Blue), Sloan's Liniment presented warden Lewis E. Lawes ostensibly in real crime tales emanating from actual prison cells. Sloan followed up by subscribing a second gritty crime-based show, *Gangbusters* (1940 to 1945, NBC Blue, Blue, ABC). In the late 1940s, Richard Hudnut was the brand of choice for concurrent musical showcases: *The Jean Sablon Show* (1946 to 1947, CBS) and the far more widely recognized *Sammy Kaye and His Orchestra* (1946 to 1948, ABC). Late in the run of *The Edgar Bergen and Charlie McCarthy Show* (1952 to 1953, CBS), meanwhile, Hudnut spent a season with the humorist and his riotous wooden dummy.

99. J. B. Williams Company

Sector: Personal care goods and over-the-counter remedies
Brand: Aqua-Velva men's fragrances, Cepacol mouthwash and sore throat remedies, Kreml hair tonic, Lectric Shave lotion, Williams shave cream
Radio: Williams bought *True or False* (1938 to 1943, MBS, NBC Blue) for its Williams shaving cream in a run that resumed and included more breaks (1948 to 1956). Quizmaster Henry Hagen asked contestants seven progressively harder queries followed by a test on current newsmakers. Winners were awarded a top prize of $2,500. Williams introduced listeners to a new private detective series, *The Adventures of Nero Wolfe* (1943, Blue) but didn't stay long enough to see it catch on. (With other sponsors, it lasted eight more years.) In the waning days of chain radio, J. B. Williams purchased insertions in the daily exhibitions of clever comics *Bob and Ray* (1955 to 1957, MBS) and their bag of zany, yet clever, characterizations.

100. William J. Wrigley Company

Sector: Chewing gum
Brand: Wrigley's
Radio: Wrigley offered many chain radio entries between 1927 and the form's final gasp. The most resilient was *Gene Autry's Melody Ranch* (1940 to 1943, 1945 to 1956, CBS). "The Singing Cowboy" interacted with ranch hands by a campfire, harmonized on prairie tunes (i.e., "Cool Water") and recalled tales of the old West. Wrigley awaited Autry's return when he signed up to serve his country in 1943. It was déjà vu in 1945, Wrigley seeing a good thing for advertiser and audience alike. Later, it underwrote a sitcom with J. Carroll Naish as an Italian immigrant who adored his new homeland, *Life with Luigi* (1950 to 1952, CBS). Between 1951 and 1958, Wrigley was a participating sponsor of *The FBI in Peace & War* on CBS. The firm's next buy was in another of radio's key crime dramas, *Yours Truly, Johnny Dollar* (1953 to 1954, CBS). John Lund played an insurance investigator with an action-packed expense account.

Appendix B: Variants That Impacted the Radio Commercial

As noted elsewhere, until 1929 the solitary voice pattern of delivering promotional copy on the air was about all that had been attempted with radio commercials. That gradually began to change as enterprising entrepreneurs adapted the sketch format to promote wares. Applying that variation, two or more individuals conversed in plausible slice-of-life exchanges in which a brand or sponsoring organization was mentioned. The departure from the tested norm set the stage for increased creativity and experimentation in successive years. By the early 1930s, the ingenuity of those resourceful pioneer marketers — aided by improved technology and an increasing array of gadgets to augment it — was obvious.

The familiar lone-voice one-on-one lecture method of audio advertising, while still dominant, was but one style for drawing a listener's attention to a client's goods and services. As radio pitchmen tested newer advances to appeal to the ears of audiences, they substituted a fresh mix of tools for the handful that fans were accustomed to. Their unabated quest was to reach and sell more goods to greater numbers of buyers.

This Appendix explores a plethora of variants that captured the imaginations of the innovators: a potpourri of contrivances — devices and alternatives apart from the traditionally accustomed pitches. Some will resonate with readers today as most persist in influencing contemporary broadcast media audiences.

In alphabetical order, they include: audience involvement, contests, cowcatchers and hitchhikes, electrical transcriptions and tape recordings, headliners as spokespersons, infomercials, institutional advertising, integrating messages within programming, jingles and other music, microphone placement and special effects, nomenclature, participating sponsorship, premiums, public service announcements, sound effects, spot announcements, sustaining programming, testimonials, and voiceovers.

Audience Involvement

Getting the studio audience to buy into the commercials was like a base runner hitting a grand slam every time at bat. Not only was the reaction of those witnesses unforgettable, their enthusiastic participation was like a ringing endorsement of the sponsoring enterprise.

Hence, when master of ceremonies Art Linkletter approached a CBS (later, ABC) microphone between 1945 to 1949 on weekday afternoons at the start of his *House Party* and inquired: "Ladies, who sponsors the next program?" the members of his live studio brigade were primed to thunderously reply: "General Electric!" Not only did they respond like that in Hollywood where the show was based but at every venue where Linkletter appeared as he randomly toured with his show across the nation. Upon the audience's exclamation of the sponsor's moniker, a pianist would break into the familiar theme and announcer Jack Slattery read some introductory copy from a script.

That unusual opening, by the way — delivered cold — instantly established who was behind the antics-filled marathon. It also helped that many of the prizes given to studio guests for appearing in the various stunts and contests conducted by Linkletter happened to be General Electric home appliances (which really wasn't a fluke at all): washers, dryers, ranges, refrigerators, radios, televisions, irons, dishwashers, mixers, toasters, blenders, fans, hairdryers and so forth — all reinforcing the sponsor's brand while depicting the image of a generous benefactor. Combined with an occasional commercial posited by Slattery, there was never any doubt about who sponsored that program, even if the fans had never reported it.

Series aimed at juveniles, in particular, were easy marks for engaging audiences. When Uncle Bill Adams, the grandfather interlocutor of *Let's Pretend*, opened that show by exclaiming "Hal-looooo, Pretenders!" and received a deafening response from a studio seasoned with wildly precocious youngsters shouting in unison "Hal-looooo, Uncle Bill!" the listeners at home knew the aging storyteller had the crowd eating from his hand.

Thus, when he whipped up enthusiasm for the sponsor's product, Cream of Wheat breakfast cereal, at appropriate intervals, the audience — well rehearsed before airtime — couldn't wait to jump in. He'd ask questions and they retorted with expected responses. Those exchanges helped drive up sales of the foodstuff from 1943 to 1952 as millions of boxes left grocers' shelves, much of it attributable to Uncle Bill and his adoring fans. At the close of every commercial, meanwhile, in his deepest basso profundo — accompanied by a whistle sliding up and down the scale — Adams reminded listeners: "It's way up in flavah ... it's way down in cost ... it's pa-lennty smooth!"

Recalling those commercials, pretender Arthur Anderson, a child actor on the show for years, averred: "Bill was the delight of the ad agency and the Cream of Wheat people. You could not help but trust what he told you about Cream of Wheat ... was the absolute truth." A weekly audience of tykes was clearly under his magic spell.

Then there was *Smilin' Ed* [McConnell] *and His Buster Brown Gang*, cajoling another batch of kiddies — this time, on the West Coast — into singing the final line of the Buster Brown theme song as he warbled and played the piano: "I got shoes ... you got shoes ... everybody's gotta have shoes ... but there's only one kind of shoes for me—[STUDIO AUDIENCE]: good ole Buster Brown shoes!" The commercials were even more remarkable as a transcribed dog barked and a voiceover juvenile exclaimed: "That's my dog, Tige ... he lives in a shoe ... I am Buster Brown ... look for me in there, too!" Audiences, in person and at home, identified with McConnell's persuasive salesmanship on several levels.

Contests

Contests created the special stir of drawing more listeners into an advertiser's lair, establishing water cooler conversations that sometimes put much of the country on alert.

In the early years, the daytime serials were a hotbed of competitive activity. Less than 15 months after *The Guiding Light* debuted, for instance, announcer Fort Pearson spelled out this treat to the show's fans on the broadcast of May 16, 1938:

> I am happy to tell our thousands of loyal listeners about this thrilling opportunity we are offering. So listen carefully, please. Every day for 30 days the makers of P&G White Naptha soap will give away 10 of the finest automatic refrigerators made. Yes, 10 beautiful new Servel Electrolux refrigerators will be given away in the easiest contest ever. That's 10 refrigerators ... every day for 30 days, beginning Friday, May 20th, and continuing through July 1st, excepting Saturdays, Sundays and holidays.

Typical of radio contests of that day, Pearson asked listeners to complete this statement in 25 words or less: "I like P&G White Naptha soap because...." To help underwrite the contest, he asked them to attach the front panels from five packages of White Naptha soap to their entries. P&G and other sponsors launched scores of similar competitions over the years to increase the fervor for their shows and wares. In subsequent contests on *The Guiding Light* during the early P&G era, the prizes were sometimes diversified but the reactions of listeners remained intense. For one similar event, a $1,000 bill, five $500 bills and 60 Servel Electrolux refrigerators were given away each week for several consecutive weeks.

The "25 words or less" scenario became one of the simplest and most repeated themes, e.g., "I like Rinso/Colgate/Tums/Rice Krispies because..." (pick a product). Mailing an entry with a boxtop or label often earned the sender a chance to be "one of those selected by the judges as among the best" or qualified him for a drawing for a generous prize. The sender might also receive a trinket by mail (a premium) for his efforts.

Possibly the ultimate radio contests, still recalled by people alive today who lived through the era, was a series of mystery identifications conducted by the producers of Ralph Edwards' *Truth or Consequences* in the 1940s. Beyond all of the zany ideas this bunch proffered over its long run, it doubtlessly gained more plaudits for the show via a series of stunts that made utterly decent sense. Over several seasons a procession of hidden celebrity identities, in conjunction with a few noble charitable causes, was introduced. A good deal of the nation's attention was riveted to the show as the sequences grabbed news headlines. One radio historiographer suggested that, through such efforts, the series "electrified the country."[1] It began when Edwards read a rhyme marinated in clues on the broadcast of December 29, 1945:

> Hickory dickory dock,
> The hands went round the clock
> The clock struck ten
> Lights out
> Good night.

A mystery subject (prizefighter Jack Dempsey) read the poem every Saturday night for several weeks. Various contestants were given an opportunity to reveal the man whom Edwards called "Mr. Hush." A small jackpot of merchandise prizes grew weekly as participants failed to get it right. Eventually a "crackpot jackpot" reached $13,500, a generous sum by the mid–1940s. At that juncture a Navy man, Ensign Richard Bartholomew of Fayetteville, Arkansas, guessed Dempsey and claimed the treasure. Radio jackpot stashes often included automobiles, travel vouchers, airplanes, motorboats, house trailers, mink coats and jewelry.

By then the Procter & Gamble Company, which had been underwriting the show since it premiered in 1940, realized that a mass of new listeners was tuning in and clamoring for more guessing games. It could hardly quit now. So the mystery person contests persevered, although from then on for charitable causes — the March of Dimes, fighting infantile paralysis, or polio, was a prime beneficiary. It appeared to audiences that P&G was also a benevolent sponsor. And by then the emphasis had shifted from the studio to the folks at home. Listeners could submit altruistic donations while — in that competition — trying to detect who "Mrs. Hush" was. In 25 words or less, they completed this statement: "We should all support the March of Dimes because...."

Out of the mailbag each week contest judges plucked a group of "best entries" which qualified their authors to be eligible for a telephone call from Edwards while on the air the following Saturday night. If no one interviewed could name the mystery celebrity, new clues were given and more prizes added to the jackpot. The March of Dimes eventually collected $545,000 directly from that appeal. By the time contestant Mrs. William H. McCormick figured out that silent screen star Clara Bow was "Mrs. Hush," the merchandise prizes were valued at $17,590.

Dancer Martha Graham was later pinpointed as "Miss Hush" by a listener claiming awards valued in excess of $21,000 as listeners sent $672,000 to the March of Dimes. When Mrs. Florence Hubbard of Chicago named comedian Jack Benny as "The Walking Man" in 1947, that contest had

Ralph Edwards (at right) loved to play games. He made a career of it, in fact, starring in or producing a handful of participatory series. It began with *Truth or Consequences* for Procter & Gamble's leading laundry detergent, Duz. The brand and the show were synonymous in listeners' minds as Edwards piqued contestants with wacky stunts. The genial emcee sometimes even trilled along with a songstress who belted out this ditty over the din of a sloshing automatic washer: *D-U-Z ... D-U-Z ... Put Duz in your washing machine ... Clothes come out so nice and clean ... When you hear this song you'll sing ... D-U-Z does everything!* P&G cleaned up with it and paid Edwards' bills for a full decade (1940 to 1950).

earned $1.5 million for the American Heart Association while Mrs. Hubbard walked away with 27 major merchandise prizes for herself. They included a Cadillac, gas range, refrigerator, home freezer, two-week all-expense-paid vacation for two to Sun Valley, Idaho, an airplane, kitchen and bath makeovers, motor coach home, speedboat, three rooms of furniture, a piano, plus more. Even a pauper could have turned into a princess with spoils like those!

Successive identity contests involved the "Whispering Woman" (vocalist Jeanette MacDonald), "Mr. Heartbeat" (poet Edgar A. Guest), "Mr. and Mrs. Hush" (musicians Moss Hart and Kitty Carlisle) and "Papa and Mama Hush" (dancers Yolanda and Velez). In all, *Truth or Consequences'* radio efforts ultimately tallied $22 million for munificent intents. In addition to the March of Dimes and the American Heart Association, recipients included the Arthritis Foundation and the Mental Health Drive.

One of the biggest winners, of course, was the Procter & Gamble Company and its Duz detergent brand. Listeners could hardly avoid one or more commercials for the laundry product when tuning in on Saturday nights. And for the non-winners, it was nail-biting anticipation for about three years.

Cowcatchers and Hitchhikes

Program developers (often advertising agencies) relentlessly sought methods of distancing their commercials from preconceived and expected norms. One way they jimmied with it was in the timing and number of messages aired. The preponderance of half-hour primetime features, for example, carried three spots set aside for advertising plugs: following the opening, near the program's middle and following the body of the show, shortly before the credits were given along with a reminder to "tune in next week." Most quarter-hour serials reserved two or three spots for advertising pitches: following the opening, following the body content and — if a third message was scheduled — most often just before sign-off, though, in a few instances, at the program's midpoint. The pattern varied from series to series so these leading conventions don't apply in every case.

There were some firms with so many different wares in their manufacturing arsenals that they cultivated techniques of squeezing in added, although briefer, commercials without loss of efficacy. An excellent example was presented weekday afternoons by Sterling Drug, Inc., which — throughout the 1940s into the early 1950s — purchased the entire four o'clock hour in the Eastern Time zone on NBC in quarter-hour segments. Sterling's extensive line of health and personal care goods included well-recognized trademarks like Bayer, Energine, Fletcher's, Haley's, Dr. Lyons and Phillips, plus dozens of less celebrated labels.

In some of those quarter hours, Sterling's inventive advertising agency — Air Features, Inc., run by the inexhaustible creative producers Frank and Anne Hummert — instituted plugs known in the industry as cowcatcher and hitchhike (or hitchhiker) commercials. The cowcatcher, lasting from 20 to 30 seconds, traditionally opened a program cold (being offered without prior show introduction) or immediately followed a pithy gateway prior to a more extensive opening. The hitchhike, on the other hand, was just the reverse. It appeared only moments before a show's network ID that instantly signaled its sign-off from the air. Using the four o'clock serial *Backstage Wife* for an illustration, the format followed by Sterling Drugs typically worked like this:

1. At 4:00:00 the network tone sounded and announcer Ford Bond exclaimed: "Next, *Backstage Wife*."
2. A live organist played three to six seconds of isolated chords.
3. Frank Gallop, engaged by Air Features to interchangeably alternate with Bond and others on a number of Sterling-backed daytime and nighttime series, read a succinct cowcatcher commercial for one of the firm's commodities. (On the serial to follow, *Stella Dallas*, aired live from an adjacent studio, Bond turned up to read the cowcatcher commercial.)
4. When Gallop finished the cowcatcher on *Backstage Wife*, the organist broke into a full canto of the drama's identifiable theme, "The Rose of Tralee," as the interlocutor for the narrative, Bond, read the opening epigraph with the music resonating behind it.
5. Following the theme, Bond read a longer commercial for a second Sterling Drug product.
6. A brief organ bridge signified the transition to the day's narrative which promptly ensued, the stage set by the announcer-turned-narrator (Bond).
7. At the close of the dialogue for that day's episodic installment — denoted by an organ bridge — Bond read a longer commercial for a third Sterling Drug commodity or a separate pitch for the item featured in the second commercial.
8. The organist played the theme through as Bond delivered the closing epigraph, the music continuing behind his words.
9. Bond read a fleeting hitchhike commercial of 20 to 30 seconds' duration for a Sterling ware not previously advertised in that quarter-hour.
10. The network ID announcer cut in with "This is NBC, the National Broadcasting Company" and the chain's signature triple tones (G-E-C) sounded.

In the early 1940s, when James Fleming was the primary interlocutor for the evening detective thriller *Mr. Keen, Tracer of Lost Persons*, the Hummerts — who also produced that crime drama feature — sent in another speaker from their battery of announcers to make the auxiliary announcements. George Ansbro arrived to bat for Sterling Drug's rival health and personal goods manufacturer American Home Products. He read cowcatcher and hitchhike blurbs for commodities bearing names like Anacin, Bi-So-Dol, Kolynos and Heet.

Of course, an advertiser could insert a cowcatcher plug and omit the hitchhike, or vice versa. Playing with the number and timing of ads was part of an innovative grandstanding in which firms with multiple commodities to push mixed their presentations in an attempt to achieve greater advantage with limited exposure.

Electrical Transcriptions and Tape Recordings

The earliest attempts to offer prerecorded material over the ether proved unsatisfactory. As a result, most airwaves voices and features presented in radio's formative era were heard live. While the technology for directly broadcasting recorded programs probably existed earlier, broadcasting didn't become aware of the promise of electrical transcriptions before 1929. (Electrical transcriptions is broadcasting jargon for a type of recording practice that was often referred to in the trade as ETs.) As the national hookups and advertising agencies fused their domination of the industry, alternative means of delivering programming emerged.

In 1932, the production firm of Kasper-Gordon, Inc., broke new ground with 15-second transcribed dramatic commercials. The following year that outfit offered transcribed musical jingles as well as longer commercials. Until the late 1930s, however, verbal commercial pitches that had been prerecorded were rare. According to one source, an influx of them was propelled as disc jockeys spinning phonograph records on the airwaves emerged. That genus of professionals derived a need for commercials that could be readily spotted between musical numbers, hence their appearance in some profusion.

On another level, electrical transcriptions allowed entire prerecorded programs to return to radio for a while in the 1930s. In most cases, small regional business enterprises with access to listeners were served. To make the transcription process happen, incidentally, engineers recorded the shows, commercials and announcements on wax discs. Then they duplicated them. At that juncture, copies were dispatched by mail to stations possessing the equipment to air them. "No microphone picks up the sound waves," a well versed scholar explained. "The transcription is immediately translated into the form of electrical impulses, amplified and broadcast, thus insuring a faithful reproduction of what originally was recorded."[2]

As a result, transcriptions sounded much better on the air than earlier recordings had. They also supplied some rewards over a prevailing costly, complex network system. By mailing transcriptions of entire programs with commercials intact to pre-selected stations, a sponsor retained absolute control over the content of its advertising plugs, the way those messages were delivered and the placement of them. Ultimately, maintained one observer, the procedure netted ample savings for both sponsors and stations.

Transcriptions favored precisely the sort of radio advertisers, performers and programs that wired chains were then distancing themselves from. Years after Clicquot Club canceled its *Eskimos* program in 1933,[3] citing economic and distribution factors, the *Eskimos* returned to the ether via transcriptions during the era of the Second World War. And in 1948, they turned up again over a regional hookup. The renewed popularity of their ensuing manifestations hinted that the *Eskimos* might have experienced still more unrelenting accomplishments had the technology for delivering national radio been different.

The webs, however, viewed transcriptions as a threat to a portion of their economic livelihood and deliberately subverted them. Accordingly, in 1933 NBC prohibited the use of electrical transcriptions by all of its owned-and-operated affiliates. The Federal Radio Commission (1927 to 1934) —

still in business under that appellation until its operation was superseded by the more all-encompassing Federal Communications Commission on July 1, 1934 — ordered an acknowledgement to be made on the air prior to running an electrical transcription. Knowing this in advance, audiences often switched off canned programming. Thus, electrical transcriptions lived on merely as adjuncts to a long-entrenched wired chain fraternity by the time the Clicquot *Eskimos* summoned ETs in the early 1940s.

The inability of recordings to afford synchronized airing of events, plus organizational confusion involved in the electrical transcription trade, permitted the national webs to retain a position of advantage. A mixed procedure, with wired networks offering live out-of-studio programming and electrical transcriptions supplying more entertainment, might have resulted in greater programming diversity. As the commercial chains gained strength, however, they abandoned public relations and persuasion as means of accomplishing desired ends (a crutch they had turned to earlier in waging a campaign to promote broadcast advertising). The nets instead traditionally resorted to governmental pressure and economic clout to bring about crushing defeat to whatever forces they collectively disdained.

Not until foremost legendary star Bing Crosby refused to play ball any longer was prerecording able to gain sufficient clout to make a real difference. Crosby's failure to be intimidated by long-standing network dictates set the industry on its heels. In one swoop, he was able to erase years of kowtowing to broadcasting moguls with whom he clearly disagreed. Commercials and programs were to be aired by some form of transcription forevermore after that watershed as a sweeping ban in existence since 1933 was lifted. Crooner Crosby broke the "sound barrier" on October 16, 1946, as *Philco Radio Time* debuted via transcription over ABC. Dubbing the alteration a "portentous premier," *The New York Times* allowed: "Mr. Crosby has delivered a major, if not fatal, blow to the outworn and unrealistic prejudice against the recorded program." Not only did aural tape recording result, that defining moment prompted the development of videotape recording, too, still in use today, revolutionizing not just broadcasting but the recording and film industries also.

The recording process initially applied by *Philco Radio Time* was at best primitive, nonetheless. Shows with commercials intact necessitated three discs per half-hour performance. They were dispersed to network affiliates coast-to-coast. For the very first time, local stations had the power to determine *when they* would air a program.

Several years before this, by the close of the 1930s, the recording process had been substantially enhanced technically. Acetate had replaced wax. Yet, according to one soap opera queen who participated — actress Mary Jane Higby — making those recordings was an onerous task that could wreak havoc still among those who performed and produced the effort.[4]

> There was still no way of editing the record or correcting a mistake once it had occurred. If we "fluffed"..., the whole disc had to be discarded. The doors of the recording studios still swung open at four in the morning to disgorge groups of bleary-eyed actors and announcers who had been there since eight in the evening....
>
> Worse than recording programs was recording commercials. Of course, all network commercials were *live*. That meant we had just one swing at the ball and if we missed we were out....
>
> Many of the commercials heard on the independent stations were recorded on sixteen-inch discs, with each commercial on a separate band. A mistake in the first two or three bands was not serious because nobody minded doing a few commercials over again, but as the tenth, eleventh, and twelfth bands were reached, the tension in the studio would reach a point approaching spontaneous combustion....
>
> There was nothing like a late-night commercial recording session to bring whatever weaknesses one had out into a glaring light. I have never forgotten the occasion when I was called, with five or six other actors, to record some dramatized plugs for a cough medicine. We all thumbed quickly through the scripts to see if we were in the last few bands. I rejoiced to note that my final commercial was number five.
>
> We had the usual hard time getting the first three on the record.... At last we cleared all hurdles; numbers four and five went smoothly, and my night's work was finished. I could not leave the studio, however, in case someone else made a mistake that would send us back to the beginning again....

I must have been more tense than I knew, for a slight tickle began to develop in my throat. I sat in my corner and slowly turned purple as I swallowed to fight the cough down. Then, just as the announcer was saying, "No need to suffer throat irritation —," I exploded in a bark that shook the building and shattered eleven perfectly recorded cough medicine commercials.

In the mid–1940s, Bing Crosby Enterprises was a six-member production unit located in San Carlos, on the San Francisco peninsula. A rather enterprising but obscure technician on its staff, John Mullin, offered a novel solution to the show's inherent transcription complexities. They seemed light years ahead of prevailing methods, in fact. Serving with Britain's Royal Air Force during the Second World War, Mullin was assigned to monitor any diversionary tactics that enemy communications had developed apart from established norms. In 1942, he learned that the Germans had perfected a superior recording device that transcended anything that those in the business had previously known. "Germany was on the air all night," Mullin reported. "We heard beautiful music and you'd swear there was a live orchestra playing. It went on and on without a break and it was obvious that they weren't using 78 rpm records because there was no scratching or surface noise."

Mullin couldn't determine the source of the Germans' high-quality system until the war ended, however. When the allies marched into Frankfurt, he learned the answer: magnetic tape. Realizing the importance of that find, Mullin dismantled two Radio Frankfurt machines. He smuggled them out of the country, literally shipping the parts to himself at his home in San Francisco, accompanied by 50 rolls of plastic tape. By the time he was released from the service and returned home, his shipments were waiting for him. Mullin put the mechanisms together and demonstrated their use to the Institute of Radio Engineers in San Francisco in April 1946. Within a year he had convincingly persuaded the producers of *Philco Radio Time* to discard its antiquated system of recording the program in favor of magnetic tape. That summer (August 1947), for the very first time, a radio show was tape-recorded. It aired on October 1, 1947, over ABC at the start of Crosby's new season.

As a result, *Philco Radio Time* could be recorded just about anywhere, then cut, pieced, edited and spliced. Not only that, it was preserved on tape for the very first time. Competing network engineers couldn't figure out how there was none of the normal needle scratch and surface noise they had long been accustomed to hearing. The horizons were suddenly infinite for assembling improved programming in ways that only a short time before hadn't seemingly existed.

An investigative journalist who supplied many of these facts offered this compelling backdrop to the budding possibilities in using tape.[5]

> Bing's involvement with tape recording came some fifty years after the Danish physicist Valdemar Poulsen invented magnetic recording in 1898. Ironically, the crooner's songs of love and peace were taped on machines developed initially as weapons of war.
>
> The Germans called them Magnetophons and they had been used by the Nazi war machine to broadcast Der Fuehrer's speeches and other propaganda throughout Europe at a time when Germany was crumbling.
>
> The Gestapo had also used them for interrogation and were able, by judicious editing, to concoct confessions from tortured prisoners.
>
> So it took a Danish physicist, a German madman and an American crooner to produce the device which changed the course of broadcasting.

Those two original Magnetophon machines couldn't maintain their reliability forever, of course. Crosby's entrepreneurial instincts kicked into gear. He formed a business relationship with the Ampex Company. Mullin worked with the firm's engineers nearly nonstop to produce an even more advanced device, the Ampex 200. When it went on the market, demand for the new apparatus was instant and phenomenal. ABC, the first to buy, ordered a dozen machines — four each for its New York, Chicago and Hollywood radio facilities. Mullin's wartime memento — cultivated by Crosby's operation — was literally spawning a multimillion-dollar commercial enterprise that was to result in a corporate behemoth known as Ampex.

That wouldn't be the end of the discoveries, however. Within four years Mullin was demonstrating a new process he called video tape recording (VTR), capable of taping and preserving television features. A short time later he was able to offer color VTR. Crosby Research Foundation would eventually amass many patents on magnetic tape recording. By 1947, Sears, Roebuck and Company was selling a model with thin wire as the recording medium for $170, opening up progress to the domestic professional and consumer market. While the fidelity was lacking and the price high for a time when the minimum wage was a quarter an hour, the new system — while heavy and cumbersome — was more portable than previous devices.

Bing Crosby Enterprises was standing on the precipice of still further accomplishment when a strong dose of reality set in. Ampex engineers had been working feverishly in their own experiments. By then the firm was overtaking Crosby. Mullin acknowledged: "Their system was so superior to ours that we recommended to Bing that he stop further development because we didn't stand a chance." As a result, in 1956 Crosby sold his electronics division of Bing Crosby Enterprises to the Minnesota Mining and Manufacturing Company (3M). That firm had earlier produced substitute tape for Crosby when Mullin's original supply of 50 German tapes was exhausted.

Crosby's trailblazing activity led the national radio chains to finally agree that taping programs did little to dilute their anticipated standard of excellence. In fact, sound quality could virtually be guaranteed without the nagging, costly repeats for the West Coast that tradition had dictated. Not only did Groucho Marx's producer John Guedel speedily jump aboard the recording bandwagon, many others were quick to follow.

For advertisers, recording their commercials meant a far greater opportunity to manifest absolute control over how and where their messages aired. For the first time on a sustained basis, quality could be relatively assured. Tapes were erased when fluffs occurred, whether missteps of voice, music or sound effects. They allowed sponsors greater hegemony in picking the exact stations where and when their perfectly-produced commercials (and programs) were broadcast. Particularly was this true of spot announcements aired on local stations. In this way, they could be more selective in who heard their advertising messages than before.

While commercials read by station personalities are still a staple of local radio now, ad agencies with national and regional accounts tend to recoil from those live spots. "They think that way ... because they feel restricted to a single voice reading straight copy," proclaimed a source. "Also they worry about consistency. On one station a live announcement could sound excellent and on another, terrible."[6]

Headliners as Spokespersons

On numerous series the headliner, star, master of ceremonies, moderator or otherwise celebrated dignitary personally delivered a sponsor's messages. The reverberating endorsement of the program's hero was considered a good thing by many advertisers. Sometimes an individual expressed a personal word of confidence in the products and services subscribing his salary. (Arthur Godfrey, whom we've met at several points, did so frequently and effectively.) To some clients, a mere recommendation from those so idolized was satisfactory.

A diversionary tactic of this technique occurred when a handful of newscasters, including Raymond Gram Swing and H. V. Kaltenborn and a few more, took a firm stand against commercials delivered by newsmen. According to radio historiographer Erik Barnouw, those electronic journalists "insisted on absolute separation of news and commercial message, at a time when the news field was vulgarized by Gabriel Heatter and others who specialized in the 'clever' integration of sales talk and news, and by sponsors who rejoiced in the practice."[7]

"Preparing his talk on the Nazi invasion of Luxembourg, Belgium, and the Netherlands, Swing was so tortured by the thought of a middle commercial for White Owl cigars that he offered to step aside for some other newsman," Barnouw reported.[8] White Owl decided to dispense with the middle commercial, however, and that dilemma didn't resurface on any Swing newsfeature. When Socony Vacuum consequently signed on to sponsor Swing, the contract ruled out middle commercials altogether. The newsman had won not just a mere skirmish but a battle royal.

Infomercials

Financial advice guru William M. Kiplinger was among the first, and possibly *the* first advertiser, to launch an infomercial on the ether. The style carried the concept of the integrated sales message in the program content one step further: in an infomercial, the *entire program*— not simply a few seconds of direct advertising — was considered the sales message. It is a popular model that has been exploited by television advertisers for years.

Kiplinger, who published a magazine originally titled *Changing Times*, hired radio announcer, host and commentator Sidney Walton to conduct weekend quarter-hour features for his organization. They appeared from 1955 to 1962, initially over NBC and then MBS, under the publication's sobriquet. Walton dealt with personal and business financial issues while at the same time incessantly pushing subscriptions to the magazine. It was truly something different that radio listeners were not accustomed to, catching many by surprise, yet tailored especially to consumer-homeowner-taxpayer interests. There was also a quarter-hour televersion of the show produced for some markets throughout the 1960s and early 1970s. Dropped into local weekend program schedules, the feature filled a niche while paving the way for video infomercials ad nauseam to follow.

Institutional Advertising

Sometimes a sponsor was interested in promoting its business enterprise as opposed to a specific commodity that could be purchased in a retail outlet or ordered from a manufacturer. The strategy might be pursued for any of a number of incentives and possibly for more than one. Institutional advertising, one of the symbols applied to that form, could be employed to raise an underwriter's visibility; to create a favorable impression with its publics; to say something about the organization behind the products it produced and the services it rendered; to establish a platform for corporate opinions on diverse issues, at times becoming a persuasive tactic; to impact the stakeholders of the business (including owners, clients, vendors, employees and industry segments); and for other diverse reasons.

Some of the exceptional expressions of institutional advertising on the air were attributable to E. I. du Pont de Nemours and Company which ended weekly discourses on *The Cavalcade of America* with its signature "Du Pont ... better things for living ... through chemistry" tagline. In the course of time, that expression became intrinsically familiar to the program's audience. The Association of American Railroads, meanwhile, turned its three-minute invective on *The Railroad Hour* into a venue promoting legislation and concerns that impacted the movement of goods and individuals by rail. And the United States Steel Corporation applied its commercial time on the *U.S. Steel Hour* to creating awareness and developing friendships within its industry and beyond. In so doing, these agencies and others were better positioned to aggressively compete in the global arena of intensifying commerce.

Integrating Messages within Programming

One of the revolutionary styles developed for proffering commercial messages in vintage radio was that of blending a portion or all of those pitches within the parameters of the feature itself. When performed shrewdly, it was an efficient and effective means of conveying a client's promotion, almost sneaking it into the program. The assimilated commercial tendered the obvious advantage of gaining the perceptible endorsement of the resident talent, whose presence hinted at a personal stamp of approval whether overtly expressed or silently. His presence or involvement tended to make the whole affair more palatable to listeners, too. The integrated message's appearance in this manner diminished or even avoided an abrupt, sometimes stiff interruption in the continuity of the entertainment flow.

The unique method appeared to work particularly well within the confines of radio comedy series, which often cast the commercial into lighter moments, thereby increasing its acceptance. Using an announcer who was well recognized by both home and studio audiences, it was simple enough to build upon a foundation that was already in existence — e.g., his rapport with the star as witnessed through ongoing interaction — and then turn a commercial into something memorable. Sidekick Harry Von Zell and comedian Fred Allen carried on this exchange one night on Allen's weekly series.

ALLEN: Someone once said that the world stands aside to make way for the man who knows where he's going, and so tonight it gives me great pleasure to make way for a man who knows what he's talking about, Harry Von Zell.
VON ZELL: Don't ever neglect a cold. At the very first sign of a cold, get after it immediately with the faster help of sparkling — er, sparkling — what's the name?
ALLEN: Fred Allen, remember?
VON ZELL: No, no, no, no. The name of the ... I'm awfully sorry. I can't remember the name of what it is that helps fight colds faster. It slipped my mind.
ALLEN: Well, it will come to you. Go ahead, Harry.
VON ZELL: Well, yes, yes, of course. Ladies and gentlemen, this famous product acts quickly, yet it's exceptionally gentle and since the progress of a cold is very fast, the greater speed of — er, er — what it is I'm talking about is especially important in fighting your cold and that's not all, this — er — the name will come to me in a minute — it also helps nature counteract the acidity that so often accompanies a cold. And, ladies and gentlemen, you can check these facts with your own doctor.
ALLEN: You'd better check the name, too, ladies and gentlemen.
VON ZELL: Oh, Fred, you know what I'm talking about.
ALLEN: Why certainly, Harry, you're talking about America's outstanding saline laxative.
VON ZELL: That's it, Fred. The name is ...
ALLEN: The name is — er, er — so many physicians recommend it ...
VON ZELL: Yes, yes, and it helps fight colds faster but what is the name?
ALLEN: Oh, here's a pretty to-do. Wait, Harry, there must be somebody around here who knows. If there is, will you please tell us confidentially ...
AUDIENCE: Sal Hepatica!
ALLEN: That's it, Sal Hepatica! Thank you, ladies and gentlemen.

In the early days of the television sitcom, following Fred Allen's retirement from radio, first Bill Goodwin and then none other than Harry Von Zell were the interlocutors for *The George Burns and Gracie Allen Show*. Each week on CBS-TV they would banter with one or both of principals about Carnation evaporated milk in a tête-à-tête that was an obvious throwback to the integrated commercial style begun on radio. While this format could be adapted by most primetime features headlined by a well-known singer or comic, it probably reached its zenith in applications by the writers of *The Jack Benny Program* and *Fibber McGee & Molly*.

In the former, comedian Benny sparred with announcer Don Wilson over whichever commodity was then sponsoring his show — Jell-O desserts, Grape-Nuts cereals or Lucky Strike cigarettes. Wilson, who was an essential member of the cast and turned up throughout the show, was simply in character as Benny's announcer while extolling the virtues of "six delicious flavors — strawberry, raspberry, cherry, orange, lemon and lime" or whatever the flavor of the night that happened to be underwriting it. Benny was usually nearby to offer a passing aside, otherwise little more than moral support during those levity-laden diatribes from the jolly fat man.

Possibly the most memorable of all the radio features deploying the amalgamated commercial, however, was the zany reactions of the head of household at 39 Wistful Vista, Fibber McGee. One could almost hear the hair stand up on the back of his neck as announcer Harlow Wilcox rang his chimes midway through every Tuesday night show. McGee (comic actor Jim Jordan) knew what was coming and feigned a strong distaste for it, a plug for Johnson Wax. His posture made the commercials all the more bearable and memorable. "What do you want, Wilcox?" McGee snarled one night. "Though as the guy said when he sat on the bee, 'I have a deep-seated suspicion.'"

Many times as Wilcox showed up McGee would be agitated already about something or be busy scheming to prove his worth to the world or to make a million dollars for Molly and "himself" (her designation for McGee). Nevertheless, he'd audibly mutter at the sight of Wilcox, whom he dubbed "Waxy." It was even worse when Molly was present for she would innocently inquire something like: "Tell us, Mr. Wilcox, why do you have such a bright shine on your face?" McGee would groan in response. "Oh Molly, now you've gone and done it!" Without missing a beat, Wilcox was off and running: "That bright shine on my face, Molly, is a reflection of the perfect job I get every time I apply Johnson's Self-Polishing Glo-Coat to my hardwood floors!" McGee interrupted the guest frequently with little rejoinders qualifying his misery: "Oh, my goodness!" or "Good grief, Waxy!" For many fans, those droll reverberations became an anticipated moment, a bona fide focal point of the show.

"Fifty years later," one wag contributed in a recent review, "ironically, sponsors would once again be seeking ways to insert their messages into the programs themselves, as viewers increasingly used technology to avoid sitting through commercials."[9] On rare occasions, the underwriters mention a client's product by name within a show's dialogue. More likely, however, they expose us to transparent references — someone drinking a can of Coke, a George Strait CD playing in the background, a package of Ritz crackers occupying a pantry shelf, checking a Bulova timepiece, using a GE blowdryer, and a Chevrolet Impala sitting in the driveway — all making their way into the sight and sound images reeling by. Their not-so-subtle appearances may seem *natural* in a film, DVD or television drama. But only in a sense: their manufacturers put them there to deliver subliminal sales pitches, and they do so quite effectively. It's a modern, less disruptive spinoff of the commercial integrated into the storyline of yesteryear.

Jingles and Other Music

"Radio babies still can sing jingles they heard half a century ago," maintained one holdover from those halcyon days. "Nearly every radio baby can still sing or whistle the peppy Rinso White tune and, like Johnny, the grinning bellhop, bellow: *Call-l-l-l for-r-r-r Philip Mor-r-r-reees!*"[10] The lyrics to zillions of radio jingles, in fact, still tinkle merrily in the brain as clearly and indelibly as vintage pop melodies.

As distant notes jog our minds and stimulate last-minute additions to shopping lists, advertising music is having an inescapable influence on our lives and on the buying patterns of radio listeners and TV watchers globally. Branding the jingle "advertising's most persuasive tool in the fight to infiltrate and conquer the American mind," an extremely successful jingle creative, Steve Karmen — who introduced us to "Sooner or Later You'll Own Generals," "For All You Do, This Bud's for You" and "We Build Excitement — Pontiac" — depicted melody's sizeable contributions to advertising.[11]

> Though no one likes a salesman, music is a part of the sales team that is welcome. A strong, unique, musical statement can add much to the success of a product. Within the daily deluge of broadcast advertising, a good music track can cut through the clutter and get attention. Sometimes the music in a commercial is the one saving element, changing mediocrity to magic. For a big-budget client, one who produces many spots during each year, a good musical image means that the agency doesn't have to reinvent the wheel each time a commercial is made. Music keeps the ads fresh with friendly nonoffensive repetition.

Who could forget the 1930s *Singin' Sam* commercials for Barbasol shaving cream, having heard them by recording or possibly live? "Bar-ba-sol ... Bar-ba-sol ... no brush, no lather, no rub in ... wet your razor, then begin."

The singing commercial is deeply embedded in America's history. Its roots may be traced nearly a century prior to radio's existence, in reality. Nineteenth century folk songs frequently referred to mercantile and industrial enterprises as in this citation of a railroad: "Oh, the Rock Island line is a mighty good road, The Rock Island line is the road to ride." The Studebaker brothers added a few words to a traditional folk tune in 1883 and dispensed sheet music that included these lyrics: "Wait for the wagon, *the Studebaker wagon*; wait for the wagon and we'll all take a ride!"

The food processing pioneering Washburn-Crosby Company (which later evolved into General Mills, Inc.), owner of Minneapolis station WCCO, summoned a barbershop quartet to introduce the music jingle. Applying the historic singing commercial concept to radio for the very first time, on December 24, 1926, the four vocalists queried: "Have you tried Wheaties? The best breakfast food in the land!"

Almost immediately advertisers began to discover an innovative and matchless method for dispatching their messages, using little songs that the public could evoke or even hum when the radio wasn't turned on. "Specially written musical selections for radio advertising,... masked a sales message in entertainment form," noted one reviewer. These lyrics were typical: "Tasty Yeast is tempting to your appetite; Creamy, wholesome candy, try a luscious bite; Vitamins are hiding in this candy bar; Pep, vim and vigor linger where they are." "As jingles became new tools for mind stimulation," another pundit acknowledged, "they began to be recognized as a foundation upon which to build a long-term advertising image. As the popularity of ad music grew, many sponsors turned to jingles to help serve their advertising needs."

Early jingles told a complete tale—including everything a consumer needed to know about a commodity. Recall the early refrain for a soft drink supplier that began "Pepsi-Cola hits the spot." The lyrics penned by durable *Pepper Young's Family* announcer Alan Kent for client Newell-Emmett advertising agency with music by Herbert Austen Johnson informed buyers how many ounces were in the bottle—twice as much as the other leading vendor's beverage—yet, still only the customary price of five cents. In a four-line verse, it was all the information required. Kent's pitch was adapted to an old English hunting song, "D'ye Ken John Peel?" and the commercial was brought to radio by The Tune Twisters, a male trio consisting of Gene Lanham, Andy Love and Bob Walker.

A pensive critic termed the finished effort "the all-time heavyweight champion of singing commercials."[12] Upon purchasing the Kent-Johnson jingle, the Pepsi-Cola Company aired the plug ad infinitum. It gave the commercial stature and created a legacy. "Running the exact same announcement many times during a concentrated period is a contemporary advertising concept that dates back to the first saturation campaign built around this Pepsi commercial," ascertained the critic.[13]

In the decade from 1934 to 1944, with General Foods Corporation as the underwriter, an unidentified singing collect introduced *The Jack Benny Program* with the lilting, scale-climbing "J-E-L-L...O!" And Henry Aldrich (actor Ezra Stone) and sidekick Homer Brown (Jackie Kelk) were going Benny one better as the same sponsor subscribed their series (*The Aldrich Family*, 1939 to 1951): the pair of youths charmed America by warbling their own high-pitched Jell-O ditty ("Oh, the big red letters stand for the Jell-O fam-i-lee..."). The advertising jingle has been an established ingredient in American marketing since its introduction in the 1920s to the present day.

In addition, as trendsetters allowed their minds to wander, they derived added means of skillfully employing music during broadcast advertising. Sometimes a tune provided a bed underneath the copy, in front of it or behind it. Such variations really came into vogue with the widespread use of transcriptions in which music was added to convey the sales message more prominently. This could include strings, a piano or organ, an instrumental ensemble, or possibly a whole orchestra backing a soloist, several individuals or possibly an entourage.

A few terms that are central to an understanding of music's possibilities include segue (pronounced seg-way), cross-fade, blending, cutting or switching, fade in and fade out.

Segue—The soft velvety movement from one sound to another, each one distinctly separate from others (one ends before the next begins).

Cross-fade—Although dissolving from one sound to another, it occurs when two sounds are crossed, one fading in as the other fades out.

Blending—Pooling two or more sounds and sending them onto the ether concurrently; this can be an amalgamation of dialogue and music, dialogue and sound effects, sound effects and music, or a mixture of the three.

Cutting or *Switching*—Abruptly discontinuing one sound while obtrusively introducing another.

Fade In and *Fade Out*—Turning the volume up or down; it's applied when fading music under the dialogue, bringing it into or taking it out of a commercial.

Microphone Placement and Special Effects

There are five basic microphone positions. When no position is indicated by the script, it is assumed that the "on mike" stance is intended. The five postures include:

On mike — The huckster (hawker, peddler, pitchman, plugger, salesman) is at the microphone.

Off mike — The huckster is some distance from the microphone, conveying the impression that the voice or sound is at a proportionate distance from the physical orientation point of the listener.

Fading on — The huckster moves slowly toward the microphone, indicating to the listener that the huckster is approaching the physical center of the action.

Fading off — The huckster moves from the microphone while speaking, moving away from the central orientation point.

Behind obstructions — It clearly sounds as if there's a barrier (a door, closed window or other object) between the huckster and the focal point of the audience's orientation.

In addition to these variants, a script might call for exploiting some clearly unique microphones. By employing a filter mike, for example, the voice or noise sounds as if it's being heard over a telephone. In such cases, the speaker at the focal point of the audience's orientation is on mike, even though the listener believes the voice is coming through a telephone. Another departure is the echo chamber which generates assorted levels of reverberation. The voice might seem as if it's originating in a never-ending cave or seemingly it could be emanating from a confining closet. Such deviations increase the possibilities for innovation in advertising, providing the copywriter (and hence, the huckster and the advertiser) with still more tools for his arsenal of imagination, inspiration and ingenuity.

Nomenclature

By the middle of the 1920s, even before the formation of the national networks, the effects of commercialization were plainly apparent. A growing number of radio features were named for the outfit underwriting them. They included *The Eveready Hour* (National Carbon Company), *The A&P Gypsies* (The Atlantic & Pacific Tea Company, a grocery chain), *The Ipana Troubadours* (Bristol-Myers, Inc., a toothpaste and other health goods manufacturer), *The Goodrich Zippers* (B. F. Goodrich Company, a tire maker), *The Clicquot Club Eskimos* (The Clicquot Club Company, a ginger ale beverage producer), *The Cities Service Concerts* (Cities Service Company, an oil firm), *The Lucky Strike Dance Orchestra* (American Tobacco Company), *The Atwater Kent Hour* (Kent Electrical Manufacturing Company, a radio maker), *The Betty Crocker Show* (General Mills, Inc.) and the *Voice of Firestone* (Firestone Tire and Rubber Company).

One of the most transient, yet adaptable, duos of the era were the performers Ernie Jones and Billy Hare, who — at the drop of a chord — plied their vocal talents as the namesake headliners of whoever was currently providing their livelihoods. They were, at different times, labeled *The Happiness Boys* (for Happiness Candy Stores), *The Interwoven Pair* (Interwoven Sock Company), *The Flit Soldiers* (Standard Oil of New Jersey), *The Tastyeast Loafers* (Tastyeast Bakers) and *The Best Food Boys* (Richard Hellman, Inc., a mayonnaise and other foodstuffs manufacturer).

Through simple identification, the classification by appellation had the unmitigated ability to constantly reinforce the sponsor's name in the minds of the shopping public. It was like an unending advertising prompt, 24–7. As time elapsed, in the 1930s, more and more organizations entered the name game. Major evening entertainment fare was recognized not for the showmen that topped them or performed steadily but for the clients whose products supported them like these examples.

Fred Astair — *The Packard Hour*
Fred Allen — *The Linit Bath Club Revue, The* [Hellman's] *Salad Bowl Revue, Texaco Star Theater*
Jack Benny — *The Canada Dry Ginger Ale Program, The Chevrolet Program, The General Tire Show, The Jell-O Program, The Grape-Nuts Program, The Lucky Strike Program*
Edgar Bergen and Charlie McCarthy — *The Chase & Sanborn Hour*

Les Brown — *The Sealtest Village Store*
George Burns and Gracie Allen — *The Robert Burns Panatela Program, The White Owl Program, The Campbell's Tomato Juice Program, Maxwell House Coffee Time*
Eddie Cantor — *The Chase & Sanborn Hour, Texaco Town, The Pabst Blue Ribbon Show*
Bing Crosby — *The Cremo Singer, Kraft Music Hall, Philco Radio Time, The Bing Crosby Chesterfield Show, The General Electric Show*
Morton Downey — *The Camel Quarter-Hour, The Coke Club*
Eddie Fisher — *Coke Time with Eddie Fisher*
Phil Harris and Alice Faye — *The Fitch Bandwagon*
Bob Hope — *The Pepsodent Show*
Al Jolson — *The Kraft Program, Shell Chateau, The Lifebuoy Program, The Colgate Program, Kraft Music Hall*
Wayne King — *Lady Esther Serenade*
Peggy Lee — *Kraft Music Hall, The Electric Hour Summer Series, The Chesterfield Supper Club*
Glenn Miller — *Chesterfield Time*
Vaughn Monroe — *The Camel Caravan*
Jack Pearl — *The Lucky Strike Hour*
Dinah Shore — *The Chase & Sanborn Program, The Birds Eye Open House, The Ford Show, The Carnation Contented Hour*
Red Skelton — *Avalon Time*
Kate Smith — *Kate Smith's A&P Bandwagon*
Jo Stafford — *The Raleigh-Kool Cigarette Program, The Colgate Program, The Chesterfield Music Shop, The Chesterfield Supper Club, The Carnation Contented Hour*
Rudy Vallee — *The Fleischman Hour, The Royal Gelatin Hour, The Drene Show*
Fred Waring — *Chesterfield Time*
Paul Whiteman — *The Old Gold Hour, The Pontiac Hour, The Buick Hour, Kraft Music Hall, Woodbury Musical Varieties, Chesterfield Presents, Philco Radio Hall of Fame*
Meredith Willson — *The Signal Carnival, Maxwell House Showboat, The Ford Show Room*
Walter Winchell — *The Jergens Journal*
Ed Wynn — *The Texaco Fire Chief*

Beyond these and shows fronted by other legendary stars, there was *The Armstrong Theater of Today, The Bell Telephone Hour, The Dreft Star Playhouse, The Hallmark Hall of Fame, The Johnson Wax Program* (with *Fibber McGee & Molly*), *The Longines Symphonette, Lux Radio Theater,* [Oxydol's own] *Ma Perkins, The Philip Morris Playhouse, The Railroad Hour* (sponsored by the Association of American Railroads), *Smilin' Ed and His Buster Brown Gang, The Tom Mix Ralston Straightshooters* and scores of additional features with similar sobriquets. Those monikers were obvious cues to the underwriters making listeners' favored features accessible.

Participating Sponsorship

In the early 1950s, one of the ingenious advertising methods that radio cultivated as it attempted to hold the line against encroaching television then starting to seriously carve up its turf was participating sponsorship. The term is sometimes used interchangeably with multiple sponsorship or dual sponsorship. After a longstanding tradition of airing series generally underwritten by solo advertisers — and almost never more than two firms, in the latter case with clients normally alternating weeks or days for their plugs — someone floated the idea of sharing advertising time on given series with two, three or more sponsors.

It could replace the increasing void left by sponsors that were picking up their marbles and moving them to the newer medium as advertising budgets were reallocated to include TV. It could also mean that many medium-sized and even smaller firms that heretofore had been locked out of network radio programming sponsorship — unable to purchase an entire quarter-hour, half-hour or hour-long series — could now enter the market and compete with their rivals. The innovation also had immediate appeal to the network brass which had sought means since the mid–1940s for reducing the programming control exercised by the advertising agencies from the early 1930s.[14]

It was a win-win situation for advertisers and the chains alike. Of course, the listeners were winners, too. Instead of abruptly abandoning the fans' programming favorites, the webs could squeeze out a little more life for many of them after the commercial backers with deep pockets pulled out and left those series behind.

A diversion of this form, partial sponsorship, often meant that an advertiser alternated broadcasts (usually weekly) with one or more non-competing firms on a continuing basis. For instance, General Electric might appear underwriting a certain feature one week and Campbell Soup the following week, then GE, then Campbell. Occasionally, a third vendor was added to such mixes. As audiences and advertisers fled radio, the chains and agencies became quite creative in how they sold and allocated their sole revenue-producing commodity, time.

Premiums

When the sermons of Dr. John Ruthledge, pastor of the nonsectarian Little Church of Five Points, were published in a single collection and offered to listeners of *The Guiding Light* in the late 1930s, Procter & Gamble received more than 250,000 requests from series fans for the complimentary volume.

Not a lot earlier, in 1937, *Teddy's Diary*, purportedly penned by a fictional character in her own handwriting, drew more than 500,000 requests when purveyed by NBC's widely-acclaimed domestic drama *One Man's Family*.

In 1934, after *Today's Children* aired for only a few months on NBC Blue, the audience was told that in return for a flour label, Pillsbury would send a brochure recalling a backstory chronicle of the narrative's central figures, the Moran clan. Within a few weeks, more than 250,000 labels arrived. The trade paper *Broadcasting* subsequently observed on March 1, 1935: "The amazing allegiance of hundreds of thousands of women not only to the members of the cast but to Pillsbury products is a constant source of wonderment even among those professional people who for years have been working with radio."

The same periodical—*Broadcasting*—nevertheless reported on June 15, 1938, that 56 percent of all network series incorporated premium offers into their production. "In 'merchandising' tie-ups the faces of radio characters smiled from cereal packages, comic strips, pencil boxes, shirts, hats, glassware, guns, holsters, lunch boxes, games, dolls," the magazine observed.[15]

With a great deal of triumph, those early enterprising radio underwriters capitalized on the premium (sometimes identified as the mailhook). The technique was applied to intensely involve the listeners in their programs. At the same time, the clients received valuable feedback on the depth of commitment of those tuning in. In the days before the ratings services furnished widespread and extensive data, that interaction became a fairly suggestive hint about how their programs were being received and by whom. Many firms with proficient sales savoir-faire made optimum use of the premium or mailhook as a method of maintaining high levels of audience contact and interest. The outcome netted maximum exposure to their commercials, a primary intent.

It took the marketing savvy of serial packager Duane Jones, who had earlier been on the staff of the Blackett-Sample-Hummert agency, to carry the premium to its definitive extreme. Jones shamelessly integrated charms of all types into the storylines of several programs that he supervised, notably those of B. T. Babbitt, the makers of Bab-O and other cleansing agents. They included the daytime serials *David Harum, Lora Lawton* and *Nona from Nowhere*. For 10 cents and a label from the sponsor's product, listeners might receive a packet of flower seeds "just like those planted by David Harum in his very own garden." The response to that bait brought about unanticipated pandemonium: the show's fanatical admirers responded with over 275,000 labels, each accompanied by a dime, all Babbitt needed to certify it was doing something right.

In the meantime, if Lora Lawton wore a new locket on a chain around her neck, several characters in the narrative made reference to it on successive days. So stunning, so provocative was this little keepsake that fans soon developed an unquenchable desire to possess a similar bauble for themselves. After a few days of whetting the appetites with this enveloping chitchat, during one of the commercials, on-the-ball announcer Ford Bond explained how — for a label from a can of Bab-O and "one thin dime" — one of those lockets "just like the one around Lora Lawton's neck" could be around milady's neck, too! Voilà! The mail pouches and the coffers instantly swelled as tens of thousands of Lawton addicts responded. For years, Babbitt announced a new offer on each of its shows every three or four months, invariably involving its fictional characters in some charade leading to a soon-to-be-announced promotion.

Occasionally a premium came along that was out of the mainstream of the normal bait supplied to listeners. One, also turning up on *David Harum*, surrounded a flake commodity that consumers could turn into their own laundry detergent at home. Lycons recipes were supplied on the product label. On one mid–1940s *Harum* broadcast, announcer Bond proclaimed:

> Now, all of you hog raisers ... helping supply America with fine pork ... accept this free offer: write today for a new 48-page book on farm sanitation. It gives practical, low-cost methods for sanitizing yards and pens. Includes methods that can help make your hogs grow sturdier ... heavier ... so you can market more pounds of pork. Write for your copy today. Address Lycons ... L-Y-C-O-N-S ... care of this station. Ask for the free Lycons farm book.

Nothing, it seemed, was beyond capturing the imaginations of premium purveyors!

Producers on other washboard weepers closely monitored Jones's exploits of premium offers. Few permitted the dramas within their trusts to become conduits serving little more than sponsors' prize giveaways. But many of them—*Aunt Jenny's Real Life Stories, Bachelor's Children, Ellen Randolph, The Guiding Light, Ma Perkins, Myrt and Marge, One Man's Family, The Romance of Helen Trent, Today's Children, Woman in White* and more — were fair game for proffering similar wares that were limited to commercials. Routinely they dangled photo albums, history books, costume jewelry, recipes, cookbooks, sheet music, Libby glasses, Christmas cards, scrapbooks and other merchandise to the faithful. None took the notion to the extremes that Jones and Babbitt did — either in frequency or in causing their heroes and heroines to ooohhh and aaahhh over a "genuine simulated" trinket. That was better held in check for the juvenile adventure series with their surfeit of masks, silver bullets, detective rings, secret mirrors, membership cards and spy thriller storybooks.

The mailhooks for the small fry worked especially well. What mother could deny her dumpling a decoder ring from *Sky King* for merely a label from the jar lid of specially-marked Peter Pan peanut butter, along with the ubiquitous dime for shipping and handling? Of course, that was only the beginning. By one estimate those adolescent-alluring advertisers shipped millions of dollars in merchandise. But the sponsor loyalty it purchased was absolutely priceless for no amount could be registered for that intangible commodity.

Media pundit Leonard Maltin observed: "Shamelessness reached its zenith on the adventure shows for children.... Here, impressionable listeners were wheedled, cajoled, and bamboozled into buying Ovaltine, Quaker's Puffed Wheat, Hot Ralston cereal, and other products because (a) they were enthusiastically endorsed by the show's dashing hero and (b) it was necessary to buy the stuff in order to send away for some swell premium."[16] Maltin pursued a typical scenario in which *Dick Tracy*, in a multi-part story in 1938, sought The Ring of Ocillis which contained a secret compartment with magical powers. "By now the bait is on the hook," explained Maltin. "The show lures its young listeners along, promising a special announcement in a day or two 'that you won't want to miss,' without actually saying that they're going to offer that very ring as a premium. All they're doing is setting the stage and whetting the appetite."[17] Shameless, indeed.

Radio historiographer Jim Harmon published a service to collectors of vintage radio memorabilia by noting hundreds — maybe thousands — of premiums dispatched by the aural kiddie features in one of his works. *Radio Mystery and Adventure and Its Appearances in Film, Television and Other Media*, initially released in 1992 and re-released in 2003, supplies data on the ornaments circulated by more than a dozen late afternoon and early evening juvenile fare, among them: *Captain Midnight, The Challenge of the Yukon, Dick Tracy, The Green Hornet, Jack Armstrong, Little Orphan Annie, The Lone Ranger, Sky King, Superman* and *Tom Mix*.

Author Gerald Nachman, meanwhile, envisioned for his readers what it was like to be on the receiving end of the plethora of merchandise spilling out of the ether that was headed the public's way. Recalling his own experience, he described those arresting long-awaited juvenile show premiums.[18]

> Out of every radio speaker tumbled a veritable cornucopia of chintzy but crucial slide-whistle rings, key rings, siren rings, magnet rings, signature rings, flashlight rings, six-shooter rings, movie rings, microscope and periscope rings, weather rings, Navajo treasure rings, flying saucer rings, Rin-Tin-Tin rings, gold ore rings, and rings with mirrors that enabled the wearer to see if the enemy was creeping up behind him....
>
>   It seemed as if every show offered a ring of some kind, or some sort of a decoding device that, of course, owed its popularity to the war effort. You often stayed tuned in less for the tale than for the cryptogram at the end, which only those owning official decoders could crack. The message, alas, always turned out to be something discouragingly stupid, such as, "Drink Your Ovaltine Today," or, "Be a Good Citizen," but all of that (as well as the fact that the item was made from some cheap wartime alloy) was overlooked in the excitement of receiving anything by mail after long weeks of unbearable patience. Finally, a small brown parcel arrived from Battle Creek, Michigan, home of Kellogg's cereals and premium paradise, you ripped open the box with hot grubby little hands, and suddenly you were the member of a secret society numbering only, say, a select few hundred thousand.

Obviously, you had to have been there.

So popular was the premium phenomenon that, by 1939, *Life* magazine reported that "American civilization has reached the point where cereal packages and soap wrappers are a form of currency." It branded the trend "the fastest-growing, most secretive and most melodramatic branch of advertising." Radio premiums, ascertained *Life*, had built a whole industry on premiums' "'excitement value' ... in comic strip ad and radio script." Those sales gurus surely had to have been doing something right.

Things did not always work without a hitch on those premium-laden promotions, however, at least not consistently the way the advertisers envisioned. In the late 1940s, daytime serial heroine Stella Dallas pursued a lecherous scoundrel to his lair in the far-off Middle East where he had carried Stella's precious adult daughter Laurel ("Lolly Baby" to Stella). That bit of nonsense provided the serial's sponsors (Sterling Drug, Inc.) with a golden opportunity to introduce a premium tied to the plot development. An "exact copy" of a necklace worn by Egypt's Queen Sit-Hat-Nor-U-Net could be any listener's prized possession for only two bits. (Inflation had set in by then.) But just as the premium was about to be announced on the air, the tiny plant that had contracted to make the trinkets temporarily shut down. During the three weeks that Laurel held the culprit at bay, a wordsmith was left holding the bag; the scribe strung out the dialogue in measured words, without any mention of the queen's precious charm, awaiting the opportune moment to introduce it. If the dialogue had proceeded at the normal pace, the sequence would have ended with Stella returning to her home in Boston long before the costume jewelry rolled off the assembly line. When its manufacture began at last, Stella tore into the harem, the narrator offered the premium for a quarter and the perspiring writer resigned from the show. It wasn't the radio premium's finest hour.

Today, nostalgia vendors do a brisk business in sales and distribution of premiums offered during old time radio's heyday. Some hard-to-find items bring top dollar (in reality, thousands of dollars) at Web sites and from dealers that have been fortunate enough to acquire — or hang on to — merchandise that moppets, in particular, patiently awaited in the golden era. For some, many of those "final sales" continue to reflect memories of the advertised brands that were associated with the trinkets. It's one of the lingering legacies of the advertising premium trade, something the originators could hardly have anticipated as they developed such powerfully potent schemes.

Public Service Announcements

A variety of public service sponsors has long existed in radio. The messages of those organizations are commonly aired without accompanying fee. And although money may not change hands in a transaction involving those commercials (for that's precisely what they are), broadcasters don't always provide time to air such "free" spots for altogether noble and selfless reasons. The Federal Communications Commission (FCC)—in existence since June 19, 1934, and preceded since 1927 by the Federal Radio Commission (FRC)—mandated that the airwaves must be open to serve the public in a responsible manner for the express benefit of the public.

Public service interests date back as far as the fourth National Radio Conference that convened in Washington, D. C., on November 9, 1925, at least. Attended by 400 delegates, that body arrived at the conclusion "a prospective licensee [must] offer more than desire and money in order to procure a license."[19] A couple of decades hence, on March 7, 1946, a new government policy manual, *Public Service Responsibility of Broadcast Licensees* (often referred to as the "Blue Book"), was released by the FCC. Directives there declared that licensees must "cater to the needs of nonprofit organizations."[20]

Apparently that could be satisfied in large measure by airing myriad public service announcements combined with a plethora of public affairs and other narrowly-focused sustained programming. As a portion of their compliance, local stations and networks — seeking to renew their licenses from time to time, which were originally issued by the federal agency — invariably documented their exposure made available to service, charitable, academic and governmental agencies on behalf of public welfare (e.g., ecology, education, health, safety, and a multiplicity of added concerns).

A riveting exhibition of the application of PSAs is discovered in the broadcast of NBC's *Young Widder Brown* on December 22, 1955, a daytime serial that is normally cited for attracting a distaff audience. By the mid-1950s, the networks appeared unconcerned with *who* was listening to some of their features. As radio attempted to compete with television for audiences — to fill the time formerly underwritten by paying commercial sponsors while complying with FCC regulations — PSAs of every stripe turned up with little regard for substance or where they aired. This one-minute spot opening *Young Widder Brown* was read by the drama's announcer, George Ansbro.

> Men, don't let time slip by. Start building for your future today as an airman in the United States Air Force. No where else will you find the opportunities open to you as an airman. It's a sure way to go places faster. The Air Force offers you more than 400 different specialized subjects for which you may qualify ... subjects that prepare you for such growing fields as aircraft maintenance ... guided missiles ... air police ... intelligence ... and many more with equal chances for advancement. In the Air Force, you'll learn from top experts. You'll receive training the like of which you couldn't get anywhere else if you paid for it. Yet all the while you learn you'll be paid ... you'll earn while you learn. So make America's future *your* future. See your nearest Air Force recruiter now and go places faster as an airman!

On that same day — December 22, 1955 — in the quarter-hour preceding *Young Widder Brown*, NBC announcer Howard Claney launched the day's chapter of *Stella Dallas* reading this public service announcement:

> Donato Mascotti is the name of man in Italy ... a man who needs your help. He has a wife and seven children. They live in one room that was once a garage. It has rust stone walls and a cement floor. All day long the family huddles around a little pan of glowing coals, their only source of heat. Donato's a junk dealer, and when he works ... well, he can earn as much as a dollar a day. When the weather's bad, he can't work. Seven children ... two adults ... living on an occasional dollar a day. Now what do they eat? Never meat. Never milk for children. Bread ... potatoes ... spaghetti ... but ... never enough of that either. Donato is one of seven million people in Italy called "the underemployed." More than two more million are not employed at all. These are among the many people around the world who need our help this winter. And for just one dollar, they can receive a 22-pound food package in your name through CARE. Join this food crusade today.

Network PSAs were exploited to encourage listeners to support the March of Dimes, the Red Cross, American Cancer Association, Community Chest, Boy Scouts and Girl Scouts of America and similar organizations, plus an absolute surfeit of war-related conservation and patriotic efforts ("Save used fats," "Save gas and rubber — drive your car only when you must," "Save tin foil," "Volunteer your services," "Safeguard energy — use only what you need," "Write to the troops," "Be sure to vote," etc.).

Topics were inexhaustible. Because PSAs were generally proffering ideas, institutions and service opportunities — even though they sometimes requested financial commitments — they may have *seemed* easier to swallow than the sales letters delivered for paying clients. Usually PSAs were of the feel good variety; the contemplative listener observed something beneficial that was greater than him, thereby giving those dispatches at least half-hearted attention.

Sound Effects

The major types of sound effects are (a) recorded and (b) live or manual. While sound technicians were employed by the major networks to provide the din needed for their programs and commercials during the golden age, some of it then — and most of it since — was or is prerecorded. Sound effects may be incorporated into commercials to determine locale or setting, direct attention and emotion by emphasizing specific noises, set time and mood, connote entrances and exits, and create unrealistic effects. The purposes and variables of sound effects seem almost endless.

Soundmen were sometimes pressed into service during the opening of a show, dramatically conveying not only what feature was coming on but — especially — who sponsored it. There was a prevailing theory among radio insiders that if listeners' interest could be drawn for the first 15 seconds of a presentation, the audience was secured for the rest of the show. Sponsors, at least, believed an ear-rousing preamble could be totally convincing for their cause. Here's an example in which the sound effects man was pressed into service, proving the point and earning his keep.

> SFX: Glass crashing followed by shrill police whistles followed by scream of police sirens followed by gunshots and machine guns followed by sneaking in marching feet
> ANNOUNCER: Sloan's Liniment presents ... *Gangbusters*!

The excitement stirred by that one, incidentally, became so notorious that it coined a phrase that found its way into the nation's lexicon: "It's/he's/she's/they're comin' on like gangbusters!"

Here's another memorable instance in which a soundman effectively purveyed the client's product.

> ANNOUNCER: So why use perfumey soaps that only cover up the problem? Use mild and refreshing Lifebuoy soap and you'll never have to worry about ...
> SFX: Foghorn (denoting two notes consistent with Beeee-Ohhhh!)

No commercial would actually mention such an offensive topic in that day. The advertising agency produced the soundman as a substitute for this dirty job. The foghorn caught the country's imagination and it seemed that everybody in the U.S.A. was doing sound effects for awhile. Pals in locker rooms and on the street chided one another about the dangers of ... BEEEEE OHHHHH! If you couldn't get a date, it might be BEEEEE OHHHH was at fault. A source acknowledged: "So identifiable was this effect with an unspeakable personal hygiene problem that the mournful fog horn was elevated out of the mist and into the glare of instant recognition. That made the people at Lifebuoy [Lever Brothers] ecstatic."

Spot Announcements

The first national freestanding spot announcement — as opposed to an integrated spot — is reported to have been sold to an advertiser in 1935 by the Schwimmer and Scott Advertising Agency. Live announcements were extremely flexible while altering them was a common and constant exercise. This is considered the main reason why single verbal radio commercials aired during the pre-television epoch haven't survived in advertising's permanent archives to any appreciable extent.

A few stations went overboard with selling spot announcements.[21] The Federal Communications Commission (FCC) discovered in 1945 that Baltimore's WBAL, an NBC affiliate, programmed 16 spot announcements — one every 2.8 minutes — in a 45-minute timeframe. The station managed to jam 507 spot announcements into a single broadcast week under study that year. It wasn't an isolated case, however. The FCC found that independent station KIEV in Glendale, California, played phonograph records and transcribed music in 88 percent of its airtime during a sample broadcast week. The remaining 12 percent was filled with 1,034 commercial spot announcements and eight public service announcements.

Yet the champion for a single week's study was San Antonio's KMAC which aired 2,215 commercial spot announcements in a 133-hour week, an average of 16.7 spots per hour. Realizing that radio commercials weren't aired then as they are now with six to 10 ads back-to-back but one at a time — the FCC designating about three minutes per primetime half-hour and three minutes per daytime quarter-hour for advertising — those numbers seem extraordinarily out of sync.

Sustaining Programming

While this text is focused on audio advertising, it would be careless to ignore the fact that a significant portion of vintage radio offered its listeners sustained (unsponsored) programming. Radio netted big profits during its halcyon days and nights (from approximately the mid–1930s to the mid–1950s) when its schedules were virtually packed to the brim with commercial features subscribed by well-heeled clients. In those pre- and post-seasons, however — when advertisers weren't nearly as prevalent — the same program hours still had to be filled. The major chains answered the need by supplying sustained series, conceived, produced and financed by the webs themselves.

"During these hours we heard some of the finest quality programs that have been produced," a critic maintained. An accumulation of musical treats, opinion forums, religious and educational features, political debates, book round-table discussions, interviews, amateur talent and public service programming of countless stripes filled the vacant niches. The topic of providing adequate time for sustained fare and at some hours that many people could tune in became an issue itself in some quarters. "Not only are programs ... inadequate in number," said one pundit in the late 1940s, "but the few we are offered actually reach only a small proportion of the listening public.... Without a sponsor, it is becoming more and more difficult for an established sustaining program (let alone a new one) to reach listeners who either are or may become interested in it." The reviewer lamented further: "Thus radio, running in double harness, has been dragged off its true course. The driver has slackened his hands on the reins and let the lead horse of advertising get away with it. The effect on the balance of programs and our diversity of choice has been disastrous."[22]

The major networks produced a handful of attractive sustained series which drew faithful audiences. Among them: *America's Town Meeting of the Air* (1935 to 1956), *The Chicago Theater of the Air* (1940 to 1955), *Church of the Air* (1931 to 1958), *The Columbia Workshop* (1936 to 1947), *Invitation to Learning* (1940 to 1964) and *The National Radio Pulpit* (1925 to 1960s).

Testimonials

Some of the earliest radio advertisers inserted endorsements into their commercials, including sports figures and entertainers, who lauded all manner of consumer goods. Tobacco firms were especially heavy users of testimonials for their assorted cigarette and cigar brands. While most early musical commercials were performed anonymously, an influx of venerated celebrities was added to radio commercials as jingle-singers especially in the years following the Second World War.

In the 1950s, for instance, Ethel Merman was married to the owner of Continental Airlines.

Presumably, it wasn't all that difficult to persuade her to plug her spouse's carrier. A couple of decades later, she was singing in Mailgram spots. Merman was then on her own. "It must be assumed," wrote one journalist about her Mailgram work, "she sang them for the money." Meanwhile, showman Arthur Godfrey blazed a trail in that area long before Merman's arrival on the horizon. The ukulele-brandishing crooner belted out the admonition: "You can search every clime, but at three for a dime, you can't beat a Cremo cigar!" The teeming directory of advertisers that have been underwriters of *Paul Harvey News and Comments* since 1950 strongly sanctions live plugs. "Harvey does the commercials and his association with his advertisers is as important as the copy itself," claimed one wag.

In her memoir, radio soap opera actress Mary Jane Higby recalled an incident that occurred in 1959, after she joined the cast of CBS's *This Is Nora Drake* daytime serial for which she played the lead.[23] She hadn't been there long when she was reminded of something that happened to her almost a quarter-century in her past. Thinking as far back as 1935, she recalled sitting by herself one day in a radio theater. She was practically unnoticed on the stage of a live broadcast of the *Kraft Music Hall* starring Bing Crosby. Momentarily she had a turn at the microphone to make a sales pitch for the sponsor's cheese.

Upon joining the *Drake* cast two dozen years hence, Higby was bemused to hear the drama's opening plug — then on tape — for Chesterfield cigarettes. It wasn't the sponsor that preoccupied her thoughts, however; it was *who* was chanting "Sound off! Sound off! Sound off for Chesterfield!" over the din of a drum and bugle corps. In the twilight of network radio's heyday, Bing Crosby and Bob Hope were trilling commercials for the cigarette maker. And in some kind of misplaced irony, Higby thought, *she* was now the star and Crosby was selling the client's commodity *for her*! For a fleeting moment there, she pondered what had transpired. Higby acknowledged that she could fully appreciate the fact that all things eventually do seem to come full circle.

Sometimes make-believe characters were powerful influencers just by being who they were. In one study, 61 percent of women claimed they used the merchandise advertised on the daytime serials they followed.[24] "I am kidded by everybody because my pantry shelf is full of radio brands," one acknowledged. "The programs help me, so I've got to help the products." A woman used a face cream purveyed on *The Romance of Helen Trent* "because she is using it and she is over thirty-five herself and has all those romances."

Voiceovers

Voiceovers are generally considered to apply to motion pictures, videos, television and other forms of unseen visualizations. But they occur in radio as well. One source noticeably expands the form, ascribing a technique "by which any disembodied voice is broadcast live or pre-recorded in radio, theater, industrial shows, fashion shows, presentations, television commercials, television programs, animation and live-action films." Defined by Webster, it is succinctly "the voice of an unseen narrator speaking." It is prevalent in the aural arena as well as the visual one, particularly in commercial delivery. Certain rules apply. Voiceovers can be jingles or buzz words a sponsor has drilled into a consumer's mind again and again. They can be the lead-in to a characterization or the unspoken voice of authority urging audience members to buy. Especially is this germane at a commercial's close, a voiceover often following a bit of narrative exchange. The voiceover announcer puts the period at the end of the sentence with possibly no more than "Lux — the soap of beautiful women." The tagline is the reinforcement for all that preceded.

Vintage radio inaugurated the voiceover. Before effective sound recording, announcers were live in the studio with the remainder of a program's cast, crew, musicians, etc. Nameless voice actors inserted a line or lines into commercials (or programming) specified in the scripts. An excellent example is the Pall Mall cigarette advertising for the American Tobacco Company heard on multiple series. In that one-minute commercial, repeated possibly hundreds of times over several seasons on a handful of primetime radio features every week, Ernest Chappell spent 55 seconds extolling the virtues of smoking Pall Malls (it "travels the smoke further," whatever that meant). After Chappell completed his hard-sell plug, voiceover announcer Cy Harrice, who had been patiently standing by the microphone, added in his deep basal timbre the seductive line: "And ... they are mild." George Ansbro, who recalled this explicit commercial in his memoir, said Chappell was "less than happy" with their compensation arrangement. "Cy Harrice received exactly the same remuneration for his 5 seconds of work as Ernie received for 55 seconds," Ansbro reported.[25]

As time passed, the art of voiceovers became a professional byproduct in itself. Today plenty of busy actors — never seen by audiences, whose names are also totally unknown to them — spend their working lives exclusively in voiceover roles. It's another subculture whose roots are deeply imbedded in radio history.

Appendix C: A Glossary of Advertising and Broadcasting Jargon

ABC (American Broadcasting Company) It originated as the Blue network of the National Broadcasting Company in January 1927. When the Federal Communications Commission ordered NBC to divest itself of one of its two webs to avoid domination, the Blue was spun off in 1943 with NBC retaining its Red hookup. The Blue network renamed itself ABC in 1945. At this writing, it is owned by the Walt Disney Company based in Burbank, California.

Account Client of an advertising agency.

Account Executive Advertising agency liaison representing the outfit to the client.

Advertisement Paid communication in which the underwriter is typically identified.

Advertising Agency A service business that creates and places client advertising; it conducts marketing and branding strategies, sales promotions and offers neutral opinions on vending services and wares.

Advertising Manager Organizational executive who administers his employer's advertising strategies.

Affiliates/Affiliated Stations Local broadcasting stations which are (or were) linked to networks that fed them programming, both commercial and sustained (unsponsored) series. Although affiliates received only a fraction of their accustomed time charges for airing a network program, they gained by selling commercial advertisements (spot announcements) immediately before and after chain-generated shows and during station break or station ID (identification) periods at elevated rates. They could do so because advertisers wished to capitalize on the sizeable audiences attracted by expensive network features.

Agent Artists' representative who lobbies for the subject's hire and fees.

AFRA (American Federation of Radio Artists) Labor union formed in 1937 of announcers, actors and added performing talent; body renamed the AFTRA (American Federation of Radio and Television Artists) in 1952.

AFTRA (American Federation of Television and Radio Artists) Labor union of announcers, actors and added performing talent in multiple broadcasting mediums growing out of the AFRA in 1952.

American Research Bureau (ARB) Surveys conducted by this market study firm are helpful planning tools for advertisers and networks.

Analog Recording broadcast material non-digitally.

ATR Audiotape recorder.

Audition Tryout for potential artists, commercials or programs in environment approximating a broadcast presentation.

Avail (Availabilities) Part of a media buy designating time that may be purchased and based on a client's total advertising commitment, readiness to obligate financially and schedule manifold commercials spread throughout a longer timeframe; entails a broader or recurring purchase to acquire select spots.

Background Music, sound effects, speech or other din behind dialogue.

Backtiming Relating the remaining time in a program to leftover script fragments; may require optional script endings to match varying lengths.

Balance Placing speakers, music and sound effects at a microphone so the desired outcome is attained.

Bed A musical underpinning.

Billboard Opening announcement; listeners learn what to anticipate during a broadcast.

Billing Mention of artists and their explicit contributions.

Billings Fees charged to clients by advertising agencies.

Bit Small part or role in a commercial or program; individual with a fleeting appearance may be referred to as a *bit player*.

Blending Combining and simultaneously airing two or more distinct sounds.

Board Fade Routine indicating lapse of time or scenery change in a script; realized by fading (turning off) microphones in the studio and — after a momentary pause — fading into the new scene.

Bridge Normally music, sound that ties two successive sectors of a radio feature together; may also indicate a lapse of time, locale change or mood shift.

Bumper Substance added to the central ingredient of a commercial, either as a frontispiece or finale (preceding or following the message content), or to the wind-up of a program with time to spare.

CAB (Cooperative Analysis of Broadcasting) A non-profit ratings service launched by the Association of National Advertisers in 1930, organized by Archibald Crossley, and popularly known as the Crossleys.

Campaign A coordinated advertising effort with a specific theme and intent; it may involve more than a solitary medium (radio, television, magazines, newspapers, billboards, product packaging, sales promotion innovations, etc.).

Cast Artists hired to function in a commercial or broadcast.

CBS (Columbia Broadcasting Company) It began as United Independent Broadcasters, Inc., on January 27, 1927. Within three months, the fledgling operation was renamed the Columbia Phonograph Broadcasting System after the latter enterprise took an interest. The arrangement collapsed almost immediately. United resumed the role of sole owner, renaming it the Columbia Broadcasting System. A short time afterward, teetering on the verge of financial ruin, the outfit was sold to cigar entrepreneur William S. Paley and his family. Paley became president and a 16-station hookup started broadcasting network programming under the Columbia banner (later, CBS) on September 18, 1927. After being under the umbrella of global media empire Viacom, CBS Radio became one of several units forming a new CBS Corporation effective January 3, 2006. Its headquarters is in New York City.

Chain A network of affiliated outlets linked by wires during radio's golden age (now by advanced technology, i.e., satellite); also known as net, hookup or web.

Chain Break Network interruption for national or local commercials.

Client's Booth (Sponsor's Booth) Soundproof space framed by a glass panel; a distinctive spot overlooking a radio studio where advertisers observe a program while listening over a speaker.

Coincidental Method A schema of audience measurement created by C. E. Hooper in the 1930s; people received telephone inquiries about their listening habits as a show aired.

Cold Speaking without verbal introduction or musical lead-in.

Cold Copy Announcement read live without rehearsal.

Commercial Broadcast advertisement.

Conflict Occurs when an artist is scheduled for multiple rehearsals or performances in tandem.

Contests Conduits for creating interaction between a sponsor's program and the home or studio audience, thereby escalating the awareness and image of advertised brands; sometimes requires purchasing a proffered commodity.

Continuity Scripted broadcast copy.

Control Board Devices that modify sound levels of all radio microphones, turntables and tapes; can blend output of multiple sources; also called switcher.

Control Booth (Monitor Booth) Soundproof room with plate glass window overlooking a radio studio where a program is directed, balanced and released to the network line (or ether).

Co-op Announcement Network commercial with more than one sponsor.

Copywriter At times limited exclusively to commercial writers; or an artist penning broadcast continuity.

Cowcatcher A pithy commercial at the beginning of a broadcast (sometimes read cold), promoting a separate commodity from one pushed elsewhere on the same show.

CPM (Cost Per Thousand) With "M" symbolizing the Roman numeral for 1,000, the CPM is figured by dividing a commercial's (or ad's) fee by the number of thousand households it reaches; sponsors apply a weighted or demographic CPM, too, sorting out an audience segment classified as primary prospects.

Credit Mention of an advertised commodity or names of those on a show.

Cross-Fade Melting from one sound into another.

Cross Plug Promotional message for a separate program aired by the network (or local station); or may be an announcement for another of an advertiser's goods or services.

Crossleys (Crossley Surveys) First national radio ratings service in the U.S., (1930) named for its founder, A. M. Crossley; fostered by the Association of National Advertisers.

Cushion Show segment that can be cut so the director can get the show off the air on time.

Cuts Show segments deleted by the director before or during a broadcast.

Cutting Shifting suddenly from one sound (or frame, in TV) to another.

Dead Mic Microphone that is turned off or disconnected.

Demographics Data revealing certain traits of listening (or viewing) audience.

Dress Last practice before air or recording; commercial or program treated as if on the air.

Drive Time Hours when a large portion of the audience is in transit; often generates higher commercial rates as the number of listeners spirals upward.

Echo Chamber (Echo) Studio section providing a hollow sound for speech or instrument; echo can be gained by a mechanical apparatus linked to radio gear, too.

Endorsement Affirmation of a commoner or celebrity in a commercial to underscore the advertised intent; sometimes referred to as testimonial.

ETs (Electrical Transcriptions) Although it had many weaknesses, a primitive method of recording commercials and programs that surfaced about 1929.

Fade/Fade In/Fade Out Measured introduction or evaporation of radio sound (or TV image).

Farm Out Occasion when an organization disperses work to an unaffiliated specialist as opposed to finishing it in its own shop.

Federal Communications Commission (FCC) Authoritative panel vested with making decisions that determine ultimate rights for all broadcasting media.

Federal Trade Commission (FTC) Authoritative panel holding some regulatory control over advertising on the airwaves, in print and other formats.

Fee Cost for services rendered to a client by an agency or advertising practitioner.

Feed Transmission from a network, from one station to another, or from a remote site.

Filter Mechanical device that distinguishes between two parties in a telephone conversation.

Fluff An error in reading; also known as a bloop, butch or boot.

Four A's Trade association: American Association of Advertising Agencies.

Freelance Self-employed advertising specialist (e.g., artist, copywriter, media buyer, photographer, musician).

Full-Service Agency Ad agency providing total advertising functions (creative services, marketing, media buying, planning, research) for clients.

Full-Service Station A contemporary radio outlet bearing multiple (two or more) formats, perhaps music, news, talk, features, sports, etc.; set apart from a narrowly-focused outlet offering a dominant format or service (i.e., music or talk). Note: Virtually all stations were full service during network radio's halcyon era although there would have been little need to certify them as such.

Golden Age Subject to individual interpretation, the heyday of network radio; often deemed the late 1920s to the early 1960s or a shorter phase of the period.

Hitchhike or Hitchhiker Pithy commercial at the very end of a broadcast, promoting a separate commodity from one pushed elsewhere on the same show.

Hooperatings Named for audience measurement specialist C. E. Hooper; a routine relying on coincidental testing (telephoning listeners as shows aired) in distinction to the earlier Crossleys, which waited a day to make similar inquiries.

Hot Mic A microphone that is on and thereby sensitive to sound.

ID (Station Identification) Pause in which local outlets give their call letters.

Image Opinion of a commodity or organization.

In-House Whatever an organization completes internally.

In the Beam Within operative reach of a microphone.

Infomercial A program-length commercial; information dispensed is a vehicle for reinforcing a product, service or idea.

Institutional Advertising Promotion for an organization that boosts its image instead of plugging the commodities or services it supplies.

Intro Customary matter introducing every program or designated segment within a program in a series; also dubbed stock opening.

Jingle Score and lyrics appearing in a commercial.

Kill Portion of speech, music or sound effects a director orders for omission.

Madison Avenue Apex of the New York City advertising commune; refers to a proliferation of agencies in the heart of midtown Manhattan, concentrated in the borough's east side.

Market Sector of the populace identified as present and impending patrons for an entity.

Marketing Actions engaged in to produce, promote, sell and distribute goods and services.

Marketing Communications Advertising, public relations and sales promotion, combined actions that promote an initiative, good or assistance.

Mass Advertising (Commercialization) Advertising aimed at the general population.

MBS (Mutual Broadcasting System) It originated in the summer of 1934 when a quartet of imposing radio stations agreed to generate programming for each other. Interconnecting by wire, they offered shows to advertisers at group rates. They included WOR (Newark), WGN (Chicago), WLW (Cincinnati) and WXYZ (Detroit). On September 29, 1934, they renamed an earlier provisional Quality Network the Mutual Broadcasting System. After MBS shifted holders multiple times, it finished its run in the portfolio of California-based syndicator Westwood One, effective September 1985. MBS operations ceased April 17, 1999, although the Mutual sobriquet remains at this writing in Westwood One's arsenal.

Media Conduits imbuing society with advertising, amusement and data.

Merchandising Actions that encourage retail sales.

Mic Microphone.

Mix Combining several sound elements in radio onto a single tape or track.

Mood Music Melody priming listeners for a scenario; can create an aura when in the background.

MOR Middle-of-the-road, a radio format uniting popular and standard music.

MU Music.

NBC (National Broadcasting Company) It was formed September 9, 1926, by three shareholders: Radio Corporation of America (50 percent), General Electric Corporation (30 percent) and Westinghouse Corporation (20 percent). The network epoch of radio broadcasting began as NBC hosted a four-hour extravaganza from New York's Waldorf Astoria Hotel plus remote locales on November 15, 1926. That inaugural gala was received by 25 outlets as far away as Kansas City. NBC added a second national chain in January 1927. The original web was designated the Red and the second the Blue. The two chains eventually became the property solely of RCA. When the FCC forced NBC to dispense with one of its hookups in the early 1940s to avoid a monopoly, NBC kept the Red (referred to exclusively as NBC thereafter) and sold the Blue (renamed ABC in 1945). In late 1986, RCA was acquired by General Electric. In July 1987, GE sold NBC Radio to California-based syndicator Westwood One. For a few years, the lingering remnants of a once robust chain persisted, furnishing news and features. While GE still licenses the NBC moniker to Westwood, it hasn't been promoted since the 1990s.

Nemo The place a broadcast airing outside a studio originates.

Nielsens Sobriquet for system developed by A. C. Nielsen Sr. that superseded the Hooperatings in the late 1940s as the primary audience measurement service.

Off Mic Speaker reads a script while faintly out of microphone beam, usually to indicate expanse between two people in a commercial or program arena.

On Mic Speaker is situated at the microphone, a location used if none other is specified.

On Speculation Work a client buys if it is acceptable and is placed into service.

Outro Repetitive matter appearing at the close of every program or in specific portions of a program in a continuing series; is also dubbed stock close.

Outtake Matter recorded in preparing a show (or commercial) but deleted in the final tape (or film).

Owned-and-Operated Station (O&O) A broadcasting outlet licensed to and managed by a firm that also controls a network.

PA (Public Address) The microphone-loud speaker schema that lets a studio audience hear voices onstage.

Pad Inserting speech, music or sound effects to fill unused air time.

Participating Announcement Commercials of more than one advertiser sharing the cost of a program; sometimes tagged multiple or dual sponsorship.

Payoff Laugh line of a joke or gag; also the final line of a scene, tale or scenario.

Per Diem Daily fee charges.

PI Per inquiry advertising for which a publisher or broadcaster is compensated based on the inquiry numbers generated by an ad or commercial.

Pick-Up Point of origination of a broadcast or broadcast segment.

Plug A paid or unpaid proclamation over the air; also known as a pitch, commercial, message, promo, announcement.

PR (Public Relations) Actions designed to net favorable perceptions without buying time (commercial) or space (ad).

Premium Incentive provided listeners for ordering or purchasing something.

Primetime Evening broadcast hours when audiences generally swell and advertising rates reach their peak.

Product Manager Official on an advertiser's staff who administers marketing and advertising functions of a product or product line; aka Brand Manager.

Promo Promotional announcement; may be paid or unpaid.

Promotion Actions beyond advertising that support sales.

Prospect Impending buyer; possesses capital, sanction and intent to purchase.

PSA Public Service Announcement.

Psychographics Listener studies that reach beyond demographics, including the attitudes, beliefs and behavior of the audience.

Puffery Embellished claims of an advertiser.

Pull Reaction derived by an advertisement or commercial.

Punch Announcement read with inflated accent.

Rate Card A grid depicting a station's charges for commercials — purchasing time based on time of day they are to air, how many and their length; rates may continue until further notice or alter daily as ratings move, or as rates at other stations and cost of buying ads in other media in the market are considered.

Ratings Percentage of all radio (or TV) households tuned to a particular series.

Ratings Services Organizations that conduct audience measurement surveys, determining who is hearing (or viewing) programming, what they are listening to (or seeing), when and possibly under what conditions.
Reach/Frequency Reach gauges how many individuals hear a commercial while frequency gauges how many times a listener may hear a pitch; advertisers plan campaigns with both figures as goals, thereby determining valid success.
Recall Method An audience measurement scheme created by A. M. Crossley; radio listeners were telephoned and asked what hey heard on the previous day — information valuable to advertisers, program creators and network schedulers.
Red Book Reference to *The Standard Directory of Advertising Agencies* or *The Standard Directory of Advertisers.*
Remote Commercial, program or other broadcast component generated from outside a studio and typically aired live.
Repeat Second show staging required by multiple time zones (until recording became widespread in the late 1940s); on the West Coast, early show aired to Eastern zone; repeat show aired from East Coast to Pacific zone.
ROI Return on investment.
Sales Promotion Marketing action in a limited timeframe netting short-term interest and applying techniques like contests, coupons, premiums, sales discounts, samples, sweepstakes, etc.
SE Sound Effects.
Segue Transitioning from one radio sound source to a new one (phonetically pronounced seg-way).
Service Announcement Pithy informational message, similar to the PSA format, though not automatically conveying public service content.
Set-Up Occurs when microphones and instruments are positioned in a studio to achieve a satisfactory balance of speech, music and sound effects.
SFX (Sound Effects) Sound creating impressions in a listener's mind (e.g., door opening and closing, traffic, footsteps, etc.).
Share Percentage of all radio (or TV) sets operating at an explicit time that is tuned to a precise program.
Sitcom Radio (or TV) situation comedy series.
Sponsored Program One underwritten by an outfit on which its ideas, wares or services are proffered.
Spot (Spot Announcement) Commercial message delivered most often between network programs during the golden age; prevalent in the modern radio environment virtually everywhere due to few solo-sponsored radio series.
Spread Stretching a commercial, announcement or program to fill time; also refers to time in a show allowed for audience reaction.
Station Representative (Rep) Ad firm that sells commercial time to national and regional advertisers on behalf of radio stations.
Stop Set Break in radio programming giving an opportunity for commercials and other station-related announcements to be aired.
Sustained Program One for which there is no paying customer, supplied by a network or station.
System Cue The words "This is _____, the _____ Broadcasting Company" (or "System") was the tip-off to local stations that the ball was in their court, signifying the end of a program except for any whose duration extended beyond 30 minutes, with IDs given at one or more intervals during those aircasts.
Tag Announcer's finale to a current installment; might promote successive chapters.
Talent Anyone in a commercial or on a show (e.g., announcer, actor, vocalist, instrumentalist, newscaster, etc.).
Talk Idiom referencing a series concentrating on interviews, conversations and other all-speech formats.
Talk-Back Microphone in the Control Booth linked to a speaker in the studio so the director and cast can converse.

Target Market/Audience Desired recipients of advertising and programming based on demographics or psychographic measurement.

TC Transcontinental, or coast-to-coast hookup.

Tease Program portion, announcement, intro or other mechanism used to build audience interest.

Throw It Away Words to be read with less stress than usual.

Universe Aggregate audience forming prospects for an idea, good or service.

Upscale Prospects in the high end of the social stratum determined by education, income and status.

VI Volume Indicator, a meter giving a graphic image of sound volume.

Voiceover Words of an unseen narrator adding to a commercial or program.

Chapter Notes

PART I

Chapter 1

1. Charles Hull Wolfe. *Modern Radio Advertising* (New York: Printers' Ink, 1949), p. 611.
2. Ibid., p. 614.
3. A preponderance of documented sources assigns 1450 as the correct date for this invention although there is debate about it. At least one historian moves it as early as 1440 while another suggests 1451.
4. Julius Caesar ordered a daily activities sheet, *Acta Diurna* (Daily Events), posted throughout Rome in 59 B.C. The earliest known printed newspaper has been traced to 748 in Beijing.
5. The preponderance of data in the timeline was adapted from several texts included in the bibliography plus these Web sites: http://adage.com/century/TIMELINE, http://www.junkbusters.com, http://www.oaaa.org, http://scriptorium.lib.duke.edu.
6. Documentation cited is from *Advertising Age*. Some sources claim this occurred in 1841 or 1842.
7. Some sources claim *Printer's Ink* did not launch until 1893 although there appears to be compelling evidence to the contrary.
8. http://www.smart90.com/nathanstubblefield
9. After constructing the first power generating station at Niagara Falls, Fessenden made the unsubstantiated claim of himself: "I invented radio, sending the first wireless voice message in the world on Dec. 23, 1900." See http://www.icce.rug.nl.
10. There is disagreement about this date, at least one source stating that Marconi sent and received his initial wireless signals across his dad's estate at Bologna, Italy, in 1895. Subsequent achievements: Marconi flashed the first wireless signals across the English Channel on March 27, 1899; and he intercepted the first transatlantic signal — the letter S — in Newfoundland, dispatched from Poldhu, England, on December 12, 1901.

Chapter 2

1. Nicholas J. Cull, and David Culbert and David Welch, *Propaganda and Mass Persuasion: A Historical Encyclopedia, 1500 to the Present* (Santa Barbara, CA: ABC-CLIO, 2003), p. 6.
2. Charles Hull Wolfe, *Modern Radio Advertising* (New York: Printers' Ink, 1949), p. 610.
3. Bruce Bliven, "How Radio Is Remaking Our World," *Century*, June 1924.
4. Wolfe, p. 620.
5. Jon D. Swartz, and Robert C. Reinehr, *Handbook of Old-Time Radio: A Comprehensive Guide to Golden Age Radio Listening and Collecting* (Metuchen, NJ: Scarecrow Press, 1993), p. 4.
6. There were other broadcast pioneers that some historians have cited for their early and historic contributions. In 1909, prolific inventor Charles David Herrold, operator of Herrold College of Engineering and Wireless at San Jose, California, opened a radio-telephone station as a promotional tool for his academic institute. His station became KQW in 1921 and then KCBS, San Francisco, in 1949. University of Wisconsin physics professor Earle Melvin Terry directed his students in voice and music transmissions in 1917 on experimental radio-telegraph station 9XM, which had been launched three years earlier. By January 3, 1919, daily weather reports began. 9XM eventually became Madison's WHA which today brands itself "the nation's oldest broadcast station." The English Cripps family, consisting of newspaper publishers and bookbinders James Edmund and William John Cripps, who changed their surname to Scripps after arriving in America, founded Detroit station 8MK, later renamed WBL, and then WWJ. The outlet purports that on August 20, 1920, it "became the first radio station in the world to broadcast regularly scheduled programs." On September 10, 1920, ex-shipboard wireless operator Fred Christian set up a five-watt transmitter in his home in Hollywood, California, and — over the airwaves — began playing recordings that he had borrowed from music stores. His station became Los Angeles' KNX in March 1922; it was sold to a newspaperman in 1924 and was purchased by CBS in 1936. In the meantime, following the WWJ and KDKA developments of 1920, the U.S. Department of Commerce licensed 32 broadcast stations in 1921 and 254 more in 1922. Radio put

down permanent roots. Source: http://members.aol.com/jeffl070/70.html

7. Bob Schulberg, *Radio Advertising: The Authoritative Handbook* (Lincolnwood, IL: NTC Business Books, 1989), p. 15.

8. Conflicting authorities are unclear on whether WBNY first went on the air in 1921 or 1922.

9. Portions of this commercial were combined from dual sources: Gleason L. Archer, *History of Radio: to 1926* (New York: American Historical Society, 1938), pp. 397–398; and Bob Schulberg, *Radio Advertising: The Authoritative Handbook* (Lincolnwood, IL: NTC Business Books, 1989), p. 16.

10. The precise fee is in question with at least one respected source intimating that the commercial time period was sold for $100 without specifying if that covered a single or multiple broadcasts. The figures in the text are provided by Erik Barnouw, widely considered one of the medium's most knowledgeable, thorough and reputable investigators.

11. Alfred Balk, *The Rise of Radio, from Marconi through the Golden Age* (Jefferson, NC: McFarland, 2006), p. 65.

12. Charles A. Siepmann, *Radio's Second Chance* (Boston: Little, Brown, 1947), p. 12.

13. Browning King had originated a *Wednesday Night Dance* series over WEAF as early as April 25, 1923, which, according to a critic, "offered pleasant entertainment accompanied by brief sponsor identification without attempt to sell specific merchandise." The feature introduced two factors that became staples of radio advertising: a sponsor identification line at the opening and a crediting line linking entertainment and sponsor by assigning the advertiser's name to the orchestra.

14. Paying celebrities big bucks for their appearances began early. WEAF compensated humorist Will Rogers with a check for $1,000 for adding colorful jesting to the more serious returns that announcer Graham McNamee gave listeners on election night in 1924. It was a check, by the way, that Rogers forgot to cash until the ad agency called his attention to it six weeks afterward.

15. Susan Smulyan, *Selling Radio: The Commercialization of American Broadcasting, 1920 to 1934* (Washington, DC: Smithsonian Institution Press, 1994), pp. 106–107.

16. The inaugural broadcast, a four-hour extravaganza aired from New York's Waldorf-Astoria Hotel with pickups from the several points east of Kansas City, occurred on November 15, 1926. It initiated a new day in delivering amusement and information to far-flung audiences tuning in simultaneously.

17. Public Law No. 632, February 23, 1927, 69th Congress. An Act for the regulation of radio communications, and for other purposes.

18. Charles A. Siepmann, *Radio, Television and Society*, (New York: Oxford University Press, 1950), pp. 44–45.

19. Smulyan, p. 103.

20. Most vaudeville performers had disregarded radio in the 1920s because it paid so little or nothing and was equipped with microphones rather than appreciative live audiences. Vaudevillians were normally nomads, having little time to remain stationary for broadcast gigs. As recognized entertainment figures, the stars of the period wouldn't and couldn't accept roles that ignored their personae.

21. Siepmann, 1947, p. 62.

22. Ibid., p. 65.

23. *Broadcasting* reported in its February 4, 1946, issue that General Mills was so satisfied with the job radio was doing for it that the firm had committed half of its $10 million advertising budget for 1946 to that medium.

24. The figures in the next three paragraphs are adapted from Christopher H. Sterling, and John M. Kittross, *Stay Tuned: A Concise History of American Broadcasting*. 2nd ed. (Belmont, CA: Wadsworth 1990), pp. 638–639.

25. Sterling and Kittross, pp. 211–212.

26. Leonard Maltin, *The Great American Broadcast: A Celebration of Radio's Golden Age* (New York: Penguin Putnam, 1997), p. 165.

27. Sterling and Kittross, p. 269.

28. Ibid., p. 333.

29. Siepmann, 1947, p. 134.

Chapter 3

1. In contemporary marketing, some advertising is produced by an advertiser's own staff, referred to as *in house*, omitting the use of a professional agency altogether. Some clients engage the services of multiple agencies, meanwhile, not the norm in the early days of advertising agencies.

2. Some scholars claim this occurred one or two years earlier while *Advertising Age* puts it at 1843.

3. JWT claims to be the first agency to invent copy and layouts, build the first full service ad agency, pioneer ad careers for women, produce the first sponsored TV program, develop account planning, and create the first international network. Recently, JWT employed more than 8,500 staff in 300-plus offices in 87 countries serving in excess of 1,200 clients. Still headquartered in New York City while under the WPP amalgamation operating in London, JWT is today ostensibly the largest advertising agency in the U.S. and the fourth largest in the world.

4. http://www.answers.com/topic/advertising

5. Erik Barnouw, *The Golden Web: A History of Broadcasting in the United States, Vol. II—1933 to 1953* (New York: Oxford University Press, 1968), p. 16.

6. *Variety Radio Directory, 1937–38* (New York: Variety), p. 731.

7. All of these statistics were supplied by Charles A. Siepmann, *Radio's Second Chance* (Boston: Little, Brown, 1947), p. 66.

8. Ibid., pp. 67, 65–66.

9. Leonard Maltin, *The Great American Broadcast: A Celebration of Radio's Golden Age* (New York: Penguin Putnam, 1997), p. 154.

10. http://www.museum.tv.htm

11. Sally Bedell Smith, *In All His Glory: The Life of William S. Paley, The Legendary Tycoon and His Brilliant Circle* (New York: Simon and Schuster, 1990), pp. 227, 258.

12. , Christopher H. Sterling, and John M. Kittross *Stay Tuned: A Concise History of American Broadcasting*. 2nd ed. (Belmont, CA: Wadsworth, 1990), p. 112.

13. Ralph Hower, *The History of an Advertising Agency: N. W. Ayer & Son at Work, 1869 to 1949* (Cambridge, MA: N. W. Ayer & Son, 1949), p. 168.
14. Adopted from Charles Hull Wolfe, Modern Radio Advertising, (New York: Printers' Ink, 1949), pp. 313–318.
15. http://www.ripleywoodbury.com

Chapter 4

1. Susan Smulyan, *Selling Radio: The Commercialization of American Broadcasting, 1920 to 1934* (Washington, DC: Smithsonian Institution Press, 1994), pp. 85–86.
2. Christopher H. Sterling, and John M. Kittross, *Stay Tuned: A Concise History of American Broadcasting.* 2nd ed. (Belmont, CA: Wadsworth, 1990), p. 126.
3. Erik Barnouw, *A Tower in Babel: A History of Broadcasting in the United States, Vol. I — to 1933* (New York: Oxford University Press, 1966), p. 270.
4. Sterling and Kittross, p. 126.
5. Ibid.
6. Ibid., p. 186.
7. The Hooper organization and *Variety*, a major published source of data surrounding the entertainment industry, were at the forefront of TV ratings information prior to 1950.
8. In the decade of the 1950s, widely considered the last of radio's golden age, just five TV shows topped the Nielsens — *Texaco Star Theater*, starring Milton Berle (1950–51, NBC); and the rest all CBS entries: *Arthur Godfrey's Talent Scouts* (1951–52); *I Love Lucy* (1952–55 and 1956–57); *The $64,000 Question* (1955–56) and *Gunsmoke* (1957–61).
9. By the late 1940s, the number of cities in which Hooper conducted research increased to 36. The specific number of calls during a half-hour broadcast was pegged at 1,470 in that era, presumably translating into 2,940 hourly. See Charles Hull Wolfe, *Modern Radio Advertising* (New York: Printers' Ink, 1949), pp. 68, 70.
10. Little was left to chance in collecting usable and bona fide information. During the 13-minute work periods, company supervisors occasionally called the homes of reporters. A busy line suggested that a reporter was on the job. Calling back during the brief rest period, the supervisor obtained the telephone numbers of a few respondents to whom the reporter had just talked, then called those respondents to verify reports.
11. *Time*, May 25, 1942; September 21, 1942.
12. In the twentieth century, and possibly to date, the highest numbers for a commercial broadcast occurred on October 19, 1948, when former radio showman Milton Berle — in his first season on television — earned a 63.2 Hooperating in metropolitan New York City. That translated into a 92.4 share of the total audience. Keep in mind that not many homes were equipped with TV sets then, not many cities could receive it and competition was relatively minor. See J. Fred MacDonald, *Don't Touch That Dial!: Radio Programming in American Life from 1920 to 1960* (Chicago: Nelson-Hall, 1991), p. 146.
13. MacDonald, pp. 113, 115.
14. Dual methods are applied today in harvesting Nielsen's television ratings. In some cases, samples are obtained via wide-ranging surveys in which viewers of assorted demographic backgrounds maintain a written record (diary) of the television programming they watch. Set Meters are another scheme for gaining samples. These are small gadgets connected to every TV set in selected homes. The gizmos gather the home's viewing habits and transmit data nightly to Nielsen through a home unit linked to a telephone line. The meters let researchers study the viewing patterns minute by minute, learning the precise moment channels are switched or sets are turned off. In 2005, Nielsen began measuring digital video recordings and early conclusions suggest that time-shifted viewing will impact future TV ratings significantly.
15. "Who Listens to What?" *Time*, January 4, 1943.
16. There were other well-known audience measurement services that competed with Nielsen and Arbitron. The Pulse, Inc., sent interviewers into homes showing householders lists of programs and asking which were heard or seen recently. Pulse contacted 67,000 family units as opposed to fewer than 1,000 contacts by some rivals. Trendex applied the coincidental method, picking names in set rotations from telephone books, inquiring which TV programs were being seen at the moment of phone calls. With interviewers in 10 key cities, Trendex delivered statistics on a show overnight. In 1948, CBS Radio's research unit instituted a high frequency radio signal based on wartime radar technology called the Instantaneous Audience Measurement Service (IAMS). A transmitter instantly reached homes having specially-equipped devices, revealing when a set was used, programs heard, family income and location. Also in 1948, the Albert E. Sindlinger Co. began collecting radio and TV data with a Transphaser, another electronic system (Radox) that beamed sound from the set by a phone line to a central switchboard. An operator tuned in one set after another to discover stations being heard in those homes right then.
17. Bob Schulberg, *Radio Advertising: The Authoritative Handbook* (Lincolnwood, IL: NTC Business Books, 1989), p. 35.
18. *Variety*, June 28, 1950, p. 25.
19. Wolfe, p. 255.

Chapter 5

1. Charles Hull Wolfe, *Modern Radio Advertising* (New York: Printers' Ink, 1949), pp. 632–633.
2. Susan Smulyan, *Selling Radio: The Commercialization of American Broadcasting, 1920 to 1934* (Washington, DC: Smithsonian Institution Press, 1994), p. 76.
3. Wolfe, p. 469. Reference is to Joseph A. Moran of Young & Rubicam.
4. Leonard Maltin, *The Great American Broadcast: A Celebration of Radio's Golden Age* (New York: Penguin Putnam, 1997), p. 29.
5. Ibid., p. 28.
6. Wolfe, p. 471.
7. Ibid.
8. Erik Barnouw, *The Golden Web: A History of Broadcasting in the United States, Vol. II—1933 to 1953* (New York: Oxford University Press, 1968), p. 111.
9. Bob Schulberg, *Radio Advertising: The Authoritative Handbook* (Lincolnwood, IL: NTC Business Books, 1989), p. 122.

10. Robert W. Bly, *The Copywriter's Handbook: A Step-by-Step Guide to Writing Copy that Sells*. 3rd ed. (New York: Henry Holt, 2005), p. 1.
11. Ibid., p. 3.
12. Ibid., p. 9.
13. Art Gilmore, and Glenn Y. Middleton, *Television and Radio Announcing*. 3rd ed. (Hollywood, CA: Hollywood Radio Publishers, 1949), p. 163.
14. Jurgen Hesse, *The Radio Documentary Handbook: Creating, Producing, and Selling for Broadcast* (Vancouver, BC: International Self-Counsel Press, 1987), p. 112.
15. Underhill, Paco. *Why We Buy: The Science of Shopping*. New York: Simon & Schuster, 1999, p. 62.
16. Schulberg, p. 110.
17. Robert L. Hilliard, *Writing for Television and Radio*. 3rd ed. (New York: Hastings House, 1976), pp. 104–114.
18. *Arthur Godfrey's Talent Scouts* broadcast, September 26, 1949, simulcast over CBS Radio and Television.
19. Words and music for *Muskrat Ramble* penned in 1926 by Ray Gilbert and Edward "Kid" Ory.
20. Charles A. Siepmann, *Radio's Second Chance* (Boston: Little, Brown, 1947), p. 193.
21. Siepmann, 1947, pp. 188–189.

Chapter 6

1. Alfred Balk, *The Rise of Radio, from Marconi through the Golden Age* (Jefferson, NC: McFarland, 2006), p. 54.
2. Bob Schulberg, *Radio Advertising: The Authoritative Handbook* (Lincolnwood, IL: NTC Business Books, 1989), p. 130.
3. Leonard Maltin, *The Great American Broadcast: A Celebration of Radio's Golden Age* (New York: Penguin Putnam, 1997), p. 128.
4. Ibid., p. 138.
5. Ibid., pp. 136–137.
6. Proverbs 25:11.
7. Charles Hull Wolfe, *Modern Radio Advertising* (New York: Printers' Ink, 1949), p. 706.
8. Ibid.
9. Art Gilmore, and Glenn Y. Middleton, *Television and Radio Announcing*. 3rd ed. (Hollywood, CA: Hollywood Radio, 1949), p. 153.
10. George Ansbro, *I Have a Lady in the Balcony: Memoirs of a Broadcaster* (Jefferson, NC: McFarland, 2000), pp. 102–104, 107.
11. This was long before the Standard Oil Company of New Jersey altered the name Esso to Exxon.
12. Adapted from Chuck Schaden, *Speaking of Radio: Chuck Schaden's Conversations with the Stars of the Golden Age of Radio* (Morton Grove, IL: Nostalgia Digest Press, 2003), pp. 365–366.
13. Gerald Nachman, *Raised on Radio: In Quest of The Lone Ranger, Jack Benny, Amos 'n' Andy, The Shadow, Mary Noble, The Great Gildersleeve, Fibber McGee and Molly, Bill Stern, Our Miss Brooks, Henry Aldrich, The Quiz Kids, Mr. First Nighter, Fred Allen, Vic and Sade, The Cisco Kid, Jack Armstrong, Arthur Godfrey, Bob and Ray, The Barbour Family, Henry Morgan, Joe Friday, and Other Lost Heroes from Radio's Heyday* (New York: Pantheon Books, 1998), p. 259.

14. Robert L. Mott, *Radio Sound Effects: Who Did It, and How, in the Era of Live Broadcasting* (Jefferson, NC: McFarland, 1993), pp. 143–144.
15. Ibid., p. 145.
16. Jim Cox, *Radio Speakers: Narrators, News Junkies, Sports Jockeys, Tattletales, Tipsters, Toastmasters and Coffee Klatch Couples Who Verbalized the Jargon of the Aural Ether from the 1920s to the 1980s — A Biographical Dictionary* (Jefferson, NC: McFarland, 2007), p. 240.
17. Cox, *Radio Speakers*, p. 204.
18. Nachman, p. 261.

PART II

American Home Products

1. Thirty years hence, in 1890, the siblings had obviously acquired a partner in their business for it was then listed under the nomenclature "John & Frank H. Wyeth & Edward T. Dobbins."
2. George Constant Louis Washington (1871 to 1946) was a Belgian immigrant who arrived in this country in 1897. Around 1906 he visited Central America to study methods of instant coffee processing. Back in New York, he sold his own coffee brand in 1909, founding a company to manufacture it in 1910. The firm underwrote multiple network radio series before Washington sold the company to American Home Products (1943). AHP discontinued the coffee in 1961 but marketed G. Washington's Seasoning & Broth from 1938–2000 when that remnant of the business was sold. Parenthetically, because G. Washington Coffee Company was an independent enterprise during a major portion of radio's golden age, an entry is included for it in Appendix A concerning its radio programming exploits.
3. In extensive case study inquisitions, there is pervasively more definitive information on AHP's relationship with these two TV dramas in *The Daytime Serials of Television, 1946 to 1960* (McFarland, 2006) by this author.
4. There are separate entries in Appendix A on both Chesebrough and Pond's which had not yet merged.
5. "Pharmacal" is obviously a coined term that was purposely misspelled; Webster does not recognize it, although some other drug manufacturers (i.e., Lambert, Norwich) also applied it.
6. The latter two ingredients were discarded by 1963.
7. Sterling Drug, under the Bayer aspirin name and many other packaged goods, backed such enduring programs as *The American Album of Familiar Music, American Melody Hour, Backstage Wife, Lorenzo Jones, Manhattan Merry-Go-Round, Mr. Chameleon, Stella Dallas, Waltz Time* and *Young Widder Brown*. Paradoxically, all of these audio series were created by the production house headed by Frank and Anne Hummert. The Hummerts were responsible for putting virtually all American Home Products features on the air, also. Thus, these competitive firms employed the same couple to establish and maintain their airwaves presence, providing the Hummerts with their two most lucrative and enduring business deals.
8. All of these radio series, and many of the others underwritten by American Home Products, were pro-

duced by Air Features, Inc., the pervasive radio program assembly unit headed by the creative team of Frank and Anne Hummert. Their exploits on behalf of AHP and other major advertisers are summarized in extensive detail in these McFarland releases, all by this author: *Frank and Anne Hummert's Radio Factory* (2003), *The Great Radio Soap Operas* (1999) and *Mr. Keen, Tracer of Lost Persons* (2004).

American Tobacco Company

1. Robert Sobel, *The Entrepreneurs: Explorations Within the American Business Tradition* (New York: Weybright and Talley, 1974), p. 152.
2. Ibid., pp. 166, 167.
3. Actually, American Tobacco faced its first antitrust action as far back as 1890, the year it was formed, when North Carolina brought the first of multiple state suits. It seemed only a matter of time before President Theodore Roosevelt ordered an investigation of an indictment in federal court after a 1904 ruling involving Northern Securities. The 1907 verdict ruled against ATC, saying it violated the Sherman Anti-Trust Act. Following appeals, the case made its way to the Supreme Court which ruled against ATC in 1910.
4. Sobel, p. 187.
5. Ironically, James Buchanan "Buck" Duke, the inheritor of the Duke legacy and organizer of the American Tobacco Company empire, who had hand-picked Percival Smith Hill as his associate and successor, died on October 10, 1925, just eight weeks prior to Hill. The Duke-Hill dynasty, extending from Washington through Washington — from the time Washington Duke began growing tobacco in 1858 until George Washington Hill died in 1946 — lasted 88 years with only four men in command: Washington Duke, 1858–1890; Buck Duke, 1890 to 1912; Percival Hill, 1912 to 1925; and George Washington Hill, 1925 to 1946. It was a phenomenon possibly unparalleled in the annals of developing American corporate manufacturing.
6. Speaking of predecessor Buck Duke, who didn't get it either, a biographer observed: "He still would not take the major step of cutting down on brands. Nor would he ever do so. Instead, he concentrated on selling all the old ones, and even introduced new cigarettes from time to time." Once the father-and-son successors saw the light, it was an extraordinary transformation that had let Reynolds (with Camels) chip away at American Tobacco's dominant position unchecked.
7. In 1930, Lucky Strike sold 43.2 billion cigarettes compared to 35.3 billion for Camel, its closest rival. Of the top five brands — encompassing 113.6 billion cigarettes — Luckies sold more than 31 percent of the volume and a much higher percentage of the *total* tobacco market.
8. According to Gene Borio's "Tobacco Timeline," while Reynolds' Camel occupied first place in 1940, after ATC introduced a king size Pall Mall in 1939, combined with Lucky Strike the two brands allowed ATC to "rule the 40s." Camel, in 1940, controlled 24 percent of the market share; Luckies had 22.6 percent. Chesterfield was third at 18 percent.
9. Would you believe? Concern over wellness issues led the Supreme Court of Tennessee (the third most productive tobacco-growing state a century hence trailing only North Carolina and Kentucky) in 1898 to ban cigarettes altogether, claiming the product was "not legitimate articles of commerce, being wholly noxious and deleterious to health. Their use is always harmful." By the turn of the century, Iowa, North Dakota and Washington state joined Tennessee in banning cigarette sales. In 1901, only Louisiana and Wyoming didn't already have anti-cigarette laws, weren't considering new or tougher legislation or hadn't witnessed heavy anti-cigarette activity.
10. For more examples of Hill's unabashed fixations, see a couple of additional McFarland releases by this author which cover those instances in sizeable detail — *The Great Radio Audience Participation Shows* (2001) and *Music Radio: The Great Performers and Programs of the 1920s through Early 1960s* (2005).

Andrew Jergens Company

1. Barry M. Horstman, "Soapmaker Built Cosmetics Giant," *The Cincinnati Post*, September 7, 1999.
2. Ms. Lansdowne created sterling ad campaigns for several commodities including Aunt Jemima pancake mix, Maxwell House coffee, Pond's cold cream and more under the J. Walter Thompson aegis. She also wed advertising executive Stanley Burnet Resor in 1917. As part owner of JWT, he became the firm's president the year before their wedding, an office he occupied until 1955 when he became chairman, retiring in 1961.
3. http://historymatters.gmu.edu/mse/ads/model.html

Brown & Williamson Tobacco Company

1. A Web site claims that Chesterfield, manufactured by Liggett & Myers Tobacco Company, was the first brand "to add a moisture-proof, overall cover to the paper and foil pack" as early as 1916.
2. As sales continued to slip dramatically, on the threshold of a new century, in the late 1990s B&W announced plans to concentrate its efforts on premium-priced brands, backing away from value-priced cigarettes, in an effort to improve market share.
3. Wigand was sued by B&W in 1995 for violating confidentiality agreements, although the company dismissed the lawsuit two years later.

Campbell Soup Company

1. It would take 67 years (1936) before the Campbell outfit began to manufacture the cans in which its contents were distributed on a mass scale. Outsourcing had solved the problem until then after Abraham Anderson was no longer in the picture.
2. Dorrance held earned degrees from the Massachusetts Institute of Technology and Germany's Göttingen University.
3. The young man reportedly turned down several university teaching roles that would have paid him substantially more in order to work at Campbell.
4. Don't feel too badly about John Dorrance's low wages. In 1932, *Every Week Magazine* observed that his salary from Campbell hovered in the range of $3.5 to $4 million annually between 1920 to 1925, much of which was untaxed. He lived in a mansion in Radnor,

Pa., with property and furnishings approaching $1 million, opulent by 1920s standards. When he died, his family inherited an estate valued at $200 million by one estimate, some of it subject to taxes. He gave nothing to charity throughout his life, it was reported, and was noted for removing the light bulbs in the servants' quarters at his manor because "they are using too much electricity."

Coca-Cola Company

1. At least one source claims this forerunner of Coca-Cola was invented in Covington, Georgia, a nearby hamlet but outside Atlanta.
2. So well respected was John S. Pemberton by Atlanta pharmacists that — on the day of his funeral — all of them closed their stores to attend in tribute to him. "On that day," wrote a biographer, "not one drop of Coca-Cola was dispensed in the entire city."
3. Among the changes Candler and Robinson's revised formula contained only a tenth of the five ounces of coca leaf per gallon of syrup.
4. Candler endowed Emory University and its Wesley Memorial Hospital with more than $8 million. The university, said one observer, "could not have come into existence without his aid." In 1907, he prevented a real estate panic in Atlanta by purchasing $1 million worth of homes and reselling them to people of moderate means at affordable prices. During the First World War, Candler helped avert a cotton crisis by using his growing wealth to stabilize the market.

Colgate-Palmolive-Peet Company

1. In a letter to its shareholders published *in The New York Times* on December 21, 1926, the Palmolive Company stated: "A large stock dividend to the holders of the Palmolive common stock will feature in the reorganization of the company so that the Peet Brothers concern can be taken over. The total number of shares issued will be approximately 900,000, of which the present stockholders of the Palmolive company will have, under the merger, 76.8 per cent, and the stockholders of Peet Brothers Company 23.2 per cent. In addition there will be issued to the latter company's shareholders approximately 14,500 shares of preferred stock." Does this insinuate that the Peets might be subordinate to the Palmolive firm after their convergence?
2. Although the "Peet" designation disappeared, the parent firm persisted in recognizing the strategic contributions of that part of the firm's heritage. In 1938, Colgate-Palmolive-Peet directors elected B. W. Railey vice president and director, responsible for the firm's soap business west of the Mississippi. He operated out of offices in Kansas City and Berkeley, California, the sites of the earlier Peet operations. Railey was an ex-vice president of Peet Brothers Soap Company, later becoming Colgate's soap sales manager for the Pacific Coast. While the "Peet" moniker vanished, Colgate-Palmolive produced soap at the celebrated Kansas City site into the twenty-first century.

Ford Motor Company

1. At least one Web site claims Ford built his first experimental gasoline-powered buggy in 1892, four years ahead of the date certified by present historians of the Ford Motor Company. According to the source, he was dissatisfied with the original vehicle's weight and sold it in 1896 to finance his "quadricycle" model.
2. While distressing economic conditions forced Ford to reduce its pay scale to $4.00 per day in 1932, as fortunes reversed, a new scale of $6.00 daily was implemented in 1935. At the same time, Henry Ford urged his employees to reject the notion of banding together in labor unions, a possibility made favorable by President Franklin D. Roosevelt's New Deal. An outspoken Henry Ford had supported Herbert Hoover for reelection in 1932, incidentally.

General Foods Corporation

1. The only remaining visible evidence of this mammoth manufacturer at this writing is as part of a brand name for a flavor-based liquid line, General Foods International Coffees.
2. The fascinating account of the Battle Creek Sanitarium operated by Dr. John Kellogg is explored in depth in this volume in the discourse on the Kellogg Company.
3. Marjorie Merriweather Post eventually wed a third time. Her husbands included (in order) Edward Bennett Close, E. F. Hutton (their only child was actress Dina Merrill) and Joseph Davies, U.S. ambassador to the Soviet Union. She "lived like a queen but also gave like a philanthropist," said the Biography Channel, claiming she gave a fortune to charity over her lifespan.
4. Of course, the Baker business in 1927 was far removed from its originators; even Walter Baker, who died in 1852, hadn't been there when the chocolate factory was launched in 1765 by Irish sweets-maker John Hannan.

General Mills, Inc.

1. As of 2001.
2. C. C. Washburn lived a colorful life. Born in Maine, he taught school there (1938 to 1939) before moving to Davenport, Iowa, where he assisted in performing a geological survey of that state. Next, at Rock Island, Illinois, he studied law and was elected surveyor of Rock Island County. By 1842, he was admitted to the bar at Mineral Point, Wisconsin, where he founded a bank a decade later. He was elected as a Republican to the U.S. Congress three times (1855 to 1861), refused to run again, and moved to La Crosse, Wisconsin in 1861. Washburn served with the Union Army (1862 to 1865) during the Civil War. He returned to the U.S. Congress for two more terms (1867 to 1871) before running for and winning the governorship of Wisconsin. He was an unsuccessful candidate for reelection in 1873. While all of this transpired, he operated commercial lumber and flour business ventures, including the latter in Minnesota.
3. Charles A. Pillsbury was successor to an uncle, John Sargent Pillsbury, who with him originated their flour-milling enterprise at Minneapolis in 1869.
4. There were most likely others playing the part of Betty Crocker besides Bucholz in later years.
5. In the text *Making Waves: The 50 Greatest Women*

in Radio and Television As Selected by American Women in Radio and Television, Inc. (Andrews McMeel, 2001, p. 139), edited by Jacci Duncan, the statement appears: "In the 1930s, the [creative radio producers Frank and Anne] Hummert team also created the 'Breakfast of Champions' slogan for Wheaties breakfast cereal." No printed attribution is supplied and the author is unidentified. The reference in our text involving Knox Reeves, meanwhile, is from the Web site http://www.wheaties.com/history/index.aspx. This is not to state that the 2001 source is incorrect. This author wishes to clarify that — as a pervasive investigator of "all things Hummert"— we have not encountered corroborating evidence that supports the 2001 assertion, and also could be guilty of publicizing a fact that is not authenticated beyond doubt. For now, that question remains unsettled, and disturbingly so.

6. More than one Pillsbury spokeswoman is cited in a reference under the company's name in Appendix A at the back of this volume.

General Motors Company

1. *The New York Times*, March 19, 1947.

2. Was Durant actually divorced from his second wife? He told the Census Bureau he was. A 1947 obituary lists Mrs. Catherine Lederer Durant, "whom he married in 1908," and a daughter, Mrs. Fitzhugh Green (not the same surname of the man who initially invested in Chevrolet, by the way). If Durant divorced his second wife, he remarried her; or they may have separated only.

Kellogg Company

1. Having fallen on hard times during the Great Depression — when many of the formerly affluent could no longer afford its skilled upscale services — the san eventually passed into government hands. As Percy Jones General and Convalescent Hospital, it treated orthopedic veterans of the Second World War and the Korean conflict. In 1954, the facility was converted into offices for federal civilian and military units.

2. Although Kellogg proclaimed to abhor the lifestyle of the rich and famous, it may be noted that — in 1925 — he purchased 377 acres in Pomona for a quarter-million dollars as the site of his Arabian horse ranch. He reportedly "acquired only the best of stock, many head coming from Lady Wentworth's historic Crabbet Stud in England." It may be observed further that the people sustaining his and his older brother's salaries at the Battle Creek Sanitarium were usually exceedingly prosperous, thereby capable of underwriting the luxurious health-giving lifestyle proffered by the Messrs. Kellogg and company. By the early 1900s, before the cereal business took off, the san maintained a staff of up to 1,000 that included 30 physicians, 200 nurses, bath attendants and other helpers, all eager to meet the whims of pampered patients who could readily afford their tender care.

3. http://www.ideafinder.com/history/inventors/kellogg.htm

4. This tale is recounted in extensive detail accompanied by its author's own appraisal in Benjamin Kline Hunnicutt's paperback *Kellogg's Six-Hour Day* (Temple University Press, 1996).

5. http://www.amazon.com/exec/obidos/ASIN/1566394481/thegreatideafind

6. Charles W. Post organized the C. W. Post Company in 1895. He had gone to Battle Creek earlier in a wheelchair as a patient in Dr. Kellogg's sanitarium. Cured of his ailments, he remained to make millions out of pre-cooked foods. His genius for advertising made Postum a popular national drink in a campaign that warned of the dangers of consuming coffee. Post Toasties nearly equaled Kellogg's Corn Flakes in sales, and when he bought the rights to Grape-Nuts from a smaller outfit, he turned it into an international sensation. His firm would later merge with others to form General Foods Company. See the separate article on that firm in this section.

Kraft Foods Company

1. An entry for National Dairy Products Corporation is included in Appendix A at the back of the book.

2. Philip Morris and General Foods are spotlighted in entries in Section 2 of this book. National Biscuit Company, meanwhile, appears in Appendix A.

Liggett & Myers Tobacco Company

1. At least one source maintains that this didn't occur before 1873, thus the date is debatable.

2. There is a separate entry for Philip Morris in Section 2 of this book.

3. Adapted from the following sources: Arthur J. Singer, *Arthur Godfrey: The Adventures of an American Broadcaster* (Jefferson, NC: McFarland, 2000), pp. 122, 205; Arts & Entertainment (A&E) Network interview with Peter Kelley, summer 1996; *The Bing Crosby Chesterfield Show*, April 5, 1950; *Arthur Godfrey and His Friends*, September 24, 1952; A&E interview with Andy Rooney, August 1996; plus some interviews conducted by Arthur Singer.

P. Lorillard, Inc.

1. Painting barn sides was an advertising practice inaugurated by Bloch Brothers Tobacco Company of Wheeling, West Virginia. From 1890 to 1992, the firm touted its Mail Pouch chewing tobacco on barn sides still found today in Indiana, Kentucky, Maryland, Michigan, Ohio, Pennsylvania and West Virginia. Some of these are identified as National Historic Landmarks by the U.S. Department of the Interior. Owners were paid a dollar or two annually for the use of their "billboards," and the company periodically repainted their entire barn exteriors.

2. http://www.historian.org

3. http://www.aliciapatterson.org

4. Iain Gately, *Tobacco: The Story of How Tobacco Seduced the World* (New York: Grove Press, 2001), pp. 273, 274.

Miles Laboratories, Inc.

1. There is an epigrammatic paperback biography of the company founder, *Dr. Miles: The Life of Dr. Franklin L. Miles (1845 to 1929)*, by Martha M. Pickrell (Indianapolis: Guild Press of Indiana, 2001).

2. Franklin Miles' educational procession included these academic institutions: Phillips Academy and Williston Seminary, both in Massachusetts; Sheffield Scientific School and Yale College, both in Connecticut; Columbia College, New York City; Medical Department of Michigan University; and Rush Medical College, Chicago Medical College, and Illinois State Eye and Ear Infirmary, all of Chicago.

3. Some of his topics: "Nervous Diseases," "The Permanent Cure of Headache without Change of Occupation," "Heart Disease," "Weak Eyes a Nervous Disease, "Headache and Other Nervous Diseases" and "The Use of Spectacles in the Treatment of Affections of the Brain and Nerves."

4. *Historic Business Register* of the Indiana Historical Society, Indianapolis, recounting the legacy of the Bayer Corporation's Elkhart area site.

5. *Historic Business Register* of the Indiana Historical Society.

Philip Morris Company

1. Iain Gately, *Tobacco: The Story of How Tobacco Seduced the World* (New York: Grove Press, 2001), p. 244.

2. Ibid., pp. 294–295.

3. Myrna Oliver, "Johnny Roventini; Bellboy Called for Philip Morris in Ads," *The Los Angeles Times*, December 3, 1998, p. 1.

R. J. Reynolds Tobacco Company

1. Robert Sobel, *The Entrepreneurs: Explorations Within the American Business Tradition* (New York: Weybright and Talley, 1974), pp. 191–192, 152, 182.

2. Ibid., p. 152.

Standard Brands, Inc.

1. Until 1941, this firm was popularly known as N.B.C. Thereafter, it adopted Nabisco, which was already a widely-recognized nickname. Even so, not until 1971 did Nabisco become the outfit's legal appellation.

2. National Biscuit Company is included in its own entry in Appendix A at the back of this book.

Sterling Drug, Inc.

1. Among references advocating the exclusivity of Diebold and Weiss is a pithy article by Mary Staley at http://www.rootsweb.com/˜wvwags/sterlingdrug.htm. In the meantime, in an incisive paper submitted to the School of Management at Boston University in January 2003, "Location and Organizing Strategy: Exploring the Influence of Location on the Organization of Pharmaceutical Research," Jeffrey L. Furman—who gathered data from as many as 75 sources while often citing *The Aspirin Wars* (Knopf, 1991) by Charles C. Mann and Mark L. Plummer—explicitly names Weiss as Neuralgyline's principal. And, for what it's worth, a Web site catering to the Wheeling Hall of Fame recognizes 1980 inductee Weiss for "*his* [italics mine] Sterling Drug Company ... the world's largest manufacturer of proprietary remedies, with plants world wide." There is no mention of an agent assisting Weiss in achieving his notoriety.

2. The information for this article by Linda Fluharty is based upon the assertions of Charles A. Winegerter in his 1912 volume, *Greater Wheeling and Vicinity* (publisher unsubstantiated, possibly self-published or by a chamber of commerce or historical society).

3. Although Bayer AG is today named for Friedrich Bayer (1825–1880), he died at 55, missing the prominence to be associated with his name. Bayer, a dye salesman, and a partner—master dyer Johann Friedrich Westkott (1821–1876)—opened a dyestuffs factory at Barmen, Germany, on August 1, 1863, out of which successors concentrated on pharmaceuticals and patent medicines. In 1897, one of the researchers there, Felix Hoffmann (1868 to 1946), was able to synthesize acetylsalicylic acid, the active ingredient in aspirin, in a chemically pure and stable form. It was registered as a trademark two years hence and widely adopted around the globe as a favorite painkiller of billions of people.

4. Taking a somewhat skeptical view, Mann and Plummer insisted: "That Sterling found it worthwhile to outbid substantially larger firms like Dupont in order to acquire Bayer's assets is a striking display of its confidence in its marketing and distribution capabilities—particularly in light of the fact that Sterling's skills in drug-making were so amateurish that it was forced to expend substantial resources soliciting assistance from Bayer simply to manufacture the products, including aspirin, that it had acquired."

5. Furman, p. 17.

Appendix B

1. Thomas A. DeLong, *Quiz Craze: America's Infatuation with Game Shows* (New York: Praeger, 1991), p. 60.

2. Herman S. Hettinger, *A Decade of Radio Advertising* (Chicago: University of Chicago Press, 1933), p. 45.

3. *The Clicquot Club Eskimos* series is considered in some detail in chapter 2.

4. Higby, pp. 52–53.

5. Charles Thompson, *Bing: The Authorized Biography* (New York: David McKay, 1975), p. 138.

6. Schulberg, p. 114.

7. Erik Barnouw, *The Golden Web: A History of Broadcasting in the United States, Vol. II—1933 to 1953* (New York: Oxford University Press, 1968), p. 148.

8. Ibid.

9. David C. Tucker, *The Women Who Made Television Funny: Ten Stars of 1950s Sitcoms* (Jefferson, NC: McFarland & Company, 2007), p. 9.

10. Gerald Nachman, *Raised on Radio: In Quest of The Lone Ranger, Jack Benny, Amos 'n' Andy, The Shadow, Mary Noble, The Great Gildersleeve, Fibber McGee and Molly, Bill Stern, Our Miss Brooks, Henry Aldrich, The Quiz Kids, Mr. First Nighter, Fred Allen, Vic and Sade, The Cisco Kid, Jack Armstrong, Arthur Godfrey, Bob and Ray, The Barbour Family, Henry Morgan, Joe Friday, and Other Lost Heroes from Radio's Heyday* (New York: Pantheon Books, 1998), p. 262.

11. Steve Karmen, *Through the Jingle Jungle: The Art*

and Business of Making Music for Commercials (New York: Billboard Books, 1989), p. 4.

12. Bob Schulberg, *Radio Advertising: The Authoritative Handbook* (Lincolnwood, IL: NTC Business Books, 1989), p. 21.

13. Ibid.

14. This concept is explored in some detail in Chapter 3.

15. *Broadcasting*, December 1, 1938.

16. Leonard Maltin, *The Great American Broadcast: A Celebration of Radio's Golden Age* (New York: Penguin Putnam, 1997), p. 162.

17. Ibid., p. 163.

18. Nachman, pp. 269–270.

19. Christopher H. Sterling, and John M. Kittross, *Stay Tuned: A Concise History of American Broadcasting*. 2nd ed. (Belmont, CA: Wadsworth, 1990), p. 85.

20. Ibid., p. 304.

21. Barnouw, 1968, pp. 227–228.

22. Charles A. Siepmann, *Radio's Second Chance* (Boston: Little, Brown, 1947), pp. 78, 79.

23. Mary Jane Higby, *Tune in Tomorrow: Or, How I Found The Right to Happiness with Our Gal Sunday, Stella Dallas, John's Other Wife, and Other Sudsy Radio Serials* (New York: Cowles Education Corporation, 1968), p. 55.

24. Barnouw, 1968, p. 97.

25. George Ansbro, *I Have a Lady in the Balcony: Memoirs of a Broadcaster* (Jefferson, NC: McFarland, 2000), p. 46.

Bibliography

Anderson, Arthur. *Let's Pretend: A History of Radio's Best Loved Children's Show by a Longtime Cast Member.* Jefferson, NC: McFarland & Co., 1994.

Ansbro, George. *I Have a Lady in the Balcony: Memoirs of a Broadcaster.* Jefferson, NC: McFarland & Co., 2000.

Apple, Terri. *Making Money in Voice-Overs: Winning Strategies to a Successful Career in TV, Commercials, Radio and Animation.* Los Angeles: Lone Eagle Publishing, 1999.

Archer, Gleason L. *History of Radio to 1926.* New York: American Historical Society, 1938.

Arnold, Frank. *Broadcast Advertising: The Fourth Dimension.* New York: John Wiley and Sons, 1931.

Balk, Alfred. *The Rise of Radio, from Marconi through the Golden Age.* Jefferson, NC: McFarland & Co., 2006.

Barnouw, Erik. *The Golden Web: A History of Broadcasting in the United States, Vol. II—1933 to 1953.* New York: Oxford University Press, 1968.

_____. *The Image Empire: A History of Broadcasting in the United States, Vol. III—from 1953.* New York: Oxford University Press, 1970.

_____. *A Tower in Babel: A History of Broadcasting in the United States, Vol. I—to 1933.* New York: Oxford University Press, 1966.

Bly, Robert W. *The Copywriter's Handbook: A Step-by-Step Guide to Writing Copy that Sells.* 3rd ed. New York: Henry Holt and Co., 2005.

Brooks, Tim, and Earle Marsh. *The Complete Directory to Prime Time Network TV Shows, 1946-Present.* 4th ed. New York: Ballantine Books, 1988.

Buxton, Frank, and Bill Owen. *The Big Broadcast, 1920 to 1950.* 2nd ed. Lanham, MD: Scarecrow Press, 1997.

Campbell, Robert. *The Golden Years of Broadcasting: A Celebration of the First 50 Years of Radio and TV on NBC.* New York: Charles Scribner's Sons, 1976.

Castleman, Harry, and Walter J. Podrazik. *505 Radio Questions Your Friends Can't Answer.* New York: Walker and Company, 1983.

Chase, Francis, Jr. *Sound and Fury: An Informal History of Broadcasting.* New York: Harper & Brothers Publishers, 1942.

Cox, Jim. *Confessions of a Moonlight Writer: A Freelancer's Guide to the Church Market.* Brentwood, TN: JMProductions, 1982.

_____. *The Daytime Serials of Television, 1946–1960.* Jefferson, NC: McFarland & Co., 2006.

_____. *Frank and Anne Hummert's Radio Factory: The Programs and Personalities of Broadcasting's Most Prolific Producers.* Jefferson, NC: McFarland & Co., 2003.

_____. *The Great Radio Audience Participation Shows: Seventeen Programs from the 1940s and 1950s.* Jefferson, NC: McFarland & Co., 2001.

_____. *The Great Radio Sitcoms.* Jefferson, NC: McFarland & Co., 2007.

_____. *The Great Radio Soap Operas.* Jefferson, NC: McFarland & Co., 1999.

_____. *Historical Dictionary of American Radio Soap Operas.* Lanham, MD: Scarecrow Press, 2005.

_____. *Mr. Keen, Tracer of Lost Persons: A Complete History and Episode Log of Radio's Most Durable Detective.* Jefferson, NC: McFarland & Co., 2004.

_____. *Music Radio: The Great Performers and Programs of the 1920s through Early 1960s.* Jefferson, NC: McFarland & Co., 2005.

_____. *Radio Crime Fighters: Over 300 Programs from the Golden Age.* Jefferson, NC: McFarland & Co., 2002.

_____. *Radio Speakers: Narrators, News Junkies, Sports Jockeys, Tattletales, Tipsters, Toastmasters and Coffee Klatch Couples Who Verbalized the Jargon of the Aural Ether from the 1920s to the 1980s—A Biographical Dictionary.* Jefferson, NC: McFarland & Co., 2007.

_____. *Say Goodnight, Gracie: The Last Years of Network Radio.* Jefferson, NC: McFarland & Co., 2002.

Cull, Nicholas J., David Culbert, and David Welch. *Propaganda and Mass Persuasion: A Historical Encyclopedia, 1500 to the Present.* Santa Barbara, CA: ABC-CLIO, 2003.

DeLong, Thomas A. *The Mighty Music Box: The Golden Age of Musical Radio.* Los Angeles: Amber Crest Books, 1980.

_____. *Quiz Craze: America's Infatuation with Game Shows.* New York: Praeger Publishers, 1991.

_____. *Radio Stars: An Illustrated Biographical Dictionary of 953 Performers, 1920 through 1960.* Jefferson, NC: McFarland & Co., 1996.

Derdak, Thomas, ed. *International Directory of Company Histories.* Vol. 1. Chicago: St. James Press, 1988.

Douglas, George H. *The Early Days of Radio Broadcasting.* Jefferson, NC: McFarland & Co., 1987.

Dun & Bradstreet Million Dollar Directory: America's Leading Public & Private Companies, 2002. Bethlehem, PA: Dun & Bradstreet, 2002.

Duncan, Jacci, ed. *Making Waves: The 50 Greatest Women in Radio and Television As Selected by American Women in Radio and Television, Inc.* Kansas City, MO: Andrews McMeel, 2001.

Dunning, John. *On the Air: The Encyclopedia of Old-Time Radio.* New York: Oxford University Press, 1998.

Durden, Robert F. *Bold Entrepreneur: A Life of James B. Duke.* Durham, NC: Carolina Academic Press, 2003.

_____. *The Dukes of Durham, 1865–1929.* Durham, NC: Duke University Press, 1975.

Eberly, Philip K. *Music in the Air: America's Changing Taste in Popular Music, 1920 to 1980.* New York: Hastings House, 1982.

Editors of TV Guide. *TV Guide Guide to TV: The Most Definitive Encyclopedia of Television!* New York: Barnes & Noble Books, 2004.

Encyclopedia of the History of St. Louis: A Compendium of History and Biography for Ready Reference. New York: Southern History Company, 1899.

Finkelstein, Norman H. *Sounds in the Air: The Golden Age of Radio.* New York: Charles Scribner's Sons, 1993.

Freedland, Michael. *Bing Crosby: The Illustrated Biography.* London: Chameleon Books, 1998.

Gately, Iain. *Tobacco: The Story of How Tobacco Seduced the World.* New York: Grove Press, 2001.

Gilmore, Art, and Glenn Y. Middleton. *Television and Radio Announcing.* 3rd ed. Hollywood, CA: Hollywood Radio Publishers, 1949.

Godfrey, Donald G., and Frederic A. Leigh, eds. *Historical Dictionary of American Radio.* Westport, CT: Greenwood Press, 1998.

Gunther, John. *Taken at the Flood: The Story of Albert D. Lasker.* New York: Harper and Brothers, 1960.

Harmon, Jim. *Radio Mystery and Adventure and Its Appearance in Film, Television and Other Media.* 2nd ed. Jefferson, NC: McFarland & Co., 2003.

Hesse, Jurgen. *The Radio Documentary Handbook: Creating, Producing, and Selling for Broadcast.* Vancouver, BC: International Self-Counsel Press, 1987.

Hettinger, Herman S. *A Decade of Radio Advertising.* Chicago: University of Chicago Press, 1933.

Hickerson, Jay. *The 3rd Revised Ultimate History of Network Radio Programming and Guide to All Circulating Shows.* Hamden, CT: Presto Print II, 2005.

Higby, Mary Jane. *Tune in Tomorrow: Or, How I Found the Right to Happiness with Our Gal Sunday, Stella Dallas, John's Other Wife, and Other Sudsy Radio Serials.* New York: Cowles Education Corporation, 1968.

Hilliard, Robert L. *Writing for Television and Radio.* 3rd ed. New York: Hastings House, 1976.

_____. *Writing for Television, Radio, and New Media.* 8th ed. Belmont, CA: Wadsworth/Thompson Learning, 2004.

Hoover's Handbook of American Business 2002. Austin, TX: Hoover's Business Press, 2002.

Hower, Ralph. *The History of an Advertising Agency: N. W. Ayer & Son at Work, 1869 to 1949.* Cambridge, MA: N. W. Ayer & Son, 1949.

Hunnicutt, Benjamin Kline. *Kellogg's Six-Hour Day.* Philadelphia: Temple University Press, 1996.

International Directory of Company Histories. Chicago: St. James Press, 1987.

Jaffe, Joseph. *Life After the 30-Second Spot: Energize Your Brand with a Bold Mix of Alternatives to Traditional Advertising.* Hoboken, NJ: John Wiley & Sons, 2005.

Johnson, Batt. *Rich and Famous in Third Seconds: Inside Secrets to Achieving Financial Success in Television and Radio Commercials.* Self published, 2000.

Jorgensen, Janice, ed. *Encyclopedia of Consumer Brands, Vol. 2: Personal Products.* Detroit: St. James Press, 1994.

Karmen, Steve. *Through the Jingle Jungle: The Art and Business of Making Music for Commercials.* New York: Billboard Books, 1989.

MacDonald, J. Fred. *Don't Touch That Dial!: Radio Programming in American Life from 1920 to 1960.* Chicago: Nelson-Hall, 1991.

MacQueen, Adam. *The King of Sunlight: How William Lever Cleaned Up the World.* New York: Bantam Press, 2004.

Maltin, Leonard. *The Great American Broadcast: A Celebration of Radio's Golden Age.* New York: Penguin Putnam, 1997.

Mann, Charles C., and Mark L. Plummer. *The Aspirin Wars.* New York: Alfred A. Knopf, 1991.

McNeil, Alex. *Total Television: The Comprehensive Guide to Programming from 1948 to the Present.* 4th ed. New York: Penguin Books, 1996.

Mott, Robert L. *Radio Sound Effects: Who Did It, and How, in the Era of Live Broadcasting.* Jefferson, NC: McFarland, 1993.

Nachman, Gerald. *Raised on Radio: In Quest of The Lone Ranger, Jack Benny, Amos 'n' Andy, The Shadow, Mary Noble, The Great Gildersleeve, Fibber McGee and Molly, Bill Stern, Our Miss Brooks, Henry Aldrich, The Quiz Kids, Mr. First Nighter, Fred Allen, Vic and Sade, The Cisco Kid, Jack Armstrong, Arthur Godfrey, Bob and Ray, The Barbour Family, Henry Morgan, Joe Friday, and Other Lost Heroes from Radio's Heyday.* New York: Pantheon Books, 1998.

Oakner, Larry. *And Now a Few Laughs from Our Sponsor: The Best of Fifty Years of Radio Commercials.* Hoboken, NJ: Wiley, 2002.

Pickrell, Martha M. *Dr. Miles: The Life of Dr. Franklin L. Miles (1845 to 1929).* Indianapolis: Guild Press of Indiana, 2001.

Plunkett, Jack W., ed. *Plunkett's Health Care Industry Almanac 1999–2000.* Houston: Plunkett Research, 1999.

Poindexter, Ray. *Golden Throats and Silver Tongues: The Radio Announcers.* Conway, AK: River Road Press, 1978.

Portrait and Biographical Record of St. Clair County, Illinois: Containing Biographical Sketches of Prominent and Representative Citizens, Together with Biographies and Portraits of All the Presidents of the United States. Chicago: Chapman Brothers, 1892.

Regent, Nancy, ed. *Hoover's MasterList of Major U.S. Companies, 2002.* Austin, TX: Hoover's Business Press, 2001.

Robinson, Marc. *Brought to You in Living Color: 75 Years of Great Moments in Television & Radio from NBC.* New York: John Wiley & Sons, 2002.

Schaden, Chuck. *Speaking of Radio: Chuck Schaden's Conversations with the Stars of the Golden Age of Radio.* Morton Grove, IL: Nostalgia Digest Press, 2003.

Schulberg, Bob. *Radio Advertising: The Authoritative Handbook.* Lincolnwood, IL: NTC Business Books, 1989.

Schwartz, Jon D., and Robert C. Reinehr. *Handbook of Old-Time Radio: A Comprehensive Guide to Golden Age Radio Listening and Collecting.* Metuchen, NJ: Scarecrow Press, 1993.

Siepmann, Charles A. *Radio, Television and Society.* New York: Oxford University Press, 1950.

_____. *Radio's Second Chance.* Boston: Little, Brown and Company, 1947.

Sies, Luther F. *Encyclopedia of American Radio, 1920–1960.* Jefferson, NC: McFarland & Co., 2000.

Singer, Arthur J. *Arthur Godfrey: The Adventures of an American Broadcaster.* Jefferson, NC: McFarland & Co., 2000.

Sloan, W. David, and Lisa Mullikin Parcell, eds. *American Journalism: History, Principles, Practices.* Jefferson, NC: McFarland & Co., 2002.

Smith, Sally Bedell. *In All His Glory: The Life of William S. Paley, the Legendary Tycoon and His Brilliant Circle.* New York: Simon and Schuster, 1990.

Smulyan, Susan. *Selling Radio: The Commercialization of American Broadcasting, 1920 to 1934.* Washington, DC: Smithsonian Institution Press, 1994.

Sobel, Robert. *The Entrepreneurs: Explorations Within the American Business Tradition.* New York: Weybright and Talley, 1974.

Sold American: The First Fifty Years, 1904 to 1954. Durham, NC: American Tobacco Co., 1954

Standard & Poor's Register of Corporations, Directors and Executives, Vol. 1, 2002. Charlottesville, VA: McGraw-Hill, 2002.

Sterling, Christopher H., ed. *Telecommunications: Special Reports on American Broadcasting, 1932–1947.* New York: Arno Press, 1974.

_____, and John M. Kittross. *Stay Tuned: A Concise History of American Broadcasting.* 2nd ed. Belmont, CA: Wadsworth Publishing Co., 1990.

Summers, Harrison B., ed. *A Thirty-Year History of Programs Carried on National Radio Networks in the United States, 1926–1956.* New York: Arno Press and *The New York Times*, 1971.

Swartz, Jon D., and Robert C. Reinehr. *Handbook of Old-Time Radio: A Comprehensive Guide to Golden Age Radio Listening and Collecting.* Metuchen, NJ: Scarecrow Press, 1993.

Swasy, Alecia. *Soap Opera: The Inside Story of Procter & Gamble.* New York: Times Books, 1993.

Terrace, Vincent. *Radio Programs, 1924–1984: A Catalog of Over 1800 Shows.* Jefferson, NC: McFarland, 1999.

Thompson, Charles. *Bing: The Authorized Biography.* New York: David McKay, 1975.

Tucker, David C. *The Women Who Made Television Funny: Ten Stars of 1950s Sitcoms.* Jefferson, NC: McFarland & Co., 2007.

Underhill, Paco. *Why We Buy: The Science of Shopping.* New York: Simon & Schuster, 1999.

Weinberger, Marc G. *Effective Radio Advertising: A Guide to Winning Customers with Targeted Campaigns and Creative Commercials.* Lanham, MD: Lexington Books, 1998.

Winkler, John K. *Tobacco Tycoon: The Story of James Buchanan Duke.* New York: Random House, 1942.

Wolfe, Charles Hull. *Modern Radio Advertising.* New York: Printers' Ink Publishing Company, 1949.

Index

A&E cable network 48, 57
The A&P Gypsies 28, 250, 286
Abbott & Costello 50, 66
A. C. Nielsen Company 29, 42, 43, 45, 47, 48, 49, 50, 300
Ackerman, William 18
The Adventures of Ozzie and Harriet 259, 260, 261–262
The Adventures of Sam Spade 271
The Adventures of Sherlock Holmes 270
The Adventures of Superman 290
Advertisers on radio, most active 2–3
Advertising definition 2
Advertising Age 32, 40, 144, 215
Advertising agencies 11, 12, 13, 14, 15, 19, 24, 26, 28, 30, 32–40, 42, 51, 52, 53, 56, 57, 60, 64, 65, 68, 83, 90, 104, 117, 138, 149, 175, 179, 202, 210, 218, 223, 277, 281, 285, 288, 293, 296
Advertising agents as intermediaries 28, 32, 36
Advertising as an indispensable tool 17
Advertising slogans 10, 33, 58, 62, 66–67, 85, 86, 87, 90, 93, 94, 98, 104, 110, 112, 117, 139, 144, 145, 166, 186, 199, 202, 206, 207, 210, 213, 214, 229, 230, 231
Adweek 48
A. H. Grebe (manufacturing concern) 22
Air Features, Inc. 64, 277
The Aldrich Family 50, 144, 285
Allan, E. C. 12
Allen, Fred 23, 45, 50, 98, 99, 134, 238, 254, 269, 283, 286
Allen, Gracie *see* George Burns and Gracie Allen
Allis-Chalmers Company 249
Allport, Gordon W. 49, 54
Altieri, Albert 210
Altria Group, Inc. 142, 173, 207, 231, 236

Ameche, Don 239
Ameche, Jim 61
American Association of Advertising Agencies 14, 33
American Broadcasting Company 4, 30, 35, 170, 175, 195, 226, 296
American Cancer Association 291
American Chicle Company 266
American Express Company 22
American Federation of Radio Artists (AFRA) 64, 296
American Federation of Television and Radio Artists (AFTRA) 296
American Home Products 3, 73–78, 124, 241, 246, 226, 278
The American Newspaper Directory 12
American Newspaper Publishers Association 13, 19, 33
American Research Bureau 49, 296
American Telephone and Telegraph Company 16, 20, 22, 23, 24, 33
American Tobacco Company 3, 25, 37, 79–87, 101, 102, 103, 184, 185, 188, 192, 193, 194, 195, 205, 228, 229, 286, 294–295
America's Town Meeting of the Air 293
Amos 'n' Andy 36, 46, 50, 83, 111, 183, 253, 264, 266
Ampex Company 280, 281
Amrhein, Jack 66
Anchor Hocking Glass Corporation 249
Andrew Jergens Company 3, 88–94
Andrews Sisters 112, 263
Announcers 60–69
Ansbro, George 61, 64, 246, 291, 278, 295
Arbitron 49
Archie Andrews 269
Armour and Company 249–250
Armour Star Jester 250
Art Linkletter's House Party 150, 257, 274
Arthur Godfrey Time 55, 56, 183, 249, 253, 263

Arthur Godfrey's Talent Scouts 56, 183, 269
Association of American Railroads 250, 287
Association of National Advertisers 44
Atlantic & Pacific Tea Company 250, 256
The Atwater Kent Hour 250, 286
Atwater Kent Manufacturing Company 250
Audience involvement 273–274
Audience measurement 29, 41–51
Audimeter 48
Audion 16
Audit Bureau of Circulations 14
Aunt Jenny's Real Life Stories 57–59, 181, 182–183, 289
Autry, Gene 272
Avalon Time 103, 104–105
Avisa Relation oder Zeitung 9
Ayer, Francis Wayland 32–33
Ayer & Son *see* N. W. Ayer & Son
Aylesworth, Merlin H. 33

Babbitt Company *see* B. T. Babbitt Company
Baby Snooks 260
Bachelor's Children 255, 289
Backstage Wife 246, 247, 268, 277
Bailey, Jack 251
Baker, Phil 250, 258
Balk, Alfred 61
Ball, Lucille 37
Banghart, Kenneth 134
Bans on commercials for certain goods 22, 38
Barbasol Company 251
Barnouw, Erik 34, 53, 281
Barnum, Phineas T. 11, 33
Baruch, Andre 61, 65, 246
Batten, Barton, Durstine & Osborn 34, 35, 40, 53
Bayer AG 10, 200, 201, 241–242, 243, 244
Beal Company 65

317

Beals, Dick 202
Beck, Jackson 61, 170
Becker, Sandy 203–204
Belk's 11
Bell, Alexander Graham 13
Bell, Jared 11
Bell Telephone Company 251
Bell Telephone Hour 251, 271, 287
Benny, Jack 23, 28, 36, 44, 50, 66, 68, 86, 87, 175, 283, 285, 286
Benton & Bowles 34
Bergen, Edgar, and Charlie McCarthy 36, 44, 50, 120, 174, 175, 238–239, 272, 286
Berle, Milton 68, 269
Best, Gordon 37
The Best Food Boys 286
The Betty Crocker Show 147–148, 154, 286
Beville, H. M. 49
BFGoodrich 257–258
Big Sister 3
Billboard 48
Billboards 12, 14
Biow, Milton 210
Blackett-Sample-Hummert 34, 219, 288
Blackwell, H. M. 21
Blanc, Mel 66
Bleyer, Archie 56
Blondie 50
Bloom, Sol 18
Bloomingdales 11
Blue network 4, 35, 170
Bly, Robert 53
Bond, Ford 61, 67, 246, 247, 251, 277, 289
Boone, F. E. 86
Borden Company 251
Boston News-Letter 9
Boston Symphony Orchestra 249
Bowery's, Inc. 251–252
Boy Scouts of America 291
Boyd, Henry 57
Brand awareness and loyalty 10, 12, 17, 24, 28, 169, 177, 234, 259, 289
Break the Bank 99, 270
The Breakfast Club 269
Brinkley, John 22
Bristol-Myers Company 74, 95–100, 283, 286
Broadcast Advertising 24, 37
Broadcasting 19, 41, 48, 54, 288
Brock, Luther 53
Brokenshire, Norman 61
Brown & Williamson Tobacco Company 3, 83, 84, 101–105, 186, 193, 194, 205, 229, 230
Brown Shoe Company 252
Browning King Orchestra 24
B. T. Babbitt Company 10, 67, 250–251, 288–289
Buckley, Homer J. 14, 15
Burdine's 11
Burnett, Leo 206
Burns, George, and Gracie Allen 28, 36, 68, 183, 257, 260, 262, 283, 287

Cable News Network (CNN) 57
Camel Caravan 188, 232–233
Campbell Soup Company 106–112, 259, 288
Cantor, Eddie 3, 28, 46, 68, 99, 232, 237, 250, 256, 262, 269, 287
Cantril, Hadley 49, 54
Captain Midnight 270, 290
CARE 291
Carlton, William James 12
Carlton & Smith 12
Carnation Company 252, 283
Carnation Contented Hour 252
Carpenter, Ken 61, 68
Carroll, Carroll 28
Carter Products 252
Case, Nelson 67
Casey, Crime Photographer 249, 269
Cavalcade of America 255, 282
C. E. Hooper, Inc. 29, 43, 45–46, 47, 48
The Challenge of the Yukon 225–226, 290
Chanel SA 252
Changing Times 282
Chappell, Ernest 68, 294–295
Chappel Company *see* P. M. Chappel Company
Charles, Judith 53
Charles B. Knox Gelatine Company 261
The Chase & Sanborn Hour 46
Chesebrough Manufacturing Company 74, 180, 253
Chevrolet Musical Moments 162, 163
The Chicago Theater of the Air 293
Chrysler Corporation 130, 132, 160, 161, 253
Church, Arthur B. 19
Church & Dwight Company 126
Church of the Air 293
Churchill, Winston 54
The Cities Service Concerts 251, 253–254, 286
Cities Service Oil Company 67, 253–254
City Hospital 252
Claney, Howard 246, 247, 291
Clark, Lloyd M. 45
Clark-Hooper, Inc. 29, 45
Clicquot Club Company 24–25, 254, 271, 286
The Clicquot Club Eskimos 24–25, 28, 254, 278, 279, 286
Clorox Company 126
Club 15 112
Coca-Cola Company 13, 14, 113–120, 264
Coincidental Method of audience measurement 46–47, 297
Colgate-Palmolive-Peet Company 1, 3, 14, 77, 83, 121–128, 179
Collier's 47
Collyer, Clayton (Bud) 61, 67, 99–100, 270
Columbia Broadcasting System 4, 22, 26, 29, 30, 31, 35, 36, 37, 49, 50, 54, 63, 65, 99, 112, 148, 170, 189, 190, 195, 203, 226, 247, 254, 297
Columbia Presents Corwin 254
The Columbia Workshop 254, 293
Commercial copywriters 52–59
Commercials, styles of 54
Communications Act of 1934 27
Community Chest 291
Como, Perry 51, 188
Compton Advertising 58
Conrad, Frank 19–20
Consolidated Cigar Corporation 254
Contests 274–277
Continuity acceptance 29–30
Coolidge, Calvin 33
Cooperative Analysis of Broadcasting (C.A.B.) 44, 45, 46, 297
Corn Products Refining Company 254
Cosmopolitan 213
County Fair 251
Cowcatcher commercial 226, 246, 277–278, 298
Crazy Water Crystals Company 254–255
Cream of Wheat Corporation 255
Creating needs through advertising 17
Crime Doctor 65
Crosby, Bing 28, 36, 44, 50, 51, 66, 68, 90, 134, 172, 173, 174–175, 188, 189, 265, 279–281, 287, 294
Crosley, Powel, Jr. 23, 43
Cross, Milton 267
Crossley, Archibald 29, 43–44, 47
Crossley Surveys 43, 45, 48, 87, 298
Cudahy Packing Company 255
Curtis Publishing Company 33

D'Arcy Advertising 117
A Date with Judy 260
David Harding, Counterspy 258, 264
David Harum 251, 288, 289
Davidson, Bill 47
Davis, Janette 55
Davis Company *see* R. B. Davis Company
Dean, Louis 65
Death Valley Days 264
De Forest, Lee 15, 16
De la Mare, Walter 41
DeLong, Tom 111
Dial Corporation 126
Dick Tracy 289, 290
Direct mail 14, 19
Direct Mail Advertising Association 14
Direct Marketing Association 14–15
Dr. Christian 253
Donald, Peter 251
Donaldson, Dan 219–220
Double or Nothing 111, 259
Dunning, John 175
Durante, Jimmy 266
du Pont de Nemours and Company *see* E. I. du Pont de Nemours and Company

Index

Eastman Kodak Company 244
Easy Aces 65, 219
Edison, Thomas A. 165
Edwards, Douglas 162
Edwards, Ralph 62, 264, 275, 276
E. I. du Pont de Nemours and Company 1, 158, 255, 282
Electric Auto-Lite Company 255–256
Electrical transcription 28, 175, 278–281, 298
Electromechanical audience analyzer 49–50
Elliot, Win 251
Emerson Drug Company 256
E. R. Squibb & Sons 22, 96–97, 267
Erwin Wasey (ad agency) 34
Esso News 64, 268
Eveready Battery Company 256
The Eveready Hour 24, 256, 286
Eversharp Pen Company 65, 256

The Fat Man 264
The FBI in Peace & War 271, 272
Federal Communications Commission 4, 27, 54, 279, 291, 298
Federal Radio Commission 25, 27, 43, 278, 291
Federal Trade Commission 34, 243–244, 298
Fessenden, Reginald Aubrey 15, 16
Fibber McGee & Molly 44, 50, 68, 261, 264, 283–284, 287
Firestone Tire and Rubber Company 133, 145, 165, 256, 286
Fisher, Eddie 119, 120, 287
The Fitch Bandwagon 44–45
Fitch Company *see* F. W. Fitch Company
Fleming, James 278
The Flit Soldiers 286
Foley's 11
Foote, Cone & Belding 35, 83
Ford, Henry 10, 129–133, 157, 165
Ford, Tennessee Ernie 134
Ford Motor Company 3, 14, 129–135, 157, 160, 161
The Ford Sunday Evening Hour 134, 162
Ford Theater 134–135
Fortune 44, 180
Franklin, Benjamin 9
Frigidaire Corporation 159
Frito-Lay Company 173, 224
F. W. Fitch Company 256–257

G. Washington Coffee Company 74, 270
Gallop, Frank 61, 68, 246, 277
Gallup, George 43, 44, 54
Gangbusters 272, 292
Garroway, Dave 250
Geller, Jack 41
General Cigar Company, Inc. 257
General Electric Company 10, 25, 161, 257, 262, 288
General Foods Corporation 3, 30, 56, 136–145, 168, 172, 206–207, 230, 236, 271, 285

General Mills, Inc. 1, 3, 29, 77, 110, 146–155, 265, 271, 285, 286
The General Mills Hour 153, 246
General Motors Corporation 1, 3, 130, 133, 156–163
George A. Hormel & Company 260
Gernsbeck, Hugo 16
Gernsbeck's Electro Importing Company 16
Gillette Company 22, 214, 257
Gilmore, Art 61, 63–64
Gimbels 11, 22
Girl Scouts of America 291
Godfrey, Arthur 55–57, 61, 62, 183, 184, 188–189, 191, 249, 269, 281, 294
The Gold Dust Twins 28
Good Housekeeping 109
Goodman, Benny 3
Goodrich *see* BFGoodrich
The Goodrich Silver Masked Tenor 28, 257–258
Goodyear Tire and Rubber Company 258
Goodwin, Bill 283
Gordon, Shirley 111
Grand Central Station 261, 269
Grand Ole Opry 232
Grauer, Ben 61
Great Depression 25, 26, 20, 48, 64, 96, 102, 123, 149, 167, 180, 210, 230
The Great Gildersleeve 50, 173, 174, 175–176
The Greatest Story Ever Told 258
Grebe manufacturing concern *see* A. H. Grebe
The Green Hornet 290
Greet, Cabell 63
Grove Laboratories, Inc. 258
Grunwald, Edgar A. 34
Guedel, John 281
The Guiding Light 153, 154, 155, 219, 274–275, 288, 289
Gulf Oil Corporation 258
Gunsmoke 31, 253
Gutenberg, Johannes 9

Hall Brothers Company 258–259
Hamilton Music Store 20
The Happiness Boys 28, 286
Happiness Candy Stores 286
Harding, Warren G. 18
Harding-Cox election returns 19–20
Harmon, Jim 289
Harrice, Cy 295
Have Gun, Will Travel 31, 257
Haymes, Dick 252
Haynes Motor Car Company 22
Headliners as spokespersons 281
Health Products Corporation 259
Healthaids, Inc. 259
Hearn's 22
Hearst Syndicate 44
Heatter, Gabriel 251, 258, 259, 281
Heinz Company *see* H. J. Heinz Company
Herlihy, Ed 61, 67
Hershey Chocolate Company 123

Hersholt, Jean 253
Hertz, Heinrich 15
Higby, Mary Jane 279–280, 294
Highway Beautification Act 12
Hilliard, Robert 54
Hilltop House 203–204, 259
Hitchhikes 202, 246, 277–278, 299
H. J. Heinz Company 110, 173, 259, 261, 265
The Hollywood Reporter 48
Hooper, Claude Ernest 43, 45, 47
Hooper, Inc. *see* C. E. Hooper, Inc.
Hooperatings 43, 45–46, 47, 48, 50, 51, 299
Hoover, Herbert 18, 167
Hope, Bob 23, 44, 50, 90, 93, 183, 189, 264, 287, 294
Hormel & Company *see* George A. Hormel & Company
(Art Linkletter's) *House Party* 150, 257, 274
Howe Company *see* Lewis Howe Company
The Hucksters 27
Hudson's 11
Hull, Warren 128, 262
Human voice use in advertising 2, 7, 18
Hummert, Frank, and Anne 64, 219, 246, 277–278

Indirect commercialization of airwaves 18–19, 22, 24, 28
Industrial Revolution 9–10, 89
Infomercial 2, 21, 22
Information Please 86
Inner Sanctum Mysteries 256
Institutional advertising 282, 299
Integrating commercials into programming 282–284
International Bill Posters' Association of North America 13
International Silver Company 260, 261
Internet 31
The Interwoven Pair 28, 286
Invitation to Learning 293
Iodent Chemical Company 260
The Ipana Troubadours 28, 97, 98, 99, 286
It Pays to Be Ignorant 65

J. Walter Thompson Company 12, 13, 14, 32–33, 34, 35, 40, 90, 179
Jack Armstrong, the All-American Boy 51, 154, 290
Jack Berch and His Boys 261, 265
James, Hugh 145
J. B. Williams Company 272
Jergens Company *see* Andrew Jergens Company
The Jergens Journal 90
Jingles and other music 1, 59, 60, 63, 96, 127, 128, 176, 186, 189, 190, 202, 203, 232, 246, 251, 255, 256, 258, 264, 266, 269, 271, 274, 276, 278, 284–285, 299

John H. Woodbury Company 89, 90
Johnson & Johnson 126, 215
Johnson & Son *see* S. C. Johnson & Son
Jolson, Al 266, 287
Jones, Duane 288, 289
Joyce Jordan 65
Just Plain Bill 219

Kaltenborn, Hans V. 266, 281
Kao Corporation 91–92
Karmen, Steve 284
Kasper-Gordon, Inc. 278
KDKA, Pittsburgh 19–20, 23
Keebler Foods Company 166
Kellogg Company 14, 136, 151, 152, 164–170, 173, 271, 290
Kelly, Pat 64
Kent, Alan 62–63, 264, 285
Kent Electrical Manufacturing Company 286
Kentucky Fried Chicken 115
KFKB, Milford, Kan. 22
KFNF, Shenandoah, Iowa 22
KIEV, Glendale, Calif. 293
Kimberly-Clark Corporation 215, 261
King, Del 104–105
King, Larry 57
Kiplinger, William M. 282
Kirby, Durward 61
Klauber, Ed 65
KMAC, San Antonio 293
Knight, Frank 65
Knox Gelatine Company *see* Charles B. Knox Gelatine Company
KPO, San Francisco 23
Kraft Foods Company 67, 110, 119, 123, 142, 152, 171–176, 206–207, 224, 230, 236, 265
Kraft Music Hall 44, 172, 173, 174, 294
Krupp, Roger 246
KYW, Chicago 23

Ladies' Home Journal 13, 33, 90, 138, 139, 179
Lady Esther Cosmetics Company 261
Lambert Pharmacal Company 261–262
Lasker, Albert D. 83
Lazar, Bill 196
Lazarsfeld, Paul F. 49, 54
Lehn & Fink 243, 262
Let's Pretend 255, 274
Lever Brothers Company 3, 30, 57–59, 121, 126, 177–183, 264, 292
Lewis Howe Company 47
Libby, McNeil & Libby 262
Life 13, 290
Life Can Be Beautiful 62, 65, 219
Life with Luigi 37
Liggett & Myers Tobacco Company 65, 82, 83, 184–191, 194, 205, 206, 229, 266
Lind, Jenny 11
Lindlahr, Victor 259

Linkletter, Art 150, 257, 274
Linotype 13
Lipton Company *see* Thomas J. Lipton Company
Lithography 9
Little Orphan Annie 270, 290
Livingstone, Mary 66
The Lone Ranger 154, 202, 290
Lopez, Vincent 20
Lora Lawton 251, 288–289
Lord and Thomas 34, 83
Lorenzo Jones 247
Lorillard, Inc. *see* P. Lorillard, Inc.
The Los Angeles Times 193
The Lucky Strike Dance Orchestra 86, 286
Luden's, Inc. 262
Lum 'n' Abner
Lumley, Frederick Hillis 49
Lux Radio Theater 44, 174, 181, 182, 183, 287

Ma Perkins 216, 218–219, 268, 289
MacRae, Gordon 250, 269
Macy's 11, 22
Madison Avenue 35, 299
Magnetophons 280
Mail order catalog 11, 12, 13, 166, 199, 213
Mailhook 288
Major Edward Bowes' Original Amateur Hour 44, 253
Maltin, Leonard 35, 61, 62, 289
Manhattan Soap Company 262–263
March of Dimes 291
Marconi, Guglielmo 15, 16
Marketing research 14
Marshall Field's 11
Martin, Charles 66
Marvin, Tony 61, 249
Marx, Groucho 36, 175, 253, 268, 281
Mass circulation magazines persuasive tool 12, 13, 17, 90, 109, 171, 179, 213
Maxwell, James Clerk 15
Maxwell Company *see* R. C. Maxwell Company
McCann-Erickson 35, 117
McCarthy, Charlie *see* Edgar Bergen and Charlie McCarthy
McFarland & Company 61–62
McNamee, Graham 24, 62
McNeill, Don 269
Metropolitan Opera 16, 51, 250, 261, 267, 269
Microphone placement and special effects 286
Middleton, Glenn Y. 63–64
Miles Laboratories, Inc. 3, 197–204
Miller, Marvin 61, 250
Millet, Art 154–155
Minnesota Mining and Manufacturing Company (3M) 281
Minute Maid Corporation 118
Mr. Keen, Tracer of Lost Persons 266, 278
Mitchell, Maurice B. 54–55
Modern Radio Advertising 54

Monitor 29, 249
Montgomery Ward Company 11, 12–13
Moorehead, Agnes 262
Morgan, Henry 56, 256
Morse, Carlton E. 52
Morse code 16
Mott, Bob 66
Moore, Garry 266
Murrow, Edward R. 68, 259
Museum of Broadcast Communications 33–34, 35–36
Mutual Broadcasting System 4, 30, 35, 99, 170, 226, 299
My Favorite Husband 37
My Friend Irma 37, 183
My True Story 262
Myrt and Marge 289

Nachman, Gerald 68, 290
Nash-Kelvinator Corporation 263
National Association of Broadcasters 54
National Biscuit Company (Nabisco) 55, 142, 173, 207, 230, 236, 263
National Broadcasting Company 4, 21, 22, 24, 25, 26, 29, 30, 31, 33, 34–35, 36–37, 62, 64, 99, 111, 144, 148, 149, 153, 170, 174, 175, 195, 226, 232, 238, 246, 247, 277, 278, 299–300
National Carbon Company 24, 286
National Dairy Products Corporation 263
The National Farm and Home Hour 249
National radio conferences 18, 19, 291
The National Radio Pulpit 293
Nelson, Ozzie, and Harriet 36
New-York Daily Times 12
The New York Sun 11
The New York Times 12, 14, 15, 18, 123, 157, 158, 234, 235, 241, 279
The New York World 14
Newell-Emmett agency 285
Newspaper supplements 14
Nick Carter, Master Detective 255
Nielsen, Arthur Charles, Sr. 43, 47, 48
Nielsen Company *see* A. C. Nielsen Company
Nielsen Food and Drug Index 48
Niles, Ken 61
Niles, Wendell 61
Nomenclature 286–287
Nona from Nowhere 251, 288
Norwich Pharmacal Company 263–264
N. W. Ayer & Son 12, 32–33, 34

Oboler, Arch 52
Office of Radio Research 49
Ogilvy, David 83
Ogilvy & Mather 40
O'Keefe, Walter 111
Omar Herth, the Swingmaker 64
Omnicom Group 40

One Man's Family 52, 203, 238, 263, 269, 288, *289*
Ortega, Santos 252, 259
Our Gal Sunday 268
Our Miss Brooks 37, 51
Outdoor Advertising Association of America 13

P. Lorillard, Inc. 3, 82, 83, 192–196, 205
Pacific Borax Company 264, 269
Painted Outdoor Advertising Association 13
Paley, William S. 22, 31, 36, 37, 56, 247
Palmer, Volney B. 11, 32, 40
The Palmolive Hour 28
Parks, Bert 99, 261
Participating sponsorship 287–288, 300
Paul, Ralph 128
Paul Harvey News and Comments 294
Payne, George Henry 34
Payne, Virginia 218
Pearson, Fort 274–275
Peary, Harold 36
Peck and Snyder 12
Pemberton, John S. 13
People's Literary Companion 12
Pepper Young's Family 62–63, 219, 264, 285
Pepsi-Cola Company 62, 118, 119, 151, 224, 264, 285
Pepsodent Company 180, 264
Perry Mason 219
Pet Milk Company 234, 264
Philco Radio Corporation 175, 264–265
Philco Radio Time 175, 264, 265, 279, 280
Philip Morris Company 3, 65, 83, 142, 172–173, 186–187, 193, 194, 205–211, 230, 231, 236, 284
Philip Morris Playhouse 65, 66, 210–211, 287
Phillips, Irna 153, 246
Pillsbury Company 146, 150, 151–152, 265, 288
Planters Nut and Chocolate Company 236
P. M. Chappel Company 253
Pond's Extract Company 12, 180, 265
Pope, Daniel 42
Poster Advertising Association 13
Posters and signs 9, 11, 12, 14, 15, 107, 149, 171, 186, 192, 209, 212, 213, 229
Pot o' Gold 45
Prang, Louis 12
Premiums 43, 58, 60, 108, 109, 117, 137, 138, 141, 166, 192–193, 198–199, 203, 226, 239, 251, 288–290, 300
Primetime 45
Print media in advertising 2, 7, 8–9, 10, 11

Printer's Ink 13
Procter & Gamble Company 3, 10, 13, 26, 30, 57–59, 65, 67, 275, 77, 88, 91, 93, 121, 122, 124, 125, 126, 141, 145, 179, 180, 181, 212–220, 275–277, 288
Prohibition 24, 25, 114, 115, 199
Protest/debate over commercialization of radio 18, 19, 27
Prudential Insurance Company 265
The Psychology of Radio 49
Public service announcements 291–292, 300
Publicis Groupe 33
Publick Occurrences Both Foreign and Domestick 9
Pulitzer, Joseph 14
Pure Oil Company 265–266

Quaker Oats Company 3, 10, 173, 221–227, 271, 289
Queen for a Day 51
Queensboro Corporation 21–22
Quiz Craze 111

Radio Act of 1927 25
Radio Broadcast 22–23, 44
Radio Corporation of America 25, 266
Radio Life 111
Radio News 18
Radio Speakers 61–62
The Railroad Hour 250, 251, 282, 287
Ralston Purina Company 266, 271
Rankin ad agency *see* William H. Rankin
Ratings and audience measurement 42
Ratings point in audience measurement 42
Rawson, Ron 61, 68
R. B. Davis Company 255
R. C. Maxwell Company 14
Recall method of audience measurement 44, 46–47
Red Cross 291
Reser, Harry 24
Rich's 11
Riggs, Glenn 262
Riggs, L. A. "Speed" 86
The Right to Happiness 219, 268
Ringling Brothers and Barnum and Bailey Circus 11, 33
R. J. Reynolds Tobacco Company 3, 33, 65, 82, 83, 84, 103, 186, 187, 193, 194, 195, 205, 206, 228–233, 236
The Road of Life 219, 268
Robbins, Fred 120
Roberts, Ken 61, 65, 66, 67
Roberts, Tony 65
Robinson, Frank 13
Rogers, Roy 226, 253, 258
The Romance of Helen Trent 219, 259, 289, 294
Roosevelt, Franklin D. 46

Roosevelt, Theodore 14
Roper, Elmo 43, 44
Ross, David 65
Roventini, Johnny 66–67, 207, 208, 209–210
Rowell, George P. 12, 13
Ruthrauff & Ryan 34, 57

Sara Lee Corporation 126, 173, 236
S. C. Johnson & Son 124, 126, 261, 264, 283
Schaden, Chuck 65
Schulberg, Bob 49, 54
Schwerin, Horace 54
Scientific American 16
Sears, Roebuck & Company 11, 13, 281
Second Industrial Revolution 10
The Second Mrs. Burton 268
Seiler, Jim 49
Senefelder, Alois 9
Seymour, Dan 57–59
The Shadow 258, 271
Sharbutt, Del 61, 111–112
Share in audience measurement 42
Shell Oil Company 266
Sherwin-Williams Company 267
Shore, Dinah 3, 51, 125, 134, 250
Shur-On Optical Company 22
Simms, Ginny 251
Sinatra, Frank 195–196
Sinclair Oil Corporation 267
Singer Sewing Machine Company 12
Singin' Sam 251, 284
Skelton, Red 36, 50, 103, 104, 287
Sky King 289, 290
Slattery, Jack 274
Smilin' Ed and His Buster Brown Gang 252, 274, 287
Smith, Kate 23, 45, 250, 287
Smith Brothers Cough Drop Company 267
Social Stratification of the Radio Audience 49 287
Socony Oil Company (Standard Oil of New York) 267, 281
Sound effects 57, 60, 292, 301
Spencer, Edith 57
Spokespersons for the aural advertiser 60–69, 111
Spot announcements 29, 36, 281, 292–293, 300
Squibb & Sons *see* E. R. Squibb & Sons
SS Avon 16
Stack-Goble 34
Stafford, Jo 252, 287
Staley Corporation 268
Standard Brands, Inc. 3, 10, 234–239
Standard Oil Company of New Jersey 268, 286
Stanton, Frank 49, 50, 54
Stark, Dick 189–190
Stars Over Hollywood 252
Stella Dallas 246, 247, 277, 290, 291
Sterling Drug, Inc. 3, 240–247, 277–278, 290

Stop the Music! 261
Strike It Rich 262
Stubblefield, Nathan B. 15, 16
Studebaker Manufacturing Company 268
Suspense 31, 253, 256, 257
Sustaining programming 37, 293
Sweeney, Warren 61
Swift & Company 269
Swing, Raymond Gram 281
Sylvania Electric Products, Inc. 269

Taft, William Howard 165
Take It or Leave It 65
(Arthur Godfrey's) *Talent Scouts* 56, 183, 269
Tastyeast Bakers 286
The Tastyeast Loafers 286
Telegraphy 10, 16
Telephone usage 13, 14, 43, 44, 46, 47, 48
Tesla, Nikola 15
Terry and the Pirates 252
Testimonials 293–294
Texas Company 269
That Brewster Boy 50, 226–227
This Is Nora Drake 65, 268, 269, 294
This Is Your Life 62
Thomas J. Lipton Company 56, 180, 183
Tidewater Oil Company 22
Time 41, 44–45, 234, 261
Today's Children 153, 154, 289
Toll broadcasting 20
Tom Corbett, Space Cadet 169, 170
Tom Mix 266, 287, 290
Toni Company 269
Topps Gum Company 12
Town crier 7, 8, 15
Transit advertising 11, 14, 108, 141, 171
Trewe Encountre 9
True or False 272
Truth or Consequences 62, 264, 275–277

Underhill, Paco 54
Unilever 14, 173, 177–183, 214, 215
U.S. Food and Drug Administration 243
U.S. Office of War Information 37
U.S. Patent Office 12, 116, 178

U.S. Steel Corporation 10, 269–270, 282
U.S. Tuberculosis Institute 15

Valiant Lady 152, 154–155
Vallee, Rudy 28, 174, 237, 238, 250, 263, 287
Variety 34, 50
Variety Radio Directory, 1937–1938 34
Vic and Sade 219
Vick Chemical Company 270
VNU 42, 48
Voice of Firestone 251, 256, 286
Voiceovers 294–295, 302
Von Zell, Harry 61, 62, 65, 68, 283
Voorhees, Donald 251, 253

Wade Advertising 202
Wakeman, Frederic 27
Wald, John 175–176
Wallington, Jimmy 61
Walton, Sidney 282
Wanamaker, John 4
Wanamaker's 4, 11, 12, 23
Wanderer Company 270
Waring, Fred 134, 258, 287
Warner & Company, Inc. *see* William R. Warner & Company, Inc.
Wasey ad agency *see* Erwin Wasey (ad agency)
Washburn-Crosby Company 1, 29, 146–149, 285
Washington Coffee Company *see* G. Washington Coffee Company
The Washington Post 13
WBAL, Baltimore 293
WBNY, New York 20
WBZ, Springfield/Boston, Mass. 23
WCCO, Minneapolis 147, 148, 149, 285
WDAF, Kansas City, Mo. 23
We, the People 258
WEAF, New York 2, 20, 21, 22, 23, 24, 25, 62, 64, 98, 194, 250, 256, 257
Weaver, Sylvester L. (Pat) 36–37
Welch Foods Company 270
Welles, Orson 26
Wendy Warren and the News 145
Wesson Oil and Snowdrift Company 270–271
Western Electric (AT&T subsidiary) 20

Western Union Company 25
Westinghouse Corporation 19–20, 23, 271
WFAA, Dallas 23
Wheatena Corporation 271
When a Girl Marries 252, 265
Whiting, Margaret 250
Wilcox, Harlow 61, 256, 261, 264, 283–284
Wildroot Cream Oil Company 271
William H. Rankin (ad agency) 22
William J. Wrigley Company 74, 77, 272
William R. Warner & Company, Inc. 271–272
Williams Company *see* J. B. Williams Company
Wilson, Don 61, 68, 283
Winchell, Walter 90, 93, 287
WJAR, Providence, R. I. 23
WJZ, New York 20, 23, 25, 64
WLW, Cincinnati 23, 43, 218, 251
WMAF, South Dartmouth, Mass. 23
WMAQ, Chicago 23
WNAC, Boston 23
Wolfe, Charles 7, 51, 53, 54
Woman in White 153, 289
Woolworth's 11
WRC, Washington, D. C. 25
Wrigley Company *see* William J. Wrigley Company
Woodbury Company *see* John H. Woodbury Company
WRVA, Richmond, Va. 254
WWJ, Detroit 23
Wyeth healthcare 73–75
Wynn, Ed 28, 62, 287

X-Minus 1 258

You Bet Your Life 253
Young, Agnes 57
Young & Rubicam 34, 35, 37, 40
Young Doctor Malone 57–59, 203, 219, 268, 269
Young Men's Christian Association 22
Young Widder Brown 64, 247, 269, 291
Your Hit Parade 86, 87
Yours Truly, Johnny Dollar 257, 272
YUM Brands 115

Zeitung 9

www.ingramcontent.com/pod-product-compliance
Ingram Content Group UK Ltd.
Pitfield, Milton Keynes, MK11 3LW, UK
UKHW050543150426
5217IPUK00026B/2046